FOURTH EDITION

# INTERNATIONAL POLITICS

## Power and Purpose in Global Affairs

## Paul D'Anieri

*University of California, Riverside*

CENGAGE
Learning·

Australia · Brazil · Mexico · Singapore · United Kingdom · United States

**International Politics: Power and Purpose in Global Affairs, Fourth Edition**
Paul D'Anieri

Product Director: Paul R. Banks

Product Team Manager: Carolyn Merrill

Senior Content Developer:
Laura Hildebrand

Managing Content Developer:
Megan Garvey

Product Assistant: Michelle Forbes

Marketing Director: Michelle Williams

Marketing Manager: Valerie Hartman

Senior Content Project Manager:
Corinna Dibble

Senior Designer: Sarah Cole

Manufacturing Planner: Fola Orekoya

IP Analyst: Alexandra Ricciardi

IP Project Manager: Farah Fard

Production Service & Compositor:
Cenveo® Publisher Services

Text Designer: Stratton Design

Cover Designer: Studio Montage

Cover Image: Istock/123ArtistImages

Icon credit: Page 12, 41, 62, 94, 142, 167, 208, 238, 275, 308, 326, 361, 389, 439, 447
**Vectomart/Shutterstock.com.**

Page 17, 26, 75, 96, 127, 179, 212, 279, 293, 330, 356, 403, 428, 453
**Allies Interactive/Shutterstock.com.**

Page 9, 29, 59, 113, 132, 164, 201, 221, 260, 304, 338, 368, 431, 408, 461
**Eman Design/Shutterstock.com.**

Page 8, 33, 81, 99, 130, 177, 196, 225, 282, 290, 335, 371, 397, 437, 457
**Khamitsevich, Vitali, Vladimirovich/ Shutterstock.com.**

Library of Congress Control Number: 2015956740

Student Edition:
ISBN: 978-1-305-63008-6

Loose-leaf Edition:
ISBN: 978-1-305-87548-7

**Cengage Learning**
20 Channel Center Street
Boston, MA 02210
USA

Cengage Learning is a leading provider of customized learning solutions with employees residing in nearly 40 different countries and sales in more than 125 countries around the world. Find your local representative at **www.cengage.com.**

Cengage Learning products are represented in Canada by Nelson Education, Ltd.

To learn more about Cengage Learning Solutions, visit **www.cengage.com.**

Purchase any of our products at your local college store or at our preferred online store **www.cengagebrain.com.**

Printed in the United States of America
Print Number: 02      Print Year: 2018

# DEDICATION

*To My Children*
*Jacey, Courtney, Zachary, Joe, and Lily*

# BRIEF CONTENTS

# CONTENTS

Dear International Politics Instructor:

The mission for the course in international politics, as I see it, is to provide students with the analytical skills and conceptual apparatus to understand and analyze international politics. Although much has changed in international politics since I began teaching the course just after the end of the Cold War, this underlying goal has not. I continue to believe the biggest benefits our students get from the course are the concepts we teach and the habits of inquiry we instill. The course is not just a course on international politics or political science; it is a central component of a liberal education. Therefore, I continue to present many of the issues addressed in the text in terms of questions or puzzles, and to examine multiple answers. I also introduce concepts that have application beyond international politics, such as collective action problems, expected utility, social construction, and the distinctions between the five paradigms of international politics we discuss. In this edition, I explore different conceptions of power much more deeply.

The themes of **power and purpose** recur throughout the text. This scheme reflects one of the main debates in contemporary theorizing—the debate between rationalist and constructivist approaches. I also want to prompt students to inquire about these two concepts when thinking about world issues. Many discussions of contemporary problems focus on the desire to achieve a particular purpose (such as "development"), without giving sufficient attention to the limitations on actors' ability, or power, to bring about that end. Similarly, we need to think about how actors' goals are formed and how they change, and why some are controversial and others go unquestioned. The notions of power and purpose are explored in depth in Chapter 1, and then are reinforced throughout the text, with a discussion focused on power and purpose at the end of each chapter.

The **five paradigms** that dominate Chapters 3 and 4 (realism, liberalism, economic structuralism, constructivism, and feminism) recur throughout the text. They arise explicitly again in Chapter 10, when they are applied to international political economy, and in Chapter 14, when they are applied to international environmental politics.

A third recurring theme is that of **continuity and change**. Chapter 2 surveys the evolution of the contemporary system, and subsequent chapters address the historic roots of many of the phenomena that concern us today. An explicit goal is to ask whether traditional concepts are adequate to understand contemporary problems, and to identify what is so new that we may not yet have the concepts needed to understand it.

## NEW TO THIS EDITION

- This edition focuses on expanding and enriching the discussion of power, based on requests from previous users.
- Chapter 1 now includes a substantive discussion on different conceptions of power: coercion, institutional power, soft power, structural power, and collaborative power.
- Subsequent chapters point out, where appropriate, how some of these different conceptions of power apply to topics under discussion.

- The text is updated throughout to use recent examples wherever possible. Although this is not primarily a course about current events, recent examples help students to engage with the material.
- The discussion of economic structuralism in Chapter 4 now includes a brief discussion of Thomas Piketty's widely read book, *Capital in the 21st Century*.
- Chapter 9, on the use of force, has evolved to address the Islamic State, which appears to blend aspects of a terrorist group and a state. There is also a brief discussion of hybrid war, based on Russia's actions in Ukraine.
- The "Connection to You" box in Chapter 5 now addresses campus activism aimed at altering foreign policies.
- The "Policy Connection" box in Chapter 7 now addresses Britain's discussion about leaving the EU.

## MINDTAP™

As an instructor, MindTap is here to simplify your workload, organize and immediately grade your students' assignments, and allow you to customize your course as you see fit. Through deep-seated integration with your Learning Management System, grades are easily exported and analytics are pulled with just the click of a button. MindTap provides you with a platform to easily add in current events videos and RSS feeds from national or local news sources. Looking to include more currency in the course? Students can access the KnowNow International Relations Blog for weekly updated news coverage and pedagogy.

Like many of my colleagues, I was inspired by talented and dedicated teachers. The best of them ignited my interest, sharpened my thinking, and raised my aspirations. As teachers, we cherish the moments we see a light bulb go on in a student's head or stand back and watch students engage in a thoughtful discussion. I have sought to provide a book that in content and style helps dedicated teachers inspire curious students.

Sincerely,

*Paul D'Anieri*

Riverside, California
August 2015
danieri@ucr.edu

Dear Student:

Unanticipated crises in international politics seem to emerge on a weekly basis. In the past few years, we have witnessed a war between Russia and Ukraine, the emergence of the "Islamic State" from conflicts in Syria and Iraq, the collapse of global energy prices, an Ebola epidemic, and an international crisis over a comedy movie. At the same time, some features of international politics—war, poverty, and the struggle for influence—seem eternal. How are we to make sense of all this? International politics presents us with many puzzles, most of which have no clear solutions. And yet the stakes are very high—responding incorrectly to these crises and challenges can lead to war, pandemic, and poverty. The puzzling nature of international politics combined with the high stakes of the issues involved make it a dramatic subject.

The book is built around the theme of "power and purpose." What goals are actors seeking to attain, and who defines those goals? Are the goals complementary or competing with those of other actors? Those are questions of purpose. Power concerns how actors pursue those goals; what resources do they have: money, weapons, prestige? The concept of power has several meanings, and exploring these will help us understand international politics, and many other areas of politics and the social sciences.

## FEATURES

- **Learning objectives** and **chapter outlines** for each chapter serve both to preview the key themes and help with review.

- **"Consider the Case"** boxes begin each chapter with a brief case study from recent or more distant history, to illustrate the real-world importance of the themes of each chapter. Each chapter then ends with a "Reconsider the Case" box that returns to the case in light of the discussion in the chapter.

- **"Policy Connection"** boxes discuss contemporary policy problems, showing how the concepts discussed in the text are applied by policy makers.

- **"History Connection"** boxes address the theme of continuity and change, tracing the origins of contemporary problems and showing how problems of today have reflections in historical cases.

- **"Geography Connection"** boxes use various kinds of maps to convey information and illustrate concepts. More broadly, these boxes help demonstrate the increasing role of geospatial tools in understanding contemporary politics.

- **"Connection to You"** boxes specifically address how the problems discussed in the text relate to today's university students. They illustrate that problems that sometimes seem very distant from our lives actually influence us considerably; and that we as individuals can seek to shape international politics in numerous ways.

- **"Power and Purpose"** discussions, at the end of each chapter, summarize how the themes of power and purpose relate to that topic. These discussions help to illustrate the different dimensions of power, and their relationship to actors' goals.

## THE BENEFITS OF USING MINDTAP™ AS A STUDENT

As a student, the benefits of using MindTap with this book are endless. With automatically graded practice quizzes and activities, an easily navigated learning path, and an interactive eBook, you will be able to test yourself in and outside of the classroom with ease. The accessibility of current events coupled with interactive media makes the content fun and engaging. On your computer, phone, or tablet, MindTap is there when you need it, giving you easy access to flashcards, quizzes, readings, and assignments.

In the time since I took my first international politics course as an undergraduate, the world has been transformed dramatically, first by the end of the Cold War, then by the terrorist attacks of September 11, 2001, and the wars that followed. It has been transformed as well by accelerating globalization, the information revolution, and the rise of China. Many of the facts I studied as an undergraduate are today irrelevant. But many of the concepts I learned—the tools for thinking about international politics—have not only remained relevant but have helped me and others make sense of the bewildering changes we have encountered in our lifetime. My aspiration for this book is that it provides you with a set of tools you can use to analyze a wide variety of new situations that you may encounter.

Sincerely,

Riverside, California
August 2015
danieri@ucr.edu

## STUDENTS...

**Access your *International Politics, 4e* resources by visiting www.cengagebrain.com/shop/isbn/9781305630086**
If you purchased MindTap access with your book, enter your access code and click "Register." You can also purchase the book's resources here separately through the "Study Tools" tab.

## INSTRUCTORS...

**Access your *International Politics, 4e* resources via www.cengage.com/login**.
Log in using your Cengage Learning single sign-on user name and password, or create a new instructor account by clicking on "New Faculty User" and following the instructions.

## MindTap

**MindTap for *International Politics: Power and Purpose in Global Affairs, 4th Edition***
ISBN for Instant Access Code: 9781305639126
ISBN for Printed Access Code: 9781305630062

MindTap for ***International Politics: Power and Purpose in Global Affairs, 4th Edition***, is a highly personalized, fully online learning experience built upon Cengage Learning content and correlating to a set of learning outcomes. MindTap guides students through the course curriculum via an innovative Learning Path Navigator where they will complete reading assignments, challenge themselves with focus activities, and engage with interactive quizzes. Through a variety of gradable activities, MindTap provides students with opportunities to check themselves for where they need extra help, as well as allowing faculty to measure and assess student progress. Integration with programs like YouTube and Google Drive allows instructors to add and remove content of their choosing with ease, keeping their course current while tracking global events through RSS feeds. The product can be used fully online with its

interactive eBook for *International Politics: Power and Purpose in Global Affairs, 4ᵗʰ Edition*, or in conjunction with the printed text.

**Instructor Companion Website for** *International Politics: Power and Purpose in Global Affairs, 4ᵗʰ Edition*— for instructors only
ISBN: 9781305639195

This Instructor Companion Website is an all-in-one multimedia online resource for class preparation, presentation, and testing. Accessible through Cengage.com/login with your faculty account, you will find available for download: book-specific Microsoft® PowerPoint® presentations; a Test Bank compatible with multiple learning management systems (LMSs); an Instructor Manual; Microsoft® PowerPoint® Image Slides; and a JPEG Image Library.

The Test Bank, offered in Blackboard, Moodle, Desire2Learn, Canvas and Angel formats, contains Learning Objective-specific multiple-choice and essay questions for each chapter. Import the test bank into your LMS to edit and manage questions, and to create tests.

The Instructor's Manual contains chapter-specific learning objectives, an outline, key terms with definitions, and a chapter summary. Additionally, the Instructor's Manual features critical thinking questions, lecture launching suggestions, in-class activities, weblinks and a listing of additional instructor resources.

The Microsoft® PowerPoint® presentations are ready-to-use, visual outlines of each chapter. These presentations are easily customized for your lectures and offered along with chapter-specific Microsoft® PowerPoint® Image Slides and JPEG Image Libraries. Access the Instructor Companion Website at www.cengage.com/login.

**IAC Cognero for** *International Politics: Power and Purpose in Global Affairs, 4ᵗʰ Edition*
ISBN: 9781305639188

Cengage Learning Testing Powered by Cognero is a flexible, online system that allows you to author, edit, and manage test bank content from multiple Cengage Learning solutions, create multiple test versions in an instant and deliver tests from your LMS, your classroom or wherever you want. The test bank for *International Politics: Power and Purpose in Global Affairs, 4ᵗʰ Edition* contains Learning Objective–specific multiple-choice and essay questions for each chapter.

## ACKNOWLEDGMENTS

This book owes its existence to wonderful teachers, students, family and friends.

Carolyn Merrill has been a wonderful friend and a supportive editor. She was instrumental in convincing me to write the first book a decade ago, and has been equally encouraging about this fourth edition. Laura Hildebrand offered persistent and positive help in thinking through this edition and bringing it to fruition. The rest of the team at Cengage has been efficient and helpful in putting the book together, including Corinna Dibble, Michelle Forbes, and Sarah Cole.

Many of the changes in this edition came from the suggestions of reviewers. In particular, they urged me to provide a more nuanced treatment of power, one of the central concepts in international politics and the book. Reviewers' advice led to many other improvements, though I did not heed all their suggestions, and the shortcomings that remain are my responsibility.

My students over the years have provided both inspiration and input. Their curiosity and optimism make teaching worthwhile, and they have offered a steady stream of suggestions about content and presentation. I am grateful as well to the University of California, Riverside, for providing a rich intellectual environment and enough time to focus on this project.

As I get older, I appreciate more than ever the teachers that I had many years ago. In particular, Michael Schechter at Michigan State and Peter Katzenstein at Cornell inspired me both with their research and their teaching. They demonstrated the impact that talented and dedicated teachers and mentors can have.

My wife Laura has always supported my scholarly endeavors, even when they take me away from home or occupy my weekends. She has been a great sounding board for my ideas about how to approach various topics, and never hesitates to point out the bad ones.

This book is dedicated to my children, Jacey, Courtney, Zachary, Joe, and Lily. As I write this, the youngest among them is leaving for college. She provided valuable feedback on the writing style of this edition. From the beginning I have been energized by the understanding that I was writing for students like them.

## REVIEWERS

We would also like to thank the instructors who have contributed their valuable feedback through reviews of this text and their participation in focus groups:

Francis Adams, Old Dominion University
Karen Ruth Adams, University of Montana
Linda Adams, Baylor University
Susan Allen, Texas Tech University
Julian Allison, University of California at Riverside
Vincent Auger, Western Illinois University
Sangmin Bae, Northeastern Illinois University
Lisa Baglione, St. Joseph's University
Ryan Baird, University of Arizona
John Barkdull, Texas Tech University
Robert Bartlett, University of Vermont
David Bearce, University of Colorado at Boulder
Henry F. Carey, Georgia State University
Ben Clansy, College of St. Rose
David Cunningham, Iowa State University
Carrie Liu Currier, Texas Christian University
Suheir Daoud, Coastal Carolina University
Jalele Defa, University of Nebraska-Lincoln
Tom Doleys, Kennesaw State University
David Edwards, University of Texas at Austin
Ophelia Eglene, Middlebury College
Traci Fahimi, Irvine Valley College
Frank Fato, Westchester Community College
William Felice, Eckerd College
Diggner Fiddner, Indiana University of Pennsylvania
Ole J. Forsberg, Creighton University
Erich Frankland, Casper College
Steve Garrison, Midwestern State University

Gregory Gause, University of Vermont
Caron Gentry, Abilene Christian University
Sean Giovanello, Elon University
David M. Goldberg, College of DuPage
Craig Greathouse, North Georgia College and State University
James R. Hedtke, Cabrini College
Timothy T. Hellwig, University of Houston
Uko Heo, University of Wisconsin at Milwaukee
Ian Hurd, Northwestern University
Marc Hutchison, University of Rhode Island
Jon Timothy Kelly, West Valley College
Patricia Keilbach, University of Colorado at Colorado Springs
Soleiman Kiasatpour, Western Kentucky University
Moonhank Kim, University of Colorado at Boulder
Douglas Kuberski, Florida State College
Donn M. Kurtz, II, University of Los Angeles at Lafayette
Lynn Kuzma, University of Southern Maine
Tobias Lanz, University of South Carolina
Mike Lebson, Johns Hopkins University-Center for Talented Youth
Howard Lehman, University of Utah
Andrew G. Long, University of Mississippi
Stephen Long, Kansas State University
Wojtek Mackiewicz Wolfe, Rutgers University
John Mercurio, San Diego State University
Harry Mokeba, Louisiana State University
Layna Mosley, University of North Carolina
Mark Mullenbach, University of Central Arkansas
Suzanne Ogden, Northeastern University
Robert Packer, Pennsylvania State University
Helen Purkitt, U.S. Naval Academy
Dan Reiter, Emory University
William M. Rose, Connecticut College
Thomas Rotnem, Southern Polytechnic State University
Stephen L. Rozman, Tougaloo College
Mark Sachleben, Shippensburg University
Kamishkan Sathasivan, Salem State College
Adriana Seagle, Wytheville Community College
Meg Shannon, Florida State University
Shalendra Sharma, University of San Francisco
Martin Slann, Macon State College
David Sobek, Louisiana State University
Patricia Stapleton, Brooklyn College
Chris Sullivan, University of Notre Dame
Alex Thompson, Ohio State University
Clayton Thyne, University of Kentucky
Karl Trautman, Central Maine Community College
Krista Tuomi, American University
Stacy D. VanDeveer, University of New Hampshire
Rossen V. Vassilev, Ohio State University

James I. Walsh, University of North Carolina at Charlotte
Julie Webber, Illinois State University
Robert Weiner, University of Massachusetts, Boston
Krista Wiegand, Georgia Southern University
Jeanne Wilson, Wheaton College
Reed Wood, Arizona State University
Wojtek Wolfe, Rutgers University
Min Ye, Coastal Carolina University
Nikolaos Zahariadis, University of Alabama at Birmingham

# ABOUT THE AUTHOR

Paul D'Anieri is Professor of Political Science and Public Policy at the University of California Riverside, as well as Provost and Executive Vice Chancellor. His teaching and research focus on politics and foreign policy in the post-Soviet states. His books include *Economic Interdependence in Ukrainian-Russian Relations* and *Understanding Ukrainian Politics: Power, Politics, and Institutional Design*, and he has published numerous articles in academic journals. He is currently studying the transnational spread of methods of political control in new democracies. Prior to coming to UC Riverside, Professor D'Anieri taught at the University of Kansas and the University of Florida. He received his BA in International Relations from Michigan State University and his PhD in Government from Cornell University.

Syrian refugees protesting in Zaatari refugee camp, Jordan, March 2014.
Anadolu Agency/Getty Images

# INTRODUCTION: PROBLEMS AND QUESTIONS IN INTERNATIONAL POLITICS

## Learning Objectives

**1-1** Identify ways in which international politics are linked to everyday life.

**1-2** Distinguish between explanatory and normative theory.

**1-3** Identify the links between theory and policy.

**1-4** Elaborate how theories are evaluated in political science.

**1-5** Apply the concept of levels of analysis in international relations.

Imagine you are president of the United States. It appears that Iran is acquiring nuclear weapons. How do you respond? Your advisers are divided. One group advocates a hard line: Threaten a military attack unless Iran proves it has stopped the program. Only the threat of a U.S. assault, these advisers contend, will persuade Iran to change course. Another group counsels a conciliatory policy: The longer we can contain the problem, they say, the more likely it is that the Iranian government will either be replaced or become less hostile. Both groups warn that if you do not take their advice, you may be responsible for prompting the use of nuclear weapons against the United States. Who is correct? How can we predict the consequences of each policy option?

Imagine you are the president of China. Other countries are increasingly insisting that you stop punishing those who speak out against corruption and human rights abuses. Your economic growth is based on huge trade surpluses with those countries, so it is important that the trade relationships be preserved. On the other hand, you fear that increasing freedom may destabilize your government, and you believe that may be the real goal of Western powers. You are not sure that those countries will ever really follow through on their implied threats. After all, their companies are desperate to sell goods to your booming market, and their governments rely on your lending to fund their deficit spending. Does participating fully in the global economy require becoming more like Western countries politically? Or is it possible to keep one's domestic political arrangements completely separate from one's international economic relations?

Imagine you are an average citizen in a democratic country voting in a national election. The candidates have similar positions on most issues but differ about how best to combat terrorism. One candidate argues that good intelligence gathering is the key to identifying terrorists before they strike and favors extensive monitoring of phone and Internet traffic. Another candidate argues that such surveillance provides relatively little benefit and constitutes an invasion of our privacy. Whom do you vote for? What are the sources of terrorism? What policies can reduce the threat?

Imagine you have joined a group devoted to alleviating poverty in Africa. A philanthropist has just given the group $1 billion to reduce poverty. How should your group spend the money? Should you focus your work on educating government decision makers to make better decisions? Should you invest in primary education to reduce the illiteracy rate? Should you spend the money on health care to reduce the drain of illness on the economy? What are the causes of global poverty? What are the cures?

These four scenarios cover a wide range of issues and views, but in each case you face difficult choices that can be made wisely only if you understand how international politics works. In each case, moreover, a bad decision will be costly. These examples illustrate an important point: International politics matters to everybody, in one way or another. It affects the daily lives even of people who know nothing or care nothing about it.

Each of these scenarios also illustrates why international politics is an interesting—even a dramatic—subject. International politics can be thought of as a set of vexing puzzles with very high stakes. Millions of lives are on the line when leaders try to avoid war or try to use war to accomplish their goals, or even when they choose policies on trade, developmental aid, or environmental collaboration. International politics involves ethical quandaries, such as whether the effort to reduce terrorism justifies torture or whether it is acceptable to stand aside in the face of famine or genocide. It involves the highest aspirations of humankind, such as the dreams of ending war and eliminating global poverty. And it involves the lowest depths to which individuals and societies sink—mass murder, terrorism, and famine.

This book seeks to help you understand the puzzles that comprise international politics today. These puzzles challenge our intellect, and the choices we make or do not make, as citizens and as societies, will have far-reaching consequences. Wise choices may help avert wars, starvation, and environmental collapse. Poor choices can lead to disaster. That combination—difficult dilemmas and high stakes—is what makes international politics an exciting subject. That we live in a rapidly changing world only increases the risks and the challenges.

# PURPOSE: THE GOALS OF POLITICS

The scenarios in the previous section bring up questions of both *power* and *purpose*, two themes that run throughout this book. Power and purpose are central concepts in understanding political behavior, and are therefore at the center of the most widely applied theories of international politics. Each approach has particular notions of what constitutes power and of what the most important goals are that actors are pursuing. It is useful to come back to these concepts again and again. Neither purpose nor power is always evident. Focusing on them prompts us to make the implicit explicit, and in doing so reveals vital characteristics of the international political process.

What are various actors trying to achieve? **Purpose** refers to the goals of political action. In this book, we consider a wide range of actors, including states, individuals, bureaucracies, firms, nongovernmental organizations (NGOs), international organizations, and terrorist groups (see Figure 1.1). Regardless of the actors, we need to consider the purposes they are trying to achieve. To what extent do the actors on a given issue have shared or competing purposes? How do the purposes of states and of the international community change, and what happens when they do? These questions are central to the study of international politics.

# THE PROBLEM OF POWER

**Power** is an essential concept in the study of politics, but how to define it, and how it works, are widely debated. For our purposes, it is sufficient to highlight five different meanings of the term *power*. These five concepts, taken together, provide some sense of the range of ways power works in political science, and the range of approaches one can take in studying it.

The simplest and most widely used meaning of the term *power* is the ability to compel another actor to do (or not to do) something. When one country uses military force or economic sanctions to compel another to surrender some disputed territory, we see power as coercion.

In many cases, institutions are given authority on certain issues, and the rules of those organizations convey power. This "institutional power" can be far reaching, but it depends on the underlying agreements on which the institution is based—which in some cases seem unquestionable and in others are fragile. In Chapter 7, we examine the United Nations (UN), which has been given authority over a variety of functions. The UN General Assembly operates according to a one-state/one-vote rule, but the Security Council allows five "great powers" to veto any resolution, assigning a different level of institutional power to those five.

Sometimes we can get others to do what we want without threatening or outvoting them. In Chapter 4, our discussion of constructivist theory examines how shared norms (values) shape behavior. To the extent that we can appeal to shared values, and to the extent we have prestige, our arguments may carry more weight. This prestige, and the ability to use it persuasively, is sometimes called "soft power." If others share our purpose, we do not need to compel them. In this conception, purpose and power begin to overlap.

**purpose**
The goals that actors pursue, including the notion of "national interest." Whether actors see themselves as having shared or competing goals is a central concern.

**power**
The ability of an actor to achieve its goals. Exactly what constitutes power and how to measure it are vexing problems in international relations.

A bomb near Colombo, the capital of Sri Lanka, tears apart a packed passenger train. The tactic of suicide bombing was developed by the Tamil Tigers in Sri Lanka. How has the advent of suicide bombing changed the kinds of questions we ask about international politics?

**FIGURE 1.1**   Political actors in the Syrian Civil War.

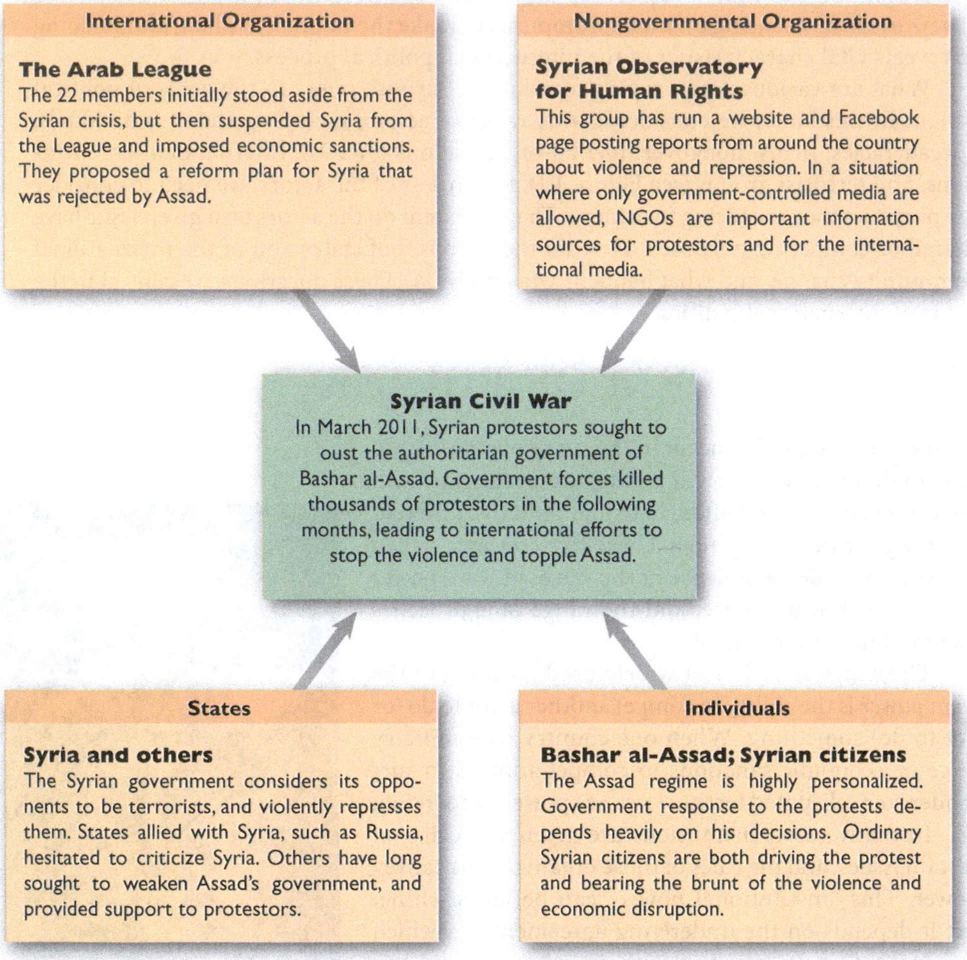

**International Organization**

**The Arab League**
The 22 members initially stood aside from the Syrian crisis, but then suspended Syria from the League and imposed economic sanctions. They proposed a reform plan for Syria that was rejected by Assad.

**Nongovernmental Organization**

**Syrian Observatory for Human Rights**
This group has run a website and Facebook page posting reports from around the country about violence and repression. In a situation where only government-controlled media are allowed, NGOs are important information sources for protestors and for the international media.

**Syrian Civil War**
In March 2011, Syrian protestors sought to oust the authoritarian government of Bashar al-Assad. Government forces killed thousands of protestors in the following months, leading to international efforts to stop the violence and topple Assad.

**States**

**Syria and others**
The Syrian government considers its opponents to be terrorists, and violently represses them. States allied with Syria, such as Russia, hesitated to criticize Syria. Others have long sought to weaken Assad's government, and provided support to protestors.

**Individuals**

**Bashar al-Assad; Syrian citizens**
The Assad regime is highly personalized. Government response to the protests depends heavily on his decisions. Ordinary Syrian citizens are both driving the protest and bearing the brunt of the violence and economic disruption.

Some assert that the ultimate power is to have social relations arranged in such a way that others serve one's interest voluntarily, and without thinking about it. This is referred to as "structural power" because it resides in the very structure of social relations. To have one's interests accepted uncritically as natural, or as the only way things can be, is to have influence that is not even noticed and, therefore, cannot be easily challenged. For example, scholars critical of capitalism (Chapter 4) point out that in capitalism most everyone accepts as natural an arrangement in which the owners of corporations make vastly more than employees, who may work equally hard. In this view, capitalism gives structural power to those who own firms.

A very different view sees power not as directed *at* other actors but *with* other actors. Put differently, this view stresses *power to* rather than *power over*. Liberal theorists (Chapter 3) and feminist theorists (Chapter 4) point out that the ability to collaborate with others to accomplish what one cannot accomplish alone is a form of collaborative power.

These five different meanings of power (and we could identify more) are summarized below:

1. The ability to compel, or coercive power.
2. Compulsion according to rules, or institutional power.
3. Persuasion, or soft power.
4. The power of unquestioned beliefs, or structural power.
5. The power gained by working together, or collaborative power.

Theorists disagree about which forms of power are most important. Those in the realist school (Chapter 3) tend to find compulsion most fundamental because it does not rely on any underlying agreement on the value of money, voting rules, or social norms. Adherents of other schools of thought argue that compulsion is a very expensive way to get things done, and that a great number of goals cannot be gained with it. They find the various kinds of power that do not rely on compulsion to be more important, and argue that most of what goes on in international politics is driven by these other notions of power. Debating which kind of power is most important is less important than recognizing that there are very different ways to define it, and very different ways in which power and purpose are linked. In compulsion, there is a clear distinction between the goal and the power used to achieve it. In structural power, having others accept one's goal is itself a form of power.

## PUZZLES WITH HIGH STAKES

International politics today is a series of puzzles with immense consequences. A great deal—including money and lives—depends on the answers and solutions we reach. Unfortunately, we are unable to answer many questions in international politics with certainty. The problem is not that we have no answers but rather that, for most important questions, we have two or more good answers, along with considerable debate concerning which is correct. A few of the questions that are most prominent today can be used to illustrate this point.

AP Photo/Tatan Syuflana

- **What are the sources of terrorism?** It seems that religion often plays an important role. But of all the religious people in the world, very few, even among the most devout, commit terrorism or support it. Therefore, some people argue that individual frustration and alienation cause specific individuals to become terrorists. Others point to the role of poverty. Ultimately, there is no simple explanation for why one person becomes a terrorist and another does not, or why one group seems to condone terrorism while another does not. Yet governments and individuals must make decisions every day on the basis of answers to these questions, even if those answers are tentative.

A polluted canal runs through Jakarta, Indonesia. Gaps between the richest and the poorest are increasing worldwide. What are the causes of poverty? Does the globalization of trade and finance help or hurt?

- **Are democracies more peaceful than countries with other forms of government?** It seems natural that they would be, and recent U.S. presidents of both parties have asserted that this is an important consideration in their policies. Although the relationship between democracy and war is complex and hotly debated, important actions such as the invasion of Iraq, intervention in the former Yugoslavia, and the provision of economic aid to Russia were justified in part by the belief that if outsiders help countries become democratic, these countries will be peaceful and war with them will be less likely. However, a pro-democratic revolution in Ukraine seems to have spurred conflict, not reduced it, and the revolution in Libya descended into civil war. What is the relationship between democracy—and democratization—and conflict?

- **What are the causes and consequences of poverty around the world?** Many people argue that global poverty is a result of the way the international economy works: Competition from advanced economies makes it impossible for poor countries to succeed. Many others, however, make the opposite argument: Competition, they say, increases efficiency and wealth. Poor countries would benefit from more international competition, not less. There is evidence for both arguments. For the lives of billions of people, making the right call on this issue is essential.

- **Should we, and could we, turn back globalization?** Is globalization a force to be feared or a force for good? Many people fear the consequences of globalization and argue that governments should take steps to limit it. Others disagree, arguing that globalization brings many benefits, including economic growth and better government. Still others argue that, whether we like it or not, globalization is an inevitable economic and social process and that those who try to fight it will be left behind.

- **Is the United States a declining power?** Is China's rise inevitable? What might slow or reverse the perceived decline of the United States or sidetrack China's rise? What are the forces that lead to the rise and decline of the power and influence of different countries? What might be the consequences when a new dominant power emerges? These questions have been applied to history as well as to contemporary cases. Leaders around the world are seeking to answer them, and to apply the answers successfully to their own states.

- **Is the international community obliged to intervene when a country's government is abusing the human rights of its own people?** Beliefs about the circumstances in which outsiders can, should, or must intervene are shifting. Traditionally, interference in others' "internal affairs" was generally prohibited, but that changed during the wars in the former Yugoslavia in the 1990s. The North Atlantic Treaty Organization (NATO) intervened in Libya in 2011 to prevent Muammar Gaddafi from massacring opposition forces. In 2012, a similar situation arose in Syria. If intervention was permitted, was it *required*? The policies adopted in one case can create difficult precedents for others.

Often we cannot delay making a decision until we have arrived at a perfect understanding of the problem. We must learn to evaluate the different arguments on a pressing question and decide which we (as individuals or as a society) find most compelling. We base our policies on answers to questions, even when we are highly uncertain about those answers. In other words, we are forced to choose a side in key debates even when we would rather delay. Academic debates, therefore, have immense practical significance.

# THE GOALS OF THE BOOK

This book aims to help you evaluate everyday arguments about international politics and foreign policy by connecting these everyday arguments to scholarly research in the field. Friends, parents, teachers, bloggers, and "experts" routinely make assertions—often with great confidence—about how international politics works and about what policies governments, groups, firms, and individuals should adopt.

Every argument about politics and policies is based on an identifiable series of assumptions. We can scrutinize those assumptions and decide whether we agree. Similarly, each argument is supported by at least some evidence. We can evaluate that evidence and identify its strengths and weaknesses. For each argument, there are competing arguments based on different assumptions and different evidence (or on a different interpretation of the same evidence). We want to be able to identify and explore the competing arguments. We want to understand where those different interpretations come from. This is the focus of the academic field of international politics.

In sum, we want to accomplish three basic goals.

- First, we want to better our own understanding of international politics. More than learning facts, this means learning how to ask the right questions and to evaluate evidence about possible answers. This will allow us to achieve our second goal.

- Second, we want to make informed evaluations about how the world works and about what choices should be made. We might use these evaluations to decide whom to vote for, where to invest, or where to volunteer.

- Third, we want to be able to engage in intelligent debate about important public policy issues. Whether the goal is to convince someone to vote for a particular candidate, to gain support for a particular policy, or simply to challenge our parents, we want to be able to bring theory and evidence together to create compelling arguments.

# THE SCIENCE OF INTERNATIONAL POLITICS

Some statements about international politics are very general, whereas others are quite specific. In either case, the goal of analysis is to decide whether to accept or to reject an assertion.

International politics is generally considered a part of the discipline of political science. The idea that there can be a science of politics is often regarded with skepticism. However, whether or not we admit it, we all behave as though we can discover patterns in politics. We form generalizations about what tends to happen in certain kinds of circumstances, and about what we might do to promote some outcomes and prevent others. Without some belief that we can explain and predict political behavior, our choices would be completely random. Political science cannot aspire to the same level of certainty as physics, but it has a crucial role to play in prompting us to make our beliefs about causes and consequences as explicit as possible, and then to subject them to scrutiny.

How do we do this? The branch of political science known as **methodology** studies how best to verify or reject different hypotheses (assertions) about politics. However, there is profound disagreement among political scientists about which methodological

**methodology**

The set of principles, strategies, and practical steps used to evaluate competing hypotheses.

# THE GEOGRAPHY CONNECTION

## PREDICTING INSTABILITY

This map shows the "political instability index" of countries, as assessed by the Economist Intelligence Unit, part of the English newsmagazine *The Economist.* We want to judge instability in the world for any number of reasons: It could affect the value of investments, the flow of migrants, the supply of goods, the security of democracy, or the need to intervene militarily. But what do we mean by "stability"? And how do we measure it? These are the kinds of questions to which academics, investment bankers, intelligence services, and humanitarian organizations devote considerable energy. Predicting unrest is difficult, but success can help actors prepare for or even prevent the worst consequences.

## Critical Thinking Questions

1. How would you define "stability" in international affairs?

2. What things that can easily be measured do you think would be the best predictors?

3. How would you figure out whether your model was better than those of your classmates?

Political Instability Index

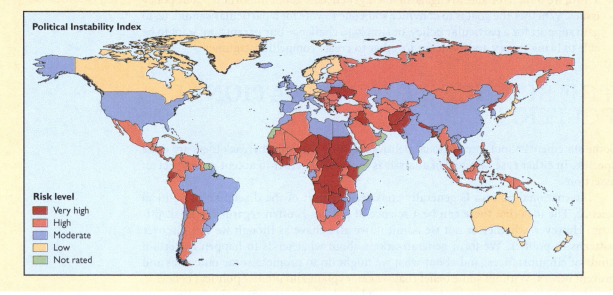

**Political Instability Index**

**Risk level**
- Very high
- High
- Moderate
- Low
- Not rated

approaches are best. There is equally profound disagreement about the extent to which the study of politics can be or should aim to be *scientific* in the way that term is used in the natural sciences.

Natural scientists perform laboratory experiments in which they isolate and control the variables they are studying. Political scientists, in contrast, are unable to perform experiments on world leaders or on the effects of different policies. Having seen the

# THE POLICY CONNECTION

## ACADEMIC AND POLICY DEBATES

The study of international politics and the practice of foreign policy are tightly linked. People study international politics because they hope to make better decisions concerning the real world. Every foreign policy is based on some understanding of how the world works and of what the results of different policies would likely be. For every headline one reads about a foreign policy debate, there is a corresponding academic debate. Every policy argument, boiled down to its essentials, is a causal argument: "If we do X, the result will be Y." The obvious follow-up question is: "How do you know?" In the public debate, we are often not very rigorous about scrutinizing these propositions.

The job of the scholar, the student, and the citizen is to examine these claims more rigorously. This means understanding the assumptions and arguments behind a particular policy position and evaluating them critically. Chapter 9, for example, considers efforts to combat terrorism and fundamentalist insurgency. If policy makers believe that terrorism is caused by poverty, they will adopt a particular set of policies. If they believe that terrorism is caused by an absence of democracy, they will adopt a very different set of policies. Because resources are limited, it is important not to waste money and effort on policies that will not work.

Chapter 11 addresses international economic crises, including the one that began in 2008 and continues today in some countries. A central dilemma for governments has been whether to borrow and spend more to help economies grow, or whether to borrow and spend less to reduce national debts. Equally important for policy makers is how to coordinate policies with other governments so that states do not enact policies that negate each other. These debates lead us into macroeconomics. What is the danger that reduced government spending will push economies into deeper recession? Is it bigger or smaller than the danger of a debt crisis? A larger question is why traditionally strong economies (United States, Western Europe) were hit harder by this crisis than developing economies we used to associate with crisis. After years of economic preaching to the developing countries, do the "advanced" economies now need to take some of their own advice?

Chapter 14 addresses international environmental problems. In the debate over the scientific evidence for global warming, we see clearly the link between scholarship, politics, and policy making. We look at the political, rather than the scientific, questions. What are the barriers to a more effective global treaty to prevent climate change? What are the economic effects of different measures? These are widely debated, and even when there is agreement on the costs, there is no agreement on who should pay those costs. Most frightening, perhaps, what are the possible international political and economic effects if little is done and climate change begins to have dramatic consequences?

### Critical Thinking Questions

1. Identify a current debate (other than those mentioned here). What are the major causal arguments in favor of one policy or another?

2. Can you envision how one might design a study to assess the validity of these arguments?

3. What obstacles do you run into?

German reaction to the election of François Hollande as President of France in 2012, we cannot run another trial in which someone else wins and then measure the different reaction. We have only the data that we can collect and observe from the real world, and we struggle to find valid comparisons and to control for factors that may skew our results. Even within the social sciences, political science offers fewer clear-cut concepts, methods, and measurements than economics or psychology. We are not seeking "laws of nature" that have no exceptions, like the law of gravity, but rather generalizable tendencies in the patterns of international affairs.

This book uses a general model of political science represented by the following process.

1.  Begin with a question, such as "What causes wars?" The question must be clearly defined. For example, the analysis should specify whether "wars" includes both civil wars and international wars, or just international wars.

2.  Identify potential answers (hypotheses). These may come from history, from political theory, from conventional wisdom, or from some observed pattern. Two prominent hypotheses about the causes of international war are: (1) war results from an imbalance in military power, and (2) war results from the choices of aggressive leaders.

3.  Determine what patterns we would observe if each hypothesis were true. What patterns would be evident if war resulted from an imbalance of power? Every time there was an imbalance of power, there would be war, and there would never be a war without an imbalance of power.

4.  Decide how to define and measure the key factors. How is power defined? How is it measured? How much imbalance is supposed to matter? Issues of definition and measurement lead to a great deal of controversy about findings. Difficulty in defining and measuring power makes it difficult to definitively resolve the relationship between power and war.

5.  Choose a research method. How will we link data to a hypothesis to reach a conclusion? We might look for a statistical pattern in a large number of cases: Is there a statistical correlation between the distribution of power and war? Alternatively, we might examine just a few cases in great depth to see if a link can be established between cause and effect. In this example, we might look closely at diplomatic records to see the role that an imbalance of power played in the thinking of key leaders. Or we might engage in a more interpretive approach. For example, to assess the role of aggressive leaders, we might analyze the rhetoric of national leaders and the ways in which they express aggression.

6.  Evaluate the findings. In politics, researchers rarely find incontrovertible support for a hypothesis. Thus, instead of asking whether a hypothesis is true or false, political scientists ask whether it is a better or worse explanation than competing explanations. For example, if we find a war in which there was not an imbalance of power, do we reject that hypothesis? Not if it fits with the data better than any other hypothesis. In that case, we would accept that an imbalance of power is an important factor in causing wars and continue to look for other factors that might explain observed deviations from this pattern.

There are many variants on the research process in political science, ranging from sophisticated computational analyses of "big data" to equally sophisticated interpretations of a single case or of a pattern of discourse. The important point is that we first ask, "What is causing this phenomenon?" Then, when we have a tentative answer, we should ask, "Why is this answer more credible than another?" Skepticism about conclusions is perhaps even more important in the social sciences than in the natural sciences. Sometimes the process is frustrating, because two contradictory ideas may seem to have nearly equally convincing support, or because it seems like every explanation for a phenomenon (such as war) has major shortcomings. This is what makes the study of politics difficult. It is also what makes it so dramatic and compelling.

In the natural sciences (and some social sciences), the ability to predict future events is the main criterion by which theories are judged. If a theory is valid, it ought to be able to predict future outcomes. In political science, and especially in international relations, consistently successful prediction is rare. Even reaching consensus on explanations of past patterns is elusive. Thus, the study of international relations is less about learning the accepted truths revealed by scientific inquiry than about understanding the ongoing debates among the most compelling theories. Progress is achieved more by eliminating explanations that seem plausible than by discovering scientific laws.

Brazilian presidential candidates Aécio Neves (L) and Dilma Rousseff at a televised debate, October 2014.

# THE ROLE OF THEORY

On the surface, academic political scientists talk about international politics very differently than do policy makers or journalists. Whereas policy makers and journalists concentrate on *specific* problems and look for specific answers, political scientists ask *general* questions about how international politics works. Despite these apparent differences, specific answers to specific questions are almost always linked to general explanations of how international politics works. These general explanations are called *theories*. Sometimes policy makers scorn the academic theories of political scientists, viewing them as too abstract to be relevant to pressing world issues.[1] Yet this superficial distinction is misleading. Even though policy makers rarely talk about theory explicitly, they use theories of international relations constantly in evaluating problems, whether they recognize it or not.

Several examples will illustrate the underlying importance of international relations theory for policy making. What is the best way to convince aspiring nuclear weapons states, such as Iran and North Korea, to give up their nuclear weapons programs? Some people argue that raising the cost of such programs—through political and economic sanctions and, if necessary, military action—will persuade potential nuclear states that the cost is simply too high. Others contend that such threats only increase the perceived insecurity of the governments in question and, therefore, increase their determination to get nuclear weapons. Still others look to domestic politics within the potential nuclear states, arguing that as long as their leaders get domestic political benefits from standing up to outside powers, there

The village of Aslam in northern Yemen. Yemen has been a source of terrorism. Is poverty an important cause?

# THE HISTORY CONNECTION

## HOW HISTORY INFLUENCES CONTEMPORARY INTERNATIONAL POLITICS

This book, like any study of international politics, makes frequent references to historical examples—ranging in time from last year to 2500 years ago. We might ask, therefore, what connection events from the distant past have with the study of international politics today, in an age of cell phones, the Internet, and global mass culture. World leaders as well as scholars constantly look back in history to try to gain insight into the current problems they are grappling with. For some, history is a source of lessons. For others, it is a source of data. Either way, history is the primary place to look in evaluating theories. The philosopher George Santayana asserted the importance of history for leaders in his frequently quoted warning: "Those who do not know history are condemned to repeat it."

History influences our thinking about international politics in three ways. First, it powerfully conditions notions of what is right and wrong, especially relating to questions of territory. For example, when Russia invaded Ukraine in 2014, Russian leaders pointed to history—large parts of Ukraine were at one time part of the Russian Empire or the Soviet Union—to justify seizing Ukrainian territory. Israel and Palestinians can both point to different times in history to support the territorial arrangements they prefer. History can also provide a strong sense of grievance, as in the view that China was exploited for many decades and now must fight for its rightful place.

History also provides analogies and lessons that we use to understand—sometimes very poorly—contemporary events. Thus, many compared Russia's tactics in annexing Crimea to Hitler's in taking over Czechoslovakia in 1938.

As Chapter 6 explores in more detail, the "lessons" taken from the rise of Hitler have been applied widely since then.

Finally, history provides data for various kinds of political science analyses of political phenomena. Statistical studies of all the wars since 1815 have been a major source of evidence for and against the democratic peace theory (Chapter 5), and case studies of the "July Crisis" that preceded World War I and the Cuban Missile Crisis of 1962 have informed much scholarship on how to resolve such crises peacefully. Those two cases are so widely studied in part because of their intrinsic importance and in part because detailed diplomatic records are publicly available.

Each chapter of this book includes a discussion showing how events in the twenty-first century are not as historically unique or fundamentally new as some believe them to be. The text also looks at the ways in which contemporary scholars and policy makers have tried to apply the lessons of the past to the problems they face today.

## Critical Thinking Questions

1. Identify a current international issue. What historical examples seem most comparable?

2. Would other students in your class likely agree? Why or why not?

3. Do you think students in Canada, China, Germany, or Russia would identify with the same relevant examples? Why or why not?

*Robert Kaplan, Warrior Politics: Why Leadership Demands a Pagan Ethos (New York Random House, 2002).*

is little that external actors can do to dissuade them. Each of these answers is based on a general explanation—a theory—of what factors drive state behavior.

Why did the United States, after World War II, spend billions of dollars building up its former enemies in Germany and Japan? Why did Western states contribute significant aid to their former enemies in the Soviet bloc after the Cold War? Why did the United States try to install a democratic rather than an authoritarian government in Iraq in 2003–2004? In each case, an underlying theory motivated these significant actions: the belief that democratic countries are much less likely to be aggressive and warlike. If this argument is true, money spent on democratization is a good investment because it will make unnecessary much larger military expenditures later.

Why did the United States fight a decade-long war in Vietnam? Many leaders believed in the "domino theory," which stated that if one state in the region became communist, others would likely follow, falling like dominoes. The theory was based partly on German aggression prior to World War II, and partly on Russian expansion into Eastern Europe after World War II.

These examples demonstrate that general notions, or theories, about causes and effects motivate all sorts of actions in international affairs. This is true whether or not policy makers recognize that their generalizations about the world can be called "theories" and whether or not those theories have been scrutinized and tested for validity. Some theories have worked out badly when applied. For example, a theory derived from the lessons of World War I, that confronting aggression could lead to unnecessary war, led to decisions that contributed to World War II.

Policy makers are concerned above all not with generalities but with specific problems at specific points in time. However, even in the context of a single case, theory is necessary for action. Without predicting the likely results of different choices, we cannot act intelligently. Thus, we theorize whether we want to or not, and any given policy can be "unpeeled" to uncover the theoretical assumptions behind it. The study of international politics aims to make those theories explicit and to subject them to scrutiny. The economist John Maynard Keynes put it bluntly: "Practical men, who believe themselves to be quite exempt from any intellectual influences, are usually the slaves of some defunct economist."[2]

## WHAT IS A THEORY?

In political science, the word *theory* is used fairly specifically: A **theory** is a generalized explanation of a set of essentially similar phenomena. Two things should be emphasized. First, a theory is an *explanation*. It answers the question, "Why?" A theory specifies a particular effect that is being explained and the causes of that effect. Second, a theory is *generalized*. It seeks to explain not a single event but a series of comparable events. Thus, political science does not advance a theory of World War I or a theory of the establishment the World Trade Organization. Rather, political scientists develop theories of how wars occur or of trade liberalization, but not of a single event. Instead, there are *descriptions* of single events. This specific usage of the word *theory* in social science differs slightly from the conventional usage, in which the term is sometimes used to label any conjecture about a single event, such as a "theory" of who killed John F. Kennedy or a "theory" of why a certain candidate won a certain election.

However, as this last example implies, there can often be a connection between a theory and an attempt to account for a particular event. To understand why a specific event occurred (such as the outcome of an election or the outbreak of a war), analysts almost always consider the factors that have been important in related cases. The question

**theory**

A generalized explanation of a set of comparable phenomena.

of why World War I occurred is related to the question "What causes wars?" Similarly, understanding the sources of the World Trade Organization is related to understanding the general causes of trade liberalization.

Thus, theory is built on an underlying assumption that specific events are not unique and do not have unique causes. Rather, we assume that most important events are single instances of broader patterns. If we want to prevent wars, we need some notion of what causes them. This requires a supposition that different wars have something in common. When stated so starkly, this idea will appear problematical to many. For example, it might seem dubious to equate the causes of World War I with the causes of World War II. However, if the lessons of the past are to be applied to the problems of today, we must assume that events in the future are somehow related to those in the past. There is a big difference between assuming that similar events have something in common and assuming that they are identical. To develop a theory of wars, we need only assume that they have some causes in common.

Historically, there have been both successes and failures in the effort to apply theory to policy. Following World War I, the dominant theories of war focused on the absence of international law. Therefore, much effort was expended on developing the League of Nations and treaties outlawing war. The problems with this approach were demonstrated at the outbreak of World War II. After World War II, however, theories of international relations were more successfully applied with the formation of the Bretton Woods trade system, which was founded on the theory that free trade would increase prosperity, and that theory was borne out in the postwar economic boom among the members of the Bretton Woods institutions.

Today, some of the most pressing policy issues are prompting new efforts to advance theoretical understanding of international politics. While police and military forces work every day to intercept specific terrorist threats, scholars seek to better understand the underlying sources of terrorism. Is terrorism based primarily in religion? In poverty? In political frustration? Answering these questions requires looking for the commonalities across different terrorist movements, even while acknowledging that they are all unique in some ways.

Egyptian antigovernment protesters on their way to Cairo's central Tahrir Square. Cairo, February 1, 2011.

## THE USES OF THEORY

Theory has three related main purposes: explanation, prediction, and prescription. First, theory is used to explain the common causes shared by a group of related events (explanation). Second, theory is used to apply such explanations to future events, to predict what might result from existing conditions or from some new event or policy (prediction). Third, theory is used to help policy makers and citizens choose the most effective policies for a given goal (prescription). In all of these tasks, theory becomes a means to simplify a reality that is extremely complex.

In evaluating different theories, it is important to keep in mind that a theory deliberately abstracts from reality, leaving much detail aside. Theories identify which parts of a complex event deserve immediate attention and which are of secondary importance. Therefore, when a particular fact or a case apparently contradicts a theory, this does not mean that the theory has no utility. Rather, the theory must be evaluated on the basis of whether, overall, it provides more or less understanding than competing explanations of the same general phenomenon.

## NORMATIVE THEORY: THE PURPOSE OF ACTION

Besides the type of theory that increases our ability to explain, predict, and prescribe, there is another kind of international relations theory with a very different goal: establishing what the purpose of political action should be. Such a theory is called a **normative theory**. Whereas explanatory theory asks, "How does the world work?" normative theory asks, "What goals should we pursue?" and "What are acceptable and unacceptable ways to behave?" Normative theory can address a wide range of moral and ethical concerns, and these will crop up repeatedly throughout this book. Many discussions assume that certain goals are worth pursuing; these normative assumptions are often taken as self-evident and therefore not discussed or debated. Sometimes these assumptions are noncontroversial, but at other times they warrant serious scrutiny.

For example, although much discussion in international politics centers on how to prevent wars, no theorist spends much time asserting that war is bad because this seems self-evident. Therefore, theorists can move on to asking how to prevent war. However, in practice, we often find ourselves agonizing over whether war, as bad as it is, is worse than other possibilities. In World War II, fighting a horrendous war with millions of casualties was seen as a lesser evil than allowing Nazi Germany to rule the world. In the 1990s, many people who generally thought of themselves as opposed to military force advocated strongly for the use of military force to prevent the "ethnic cleansing" taking place in the former Yugoslavia. Although they still believed war was bad, they believed genocide was worse. Thus, even normative arguments that seem self-evident often are not. Some theorists believe that unquestioned normative beliefs often serve the interests of the powerful and that a primary goal of research should be to investigate how some goals come to predominate over others.

**normative theory**
A theory that aims to establish the proper goals of political action.

## LEVELS OF ANALYSIS

This book considers a variety of explanations of how international politics works and how states behave. At times you may find the range of theories bewildering. Unfortunately, it is not easy to reduce the number of plausible explanations down to one or two. To envision how explanations relate to one another, it is useful to group them into different schools of thought.

ARPL HIP/The Image Works

Adolf Hitler speaks at a rally. Are the decisions of individual leaders responsible for different international outcomes? If so, the individual level of analysis is important.

An initial way to categorize theories is according to their **level of analysis**. Level of analysis identifies where the analysis focuses—where the most important variation occurs. Is the main actor in the model a single individual, a larger aggregation such as a bureaucracy, or an even larger aggregation such as the state? Every analysis focuses on one aggregation and holds the other aggregations constant for the purposes of analysis. In an influential study on the causes of war, Kenneth Waltz argues that one can explain wars at any of three levels of analysis.[3] Individual-level theories see the cause of war in individuals, either generally (for example, in human nature) or specifically (in the characteristics of specific leaders). State-level theories locate the cause of war in the nature of states. For example, some types of governments might be more prone to war than others, or some states might have profound grievances that cause them to seek redress through war. System-level theories, which Waltz prefers, see the causes of war in the characteristics of the international system. War, in this view, is caused by factors that extend beyond any single state, such as the distribution of power and the number of "great powers" in the system.

Other theorists have proposed four or even five levels of analysis because they break the state level down into more than one level.[4] This book also explores explanations at a fourth level, the "substate" level, between the state and individual levels. Analyses at the substate level examine the bureaucracies and small groups that make foreign policies, as well as the influence of interest groups and public opinion on those policies (see Chapters 5 and 6). Debating the "right" number of levels is less important than understanding the concept. Thinking about the level of analysis helps illuminate where different theories look for answers; it shows what they focus on and what they de-emphasize. More important, it helps explain why theories that are compelling sometimes tend to speak past one another. It is fairly easy, for example, for theorists who hold two different system-level theories to debate each other. It is more difficult for a theorist who prefers a system-level theory to debate one who prefers an individual-level theory, because the questions they ask and the evidence they look at are different.

Following this introduction, Chapter 2 surveys the history of international politics. Chapters 3 and 4 investigate theories of international politics. With important exceptions, the main schools of thought covered in these chapters tend to seek explanations at the system level, bringing in theories at other levels where needed to add detail. Chapter 5 presents explanations primarily at the state level, examining the argument that democracies are more peaceful than other states, as well as the role of interest groups, public opinion, and the media. Chapter 6 presents explanations at the substate and individual levels. These include the various branches of government, bureaucracies, the small groups of advisers on whom leaders often rely, and the individual leaders themselves. Chapter 7 examines

**level of analysis**

The unit (individual, state, or system) that a theory focuses on in its general explanation.

## THE CONNECTION TO YOU

# HOW DOES INTERNATIONAL POLITICS INFLUENCE YOUR LIFE?

How does international politics influence your life? And how do you influence international politics? For many people, the subject may seem distant from everyday life. Here we consider the ways in which an average college student is connected to international politics.

Start with the clothes you are wearing. Were any of them made in the country you live in? Probably not if you live and shop in North America or Europe. What makes it possible for those clothes, and other consumer goods, to get from Asia, where most are made, to the rest of the world? Trade, of course. But international trade rests upon a dense web of international agreements and institutions. These include trade agreements that provide for the movement of goods and financial agreements that allow for the movement of money, as well as legal practices that facilitate fulfillment of contracts. Your grandparents did not consume vast amounts of consumer goods made in China, because until the 1970s China was isolated both diplomatically and economically from the rest of the world, much as North Korea is today. In sum, our access to cheap and plentiful consumer goods is a direct result of changes in international politics in recent decades.

Have you experienced war, either as a combatant or a bystander? Although much violence in the world today is rooted in civil conflicts, international war is still a prominent threat. The United States has been involved in Afghanistan since 2001, making this the longest period of warfare in the nation's history. Many other states have been involved in that conflict or in others. What have been the effects of these wars on combatants? What have been the effects on their families? What are the indirect economic effects?

How do you influence international politics? What is the economic and political impact of your consumption of goods produced in one country versus another? Each purchase has an infinitesimal influence on wages, exchange rates, and tax revenues in different countries.

Have you taken conscious steps to influence affairs in other countries? Have you undertaken a mission trip? Donated to an organization dedicated to aiding people in another country? "Liked" a Facebook post or forwarded a link on a foreign policy issue?

Have you sought to directly influence your country's foreign policy? How? In some cases, one might take foreign policy positions into account in voting for a candidate (or working on a campaign). One might also donate money to organizations promoting a particular policy or supporting a foreign country.

How would the answers to all of these questions change if you lived in a country very different from the one you live in? If you lived in Afghanistan, for example, how might you answer questions relating to buying cell phones, to experiencing war, or to international aid efforts?

In subsequent chapters, we continue to ask you to think about the connection to you.

## Critical Thinking Questions

1. How would your parents or grandparents have answered these questions when they were your age?

2. How do you think people will answer them twenty-five or fifty years from now?

3. Do most of your peers view themselves as participants in international affairs, as bystanders, or as completely disconnected?

transnational actors and international organizations, complementing the focus on domestic actors in Chapters 5 and 6. The book then turns to specific issues, including security (Chapters 8–9), international political economy (Chapters 10–12), international law and norms (Chapter 13), and international environmental issues (Chapter 14). The conclusion (Chapter 15) looks to the future in light of the theories introduced and the issues discussed.

By the end of the book, you will be able to see how the approaches developed in the early chapters can help address current and emerging issues. Although a goal of any such book is to teach a certain amount about what the world looks like today and about the main approaches to understanding it, these are means to a greater end. The ultimate goal is to be able to tackle new and unfamiliar problems and to become a critical participant, whether as citizen or as policy maker.

## SUMMARY

- International politics is a subject about which we constantly debate what we know and how we know it. These are debates with high stakes because policy making requires acting on current knowledge, even when that knowledge is imperfect.

- Power and purpose are central concepts in understand political behavior, and are central to most major theories of international politics. Power is a concept that is extremely difficult to understand as what counts as power differs from situation to situation.

- Theories are used to explain, predict, and prescribe political behavior. Political scientists disagree about what is the best methodology to use to verify or reject hypotheses. Many approaches begin with a question,

identify potential answers, determine patterns, decide how to define and measure key factors, choose a research method, and evaluate the findings. Normative theories establish what the purpose of political action should be. Theories of international politics are, therefore, not merely of academic interest. The study of international politics aims to make these theories explicit and to subject them to scrutiny so that they can help provide the best possible answers to the urgent questions facing governments, societies, and individuals.

- Levels of analyses are the unit (individual, substate, state, or system) that a theory focuses on to explain a political behavior.

## KEY CONCEPTS

1. Purpose
2. Power
3. Methodology

4. Theory
5. Normative theory
6. Levels of analysis

## STUDY QUESTIONS

1. A theory that aims to establish the proper goals of political action is
   a. a level of analysis
   b. an explanatory theory
   c. power
   d. a normative theory

2. The goals that actors pursue, including the notion of "national interest" is
   a. a purpose
   b. power
   c. an explanatory theory
   d. a methodology

3. Thinking scientifically about international politics requires assuming
   a. politics follows the same rigid laws as physics.
   b. international events can be compared scientifically even if they are not identical.
   c. testing hypotheses about international politics can reliably determine if they are true or false.
   d. None of the above.

4. Which of the following is an example of a theory?
   a. Nationalism causes wars.
   b. Economic distress caused the French Revolution.
   c. Power is the ability of an actor to achieve its goals.
   d. All of the above.

5. Which of the following represents the proper order of steps a political scientist would need to test a hypothesis?
   a. Ask a question, evaluate the findings, decide how to define and measure key factors, and choose a research method
   b. Determine patterns, ask a question, decide how to define and measure key factors, identify potential answers, and choose a research method
   c. Choose a research method, determine patterns, decide how to define and measure key factors, and evaluate the findings
   d. Ask a question, identify potential answers, determine patterns, decide how to define and measure key factors, choose a research method, and evaluate the findings

6. Which of the following is a level of analysis of international relations theories?
   a. individual
   b. state
   c. system
   d. All of the above.

7. What purposes do theories and normative theories serve?

8. What are the limitations of the "science" of international politics?

9. How do theories of international politics relate to the policies that various actors adopt?

10. How does the level of analysis we choose influence the kinds of answers we get?

11. In what ways can the study of international politics take a scientific approach?

12. What are the limitations of the "science" of international politics?

13. How do theories of international politics relate to the policies that various actors adopt?

14. What is a theory?

15. How does normative theory differ from explanatory theory?

16. How does the level of analysis we choose influence the kinds of answers we get?

[Correct answers: 1 d; 2 a; 3 b; 4 a; 5 d; 6 d]

## END NOTES

1. Harvard professor turned member of the Canadian Parliament Michael Ignatieff is one who holds this view. See "Getting Iraq Wrong," *New York Times Magazine*, August 5, 2007, at http://www.nytimes.com/2007/08/05/magazine/05iraq-t.html.

2. John Maynard Keynes, *The General Theory of Employment, Interest, and Money* (New Delhi: Atlantic Publishers, 2007 [1936]), p. 351.

3. Kenneth N. Waltz, *Man, the State, and War* (New York: Columbia University Press, 1959).

4. Arnold Wolfers, "The Actors in International Politics," in W. T. R. Fox, ed., *Theoretical Aspects of International Relations* (South Bend, IN: University of Notre Dame Press, 1959), pp. 83–106; Robert Jervis, "Perception and the Level of Analysis Problem," in *Perception and Misperception in International Politics* (Princeton, NJ: Princeton University Press, 1976), pp. 13–31; and James Rosenau, "Pre-Theories and Theories of Foreign Policy," in J. Rosenau, ed., *The Scientific Study of Foreign Policy* (New York: The Free Press, 1971), pp. 95–151.

# 2

## CHAPTER OUTLINE

The Dome of the Rock, Jerusalem. History has an enormous impact on contemporary international politics.

Peter Zaharov/Shutterstock.com

# THE HISTORICAL EVOLUTION OF INTERNATIONAL POLITICS

## Learning Objectives

2-1 Describe the major developments in the history of international politics.

2-2 Understand the evolution of the international system.

2-3 Explain the significance of the Westphalian system.

2-4 Interpret the role of colonialism in transforming the international system.

2-5 Summarize the causes and significance of World War I, World War II, and the Cold War.

2-6 Identify the major developments of the post–World War II system.

2-7 Discuss the extent to which the international system is characterized by continuity and change.

## CONSIDER THE CASE

# CHINA'S HISTORY AND FUTURE

The rise of China is one of the most important developments in recent years. In the context of recent decades, China is a new player on the world stage. But China has a remarkable history stretching back 5000 years. How did such an ancient civilization become a new player on the world stage? And how does that mix of old and new influence China's role in the world?

For many centuries, China's major external interactions were with nomads from the Central Asian steppes, against whom the Great Wall was built for protection. As Europe began expanding around the world in the sixteenth century, contact with China grew, and Portugal founded a colony at Macao in the 1560s. China remained relatively isolated, however, until the weakening of the Qing dynasty in the nineteenth century left China open to exploitation by Western colonial powers.

By the early nineteenth century, British merchants were buying increasing amounts of merchandise (much of it tea) from the Chinese for resale in Britain. Then, as today, China was a potentially lucrative market, and the British profited from selling opium produced in their colony in India to China. The Chinese sought to limit this trade because of its negative influence on their society and economy, but after defeat by the British Navy in the Opium War, the Chinese were compelled in 1842 to sign the treaty of Nanjing, which handed control of Hong Kong to Britain (which held it until 1997) and opened other port cities to unlimited British imports of opium and other goods. Other European powers and the United States then forced similar concessions, known as the "unequal treaties."

Internal division and external domination continued after the overthrow of the Qing Dynasty in 1911. In the 1930s, large parts of China were colonized by Japan, which committed massive atrocities against civilians. Throughout the Japanese occupation, an internal battle continued between the Chinese Communist Party under Mao Zedong and the Nationalist (Koumintang) Party. When the Communists finally defeated the Koumintang in 1949, establishing the People's Republic of China, the Koumintang retreated to the offshore island of Taiwan and formed the independent Republic of China with Taipei as its capital.

The United Nations, dominated by the United States and its allies, refused to recognize the communist government in Beijing and instead recognized the government of Taiwan as the government of "China." Thus, China was completely isolated diplomatically. Mao's imposition of a totalitarian version of peasant communism impoverished the country, caused millions of deaths, and furthered China's international isolation. By the 1960s, China was as much at odds with the communist Soviet Union as with the capitalist United States. China's isolation began to ebb in 1972 when U.S. President Richard Nixon shocked the world by traveling to China to meet its leaders. In 1977, the United States recognized the government in Beijing as the government of China.

Even after this, however, the move toward global power started slowly. After Mao died in 1976, his successor Deng Xiaoping gradually allowed markets to take hold in China, but the Communist Party maintained control of the state and the economy. Western firms sought access to China's gigantic and cheap workforce and to the huge number of potential consumers there. China sought access to world markets and to investment but insisted on trading on terms that preserved China's sovereignty and the control of the Communist Party. China's admission to the World Trade Organization in 1995 further accelerated China's integration into the world economy.

In less than fifty years, China has gone from an impoverished and isolated country to a major global economic and political power. Yet it remains deeply cautious both about internal division and about exploitation from outside. Internally, China maintains a highly authoritarian political system and severely limits human rights. Externally, China guards its sovereignty closely. Consciously or unconsciously, understandings of history influence the way people view problems—the grievances they feel, the goals they set, and the policies they adopt to pursue those goals. An understanding of the historical context of international politics is, therefore, essential to comprehending today's issues.

Construction cranes in Beijing, 2014. Beijing and other Chinese cities are rapidly being transformed.

WANG ZHAO/Getty Images

Where did today's international system come from? Why is the system divided into nation-states, and why has Europe been dominant in recent centuries? In this chapter, we provide general answers to these questions along with a summary of the historical development of the international political system. The chapter does not attempt to provide a complete history of international politics—that would make for a very long book.[1] Nor does it provide equal treatment of all events or of all parts of the world. Instead, the goal is to provide a cursory overview of the evolution of the contemporary international system.

The evolution of the international system has been dominated by the emergence and spread of the sovereign state system. The system of sovereign states emerged in early modern Europe and spread over the next 500 years to the rest of the world through colonialism. By the end of the 1970s, the entire world was contained in a single system of sovereign states. Today that system is being challenged by the rise of international organizations and nonstate actors, and by the weakness of states around the world.

## THE BIRTH OF INTERNATIONAL POLITICS

**city-state**

A state that centers on a single city, rather than a larger territory or a nation.

**Peloponnesian War**

A war between Athens and Sparta from 431 BCE to 404 BCE. Thucydides's study of this war has been influential on later thinking about international relations.

Many histories of international politics begin with developments in the Greek **city-states** in the fifth century BCE. This Greek period is important because it is one of the earliest examples of what later came to be viewed as a system of independent states. Moreover, this period gave rise to one of the earliest known analyses of international politics: *The History of the Peloponnesian War*, by the Athenian general Thucydides.[2] His analysis was the first known attempt to advance a general understanding of how international politics works, and his fundamental assertions continue to be influential today.

In 431 BCE, Sparta and Athens, two Greek city-states, went to war. Although the details of the **Peloponnesian War** are not essential here, Thucydides's explanation of the causes is. Thucydides asserted that the war was caused by the changing distribution of power between Athens and Sparta. As long as Sparta was considerably more powerful than Athens, there was no cause for war. However, as Athens' power approached that of Sparta, the Spartans feared that Athens would soon become strong enough to attack and defeat Sparta. To avoid that, Sparta attacked Athens first.

In this explanation of the Peloponnesian War, Thucydides provided an embryonic theory of international politics that has persisted to this day. The key actors were states. The key factor in international politics was the distribution of power, upon which war and peace depended.

Thucydides also argued that discussions of justice had no place in international politics. Arguments about morality, he said, were simply disguises for the ambitions of states. He famously stated that "the strong do what they can and the weak suffer what they must." For 2500 years, people have debated whether, as Thucydides said, international politics is beyond morality. One could cast discussions of many contemporary developments in terms Thucydides would find completely familiar.

# FROM CITY-STATES TO NATION-STATES

Many histories of international politics begin in the seventeenth century CE. Why do they skip the preceding history? Between the fall of the Greek city-states and the rise of Western European sovereign states, two very different kinds of international system existed. First, for several centuries, the Roman Empire dominated much of what Europeans considered the known world. In that system, a single empire dominated international politics. This situation contrasts sharply with the system of multiple states that later arose, and it is seen as a fundamentally different kind of politics. By most accounts, the Roman Empire was not an international system at all.[3] Therefore, it is seen as having little relevance for understanding modern international politics.

Following the collapse of the Roman Empire in the fifth century CE, political power and authority in Europe were highly fragmented, and over time a **feudal system** emerged (Figure 2.1). In a feudal system, political authority was defined personally and religiously rather than territorially. A given territory was subject to several different rulers, depending on which inhabitants were being considered or what the issue was. Most notably, authority to rule was divided among three kinds of rulers: local nobles; kings, whose power had a wider geographic scope but whose local authority was limited; and the Roman Catholic Church, which claimed religious authority over all of Europe but whose practical power was limited. These different bases of power often clashed with one another as each actor tried to expand its own territorial control, political authority, and wealth. Despite the fragmentation of power, however, medieval Europeans shared the view that Europe *should* and *could* be a single political and religious entity. The only question was who would renew the role of the Roman Empire.

**feudal system**

A political system in which legal and political subservience is owed to multiple overlapping authorities, such as local nobles, emperors, and the Pope, rather than being defined territorially.

# THE WESTPHALIAN SYSTEM

The modern sovereign state system is often called the **Westphalian system**, after the Treaty of Westphalia, signed in 1648. The Treaty of Westphalia, which ended the Thirty Years' War, is seen as enshrining the status of sovereign states, though this sovereign state system actually emerged gradually.

**Westphalian system**

The system of sovereign states that was recognized by the Treaty of Westphalia in 1648.

**Europe in 1100 CE.** For much of recorded history, global politics was not "international" politics in that it did not consist of relations between clearly delineated states. Empires were the rule, their borders were fluid, and they tended not to have extensive relations with anyone other than their closest neighbors.

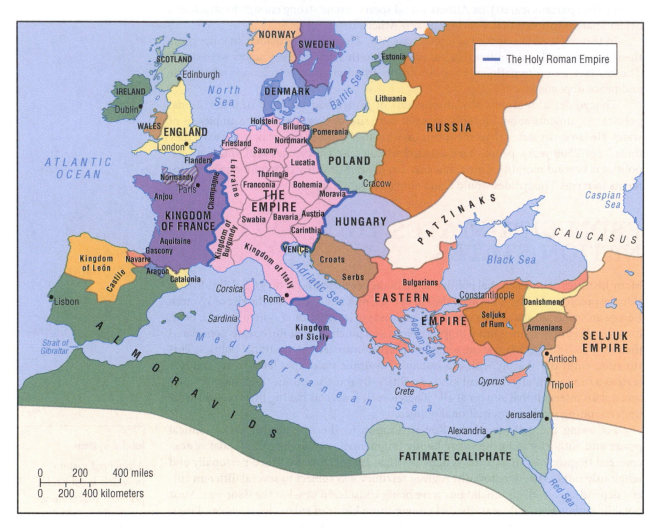

Source: http://www.culturalresources.com/MP_Muir6.html, from Ramsay Muir, *Philips' New Historical Atlas for Students* (London: The London Geographical Institute, 1911).

The Thirty Years' War was motivated both by religious conflict and by a contest for political control over Europe. Catholic leaders sought to defeat Protestant states to restore the "true faith." States also battled to increase their power at the expense of their rivals. Both perspectives shared the prevailing assumption that Europe was naturally a single political and religious space.

The Thirty Years' War lasted much longer and was much more devastating than anyone expected. In central Europe, roughly one-third of the population died as a result of the war, a higher death rate than during World War I or World War II. Exhausted, the European powers gathered in Westphalia (in today's Germany) in 1648 to make peace (Figure 2.2).

**FIGURE 2.2**    **Europe in 1648.** At the end of the Thirty Years' War in 1648, a plurality of independent states existed in Europe. However, as this map shows, some were quite large and others were tiny. Over the ensuing centuries, borders continued to change, usually through warfare or the threat of it.

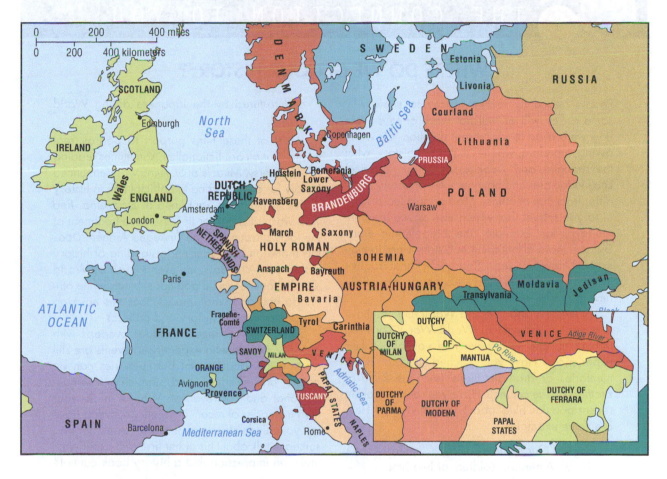

## STATE SOVEREIGNTY

By recognizing the existence of sovereign states and clarifying their rights, the Treaty of Westphalia established principles that defined the system from then until now. The monarchs of Europe accepted that renewing the Roman Empire was impossible and that pursuing that goal would lead to continuous war. This meant acknowledging Europe as a system of multiple **states**. How would these states relate to one another? The principle of **sovereignty** answered this question. Sovereignty meant that each state had complete authority over its territory, at least in theory.

Sovereignty had both internal and external dimensions. Internally, it meant that no one within a state had the right to challenge the ruler's power. Any challenges that occurred were regarded as illegitimate. This principle gave kings authority over lesser nobles, recognizing a trend toward the consolidation of state power that had been under way for decades. Continuous warfare as well as advances in taxation and administration had slowly strengthened monarchs at the expense of lesser nobles. France under Louis XIV (ruled 1643–1715) was emblematic of the strengthening of the modern absolutist state.

**states**

An entity defined by a specific territory within which a single government has authority.

**sovereignty**

The principle that states have complete authority over their own territory.

## THE CONNECTION TO YOU

### WHERE DO WE GET OUR HISTORY?

People frequently invoke history to show why some policy will or will not work or to explain how we arrived at our current situation. It is worth asking, therefore, where we get our history, what the strengths and weaknesses in our historical knowledge are, and how our view of history might differ from that of others. Most people learn some history in school, but where else do we learn it?

Take, for example, the Napoleonic wars. Did you learn about them in history class in high school? Have you read Tolstoy's fictional account in *War and Peace*? Or is this period essentially new to you? If so, does it matter?

Now think about World War II. Do you have relatives who fought in World War II, or lived through it, and who have told you about their experiences? Have you watched television documentaries or dramatizations (such as *Band of Brothers* or *The Pacific*)? Have you seen any of the recent popular films about World War II? Here are some examples.

- *Flags of Our Fathers* (2006), Clint Eastwood's film on American soldiers at Iwo Jima
- *Letters from Iwo Jima* (2006), Eastwood's film about the Japanese at Iwo Jima
- *Defiance* (2008), about Jewish partisans fighting the Nazis in occupied Poland
- *Miracle at St. Anna* (2008), about African American soldiers and a Nazi atrocity in Italy
- *Valkyrie* (2008), a dramatization of a plot to assassinate Hitler
- *Inglorious Basterds* (2009), about Jewish American soldiers trying to assassinate Nazis leaders
- *Red Tails* (2012), about the Tuskegee Airmen, a pioneering group of African American pilots
- *Unbroken* (2014), Angelina Jolie's film about a former American Olympian captured and tortured by the Japanese during World War II

Most of these films purport to portray real events. But all are fictionalize, sometimes leading to controversy. *Miracle at St. Anna* was denounced in Italy for contradicting the official Italian history of the massacre at Sant'Anna di Stazzema. *Red Tails* was criticized for its very loose treatment of the facts surrounding the Tuskegee Airmen. Does this matter in how your understanding of history is formed? Why do some events, such as World War II, continue to be popular subjects while others do not, and what impact does this have on our perceptions of history and politics?

The history of recent decades overlaps with memory. People who experienced events are still alive to talk about them, but memories can be painful and selective, and many issues remain personal and controversial. What role do your own memories of recent international events have for your understanding of them? Does hearing someone talk about his or her firsthand experience make an impression that a history book cannot?

### Critical Thinking Questions

1. Consider an important international event from decades ago, such as the Vietnam War. How much do you know about it, and where does that knowledge come from? How much of your "knowledge" comes from works of fiction?

2. Consider a more recent event, such as the war in Afghanistan. How much do you know about it, and where does your knowledge come from? How does your view of events you lived through differ from your view of events before you were born?

3. How would the history you know differ if you grew up in a different country?

The external dimension of sovereignty was that no one outside a territory had the right to say what should go on within that territory. This principle, often known as the *principle of noninterference in the internal affairs of other states*, was especially important in religion. In particular, the Treaty of Westphalia reaffirmed the power of rulers to determine the religion of the people in their territory.

The treaty acknowledged the reality of political and religious **pluralism**. In political terms, pluralism meant accepting that Europe would not be a single empire based on a single religion. Instead, it would be divided territorially into states, with each state having immense authority within its territory and none outside of it. In religious terms, pluralism meant acceptance of more than one religion rather than an attempt to establish a single "true" religion. Religious authority would also be segmented territorially, with individual leaders determining the religions of their own states but recognizing the rights of other monarchs to impose different religions in their states. This was not exactly a recipe for religious tolerance; within individual states, persecution of minorities continued to be widespread and brutal.

It must be emphasized that sovereignty is a principle, not a statement of fact. Although there have been many violations of the principle over the years, the principle itself remains the underpinning of the international system today. Moreover, sovereignty is not an objective trait of states; rather, states are treated as sovereign only when other states officially recognize their sovereignty. **Recognition** is important in this system. Political entities that are recognized as sovereign by other sovereign entities have greater legitimacy, and hence a greater chance of surviving, than those that are not recognized.

**pluralism**
The presence of a number of competing actors or ideas.

**recognition**
The acceptance by the international community of a state's sovereignty over its territory.

## THE BALANCE OF POWER SYSTEM: 1648–1800

The principles of the Westphalian system did not prevent states from pursuing their interests, and states often used war as a tool to achieve those interests. Nor did the principle that Europe would be a system of multiple states prevent periodic attempts by one state or another to assert total dominance over Europe.[4]

Sovereignty had important implications for international politics. If no higher power could tell states what to do, then no one could prevent states from attacking one another. Nor was there any international organization to compel or even persuade states to limit their aggression. A situation in which there is no central ruler or government above the separate actors is termed **anarchy**. Note that *anarchy* does not mean *chaos*, a term with which it is sometimes confused. A central issue in international politics is the possibility of establishing order within a system that is anarchic. This term is of central importance in understanding international politics and will be explored further in Chapter 3.

In the situation of anarchy that followed Westphalia, larger states could and often did attack and absorb smaller states, so that the number of European states declined steadily over time. In this sense, the Westphalian system was perhaps little different from what preceded it, even if the principles had changed.

Thus, the history of Europe from 1648 until the beginning of the nineteenth century was characterized by what is sometimes called the *classic balance of power system*. There was little other than prudence to prevent states from waging war against each other. Yet warfare in this era was in many ways more limited than it had been during the Thirty Years' War that preceded it or the Napoleonic wars that followed. In part this was because of the distribution of power. A rough **balance of power** meant that no single state was sufficiently powerful to defeat the others. This balance of power was both a fact and a policy. No individual state could gain enough power to conquer all the others, and many states made the maintenance of a balance an explicit goal of policy.

**anarchy**
A condition in which there is no central ruler.

**balance of power**
A system in which no single actor is dominant; also, the distribution of power in such a system, which is not necessarily equal.

Moreover, the nature of the states themselves placed important limitations on the size of armies. All of these states were monarchies, in which the vast majority of the population had no citizenship. There was little reason for peasants with no rights to fight for rulers of countries of which they were not citizens. Modern notions of nationalism and patriotism had not yet emerged. The only people with a "stake" in whether a territory was ruled by one king or another were the nobles, from whose ranks armed forces were drawn. Mercenaries were sometimes used, but this too had limiting effects. Mercenaries were expensive, and they tried very hard to avoid actual battle, where they might be killed. Furthermore, before modern manufacturing techniques were developed, armaments such as cannon and guns were extraordinarily expensive. In sum, the expense of building armies and armaments kept forces small and made leaders wary of risking them in battle.

Finally, despite religious divisions in Europe, there existed a **law of war**, based on Christian doctrine, which raised moral objections to unlimited war, and particularly to the targeting of noncombatants (civilians).[5] These limitations, which did not apply to non-Christian groups such as the Turks, helped make war in Europe less lethal than it might otherwise have been.

**law of war**

A doctrine concerning when it is permissible to go to war and what means of conducting war are (and are not) permissible.

## EUROPE AND THE REST OF THE WORLD

What was happening in the rest of the world while the modern state system was emerging in Europe? In China in the first millennium BCE, the system varied between an empire with a single dominant leader (roughly analogous to Rome during its heyday) and a pluralistic system roughly analogous to the Westphalian system. Normative debates over what system should prevail helped distinguish doctrines such as Taoism and Confucianism that continue to wield influence today. For most of the past 2000 years, China has existed as a single state, although the territorial extent and the strength of that state have varied. In some periods, China expanded its political and cultural influence into adjacent regions, including Xinjiang, Mongolia, Tibet, Korea, Vietnam, and Japan. During other periods, Chinese territory was controlled by outsiders, as when the Mongol emperor Kublai Khan conquered China in the thirteenth century CE.

In the Middle East and North Africa, the rise of Islam beginning in the seventh century CE led to the establishment of the Caliphate—a unified political area governed by Islam—the geographic extent of which varied over time. Eventually, however, various groups such as the Berbers in North Africa and the Mamluks in Egypt broke away from the Caliphate. Here, as in medieval Europe, there was tension between the principle that political authority should be unified and the reality that it was fragmented among competing authorities. By the sixteenth century, the Ottoman Empire became the most powerful claimant to the authority of the Caliphate.

One marauding group, the Mongols, played a role in upending existing arrangements in three distinct regions: in China, where it ended the Song Dynasty; in the Middle East, where it ended the Abbasid Caliphate; and in Europe, where it conquered the nascent Russian state, with far-reaching effects.

In India, feudal systems dominated, and no mutual recognition of sovereignty emerged.[6] Most of what is today North and South America was sparsely populated, so relations between distinct polities—international politics—were not as pressing an issue as they were in more heavily populated regions. In Africa, a great diversity of empires rose, expanded, and fell in different places at different times, so that the consolidation of political authority into a small number of large entities did not occur.

# THE POLICY CONNECTION

## EXPLAINING THE RISE OF EUROPE AND LEARNING LESSONS FROM IT

In 1500, Europe was neither wealthier nor more powerful than any other part of the world, but by 1900, Europe and the United States had colonized nearly the entire planet. How? The sources of Europe's rise engender debate among academics in several disciplines. For policy makers seeking to bring the "recipe" of Europe's success to the rest of the world, the debate is equally relevant.

The German sociologist Max Weber attributed Europe's success to its values. In *The Protestant Ethic and the Spirit of Capitalism* (1905), Weber argued that the adoption of Protestant religious beliefs reshaped the relationship between religion and economics in a way that promoted capitalism.* In non-Protestant faiths, Weber argued, religious devotion was equated with a rejection of worldly goods; hence, one could not be both pious and wealthy. Protestantism supported the notion that success on earth was an indicator of the likelihood of being "saved" after death.

More recently, in *Guns, Germs, and Steel*, geographer Jared Diamond attributes Europe's success to environmental factors that gave it an advantage in competition with the rest of the world.[†] Diamond contends that species of animals and plants suitable for domestication and agriculture were more prevalent in Europe than elsewhere. Because Eurasia stretches mostly east–west and has a roughly similar climate across its expanse, agricultural successes in one place could be adapted elsewhere. Agricultural surplus allowed cities to develop and allowed labor to be diverted into other fields. Moreover, the concentration of population in cities helped the spread of disease, so that Europeans developed resistance to many diseases that were devastating elsewhere. Concentration of population also meant that the states of early modern Europe were constantly at war, which led them to develop the superior military technology and organizations with which they then conquered the world. Diamond claims

to have produced an explanation of Europe's dominance that is not based on any notion of European cultural superiority.

The sociologist Immanuel Wallerstein argues that a very small economic advantage in economic development at the beginning of the modern era allowed England and France, and subsequently other European states, to get ever further ahead of other states.[‡] He contends that in a world of capitalist exchange, each exchange provides greater benefit to the wealthier. As a result, the initially small gaps between Europe and other states inevitably grew over time. This view, inspired by Marxist economics (see Chapters 4 and 10), sees Europe's advance as inseparable from, and enabled by, the spread of poverty over the rest of the planet.

These competing perspectives motivate intense debate because they lead to competing implications for two very contemporary questions: Who is to blame? and What is to be done?

### Critical Thinking Questions

1. What different implications do the theories of Weber, Diamond, and Wallerstein have with regard to assessing blame for the relative poverty in much of the world?

2. To what extent can the sources of Europe's success cited by each theory be controlled by contemporary governments?

3. To what extent does each approach see one society gaining only at the expense of others?

---

*Max Weber, The Protestant Ethic and the Spirit of Capitalism, trans. Talcott Parsons (New York: Scribner, 1976).

[†]Jared Diamond, Guns, Germs, and Steel: The Fates of Human Societies (New York: W. W. Norton, 1997).

[‡]Immanuel Wallerstein, The Modern World-System 1: Capitalist Agriculture and the Origins of the European World-Economy in the Sixteenth Century (New York: Academic Press, 1974).

The emergence of the modern state in Europe coincided with increased European contact with the rest of the world, which accelerated dramatically after European contact with the Americas in 1492. Until then, different systems of international relations existed largely unconnected to one another. Over the next 400 years, Europe forcibly integrated the rest of the world into the modern state system, first as colonies of European states and then, after European powers surrendered their colonies, as sovereign states.[7]

How did this happen? Why were European countries able to dominate the rest of the world? Why didn't some other country or group or some other system of principles become dominant? Why was resistance to European imperialism generally unsuccessful? These questions are widely debated, and there are no definitive answers.[8] Several factors likely played a role. Europeans developed superior agricultural, industrial, and especially military technology. Some scholars contend that the constant warfare among European states in the early modern period strengthened European states to compete with the rest of the world. Others point to the development of capitalism as a key source of European domination. Capitalism may have provided both the means for expansion, in terms of surplus profit to invest in overseas business ventures, and the incentive, in terms of the lust for private wealth. Finally, some point to ideology. The varieties of Christianity that predominated in modern Europe provided justification for expansion for the purpose of converting non-Christians.

European domination did not just mean that European states dominated other societies. It meant that the European *system* of sovereign states and subservient colonies came to dominate, and that European principles, "rules of the game," and interpretations of history dominated. For this reason, the development of the modern state system in Europe receives disproportionate attention in the study of international relations; for better or for worse, this is the system that came to dominate international politics.

## NAPOLEON AND NATIONAL WARFARE

By 1800, substantial changes had taken place in Europe that fundamentally altered the nature of international politics. These changes were embodied in the rise to power in France of Napoleon Bonaparte and in the wars he waged.[9] Napoleon sought to overthrow the Westphalian system in Europe by taking control of the entire continent. In this he failed. However, in the process, he overthrew many of the limitations on war that had characterized the classical balance of power era.

Two important developments in European politics made possible Napoleon's rise: nationalism and democracy. **Nationalism** is the doctrine that "nations"—large groups of people who perceive themselves to be fundamentally similar to each other and distinct from other groups—are and should be a basic unit of politics. Closely linked to nationalism is the principle of **national self-determination**, the idea that each state should consist of a single nation and each distinct nation should have its own state. **Democracy** is the doctrine that the entire population of a nation, rather than a small elite or a single monarch, should control government. All of these doctrines were fairly new at this point in European history.

The French Revolution of 1789 overthrew the French monarchy and replaced it with a regime that claimed to be democratic. The doctrines of nationalism and democracy gave, in theory, every French resident a stake in the welfare and in the glory of France. In revolutionary France, every adult male (women's rights were still limited) was considered a citizen, with a voice and an interest in government. Moreover, thanks to the doctrine of nationalism, every citizen of the French state was a "Frenchman." No longer were the masses cut off from government and from each other.

**nationalism**
The doctrine that recognizes the nation as the primary unit of political allegiance.

**national self-determination**
The doctrine that each state should consist of a single nation and each distinct nation should have its own state.

**democracy**
The doctrine that the entire population of a nation, rather than a small elite or a single monarch, should control government.

When Napoleon Bonaparte came to power in 1799, he harnessed democracy and nationalism for military purposes, and he sought to expand French influence across Europe and beyond. The crucial military innovation in revolutionary France was the institution of a draft, known as the **levée en masse**, which conscripted hundreds of thousands of ordinary French peasants into the French military. Whereas the armies of his more traditional monarchical neighbors were still based on feudal principles, Napoleon was able to harness the entire French nation—both its industry and its population—in support of his war effort. Peasants who in earlier generations had resisted fighting for kings were more willing to fight for a "fatherland" in which they were citizens. Napoleon's tactical innovation was to develop ways of dividing and recombining forces that made the huge numbers of troops manageable on the battlefield.

By 1812, Napoleon had conquered Austria and Prussia (one of the forerunners of modern Germany), the leading European powers of the day, and had reached Moscow, where he stabled his horses in the Kremlin. Ultimately, he failed to conquer Russia and was defeated so badly there that he was pushed all the way back to France. Napoleon was beaten partly because Russia and others began to adopt his strategies, using nationalism to mobilize masses of common people into the army. Russia's huge armies, coupled with its vast territory and frigid winters, were more than Napoleon's armies could conquer.

Napoleon's defeat, however, did not undo the revolution in international affairs he had initiated. Gone were the days of the small professional army and of the clear distinction between the military and mass society. After Napoleon, war became *national* war, which engaged entire populations against one another. This "democratization of war," coupled with industrialization, led to a massive increase in the size of armies, the scale of combat, and the number of casualties. The 1812 Battle of Borodino, near Moscow, involved more than 250,000 soldiers and caused 70,000 casualties.

**levée en masse**

A draft, initiated by Napoleon following the French Revolution, that allowed France to vastly expand its army.

Fine Art Images/Age Fotostock

Napoleon Bonaparte in Moscow, 1812. Napoleon sought to unify all of Europe under French rule. When he took Moscow, the Russians set the city alight, leaving Napoleon's troops without supplies in the cold Russian winter.

## THE CONCERT OF EUROPE

The Napoleonic wars of the early nineteenth century changed not only how wars would be fought but also how peace would be sought. At the Congress of Vienna in 1815, the victorious powers put into place a mechanism intended to prevent a country such as France from again seeking to dominate the continent. This agreement, known as the **Concert of Europe**, was the first of its kind in modern history and is in many ways the predecessor of the League of Nations, formed after World War I, and the United Nations (UN), formed after World War II.[10]

The Concert of Europe was based on an understanding that the inability of Austria, Prussia, Britain, and Russia to form an early alliance against Napoleon made it considerably easier for him to succeed both politically and militarily. To prevent any future recurrence, the four powers agreed to work together to preserve the status quo in European international politics and to confer periodically. In contrast to later efforts, there were no formal procedures or legal documents. Instead, the Concert of Europe was a statement of intentions, based on a shared understanding on the part of the major powers that peace could be better preserved if active collaboration supplemented traditional balance of power politics.

From a theoretical perspective, the Concert of Europe marks the first attempt to put into practice the emerging **liberal approach** to international affairs (explored in depth in Chapter 3). It is not coincidental that this first attempt occurred when it did; the American Revolution and the writings of European philosophers such as Immanuel Kant and Jean Jacques Rousseau, in the last part of the eighteenth century, had advanced the notion that there was an alternative to anarchy other than domination by a single dominant power.

There is considerable disagreement concerning the effects of the Concert of Europe. On one hand, the era following the establishment of the Concert was the most peaceful century in Europe's history. From 1815 to 1914, only relatively limited wars occurred, such as the Crimean War (in which Russia fought England, France, and Turkey from 1854 to 1856) and the Franco-Prussian War (in which Prussia fought France from 1870 to 1871). On the other hand, the mechanism of the Concert broke down quickly. The more authoritarian powers (Austria and Russia) wanted the Concert to preserve the domestic status quo (autocratic politics) as well as the international status quo, especially during the revolutions of 1830 and 1848. England objected to these efforts and did not participate. Skeptics assert that the Concert had little effect; the traditional balance of power and effective diplomacy, not the Concert, dissuaded potential aggressors and preserved peace.

# NATIONALISM AND IMPERIALISM

The nineteenth century saw the dramatic rise of two phenomena that had originated earlier: nationalism and **imperialism**. Imperialism refers to a situation in which one country controls another country or territory. Imperial control was exercised either formally, through the establishment of colonies (territories that are governed from the imperial center rather than having their own government), or informally, using economic means or military threats to control the government of another country. Within Europe, the forces of nationalism unleashed a far-reaching revision of domestic and international politics. Beyond Europe, the competition inspired by nationalism helped justify the extension of European imperialism to cover nearly the entire globe.

Nationalism led to a redrawing of the map of Europe. The notion that state boundaries should coincide with ethnic, linguistic, or national boundaries meant that many of the boundaries in the mid-nineteenth century seemed inappropriate or unjust. In the areas that today comprise Italy and Germany, there were a large number of small, distinct states

**Concert of Europe**

An agreement reached at the Congress of Vienna in 1815 in which major European powers pledged to cooperate to maintain peace and stability.

**liberal approach**

Political approach focusing on the ability of actors to govern themselves without surrendering their liberty. International liberal theory focuses on the ability of states to cooperate to solve problems.

**imperialism**

A situation in which one country controls another country or territory.

# THE GEOGRAPHY CONNECTION

## SHIFTING BORDERS, CHANGING POLITICS: EUROPE IN 1815 AND 1914

A map of the world generally shows us a static picture. But if we compare maps over time, we see that the map at any one time is just a snapshot of a changing reality. These two maps show the boundaries of Europe in 1815 and in 1914.

Europe in 1815

## Critical Thinking Questions

1. What were the causes of the differences between the two maps?

2. How has the map changed between 1914 and today, and what drove these changes?

3. How might we expect the map to change in the future, and what forces will drive those changes? Or have we reached an end to boundary changes?

Europe in 1914

Source: http://.lib.utexas.edu/maps/historical/shepherd/europe_1911.jpg, from http://www.lib.utexas.edu/maps/historical/history_europe.html. Courtesy of the University Libraries, The University of Texas at Austin.

(such as Piedmont, Naples, and Veneto in Italy; and Pomerania, Bavaria, and Westphalia in Germany). The doctrine of nationalism convinced people in both regions that those smaller states should be combined into single, large, ethnically and linguistically defined states. The results fundamentally altered European international politics because a unified Germany, with great industrial power, seemed to have the capacity to take over the continent, a concern that dominated the period from 1900 to 1945.

In the multinational Russian, Austro-Hungarian, and Ottoman Empires, nationalism created pressure to break large states into smaller parts. Each of these empires encompassed multiple nations that perceived themselves as deserving their own nation-states. In the Russian Empire, these included Poland, Ukraine, Latvia, Lithuania, Estonia, Georgia, and Chechnya. In the Austro-Hungarian Empire they included territories that today comprise parts of the Czech Republic, Slovakia, Hungary, Ukraine, Romania, Slovenia, Croatia, Serbia, and Bosnia-Herzegovina. The Ottoman (Turkish) Empire contained much of the modern Middle East (including Israel/Palestine, Syria, Iraq, Jordan, and Lebanon) as well as parts of southeastern Europe (Bulgaria, Macedonia, Bosnia-Herzegovina, and Albania).

The doctrines of nationalism, self-determination, and democracy had profound effects in the Americas as well. In the Caribbean and Latin America, nationalism led to the world's first wave of decolonization. In Haiti, a revolution overthrew slavery, instituted a democratic constitution, and declared independence from France in 1804. In South America, liberation movements led by Simón Bolívar and José de San Martín led to a series of declarations of independence between 1810 and 1825. Similarly, Mexico fought a successful war of independence ending in 1821, and Brazil declared independence from Portugal in 1822. Great Britain's colonies in Canada formed the Canadian Confederation and became autonomous in 1867. In sum, although several territories remained colonies until the twentieth century, nearly the entire Western Hemisphere became independent between the U.S. Declaration of Independence in 1776 and the Canadian Confederation in 1867.

Nationalism helped spur a new wave of **colonialism** in the second half of the nineteenth century, driven by the idea that soon all the territory would be taken and slow movers would be forever at a disadvantage.[11] Most of Africa and Asia were colonized during this period. In most cases, imperialism took the form of direct control of a territory, along the model the Spanish had implemented in South America and the British had established in India. In some cases, such as in the Belgian Congo, this model led to brutality toward indigenous populations on a horrendous scale. In other instances, imperialism was exercised through indirect control but still achieved the goal of harnessing the local economy for the benefit of external powers. Twice, in 1839 and again in 1856, European powers waged war on China to force its government to allow Europeans (and Americans) to sell their goods in China. The resulting "unequal treaties" created economic advantages in China for Western states without requiring them to take over the territory directly. The treaties are a source of Chinese resentment to this day.[12] Many people believe that the colonized countries have never fully recovered from the disadvantages forced on them during the colonial era.

Although this last onslaught of European colonialism was inspired partly by European nationalism, it also sowed the seeds for the nationalism that was to manifest itself in many of the colonies during the twentieth century. Just as the doctrine of national self-determination undermined Europe's multinational empires, it undermined Europe's overseas empires as well. Resentment among colonized societies over political domination and economic exploitation helped inspire their own national liberation movements. The struggles against colonial rule were, in many cases, long and brutal, as in the Vietnam War. Nationalism played an important role right up to the end of the twentieth century, spurring the disintegration of the Soviet Empire in 1989–1991, and the violent collapse of Yugoslavia in the 1990s.

**colonialism**

A type of imperialism in which the dominating state takes direct control of a territory.

# THE ROAD TO WORLD WAR I

By the beginning of the twentieth century, the increased power and ambitions of the newly unified Germany made the existing state of affairs in Europe appear unsustainable. Increasingly, each major European power sought to tilt the very precarious balance of power in its own favor. In part, this was manifested in the rush to colonize the Southern Hemisphere. It resulted also in a naval arms race between Germany and Great Britain, and in a growing sense that a European war was inevitable.

The situation was made especially unstable by the erosion of two of Europe's great empires. The Ottoman Empire was slowly losing control of territories in what are today Bosnia-Herzegovina, Serbia, and Bulgaria, an area generally known as the Balkans. National independence movements plagued the Austro-Hungarian Empire as well. The other great powers competed to gain influence at the expense of the declining empires and each other. Many people believed that the outcome of this competition would determine the long-term winners and losers in European power politics.

Russia, lying to the north and east of the Balkans, seemed most likely to gain from the disintegration of the Ottoman Empire. It sought to control the Ottoman capital, Istanbul, for both religious and geopolitical reasons. Istanbul had been the traditional home of the Orthodox Christian Church until its conquest by the Muslim Turks in 1453. Through Istanbul's straits, Russia could gain year-round access to the open sea, which it otherwise lacked. Germany sought to deny Russia this victory by bolstering Austria and the Ottoman Empire. France, fearing Germany after the Franco-Prussian war, saw Russia as a potential ally. Great Britain saw its place as the most powerful military and economic player on earth jeopardized by the rapid rise of Germany. German economic growth, weapons programs, and rhetoric convinced many people that Germany sought to supplant Britain as Europe's dominant country. Britain's willingness to go to war in 1914 rested on logic similar to that which Thucydides attributed to the Spartans: If war was likely, it was better to fight it before the enemy became even stronger.

By 1914, Europe was delicately balanced between two great alliances, The **Triple Alliance**, consisting of Germany, Austria-Hungary, and Italy; and the **Triple Entente** of Britain, France, and Russia (Table 2.1). A more complex web of alliances connected these larger powers to smaller ones, such as Serbia and the Ottoman Empire.

To the flammable situation that existed in 1914, a spark was provided by Serbian nationalists, who assassinated Archduke Franz Ferdinand, the heir to the Austro-Hungarian throne, in July 1914. In the "July Crisis" that ensued, Austria issued an ultimatum insisting that Serbia submit to Austrian intervention or face war. Russia pledged to defend Serbia, fearing for its position in the region if Serbia fell under Austrian control. Germany, seeing that its position would be ruined if Russia defeated Austria, backed Austria. France, fearing its position should Germany defeat Russia, backed Russia. Finally, Britain, fearing that Germany might defeat both Russia and France and therefore rule all of Europe, backed its allies. As a result of these overlapping fears, all of Europe went to war, and eventually the United States was drawn in as well.

Contrary to expectations, World War I was not over quickly. Moreover, it was far more destructive than any previous war. The trend toward total warfare started by Napoleon

**Triple Alliance**

A pre–World War I agreement by Germany, Austria-Hungary, and Italy that if one state were to be attacked the others would come to its aid.

**Triple Entente**

A pre–World War I agreement by Britain, France, and Russia that if one state were to be attacked the others would come to its aid.

**TABLE 2.1   World War I: Major Players**

| Alliance Powers | Entente Powers |
|---|---|
| Germany | Great Britain |
| Austria-Hungary | France |
| Ottoman Empire | Russia |
| Italy (until 1915) | Italy (after 1915) |
|  | United States (after 1917) |

a century earlier had been strengthened by the industrial revolution. Weapons were manufactured on a vastly larger scale, and new technologies such as the machine gun, barbed wire, and poisonous gas made it much easier to defend territory than to attack it. As a result, the war quickly bogged down into hellish trench warfare, and the youth of Europe were butchered in terrifying numbers. On July 1, 1916, at the Battle of the Somme, the British army took 58,000 casualties in a single day. By the end of that battle, in September 1916, total British, French, and German casualties surpassed 1 million, but the lines between the sides had barely budged.

The stalemate was broken only in 1917 when the United States intervened on the side of Britain, France, and Russia. The war ended in November 1918, but not until four major empires (German, Austro-Hungarian, Ottoman, and Russian) had collapsed, the communists had come to power in Russia, and more than 8 million soldiers had died.

The **Treaty of Versailles**, which officially ended World War I, was signed on June 28, 1919. It created the **League of Nations**, redrew Germany's boundaries, required Germany to pay substantial "reparations" for the harm it had caused in starting the war, and specified numerous limits on Germany's ability to rearm in the coming years. Out of the rubble of the collapsed empires, the Treaty of Versailles established several countries, including Czechoslovakia, Yugoslavia, Poland, and the **Baltic states** in Europe. Granting independence to these Eastern European countries was a major commitment of U.S. President Woodrow Wilson, who strongly supported national self-determination. Wilson believed that if free democracies could be built in a region traditionally devoid of democracy, then peace would be guaranteed there. The same principle was not applied outside of Europe: the Middle Eastern, African, and Asian colonies of the defeated powers were simply transferred to the control of the victors.

World War I caused a fundamental shift in global power. Although the war had been fought in part to determine whether Britain or Germany would dominate Europe, both were devastated. At the same time, the war demonstrated and contributed to the rise of the industrial, military, and financial power of the United States.

Print Collector/HIP/The Image Works

The industrialization of warfare made World War I more destructive than its predecessors. The Battle of Verdun, shown here, lasted ten months and claimed an estimated 700,000 lives. At the end of this longest battle of World War I, the lines of the two armies had moved only a few hundred yards.

**Treaty of Versailles**

The agreement ending World War I that set up the League of Nations.

**League of Nations**

An international organization formed after World War I intended to resolve disputes without force, and to use military force against aggressors.

**Baltic states**

Refers collectively to Estonia, Latvia, and Lithuania, which lie on the Baltic Sea in northern Europe, just to the west of Russia.

# THE ROAD TO WORLD WAR II

Woodrow Wilson called World War I "the war to end all wars." The unprecedented destruction of that war convinced many that new ways had to be found to avoid wars in the future. It seemed that the memory of that war would motivate leaders to take the necessary steps. Yet a mere twenty-one years later, in 1939, World War II began, and it was to be even more brutal than World War I.[13] Why did this intense desire to avoid another war fail to prevent World War II? The reasons are complex and still debated today, but a few important factors can be identified.

# COLLECTIVE SECURITY AND ECONOMIC NATIONALISM

**collective security**

A doctrine nominally adopted by states after World War I that specified that when one state committed aggression all other states would join together to attack it.

**isolationism**

The doctrine that U.S. interests were best served by playing as little role as possible in world affairs. From the founding of the republic until the Spanish-American War of 1898, the doctrine was largely unquestioned, but the Japanese bombing of Pearl Harbor in 1941 is widely viewed as destroying any credibility that the doctrine had left.

**Munich Crisis**

A crisis in 1938 precipitated by Germany's demand that it be allowed to occupy part of Czechoslovakia. War was averted when Britain and France agreed to Germany's demands.

**appeasement**

A strategy of avoiding war by acceding to the demands of rival powers.

The major method by which leaders after World War I envisioned preventing war was **collective security**, whereby all states would agree that if any state initiated a war, all the others would come to the defense of the state under attack. This policy was an updated version of the liberal doctrine that inspired the Concert of Europe. With the old balance of power system having failed so miserably to prevent World War I, many states saw the need for a collaborative solution. The theory was compelling. Any state would know that if it started a war, it would face retaliation from every other country. Therefore, it could not possibly hope to gain anything from starting a war. If collective security worked well, the threat would never have to be carried out.

The problems arose in practice. Collective security relied on the promise that any aggression would be countered by attacks from all the other states, but after World War I, leaders were determined to avoid another war. This was particularly true of the United States, where participation in World War I had met serious opposition and many people sought a return to the traditional U.S. policy of **isolationism**. The U.S. Senate refused to ratify the Charter of the League of Nations because many senators rejected the commitment to go to war if needed. When Japan invaded the Chinese territory of Manchuria in 1931, many people saw this as the first big test of collective security. The League of Nations demanded that Japan withdraw, but when Japan continued the invasion, other states did nothing. Similarly, when Italy invaded Abyssinia (today Ethiopia) in 1935, the major powers, working through the League of Nations, chose to impose only relatively trivial economic sanctions against Italy.

The great powers sought desperately to avoid going to war, and without their support, the League of Nations could do little. Ironically, the determination of most leading states to avoid war at all costs probably made war more, not less, likely.

When Germany first violated the Treaty of Versailles in 1936, other countries again hesitated to respond with force. The initial violations were not extremely consequential, and no one wanted to replay World War I in response. Moreover, each country hoped that it could stand aside and let others bear the burden of keeping Germany in line. Germany's demand that it be allowed to occupy the Sudetenland, a part of Czechoslovakia with many ethnic Germans, precipitated the **Munich Crisis** of 1938. British Prime Minister Neville Chamberlain advocated **appeasement**, a strategy of avoiding war by acceding to the demands of rival powers (in this case Nazi Germany). Germany was given permission to occupy part of Czechoslovakia, and Chamberlain celebrated having secured "peace in our time." In later years, "Munich" and "appeasement" became synonyms for weakness in situations requiring a firm stand.

The United States, France, and Britain, all of which were hostile toward the Soviet Union, hoped that Germany would attack eastward (toward the Soviet Union). The Soviet Union signed a peace treaty with Germany in 1939, hoping to turn German aggression westward. By playing the potential allies against each other, the German leadership was able to divide and conquer. In the United States, many leaders and much of the public continued to oppose U.S. involvement in Europe's war, even after Hitler attacked Poland, France, and the United Kingdom in 1939 and 1940. Only after Germany declared war on the United States in 1941 did the United States join the war. Germany was defeated only when Hitler chose to go to war with all of these countries simultaneously (see Table 2.2). Like Napoleon's France, Hitler's Germany found Russian territory too vast and Russian winters too cold.

**TABLE 2.2**    **World War II: Major Players**

| The Axis Powers | The Allied Powers |
|---|---|
| Germany | France |
| Italy | Great Britain |
| Japan | Soviet Union |
| | United States |

# ECONOMIC ROOTS OF WORLD WAR II

World War II, by most accounts, had important economic roots. The 1930s was a period of economic depression around the world. As economies collapsed, most countries adopted selfish strategies to try to boost employment. A common strategy was to increase barriers to imports in order to keep more jobs at home. However, when every country took this strategy, world trade collapsed and all economies became less efficient.

Prior to World War I, Great Britain had played a leading role in organizing the world economy. Because of its considerable naval and financial power, it was able to facilitate trade around the world. This was seen as advantageous both to Great Britain and to other countries. World War I, however, substantially undermined Great Britain's ability to play this role. The new big player in the world economy was the United States. Because of the doctrine of isolationism, however, the U.S. government declined to take up Britain's leadership role. As a result, there was no effective international collaboration to maintain trade under the stress of the Great Depression.

This lack of international economic cooperation played an important role in helping Hitler come to power in Germany. Germany after World War I was a new and unstable democracy. The financial burden of **reparations** required by the Treaty of Versailles further undermined a German economy that had already been ravaged by war. On top of these difficulties, the Great Depression brought the German economy, traditionally one of the strongest in the world, to the brink of collapse. The failure of democratically elected governments to avert this disaster, along with seething resentment at the economic restrictions placed on Germany by the Treaty of Versailles, provided fertile ground for a fascist such as Hitler to come to power. Although Hitler was no democrat, he first became chancellor (prime minister) of Germany through a democratic election.

**Fascism** took nationalism, which had been growing since the late eighteenth century, to a militant extreme. As it developed in Italy and Germany, the doctrine saw the strengthening of the nation, as represented by the state, as the most important political goal. In fascism, the rights or goals of individuals are subservient to those of the nation, which is viewed as a single organism. This doctrine justified political authoritarianism, economic centralization, and the belief that one nation was superior to all others. Fascism can be viewed as a mixture of the doctrines of nationalism and socialism. This virulent nationalism had its ultimate expression in the Holocaust, the systematic murder of approximately 6 million Jews by Germany and its allies.

In Japan, which had limited supplies of raw materials, the economic devastation of the Great Depression hit especially hard. Japan had started industrialization later than the European powers and the United States and was racing to catch up. Like European imperialism, Japanese imperialism in Korea and China was motivated by economic

**reparations**

Payments that Germany was forced to make as a result of starting World War I. Reparations caused serious economic problems in Germany and were deeply resented by the German people.

**fascism**

A doctrine in which the rights or goals of individuals are subservient to those of the nation, which is viewed as a single organism.

**FIGURE 2.3**   **Japanese expansion prior to World War II.** Japan, a relative latecomer to the practice of colonization, expanded its political and economic control in East Asia and the Pacific, threatening British, French, and U.S. colonies.

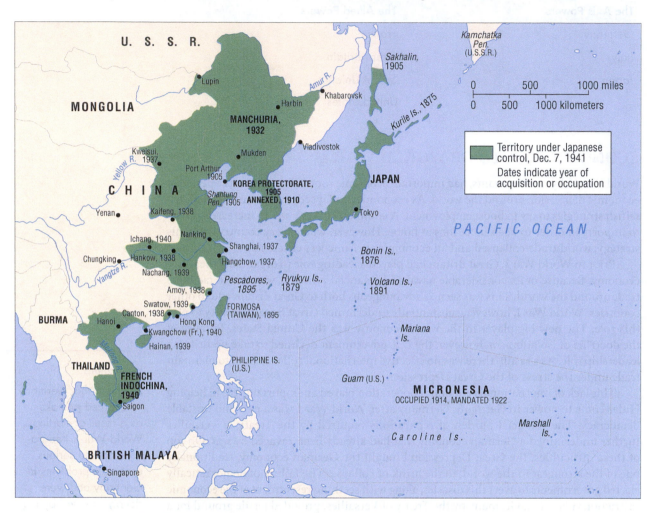

Source: http://www.lib.utexas.edu/maps/map_sites/hist_sites.html for link to http://www.shsu.edu/~his_sub/map–imperial%20japan.jpg.

pressures combined with intense nationalism (see Figure 2.3). The United States, France, and Great Britain saw Japanese expansion as a threat to their own economic and imperial interests in Asia. To weaken Japan and to impede further expansion, the United States cut off sales of key raw materials such as scrap metal. This embargo convinced the Japanese leadership that pursuing its interests would require ejecting the United States, Britain, and France from the Far East. In December 1941, Japan sought to force the United States from the Pacific region by bombing the U.S. Pacific Fleet at its base at Pearl Harbor in Hawaii.

Two related lessons were learned from World War II. First, many people believed that the immediate cause of the war was the rise to power of intensely nationalistic and undemocratic regimes in Germany, Italy, and Japan. World War II thus reinforced the lesson Woodrow Wilson took from World War I: that democracy is a key underpinning of peace. Second, many concluded that democracies would be under threat if economies performed badly and that more effective governance of the global economy was needed

# THE HISTORY CONNECTION

## THE USES AND ABUSES OF HISTORY IN FOREIGN POLICY

The nineteenth-century Prussian statesman Otto von Bismarck is reported to have said that fools learn from experience but wise men learn from other people's experience.* Throughout the centuries, policy makers faced with difficult choices have sought to learn from their own experience and that of prior generations. To ignore such experience would seem foolish.

However, it is difficult to know which historical experiences provide the best model for a current problem, and history is replete with examples of policy makers relying on historical analogies, only to be misled by them. Political scientist Robert Jervis has pointed out that people tend to overestimate the importance of certain types of historical events.† The following are among the sources of such overemphasis:

- **Personal experience**. It appears that people give especially heavy emphasis to historical events that they experience firsthand. Because many people have only a limited knowledge of history, it makes sense that they would place disproportionate emphasis on the events with which they are familiar. Especially when such experiences are extremely negative, they can create a profound desire to avoid repeating the same mistakes. Thus, leaders in the 1930s, who had witnessed the rush to war in 1914, sought to find ways to avoid war with Germany and Japan. In the decades after the Vietnam War, many policy

debates in the United States continued to be informed by the perceived mistakes made in that conflict.

- **Generational effects**. Not only do people overemphasize their personal experience, but experiences at a particular time in life seem to be especially salient. Thus, it is argued, many people form strong belief systems during young adulthood and maintain them for the rest of their lives. As a result, we may see "generational effects," in which a wide range of people who grew up during an especially difficult or triumphant time develop similar views. For those who came of age during the Vietnam War, for example, that conflict and the controversy that accompanied it may be especially salient. This might explain why, as that generation came to hold the key political offices in the United States, the issues of that era were debated all over again.

That policy makers would seek to learn from those events that made the biggest impression on them should probably not be surprising. But this tendency has a substantial impact on what kind of lessons can be learned. One thing is clear: People cannot learn anything at all from historical events of which they are ignorant.

### Critical Thinking Questions

1. What events have had the most influence on your thinking about international politics?

2. What events had the most influence on your parents or grandparents?

3. Have you learned different lessons from those your parents or grandparents learned? Do they view current events differently than you do? Do you evaluate the events of their formative years differently?

---

*Kenneth Waltz, Man, the State, and War (New York: Columbia University Press, 1959), p. 220; cited in Robert Jervis, Perception and Misperception in International Politics (New York: Columbia University Press, 1976), p. 239.

†Robert Jervis, Perception and Misperception in International Politics (New York: Columbia University Press, 1976), pp. 239–243.

to prevent the sort of economic chaos that facilitated the rise of authoritarianism in Germany, Italy, and Japan.

The political and military lessons taken from World War II were almost the opposite of those taken from World War I. World War I had shown the foolishness of going to war before diplomacy was exhausted, whereas World War II showed the foolishness of neglecting to confront expansionist powers. It was this lesson that guided both the United States and the Soviet Union in the Cold War that followed World War II.

World War II also unleashed a new force into international politics: nuclear weapons, which the United States dropped in August 1945 on Hiroshima and Nagasaki. The enormous power of these weapons, and the indiscriminate destruction they caused, changed how military strategists and political leaders thought about war. The advent of nuclear weapons, as much as the memory of two world wars, dominated thinking about international politics in the postwar era.

# THE COLD WAR

**Cold War**

A conflict between the United States and the Soviet Union during which no actual war broke out between the two superpowers. The Cold War dominated world politics from 1946 until 1991.

World War II further weakened the traditionally powerful European states of Germany, France, Britain, and Italy and elevated to top status two relative newcomers: the United States and the Soviet Union. These two countries had been allies against Germany, but they mistrusted each other intensely and had incompatible plans for postwar Europe. The period from 1946 through 1991 is known as the **Cold War** because, despite the intense conflict between the superpowers, actual "hot" war never broke out between them. The Cold War conflict dominated world politics over that period, and its after effects are widely felt today.[14]

Both the Soviet Union and the United States were intent on not repeating mistakes of the 1930s. Having learned the "lesson of Munich," each side strived to convince the other that the slightest aggression would be countered. For example, there was a series of crises over the status of Berlin, which was surrounded by communist East Germany but had been left under joint control of the Soviet Union, the United Kingdom, France, and the United States after World War II. The Soviet Union repeatedly sought to force the Western allies out of Berlin, precipitating crises in 1948, 1958, 1960, and 1961. Berlin was nearly impossible to defend in conventional military terms, but the United States and its allies maintained that any attack on Berlin would lead to a nuclear war.

These attempts at deterrence were strongly influenced by the development of nuclear weapons, which fundamentally changed the nature of military security by raising the potential death toll of the next major war to unimaginable levels. The nuclear arms race came to define Cold War security strategies, and fear that one side might seek a decisive victory through a surprise attack led to a high state of military readiness.

## THE CUBAN MISSILE CRISIS

The period of highest tension culminated in the Cuban Missile Crisis in 1962. Fearing that it was falling behind in the arms race, the Soviet Union began to install medium-range missiles in Cuba, less than one hundred miles from the U.S. coast. The United States threatened military attack and blockaded Cuba to prevent the missile installations from being completed. After a tense standoff, in which U.S. President John F. Kennedy estimated the chances of nuclear war were "between one out of three and even," the Soviet Union agreed to withdraw the missiles in return for concessions by the United States.[15]

The Cuban Missile Crisis ended the period of greatest danger in the Cold War for two reasons. First, it frightened both sides into taking steps to reduce the chances of such a crisis in the future. In historical terms, the Cuban Missile Crisis forced leaders to focus a bit less on the lessons of the 1930s and a bit more on the lessons of 1914. One measure taken was the installation of a "hotline" enabling immediate communication between leaders in Washington and Moscow. The first major arms control agreement between the United States and the Soviet Union followed shortly thereafter. Second, as both sides built more nuclear weapons and more missiles and aircraft to deliver them, the chance that either side could win a nuclear war, even if it waged a successful surprise attack, diminished. This situation was known as **mutual assured destruction (MAD)**. The fact that neither country could get away with a surprise attack—and that both U.S. and Russian leaders understood this—increased stability. The military competition between the United States and the Soviet Union continued for three decades after the Cuban Missile Crisis, with alternating periods of increased and decreased tension, but never again did the two sides come so close to war.

## THE GLOBAL ECONOMY

Among the lessons learned from World War II was that states needed to collaborate to avert global economic crises. For the Western powers, the importance of international economic collaboration was increased by the communist challenge. The long-term fear was that international economic instability would weaken the West relative to the Soviet Union. The immediate fear in the late 1940s was that if key European states such as France and Italy did not quickly recover economically from World War II, their own domestic communist parties might be able to win power.

Japan's bombing of Pearl Harbor had forced the United States to abandon its traditional doctrine of isolationism; it could not remain apart from the world's problems. A new internationalist consensus emphasized both active military confrontation with the Soviet Union and leadership in the global economy. Economic leadership was intended to increase global prosperity and to strengthen U.S. security. It also served the economic interests of the United States, which, as the major economy least damaged by the war, was best positioned to profit from a thriving international economy. The main institutions of international collaboration were formed at a conference in Bretton Woods, New Hampshire, in 1946, and the postwar economic system is therefore often referred to as the Bretton Woods system.

A major goal of the system was to foster expanded international trade in order to increase prosperity. The mechanism was the General Agreement on Tariffs and Trade (GATT), which in 1995 evolved into the World Trade Organization (WTO). The GATT was a multilateral agreement on **tariff** levels (see Chapter 11). Over time, successive rounds of negotiations lowered tariffs on many categories of goods. Although some key sectors, such as agriculture and services, were left out, GATT is widely credited with having increased trade and prosperity among its members.

A second goal of the Bretton Woods system was to provide stability in the international financial system. This was accomplished through the development of an international currency system based on the U.S. dollar, which in turn was linked to the value of gold. This system was managed by the International Monetary Fund (IMF). Agreements on exchange rates between different currencies provided stability and predictability, and a system of IMF loans helped countries overcome short-term imbalances in their international financial positions.

A related goal of postwar economic arrangements was to promote economic development. The International Bank for Reconstruction and Development (IBRD), commonly

**mutual assured destruction (MAD)**
A situation in which each side in a conflict possesses enough armaments to destroy the other even after suffering a surprise attack.

**tariff**
A tax on imports, used to protect domestic producers from foreign competition.

known as the World Bank, was founded in 1944 to promote the postwar reconstruction of Europe. In 1947, the United States initiated the Marshall Plan, intended to rebuild Europe, ensure the success of market economies, and reduce the attractiveness of communism. The success of the Marshall Plan validated international development lending as the World Bank shifted its focus from Europe to the developing world.

The Bretton Woods system is widely credited with spurring rapid economic growth among advanced industrial states in the second half of the twentieth century, but it is important to recognize that membership in these institutions was limited to a relatively small number of wealthy industrialized states. The Soviet Union and its allies chose not to participate. Many poor countries did not meet the requirements for membership and believed that the system exploited them. Thus, for much of the period in question, the global economy consisted of three groupings. One was centered on the United States and was organized by the Bretton Woods system. A second group was centered on the Soviet Union and consisted of states with communist systems and trade largely based on bilateral agreements. The third group consisted of the developing states, which traded on whatever terms they could negotiate. These groups were known as the First World, the Second World, and the **Third World**, respectively. Over time, more and more states joined the Bretton Woods institutions and the "Second World" vanished with the collapse of communism, so that today, although inequalities remain enormous, the global economy is not so clearly separated into groups.

# DECOLONIZATION, DEVELOPMENT, AND UNDERDEVELOPMENT

Following World War II, a wave of **decolonization** from 1945 until 1975 disbanded nearly all of the colonial relationships that had been established over the previous five centuries (Figure 2.4).[16] Several factors contributed to decolonization. First, the major colonial powers (especially Britain and France) had been severely weakened by World War II and were less able to resist independence movements. Second, the independence movements themselves grew stronger as a result of the doctrine of national self-determination and the democratic ideals that were the rallying cries in World War II. In India, a nonviolent Indian nationalist movement led by Mahatma Gandhi used the ideals of liberal democracy to show the hypocrisy of Britain's colonial empire. In China and French Indochina (later Vietnam), Mao Zedong and Ho Chi Minh used communist ideology to bolster their independence movements. Third, the United States, which had few formal colonies but was now the leading power in the West, disapproved of colonialism and sought to undermine it.

The U.S. position on colonialism was motivated in part by the understanding that the battle with the Soviet Union would be global in scope and ideological in nature. It was, therefore, crucial for the United States to gain friends and allies among the poor countries of the world because the Soviet Union would be making similar efforts. When communist revolutionaries triumphed in China in 1949, creating the (incorrect) perception that the world's most populous country would be controlled by the Soviet Union, competition for the loyalty of new states (and the remaining colonies) intensified. In some cases, this competition led to extensive financial aid, such as that which Japan and Korea received from the United States, and Egypt and China received from the Soviet Union.

In other cases, the competition took a military turn. When Vietnamese nationalists sought to gain independence from France after World War II, the United States feared that Vietnam would join China in the communist camp. As a result, the United States joined anticommunist South Vietnamese forces fighting a civil war against procommunist

## Third World

A term coined during the Cold War to describe those states that were neither in the group of advanced industrial states nor in the communist bloc; typically, it refers to the many poor states in the Southern Hemisphere. The term is generally considered synonymous with "underdeveloped."

## decolonization

The disbanding of nearly all colonial relationships between 1945 and 1975.

**Decolonization, 1945–1975.** In the decades following World War II, many of the colonies formed in the eighteenth and nineteenth centuries became independent sovereign states, a process that had occurred earlier in much of Latin America.

### Dates of independence of African countries

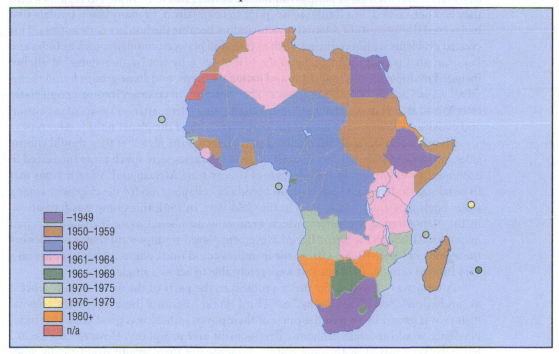

Source: http://www.saylor.org/site/wp-content/uploads/2011/04/Decolonization-of-Africa.pdf.

North Vietnamese forces. The Vietnam War had repercussions far beyond Southeast Asia. The fact that a nationalist movement consisting mainly of poor peasants could resist and eventually defeat the most powerful country in the world inspired other such movements. Moreover, it encouraged the belief in the Soviet Union that communist ideology combined with Soviet support could turn the tide in the developing world. It also had profound and lasting effects on the politics of Western Europe and the United States by undermining consensus about the conduct of the Cold War and the assumption that the United States was always a force for good in the world.

The superpowers in the Cold War avoided direct combat with each other, but they often waged it through allies, or "proxies," in the developing world. In addition to the Vietnam War (1954–1975), other regional wars that drew the superpowers in included the Korean War (1950–1953), the 1973 Arab-Israeli War, the Ogaden War between Somalia and Ethiopia (1978), and the Soviet-Afghan War (1979–1989). By involving themselves in these proxy wars, the United States and the Soviet Union sought to win allies in key regions, to harm each other's allies, and to demonstrate to the world their relative superiority over the other. Vietnam played an important role in weakening the United States, and Afghanistan was equally damaging to the Soviet Union.

As Africa and Asia decolonized, they did not revert to precolonial territorial and political arrangements (which varied from place to place). Rather, newly independent territories were integrated into the sovereign state system, a system developed and maintained by Europe. New states were formed, their borders were demarcated, and they were recognized as sovereign through membership in the UN. Possessing a sovereign state was the central goal of most nationalist movements, but integration of decolonized territory into the state system was fraught with difficulty. The sovereign state system is based on a strict territorial division of political authority. Borders had to be drawn in regions where they had not existed, in a formal sense, prior to colonialism. In many cases, borders that had served the interests of colonial administrators became the borders of new states. This created problems within countries, such as Iraq, and between countries, such as India and Pakistan, that persist today. Many of the new states were not "nation-states" at all, but included multiple ethnic, linguistic, and national groups, and some groups found themselves spread across two or more states. The transition of colonies into sovereign states after World War II meant that the Westphalian state system, after 500 years of expansion and evolution, now covered almost the entire territory of the planet outside Antarctica.

Many leaders of newly decolonized states rejected the idea that they should choose sides in the Cold War. Leaders in most of these countries were much more interested in economic development. In 1955, leaders of twenty-nine African and Asian nations met in Bandung, Indonesia, to establish an agenda of collaboration for development among states hoping to avoid taking sides in the Cold War. In 1961, this group was formalized in the Non-Aligned Movement, which eventually numbered more than one hundred members. Although the Non-Aligned Movement played an important role in broadening the agenda of international affairs, the members could find common interests only on a very limited number of issues and were rarely able to act as a single bloc.

Poverty was viewed as the major problem in the parts of the world usually labeled as "underdeveloped," "developing," or "Third World." Because these new states' colonial history was generally seen as the cause of their poverty, there was great hope that independence would increase economic development and prosperity. However, the record has been very mixed, with some countries increasing their wealth dramatically since the 1950s, while many others, especially in Africa, have stagnated. Which factors were responsible for the successes (and the failures) of these states has been a major source of debate to this day and remains a central concern in the study of international politics and economics (see Chapter 12).

By the 1970s, poor countries were trying new strategies of economic development. The ability of oil-producing countries to band together into the Organization of Petroleum Exporting Countries (OPEC) to force global oil prices higher was seen as a major victory for some poor countries. For others that had no oil and needed to buy it on the world market, the price hikes were a disaster. Efforts to form cartels to boost prices of other raw material exports, such as copper, coffee, and cocoa, generally failed. Another strategy sought to create a "new international economic order" that would change the rules of international trade to help redistribute power and wealth from the wealthy countries to the poorer ones. However, this project was rejected by wealthier countries, partly because they believed it was based on a faulty understanding of economics and partly because it was not in their interest.

# THE WORLD TODAY

## THE RISE OF NONSTATE ACTORS

**nonstate actors**

A political actor that is not a state, such as an advocacy group, charity, corporation, or terrorist group.

Throughout modern history, discussion of international affairs was essentially a discussion of states, which were widely viewed as the only important actors in international affairs. However, in the post–World War II era, new kinds of actors were recognized as having important impacts on international politics. Collectively, they are known as **nonstate actors**, but this is a misleading category because the variety of nonstate actors is immense. One of the first nonstate actors to gain widespread notice was the **multinational corporation (MNC)**, a company with operations in more than one country. Today, such corporations are a part of everyday life, but prior to the 1960s, they were the exception rather than the rule. Especially in relatively poor states, it often seemed as though these global corporations had more power than local governments. There was also considerable concern about the links between these large companies and their "host" governments in North America and Europe.

Attention also became focused on **international organizations (IOs)**—organizations formed by governments to help them pursue collaborative activity. These too proliferated after World War II. The UN is perhaps the best known of these, but economic IOs, such as the World Bank and the IMF, also attracted intense interest, as they were becoming very influential actors in the world economy. More recently still, international advocacy groups, often known as **nongovernmental organizations (NGOs)**, have proliferated and taken a higher profile on many international issues.[17] Today, there is considerable debate about the relative importance of nonstate actors versus traditional states (see Chapter 7).

Perhaps the most striking development with regard to the emergence of nonstate actors was the rise of the European Union.[18] Having started with six members in 1950, the European Union now has twenty-eight members, including almost every state in Western, Central, and Southern Europe (Norway and Switzerland are prominent exceptions). The members of the European Union have granted more and more political authority to common decision-making bodies based in Brussels, Belgium. The willingness of the "original" sovereign states to surrender key aspects of sovereignty has been seen as proof that IOs can be as important as states. The fact that Germany and France, after fighting three wars between 1870 and 1945, now consider war between themselves unthinkable is seen by some as evidence that IOs can significantly mitigate the problems of anarchy in international affairs.

## THE END OF THE COLD WAR

On November 9, 1989, the East German government opened the **Berlin Wall** and then stood aside as overjoyed citizens spontaneously destroyed it. Symbolically, tearing down the wall ended the Cold War, which had divided the Soviet-controlled regions of Eastern Europe from Western Europe since World War II. The definitive end to the Cold War came in 1991, when the Soviet Union fragmented into fifteen separate states.

To some observers, it seemed that without the clash between liberal democracy and authoritarian communism, there was no longer a significant cause for conflict in the world. The possibility of a fundamentally more peaceful world was illustrated when the Soviet Union tacitly supported the U.S. military campaign to eject Iraq from Kuwait, which it had invaded in 1990. U.S. President George H. W. Bush declared that a "new world order" was emerging.

The rest of the 1990s, however, belied those hopeful expectations. It became clear that nationalism had been suppressed, but not extinguished, in areas under communist control. Eastern Europe went through a period of nationalist resurgence that led to the fragmentation of three states: the Soviet Union, Czechoslovakia, and Yugoslavia (see Figure 2.5). This process demonstrated the tension between two important principles: national self-determination (of groups that wished to secede) versus sovereignty (of the existing countries). Only Czechoslovakia managed this process without sustained violence. After forty-five years of Cold War in which there had been no war in Europe, civil wars

**multinational corporation (MNC)**

A company with operations in more than one country; a type of nonstate actor; also called a transnational corporation.

**international organizations (IOs)**

Organizations formed by governments to help them pursue collaborative activity; a type of nonstate actor. More specifically known as international governmental organizations (IGOs).

**nongovernmental organizations (NGOs)**

A broad category of diverse organizations, including groups similar to domestic interest groups but with transnational concerns and organizational structures, and groups that focus not on influencing government but on conducting activities in different countries.

**Berlin Wall**

Erected in 1961 to prevent citizens of communist East Germany from migrating to West Germany, the Berlin Wall became a symbol both of the division of Europe and of the lack of freedom in the communist-controlled areas.

**FIGURE 2.5** Yugoslavia was formed out of several smaller independent countries and former parts of the Austrian and Ottoman Empires at the end of World War I. It fragmented in a series of conflicts beginning in 1991.

Source: http://www.lib.utexas.edu/maps/europe/fm_yugoslvia_po196.jpg. Adjusted to show dates of secession/independence. From: chttp://www.lib.utexas.edu/maps/serbia.htm. Courtesy of the University Libraries, The University of Texas at Austin.

broke out in the former Yugoslavia and in Russia (Chechnya), and ethnic cleansing in Yugoslavia brought back memories of genocide during World War II.

The collapse of communism also led to a new wave of democratization. Around the world, authoritarian regimes were replaced with elected ones, and many people believed that the spread of democracy would help to reduce conflict. Although some aspiring democracies have made the transition successfully, many others have found themselves with new variants of authoritarianism, and other governments, such as those in China and Cuba, have successfully resisted calls for greater democracy. Similarly, the hope that adopting free market economic principles would quickly increase prosperity has worked out splendidly in some countries and poorly in others.

The 1990s also witnessed an increased willingness to tackle global problems through international collaboration. The GATT was turned into a much stronger WTO in 1995. The North Atlantic Treaty Organization (NATO) and the UN struggled to manage the conflict emerging in Yugoslavia, but eventually, when the UN could not agree on action, NATO used military force in Bosnia in 1995 and in Kosovo in 1999. An agreement to limit global warming, the Kyoto Protocol, was reached. By the end of the decade, it was clear that the post–Cold War world was not going to be as simple and kind as some had hoped. At the same time, however, there was a widespread belief that the problems ahead were much less daunting than those behind.

## NEW WORLD ORDER? OR NEW WORLD DISORDER?

The attacks on New York City and Washington, D.C., on September 11, 2001, undermined sanguine assessments of security in the post–Cold War world. Suddenly, a key tenet of the Westphalian system, the idea that the main challenges to state security came from other states, was undermined. Overnight, the world's attention shifted to focusing on nonstate transnational terrorist organizations such as Al Qaeda.

Initially, the threats from terrorist groups catalyzed a new sense of common purpose among many of the world's states, for most perceived a common threat. However, disagreement over the best means of combating terrorism quickly undermined the emergent consensus. That acrimony was manifested intensely and publicly by the debate around the world on the U.S.-led invasion of Iraq in March 2003. Two major issues divided countries in this debate. First, what should be the relative importance of unilateral versus multilateral action in combating terrorism? Second, what is the role of traditional warfare versus less violent actions (such as policing and intelligence) in combating terrorism? Are the lessons of World War I, World War II, and the Cold War applicable to the "global war on terrorism?"

While the problems of terrorism and the wars in Afghanistan and Iraq dominated headlines in the post–September 11th era, other international problems and challenges did not disappear. An outbreak of the Ebola virus in western Africa in 2014 highlighted a

Protesters in the kasbah of Tunis, Tunisia, on February 25, 2011. Tunisia's revolution was the first of several in the "Arab Spring," which saw long-serving autocrats ejected in several states. Would these countries adopt democracy, and if so, what would be the effects on regional and global politics?

James Doberman/Getty Images

new danger of a global epidemic. The disease caused suffering and havoc in the countries to which it spread, and immense fear elsewhere. The danger of the pandemic led to an unusual degree of international collaboration to monitor and study the virus and impede its spread. Ultimately, the spread of the disease was contained, which some saw as a sign that national and international efforts to combat the virus were a success.

The expansion of the European Union to twenty-eight members provided renewed optimism in Europe but also raised questions about how large the organization could grow without becoming ineffective. People continue to debate whether the most powerful country in the world today, the United States, can or should attempt to establish global leadership, which in some ways would return the world to the pre-Westphalian dream of a single political leadership over all states. Some view that as a dream, others see it as a nightmare, and some believe it is impossible. Many anticipate that China will soon challenge the United States for global leadership, for better or for worse.

The global economic crisis that began in 2008 further upended prevailing conceptions about international politics. The wisdom of putting more faith in the free market was thrown into doubt as governments around the world tried to rescue their economies from markets that had induced chaos and collapse. The absence of a mechanism to coordinate global economic policy was felt keenly, as countries struggled to dampen a crisis that spread rapidly around the world. The U.S. debt crisis prompted many to argue that the financial basis for U.S. global power had largely vanished. The crisis also spurred acrimony within the European Union and created a real danger that the single currency, the euro, could not be maintained.

Economically, global interaction has increased. The past half-century has seen the growth of free trade and growing agreement on the important role of market mechanisms in increasing wealth. Yet the benefits of those developments have been spread unevenly, both around the globe and within individual countries. Simultaneously increasing wealth and equality continues to be an elusive goal.

Looking at the events and trends discussed in this chapter, we can see how they condition the background of today's events, how they shape political purpose, and how they might provide evidence for various assertions about international politics. Conversely, we can look at any issue today to uncover the understandings of history that influence thinking about that problem. There is often much debate about what history tells us. What is indisputable is that thinking about history powerfully influences what we think about international politics, and therefore what we do.

## RECONSIDER THE CASE

## THE RISE OF CHINA

When China joined the World Trade Organization in 1995, it was a watershed moment. China reversed fifty years of isolation from the global economy and a much longer tradition of political, economic, and cultural isolation, but it appeared determined to do so on terms that ensured it would remain powerful with respect to its trading partners and retain strong control internally.

China joined the WTO on the basis of a carefully negotiated agreement that allows it to limit foreign competition for all of its state-run organizations (SROs), including most manufacturing industries, such as steel,

*(Continued)*

mining, and energy, as well as publishing, film, and computers. For China, the goal is to avoid becoming a large importer; it plans to produce what it consumes and to export to other countries. For example, in 2011 Chrysler sold fewer than 300 vehicles per year in China because taxes and tariffs raised the price of a Jeep Cherokee from $27,000 to more than $85,000. China now produces more automobiles than any other country in the world. Meanwhile, China can export almost unlimited goods to Western countries. As a result of these provisions, China runs a large trade surplus with the United States and Europe and has accumulated more than a trillion U.S. dollars in reserves. These results are very different from those of China's last major trade interaction with the West in the nineteenth century.*

Western countries agreed to these terms in part because their firms were desperate to access Chinese markets and in part because leaders believed that, over time, trade with the West would naturally erode authoritarianism in China and cause China to drop some of these limits.

China also tries to prevent the intrusion of Western "soft" values or "propaganda" by limiting access to foreign intellectual property, such as film, the Internet, and Western books. The Chinese government allows licenses for only twenty foreign films per year to be shown in China. This significantly undermines efforts of global media companies to compete in China.

## Critical Thinking Questions

1. To what extent can we attribute Chinese policies to lessons of history as opposed to contemporary interests?

2. Do we see evidence that the Western states' policy toward China is guided by history? If not, why would some countries be guided by history more than others?

3. What lessons are being learned today that might guide future policies?

---

*Keith Bradsher, "China's 10-Year Ascent to Trading Power-house," New York Times, December 8, 2011, www.nytimes.com/2011/12/09/business/global/ chinas-10-year-ascent-to-trading-powerhouse.html?pagewanted=all.

# POWER AND PURPOSE IN INTERNATIONAL HISTORY

The themes of power and purpose recur throughout this brief overview of international history. It would be nearly impossible to tell the story without them. Much of international history concerns the efforts of states to gather and wield power, and changes in the distribution of power play an important role in driving change. For example, it is hard to discuss World War I or the Cold War without discussing the distribution of power. At the same time, we see evolution in the purpose for which power is exercised, and in the uses of power that are considered legitimate or illegitimate. The emergence of the sovereign state system is as much about shared purpose—acceptance of plurality and sovereignty—as about the distribution of power. The rise of nationalism fundamentally shifted the purpose of political action, and in turn created new sources of power and new constraints on power. The emergence of the Concert of Europe saw a near merger of power and purpose, as states sought to preserve a particular distribution of power that they believed would preserve stability. The Cold War was both a naked competition for power and an intense ideological competition between communism and free market democracy concerning the proper goals of government. In today's world, power and purpose overlap in debates about the effective and acceptable ways to solve international political and economic problems.

## SUMMARY

- History helps us understand the roots of contemporary problems, shapes our understanding of the purpose of policies, and provides much of the evidence used to evaluate hypotheses, arguments, and assertions about the nature of international politics.

- The Greek city-states provide one of the earliest examples of what later came to be viewed as a system of independent states.

- A feudal system, in which political power and authority were highly fragmented, arose in Europe after the collapse of the Roman Empire. The Treaty of Westphalia established principles that gave rise to today's system of sovereign states.

- A classic balance of power system prevailed in Europe until the early nineteenth century. The nineteenth century witnessed the rise of nationalism and imperialism.

- The political and military lessons taken from World War II are almost the opposite of those taken from World War I. World War I showed the foolishness of going to war before diplomacy was exhausted, whereas World War II showed the foolishness of neglecting to confront expansionist powers.

- World War II weakened Western Europe, leaving two superpowers, the United States and the Soviet Union, which engaged in the Cold War. A wave of decolonization created many new developing states that were not "nation-states."

- The twentieth and early twenty-first centuries have seen the state-centered model of international politics eroded both from above (through the increased role of IOs such as the UN and the European Union) and from below (through the increased role of a wide range of nonstate actors as varied as Microsoft, Greenpeace, and Al Qaeda). Yet the importance of sovereign states remains undeniable.

## KEY CONCEPTS

1. Peloponnesian War
2. Westphalian system
3. Sovereignty
4. Anarchy
5. State
6. Balance of power
7. Nationalism
8. Concert of Europe
9. Imperialism
10. Treaty of Versailles
11. League of Nations
12. Collective security
13. Isolationism
14. Cold War
15. Bretton Woods system
16. Nonstate actors

## STUDY QUESTIONS

1. An analysis of which war gave rise to the first known attempt to advance a general understanding of how international politics works?
   a. The Peloponnesian War
   b. The Thirty Years' War
   c. World War II
   d. The Cold War

2. How did the Westphalian system differ from the medieval system that preceded it?
   a. It gave rise to sovereign states.
   b. It created a feudal economy.
   c. It initiated a race to colonize Africa and Asia.
   d. It led to the rise of nonstate actors.

3. How did the Napoleonic wars change the way wars were fought?

   a. They greatly increased the size of armies.

   b. They expanded the scale of combat.

   c. They increased the number of casualties.

   d. All of the above.

4. What was the major lesson taken from World War II?

   a. Exhaust all avenues of diplomacy before going to war.

   b. Expansionist powers should be confronted without delay.

   c. The only way to win a nuclear war is to strike first.

   d. Do not fail to recognize threats from nonstate actors.

5. What event led to the end of the Cold War?

   a. The Treaty of Westphalia

   b. The rise of Napoleon

   c. The colonization of Asia and Africa

   d. The fall of communism in Eastern Europe

6. What event led people to wonder whether the financial basis for U.S. global power had largely vanished?

   a. The Treaty of Westphalia

   b. The Concert of Europe

   c. The establishment of the Bretton Woods system

   d. The international financial crisis that began in 2008

1. How did the system that arose in modern Europe spread to the rest of the world?

2. Is the Concert of Europe best viewed as a variant of traditional balance of power politics or as a new form of international politics?

3. How did "collective security" work between World War I and World War II?

4. What role did economics play in the outbreak of World War II?

5. What arrangements were made to govern the international economy after World War II?

6. How did the process of decolonization influence international politics?

[Correct Answers: 1. a; 2. a; 3. d; 4. b; 5. d; 6. d]

## END NOTES

1. There are few, if any, comprehensive histories of international politics. Most studies focus on a particular period, a particular issue, or both. One study that begins even before the Greek city-states is Adam Watson, *The Evolution of International Society* (London: Routledge, 1992). K. J. Holsti, *Peace and War: Armed Conflicts and International Order, 1648–1989* (Cambridge, UK: Cambridge University Press, 1991) covers the modern era but focuses primarily on war.

2. Thucydides, *History of the Peloponnesian War*; Donald Kagan, *The Peloponnesian War* (New York: Penguin, 2003).

3. On the Roman Empire and the *pax Romana*, see Watson, *The Evolution of International Society*, Chapter 9, and Michael Doyle, *Empires* (Ithaca, NY: Cornell University Press, 1986), Chapter 4.

4. Gordon A. Craig and Alexander L. George, *Force and Statecraft: Diplomatic Problems of Our Time* (New York: Oxford, 1990), Chapters 1–3.

5. See Michael Howard, George Andreopoulos, and Mark R. Shulman, eds., *The Laws of War: Constraints on Warfare in the Western World* (New Haven, CT: Yale University Press, 1997).

6. The evolution of international politics in non-European parts of the world is discussed in Watson, *The Evolution of International Society*.

7. The bringing of the rest of the world into the Westphalian state system is discussed in Watson, *The Evolution of International Society*, Chapter 22.

8. One compelling, though debated, explanation is that of Jared Diamond in *Guns, Germs, and Steel: The Fates of Human Societies* (New York: Norton, 1999).

9. On Napoleon's revolution in warfare, see David A. Bell, *The First Total War: Napoleon's Europe and the Birth of Warfare as We Know It* (New York: Houghton Mifflin, 2007).

10. See Louise Richardson, "The Concert of Europe and Security Management in the 19th Century," in Helga

Haftendorn, Robert O. Keohane, and Celeste A. Wallander, eds., *Imperfect Unions, Security Institutions over Time and Space* (Oxford: Oxford University Press, 1999), pp. 48–79.

11. For a brief survey of late nineteenth-century imperialism, see Andrew Porter, *European Imperialism 1860–1914* (New York: Palgrave Macmillan, 1996).

12. A good survey of this period is Jonathan D. Spence, *The Search for Modern China* (New York: W. W. Norton, 1999), especially Chapters 6–7.

13. On the interwar period, see Edward Hallett Carr, *The Twenty Years' Crisis, 1919–1939* (New York: Harper & Row, 1964 [1939]). On the war itself, see Martin Gilbert, *The Second World War: A Complete History* (New York: Henry Holt & Co., 1989).

14. For a comprehensive history of the Cold War, see John Lewis Gaddis, *The Cold War: A New History* (New York: Penguin, 2005).

15. Despite having lasted barely two weeks, the Cuban Missile Crisis has generated an immense literature.

For a participant's view, see Robert F. Kennedy, *Thirteen Days: A Memoir of the Cuban Missile Crisis* (New York: Norton, 1971). For a historical treatment, see Don Munton and David A. Welch, *The Cuban Missile Crisis: A Concise History* (Oxford: Oxford University Press, 2006).

16. John Springhall, *Decolonization Since 1945: The Collapse of European Overseas Empires* (New York: Palgrave Macmillan, 2001).

17. Margaret E. Keck and Kathryn Sikkink, *Activists Beyond Borders: Advocacy Networks in International Politics* (Ithaca, NY: Cornell University Press, 1998); Sanjeev Khagram, Kathryn Sikkink, and James V. Riker, eds., *Restructuring World Politics: Transnational Social Movements, Networks, and Norms* (Minneapolis: University of Minnesota Press, 2002).

18. Desmond Dinan, *Europe Recast: A History of European Union* (Boulder, CO: Lynne Rienner, 2004).

German Chancellor Angela Merkel and Russian Prime Minister Vladimir Putin address the media in Berlin, 2009. Is their relationship defined primarily by conflict or by cooperation?

iStockphoto.com/EdStock

# THEORIES OF INTERNATIONAL RELATIONS: REALISM AND LIBERALISM

## Learning Objectives

**3-1** Identify the major assumptions of the realist and liberal approaches.

**3-2** Distinguish the major strands of theory within each approach.

**3-3** Understand the normative positions of realism and liberalism.

**3-4** Summarize the major critiques of each approach.

**3-5** Identify ways in which each approach can be linked to policy problems.

**3-6** Articulate and defend an argument concerning the relative merits of the different approaches.

## CONSIDER THE CASE

## SHOULD IRAN OBTAIN NUCLEAR WEAPONS?

Will Iran be more secure if it obtains a usable nuclear weapons arsenal? Many people in the Middle East and beyond see an Iranian nuclear arsenal as a threat to others, but presumably the Iranian government's primary concern is making itself more secure. Iran continues to fear attack by the United States or Israel, both of which have nuclear weapons. The success of U.S. air power in Iraq in 1991 and 2003 and in Yugoslavia in 1999 may have increased Iran's fears that it could neither defeat nor deter a U.S. attack. Moreover, the United States, in naming Iran part of an "axis of evil," along with North Korea and Iraq, appeared to be contemplating using force to accomplish "regime change." The U.S. invasion of Iran's neighbors Iraq and Afghanistan may have appeared especially threatening. Iran may calculate that its adversaries will be less likely to attack if they face the possibility of nuclear retaliation. This argument reflects the traditional theory of realism: In an insecure world, states gain security only by having enough power to defeat, or at least deter, their enemies. Surely Iran cannot base its security on the hope that, if the United States were to attack, some other country or countries could or would successfully protect it. In this view, nuclear weapons are a "no brainer" for Iran and for any other country whose leaders believe that it faces powerful adversaries.

But what responses has Iran's nuclear program provoked? It has inspired fear, and states have taken action in response. Israel and the United States have developed plans for a potential attack on Iran to destroy the weapons preemptively. European states have enacted tough economic sanctions on Iran. Meanwhile, Arab states in the region, such as Egypt and Saudi Arabia, might be tempted to develop their own nuclear weapons in response (and both have the resources to do so). In sum,

Iran's nuclear weapons program might mean that it faces more adversaries armed with nuclear weapons, not fewer, and that the United States or Israel is more likely to attack, not less.

The same dilemma exists for Israel: Having fought three wars with its neighbors since its founding in 1948, Israel remains profoundly insecure. To deter further attack, Israel procured nuclear weapons in the 1970s. With Iran's former President Mahmoud Ahmadinejad having denied Israel's right to exist, nuclear weapons may be all that deters an attack. At the same time, however, Israel's neighbors might view Israel's nuclear arsenal as a reason they need nuclear weapons too.

Thus, Iran faces a dilemma. If it does not build nuclear weapons, it might be attacked or threatened by more powerful actors such as the United States. But if it does build nuclear weapons, it might increase the incentives for Israel and the United States to attack and prompt other neighbors to acquire nuclear arms. Either way, it seems difficult for Iran to guarantee its security. Is there any way out of this dilemma? Some theorists say there is not. Such insecurity is the essence of international politics, many believe, and the smart state procures as many weapons as is feasible to protect itself. Others say that there is a way out. If the United States threatens Iran because of its nuclear program and Iran seeks nuclear weapons because it feels threatened by the United States, the two could come to an agreement whereby Iran would commit to neither attacking Israel nor obtaining nuclear weapons and the United States and Israel would commit to not attacking Iran. That approach was reflected in an agreement reached in early 2015, under which Iran would undergo strengthened inspections to ensure that it was not procuring nuclear weapons, and the US and Europe would end economic sanctions.

What are the driving forces of international politics? What underlying patterns do we see in the variety of issues and events that interest us? When we seek to explain a policy or a trend, where should we begin? These questions are answered by theories of international politics—that is, by generalized explanations of what drives states to do what they do.

As Chapter 1 stressed, theory underpins action, whether we admit it or not. When we hear policy makers arguing about the best policy on some issue, we can almost always find competing theories of international politics behind the specific policy disagreement. A central goal of this text is to help you identify the connections between theories and policy prescriptions and the corresponding links between theoretical debates and policy debates.

Theory in international politics is characterized above all by disagreement and debate. On almost every question that matters, there is significant theoretical disagreement. There are virtually no theories that allow reliable predictions, and few if any theories provide explanations that satisfy a wide range of scholars or practitioners. In these ways, international relations differ from the rigorous and empirically tested theories in economics.

This multiplicity of theories is an asset as well as a weakness. Different theoretical approaches provide different "lenses" through which we see events. Each lens brings certain aspects of international politics into sharp focus, while giving less emphasis to others. If we are able to see the same problem from multiple perspectives, we can understand it more thoroughly, and perhaps make more effective policies. Thus, although we often see different approaches as competing with one another, in practice they are often complementary.

This chapter considers the two oldest and most widely articulated approaches: realism and liberalism. Realism is an approach that focuses almost exclusively on the role of state power in an anarchic world where insecurity is high. Realism sees power as the main determinant of outcomes and sees the pursuit of power as the main determinant of policies. Liberalism is concerned with purpose as well as power; it asserts that states have a range of goals beyond accruing power and that cooperation is often as important

Iran's Bushehr nuclear power plant, which could provide materials for a nuclear weapons program. What are Iran's incentives to obtain nuclear weapons, and what would the consequences be?

as power in achieving state aims. First, however, the chapter examines the ways in which compatible theories are grouped together into paradigms.

# PARADIGMS OF INTERNATIONAL RELATIONS

Chapter 1 introduced four levels of analysis in international relations: the system, the state, the substate, and the individual. Theories of international politics can also be categorized according to their philosophical underpinnings. Every theory makes certain simplifying assumptions in order to focus on some central concern. Scholars differ on what the central concerns are and on what matters can be set aside with these simplifying assumptions. For example, in many theories of international politics, the central concern is the behavior of states, and the actions of other kinds of actors are assumed to be less important. This assumption allows the scholar to focus on a single actor, rather than going in ten directions at once.

This book discusses five paradigms of international politics: realism, liberalism, economic structuralism (Marxism), constructivism, and feminism. Note that these are called "theoretical approaches" or "paradigms" rather than "theories." Each paradigm is broader than a single theory and may encompass many theories. Those theories may contradict each other in some ways, but if they are based on similar philosophical assumptions, we group them together. For example, some theorists argue that the existence of many great powers in the international arena is most conducive to peace, whereas others argue that having only two great powers is most conducive to peace. In some respects, these are contradictory theories. However, because both theories view the problem of war and peace as based on the distribution of power in the system, they are viewed as part of a single theoretical approach (realism).

The term **paradigm** describes an approach to a problem shared by a group of scholars. Within a given paradigm, there is agreement concerning which assumptions are uncontroversial and which are debatable. In other words, a paradigm determines which questions are asked and which questions are not asked. An issue that one group of scholars considers unimportant and ignores may be identified by another group as the central problem. Thus, it is often valuable to view a problem from more than one perspective.

Understanding the relationship among paradigms, levels of analysis, and theories is important. A *paradigm* is a set of beliefs about what should be taken for granted and what needs to be investigated, about what sorts of forces are most important in the world, and about what assumptions should begin the analysis (for example, human nature is aggressive, or states are the main actors in international politics). More than one theory can exist within each paradigm. A *level of analysis* is a "place" where the analysis takes place. Every analysis focuses on one aggregation—the individual, the group, or a collection of groups—and holds the other aggregations constant for the purposes of analysis. More than one theory can exist at each level of analysis. A *theory* is a specific statement about how international politics works. It is based on assumptions, such as what level of analysis matters most and what the most important questions are.

To clarify the relationship of these three concepts, Table 3.1 shows how different theories can be classified according to their paradigm and level of analysis. Such a classification scheme is a matter of judgment, and to put theories in boxes like this might exaggerate their differences, but this kind of exercise is useful in considering the relationship among different theories.

**paradigm**

A theoretical approach that includes one or more theories that share similar philosophical assumptions.

**TABLE 3.1**    **Theories of International Politics Categorized by Paradigm and Level of Analysis**

| Paradigm | Level of Analysis | | | |
|---|---|---|---|---|
| | **System** | **State** | **Substate** | **Individual** |
| Realism | Balance of power theory; hegemonic stability theory | Revisionist versus status quo powers | | Human nature as inherently aggressive |
| Liberalism | Liberal institutionalism; regime theory | Democratic peace theory* | Complex interdependence theory | Human nature as inherently peaceful |
| Economic structuralism* | World systems theory; dependency theory | State working on behalf of the capitalist class | Firms dominating politics | |
| Constructivism* | Systemic norms (for example, sovereignty) | Identity politics | Transnational actors, NGOs | |
| Feminism* | Gendered nature of systemic international relations theory | State as a gendered construction | Effects of separating public from private | Effects of international politics on women |

*Regime theory, democratic peace theory, economic structuralism, constructivism, and feminism are discussed in later chapters.

# THE POLICY CONNECTION

## WHAT IF ACADEMICS MADE FOREIGN POLICY?

The theories discussed in this book sometimes seem detached from the real world of policy making. However, academics do make foreign policy when they are brought into government. In the United States alone, there are several prominent examples.

- Woodrow Wilson, president of the United States from 1913 to 1921, was a political scientist and international relations scholar. He taught at Bryn Mawr, Wesleyan, and Princeton. As an academic, Wilson was highly regarded for his analysis of the U.S. Congress, as well as for his work on the British cabinet system. As president, Wilson is known for putting liberal theory into practice and trying to establish international peace through democratic government, ideas developed in his earlier scholarly writings.

- Henry Kissinger was a professor of government at Harvard before becoming national security

adviser in the Nixon and Ford administrations (1969–1977) and secretary of state under President Ford. As an academic, he was known primarily for his writing on realism and on balance of power as a policy. As secretary of state, he is credited with having achieved important agreements with the Soviet Union, and is criticized for his mistrust of democracy.

- Condoleezza Rice was a specialist on the Soviet military as a professor at Stanford before becoming national security adviser (2001–2005) and secretary of state (2005–2009) for President George W. Bush. Her most important work as an academic dealt with civil–military relations in the Soviet bloc.* By the time she became national security adviser, the Soviet Union was long gone, so it is hard to identify any clear link between Rice's academic writings and her policies. Interestingly,

(Continued)

she coauthored a political science book while serving as secretary of state.[†]

- The position of national security adviser seems particularly suited to academics. In addition to Kissinger and Rice, Zbigniew Brzezinski (Carter Administration, 1977–1981) and Anthony Lake (Clinton Administration, 1993–1997) moved into it from teaching international politics.

- In Brazil, former sociology professor Fernando Enrique Cardoso served as minister of finance and then president from 1995 to 2003. As a sociologist, Cardoso was a central figure in the development of dependency theory, a Marxist approach to international political economy. As finance minister and president, however, he oversaw Brazil's embrace of free market economics.

- In 2015, Yanis Varoufakis, an economist at the University of Texas, was named finance minister in Greece, charged with renegotiating Greece's bailout agreement with the European Union. A self-described Marxist, Varoufakis resigned after a few months over his opposition to the terms of a bailout for Greece.

## Critical Thinking Questions

1. The practice of appointing academics to leading foreign policy positions seems to be more prevalent in the United States than in other countries. Why might this be the case?

2. What strengths and weaknesses might an academic bring to the task of devising and implementing foreign policy?

3. What kinds of traits should leaders seek in their foreign policy advisers?

*Condoleezza Rice, The Soviet Union and the Czechoslovak Army, 1948–1983: Uncertain Allegiance (Princeton, NJ: Princeton University Press, 1984).

†Bruce Bueno de Mesquita, Kiron Skinner, Serhiy Kudelia, and Condoleezza Rice, The Strategy of Campaigning: Lessons from Ronald Reagan and Boris Yeltsin (Ann Arbor: University of Michigan Press, 2007).

# REALISM

Bust of Thucydides (c.471-400 BC), engraved by Barbant (engraving) (b&w photo), Lacaille, Felix Jules (19th century) (after)/Private Collection /The Bridgeman Art Library

The analysis of the Peloponnesian War by the Athenian general Thucydides has influenced realist theory for nearly 2500 years.

In his *History of the Peloponnesian War*, written in the fifth century BCE, Thucydides made several famous generalizations about relations between Greece's city-states.

- "The strong do what they can and the weak suffer what they must."
- "Of gods we trust and of men we know, it is in their nature to rule whenever they can."
- "What made war inevitable was the growth of Athenian power and the fear that this caused in Sparta."
- "So far as right and wrong are concerned … there is no difference between the two."[1]

In this ancient text, Thucydides laid out the philosophical underpinnings of the school of thought later known as realism: International politics is about the exercise of power by states, unconstrained by moral limits. The first quotation indicates that the distribution of power determines the options open to states; the second asserts that striving to dominate others is a primordial human motivation; the third contends that the distribution of power is the primary cause of war and peace. The final quotation warns that in international politics there is no shared morality, and hence, morality cannot be the basis for action. This rather bleak view of international politics continues to be influential to the present day. Some of the most prominent figures in the history of Western thought, including **Niccolò Machiavelli** and **Thomas Hobbes**, have contributed to its evolution.

As an approach to international politics, realism focuses on the problems of international conflict. Above all, realists seek to account for the fact that international politics over all of recorded history has seen a succession of wars. Despite progress in science and technology, the demise of monarchies and the rise of democracies, the rise and decline of colonialism, and the evolution of weaponry from spears to cannon to nuclear weapons, wars have recurred, and the possibility of war has been a constant. Why?

## CENTRAL ASSUMPTIONS

Realist theories share four central assumptions.

**Anarchy**    Realism places immense emphasis on the idea that international politics is *anarchic*, because there is no world government to rule over the states.[2] Thus international politics is fundamentally different from domestic politics. **Anarchy** follows logically from state sovereignty and is the defining element of the Westphalian system. For realism, anarchy predisposes international politics toward conflict.

**States as the Central Actors**    Realism sees states as the central actors in international politics.[3] Realists argue that international organizations in the contemporary era primarily reflect the interests of the states that create them. Similarly, realists assert that states can control actors such as multinational corporations when they really want to. Thus international politics is politics between states.

**States as Unitary Actors**    When realists look at the state, they see a single coherent entity. This assumption has worked its way into much of the popular journalistic treatment of international politics, as well as into many history books, which treat history as a history of countries (states). When journalists or historians write "Russia did X" or "Washington believes Y," they are implicitly advancing this state-centered view.

**States as Rational Actors**    Realists assume that state behavior is rational. This is perhaps the most widely debated assumption of realism. Rationality does not mean that states always make the best or the "right" decisions, but rather that states "have consistent, ordered preferences, and that they calculate the costs and benefits of all alternative policies in order to maximize their utility."[4] The rationality *assumption* is not meant to be an accurate *description* of how states behave all the time; every realist understands that states sometimes make bad decisions. In practice, realists often criticize state policies as being counter to the national interest.

Obviously, the notion of states as unified, rational actors is a simplification. Every country contains many individuals and groups, and every government contains a complex array of organizations and decision-making procedures. Realists argue that in most of the important matters, states are highly constrained by their circumstances.[5] In this view, foreign policy is a rational response to external conditions, and different leaders in the same situation could be expected to behave similarly. It does not much matter if a liberal or a conservative is in power, or even if the government is democratic or authoritarian. In a commonly used metaphor, states are like billiard balls on a table. We do not need to look inside them to see how they behave; we only have to understand the external forces to which they are subject. For this reason, realism is characterized primarily as a system-level paradigm: behavior is driven by the conditions in the system, not by internal politics of the individual states.

**Niccolò Machiavelli (1469–1527)**

A government official in the medieval city-state of Florence who wrote about the "laws of politics" for the "wise statesman," focusing on how the state could defend itself from domestic and foreign enemies.

**Thomas Hobbes (1588–1679)**

Author of the influential work *Leviathan*, in which he argued that government had to be autocratic to prevent a slide back into anarchy.

**anarchy**

A condition in which there is no central ruler.

# THE HISTORY CONNECTION

## REALISM AND LIBERALISM, AND WAR IN EUROPE, 1939 TO 2015

In 1939, Germany invaded Poland, kicking off World War II, and the English historian E. H. Carr published *The Twenty Years Crisis*, a scathing indictment of interwar policy and a powerful attack on liberal international relations theory, which he called "idealism." Carr's critique of the post–World War I order was simple: Efforts to prevent war by resort to treaties, as embodied by the League of Nations, were an attempt to base policy not on international politics as it was but as people hoped it could be. Carr advocated "realism," and realism dominated scholarship on international politics in the following decades.

By the 1970s, however, new phenomena emerged that left many scholars believing realism was missing a lot. The emergence of international organizations and multinational corporations led scholars to question the dominant role of the state. The prominence of international economic issues led scholars to question whether military security was the only important issue in global politics. Scholars Joseph Nye and Robert Keohane coined the term *complex interdependence* to characterize this much more nuanced array of issues and actors. The deepening of economic cooperation, the success of European integration, and the moderation of the Cold War, all contributed to the rise of liberal theory in the 1970s and 1980s. Although realists countered with arguments of their own, liberalism came to rival realism as an academic theory and as a guide to policy.

For many opponents of realism, the end of the Cold War (1989–1991) signaled the burial of realism as a viable theory. How could realism explain that one of the superpowers had decided not to compete any longer? The spread of democracy in eastern Europe and elsewhere led to the belief that the problem of security in Europe had moved from the realm of military competition to cooperation.

Russia's invasion of Ukraine in 2014 reenergized realist analysis. John Mearsheimer, a prominent realist, argued that Russia's invasion was the fault of Western governments and the liberalism that guided them.* Thinking that territorial control and security were no longer important, they extended the NATO alliance and the EU ever closer to Russia, and provoked a Russian response. Realism, he said, would have told the West to play politics the old way by respecting Russia's need to control the region directly to its west. Mearsheimer seemed to be reprising Carr's earlier critique. Many found that Mearsheimer's argument was not only a poor analysis of the Russia–Ukraine war, but a poor application of realism—why wouldn't a realist have urged the West to seize territory from Russia while it was weak; and why shouldn't the West now arm Ukraine in order to undermine Russia's power?

Whether Mearsheimer's argument accurately represented realism or not, Russia's invasion of Ukraine was an unpleasant reminder that traditional warfare, in which one state simply decides to invade another, is not a thing of the past. Many in Europe lamented that in the years since the end of the Cold War they had dramatically reduced the sizes of their armies and defense budgets, leaving them vulnerable to a newly aggressive Russia. Again, the debate about security in Europe was being carried out largely in realist terms.

### Critical Thinking Questions

1. What factors account for the rising and sinking popularity of theories such as realism and liberalism?

2. Does it make more sense to debate which theory is true, or to try to figure out why each of them seems valid in different situations?

3. Can we apply to the world of today the same theories that were used to examine the 1930s?

---

*John J. Mearsheimer, "Why the Ukraine Crisis Is the West's Fault: The Liberal Delusions That Provoked Putin," Foreign Affairs (September/October 2014): 1–12.

The notion of a state that is unitary and rational leads directly to the concept of the **national interest**—a foreign policy goal that is objectively valuable for the overall well-being of the state. The term *national interest* implies that the state is a single entity (rather than a collection of actors and interests), that it has a single interest, and that the interest can be objectively determined. Policy makers and commentators often justify particular policy prescriptions with the argument that they are in the "national interest."

## THE SECURITY DILEMMA

Realism begins with anarchy and then deduces its implications. First, anarchy leads to insecurity. In anarchy, there is no one to stop one country from attacking another. In other words, realists see a "self-help world." If states are to survive, they must rely on their own means, because there is no international police force to protect them or to punish aggressors.

Second, insecurity leads states to arm themselves. States that want to survive must be able to defeat potential attackers or deter them from attacking in the first place. The problem is that when state A arms, even if only to protect itself, states B, C, and D view the action as a threat. States B, C, and D then increase their armaments. Now state A faces a bigger threat than before, so it increases its armament. The other states then respond to this threat, and so on. The result can be an arms race, as occurred between Britain and Germany prior to World War I and between the United States and the Soviet Union during the Cold War.

The tendency for one state's efforts to obtain security to cause insecurity in others is known as the **security dilemma**. If a state refrains from engaging in the weapons competition with other states, it leaves itself vulnerable to attack. But if it builds new weapons, it creates insecurity for others. The others' natural response is to arm, making the first state less secure. The dilemma is that either way, the state ends up less secure. Today, Iran's interest in nuclear weapons—and the fear this causes in other states—can be understood in terms of the security dilemma. Iran contemplates acquiring nuclear weapons because it fears attack, but its efforts to gain nuclear weapons may make it more likely to be attacked. Although some people suggest reaching an agreement to stop building weapons (see the discussion of liberalism later in the chapter), realists contend that agreements can always be broken and that states are unlikely to stake their survival on agreements with other states. Therefore, insecurity leads states to arm, but arms create more insecurity.

## THE SECURITY DILEMMA AND THE PRISONER'S DILEMMA

A branch of mathematics called *game theory* has been widely applied in efforts to understand various aspects of international politics, including the security dilemma. Simple game theory provides a provocative insight into the challenges of cooperating in a wide range of social situations. One particular model known as the **prisoner's dilemma** game has been used to represent a wide variety of social and political problems, and you will encounter it repeatedly in this book.[6]

The basic story that gives the model its name is familiar to anyone who has watched television crime shows. The police detain two people suspected of a crime. They separate the two for interrogation and try to get each one to "rat out" the other in return for a lighter sentence. If they cooperate with each other and refuse to talk to the police, both may escape with a light sentence. However, each of the suspects has an incentive to "defect" on the partner by confessing to the police, and each knows that the other has the same incentive.

**national interest**
A foreign policy goal that is objectively valuable for the overall well-being of the state. The concept is important in realist theory and in foreign policy discussions, but some dispute that there is any single national interest.

**security dilemma**
The difficult choice faced by states in anarchy between arming, which risks provoking a response from others, and not arming, which risks remaining vulnerable.

**prisoner's dilemma**
A game theory scenario in which noncooperation is the rational strategy but leads to both players being worse off than if they had cooperated.

**TABLE 3.2** Payoffs in the Prisoner's Dilemma

| | | Player A | |
|---|---|---|---|
| | | Cooperate | Defect |
| Player B | Cooperate | (3, 3) | (1, 4) |
| | Defect | (4, 1) | (2, 2) |

The dilemma is represented in Table 3.2. Each player's "payoff" (in this case, the sentence he or she will have to serve) can be ranked from best (4) to worst (1). In this example, "cooperate" means to cooperate with one's partner, not the police, and "defect" means to betray one's partner by confessing to the police. If one player cooperates and the other defects, the one who defects gets the best possible outcome (4, the benefits of a deal) while the one who cooperates gets the worst payoff (1, being implicated by his or her partner). If both players cooperate, the police can only charge them with a lesser offense, and they get the second-best outcome (3). If both defect, each gets some benefit from a lighter sentence but not as much as if the partner had cooperated (2). The model might not perfectly capture the way criminal sentencing works, but it illustrates a problem that recurs in a wide variety of social relations.

What strategy should each player choose: cooperate or defect? Analyzing the payoffs reveals a paradox that has far-reaching consequences for social interaction. At first glance, it might appear that the strategy one should choose would depend on what the other actor does, but this turns out not to be the case. Look at the problem from the perspective of player A. If player B defects, A can get the worst outcome by cooperating or the second-worst outcome by defecting, so A is better off defecting. But what if B cooperates? Then A can get the best outcome by defecting or the second-best outcome by cooperating. *Regardless of what B does, A scores better by defecting.* Because the game is symmetric, B is also better off defecting, regardless of what A does. If both players are rational, both will defect and both will receive the second-worst outcome. But both players could be better off, at the same time, if both cooperated. This is the paradox of the model: *Individual rationality leads to collective irrationality.*

This paradox, also known as the *collective action problem*, directly parallels the realist understanding of the security dilemma. For the realist, the dilemma is whether or not to arm (or to arm further). Arming is equivalent to defecting; not arming is equivalent to cooperating. Realists argue that, in anarchy, the rational state will arm, regardless of what its neighbor does. However, when both states arm, both end up less secure (because war will now be more destructive) and less wealthy. Again, individually rational behavior leads to collective irrationality. The dilemma is that the state faces diminished security whether it arms or not. For the realist, overcoming this dilemma is extremely difficult. Because there is no one to enforce agreements, cheating can leave a state that cooperates vulnerable. Therefore, prudent states consistently "defect," acquiring more and more arms.

The model embodies a great number of assumptions, including that states are unified actors, that they behave rationally, that the game is played only once, that different issues are not connected, and that payoffs are symmetric. These assumptions make it hard to apply the model to the real world, but scholars widely agree that it captures a basic problem in international politics and many other situations.

## POWER IN REALIST THEORY

In the realist view, the distribution of power is the central force in international politics. The prominent realist Hans Morgenthau wrote, "International politics, like all politics, is a struggle for power."[7] Powerful states are safe; weak states are not. Relatively powerful states are able to shape the behavior of others (through threats or bribes). Because power is necessary to obtain any other goal, Morgenthau reasoned, every state's national interest boils down simply to getting more power. The alternative, Kenneth Waltz writes, is "probable suicide."[8]

Power in realism is defined largely in terms of coercion. Morgenthau famously defined power as "man's control over the minds and actions of other men."[9] To John Mearsheimer, power "represents nothing more than specific assets or material resources that are available to a state."[10] A preponderance of such resources does not guarantee victory in conflict, Mearsheimer says, but states nonetheless would always rather have more assets or resources than less because, other things being equal, the more powerful state will prevail.[11] Like many realists, he defines "power" as military power, because "force is the *ultima ratio* [last resort] in international politics."[12] For realists, therefore, the relative power of various countries is measured primarily by their military arsenals.

*"But how do you know for sure you've got power unless you abuse it?"*

However, realists also stress that economic power is an essential underpinning of military power, especially in the long term. The size of a state's economy determines the potential to procure weapons. Moreover, in terms of creating threats and inducements, economics can be a power resource all by itself. There is a large literature on the use of economic sanctions to achieve goals. However, wealth does not translate directly into military power. Some countries (for example, Japan) may choose to spend a small part of their wealth on the military; others (such as North Korea) may choose to spend a great deal. Additionally, better technology may yield greater military effect for less money (although in practice, better technology often requires greater spending).

U.S. soldiers fire a mortar at Taliban forces, Kandahar province, Afghanistan. Realists stress the importance of military force, but warn that it may not be suitable for all purposes.

Because power is so hard to define, realism's reliance on that concept is one of its central weaknesses. To the extent that power can be measured, it is clear that the most powerful do not always prevail in conflict. Despite those limitations, realists assert a larger point: States pursue power because they know it is central to their ability to pursue their interests, whether those interests are defined as survival, expansion, or acquisition of wealth.

## NORMATIVE CONCERNS: PURPOSE IN REALIST THEORY

Realism is often considered an amoral theory in two different respects. First, realism finds that morality plays little or no role in relations between states. States do what is in their interest. States that are altruistic risk being annihilated. When a leader advocates some standard of international morality, realists say, it is usually a standard that serves the interests of that leader's country. In other words, normative arguments are just another weapon in power politics.

Second, realist policy recommendations are often seen as amoral. Realists contend that the international system is a harsh realm and that only a hardheaded pursuit of self-interest will prevent ruin. One question that often arises is whether a country should ally itself with another country that it finds morally objectionable. The realist position was captured colorfully in a quotation usually attributed to Cordell Hull, U.S. secretary of state under Franklin Roosevelt, when considering the case of Dominican dictator Rafael Trujillo: "It doesn't matter if he's a son-of-a-bitch, as long as he's *our* son-of-a-bitch."

However, realism's position on morality is in fact a bit more nuanced. Following Machiavelli, realists emphasize that the role of a state's government is to serve the national interest of *that* state and that the government has no moral obligations to other states.[13] In this view, pursuing the national interest at the expense of other states is, in a democratic sense, moral. Realists acknowledge that policy makers often refer to common standards of behavior, but stress that they should not do so if it undermines the national interest.[14]

Realists fear that in a dangerous world, efforts to be moral can lead to immoral results, while unethical behavior might avoid much larger evils. Realists point in particular to the era between World War I and World War II, when many leaders sought to replace power politics, which was seen as immoral, with appeasement, which was seen as moral. When faced with a leader like Hitler, who rejected all standard notions of morality and had no desire for international peace, these policies, realists contend, were not moral. By failing to confront Hitler earlier, those who pursued a more "moral" solution to international conflict may have inadvertently cost millions of people their lives. In the realist view, power politics is moral because it most effectively prevents such aggressors from doing evil on a huge scale. Thus, the realist normative approach is strongly conditioned by the belief that power politics cannot be transcended.

## VARIANTS OF REALISM

**Balance of Power Theory**   The most widely known realist theory of international politics is balance of power theory. This theory asserts that the likely result of the assumptions discussed previously will be a relatively even distribution of power among the most powerful states (the so-called great powers). Why? Although individual states will often seek to dominate, superiority will be almost impossible to achieve because states will counter each other's attempts to dominate. Historical examples include Spain under Charles V (1516–1556), France under Louis XIV (1643–1715), France again under Napoleon (1800–1815), and Germany in World War I and World War II. Many see the

United States after the Cold War as pursuing global dominance. Realists consider it inevitable that powerful states will seek to dominate. But balance of power theorists consider it equally inevitable that other states will strive to prevent gaps from emerging because their security depends on being able to fend off the most powerful. A balance will naturally result.

According to balance of power theory, war can begin in two ways. First, if states do not balance as they should, then power can become unbalanced, encouraging the powerful to attack. Thus Napoleon could entertain dreams of conquering Europe because other countries failed to unify to oppose him. Second, states may initiate war in the pursuit of power, either to augment their own power, as in Germany's expansionist aims in World War II, or to prevent another state from becoming too powerful, as in Israel's attack on Iraqi nuclear facilities in 1981. This was how leaders in all the countries involved in World War I perceived the necessity of going to war in 1914; they went to war to preserve the existing balance of power. Similarly, some analysts have interpreted Russia's invasion of Ukraine in 2014 as driven by a Russian need to prevent the United States and its allies from becoming too dominant in Europe.

**Hegemonic Stability Theory**    In contrast to balance of power theory, hegemonic stability theory finds that stability results not from a balance among the great powers, but from unipolarity, in which one dominant state ensures some degree of order in the system (Figure 3.1). The word *hegemon* means "leader" or "dominant actor." The term *hegemonic*

**FIGURE 3.1**  **Polarity in international politics.**

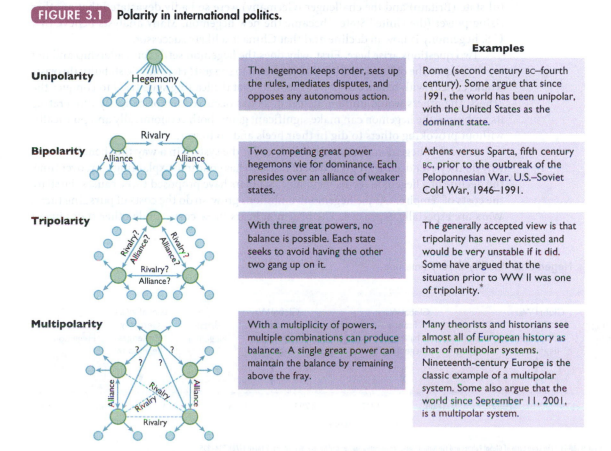

| | | Examples |
|---|---|---|
| **Unipolarity** — Hegemony | The hegemon keeps order, sets up the rules, mediates disputes, and opposes any autonomous action. | Rome (second century BC–fourth century). Some argue that since 1991, the world has been unipolar, with the United States as the dominant state. |
| **Bipolarity** — Rivalry / Alliance | Two competing great power hegemons vie for dominance. Each presides over an alliance of weaker states. | Athens versus Sparta, fifth century BC, prior to the outbreak of the Peloponnesian War. U.S.–Soviet Cold War, 1946–1991. |
| **Tripolarity** — Rivalry? Alliance? | With three great powers, no balance is possible. Each state seeks to avoid having the other two gang up on it. | The generally accepted view is that tripolarity has never existed and would be very unstable if it did. Some have argued that the situation prior to WW II was one of tripolarity.[*] |
| **Multipolarity** — Alliance / Rivalry | With a multiplicity of powers, multiple combinations can produce balance. A single great power can maintain the balance by remaining above the fray. | Many theorists and historians see almost all of European history as that of multipolar systems. Nineteenth-century Europe is the classic example of a multipolar system. Some also argue that the world since September 11, 2001, is a multipolar system. |

[*]Tripolarity is discussed in theory and applied to World War II by Randall Schweller, *Deadly Imbalances: Tripolarity and Hitler's Strategy of World Conquest* (New York: Columbia University Press, 1998).
Source: Paul D'Anieri.

*stability* points to the main argument of the theory: stability results from a situation of hegemony, in which one great power dominates the others. Hegemony, it is argued, leads to peace because states are not irrational enough to tangle with the hegemon unless it is absolutely necessary. The hegemon, therefore, can act as the "global cop," in effect reducing the degree of anarchy in the system. The hegemon can solve the prisoner's dilemma because it has the ability to punish those who defect.

According to hegemonic stability theory, war is most likely when the dominant position of the leader erodes, giving other states the temptation to seek dominance. War can begin either if the rising second-place state seeks to assert its power or if the hegemon attacks preemptively to crush the rising threat before it becomes even more powerful.

These hypotheses contradict those of balance of power theory. Whereas balance of power theory sees stability in balance and sees the chances of war increasing as one state seeks to dominate the others, hegemonic stability theory sees stability in dominance and sees the chances of war increasing as the situation moves toward equality.

Hegemonic stability theorists interpret the history of modern Europe as a succession of hegemonies, punctuated by "hegemonic wars" that mark the fall of one hegemon and the rise of another (Figure 3.2).[15] British dominance, based on its naval supremacy, characterized the eighteenth century. At the beginning of the nineteenth century, Napoleon's France challenged British hegemony but failed, and a new era of British hegemony lasted until Germany challenged it in World War I. In that hegemonic war, both the most powerful state (Britain) and the challenger (Germany) were so badly devastated that another rising power (the United States) became the new hegemon. Many analysts believe that U.S. hegemony is now in decline and that China is a likely successor.

Two questions arise here. First, why does the hegemon settle for leadership and not try to conquer the others, as realist theories seem to suggest? Hegemonic stability theorists would concur with balance of power theorists that if a leading state tried to conquer the others, the others would unite to defeat it, as has occurred historically. By moderating its ambition, the hegemon can make significant gains, both economically and politically, without provoking others to dig in their heels and go to war.

Second, if hegemonic states are able to order the system in a way that benefits them, why do they ever decline? A great deal of research has gone into explaining why, over time, the decline of a hegemon seems inevitable. Scholars have proposed three causes. First are the costs of "empire." As the hegemon's ambitions grow, so do the costs of pursuing them. Wars are especially expensive. The hegemon bears these costs, while other states invest

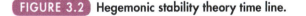

**FIGURE 3.2**   Hegemonic stability theory time line.

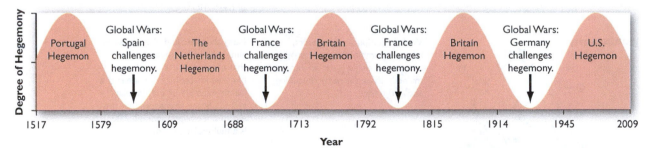

Source: Based on George Modelski, "The Long Cycle of Global Politics and the Nation State," *Comparative Studies and History*, Vol. 20, No. 2 (April 1978): 214–235.

in their economies and grow at a faster rate. Second is the potential for internal decay. If "lean and mean" states rise to hegemony, they eventually become "fat and happy," spending more and investing less. Third, technological advantages diffuse from the hegemon to other states, and new leading economic sectors may rise in other countries. All of these explanations place the underlying cause in the economic realm. Hegemony erodes when the economy underlying it becomes less productive than those of its competitors. Those who see the United States today as a declining hegemon identify all three factors at work.

**Realism at the State Level**   So far, our discussion has considered system-level theories within the realist paradigm, for which the primary characteristic of interest is the distribution of power, a characteristic of the system. However, many realists examine the intentions of individual states as well. Given a particular distribution of power, they argue, whether a state accepts the status quo or seeks to overturn it is crucial to anticipating that state's policy and to assessing the chances of war. Henry Kissinger, who was a prominent realist theorist before becoming a policy maker and then a pundit, interpreted much of the history of European politics through a lens of status quo versus revolutionary powers. When all the major powers accepted the status quo, such as after the Napoleonic wars and in the later stages of the Cold War, stability was assured. However, a revolutionary state—one that rejects the existing order—might be predisposed to attack other states, as in the cases of Napoleonic France and Nazi Germany.[16] A revolutionary power is particularly important in hegemonic stability theory, which expects that, as a secondary power narrows the gap with the hegemon, it might be inclined to challenge the existing order.

From this perspective, some have questioned today whether China is a revolutionary power. While system-level realists look primarily at China's growing military power and at the future potential of its economy, state-level realists ask whether China is satisfied with the existing international order or likely to seek to overturn it. One careful analysis of China's intentions concludes that, contrary to conventional wisdom, China is not clearly a "revolutionary" power.[17] Similarly, Russia's invasion of Ukraine has been interpreted in terms of status quo versus revolutionary powers—some see Russia as trying to overthrow the post–Cold War status quo in Europe; others see the United States as trying to overthrow that status quo by wooing Ukraine away from Russia.

## REALIST PRESCRIPTIONS

Realist prescriptions follow directly from the theories. Balance of power and hegemonic stability theorists both advocate that their governments pursue increased power and that they be especially sensitive to losses in power. For example, following the collapse of the Soviet Union, realists around the world advocated that others take steps to prevent the United States from dominating the world. Although realists see war as a useful tool of foreign policy, they may oppose it when they believe that a particular war will undermine, rather than strengthen, their country's power. Thus John Mearsheimer and Stephen Walt, two prominent American realists, argued against the 2003 invasion of Iraq, believing that it would decrease U.S. security.[18] The concept of national interest is crucial to realist policy prescriptions, but there is often considerable debate about what the national interest is at a given point in time.

## CRITIQUES OF REALIST THEORY

Each of the major assumptions of realism has come under fire. Whereas realists focus on anarchy as a basic condition that predisposes international relations to conflict, others see anarchy as only one of many characteristics of international politics, and a characteristic that

Destroying poached elephant tusks. What does realism's focus on power politics tell us about international problems such as protection of endangered species?

Andrew Holbrooke/Corbis News/Corbis

does not necessarily result in conflict. According to this view, international organizations and international law reduce the degree of anarchy. Similarly, many argue that the system from which anarchy emerged, the Westphalian state system, is itself evolving in a way that substantially limits sovereignty and thus the extent of anarchy. Even some scholars who agree that the system has traditionally been anarchic believe that it has changed over time. In this view, anarchy is simply a historical circumstance, and it could be replaced by another condition.

The assumption of the state as the fundamental unit of analysis is criticized for similar reasons. An increasing number of nonstate actors have influence on a wide variety of issues. If the conduct of major international wars is the focus of study, it may still make sense to regard the state as the unit of analysis. However, critics say, an increasing amount of what is interesting and important, from human rights to terrorism, concerns actors ranging far beyond the state.

Another series of critiques targets the assumptions that the state is unitary and rational. These assumptions imply that, with regard to foreign policy, it simply does not matter what kind of government or society a country has. Many critics reject this assumption. We routinely assume that with a different party in power, or a different form of government, a state's foreign policy would be different.

Critics also attack realism on the basis of its usefulness—the extent to which it can be applied practically. Realism does not predict when wars will occur, critics charge. It merely tells us that when they occur, the distribution of power was the ultimate cause. To the extent that theories are evaluated on their ability to create clear, testable predictions, realism appears weak.[19]

With its fixation on power, realism is also criticized for its tendency to ignore the purposes to which power is applied. This is the central concern of constructivist theory, addressed in Chapter 4. However, some traditional realists also raise this concern. E. H. Carr found that without some ultimate purpose, the pursuit of power becomes meaningless.[20] Similarly, Kissinger's emphasis on revolutionary versus status quo states shows a concern with states' goals. However, most contemporary realists, in their pursuit of a rigorous scientific theory, have assumed that states' intentions can be reduced to the pursuit of power. Kenneth Waltz, recognizing that the pursuit of power could be counterproductive in the nuclear age, posited "security" as the primary state goal but did not investigate the problem of defining security.[21]

The last and most significant problem is the concept of power. Realist theory is a theory of power politics, but defining power in a meaningful way is difficult (see Figure 3.3).

**FIGURE 3.3**  **What factors make a state powerful?** The three tables below list the top ten states (including the European Union as a single state) in three different categories that might be used to assess power. The Venn diagram shows which states are in the top ten in one, two, and three categories. What does this kind of analysis show us? What does it obscure? What other categories might be used to assess power? Are the different categories of equal importance? All these questions complicate efforts to assess the role of power in international politics.

| Rank | Country | Nuclear Warheads |
|------|---------|------------------|
| 1 | Russia | 7500 |
| 2 | United States | 7260 |
| 3 | European Union UK France | 515 215 300 |
| 4 | China | 250 |
| 5 | India | 90–110 |
| 6 | Pakistan | 100–120 |
| 7 | Israel | 80 |
| 8 | North Korea | 6–8 |

| Rank | Country | Oil Exports (bbl/day) |
|------|---------|-----------------------|
| 1 | Saudi Arabia | 8,900,000 |
| 2 | European Union | 6,971,000 |
| 3 | Russia | 5,080,000 |
| 4 | Norway | 3,018,000 |
| 5 | United Arab Emirates | 2,540,000 |
| 6 | Iran | 2,520,000 |
| 7 | Canada | 2,274,000 |
| 8 | Mexico | 2,266,000 |
| 9 | Venezuela | 2,203,000 |
| 10 | Kuwait | 2,200,000 |

| Rank | Country | GDP in Trillions of U.S. dollars Rank (purchasing power parity) |
|------|---------|-----------------------------------------------------------------|
| 1 | European Union | 14.45 |
| 2 | United States | 13.86 |
| 3 | China | 7.04 |
| 4 | Japan | 4.42 |
| 5 | India | 2.97 |
| 6 | Russia | 2.08 |
| 7 | Brazil | 1.84 |
| 8 | Mexico | 1.35 |
| 9 | Canada | 1.27 |
| 10 | South Korea | 1.21 |

Source: http://www.sipri.org/research/armaments/nuclear-forces

Military capability, economic capacity, and prestige or cultural power are important components. Combining all of these factors in a way that allows researchers to determine which countries are more powerful than others is impossible, yet realist analysis relies on the ability to do so. Realism also tends to ignore other manifestations of power, such as institutional power, "soft" power, structural power, and collaborative power (see Chapter 1).

# LIBERALISM

Political liberalism arose in the eighteenth century and took a practical form when it inspired the American Revolution and was embodied in the U.S. Constitution. Liberal theory took hold more slowly in the international realm than in the United States, but its influence has gradually increased over time.

Both international and domestic liberalism were responses to the problem of anarchy that had been set out by theorists such as Thomas Hobbes. Hobbes argued that in order to solve the problem of domestic anarchy, a powerful monarch, the "Leviathan," was necessary. In the international realm, with a single international "monarch" (a global empire) or world government viewed as impossible, realists argue that anarchy, with all its consequences, is unavoidable. Although liberal theories vary considerably, all share a rejection of the realist notion that the consequences of anarchy cannot be mitigated.

Liberal domestic theory centers on the rights (liberties) of the individual. The political theorist John Locke and later liberals argued, contrary to Hobbes, that individuals could freely join together to form governments that would protect them from anarchy without resorting to authoritarianism. The limitation of state power and the guarantee of the rights of individuals are still the core of liberalism (which, in contemporary usage, is often simply called *democracy*).

The central philosophical insight of liberal international theory is that it is possible to overcome the worst aspects of the realist world. Indeed, liberals argue, because the world described by the realists is so dangerous, states and other actors have a powerful incentive to try to escape from that system, or at least to moderate its worst effects. Whereas realists are utterly pessimistic about the possibility of doing so, liberals are a bit more optimistic. They do not necessarily see people as "good" or inherently peaceful, but they do see people as being smart enough to recognize the problems created by international anarchy and to work to overcome them.

The most prominent assumption shared by all liberals is that people are rational and understand their interests. This faith in human reason leads domestic liberals to believe that liberal democracy is the best form of government and leads international liberals to believe that rational, self-interested states and leaders can overcome the problems of anarchy.

Liberalism is a much more diverse body of theories than realism, however, and is therefore more difficult to summarize coherently. This book highlights three different strands of liberal theory, each of which departs from realism in a different way and each of which focuses on a different level of analysis.

One way to depart from realism is to rethink the implications of anarchy. This school, known as liberal institutionalism, agrees with realism that anarchy creates a security dilemma in which states' efforts to gain security cause insecurity instead. According to liberal institutionalism, however, the danger of the security dilemma provides states with strong incentives to find a way out. It makes them willing to negotiate formal and informal agreements to overcome the counterproductive behaviors that result from anarchy.

International institutions help increase confidence that agreements will be followed. Like the balance of power and hegemonic stability theories, liberal institutionalism operates primarily at the systemic level.

A second way to depart from realism is to discard the focus on the state as the central actor. Opening up the analysis to the whole range of actors also opens up a range of potential motivations. Firms, for example, are primarily driven not by international security motives but by the profit motive. Focusing on multiple actors leads to a view of politics that, instead of being simple, stark, and conflictual, is complex, multifaceted, and often characterized by collaboration. Scholars Robert Keohane and Joseph Nye call this school of thought complex interdependence theory.[22] This perspective can cut across levels of analysis, but because it focuses on nongovernmental actors, much of its focus is at the substate level.

A third liberal school of thought attacks the realist notion that all states are unitary rational actors. That assumption, in realist theory, implies that a state's form of government does not affect its behavior. The democratic peace theory asserts just the opposite—that the characteristics of governments are crucial to understanding international relations. Some kinds of states—liberal democracies—are able to escape the conflictual dynamics of anarchy. This theory operates at the state level. Democratic peace theory is among the most influential schools of thought today, especially in the United States.

As illustrated in Table 3.3, these are three very different theories. However, they are all essentially "liberal" in their belief that cooperation and order are possible in international affairs. International politics, in the liberal view, concerns the struggles to find solutions to the problems of anarchy. Liberalism is not simply naïve. It does not see collaboration as simple or unproblematic, but neither do liberals share the realist view that cooperation is inherently limited.

None of these approaches rejects power politics as completely irrelevant. Instead, they argue that the world is *contingent*. Sometimes states compete for power, and this drives international politics. But some goals require collaboration, so states often join to pursue mutual goals. Additionally, actors other than states are concerned with a vast array of goals. For liberals, realist theory falls short because it does not acknowledge that various conditions exist in international affairs and that some of these create incentives to cooperate. Because realism does not take this contingency seriously, it cannot explain why international politics at some times appears conflictual and at other times does not.

The rest of this chapter focuses on liberal institutionalism and complex interdependence theory; democratic peace theory is treated in detail in Chapter 5 with other

**TABLE 3.3**    **Three Strands of Liberal Theory**

| Variant of Liberalism | Level of Analysis | Departure from Realism |
|---|---|---|
| Liberal institutionalism | System; retains basic assumption of balance of power theory. | Anarchy does not necessarily lead to conflict; cooperation is possible. |
| Complex interdependence theory | Substate, but not exclusively; focuses on individuals, firms, non-governmental organizations (NGOs), and organizations within governments as key actors. | States are not the only important actors. Actors have diverse interests in international politics. Much of international relations have little to do with military security. |
| Democratic peace theory (Chapter 5) | State; focuses on what kind of government a state has. | States are not all essentially the same; liberal (democratic) states can solve disputes without war. |

state-level approaches. A major difference between complex interdependence theory and liberal institutionalism is their view of realist assumptions. Liberal institutionalism accepts realist assumptions but contends that they do not necessarily lead to the conclusions specified by realism. Complex interdependence theory finds fault with realist assumptions and argues that if the assumptions are flawed, the theory built on them must be flawed.

## LIBERAL INSTITUTIONALISM

Liberal institutionalism accepts many realist premises but arrives at different conclusions. It shares realist views on the nature of international anarchy, the problem of insecurity, and the notion that states can be seen as unitary rational actors. In adopting all these realist assumptions, liberal institutionalists want to avoid the accusation that their different conclusions stem from unrealistic assumptions. As the theorist Robert Keohane writes, "I propose to show, on the basis of their own assumptions, that the characteristic pessimism of realism does not necessarily follow. I seek to demonstrate that realist assumptions about world politics are consistent with the formation of institutionalized arrangements, containing rules and principles, which promote cooperation."[23]

The security dilemma as portrayed by realists offers no good choice, but liberal theorists offer a partial solution to this problem. They argue that if everyone could stop building arms at the same time, the security dilemma could be partly overcome, and everyone would be better off. If states cannot completely escape the security dilemma, perhaps they can, through agreements, help maintain a stable balance of power. In such a situation, security would be increased, and states could give more attention to other concerns, such as increasing prosperity.

**Liberalism and the Prisoner's Dilemma**    Liberal institutionalists also use the prisoner's dilemma model, and it helps to illustrate how they diverge from realists. For liberals, the prisoner's dilemma demonstrates that it is possible for two states to become better off at the same time. By moving from mutual defection to mutual cooperation, both actors can move from 2 to 3. This possibility undermines the realist assumption that international politics is a **zero-sum game** in which one state can gain only at the expense of another. For liberals, states have powerful incentives to overcome the security dilemma, and some ability to do so. Following is a summary of some, but not all, liberal institutionalist arguments with respect to the prisoner's dilemma.

**zero-sum game**

A situation in which any gains for one side are considered losses for the other.

- Shared norms or values can provide an extra incentive to cooperate. The norms of criminals, for example, create powerful incentives not to "rat out" a colleague. Liberals, therefore, study how shared norms can make it easier to solve the prisoner's dilemma in international politics.

- In interactions with multiple countries, cooperation between two or more members against others (that is, alliance) becomes an asset for preserving security. The incentive to defect, on which realism is based, holds only for a two-player model.

- The logic of the game changes considerably if the game is played repeatedly.[24] Over time, the difference between benefits to those who cooperate and those who fail to collaborate continues to mount. In economics, for example, those who fail to collaborate will, over time, become poorer than those who solve the prisoner's dilemma. That, in turn, can leave a country weaker militarily.

**reciprocity**

The strategy of matching the other player's previous move.

- Playing the game repeatedly can increase the actors' ability to solve the prisoner's dilemma. The strategy of **reciprocity**, in which one cooperates only as long as one's partner cooperates, can persuade even selfish states to cooperate.

# THE CONNECTION TO YOU

## THE PRISONER'S DILEMMA IN EVERYDAY LIFE

The prisoner's dilemma is an abstract model, but it is meant to capture a real-world dynamic, known as a collective action problem, that arises whenever two or more individuals must collaborate to achieve a goal. One hopes not to have too much direct experience with being interrogated by the police, but you do encounter collective action problems on a daily basis. How do you resolve them?

If you are in a bar with friends and agree to share a pitcher of a cold beverage, who pays? And who drinks how much? Both of these are collective action problems. Each friend has an incentive to let someone else throw down the money for the pitcher. Can't you just agree to split the cost? Yes. But then each person has an incentive to make sure he or she gets the most out of the pitcher—perhaps reaching quickly for the pitcher to refill his or her glass when it is running low.

What ways do we find to overcome the collective action problems inherent in the sharing of cold beverages? One solution is to "privatize" the supply so there is no more collective sharing to worry about. If we each order beverages in single servings, then we can each pay for only what we drink (though if the server is going to bring a single check, the collective action problem may reemerge). Privatization occurs in solving certain environmental problems: By declaring the seas within 300 miles of shore sovereign territory, states take those seas (and their fish) out of "international" (shared) waters and into state jurisdiction where one state bears all the costs of consumption. Privatization still relies on a rational approach, but approaches that rely on norms rather than rationality are also available.

Much of the time we solve the pitcher problem through norms of sharing. You pay for the first one and assume someone else will pay for the next one, and that it will even out over time. Norms in favor of generosity and against shirking responsibility can have a strong influence on behavior. Offering to pay for the first one, offering the last drink to someone else, and offering to pick up the check at the end of a meal are actions that are often viewed favorably, sometimes even leading to an argument over who will pay. Such behavior appears to overturn the assumptions of the collective action problem.

A collective action problem also arises when instructors assign a group project. Each member of the group will get the same grade, regardless of how much he or she contributes to completing the project. The incentives are obvious: shirk and let someone else do most of the work. But when everyone shirks, the work gets done poorly, and everyone gets a bad grade. Ironically, the students who care least about their grades have more power. This situation is analogous to questions of enforcement of collective security prior to World War II, in which each state sought to let someone else pay the cost of confronting aggression by Germany, Japan, and Italy.

How do we solve this problem? We may try to arrive at an agreement early in the project about who will do what, but each actor still fears that the others will not live up to their commitments. We are likely to try to form a group with our friends, because nonrational positive incentives (friendship) and negative incentives (shame) can have powerful effects among friends, just as in international affairs cooperation between like-minded states is often easier than between those with conflicting ideologies or domestic systems.

### Critical Thinking Questions

1. What other situations in your life mirror the dynamics of the prisoner's dilemma? What ways do you find to deal with them?

2. Do you find that solving the problem is easier in situations in which the interaction is repeated many times?

3. What do our everyday ways of dealing with prisoner's dilemmas tell us about the potential of mitigating the security dilemma internationally?

• Cheating is less of a problem than realists believe. States can agree on monitoring mechanisms to reduce the benefits of cheating. Moreover, a state that cheats in one area will damage its reputation as a partner across all areas, increasing the cost of defection.

Realists, of course, have responses to all of these arguments. They see the prospects for cooperation as severely limited in the real world by concerns about cheating and by concerns that one side will gain more than the other (known as the "relative gains problem").[25] They also believe that much cooperation in the world is not bargained fairly among equals, but imposed by the strong on the weak.[26]

**Institutions and Anarchy**   The effort to use institutions to overcome the worst aspects of anarchy is, for liberal institutionalists, what international politics is all about. **Institutions** are sets of agreed upon norms, rules, and practices. They can be formal, such as those embodied in a treaty, or they can be informal, such as the annual meetings of leaders of the so-called **G-7** countries. In some cases, the institution may be an undeclared principle that is widely shared. International agreements can be supported by formal organizations (there are thousands of these, including the United Nations, the World Trade Organization, and the World Bank), or they can be carried out without any international organizational structure (as are many bilateral agreements). Some theorists use the term *international regime* (see chapter 13) to encompass the whole range of cooperative activity, from formal institutions to unstated principles.[27] The historical establishment of rules of diplomacy, in which ambassadors were given "diplomatic immunity" and embassies were protected, is one example of a set of norms and practices that states found advantageous, even (or especially) when dealing with bitter rivals.

Particularly in the economic realm, collaboration among states can increase benefits without threatening survival. If states agree to trade freely rather than erect protectionist barriers to trade, all can become wealthier at the same time. But most liberal institutionalists contend that such cooperation can occur even among great powers and even among the most intense rivals, as between the United States and the Soviet Union during the Cold War, or the United States and China today.

Whereas realism focuses on power as coercion, liberal institutionalism focuses on collaborative and institutional power. States that collaborate are likely to become wealthier and, therefore, more powerful in terms of coercion than those who do not. The formation of institutions creates institutional power that can supplant coercive power as a means for resolving disagreements.

**Institutionalism in Practice**   Probably the first conscious attempt to put liberal theory into practice was the Concert of Europe that followed the Napoleonic wars. This system was still anarchic and still driven largely by the balance of power, but the great powers at that time believed that the previous uncoordinated system of diplomacy had made all of them less safe. By agreeing on certain principles of engagement and meeting periodically to revise the arrangements, the states of that period were able to usher in an era of considerable peace and prosperity.[28] Skeptics point out that this system eventually degenerated and did not prevent World War I. Liberal institutionalists reply, "That is exactly our point: When collaboration broke down, everyone ended up worse off."[29]

The Cold War between the United States and the Soviet Union, liberal institutionalists assert, demonstrated that even the most bitterly opposed and mistrusting enemies could cooperate to limit the chances of conflict. As the number of nuclear warheads rose, it became clear that the next war would be even more devastating than World War II. By the mid-1960s, each side could match any increase by the other, and neither side could gain any military or diplomatic advantage in this competition. But neither side believed that it could stop, for fear that the other would gain an advantage. This seemed to be a

---

**institutions**

Sets of agreed upon norms, rules, and practices.

**G-7**

Shorthand for the "Group of Seven" industrial countries formed in the 1970s to coordinate economic policies. Members are Canada, France, Germany, Italy, Japan, the United Kingdom, and the United States. Russia was added in 1997 and removed in 2014.

classic security dilemma. In a series of agreements, including the **SALT-I** agreement of 1972 (SALT stands for Strategic Arms Limitation Talks) and the **SALT-II** agreement of 1977, the two sides agreed to limit the building of new weapons (see Figure 3.4). More significantly, they agreed to limits on certain kinds of weapons that were perceived to be especially dangerous.[30]

An equally telling example is that of Argentina and Brazil. In the 1970s, both countries, ruled by military dictatorships, were developing nuclear weapons, largely in response to a perceived mutual threat. In 1980, however, the two countries signed the Brazilian-Argentine Agreement on the Peaceful Use of Nuclear Energy, an agreement to end their nuclear weapons programs, based on a mutual perception that the nuclear arms race on which they were poised to embark would substantially diminish their security and undermine the economies of both countries.[31]

These examples all concern military strategic affairs. Liberal institutionalists contend that if states find it in their interest to collaborate even on issues that have a direct impact on state survival, it makes sense that collaboration will be more extensive in other areas. They point to the ever-expanding web of economic agreements as evidence that collaboration is much more representative of international politics than is the narrow competition for power on which realism focuses. Issues such as global

**SALT-I and SALT-II**
Agreements between the United States and the Soviet Union to limit nuclear weapons.

**FIGURE 3.4**   The graph shows the numbers of U.S. and Soviet strategic nuclear weapons launchers over time, along with key events in the relationship. Can you assess the relative importance of arms control versus other factors in influencing weapons building?

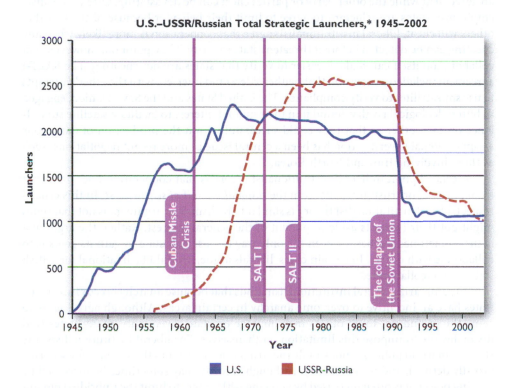

U.S.–USSR/Russian Total Strategic Launchers,* 1945–2002

■ U.S.          ■ USSR-Russia

*Launchers include any vehicle capable of delivering a nuclear weapon across continents. Each single missile (land- or sea-based) or long-range-bomber counts as a single launcher, even if it carries more than one nuclear warhead.
Source: http://www.nrdc.org/nuclear/nuguide/nrdcnuc.asp.

Colombia president Juan Manuel Santos (L) and his Chilean counterpart Michelle Bachelet attend a session of the UN Climate Change Conference in Lima, Peru, December, 2014. Can international cooperation help deal with climate change?

Martin Bernetti/Getty Images

warming, terrorism, and disease, liberals contend, will require cooperation and are not solvable by coercion.

**Cheating and Enforcement**   The possibility of cheating arises often in liberal institutionalist theory and in realist critiques of it. Especially when survival is at stake, adhering to an agreement while the other party or parties cheat can be devastating. Often, as realists emphasize, states are reluctant to agree to limit their behavior because of the fear that others will cheat. Liberal institutionalists agree that cooperation is more likely when any cheating can be detected before it threatens state security. They point out, however, that collaboration itself can make it easier to verify that states are not cheating. The SALT-I agreement included a provision that neither side would interfere with the other's attempts to use spy satellites to verify compliance. The United States and the Soviet Union, engaged in bitter ideological rivalry, found it in their mutual interest to facilitate satellite surveillance on each other so that they could successfully limit the production of dangerous weapons. Reliable verification has been a central issue in more recent negotiations, such as those involving Iran and North Korea.

A central point in liberal institutionalist theory is that cooperation does not result from altruism or trust. It results from the *rational pursuit of self-interest*. In this crucial respect, liberal institutionalist theory is similar to realism. The argument is not that states might put their interests aside in pursuit of the general interest. Rather, the argument is that sometimes the best or even the only way for a selfish state to gain its goals is to collaborate with others. In certain cases, liberals argue, it would be irrational for selfish states *not* to collaborate.

To summarize, liberal institutionalism finds that because anarchy breeds insecurity, states have an incentive to overcome anarchy in certain areas. Although agreeing to do some things and not to do others may impinge on state sovereignty, many states find it worthwhile to impose this limitation on themselves. For liberal institutionalists, the struggle of world politics is not simply the struggle for power but the struggle for security, broadly defined, and for prosperity. Although security may sometimes be increased by gaining power, it is often increased by agreeing with others to limit the unbridled pursuit of power or to collaborate to deal with common threats, such as climate change.

# COMPLEX INTERDEPENDENCE THEORY

According to Keohane and Nye, complex interdependence has three essential traits.

1. *Multiple channels connect societies.* There is much more going on than government-to-government interaction. Bureaucratic contacts below the level of national leadership, which they label **transgovernmental relations**, are significant, as are **transnational relations** between societal actors across nation-states, including firms, NGOs, and individuals.
2. *There is no clear hierarchy of issues.* Security, which realists see as dominant, is not always the most important agenda item, especially in economic, human rights, or environmental relations, and especially for nonstate actors.
3. *Military force is often not considered a viable tool of policy.* In dealing with allies or with issues that have little to do with security (health crises, for example), military force would be inappropriate if not counterproductive.[32]

Complex interdependence theory rejects realism's (and liberal institutionalism's) narrow focus on the state. By defining a broader range of actors, the theory identifies a broader range of interests. In contrast to the stark simplicity of realism, a more complicated and nuanced view of the world emerges. Where realist theory sees a single actor (the state), a single goal (security), and a single driving force (power), complex interdependence theory sees multiple actors, diverse goals, and a variety of driving forces. Whether a simple or a complex theory is preferable will depend largely on the questions asked.

**Variety of Actors**   The assumptions of complex interdependence theory are as different from those of liberal institutionalism as from those of realism. Complex interdependence assumes that international politics encompasses a wide array of actors. This array includes states, but it goes far beyond them. Within states, actors such as bureaucracies, companies, political parties, interest groups, and voters are considered to be important. Beyond states, the list of actors includes a wide variety of international organizations and transnational actors. This focus on multiple actors is sometimes referred to as **pluralism**.

**Variety of Goals**   Because complex interdependence assumes a variety of actors, it logically follows that there would be a wide variety of goals. Complex interdependence does not see security dominating all other goals. As Henry Kissinger, a noted realist, argued when he was U.S. secretary of state in 1975, "Progress in dealing with the traditional agenda is no longer enough.... The problems of energy, resources, environment, population, the uses of space and the seas now rank with questions of military security, ideology and territorial rivalry which have traditionally made up the diplomatic agenda."[33] Whereas both realism's and liberal institutionalism's belief in the importance of state security means that all other goals are seen through the lens of state security, complex interdependence theory does not assume that there is a **hierarchy of goals**. States have economic, environmental, and other goals that have no substantial interaction with the pursuit of national security. In this view, when states are negotiating about banana tariffs, pollution limits, or preventing the spread of HIV, they are not worried about the balance of power.

**transgovernmental relations**
Direct interaction between bureaucracies in different countries without going through their heads of state.

**transnational relations**
Interaction between societal actors across nation-states.

**pluralism**
The presence of a number of competing actors or ideas.

**hierarchy of goals**
A clear ranking of goals.

Facebook CEO Mark Zuckerberg meeting with Japan's Prime Minister Yoshihiko Noda, March 2012.

Similarly, for many of the other actors involved in international politics, the goals are not primarily security. Greenpeace is concerned with environmental issues, the World Health Organization (WHO) with the spread of disease, and Toyota with selling cars. Within governments, ministries of economics and finance are primarily concerned with economic affairs, not security. It is not so much that these actors do not care about military security issues, but rather that they leave them aside while they pursue other goals. Moreover, to the extent that the issues they are concerned with overlap with military security issues, these other actors are likely to view military security very differently. Greenpeace, for example, might view war primarily as something that causes vast amounts of environmental damage, whereas WHO may view it as something that destroys the infrastructure needed to combat disease.

**The Web of Relationships**  Realism views states as billiard balls colliding with one another. In contrast, because it sees multiple actors concerned with multiple goals, complex interdependence theory views the world as interconnected by a thick web of many relationships among many actors (see Figure 3.5).

Of the wide range of goals being pursued by many actors in world politics, very few can be attained through the exercise of military force. Rockets and bombs might be valuable in a military conflict, but they are largely irrelevant when the goal is to limit production of polluting gases or to increase trade. Therefore, each separate issue has its own distribution of power and its own definition of what constitutes power. Russia, for example, remains powerful in the military realm, but it is less influential in financial affairs. Japan, in contrast, is much more influential in economic affairs than in security (although that is changing). Saudi Arabia is powerful in the arena of petroleum production but not in other economic areas, such as high technology.

**Cooperation**  Because there are many actors concerned with much more than state security, much of international politics, according to complex interdependence theory, is not so conflictual. This position on cooperation overlaps significantly with liberal institutionalism and places complex interdependence theory within the liberal paradigm. Where liberal institutionalism sees the possibility of collaboration even among actors with security concerns, complex interdependence sees many more actors focusing on

**FIGURE 3.5**  Number of telephone subscriptions and Internet connections per 100 people, world, 1990 to present.

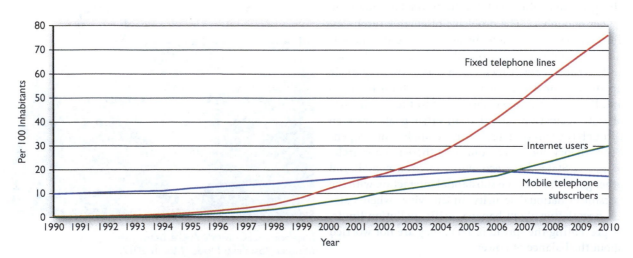

Source: ChartsBin statistics collector team 2011, ChartsBin.com, viewed May 22, 2012, http://chartsbin.com/view/184.

# THE GEOGRAPHY CONNECTION

## THE GLOBAL CONNECTIVITY AND COMPLEX INTERDEPENDENCE THEORY

The globalization of transportation networks represents the kind of connectivity that complex interdependence theory asserts is changing the nature of world politics. This global transportation map shows how cities are connected by roads, flight paths, and shipping routes.

### Critical Thinking Questions

1. Do these transportation networks actually change international politics, or just the way

we talk and write about the subject? What concrete changes can you point to?

2. What is going on in the darker regions of this map? If complex interdependence depends on connectivity, will the effects of complex interdependence vary with the density of connections?

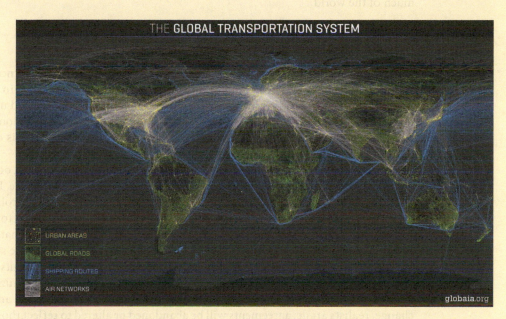

The global transportation system.

issues less difficult than security. For the vast majority of issues, state survival is not at stake, and although cheating is still a concern, it has less dire consequences and is often easy to detect. Therefore, using a logic different from that of liberal institutionalism, complex interdependence arrives at a similar conclusion in that it expects to see much cooperation in the world.

What specific predictions does complex interdependence theory make about the world? Generally, complex interdependence theory is more optimistic about the chance for peace because other goals compete with security. War appears more costly when seen as undermining other key goals than when seen simply in terms of power politics. Moreover, there are many actors, in this view, who might see their interests injured through war and therefore work to prevent it.

## LIBERALISM'S NORMATIVE POSITION

The normative position of the liberal paradigm follows straightforwardly from its explanatory theories. If the perils and problems of anarchy can be mitigated through collaboration, liberals contend, leaders should attempt to achieve these benefits. Liberals reject the realist notion that progress in international affairs is impossible.[34] They argue that collaboration can make all participants better off and that it should therefore be a priority in international affairs. Much of the substantive discussion of issues in contemporary international politics, including security, economic, health, and environmental affairs, concerns what international collaboration should look like and how best to promote it.

Although there are no guarantees of peace or progress, liberals of different schools believe that both are attainable by intelligent and reasonable actors. Nowhere can this be seen more clearly than in the international economy. Since World War II, increasing collaboration on free trade has yielded an enormous increase in prosperity throughout much of the world.

## THE REALIST REPLY

Historically, realists have derided liberal theory as "idealism" and have warned that policies based on trust in international collaboration make states less secure in the face of potential aggression. This is the realist interpretation of the events that led up to World War II.[35] To the realist, anarchy is the immutable condition of international politics, and inevitably causes the struggle for power. They view the belief that this can change as idealistic, or even hazardous.

Realists do not dispute that liberalism captures certain aspects of what occurs in the world. However, realists argue that liberalism fails to capture the big picture. In response to liberal institutionalism, realism accepts certain arguments about collaboration. Indeed, the concept of alliances in balance of power theory is equivalent to the liberal notion of providing security through collaboration. Similarly, the view that hegemony can lead to stability is in many respects a recognition that anarchy is more successfully dealt with in some situations than in others. In the realist view, agreements reflect the balance of power but do not alter it. In other words, international organizations and agreements are set up to serve the interests of the powerful. When power and interests change, realists argue, agreements will be abandoned or altered to reflect those changes. Ultimately, realists say, states that put their faith in institutions rather than in self-help will eventually regret it.

In responding to complex interdependence theory, realists make two arguments. First, realists accept the extensive list of actors, goals, and relationships emphasized in complex interdependence theory as a description of the world. Their goal, however, is not to provide an accurate description of the world today but to explain the major underlying dynamics that have existed for centuries. Realists say that complex interdependence theory, with its highly nuanced and complex view of the world, loses the big picture. The theory is not wrong; rather, it answers a very different set of questions.

## R E C O N S I D E R   T H E   C A S E

## SHOULD IRAN OBTAIN NUCLEAR WEAPONS?

The question "Should Iran get nuclear weapons?" has a strong normative underpinning. Any answer to the question requires stating what the goals are and whose goals we are talking about. Iranian leaders would likely approach the "should" question differently than U.S. leaders. Beyond this normative question, however, are the questions of what might ensue if Iran acquires nuclear weapons and what might convince the Iranian government that its security is better enhanced through other measures.

In 2012, speculation mounted that Israel would attack Iran, either alone or together with the United States. Israeli Prime Minister Benjamin Netanyahu called Iran's possession of a nuclear weapon an "existential threat" to Israel. Debate raged in Israel and the United States over the relative dangers of attacking Iran versus relying on negotiations, which might fail. Some people argued that the costs of attacking Iran would be high, polarizing world opinion and solidifying internal support for the Iranian government. Moreover, the results of an attack were uncertain because Iranian facilities were widely dispersed and well protected. Opponents of an attack contended that diplomacy could yield a solution that would assure the world that Iran was not getting nuclear weapons, without resorting to a military attack. This would require agreement by Iran to allow inspectors from the International Atomic Energy Agency (IAEA) unfettered access to all of its suspected nuclear facilities. Iran is a signatory of the Non-Proliferation Treaty, but has repeatedly circumvented the inspection process or simply denied inspectors access.

Skeptics of negotiating with Iran saw the negotiation process as a means by which Iran could delay action by Israel or the United States until it had obtained nuclear weapons, making an attack much more risky. In 2015, the Republican majority in the U.S. Senate took the unprecedented step of sending a letter to Iranian leaders saying that they would not support an agreement. An agreement was subsequently reached in which Iran would submit to increased inspections, while others would reduce economic sanctions. Both in Iran and in other countries, there was considerable disagreement over whether the agreement would increase security.

Talk of an attack alarmed many people, but it may have made Iran more willing to seek a negotiated solution, and it also likely helped increase support in Europe for economic sanctions as an alternative to war. These sanctions caused significant damage to Iran's economy, and it appears that Iran's interest in negotiations was driven in large part by the desire to have the sanctions lifted.

### Critical Thinking Questions

1. Imagine liberals and realists in the Iranian government. How might they frame Iran's goals differently?

2. How would balance of power theory and liberal institutionalism view the prospects for solving this problem without war?

3. To what extent are tensions between Iran and the West driven not by the security dilemma but by competing purposes? If the states had different goals, would the security dilemma moderate or disappear, or is it completely unavoidable?

Second, realists are skeptical about complex interdependence theory's assertions that military security issues hold no special place above other goals. This idea may be easy to assert in times of peace, they say, but not when security is actually threatened. For example, after September 11, 2001, a whole range of goals suddenly receded in importance when security was threatened. When the United States went to war with Iraq in 2003, almost no one was overly concerned with the effect of military activity on the environment or the economy. The goal on both sides was to win the war, and with security on the line, other goals took a back seat.

# ★ POWER AND PURPOSE IN REALISM AND LIBERALISM

Realism is a paradigm heavily focused on power defined as coercion. Some realists argue that because the main currency of international politics is military power, the main goal of states is simply to get more of it. In that sense, they subsume purpose completely within power, so that purpose essentially disappears from their analysis. Other realists are more nuanced, including those who examine state-level factors such as states' orientation toward the status quo in the system.

Liberal theories separate power and purpose much more distinctly than does realism. Liberal institutionalism asks about state goals and examines how these goals may be achieved cooperatively. Complex interdependence theory questions purpose even more explicitly, positing that different actors have different goals and that these cannot be achieved by coercion. Thus, liberal approaches focus much more on other dimensions of power, most importantly on the power to collaborate and the power created by institutions.

## SUMMARY

- Even though hegemonic stability theory and balance of power theory contradict each other on essential questions, both theories fit within the realist paradigm. Both theories see anarchy as the central condition constraining state behavior. Both theories see states as the fundamental actors in the system and view states as rational, unitary actors. Both theories argue that anarchy inexorably pushes states to seek power in order to survive, and both find that what happens in the system results from the distribution of power. Realist theories share a stance of moral aloofness, arguing that it is more dangerous to try to change the system than to live intelligently within its constraints.

- The liberal paradigm includes theories such as liberal institutionalism, complex interdependence theory, and democratic peace theory. Liberal institutionalism shares the realist assumptions about anarchy and the central importance of states, but argues that states can cooperate even in anarchy. Complex interdependence theory differs from liberal institutionalism primarily in that it recognizes substate entities, such as individuals, firms, nongovernmental organizations, and government agencies, as key actors in international politics. Liberalism provides a much less pessimistic outlook on international politics, believing that states can find a way out of the security dilemma. Whereas realism finds that the basic characteristics of international relations have not changed over the past 2500 years, liberalism finds that progress is possible. Liberals contend that their view is more "realistic" than realism because it helps us understand the extensive range of collaboration that exists in the world today.

## KEY CONCEPTS

1. Paradigms
2. Realism
3. Liberalism

4. Anarchy
5. Security dilemma
6. Prisoner's dilemma

7. Hegemonic stability theory

8. Liberal institutionalism

9. Complex interdependence theory

## STUDY QUESTIONS

1. Which of the following is a realist theory?

   a. Balance of power theory

   b. Liberal institutionalism

   c. Complex interdependence theory

   d. Democratic peace theory

2. What do political scientists call the difficult choice states face when trying to decide whether or not to arm themselves?

   a. National interest

   b. The security dilemma

   c. The prisoner's dilemma

   d. Reciprocity

3. What do political scientists call a game theory scenario in which noncooperation is the rational strategy but leads to both players' being worse off than if they had cooperated?

   a. National interest

   b. The security dilemma

   c. The prisoner's dilemma

   d. Reciprocity

4. What do hegemonic stability theory and balance of power theory have in common?

   a. Both are liberal theories.

   b. Both focus on the distribution of power.

   c. Both believe that an even distribution of power is conducive to peace.

   d. Both reject the assumption that states are unitary actors.

5. What common assumption unites liberal theories?

   a. International politics is anarchic.

   b. States are unitary, rational actors.

   c. Collaboration among states is possible.

   d. Substate actors play a major role in international politics.

6. What common assertion(s) do realist theories share?

   a. International politics is anarchic.

   b. States are unitary, rational actors.

   c. States cannot escape the security dilemma.

   d. All of the above.

7. In realist theory, what are the logical links between anarchy and the balance of power?

8. What are the major critiques of realism?

9. How do realism and liberalism use the prisoner's dilemma model to advance their claims?

10. In the liberal paradigm, how does anarchy create incentives to cooperate?

11. How does complex interdependence theory differ from liberal institutionalism?

12. What are the major realist critiques of liberalism?

[Correct answers: 1. a; 2. b; 3. c; 4. b; 5. c; 6. d]

## END NOTES

1. Thucydides, *History of the Peloponnesian War*. The third quotation is from the introduction (Book I, Section 23). The other quotations are from the "Melian Dialogue" (Book V, Sections 89, 105, and 97, respectively).

2. Kenneth Waltz, *Theory of International Politics* (New York: McGraw Hill, 1979), Chapter 6.

3. Waltz, *Theory of International Politics*, pp. 95–97.

4. Robert O. Keohane, "Realism, Neorealism, and the Study of World Politics," in Robert O. Keohane, ed., *Neorealism and Its Critics* (New York: Columbia University Press, 1982), p. 11.

5. Waltz, *Theory of International Politics*, pp. 107–111.

6. To see how a variety of simple game theory models can be applied to international politics, see Arthur A. Stein, "Coordination and Collaboration: Regimes in an Anarchic World," in Stephen D. Krasner, ed., *International Regimes* (Ithaca, NY: Cornell University Press, 1983), pp. 115–140.

7. Hans J. Morgenthau, *Power among Nations: The Struggle for Power and Peace*, 5th ed. (New York: Alfred A. Knopf, 1978), p. 27.

8. Kenneth N. Waltz, *Man, the State, and War* (New York: Columbia University Press, 1959), p. 205.

9. Morgenthau, *Power among Nations*, p. 28.

10. John Mearsheimer, *The Tragedy of Great Power Politics* (New York: W. W. Norton, 2001), p. 57.

11. Mearsheimer, *The Tragedy of Great Power Politics*, p. 58.

12. Mearsheimer, *The Tragedy of Great Power Politics*, p. 56.

13. Edward Hallett Carr, *The Twenty Years' Crisis, 1919–1939* (New York: Harper & Row, 1964 [1939]), p. 153.

14. Carr, *The Twenty Years' Crisis*, pp. 155–156.

15. Paul Kennedy, *The Rise and Decline of Great Powers* (New York: Random House, 1987).

16. Henry Kissinger, *A World Restored* (London: Wiedenfeld and Nicholson, 1957).

17. Alistair Ian Johnston, "Is China a Status Quo Power?" *International Security*, Vol. 27, No. 4 (Spring 2003): 5–56.

18. John J. Mearsheimer and Stephen M. Walt, "Keeping Saddam in a Box," *New York Times*, February 2, 2003, p. 15.

19. See John A. Vasquez, "The Realist Paradigm and Degenerative versus Progressive Research Programs: An Appraisal of Neotraditional Research on Waltz's Balancing Proposition," *The American Political Science Review*, Vol. 91, No. 4. (Dec. 1997): 899–912.

20. Carr, *The Twenty Years' Crisis*, Chapter 6.

21. Waltz, *Theory of International Politics*, Chapter 6.

22. Robert O. Keohane and Joseph S. Nye, *Power and Interdependence*, 2nd ed. (New York: HarperCollins, 1989).

23. Robert O. Keohane, *After Hegemony: Cooperation and Discord in the World Political Economy* (Princeton, NJ: Princeton University Press, 1984), p. 67.

24. There is an immense literature on the "iterated" (repeated) prisoner's dilemma. For a fun and provocative introduction, see Robert Axelrod, *The Evolution of Cooperation* (New York: Basic Books, 1984). See also Keohane, *After Hegemony*, pp. 67ff; and Kenneth Oye, *Cooperation under Anarchy* (Princeton, NJ: Princeton University Press, 1986).

25. See Joseph Grieco, "Anarchy and the Limits of Cooperation: A Realist Critique of the Newest Liberal Institutionalism," *International Organization*, Vol. 42 (Summer 1988): 485–508.

26. See Stephen Krasner, "Global Communications and National Power: Life on the Pareto Frontier," *World Politics*, Vol. 43, No. 3 (April 1991): 336–366.

27. Stephen D. Krasner, in a widely cited definition, defines regimes as "sets of implicit or explicit principles, norms, rules, and decision-making procedures around which actors' expectations converge in a given area of international relations." See "Structural Causes and Regime Consequences," in Stephen D. Krasner, ed., *International Regimes* (Ithaca, NY: Cornell University Press, 1983), p. 2.

28. Robert Jervis, "From Balance to Concert: A Study of International Security Cooperation," in Oye, *Cooperation under Anarchy*, pp. 58–79.

29. Stephen van Evera, "Why Cooperation Failed in 1914," in Oye, *Cooperation under Anarchy*, pp. 80–117.

30. George W. Downs, David M. Rocke, and Randolph M. Siverson, "Arms Races and Cooperation," in Oye, *Cooperation under Anarchy*, pp. 118–146.

31. See Leonard Spector, *The New Nuclear Nations* (New York: Carnegie Endowment, 1985), Chapter V; and http://www.fas.org/nuke/guide/brazil/nuke/index.html.

32. Keohane and Nye, *Power and Interdependence*, pp. 21–25.

33. Quoted in Keohane and Nye, *Power and Interdependence*, p. 22.

34. On the concept of progress in international affairs, see Emanuel Adler and Beverly Crawford, *Progress in Post-War International Relations* (NY: Columbia University Press, 1991); and Ernst Haas, *Nationalism,* *Liberalism, and Progress: The Rise and Decline of Nationalism*, Vol. 1 (Ithaca, NY: Cornell University Press, 1997).

35. Carr, *The Twenty Years' Crisis.* For a more modern version of the same argument, see John Mearsheimer, "The False Promise of International Institutions," *International Security*, Vol. 19, No. 3. (Winter 1994/1995): 5–49.

# 4

Fidel Castro, who led Cuba's communist revolution in 1959 and ruled the country until 2008, in New York in 1960. Under Castro, Cuba became a symbol, both to supporters and to detractors, of communism in practice in Latin America.

New York Times Co./Archive Photos/Getty Images

# THEORIES OF INTERNATIONAL RELATIONS: ECONOMIC STRUCTURALISM, CONSTRUCTIVISM, AND FEMINISM

## *Learning Objectives*

**4-1** Identify the major assumptions of economic structuralist, constructivist, and feminist approaches.

**4-2** Distinguish the variants within each approach.

**4-3** Understand how these approaches relate to one another and to realism and liberalism.

**4-4** Summarize the major critiques of each approach.

**4-5** Identify ways in which each approach can be linked to policy problems.

**4-6** Articulate and defend an argument concerning the relative merits of the different approaches.

# CONSIDER THE CASE

## CAPITALISM AND ITS DISCONTENTS: IS SOCIALISM MAKING A COMEBACK?

In January 2015, Greek voters elected the Syriza party, whose name is an acronym for "Radical Coalition of the Left." Its leader, Prime Minister Alexis Tsipras, appointed a self-described Marxist as finance minister. Syriza and Tsipras vowed to overturn the fiscal austerity measures that had been part of a "bailout" plan that prevent Greece from defaulting on its massive debt.

The results in the Greek election, which were repeated in a second election in September 2015, were an extreme instance of a broader trend in Europe. In 2012, for the first time in seventeen years, the people of France elected a Socialist president. President François Hollande proposed a 75 percent tax on the wealthiest citizens, with the proceeds to be used to create jobs and avoid spending cuts. He advocated shifting from a policy of austerity to one of government spending to lift Europe out of its economic crisis. Many feared that the austerity measures would lead to the end of benefits, such as free college education and universal health care, that contribute to the high quality of life in Europe. In Portugal, France, and Italy, workers shut down railways, airlines, and other industries. In Spain, the *indignados* (indignants) set up camps in parks before eventually being ejected by police. In the United States, the "Occupy" movement expressed outrage at political and economic arrangements that the protestors blamed for growing gaps between the rich and poor.

In Latin America, the tide toward socialism had emerged earlier. Hugo Chavez, president of Venezuela from 1999 to 2013, accused the United States of trying to "preserve the current pattern of domination, exploitation, and pillage of the peoples of the world."* Chavez established state control over Venezuela's lucrative oil industry, rejecting commitments to international energy firms. He instituted a program of providing subsidized food and medical care in the poorest areas of a very poor country. Chavez's supporters saw this as a successful attempt to achieve socialist goals; his critics viewed these policies as cynically spending Venezuela's oil wealth to boost Chavez's political power.

In Bolivia, President Evo Morales nationalized the country's oil and gas industries and joined Chavez's "Bolivarian Alternative for the Americas," an attempt to form an anti-U.S. trade bloc. Morales, like Chavez, sees the involvement of foreign firms in the lucrative energy industry as exploitative. In Ecuador, President Rafael Correa echoed Chavez's call for "twenty-first-century socialism."[†] Argentina, reeling from a financial crisis, turned away from the market-oriented policies advocated by the International Monetary Fund and mainstream economists. It defaulted on its $93 billion international debt in 2001, rejecting international capital markets, but after restructuring its economy was able to repay its debt fully in January 2006. This was seen as evidence of a genuine alternative to the international liberal economic consensus.

At the practical as well as the ideological level, the role of the state in the economy is being rethought. State ownership of firms, long viewed as a recipe for bloat and inefficiency, has made a comeback: "State-run enterprises have recovered from the wreck of communism and now include the world's biggest mobile-phone company (China Mobile), its most successful port operator (Dubai World), its fastest-growing big airline (Emirates), and its thirteen biggest oil companies."[‡]

This resurgence in anticapitalist rhetoric and in state ownership follows a long period in which states around the world were gravitating toward free market approaches. Beginning in the United Kingdom and the United States in the early 1980s, faith in government's ability to manage economies and to provide for welfare diminished, and faith in the market's ability to do these things increased. The end of communism in Europe accelerated the global shift away from state control. By 1997, Britain's Labour Party had rejected its historic commitment to socialism and recast itself as a promarket "New Labour," demonstrating a broad consensus in favor of the market. This shift signaled a reversal of the growth, since the early twentieth century, of welfare capitalism as a compromise that sought to provide both economic growth and equity.

---

*"Chavez: Bush 'devil'; U.S. 'on the way down,'" *CNN.com*, September 21, 2006, at www.cnn.com/2006/WORLD/americas/09/20/chavez.un/index.html.

†"Correa's Victory," *The Economist*, October 6, 2007.

‡"The Endangered Public Company," *The Economist*, May 19, 2012.

Agencia Boliviana de Informacion/Handout/Reuters

Bolivian President Evo Morales (center right) accompanies soldiers as they occupy Bolivia's natural gas fields, March, 2006. Morales threatened to evict foreign firms unless they gave the state more control over production.

This chapter continues to explore the questions raised in the previous chapter. What are the driving forces of international politics? What underlying patterns do we see? When we seek to explain a policy or a trend, where should we begin?

This chapter will discuss very different answers to these questions by examining three approaches that critique both realism and liberalism. Economic structuralism, also known as "Marxism," focuses on the role of economic power and exploitation and sees international politics as a struggle between capitalists and workers over the profits generated by workers' labor.

Constructivism and feminism go much further than economic structuralism, liberalism, or realism in focusing their attention on *purpose* in international politics. Constructivism argues that much of the variation in the behavior of states and other actors cannot be accounted for by changes in the distribution of material power, as defined by realists, liberals, and economic structuralists. Rather, they say, change is explained by the evolution of the goals of actors, and in particular by the emergence of shared purpose across actors in the global arena. Feminism questions conventional notions of purpose as well as of power. It sees the exercise of power in the international arena as connected to the exercise of power in the domestic arena that leads to the economic and political disempowerment of women. Feminist international scholars seek to make remedying this disempowerment a central purpose of the conduct and study of international politics.

# ECONOMIC STRUCTURALISM

Just as liberalism was a response to realism, economic structuralism is, in many respects, a response to liberalism. Like liberalism, economic structuralism first arose as a theory of domestic politics and only later was applied to questions of international politics.

Economic structuralism has its roots in the critique of capitalism leveled by Karl Marx, but the label "economic structuralism" is used both because it more clearly describes the theory itself and because there are other Marxist theories that will not be covered here.[1]

Economic structuralism is a theoretical approach that focuses above all on *economics*, both as a motivation in politics and as a source of power. Wealth plays as important a role in economic structuralism as military power does in realist theory. Whereas realism examines the distribution of military power, economic structuralism explores the distribution of wealth (which it sees as essentially identical to power).

Economic structuralism has a strong normative component, finding that economic inequality is a double evil. In addition to creating poverty, it leads to political inequality because political power is built largely on economic power. Advocates of the economic structuralist approach seek not only to expose the sources and effects of economic inequality but also to provide some guidelines as to how such inequality might be overcome. As with realism and liberalism, it is easier to see the contribution that economic structuralism makes to understanding international politics than it is to use it as a guideline for policy.

## ASSUMPTIONS

At the core of economic structuralism is the belief that economics drives politics. This **economic determinism** is very compatible with the standard economics taught in every university economics department. Economic determinism assumes that political behavior is motivated by economic goals and that political outcomes are determined by economic power. This approach also assumes that wealth is a *fungible* resource. This means that it can be converted into other resources. With money, one can buy other things, such as territory, bombs, or politicians.

In general, economic structuralism sees the fundamental actors in politics not as individuals or states but as *classes*. The term **classes** refers to groups of people at different places in the economic hierarchy. At the top are those who own **capital** (such as factories, stores, shares in corporations, land, and money). At the bottom are those who must sell their labor to others to earn money. This includes the majority of people, those commonly called *workers*. In Marxist jargon, the owners of capital are known collectively as the **bourgeoisie**, and the workers are known as the **proletariat**. According to economic structuralism, the world is divided not simply into countries but into classes with opposing economic interests, and people have more in common with members of the same class in another country than with people of a different class in their own country.

However, economic structuralists say, the workers do not always realize this, partly because the owners of capital, who control the means of mass communication, do not want workers to know this. At the core of the structural conception of power is the idea that people are deceived about their true interests. Marx saw ideas such as religion and nationalism as methods by which members of the working class were distracted from seeing their true (class) interests. Economic structuralists have hoped, usually in vain, for an international movement of workers based on their common interests and have lamented what they see as the well-organized collaboration of the capitalist class across boundaries. For example, when World War I broke out, Vladimir Lenin, leader of the Russian communist movement, advocated and expected that workers in the various countries of Europe would see the war as serving the interest of the capitalists at the expense of the workers and would therefore refuse to participate. As it happened, however, an upsurge in nationalist sentiment caused even the dedicated German socialists to embrace their country's war effort. Today, activists seek to build a transnational alliance of labor unions to increase workers' power relative to corporations.

**economic determinism**

The assumption that political behavior is driven by economic motivations and that political outcomes are determined by economic power.

**classes**

In economic structuralist theory, groups of people at different places in the economic hierarchy.

**capital**

Resources that can be used to produce further wealth.

**bourgeoisie**

In Marxist jargon, the owners of capital.

**proletariat**

In Marxist jargon, the working class.

As economic structuralist theory is applied to international politics, analysis of classes and states is often blurred so that the focus on classes loses some of its emphasis. Instead of examining poor people across the world, many analysts simplify by referring to poor *states*. As states like China and India become wealthier—and gaps *within* societies become as striking as those between societies—this formulation becomes more problematic.

## PROPOSITIONS

Economic structuralism is based on the central concept of surplus value, as developed in Karl Marx's theory of economic exploitation. The main point is that when companies make a profit the workers get a much smaller share than the owners, even though it is the workers who are actually producing the product. When a worker applies labor to some set of raw materials, value is added. Leather becomes a shoe, steel becomes a car, and so on. The difference between the value of the leather and the value of the shoe has been added by workers (using tools supplied by the factory owner). Marx called this difference the **surplus value**, and he asked a simple question: How is this "profit" divided between the person who does the work ("labor") and the person who owns the factory and tools ("capital")? Marx pointed out that the worker receives a fixed amount (a *wage*) regardless of how much value is added. Inevitably, Marx argued, the greater share of surplus value goes to the owner (see Figure 4.1).[2] To many, this is obvious, logical, and fair. But Marx and others who followed this line of thinking found some disturbing implications. In particular, they concluded that in such a system, the wealthy will get ever wealthier while the poor will be left even further behind. In recent years, this concern has been raised in debate over the issue of "sweatshops," in which workers desperate for any job accept low wages and poor working conditions. Economic structuralists often note the growing gap between rich and poor in countries such as the United States.

Economic structuralists ask how the division of profits is determined. They argue that it is determined by the relative bargaining power of the owner and the worker. In most circumstances, the theory asserts, there are fewer jobs than people looking for work. The owner or the manager can use the threat of replacing one worker with another to drive wages down. The owner of capital has what economic structuralist theorists call *structural power*. Note that this is a very different notion of power than that used by many realists, who define *power* as direct coercion through the threat or application of violence. By controlling the means by which labor is added to materials (tools, land, the factory), the owner inevitably has power to extract from the worker a disproportionate share of the profit. Economic structuralist theorists are concerned about the inequality and injustice that result.

Because the ability to extract a favorable deal from workers depends on the workers' needing jobs, poverty is actually in the interest of owners. The more desperate workers are, the more cheaply they

**surplus value**

In economic structuralist theory, the difference between the value of raw materials and the value of the final product; presumably this is the value added by laborers.

**FIGURE 4.1**   Distribution of value of an Apple iPad. Of the $500 or so a consumer pays for an iPad, how much goes to the workers who build it? For economic structuralists, this is a crucial question.

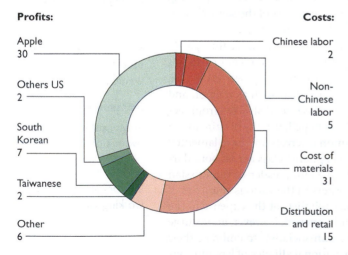

Distribution of value for an Apple iPad
2010, % of total

**Profits:**

Apple
30

Others US
2

South
Korean
7

Taiwanese
2

Other
6

**Costs:**

Chinese labor
2

Non-
Chinese
labor
5

Cost of
materials
31

Distribution
and retail
15

Source: Personal Computing Industry Centre, http://www.economist.com/node/21543174.

CHAPTER FOUR: Theories of International Relations: Economic Structuralism, Constructivism, and Feminism  **93**

will work. Thus, firms around the world save money by hiring economically desperate illegal aliens or by shifting manufacturing to poor countries where workers will accept lower wages. Similarly, in this view, a certain level of unemployment is helpful for owners because it helps keep wages down. Economic structuralist theorists also see free trade as a way for owners of capital to increase their bargaining power over workers, because they can threaten to move production abroad if wages are too high. In the contemporary world, this threat is reflected in concerns over the "outsourcing" of jobs.

In 2013, Thomas Piketty, a French economist, advanced a new Marxist argument about how global capitalism generates inequality.[3] Piketty argued that wealth tends to grow faster than economic output (which drives wages), and that the rich therefore tend to get wealthier faster than others. If the return on investments grows faster than do wages, then those whose income depends heavily on investments (that is, people with the most excess wealth to invest) will gain new wealth faster than those who rely on wages. For Piketty, this explains why, contrary to the expectations of conventional economic theory, income inequality has been growing since the 1970s. In Piketty's view, this source of inequality is inherent in the structure of capitalism, and only a global tax on high wealth and incomes can offset it. Although Piketty's academic arguments and policy recommendations both drew criticism, the popularity of his book demonstrated that growing inequality is a major concern today.

## SURPLUS VALUE AND INTERNATIONAL POLITICS

What does all this have to do with international politics? When economic structuralists apply the domestic concept of surplus value internationally, it leads them to question how international politics affects the distribution of wealth in the world, which is their central concern.

To understand international politics, economic structuralists look first at the interests and actions of different economic classes, and especially at the most powerful class, the owners of capital. Economic structuralist theorists assert that behind every government is a class of owners in whose interests the government usually acts. Owners influence or even control governments through campaign contributions and lobbying and by promoting the general idea that what is good for business is good for the country. According to economic structuralist theory, owners of capital eventually exhaust the opportunities to invest profitably at home, and therefore they look abroad for further prospects. This drive for economic expansion, economic structuralists contend, drives international politics. A primary goal of governments of wealthy countries is to keep markets abroad open so that companies in those countries can invest and trade profitably.[4]

Historically, the theory argues, this goal was the impetus for colonialism. Almost every colonial arrangement had specific investment and trade provisions aimed at giving firms in the colonizing country an advantage over those in the colony. In Latin America, wealth in the form of gold and silver was exported to Spain. The Stamp Act and the Navigation Acts that spurred the American Revolution were policies intended to enrich Great Britain at the expense of the colonies. In India, the British suppressed the vibrant Indian textile industry to increase the market for Britain's own rapidly industrializing textile firms. The overall argument is that powerful states and wealthy capitalists use what power they have to gain even more, forcing weaker actors into the parts of the production process that yield relatively little reward and saving the lucrative parts for themselves.

# THE HISTORY CONNECTION

## THE RISE AND FALL OF MARXISM IN THEORY AND IN PRACTICE

Today's economic structuralism has its roots in the writing of the German economist Karl Marx (1818–1883). Marx was disturbed by the poverty and the growing inequality of wealth he saw during the industrial revolution, both in his native Germany and in England, to which he emigrated. At the time Marx wrote and for many years afterward, Marxism was essentially an academic theory, although broader ideas of socialism gained popularity throughout Europe and North America in the late nineteenth century. In March 1871, following France's defeat in the Franco-Prussian War, rebelling French workers established an alternative government known as the Paris Commune. It lasted only a few months but symbolized increasing efforts among European workers to move revolution from theory to practice.

When a group of revolutionaries led by Vladimir Lenin took over Russia in 1917 and declared that they were putting Marxism into practice, the theory came to play a central role in international politics. To some people, the introduction of Marxism in the Soviet Union showed that progress and revolution were inevitable, as Marx had predicted. Others saw the same possibility of revolution but regarded it as an existential threat, particularly after the Chinese Communist Party, led by Mao Zedong, took over China in 1949. For most of the twentieth century, almost everyone took Marxism seriously, both as a doctrine and as a set of political practices.

This was the case despite the fact that the Soviet Union and China, by most criteria, did not look anything like the communist paradise Marx had envisioned. He certainly had not argued in favor of totalitarianism and violent repression. To some people, this meant that the Soviets and Chinese had perverted or digressed from the true

doctrine of Marxism. To others, it indicated that Marxism could not possibly work—that it was destined to lead to dictatorship.

In the academic realm, work inspired by Marx continued to develop in new ways that moved ever further away from Marx's ideas. In Latin America, the failure to achieve economic development after World War II led scholars to advance a new version of the theory, known as "dependency theory," which would explain how their countries continued to be underdeveloped even though formal colonialism was long gone. Another variant, "world system theory," stressed that the world economy is a single entity, rather than a series of independent economies, and that the European countries had gradually become wealthier over time by subjecting others economically.

Ultimately, however, the popularity of Marxism as a doctrine hinged on the fate of the country with which it had come to be identified. When the Soviet Union collapsed in 1991 (and China abandoned much of its communist rhetoric), Marxism became widely viewed as a dead ideology, no longer worth taking seriously. Marx's words about the future of capitalism—that it would be consigned to "the dustbin of history"—were ironically applied to his own theory. Marx's writings, once considered essential reading for undergraduates, have largely vanished from university syllabi.

After a century in which it generated both immense hopes and fears, Marxism as a prescription for how to build a society appeared to have died in 1991. Yet the theoretical descendants of Marxism remain alive and well. Many of Marx's ideas have been appropriated into mainstream thought. Marx's central concern, that growth in wealth can also lead to greater inequality, has become a central focus of economic research

*(Continued)*

today. Moreover, the recent upsurge in Marxist thinking in Latin America and arguments about the distribution of wealth indicate that Marx's ideas have not disappeared altogether from policy makers' minds.

## Critical Thinking Questions

1. Which of the ideas connected in this chapter with economic structuralism seem most "mainstream," and which seem most radical?

2. What is your impression of how Marxism is seen today by those outside academic circles?

3. Why did it make sense for Marx's writings to be compulsory reading for undergraduates during the Cold War? Is there any reason to read Marx today?

Chinese workers make Nike shoes at a factory in Guangdong province. When labor is added to material, the product is worth more than the material. How is this increased value divided between those who do the work and those who own the factory?

In this respect, economic structuralism fully agrees with the realist statement that "the strong do what they can and the weak suffer what they must."[5] Yet there are two crucial differences. First, realist theories explore politics between the "great powers" because the most powerful drive the system, whereas economic structuralists focus on relations between the strong and the weak. Second, realists assert that the exploitation of the weak is simply a fact of life that must be accepted, whereas economic structuralist theorists consider it an unacceptable fact that must be changed somehow. Karl Marx asserted that capitalism, and the exploitation that accompanies it, would *inevitably* be overthrown in a worldwide revolution. Few theorists today believe this.

# THE CONNECTION TO YOU

## CURRENT DEBATES ON INEQUALITY

In early 2015, as the wealthy of the world were preparing to convene at the World Economic Forum in the exclusive Swiss ski resort at Davos, Oxfam, a British NGO, released a report asserting that *half* of the wealth in the world was controlled by only *1 percent* of the people, while the poorest 80 percent of people control just 5.5 percent of the wealth. Oxfam's analysis showed that the share of wealth controlled by the wealthiest 1 percent had increased by 4 points since 2009.

Economic inequality has become a hot topic in recent years in North America and Europe. The "Occupy" movement in the United States, which organized major protests in 2011, focused heavily on the contrast between the "1 percent" at the top of the economic ladder and everyone else, the "99 percent." Anger over the pay and bonuses of executives and the stagnation of working-class incomes also motivated protests in Europe, where economic austerity programs caused significant hardship.

The result is that, in most countries, assertions relating to the causes and effects of economic inequality are in popular consciousness today as much as ever. If you watch or read news reports in many countries, you will see the sources and implications of inequality raised repeatedly.

Much debate concerns the causes of economic inequality within societies. The Occupy movement criticized what is seen as the undue political power accrued by a small number of people to structure the economy and the laws in ways that benefit them and concentrate wealth, rather than dispersing it. In Europe, critics focused their ire on government austerity programs that cut social programs rather than increasing government spending to stimulate growth.

Related to the argument about causes is an argument about how to remedy the situation.

For those who see inequality as rooted in unfair rules of the game, in which bankers reap huge bonuses when they make money but are bailed out by governments and taxpayers when they lose money, the solution is to change the rules of the game. Recommended policies include strengthening the rights of labor unions, changing the rules for financing political campaigns, and increasing support for public education by raising taxes on the wealthiest.

Those with more confidence in the free market advocate eliminating or weakening unions, reducing regulation, and lowering taxes. Businesses, they argue, do not want to hire workers if rules make it impossible to lay them off if they perform poorly or if needs change. Thus, many argue, the rules intended to help workers actually keep unemployment higher. Much of the debate we hear about whether taxes should be higher or lower is linked to questions about the causes of economic inequality: Some people assume that higher taxes will reduce inequality through social programs such as education and health care; others assume that higher taxes squelch investment and reduce job opportunities.

Underlying the debate about what causes inequality and what reduces it, however, is a normative question about how much inequality is acceptable. In contrast to arguments about taxes, bankers' bonuses, and campaign finance, this question receives relatively little public debate. This is true even though many debates about taxing and social programs are at least in part disagreements about how much inequality we should tolerate.

For the likely readers of this book, these theoretical issues in fact hit close to home. Tuition rates at public universities, loan subsidies for higher education, and the availability of health

*(Continued)*

insurance are all topics that have arisen in the United States and Europe in conversations about appropriate government spending. At the same time, high unemployment rates, especially for people in their twenties—which in 2012 reached as high as 50 percent in Spain—are also a major concern.

### Critical Thinking Questions

1. What kinds of arguments about economic inequality do you hear most often?

2. How much economic inequality is acceptable?

3. What factors influence people's answers to these questions?

## WAR AND PEACE

Although there is consensus among economic structuralist theorists that unbridled free markets lead to economic exploitation and to the expansion of wealthy states into poorer ones, there are two schools of thought about what this means for war and peace (an issue that is generally of less interest to economic structuralist theorists).

One school of thought, advanced by the Russian revolutionary leader Vladimir Lenin, is that capitalism inevitably leads, through imperialism, to war. Lenin asserted that the pursuit of access to economic markets and sources of cheap labor and raw materials will inevitably lead the great powers to clash with one another. He viewed the scramble for colonies by European powers in the late nineteenth century as a prelude to World War I. After that wave of colonization, there was little territory left in the world for economic expansion. The great powers could expand only at each other's expense, so they were driven to wage war with each other.

Another school of thought fears that the opposite is true. In this view, the owners of capital and the governments of powerful states are smart enough to recognize that, rather than fighting each other, they are better off collaborating to exploit the weak. This view echoes the liberal institutionalist perspective, finding that, in economic terms, powerful states have many reasons to collaborate and can do so. Whereas liberal institutionalism sees this collaboration as desirable, economic structuralism sees it as paving the way for ongoing exploitation of the poor.

Today, economic structuralist theorists are skeptical of the web of collaborative institutions that is increasingly governing the world economy, such as the World Bank and the World Trade Organization (WTO). They assert that these are sponsored by governments of wealthy countries and serve the interests of the wealthy owners of capital who influence them. Whereas liberals see these agreements as providing a level playing field on which all can compete, economic structuralist theorists point out that in the race being run on this playing field, some countries got a head start of several hundred years through colonialism. Until that initial difference in positions is resolved, they say, free trade will always favor those already ahead.

# CONSTRUCTIVISM

Constructivist approaches differ fundamentally from the realist, liberal, and economic structuralist approaches. They examine factors that those theories largely ignore, and they make fewer categorical statements about international politics. There are many different constructivist approaches, but they all share a focus on how *ideas* influence international politics.

From the constructivist perspective, realist, liberal, and economic structuralist approaches are all essentially similar in that they are strongly *materialist*. Materialist theories are those that see *material* factors, such as money, territory, and weapons, as driving international politics. Realism focuses primarily on the distribution of military power; economic structuralism centers on the distribution of economic power; liberalism involves both military and economic factors. Even the liberal institutionalist explanation of cooperation is based on a material argument—that concrete incentives will lead to cooperation, even under anarchy.

In contrast, constructivism looks at the powerful role that *ideas* play in international politics. Although they do not deny the importance of material factors such as money and weapons, constructivists argue that the effects of these factors are not predetermined. Instead, the effects of these factors depend on how we think about them. In contrast to the dominant focus (especially in realism and economic structuralism) on *power* in international politics, constructivism seeks to investigate *purpose*—the goals that actors pursue with the power they have, however power is defined.

A simple illustration demonstrates this very sweeping notion. Consider the distribution of nuclear weapons. Presumably, it is important to any country that other countries have as few nuclear weapons as possible. But contrast perspectives on British nuclear weapons with those on Iranian or North Korean nuclear weapons. Britain has far more nuclear weapons than either of the other two (North Korea may have as many as ten; Iran currently has zero), yet most countries consider North Korea's tiny arsenal and Iran's potential arsenal to be far more threatening than the much larger British arsenal (see the "Geography Connection: Identity and Insecurity: Iran's Nuclear Program"). From a material perspective, this cannot be explained; one nuclear weapon should be just as dangerous as the next. As the constructivist theorist Alexander Wendt points out, variation in the importance of nuclear weapons can be explained only by the fact that Western states consider Iran and North Korea *enemies* and consider Britain a *friend*. Friendship and enmity, however, have no basis in the distribution of power.[6] They are *ideas*, existing only in the collective beliefs of populations and leaderships.

There is a huge variety of constructivist approaches, and they are not easily broken down into discernible "schools of thought." Nevertheless, constructivism in general focuses on three key kinds of ideas: interests, identities, and norms.

## INTERESTS

**interests**

In constructivist theory, socially constructed goals that groups of people together define for society.

Most international relations theories connect actors' behavior to their interests. If we understand actors' **interests** (their goals) and the constraints they face, then we can predict their behavior. Although realist, liberal, and economic structuralist theories do not agree on who the key actors are or how their interests are derived, they all follow this simple logic. For realism, a state's interest is dictated by its place in the distribution of power. In economic structuralism, the interests of actors (whether states, classes, firms, or workers) are dictated by the actors' place in the economic hierarchy.

As the example of nuclear weapons previously cited indicates, constructivists find these simple assumptions about interests highly unsatisfactory. Rather than assuming interests and then connecting them to behavior, constructivists ask *where interests come from*. Why does behavioral change often result from relatively minor changes in material factors? Constructivists posit that interests do not follow simply and automatically from

# THE GEOGRAPHY CONNECTION

## IDENTITY AND INSECURITY: IRAN'S NUCLEAR PROGRAM

Constructivists assert that the identity of a country, and whether it is perceived as a "friend" or an "enemy," is as important as material considerations (such as the number of weapons it possesses) in determining whether the country is seen as a threat. This table shows public opinion data for different countries regarding the threat posed by Iran's nuclear weapons program (which as of mid-2015 had produced no weapons). How would a constructivist interpret these data?

*Do you think that Iran's nuclear program is a major threat, a minor threat, or not a threat? (2013)*

| Country | Major Threat | Minor Threat | Not a Threat | Don't Know |
|---|---|---|---|---|
| Argentina | 38 | 17 | 23 | 23 |
| Australia | 44 | 37 | 12 | 7 |
| Bolivia | 36 | 15 | 16 | 33 |
| Brazil | 56 | 22 | 15 | 7 |
| Britain | 42 | 39 | 11 | 8 |
| Canada | 44 | 36 | 13 | 6 |
| Chile | 55 | 18 | 12 | 15 |
| China | 18 | 36 | 29 | 18 |
| Czech Rep. | 46 | 37 | 10 | 7 |
| Egypt | 42 | 35 | 17 | 5 |
| El Salvador | 46 | 24 | 24 | 6 |
| France | 58 | 31 | 11 | 0 |
| Germany | 57 | 32 | 7 | 4 |
| Ghana | 41 | 21 | 17 | 20 |
| Greece | 64 | 14 | 15 | 6 |
| India | 34 | 21 | 12 | 33 |
| Indonesia | 36 | 27 | 24 | 13 |
| Israel | 85 | 10 | 3 | 1 |
| Italy | 70 | 17 | 5 | 8 |
| Japan | 56 | 30 | 9 | 4 |
| Jordan | 41 | 32 | 22 | 5 |

| Country | Major Threat | Minor Threat | Not a Threat | Don't Know |
|---|---|---|---|---|
| Kenya | 40 | 29 | 21 | 10 |
| Lebanon | 51 | 9 | 38 | 2 |
| Malaysia | 44 | 24 | 15 | 18 |
| Mexico | 39 | 26 | 21 | 14 |
| Nigeria | 18 | 19 | 39 | 24 |
| Pakistan | 7 | 15 | 38 | 40 |
| Palest. Ter. | 31 | 33 | 27 | 9 |
| Philippines | 57 | 25 | 12 | 6 |
| Poland | 56 | 28 | 10 | 6 |
| Russia | 40 | 34 | 14 | 12 |
| S. Africa | 28 | 21 | 24 | 27 |
| S. Korea | 63 | 25 | 8 | 4 |
| Senegal | 42 | 9 | 21 | 28 |
| Spain | 49 | 31 | 15 | 5 |
| Tunisia | 26 | 17 | 36 | 21 |
| Turkey | 36 | 35 | 14 | 14 |
| Uganda | 47 | 15 | 11 | 27 |
| U.S. | 54 | 33 | 7 | 6 |
| Venezuela | 32 | 14 | 38 | 16 |

Source: Pew Research Center, at http://www.pewglobal.org/question-search/?qid=1667&cnt IDs=&stdIDs=.

Missiles on Parade at Army Day in Tehran, Iran, April 2012. How dangerous are they? Constructivists stress that ideas of friendship and enmity are as important as weapons themselves in creating security and insecurity.

AHMAD HALABISAZ/Xinhua /Landov

**apartheid**

A system of official discrimination in South Africa in which the African majority was controlled by the white minority.

material factors such as wealth or weapons. Rather, they find that interests are "socially constructed," meaning that groups of people together define what is good and bad and what the goals of society are. One example during the Cold War was that the United States and most European countries shifted from viewing South Africa as a friend and ally to seeing that country as a pariah. As Audie Klotz has shown for the U.S. case, interests changed because attitudes toward South Africa's **apartheid** system changed.[7] Apartheid was dismantled in the 1990s.

Another version of this problem involves how enemies become friends without much change in economic or military factors. For example, how do we explain the emergence of the Franco-German friendship after World War II? The two countries had fought three wars in the space of seventy-five years. Yet, after World War II, leaders in both countries chose to build a fundamentally different kind of relationship. For this to happen, each country had to define its well-being as closely connected to that of the other, rather than seeing the two states' interests as necessarily conflicting. Although some degree of cooperation may be seen as driven by economic and security interests, the extent of European integration since World War II, constructivists argue, can be explained only by the salience of the *idea* of European integration, which came to have a powerful influence.[8]

## IDENTITIES

**identity**

In constructivist theory, actors' and others' perceptions of who they are and what their roles are.

**Identity**, in constructivism, means who the actors are and what they and others perceive their role to be. Realist, liberal, and economic structuralist theories all take the identities of the actors as given: for realists, they are states; for liberals, they range from states to substate and nonstate actors; for economic structuralists, they are classes and states. For constructivists, a key question is how identities change. It stands to reason that as identities change interests and behavior change as well. Theories that ignore the role of identity, therefore, will miss an important source of change. Two examples help illustrate this argument.

First is the centerpiece of the Westphalian system, the sovereign state. Whereas other approaches take the state as a fundamental and unchanging actor, constructivists assert that what it means to be a "sovereign state" changes over time. For example, prior to the seventeenth century, there was no widespread recognition of "state sovereignty" and the rights that accompany it. When states began recognizing each other's sovereignty and legalizing it in the Treaty of Westphalia, they then behaved differently toward each other. If the sovereign state did not always exist, there is no reason to believe that it must always exist or that it must always exist as it did then. For much of the planet, the process of being integrated (usually unwillingly) into the Westphalian system changed the identities of the actors from local, tribal, imperial, or other systems into sovereign states.

Moreover, what it means to be a sovereign state is itself changing. For example, in 1999, UN Secretary General Kofi Annan asserted that the doctrine of "noninterference in the internal affairs of sovereign states" was obsolete. He was concerned about the atrocities being committed by various governments against their own citizens. Preserving human rights, he asserted, was a higher priority than noninterference. This may seem like a theoretical point, but it is much easier to gain support for "humanitarian intervention" when doing so does not appear to violate important international principles. Under this new interpretation, many people deemed armed interventions in Somalia, Bosnia-Herzegovina, and Kosovo in the 1990s and Libya in 2011 to be acceptable. A change in the identity of the sovereign state altered international rules of behavior. Countries such as Russia and China have strongly opposed weakening this norm, and the controversy demonstrates that countries take this issue very seriously. In other words, as constructivists stress, ideas matter, and the evolution in the identity of sovereign states matters a lot.

Constructivists also explore identity in a different sense. Other approaches assume that each state has a single identity and that this identity is distinct from that of other states. Constructivists investigate the extent to which different states might develop shared identities. One prominent example is the European Union, where there may exist a "European" identity in addition to the identities of the separate states. The extent to which leaders (and voters) in different European states view themselves as "European" and essentially like one another, constructivists argue, is likely to influence policy positions (see Figure 4.2). In some cases, these merged identities can be formally institutionalized. Europe, for example, has an extensive bureaucratic apparatus in Brussels. In international trade forums such as the WTO, Europe participates not as twenty-eight sovereign states but as a single entity.

The same can be true in a region characterized by conflict. Michael Barnett has shown that alliance patterns among the Arab states are explained more completely by identity politics than by the balance of power. When identities shifted in response to evolution in the agenda of "Pan-Arabism," alliances shifted as well. Similarly, Barnett argues that the Israel–U.S. alliance is best explained neither by the balance of power nor by domestic politics but by the perception of shared values.[9] More recently, the war in Ukraine is complicated by Ukraine's relatively recent (1991) emergence as a sovereign state, and questions in Russia and elsewhere about how distinct Ukraine is from Russia and where the line between those societies ought to exist. Separatist conflicts are at some level all about identity.

In one of the most widely read (and widely disputed) books in recent decades, *The Clash of Civilizations*, Samuel Huntington argues that identity issues are just as likely to create conflict as unity. He hypothesizes that fundamental cultural differences in different parts of the world create a permanent barrier to a further homogenization of global interests.[10] Thus, for example, the wars in the former Yugoslavia in the 1990s, as well as

**FIGURE 4.2** **Constructivists emphasize the possibilities that international identities can change.** This chart shows Europeans' responses to survey questions about whether they identify with Europe, their nation-state, or both. In what ways can these data be used to support or challenge the constructivist perspective?

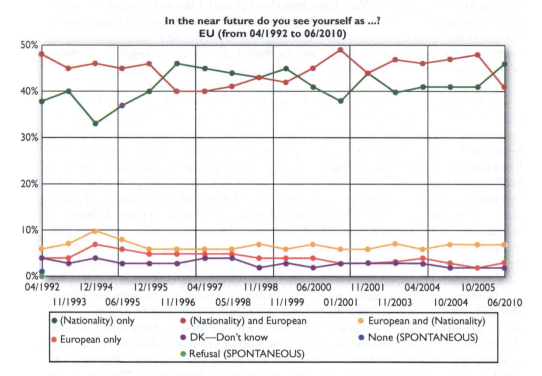

**In the near future do you see yourself as ...?**
**EU (from 04/1992 to 06/2010)**

- ● (Nationality) only
- ● (Nationality) and European
- ● European and (Nationality)
- ● European only
- ● DK—Don't know
- ● None (SPONTANEOUS)
- ● Refusal (SPONTANEOUS)

Source: Eurobarometer Interactive Search, http://ec.europa.eu/public_opinion/cf/index_en.cfm. Reprinted by permission of EB Team.

the Rwandan genocide, appear to be about identity conflicts between competing religious, ethnic, and linguistic groups. Moreover, he sees identity differences between Orthodox Christian, Western Christian, Muslim, Buddhist, and other cultural groupings as leading to a "clash of civilizations." Although a bit of scrutiny reveals serious problems with this hypothesis, it has gained adherents because of the seemingly fundamental nature of the conflict between "the West" and "radical Islam" (both categories are defined by identities rather than states). To the extent that Huntington's argument is correct, the source of this conflict would be difficult to understand using theories that treat identity as irrelevant.

## NORMS

**norms**

Shared rules or principles that influence behavior.

Much of the attention of constructivist approaches has centered on the role of norms in international affairs. **Norms** are defined as shared rules or principles that influence behavior. More specifically, they can be viewed as "collective expectations for the proper behavior of actors."[11] An example discussed previously is the norm of noninterference in the internal affairs of other states. Although it is clear that norms (like any other rules) are sometimes violated, constructivists contend that norms play an important role in shaping behavior, in part because those who violate shared norms pay a price in terms of losing moral influence over others. Therefore, constructivists inquire into both the effects and the causes of norms.

In terms of effects, constructivists see norms shaping the way that states define their interests, a key concern in constructivist thought. In terms of causes, constructivists ask how new norms arise and how norms change. Chapter 2 discussed how the norm of noninterference arose from the religious wars of the seventeenth century, and we might explain the decline of this norm in terms of the increasing power of a competing norm in the twentieth century: human rights. The notion of an international commitment to human rights was vaguely held prior to World War II, but the horrors of the genocide that accompanied that conflict led to a series of agreements signaling that states were willing to elevate human rights to a level that rivaled noninterference in importance.

Franklin D. Roosevelt Library

Eleanor Roosevelt, who campaigned for adoption of the Universal Declaration of Human Rights. To what extent do shared norms such as human rights influence the goals that states and other actors pursue?

## IMPLICATIONS OF CONSTRUCTIVIST THEORY

Like realist, liberal, and economic structuralist theories, constructivist theory makes few unambiguous predictions about what will happen in international politics. One important criticism of this theory is that constructivism's main argument, that "ideas matter," provides no general rules about how they matter, when they matter, or which ideas will come to dominate a particular problem.

However, when combined with one of the other perspectives, constructivism can yield practical insights. Liberal theorists see constructivism supporting liberal arguments about the possibility of cooperation in an anarchic world. The notion that internationally shared norms or identities may arise over time would help explain why we see more cooperation than realism would lead us to expect. Norms and identities may evolve in a way that makes interests overlap more than they have in the past. Norms can also help solve the prisoner's dilemma (as when two members of a gang refuse to talk to the police), or they can change the actors' interests so that the situation is no longer a prisoner's dilemma.

Constructivism also has important implications for activists seeking to promote cooperation. If norm change can increase the likelihood of cooperation, then activists can work to promote norms that, if accepted, will likely lead to cooperation on certain issues. Examples of this in recent years include the support by a global network of activists of the **Convention on Anti-Personnel Mines** in 1997 and the movement in various countries in the 1980s to promote sanctions against South Africa to overcome its apartheid system of institutionalized racism. Much of the work of international nongovernmental organizations consists of trying to promote new norms.

For economic structuralist theorists, constructivism helps explain why global capitalism is so difficult to overthrow. A powerful set of ideas and norms has developed to support the notion that capitalism and international free trade are neutral and fair arrangements that effectively increase global prosperity. Economic structuralist activists fear that these beliefs, which Marx called "false ideology," help convince people that these arrangements are good, even when they increase inequality.

A significant literature, based in large part on the work of the Marxist theorist Antonio Gramsci, seeks to show that the capitalist system promotes a whole range of ideas that make capitalism appear normal and just.[12] In this structural view of power,

**Convention on Anti-Personnel Mines**

Agreement signed in 1997, officially called the Convention on the Prohibition of the Use, Stockpiling, Production and Transfer of Anti-Personnel Mines and on Their Destruction. Also known as the Ottawa Convention.

purpose and power become nearly interchangeable. The ability to influence how goals are defined and what seems "normal" is seen as more consequential than the ability to coerce, because defining the purpose of action gains the acquiescence of the exploited without their recognizing that they are being exploited.

For some realists, constructivism is important because it helps explain state goals. These realists recognize that states often have ambitions that are not dictated simply by the distribution of power. Realists operating at the state level consider it crucial to understand whether a powerful state is a "revolutionary" or a "status quo" power. Whether a state is revolutionary or status quo–oriented does not depend solely or even primarily on the distribution of power. One of Kissinger's major arguments was that as the Cold War progressed, the Soviet Union evolved from a revisionist to a status quo power, making it possible to reach agreements on key issues. The British historian E. H. Carr, one of the most prominent realist scholars of the twentieth century, insisted that power alone cannot explain international politics.[13] Studying power, he warned, without studying the *purposes* for which states seek to use power, encourages a dangerously one-dimensional view. He stridently rejected the notion that interests are obvious, "given," or nonproblematic. His realism stems from the argument that we must deal with the world that is, rather than the world we wish to see, but he argues that we must nonetheless be motivated by the world we wish to see. Carr's views are intensely realist, but at the same time, they emphasize the questions raised by constructivists.

# FEMINIST INTERNATIONAL RELATIONS THEORY

Although the field of international relations has been slow to bring feminist perspectives into its mainstream, they have become important in a wide range of issue-oriented subfields, from international security to global development and the environment.[14] Indeed, feminist approaches have had a greater impact in the practice of international politics than in the study of it.[15] Like the other approaches we have examined, feminist theory does not provide a unified, comprehensive approach to understanding international politics, but it does provide an increasingly influential "lens" through which we can examine the practice and theory of international relations. As one feminist scholar asserts, "accurate, rigorous, and ethical scholarship cannot be produced without taking account of women's presence in or the gendering of world politics."[16]

**gender**

A set of ideas that society has attached to the biological categories of male and female.

Feminist approaches to politics examine how ideas about **gender** shape political problems and our thinking about them. "Gender" is distinguished from "sex" in that sex is a *biological* category, referring to genetic and physiological traits, whereas gender is a *social construction*—a set of ideas that society has attached to those genetic and physiological traits.[17] Whereas sex is generally defined unambiguously and dichotomously, gender allows for the blending or overlap of different characteristics.

There are so many different strands of feminist theory, and they are based on such different assumptions that it is difficult to treat feminism as a single coherent body of theory. What unites the range of feminist theories is a common belief that international politics cannot fully be understood without taking gender into account. Feminist theory asserts that mainstream theory is distorted by **gendered ideas**—ideas that artificially distinguish between "masculine" and "feminine" roles. Such gendered ideas, according to feminist theory, include traditional definitions of power, security, the state as a central actor, and the distinction between "high" and "low" politics. Feminist theory is concerned that this "masculinized" theory not only distorts our understanding but guides our behavior in

**gendered ideas**

Ideas that take "masculine" perspectives as "normal" and neglect "feminine" perspectives.

ways that are destructive, especially to women. All variants of feminist theory also share a normative agenda, improving the status of women, although different strands of theory differ considerably on what constitutes improvement.

In one of the early landmarks of feminist scholarship, Simone de Beauvoir showed how philosophers who shaped much of modern thought, such as Aristotle and Thomas Aquinas, defined "woman" in a way that viewed women's differences from men—both biological and perceived—as deviations from an ideal standard.[18] Feminists question the tendency to automatically connect "feminine" traits to women and "masculine" traits to men. Moreover, they argue that "masculine" characteristics have usually been viewed as positive, whereas "feminine" characteristics have been seen as less desirable. Several problems result. First, if a set of characteristics is artificially ascribed to women and those characteristics are defined as less desirable or less

*"How is it gendered?"*

important, then justification exists for subordinating women. In political terms, this results in widespread discrimination against women. In scholarly terms, it means that we tend to see those issues that are identified with women as being less important, and we therefore tend to ignore them.

Second, the practice of preferring "masculine" traits (including autonomy, rationality, and aggression) over "feminine" traits (including interdependence, emotion, and pacifism) limits our understanding of international politics. Because we tend to see all actors in masculine terms (power seeking, competitive, willing to fight), feminists contend, we underestimate the prospects for cooperative or even altruistic behavior. In practical terms, this means that war and conflict are viewed as normal, and collaboration is derided as "utopian" or "idealist." In scholarly terms, it means that international relations theory tends to be based on a series of biased masculine concepts that lead to biased analysis.

Third, gender distinctions lead to the artificial division of life into a "public" sphere, which is the realm of politics and policy, traditionally dominated by men, and a "private" sphere, which is the realm of families, to which women have traditionally been confined. This, feminists contend, causes a whole range of issues of concern to women, including abuse, women's rights, and children's welfare, to be excluded from discussion and analysis. For example, the work women do in raising children is not "counted" in economic statistics and therefore is invisible to policy makers.

Feminist theory is often divided into three basic schools of thought, following a typology developed by Sandra Harding (though there are other classification schemes as well).[19] *Feminist empiricism* focuses on the practical issues of women in the real world—including the effects of war and globalization on women—which are often ignored in mainstream scholarship. Feminist *standpoint theory* goes beyond "women's issues," arguing instead that every issue can be better understood if examined from a "feminine" perspective in

**FIGURE 4.3** Women's rights time line.

**1792**
Mary Wollstonecraft publishes *A Vindication of the Rights of Women*, seen as the first modern feminist text.

**1848**
The Seneca Falls Convention, seen as the birth of the women's movement in the U.S., adopts a "Declaration of Sentiments" including the statement: "We hold these truths to be self-evident: that all men and women are created equal..."

**1893**
New Zealand becomes the first state to allow women the right to vote.

**1916**
Margaret Sanger opens the first birth control clinic in the US. She is arrested and the clinic shut down. After pursuing her case successfully in the courts, she opens a new clinic in 1923.

**1920**
The US adopts the 19th Amendment to the Constitution, stating: "The right of citizens of the United States to vote shall not be denied or abridged by the United States or by any State on account of sex."

**1949**
Simone de Beauvoir publishes *The Second Sex*, a formative text for 20th-century feminism.

**1960**
In the U.S. the Food and Drug Administration approves the birth control pill, ushering in the sexual revolution.

**1960**
The first female head of state, Sirimavo Bandaranaike, comes to power in Sri Lanka.

**1965**
In the case of *Griswold v. Connecticut*, the U.S. Supreme Court strikes down state laws banning the use of birth control by married couples.

**1972**
The U.S. adopts Title IX prohibiting sex discrimination in education. Among the prominent effects is the opening of interscholastic and intercollegiate athletics to girls and women.

**1972**
The Equal Rights Amendment passes the U.S. Congress, but will fail to gain ratification by the states. The amendment reads "Equality of rights under the law shall not be denied or abridged by the United States or by any State on account of sex."

Timeline markers: 1780, 1790, 1800, 1810, 1820, 1830, 1840, 1850, 1860, 1870, 1880, 1890, 1900, 1910, 1920, 1930, 1940, 1950, 1960, 1970, 1980, 1990, 2000, 2010, 2020

**1973**
The U.S. Supreme Court, in *Roe v. Wade*, rules that the right to privacy gives women the right to abortion (with limitations).

**1973**
Harvard College admits female undergraduate students.

**1977**
In Argentina, the "Mothers of the Plaza de Mayo" begin a human rights campaign to find out what happened to children who disappeared in Argentina's "dirty war."

**1979**
Margaret Thatcher becomes Britain's first female Prime Minister.

**1979**
The UN General Assembly adopts the Convention on the Elimination of All Forms of Discrimination against Women, an international bill of rights for women.

**1982**
British women gather at the Greenham Common air base to protest Cold War weapons deployments; the encampment lasts 19 years and represents the connection between the women's and peace movements.

**1994**
Rape in marriage is made a criminal offense in Britain.

**2000**
A census in China reveals that 116.9 males are born for every 100 females. Selective abortion and infanticide are suppressing the number of females born.

**2008**
Thailand, an international center of sex-trafficking, passes its first antitrafficking law.

**2010**
A new Kenyan constitution guarantees women the eligibility to serve in the legislature and defines a minimum quota for female membership in the National Assembly, Senate, and Parliament.

**2012**
Two female U.S. soldiers file a lawsuit against the restriction on women in military combat roles.

addition to the traditional "masculine" perspective. Feminist *postmodernism*, like other postmodern theories, finds that all attempts to analyze politics are, consciously or not, products of a specific power position. In this view, it is necessary to constantly scrutinize the interests behind even feminist analysis, and it is important to recognize that no single theory will ever be completely valid.

## FEMINIST EMPIRICISM

Feminist scholars and activists note that women have tended to be "invisible" in thinking about international politics. The focus on activities traditionally dominated by men, such as war and diplomacy, has led observers to neglect how international politics profoundly influences spheres traditionally associated with women, such as raising a family and working in low-wage jobs (see Figure 4.4). This emphasis follows a pattern long observed in broader feminist theory: Jobs that are identified with women, such as "housewife," are devalued and hidden compared to those associated with men, such as "businessman." Women are neglected subjects.

In one influential study, Cynthia Enloe studied the effects on local women of placing U.S. military bases in foreign countries. She found that the establishment of U.S. military bases in the Philippines changed the entire context of local women's lives. The influx of U.S. soldiers, with a new set of "needs" and the money to pursue them, changed the traditional economic roles of women.[20] In particular, the demand for sex workers

**FIGURE 4.4** **Why are literacy rates different for men and women and why is the gap bigger in some cases than in others?** Feminist scholarship tries to understand these differences to assess how much other inequalities (such as those in income and political rights) are linked to inequalities in education.

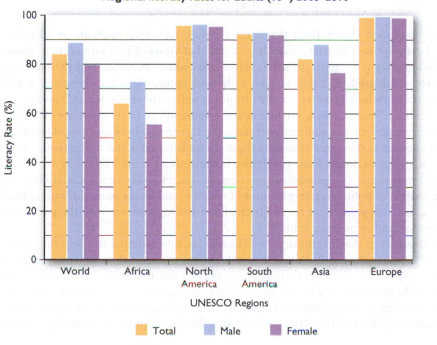

Regional literacy rates for adults (15+) 2005–2010

Legend: Total, Male, Female

Source: UNESCO Institute for Statistics. Reprinted by permission.

skyrocketed. When NATO forces were deployed in Bosnia and then in Kosovo, many young women were led into prostitution through the combination of desperate poverty, organized crime, and high demand by the soldiers for sexual services. These women and their communities became dependent on this economy for their survival. This is but one example of how women's lives are profoundly affected by international politics in ways that few people ever consider.

A related issue is how war affects women. A great deal of attention is given to those, traditionally men, who fight in wars, but less attention is given to the women and children left behind to survive without those who had previously served as breadwinners. Women left in war zones encounter even greater problems, including frequently being the victims of rape. Sometimes this is an "unintended consequence" of war, but in many cases around the world rape has been used deliberately, as a tactic intended to demoralize and terrorize civilian populations in contested territories.[21] More broadly, feminist scholarship shows how women are increasingly involved in international conflict in roles traditionally assigned to men, including as soldiers, terrorists, insurgents, and even war criminals.[22]

Feminist scholars have also studied the individual-level effects of global trade agreements.[23] Because women are often the primary breadwinners in their families and often work in the factories that mass-produce goods for the world market, they are disproportionately affected by changes in global trading rules. Some people argue that globalization, by increasing the demand for such labor, will tend to benefit women. Others fear that the competition induced by globalization, combined with weak regulations in many countries, leads to intensified exploitation of women, many of whom are desperate to earn enough to feed their families.

A broad effort in the feminist empiricist agenda is to improve the collection of data on the status of women, to render them less "invisible." One example is the Woman Stats project (www.womanstats.org), which seeks to collect detailed statistical data on the status of women around the world and to connect those data with data on the security of states.

## FEMINIST STANDPOINT THEORY

Feminist standpoint theory finds that some theories, especially realism, are based on gendered assumptions. In particular, they charge that views of human nature as prone to conflict are based on generalizations about "masculine" behavior and therefore are incomplete and biased. A complete view of human nature, feminists contend, would include traits traditionally defined as "feminine" as well as those defined as "masculine." These "feminine" traits include nurturing and collaboration, factors that are viewed as inherent in females' roles as mothers, nurturers, and caregivers. To be clear, most feminists do not argue that women are fundamentally different from men, but rather that a group of traits has been excluded from theorizing because these traits have been *artificially* associated with women. "The whole theoretical approach to international relations rests on a foundation of political concepts, most of which would be far more difficult to hold together coherently were it not for the trick of eliminating women from the prevailing definitions of man as political actor."[24]

Feminists assert that, beginning with Thucydides, international relations theory has confused "human nature" with "masculine nature." For example, there is another ancient Greek view of war very different from Thucydides's view that human nature leads to conflict. In the play *Lysistrata* by Aristophanes, the women of Greece's warring city-states refuse to have sex with their husbands until the men end the Peloponnesian War. Modern feminists see this as a refutation of the notion that "mankind" is essentially warlike.

Women fleeing a rebel advance in Congo. Feminist scholarship points out that the role of women in war is often ignored by casualty figures that focus only on combatants, who historically have been overwhelmingly male. What costs do women pay as they are caught on the battlefield or left behind to fend for themselves and their children?

WALTER ASTRADA/Stringer/Getty Images

Similarly, the division of life into a "private" women's sphere (the household) on one hand and a "public" men's sphere (the state) on the other creates the necessary basis for conventional views on war and the security dilemma. Because the private household sphere, which is often delegated to women, is excluded from the realm of power politics, the household-level costs of war are rarely discussed by policy makers or international relations theory. For example, as feminist empiricists point out, casualty statistics in warfare include killed and injured soldiers, but not the battle deaths of noncombatants, the starvation of children, and the rape of women that almost always accompany war.[25] These costs can be overlooked, feminists stress, only if they are ruled out of consideration prior to the analysis. More broadly, the notion of the "state," on which so much international relations theory relies, itself relies on an artificial separation of private and public that feminists argue is gender-based and gender-biased.[26] The study of international politics therefore misses not only the violence done to women in war, but also the fact that even more violence is done to women within the everyday confines of the family, an arena that is considered "private" and therefore beyond the concern of political analysis.

We might then ask, what view of international politics would have emerged over the centuries had Thucydides written not "of gods we believe and of men we know, it is their nature to rule whenever they can," but "of women we know and of goddesses we trust, it is in their nature to work together whenever they can?" Had this view been advanced in Thucydides's influential text and picked up by later theorists, feminists speculate, both our understanding of international affairs and our conduct of it might be quite different.[27]

Scrutinizing more modern literature, J. Ann Tickner shows how Hans Morgenthau's principles of realism (discussed in Chapter 3) are based on gendered notions of what is "natural." Tickner then reformulates Morgenthau's principles to show how nongendered assumptions lead to a very different kind of international relations theory.[28] Reformulating Morgenthau's definition of power as "man's control over the minds and actions of other men,"[29] Tickner provides a perspective that emphasizes context and contingency more than universal law; gives no single definition of power, viewing power as varying with context; views all action as having moral implications, rather than putting morality aside; and obscures the boundaries of what is political and what is nonpolitical.[30] To cite just one example, Tickner asserts that the threat to survival posed by poverty should be considered as important as the danger that arises from weapons.[31]

In contrast to the common understanding of "power" as the ability of one actor to compel another to do something he or she does not wish to do (coercive power), some feminist scholars define "power" as the ability of two or more actors to work together to achieve what they cannot achieve alone (collaborative power).[32] In other words, the ability to solve the prisoner's dilemma—and get the higher payoffs associated with mutual cooperation—can be thought of as a form of power within a group. With power viewed this way, "power politics" and collaboration do not look contradictory. This strand of thinking overlaps with liberal theories of all varieties.[33] Liberal feminists are concerned that the lack of emphasis on the possibility of collaboration becomes a self-fulfilling prophecy. If people are convinced that cooperation is limited and that they must constantly be ready for conflict, they will be less likely to put effort into cooperative solutions.

## FEMINIST POSTMODERNISM

Postmodernism is a broad school of thought that is skeptical of all claims of objective truth. Postmodernists find that all inquiry is biased by the questions asked (and the questions ignored), the assumptions made, and the way evidence is interpreted. Therefore, they stress that all knowledge is partial at best and that all knowledge serves someone's interest (and therefore tends to oppress someone else). Feminist postmodernism shares its basic concerns with other forms of feminist international relations scholarship— namely, a focus on the consequences of hidden gender biases and a normative concern with emancipation. However, it frames the problem in a very different way, which in important respects leads it to contradict feminist empiricism and feminist standpoint theory. Like other postmodern approaches, feminist postmodernism rejects the possibility of creating a more truthful analysis, a possibility that both feminist empiricism and feminist standpoint theory embrace.

From the postmodernist perspective, *all* claims about truth, and especially claims about truth involving social relations, are social constructions. Therefore, postmodernists reject the goal of feminist empiricists and standpoint theorists to create a more complete or accurate theory of international politics. Whereas standpoint theorists argue that our view of reality has been distorted because it focuses on the masculine at the expense of the feminine, postmodern theorists insist that the categories "masculine" and "feminine," and all other categories of analysis, are artificial constructions.

Postmodern feminists worry that analyses based on "improved" understandings of gender may themselves become part of a more subtle pattern of oppression. Two specific examples of this type of argument help illustrate the point.

Feminist empiricists and standpoint theorists agree that certain aspects of women's oppression in poor countries ought to get more attention, but cannot because of the way the discipline of international relations is constructed. Postmodern feminists raise two different kinds of concerns about these arguments. First, by dwelling on oppression based on gender, such analysis naturally gives less attention to oppression based on race, class, and colonial status. For many postmodern analysts, gender is merely one dimension in a broader pattern of oppression, and to separate it out from others is to reflect the bias of white, wealthy women from states that were colonizers rather than colonized. More broadly, Jean Bethke Elshtain cautions feminists against too ardently identifying "feminine" qualities with peace, because doing so subtly reinforces the binary categories of good and bad on which all oppression—including the oppression of women—is based.[34]

Second, and perhaps more vexing, is the assumption, implicit in feminist empiricism and standpoint theory, that clear judgments can be made about what constitutes oppression of women. For example, many feminists in Western countries take it for granted that practices such as the veiling of women, the restriction of women's political rights, and female genital mutilation are violations of women's rights and ought to be stopped. Postmodern scholars reject all universal statements about moral values and consider whether women in other cultures, with different moral codes, might be more oppressed by having to conform to Western standards of morality than by having to conform to their own culture's standards. For example, are Muslim girls in France liberated or oppressed by laws forbidding them to cover their heads in schools (see Figure 4.5)?

This sort of argument has led many people to argue that postmodernism in general, and postmodern feminism in particular, goes too far. The notion that all truth and all

**FIGURE 4.5**  **Western liberal approaches to human rights emphasize equality of the sexes.** Postmodern feminists argue that this may impose Western values on other cultures, including on their women. In recent decades, Turkey's focus on secular values has led it to forbid women from wearing the traditional head scarf. Does this liberate women or oppress them? This graph shows Turkish women's responses to survey questions on Muslim dress.

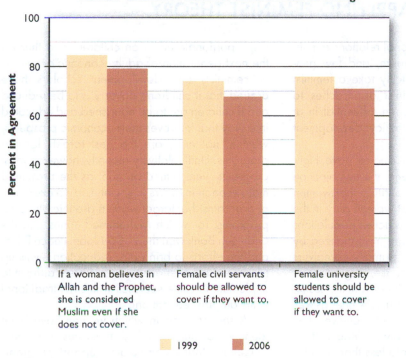

Source: http://www.tesev.org.tr/eng/events/RSPTurkey.pdf.

moral views are socially constructed, critics point out, brings us to a situation in which we cannot say anything about truth and have no basis for deciding what we should agree upon. Most postmodernists reject this critique. They assert that greater understanding can be reached by constantly "deconstructing" claims of truth to uncover hidden biases and their potential to be used for oppression. The postmodernists' point is not that there is no truth, but that there are multiple truths. These truths depend on how questions are framed, and even more so on which issues are considered central (and therefore are "foregrounded") and which are considered less important (and therefore are left in the "background").

## FEMINIST INFLUENCE

Feminist approaches to international relations are gradually being integrated into the field. For example, the pivotal role of women has come to be widely accepted in discussion of two major trends in international affairs today (see "The Policy Connection: Women, Development, and Democratization: Applying Feminist Theory"). There is also an increasing recognition that feminist approaches are not just about women—that the entire field, and all the issues it contains, are better understood when the role of gender is taken into account.

# THE POLICY CONNECTION

## WOMEN, DEVELOPMENT, AND DEMOCRATIZATION: APPLYING FEMINIST THEORY

Feminist theories of international relations remain on the edge of the mainstream, and few general policy discussions explicitly take a feminist perspective. However, feminist approaches to international politics have been influential in at least two important areas of policy: development and democratization.

In development, feminist studies have highlighted two related phenomena: the combination of economic and social exploitation that women face, and the central role that women play in the economic welfare of poverty-stricken populations around the world. Women are marginalized by being forced to become the primary caregivers for children. When war, disease, migration, or other causes have removed fathers from the scene, women fill the function of sole breadwinner as well as sole caregiver. At the same time, however, they tend to be excluded from many profitable areas of the economy and to be paid less than men for the work they do. The poverty of women has a

disproportionate effect on children, and thus on the next generation of adult economic actors.

Feminists and development scholars have argued that if children's poverty is to be reduced and if children are to be nourished and educated in a way that improves their economic prospects, women, not men, are the best targets for aid programs. Until relatively recently, however, most programs were aimed at men, as the presumed main economic actors in societies. Two examples of programs that target women are microlending programs, for which Muhammed Yunus and the Grameen Bank won the 2006 Nobel Peace Prize, and the efforts to bring girls' education levels up to those of boys (efforts that have been difficult to implement in some societies with strict traditional limits on girls' education).

A second area in which women have been identified as important keys to success is democratization. Many democracy support programs led by Western states have strongly emphasized

*(Continued)*

women's participation. One goal is simply to reduce the traditional disadvantages that women in every country face in political participation. In some cases, participation of women in a system previously closed to them is seen as a means of transforming a system that is resistant to democratic norms. Thus, external actors insisted that women be given an increased role in the new institutions put into place in Afghanistan after the Taliban government was ejected in 2001. Such policies highlight the tensions between postmodern feminism and other variants. Postmodernists are more wary of insisting on the universality of Western notions of democracy and of the proper role of women in politics, and therefore give more credence to those women who say that they do not believe women and men should play the same roles and who do not want to do so.

The influence of feminism on policy should not be exaggerated; women remain economically exploited and politically marginalized around the world. Still, feminism has influenced policy and served as a "practical" approach to international politics.

## Critical Thinking Questions

1. In looking at public policy in general, should feminist approaches get more attention than they do now? What problems might be more effectively addressed by feminist approaches? What issues might not benefit from a greater focus on feminism?

2. What aspects of feminist thought seem most valuable in policy making?

3. Should Western countries promote universal values of women's rights, or should they accept the argument that women in some countries might be more liberated by being free to choose a limited political, economic, and social role?

# POWER AND PURPOSE IN ECONOMIC STRUCTURALISM, CONSTRUCTIVISM, AND FEMINISM

The three paradigms discussed in this chapter offer a wide range of perspectives on power and purpose in international affairs. Economic structuralism, in its most traditional formulation, focuses exclusively on economic power, and defines power in terms of coercion; it assumes that purpose is dictated by class interests and therefore does not require extensive analysis. More modern economic structuralist analyses define power more in structural terms, focusing on how the ideology of capitalism makes exploitation seem normal. By shaping notions of purpose, in this view, capitalism exerts power over the weak.

Constructivism puts a very heavy emphasis on purpose rather than power. It does not deny the importance of power but focuses on a different question: What are the purposes to which power is put, and how do those purposes change? Interests, identities, and norms all represent different ways of examining how actors understand their goals. For constructivists, changing conceptions of purpose tell us much more about world politics than changes in material power.

Most versions of feminism take a position on purpose that is compatible with that of constructivism. The social construction of gender roles, they contend, is central in understanding all politics. At the same time, feminists remain intently focused on questions of power—which they define broadly, often invoking structural and collaborative as well as coercive understandings of power. Postmodern feminism stresses that the ability to influence how actors view problems is itself a crucial power. In contrast to realism and economic structuralism, which see purpose as being determined by power, most feminists (and many constructivists) believe that ideas create their own power, which can be used both to liberate and to oppress.

# RECONSIDER THE CASE

## IS SOCIALISM MAKING A COMEBACK?

Protest and advocacy of an increased role for the state have not been the only responses to recent economic woes in the United States and Europe. In both places, we now see intense debates about the sources of wealth, the proper role of state and market, and the appropriate level of regulation of financial markets. Around the world, these questions concern not only wealth and inequality within societies, but efforts of poor countries to catch up and compete with the wealthy states of the world. Is the free market truly in retreat, and if so, what are the implications for global politics?

In Europe, the election of socialists has not been the only response to the crisis. In Italy, a sitting prime minister resigned to be replaced by a "technocrat," a nonpartisan expert given a mandate to implement austerity measures without engaging the larger ideological differences between left and right. In Spain, the People's Party (a conservative party) defeated the incumbent Socialist Party by a landslide in late 2011, and the United Kingdom re-elected a Conservative government in 2015.

Moreover, the far right and anti-immigrant parties have also performed well in recent elections. In France's 2012 election, the far right National Front candidate Marine Le Pen achieved her party's best result ever, taking 18 percent of the vote, and by 2015 she was polling over 30 percent (France's next presidential election is scheduled for 2017). The radical left Syriza party won election in Greece in 2015, but the fascist Golden Dawn party finished in third place with 6 percent of the vote. Rather than a decisive shift to socialism, the results seem to demonstrate frustration with incumbents and movement of votes out of the center to both left and right. In sum, it may be appropriate to say that many ideologies and ideas are making a comeback in an era in which economic crisis has people around the world looking for new answers.

### Critical Thinking Questions

1. Which aspects of economic structuralism resonate most (and least) strongly with you? What sorts of policy prescriptions might emerge from them?

2. How might a constructivist or feminist view the current debate over economic arrangements?

3. To what extent do people's views on economic issues follow the rise and fall of their country's economic situation?

## SUMMARY

- The five paradigms discussed in this book (see Table 4.1) should be viewed as different tools for understanding international politics, not as ideological positions among which one must choose. There are important overlaps among the different approaches as well as contradictions.

- Realism and liberal institutionalism share the same assumptions concerning the centrality of states as actors and the problems created by anarchy. They disagree primarily on the extent to which states

are able to transcend these problems through collaboration.

- Complex interdependence theorists sometimes disagree almost as much with liberal institutionalists as they do with realists, because the complex interdependence theory sees the state as only one actor among many in international politics.

- Liberalism and economic structuralism agree to a large extent about how the world works, including that there is a great deal of collaboration among states.

**TABLE 4.1**    **Paradigms of International Politics**

| | Main Variants | Essential Concepts | Key Actors | Key Processes | Normative Commitment |
|---|---|---|---|---|---|
| Realism | Balance of power theory, hegemonic stability theory | Anarchy, security dilemma, self-help | States | Changes in the distribution of power, internal and external balancing | State interest should be priority; protect the state rather than improve the world |
| Liberalism | Liberal institutionalism | Anarchy, security dilemma, cooperation | States | Cooperation to overcome problems of anarchy | Promote collaboration to bring peace and prosperity |
| | Complex interdependence theory | Multiple actors, multiple goals, nonhierarchical interests | Wide range of actors | Emergence of a complex web of cooperative relationships | |
| Economic structuralism | | Surplus value of labor, division of gains from trade, inequality | Classes (owners of capital and workers), states | Unequal bargaining, imperialism, widening of inequality | Reduce economic and political inequality |
| Constructivism | Many variants, none dominant | Ideas, interests, identities, norms | States, NGOs that try to shape norms | Evolution of new interests, norms, identities | Varies; compatible with others |
| Feminism | Empiricism, standpoint theory, postmodernism | Gender, gender hierarchy, partial truth | Marginalized people, especially women; reproducers of gender hierarchy | Creation of gender bias; oppression; revealing of gender bias | Liberation of women; less masculinized view of world politics |

They disagree on their normative assessment of the system—that is, on whether international cooperation leads to increased good for everyone or to exploitation of the poor by the rich.

- Economic structuralism's emphasis on economic motivations is compatible with any version of liberalism. Economic structuralism and complex interdependence theory agree that many actors have an influence over the state.

- When economic structuralism identifies states rather than classes as the primary actors, or when realism

analyzes strong/weak interactions rather than great power politics, the two approaches look very similar.[4] Realism and economic structuralism disagree in their definition of power and their assessment of whether the international system can be changed. Whereas economic structuralists hope to transform a system they see as inherently unfair, realists assert that the system cannot be changed and that policy should be focused on winning the competition.

- Constructivism is not compatible with the dominant strands of realism today, which place a heavy emphasis on inferring interests directly from the structure of the system. It is more compatible with older versions of realism, which consider intentions, along with capabilities, to be important variables in determining how states behave. Realists of all kinds are highly skeptical of the notion that shared norms can have an important effect on state behavior. Such norms will be followed, they contend, only when doing so serves other state interests.

- Constructivism's focus on the sources of interests and identities contradicts the assumption in liberal institutionalism that state interests can be objectively determined from the structure of the international system. Liberals generally view constructivism as supporting their arguments because it shows how shared interests, identities, and norms can emerge and can make cooperation easier than realism would have us believe.

- A strict Marxist version of economic structuralism holds that only material factors (for example, money) influence actors' behavior and that ideas and beliefs are dictated by economic interest. However, many economic structrualists include ideologies as part of the structure of domination. This type of argument is compatible with constructivism, because it sees beliefs and ideas as contingent on many factors, not

just determined by material factors. Activists working from an economic structuralist perspective hope to help workers overcome national identities, which in their view allow workers in different countries to be pitted against one another rather than uniting to pursue their common interests.

- Feminist theory rejects the basic tenets of realism, including the anarchic nature of the system, the view of the state as an unproblematic concept, and the focus on conflict. Feminist standpoint theorists argue that realist theory overestimates the likelihood of conflict and underestimates the potential for collaboration. They agree with liberal institutionalists that cooperation is more likely, and indeed more evident, than realists admit.[31] The feminist insistence that theorists not dwell on one set of actors or issues to the exclusion of others fits well with complex interdependence theory. Economic structuralist approaches see gender bias as just one part of the broader pattern of economic oppression endemic under capitalism.[25]

- The idea that many categories of analysis are socially constructed is shared by both constructivist and feminist scholars; feminist scholars simply examine one particular way in which social construction leads to bias.

## KEY CONCEPTS

1. Surplus value
2. Classes
3. Structural power
4. Capital and labor
5. Economic determinism
6. Materialist versus constructivist theories
7. Social construction
8. Interests, identities, norms
9. "Sex" versus "gender"
10. Feminist empiricism
11. Feminist standpoint theory
12. Postmodernism

## STUDY QUESTIONS

1. Which paradigm assumes that political behavior is driven by economic motivations?
   a. Feminism
   b. Constructivism
   c. Economic structuralism
   d. Liberalism

2. Which paradigm views norms and identity as playing a powerful role in international politics?
   a. Feminism
   b. Constructivism
   c. Economic structuralism
   d. Realism

3. Which paradigm examines how gender shapes international political problems?

   a. Feminism

   b. Constructivism

   c. Economic structuralism

   d. Liberalism

4. What does economic structuralism predict will happen to gaps in wealth?

   a. They will widen.

   b. They will narrow.

   c. They will stay the same.

   d. They will narrow and then widen.

5. Which of the following is NOT asserted by feminist theory?

   a. Women are more peaceful than men.

   b. Gender roles are socially constructed.

   c. Women's roles have tended to be undervalued.

   d. Cooperation is an important form of power.

6. How does economic structuralism's normative position differ from that of liberalism?

a. Economic structuralism does not believe that cooperation is possible.

b. Economic structuralism sees more cooperation in international politics.

c. Economic structuralism views cooperation in a positive light.

d. Economic structuralism sees cooperation as leading to exploitation.

1. How do economic structuralists explain the outbreak of war?

2. How do economic structuralists view the role of international organizations?

3. How does the constructivist understanding of the Westphalian system differ from the realist understanding?

4. How can changes in identity influence international politics?

5. In what ways can constructivism complement realist, liberal, and economic structuralist approaches?

6. What are the differences between empiricist, standpoint, and postmodern versions of feminist international relations theory?

[Correct answers: 1. c; 2. b; 3. a; 4. a; 5. a; 6. d]

## END NOTES

1. I do not use the label "Marxism" in part because it is such a politically loaded term and in part because it is somewhat meaningless to many students today. Also, there are important parts of Marxist theory, most notably the philosophy of historical materialism, that are soundly rejected by most contemporary economic structuralists. At the same time, there are important contemporary theories that are Marxist but are not structural or even materialist, most notably Gramscian approaches. I have chosen the label "economic structuralism" because it simply describes the content of the approach and therefore should help readers grasp the concepts.

2. Karl Marx, *The Grundrisse*, excerpted and translated in Robert C. Tucker, ed., *The Marx-Engels Reader*, 2nd ed. (New York: W. W. Norton, 1978), pp. 247–250.

3. Thomas Piketty, *Capital in the 21st Century*, Translated by Arthur Goldhammer, (Cambridge: Harvard University Press, 2014).

4. This thesis was developed by the English economist John Hobson in *Imperialism* (1902) and was given an explicitly Marxist formulation in Vladimir Lenin's *Imperialism: The Highest Stage of Capitalism* (1916).

5. The links between realism and Marxism are stressed by two prominent realists, Albert Hirschman and Robert Gilpin. See Albert O. Hirschman, "Beyond Asymmetry: Critical Notes on Myself as a Young Man and on Some Other Old Friends," *International Organization*, Vol. 32, No. 1 (Winter 1978): 45; and Robert Gilpin, *The Political Economy of International Relations* (Princeton, NJ: Princeton University Press, 1986), p. 42. Robert O. Keohane, generally regarded as a proponent of liberal international relations theory, makes a similar point in *After Hegemony: Collaboration and Discord in the World Political Economy* (Princeton, NJ: Princeton University Press, 1984), p. 44.

6. Alexander Wendt, "Anarchy Is What States Make of It: The Social Construction of Power Politics," *International Organization*, Vol. 46, No. 2 (Spring 1992): 391–425.

7. Audie Klotz, *Norms in International Relations: The Struggle against Apartheid* (Ithaca, NY: Cornell University Press, 1995).

8. Craig Parsons, "Showing Ideas as Causes: The Origins of the European Union," *International Organization*, Vol. 56, No. 1 (Winter 2002): 47–84.

9. Michael Barnett, "Identity and Alliances in the Middle East," in Peter J. Katzenstein, ed., *The Culture of National Security: Norms and Identity in World Politics* (Ithaca, NY: Cornell University Press, 1996), pp. 400–447.

10. Samuel Huntington, *The Clash of Civilizations and the Remaking of World Order* (New York: Simon & Schuster, 1996).

11. Peter J. Katzenstein, "Introduction: Alternative Perspectives on National Security," in Katzenstein, ed., *The Culture of National Security*, p. 5.

12. For an example of this approach, see Mark Rupert, *Ideologies of Globalization: Contending Visions of a New World Order* (London: Routledge, 2000).

13. Edward Hallett Carr, *The Twenty Years' Crisis, 1919–1939* (New York: Harper & Row, 1964 [1939]), Chapter 6.

14. I am grateful to Laura Sjoberg for the detailed critique she provided on this section.

15. Laura Sjoberg, "Introduction to *Security Studies*: Feminist Contributions," *Security Studies*, Vol. 18, No. 2 (2009): 185.

16. Sjoberg, "Introduction to *Security Studies*," p. 186.

17. The classic exposition of this idea is in Simone de Beauvoir, *The Second Sex*, trans. and ed., H. M. Parshley (New York: Vintage, 1989) [originally published 1949].

18. de Beauvoir, *The Second Sex*, p. xxii.

19. See Sandra Harding, *The Science Question in Feminism* (Ithaca, NY: Cornell University Press, 1986). Harding's typology is applied to international relations by Christine Sylvester, *Feminist Theory and*

*International Relations in a Postmodern Era* (Cambridge, UK: Cambridge University Press, 1994), Chapter 1, pp. 30–67. Laura Sjoberg provides a different typology, identifying feminist approaches according to how they overlap with other perspectives (realist, liberal, constructivist, etc.). See Sjobert, "Introduction to *Security Studies*."

20. Cynthia Enloe, *Bananas, Beaches and Bases: Making Feminist Sense of International Politics* (Berkeley: University of California Press, 1990).

21. See: Claudia Card, "Rape as a Weapon of War," *Hypatia*, Vol. 11, No. 4 (Fall 1996): 5–18.

22. See Laura Sjoberg and Caron E. Gentry, *Mothers, Monsters, Whores: Women's Violence in Global Politics* (London: Zed Books, 2007).

23. See Jill Steans, *Gender and International Relations: An Introduction* (New Brunswick, NJ: Rutgers University Press, 1998), Chapter 6, pp. 130–157; and Leslie Salzinger, *Genders in Production: Making Workers in Mexico's Global Factories* (Berkeley: University of California Press, 2003).

24. Rebecca Grant, "The Sources of Gender Bias in International Relations Theory," in Rebecca Grant and Kathleen Newland, eds., *Gender and International Relations* (Bloomington: Indiana University Press, 1990), p. 9.

25. Sylvester, *Feminist Theory and International Relations in a Postmodern Era*, p. 36.

26. Steans, *Gender and International Relations,* pp. 46–53.

27. See Grant, "Sources of Gender Bias," p. 15.

28. J. Ann Tickner, "Hans Morgenthau's Principles of Political Realism: A Feminist Reformulation," *Millennium: Journal of International Studies*, Vol. 17, No. 3 (1988): 429–440.

29. Hans J. Morgenthau, *Power among Nations: The Struggle for Power and Peace*, 5th ed. (New York: Alfred A. Knopf, 1978), p. 28.

30. Tickner, "Hans Morgenthau's Principles of Political Realism," pp. 437–438.

31. Tickner, "Hans Morgenthau's Principles of Political Realism," p. 435.

32. Hannah Arendt, *On Violence* (New York: Harcourt Brace and World, 1969), p. 44, cited in Tickner, "Hans Morgenthau's Principles of Political Realism," p. 434.

33. This connection is made explicit and developed in Robert O. Keohane, "International Relations Theory: Contributions of a Feminist Standpoint," *Millennium:*

*Journal of International Studies*, Vol. 18, No. 2 (1989): 245–253.

34. Jean Bethke Elshtain, "The Problem with Peace," *Millennium: Journal of International Studies*, Vol. 17, No. 3 (1988): 441–449.

Demonstrators opposing an international bailout agreement hold a banner reading "No to the Euro" in front of the Greek parliament in Athens on August 13, 2015. What roles do citizens and parliaments play in shaping foreign policy?
Louisa Gouliamaki/Getty Images

# THE STATE, SOCIETY, AND FOREIGN POLICY

## Learning Objectives

**5-1** Explain democratic peace theory and the major arguments in support of it.

**5-2** Evaluate the evidence for and against the theory.

**5-3** Identify the links between democratic peace theory and foreign policy.

**5-4** Understand the influence of state structure on foreign policy.

**5-5** Articulate different views on the role of public opinion in foreign policy.

**5-6** Evaluate the interaction among public opinion, media, and government in making foreign policy.

## WAR, REVOLUTION, AND DEMOCRATIZATION IN THE MIDDLE EAST

"The United States has adopted a new policy, a forward strategy of freedom in the Middle East. This strategy requires the same persistence and strategy as we have shown before. And it will yield the same results. As in Europe, as in Asia, as in every region of the world, the advance of freedom leads to peace."* In this 2003 speech, U.S. President George W. Bush linked the promotion of democracy to peace. The United States had recently invaded Iraq, and at the time, many were still optimistic that the United States might soon leave a functioning democracy in place there.

Bush's policy of democracy promotion fit into a long U.S. tradition. His predecessor, Bill Clinton, had stated: "Ultimately, the best strategy to ensure our security and to build durable peace is to support the advance of democracy elsewhere."† Woodrow Wilson had made democracy promotion a central goal of U.S. involvement in World War I, and the installation of working democracies in post–World War II Japan and Germany was seen as a great triumph. What was new, however, was the argument that the benefits of democracy were a reason to use war to overthrow nondemocratic regimes.

The 2003 U.S.-led invasion of Iraq was motivated by various factors, but among the most important was the goal of transforming Middle East politics by introducing democracy to the region. U.S. leaders believed that building democracy in Iraq would provide an example that other peoples in the region would seek to follow. With democratic governments, the reasoning went, these states would be much more amenable to making peace with Israel and the United States and less likely to harbor terrorists. In 2005, Bush succinctly stated the conventional wisdom: "Democracies don't war with each other."‡ Secretary of State Condoleezza Rice stated directly that realism had been rejected: "The fundamental character of regimes matters more today than the international distribution of power."§

Beginning in late 2010, a new wave of political change, known as the "Arab Spring," swept across the Middle East and North Africa. This wave of protest was driven primarily by actors and grievances within the region, not from outside. Rulers who had held power for decades in Tunisia, Egypt, Libya, and Yemen were swept aside by popular protests, and the process of democratization began. Western leaders praised these changes, and in some cases actively supported them. U.S. President Barack Obama said "A democratic Egypt can advance its role of responsible leadership not only in the region but around the world."¶

But these democratic revolutions raised serious concerns in the same Western countries that voiced support for democracy. Egypt's Hosni Mubarak was authoritarian, but he stood by his country's peace agreement with Israel and was a U.S. ally in the region. Would democratic elections bring the Islamic Brotherhood to power in Egypt, and would it lead to a radicalization of policy? Would the fall of Muammar Gaddafi in Libya lead to democracy or create chaos from which Al Qaeda might gain? If Bashar al-Assad fell in Syria, would the result be a wave of bloody interethnic warfare?

Although democracy remained desirable in principle, the process of democratization seemed to entail considerable danger. By 2012, there was much less confidence than there had been a decade earlier that ousting authoritarian governments would lead smoothly to the adoption of liberal democracy. Inspiration at the bravery of protestors in the region was tempered by fears that the fall of stable authoritarian regimes might

---

*"President Bush Discusses Freedom in Iraq and Middle East," remarks by the President at the twentieth anniversary of the National Endowment for Democracy, Washington, D.C., November 6, 2003.

†Bill Clinton, "Address before a Joint Session of the Congress on the State of the Union," January 25, 1994, www.gpoaccess.gov/sou/index.html.

‡"President and Danish Prime Minister Rasmussen Discuss G8, Africa," White House Press Release, July 6, 2005.

§Condoleezza Rice, "The Promise of Democratic Peace: Why Promoting Freedom Is the Only Realistic Path to Security," Washington Post, December 11, 2005, p. B7.

¶BBC, February 11, 2011, www.bbc.co.uk/news/world-us-canada-12437116.

(Continued)

lead to something worse, such as populist radical anti-Western governments or state collapse.

The experience of the Middle East in the past decade raises difficult questions about the relationship between domestic and international politics. Is it true that democracies have different foreign policies than nondemocracies? Do democracies never go to war with one another? Should policies be based, as Rice asserted, not on the balance of power but on the character of domestic government? In sum, do state-level variables explain international affairs better than systemic factors do?

# CHANGING THE LEVEL OF ANALYSIS

Any analysis of international politics begins by making assumptions about where to look—about which level of analysis is the most appropriate starting point. Some theories examine the nature of the international system. If the system tightly constrains the state, then the state has a very narrow range of options. In this view, the system explains most of what states do, and we do not need to know much about the states themselves. To apply realist balance of power theory, one needs only to know a state's position in the distribution of power (whether it is strong or weak compared to other countries). To apply economic structuralist theory, one needs only to know a state's position in the global economy. In these theories, variation internal to the state—what kind of government and society the country has, or how the government works—is not an important explanation of different outcomes.

Other theories assert that states retain a significant amount of room for choice within the constraints of the system. If states have a range of choices, how and why do states choose the policies they do? To address this question, we need more detailed theories, at the state and substate levels of analysis, to account for behavior.

In casual usage, the word *state* is used interchangeably with the word *country*; both are inclusive terms that refer to a country's geographical territory, its population, and its government. This chapter uses **state** more specifically to mean "the government and political system of a country." This definition includes not only executives, bureaucracies, legislatures, and armed forces but the entire *system* of government, including the constitution and laws.

State and substate approaches reject the system-level analysis, which assumes that different states will behave the same in similar international circumstances, but they differ in what factors they believe to be driving state behavior. In contrast to the theories discussed in the previous chapters, state and substate approaches do not claim to offer a general theory of international politics. Rather, these are theories of **foreign policy**. Although the distinction may seem semantic, there is an important point here: Theories differ in the kinds of questions they seek to answer. Theories of international politics ask, "What is the nature of international politics?" Theories of foreign policy ask, "What explains foreign policies?" There is some overlap in these questions, but a great deal of difference in the answers. Systemic theories provide answers that are presumably valid regardless of the country; state- and substate-level theories assume that countries differ from one another and that they change over time.

Are there important variations in the kinds of states that populate the world? If so, do different states behave differently? Only if the answer to both of these questions is yes do theories need to examine this level.[1]

**state**

The government and political system of a country.

**foreign policy**

Policy (actions or statements intended to change behavior or outcomes) aimed at problems outside of the policy-making state's borders.

# DEMOCRATIC PEACE THEORY

Democratic peace theory asserts that it matters profoundly what kind of states are involved in any interaction. Democratic states, the theory contends, behave very differently than nondemocratic, or autocratic, states do. The argument is supported by a considerable body of evidence, but many scholars remain deeply skeptical. This is an area in which academic research has far-reaching implications for public policy. If democracies are truly more peaceful, then promoting democracy can be equated with promoting peace. In recent decades, this argument has been cited in support of using economic aid as well as military force to promote democracy.

Ironically, the argument that democracies are more peaceful might provide a rationale for war, because a war that installs a democracy might reduce the chances of war in the long run. This logic was the basis of Woodrow Wilson's argument for involving the United States in World War I and was part of George W. Bush's justification for invading Iraq in 2003. It is essential, therefore, that we assess the validity of this theory. Whether it is worthwhile to bear the cost of building democracy in other countries, particularly if this cost involves waging war, will depend in part on whether peace is a likely result. Therefore, we must first consider the theoretical reasons why there *should* be a connection between regime type (democratic versus autocratic) and war. We then need to examine the evidence. Finally, we need to consider the implications in depth.

An Iraqi woman flashes the victory sign with a purple finger, indicating she has already voted, at a polling station in Az Zubayr, southern Iraq, January 2005. U.S. policy was based on the belief that elections would help make Iraq democratic and peaceful.

## DEMOCRATIC PEACE THEORY: TWO VERSIONS

It is very important to distinguish between two versions of democratic peace theory. Only one version stands up to scrutiny, but the two are easily confused. The "individual" model, which has been discredited, argues that democracies in general are more peaceful. This model looks at the behavior of *individual* states. The second, "dyadic" (focusing on pairs) model holds that toward autocracies democracies are just as warlike as autocracies, but that democracies do not fight *each other*. This argument is not about individual democracies but about *pairs* or *groups* of them. The individual democratic peace model has been refuted, but the dyadic model is considered valid by many scholars and policy makers. Both fit into the liberal paradigm, in arguing that peace is easier to attain than realists (or economic structuralists) would have us believe.

**The Individual Democratic Peace Model**   The individual democratic peace argument is intuitively plausible and normatively attractive. It is based on two notions. First, it is believed that publics are generally disinclined to go to war and will stop it if allowed. Second, it is believed that authoritarian leaders sometimes start wars to distract the public from their authoritarianism, a motivation that democratic leaders do not have.

*The Cost of War and Public Opposition*   The origin of the democratic peace theory is widely attributed to the German philosopher Immanuel Kant, who wrote in 1795 of the possibility of an international federation of republics that would usher in *Perpetual Peace* (as his book was titled). Kant and those following him have argued that ordinary citizens are inherently peaceful because they are the ones who have to fight the wars. In Kant's view, power-hungry governments make the choice to go to war against the wishes of their citizens.

In democracy, it is argued, citizens can use the vote to control politicians. Those who will suffer most from war can therefore prevent it. In autocratic regimes, the people who suffer war have no such voice. There is some anecdotal evidence of such democratic pacifism in recent years. In 2003, Spanish voters unseated a prime minister, otherwise very popular, who chose to contribute 1300 troops to the U.S. occupation of Iraq. Similarly, voter dissatisfaction with the Vietnam War in the United States led to U.S. President Lyndon Johnson's decision not to run for a second term.

*War as a Diversion*   A related argument asserts that autocratic regimes have a reason to go to war that democracies do not have. In democracies, the legitimacy of rulers derives from their having been elected in free and fair elections. Governments in autocratic countries have no such source of legitimacy. Citizens often rally around their country's leadership in times of war, raising the popularity even of unpopular leaders. Therefore, it is argued, autocratic leaders sometimes seek to use a successful military campaign to bolster their support among the public (and the elite). The cynical leader can take advantage of this **rally around the flag effect**. In early 2010, a North Korean torpedo attack on a South Korean ship, viewed as a highly provocative act, was attributed to the need of North Korea's ailing president, Kim Jong Il, to show his toughness to other elites in order to ensure that his son would be chosen to succeed him. Such distractions, it is argued, are not needed in democracies because their leaders, subject to periodic elections, automatically have a certain level of popularity and a great deal of legitimacy. One problem with this argument is that many scholars see diversionary war occurring in democracies as much as in autocracies.

### The Dyadic Model: Democracies Do Not Fight Democracies
Many studies have shown that democracies go to war just as often as other countries, and that they initiate war as often as other countries, refuting the individual version of the democratic peace theory. However, it appears that democracies rarely, if ever, fight with each other. Therefore, a more refined hypothesis argues that democracies do not go to war with each other. Peace is not a characteristic of individual states but of dyads (pairs), or groups of democracies. This model must explain *both* why democracies are unlikely to go to war with each other *and* why democracies and nondemocracies do go to war. Three arguments support this view. A structural argument focuses on ways in which democracies find it easier to reach compromises with each other. A normative argument asserts that democracies respect each other more than they respect nondemocracies. An institutional argument, based in **rational choice theory**, finds that democracies are very successful at fighting wars and that democratic politicians are especially vulnerable if they lose a war; this combination makes democratic leaders fear going to war with other democracies.

*The Structural Argument*   In democracies, it is argued, political disputes are resolved by compromise, and this pattern carries over into foreign relations in two ways. First, it is argued, when two democracies bargain in a dispute, they bargain the same way they do domestically, through a politics of compromise that searches for a mutually acceptable solution. This kind of bargaining, which rules out force as an option, cannot take place between two autocracies or even between a democracy and an autocracy, because both sides must operate in this way.[2]

**rally around the flag effect**

The increase in popular support often gained by leaders of a country in times of war.

**rational choice theory**

A theory that bases explanations of decisions on the assumption that decision makers have clear goals, calculate the costs of various courses of action, and pick the policy that will best serve their goals.

Second, some theorists point out that since policy making in democracies requires reconciliation of a range of political views, it is very difficult to adopt an extreme policy. Policies are usually watered down in the process of gaining majority support. When two democracies are negotiating with each other, even in an intense conflict, neither of them will tend toward extreme solutions, such as war. Rather, the domestic processes of democracies carry over into the international arena and lead to moderate solutions.

Third, some argue that democracies are less likely to fight not only because they can reach compromises but also because they keep their promises. Once a commitment is made, it may be difficult to break it because democracies have institutions such as courts and legislative minorities that allow even a small minority to force a government to live up to its commitments.[3] Moreover, because leaders must campaign publicly for office, they may pay a higher penalty for reneging on their commitments. This cost of reneging is known as **audience costs**. Authoritarian leaders have low audience costs because they are less accountable to the citizenry. Because leaders of democracies understand that other democracies are more likely to honor their commitments, they are more willing to enter into agreements and make the concessions needed to avoid war.

**The Normative Argument**   The simplest explanation of a dyadic democratic peace is that democracies do not go to war out of mutual respect. This view holds that citizens and leaders in democracies respect the institutions of democracy not only in their own country but in other countries as well.[4] They reject the idea of forcibly conquering another democracy. They expect other democracies to treat them with the same respect. In other words, both sides in a dispute reject the idea of using force, respect differences that are derived from democracy, and expect to work out problems peacefully. This is essentially a constructivist explanation based on the emergence of a shared identity among democracies and a shared norm that destroying another democracy is bad.

One strength of this normative argument is that it may explain why war between democracies and nondemocracies is more frequent than war between two nondemocracies. Although democratic states have immense respect for each other, they have disdain (not simply a neutral attitude) toward autocratic states. Therefore, a democracy in a dispute with an autocracy may be especially disrespectful of the other side and may view favorably the prospect of destroying the autocracy and replacing it with a democracy.

**The Institutional Argument**   Proponents of rational choice theory argue that democratic political institutions have two effects on their leaders that, when combined, make them very cautious about going to war with one another.[5] The first effect is that democratic states are more likely to win wars. This point was originally made by Machiavelli, but it has received empirical substantiation in recent research.[6] The reason, apparently, is that citizens in a democracy are more likely to support their government's war efforts. The second effect is that leaders in a democracy are more sensitive to the political costs of losing a war, because they are more likely to be turned out of office if the war fails. The combination of these two effects, it is argued, makes war between democracies especially unlikely. If democracies are hard to defeat, and democrats are especially afraid of defeat, then the combination should make democrats especially unwilling to attack other democracies. This does not mean that they do not coerce one another. When democracies are in conflict, the weaker state, being especially sensitive to possible defeat, is expected to give in.[7]

This institutional explanation, like the normative explanation, also explains why war between democracies and autocracies is more likely, and especially why democracies seem inclined to initiate war against autocracies. Democratic leaders may perceive a high likelihood of winning a war with an autocracy. They may expect that the army

**audience costs**
The costs in loss of public support paid by leaders of democracies when they renege on a commitment.

and/or the citizenry in an autocratic state will refuse to fight, leading to an easy victory for the attacker.

## EVIDENCE FOR THE DEMOCRATIC PEACE THEORY

Much of the evidence supporting the democratic peace argument comes from statistical analyses of large data sets of all wars since the early nineteenth century. These data sets list each war (usually defined as a conflict between states resulting in more than 1500 battle deaths), data about the states involved, and the outcome of the conflict. A second kind of evidence comes from specific cases. Some scholars have looked in depth at crises between democracies and argue that there is evidence that leaders and citizens alike hesitate to initiate war with a country they recognize as a democracy and have confidence that compromise can be reached with other democracies.[8]

Scholars generally agree about two major findings.[9] First, there is *no* statistical evidence that democracies go to war less frequently than autocracies.[10] Moreover, studies that seek to determine which state is the initiator of a given war show that democracies are *not* averse to starting wars. This observation has caused the "individual" democratic peace hypothesis to be widely rejected.

Second, there are very few, if any, cases of war between democracies in all of history. Michael Doyle looked at all the wars from 1815 to 1980 and found that none were fought between liberal democracies.[11] In a field as ambiguous as international politics, this stark result is highly unusual, and this pattern has contributed to the notion that war between democracies is practically impossible. There is disagreement about a few cases. For example, Germany had many democratic institutions prior to World War I. Therefore, World War I could be said to have involved several "democratic war" dyads (Germany vs. Great Britain, Germany vs. France, Germany vs. the United States). However, whether the number of wars between democracies is zero or very close to it, the result remains striking. One scholar has asserted, based on this evidence, that the democratic peace theory "comes as close as anything we have to an empirical law in the study of international politics."[12]

## CRITIQUES OF DEMOCRATIC PEACE THEORY

Although democratic peace theory has been widely influential, it has attracted serious criticism as well. The critiques can be broken into three categories. Some assert that the theory is not clearly defined and that its supporters use this vagueness to misinterpret evidence. Others assert that the pattern that exists is not surprising and, in fact, does not show the powerful influence of democracy. Many argue that the pattern is genuine but is more plausibly explained by factors other than democracy.

**Defining Democracy**   The central critique of democratic peace theory is that the key factor, "democracy," is defined poorly and in contradictory ways. Democracy is a concept easily defined as "rule by the many," but identifying democracy in practice—what political scientists call **operationalizing** the concept—is difficult. By many definitions, Germany was a democracy prior to World War I, but if Germany is classified as such, one of the most important wars in history suddenly provides important evidence against democratic peace theory. Thus, one of the most prominent advocates of democratic peace theory, Michael Doyle, has to violate his own classification scheme to call Germany a nondemocracy.[13] One scholar has even shown that Woodrow Wilson himself considered Germany an admirable democracy when he was a scholar and changed his view only after

**operationalizing**

Translating a theoretical concept into attributes that can be measured.

# THE CONNECTION TO YOU

## WHY DON'T YOUNG PEOPLE VOTE?

Democracy is a complex set of norms and institutions, but at its center are elections—the ability of people to choose who will govern. Few debate the value of democracy, and we praise those who struggle for free and fair elections around the world. Throughout the Arab Spring, young people led street protests that brought free elections to these countries for the first time in decades. Why, then, do young people who can take the right to vote for granted rarely exercise it?

Across the developed world, voting participation increases with age. In the 2010 elections in the United States, roughly 21 percent of people between the ages of 18 and 29 voted.* In Germany's 2009 parliamentary elections, more young people voted (59 percent of people ages 21–24) than in the United States, but there was still a large gap between young and old (80 percent of people ages 60–69 voted).[†] In Canada's 2011 federal general election, 39 percent of voters ages 18–24 voted, compared to 75 percent of those ages 65–74.[‡]

Why do young people vote at lower rates than their elders, and what are the implications? Several explanations for low voter turnout among the young can be advanced. It may be that the notion of voting as a duty has decreased over time, so that young people feel a weaker obligation. The overall decline in voter turnout in many countries may support this argument. Others point to a vicious cycle: Politicians do not address the issues of interest to young people, so young people don't vote; and because young people don't vote, politicians have less incentive to address their concerns.

Many organizations seek to address low voting turnout, and low civic engagement more generally, among the young. In the United States, programs such as Rock the Vote use entertainers to encourage the young to vote, and foundations support organizations such as CIRCLE to promote civic engagement among the young. In 2011, the German city-state of Bremen reduced its voting age for state elections to 16. In some countries—including Argentina, Australia, Brazil, Ecuador, Peru, Singapore, and Uruguay—voting is compulsory for people of all ages and is enforced with fines. In Brazil, eligible voters who fail to vote cannot get a passport.

Does it matter that young people vote less than their elders? There are often significant differences between the preferences of young and old, but does low turnout influence foreign policy? One can identify some particular cases, such as the Vietnam era in the United States, in which young people were deeply involved on one side of a major foreign policy question.

The democratic peace theory casts the issue of voter turnout in a new light. To what extent does the quality of democracy influence the validity of the democratic peace theory? If voter turnout is lower, or is skewed away from younger generations, will the mechanisms by which democracy is supposed to cause peace be affected?

### Critical Thinking Questions

1. What does low voter turnout say about the state of democracy?

2. Do young people have alternative ways of being politically influential?

3. Does low voter turnout among young people influence the propensity of states to go to war or to compromise?

---

*The Nation.com, November 16, 2010, www.thenation.com/blog/156470/young-voter-turnout-fell-60-2008-2010-dems-wont-win-2012-if-trend-continues.

[†]The Federal Returning Officer, "Representative Electoral Statistics of the 2009 Bundestag Election," February 5, 2010, www.bundeswahlleiter.de/en/bundestagswahlen/BTW_BUND_09/presse/77_Repr_WStat.html.

[‡]Elections Canada, "Estimation of Voter Turnout by Age Group and Gender at the 2011 Federal General Election," at http://www.elections.ca/content.aspx?section=res&dir=rec/part/estim/41ge&document=report41&lang=e

the country became a rival.[14] But in scholarly terms, the point of objective definitions is to prevent us from interpreting the evidence to fit the theory.

A related problem is that the definition of democracy in the theory appears to change over time. No one today would consider a state a democracy if it enslaved a large portion of its population or denied half the adult citizens (women) the right to vote. But if slavery is incompatible with democracy, then the United States was not a democracy until 1863, and by the standard of universal adult suffrage, the United States was not a democracy until 1920. Yet the United States is considered to have been a democracy throughout its entire history. By classifying states as democracies for more years, the period of time in which democracies did not fight each other looks much longer. This becomes important in assessing the significance of the evidence.

**How Significant Is the Absence of War between Democracies?**   Critics of democratic peace theory assert that the absence of war between democracies is not surprising, for two related reasons. First, for most of recorded history, there have been very few democracies. The first state to consistently meet the definition, the United States, arose in 1789 (or perhaps much later). Using widely accepted definitions, there has been a significant number of democracies in the world only since World War II.

Second, the incidence of war is also fairly rare throughout history. In any given year, only a small number of states are at war with each other. This fact, combined with the small number of democracies at most points in history, makes the likelihood minuscule that any pair of states is both at war and democratic. Thus, one critic argues that the evidence supporting the theory is "statistically insignificant," meaning that the pattern we observe is not substantially different from what we would observe if democracy and war were unrelated.[15]

**Other Explanations for the Observed Pattern**   Finally, when looking at the period in which there were more democracies in the world (after World War II), skeptics point out that there is a much simpler explanation for the absence of war between democracies: the Cold War. From 1945 until 1991, all the world's democracies were threatened by Soviet expansionism, so all were allied to combat that threat. In this view, the balance of power, not the nature of states, explains the absence of war.

In sum, although the evidence supporting the argument that democracies do not go to war with one another is compelling, the critiques of that evidence are also compelling. To some, the critiques indicate a need to reject the theory; to others, they indicate a need for caution; and to still others, the critiques are not persuasive at all. The debate, therefore, continues, and the stakes are high, because the theory has profound implications for policies involving war and peace.

## APPLICATIONS OF DEMOCRATIC PEACE THEORY

The idea of a democratic peace creates a tantalizing prospect: If all the states in the world were democratic, there would be no war. In this respect, democratic peace theory is entirely at odds with realism, which sees the possibility of war as an unavoidable fact of international life. Even if a world full of peaceful democracies is not possible in the very near term, many believe that a zone of peace already exists, consisting of North America, Western Europe, and other areas, and they hope that this zone of peace can gradually expand to include more countries. Such a process, in which a limited region of peaceful democracies gradually expands to cover the earth, is precisely what Kant envisioned in writing *Perpetual Peace* more than 200 years ago.

**zone of peace**

A group of states that tend not to go to war with each other because they are democratic.

**Woodrow Wilson's War to End All Wars**   When World War I started in Europe, most people in the United States were determined to stay out of it. The war was widely viewed as a quarrel among the old, nondemocratic, corrupt empires of Europe. Therefore, many in the United States perceived no real reason to go to war on either side. Woodrow Wilson (president from 1913 to 1921) took a different approach, based largely on democratic peace theory. He argued that, by getting involved in the war on the side of the democratic states (Britain and France were democratic, although their ally Russia was far from it), the United States could help transform Europe into a region of peaceful democracies. In particular, Wilson contended, if Austria's empire in east-central Europe was disbanded, democracy would flourish, and the states in the region would have no reason to go to war with one another. Wilson was perhaps the first to argue that war could be used to promote democracy, thereby reducing the chances for future conflicts.

In Wilson's view, an international organization to maintain the peace could work only if its members were democracies. "No peace can last, or ought to last, which does not recognize and accept the principle that governments derive all their just powers from the consent of the governed."[16] Therefore, two of Wilson's main goals, enshrined in the Treaty of Versailles, were to break up empires to allow for "national self-determination" and to replace autocratic rule with democracy.

Ironically, the biggest democracy of that period, the United States, did not take part in the new League of Nations because the U.S. Senate refused to ratify the charter. However, both the entry of the United States into World War I and the diplomacy involved in ending the war were largely driven by the democratic peace theory.

**Post–Cold War Europe**   The idea that an existing zone of peace can be enlarged by adding new democracies has been put into practice by the states of Western Europe since the end of the Cold War. These states have sought to decrease instability in the formerly communist region and to expand the existing zone of peace by engaging in a vigorous program to promote democracy in new states and to integrate them into the institutional arrangements that help build security in Europe: the European Union (EU) and the North Atlantic Treaty Organization (NATO).

Faced with roughly twenty states in transition in Eastern Europe, both organizations have sought to put democratic peace theory into practice. Their goals are to expand the group of countries among whom war is essentially unthinkable, to increase economic influence, and to create a barrier against potential future Russian expansion.

The EU and NATO have pursued these goals with roughly similar strategies of *conditionality*. Each organization has established numerous criteria for membership. In keeping with the democratic peace theory, most of the conditions for membership concern democratic governance, both generally, in terms of holding elections, and more specifically, in terms of the functioning of judicial systems, civilian control of the military, and so on.[17] The potential benefits of joining the EU and NATO, in terms of security, economics, and technical assistance, are powerful motivators to many formerly communist countries, creating a political will for changes that otherwise would have been difficult to promote.

The strategy appears to have worked. The EU, which had twelve members at the time of the fall of the Berlin Wall, now has twenty-eight; NATO has grown from sixteen to twenty-eight members. Some of these countries are not yet fully consolidated democracies, but the new Eastern European members, who until 1989 were part of an alliance against which NATO was constantly preparing for war, are now part of a single, peaceful Europe. Those countries that have not yet been admitted to this zone of peace, including Turkey, Russia, and the Ukraine, have voiced considerable resentment.

# THE GEOGRAPHY CONNECTION

## THE SPREAD (AND RETREAT) OF DEMOCRACY IN EASTERN EUROPE

Freedom House is a Washington-based nongovernmental organization (NGO), funded in part by the U.S. government, that assesses the state of democracy around the world. These maps show Freedom House's 1986, 2002, and 2012 rankings for the level of democracy in central Europe and the surrounding regions, based on a set of criteria determined by experts selected by Freedom House.

### Critical Thinking Questions

1. What have been the trends in democratization in this region?

2. According to the empirical findings we have discussed, where are we most likely and least likely to see conflict in coming years?

3. Examine particular countries with which you are familiar. Do you agree with the rankings? How might the maps look different if they were produced in Beijing, Moscow, or Tehran?

Democracy in Eurasia, 1986

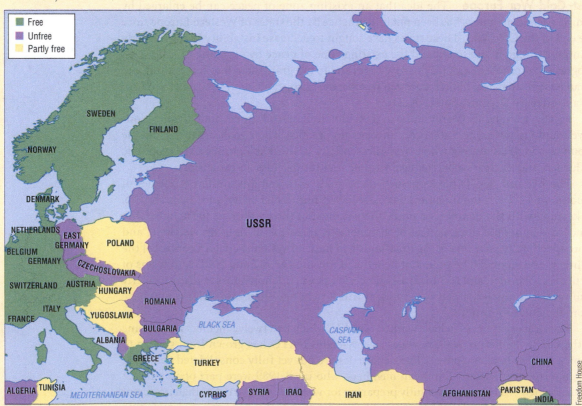

In 1991, the USSR split into 15 separate states.

Democracy in Eurasia, 2002

- Free
- Unfree
- Partly free

Freedom House

Democracy in Eurasia, 2012

- Free
- Unfree
- Partly free

Freedom House

# THE POLICY CONNECTION

## DEMOCRATIZATION AND REALISM: THE VIEW FROM MOSCOW

Democratic peace theory holds that the effects of anarchy can be mitigated in a world of democracies. In this respect, democratic peace theory is entirely contrary to realism. But there is another view about democratization—not an academic view—that sees democratic peace theory in very realist terms, and this has significant consequences for politics and policy.

As this chapter has discussed, governments in the West, and especially in the United States, have seen the spread of democracy as advancing everyone's interest at the same time. In this view, democracy is a better system of government—indeed, the only legitimate system of government—and reduces international conflict. That appears to be good for everyone.

Countries such as Russia and China, however, have argued that the promotion of democracy is not good for everyone and is not meant to be. They see democracy promotion as a hostile tactic in a traditional competition for power. In this view, spreading democracy is not meant to advance them as equal partners but to weaken them by removing governments that have the determination and the means to stand up to the United States. This sentiment appears to be held in places as diverse as Russia, China, Iran, Cuba, and North Korea.

This has been articulated most forcefully in Russia, where Vladimir Putin sees the democratic "colored revolutions" that have occurred in the region as a security threat to Russia: "In the modern world extremism is being used as a geopolitical instrument and for remaking spheres of influence. We see what tragic consequences the wave of so-called color revolutions led to. For us this is a lesson and a warning. We should do everything necessary so that nothing similar ever happens in Russia."* Many Russians look back at the 1990s as a period in which Russia's effort to end the Cold War and adopt free market democracy was exploited by the West to weaken Russia and to expand NATO into eastern European countries formerly controlled by the Soviet Union.

In response, Russia and others have tried to turn the rhetoric of democracy back on the West, arguing that for the international system to be truly democratic, different political systems should be tolerated. Just as the West advocates domestic pluralism (tolerance of various political viewpoints), Russia and China advocate international pluralism (tolerance of different governing models). Thus, the Shanghai Cooperation Organization, a group containing Russia, China, and many of the post-Soviet autocracies in Central Asia, advocated "democratization of international relations" and "respect for diversified civilizations."[†]

These arguments by nondemocratic leaders may simply be aimed at tarnishing the idea of democratization, which would likely drive them from power, but they do point to some dilemmas for those who promote democracy internationally. If democratization is seen as a security threat by other states, should the promoters of democracy back off? That is what some advocated in response to Russia's invasion of Ukraine in 2014. If democratization becomes associated with the spread of American influence in the world, is there a danger that the idea of democracy will be viewed less favorably? These are the kinds of questions that arise when one takes seriously the idea that democracy promotion serves realist policies rather than undermining realism altogether.

### Critical Thinking Questions

1. Is there validity in the view that democratization, rather than being a universal good, is a threat to some countries?

(Continued)

2. Should the United States and its allies deliberately promote democracy as a means of undermining hostile regimes?

3. If other countries see democratization as a threat, should Western states end their support for democratization movements in those countries?

*Quoted in Darya Korsunskaya, "Putin says Russia must prevent 'color revolution'," Reuters, November 11, 2014, http://www.reuters.com/article/2014/11/20/us-russia-putin-security-idUSKCN0J41J620141120.

†Quoted in Paul D'Anieri, "Autocratic Diffusion and the Pluralization of Democracy," in Bruce Jentleson and Louis Pauly, eds., Power in a Complex Global System, p. 90. (London: Routledge, 2014).

In 1991, following a failed coup attempt by hardline communists in the Soviet government, the Soviet Union collapsed. Russia began a massive internal transformation, with President Boris Yeltsin pledging a shift to Western-style democracy. U.S. policy makers had to decide whether to treat Russia as an enemy because of its undiminished military power, or as a friend because of its domestic reforms.

At first, the administration of George H. W. Bush (president from 1989 to 1993) and then that of Bill Clinton (president from 1993 to 2001) followed the democratic peace theory, believing that if Russia became democratic, its arsenal would be no threat to the United States. Therefore, the U.S. government (and other Western governments) initiated programs to aid Russia's transition to a market economy and democratic rule. However, the amount of money was meager compared to the size of Russia's economy and the scope of the envisioned transformation. Some people opposed even this limited aid, seeing Russia as a threat based on its military strength, not its intentions or form of government. Ultimately, U.S. efforts to democratize Russia failed. Russia became progressively less democratic under President Vladimir Putin, and rising oil prices increased Russian wealth, making Western economic aid unnecessary.

Russia has viewed this democratization in post–Cold War Europe not in terms of the democratic peace but in terms of traditional geopolitics. It sees the eastward spread of NATO and the EU as directed against Russia, and sees the promotion of democracy not as altruism on the part of the West but as a tool to topple independent or pro-Russian governments and replace them with pro-Western ones. China has viewed democracy promotion in much the same terms.

# STATE- AND SUBSTATE-LEVEL THEORIES

Democratic peace theory has received a vast amount of attention in recent years, but it is not the only school of thought to find important variation at the level of the state. Many authors find important variations in the way states are organized and in the way states relate to their societies. Unlike the democratic peace theory, models of **state structure** and **state strength** have the virtue of being applicable to the whole range of foreign policy issues, not just war and peace.

For example, an influential study by Peter Katzenstein and others compared various states' responses to the oil shortages of the early 1970s. All the advanced industrial states were faced with the same external shock to their economies, but they responded in very different ways.[18] Why? Katzenstein and his colleagues found that different states had different policy instruments for influencing their economies. For example, Japan's

**state structure**

The form and function of state institutions.

**state strength**

The degree to which a state is independent of societal influences.

Ministry of International Trade and Industry was set up to provide very specific, sector-level support to specific industries in Japan.[19] In contrast, the United Kingdom and the United States tend to use more blunt instruments, such as the overall level of interest rates, to govern their economies. The point is not that one type of arrangement is better than the other (although there has been much debate on this question), but rather that these different state structures will naturally lead to different policies.

Moreover, the Katzenstein study found that different states had different relationships with their societies, with some being tightly constrained and others being more autonomous. In the United States, the state was seen as "weak" because it is heavily influenced by interest groups that are given a prominent role in developing policies. In France and Japan, which are typically regarded as "strong" states, the state has a greater degree of autonomy from interest groups. In still other states, including Germany, the state negotiates major economic policies with broad associations of industry and labor groups.[20]

The issue of state strength has also received considerable attention in the literature on economic development. An important question is why certain countries, most notably the "Asian Tigers" (Hong Kong, Singapore, South Korea, Taiwan), moved from poverty to wealth while others were left behind (see Chapter 12). One argument focuses on the strength of states. These governments, it is argued, were able to raise capital for investment, funnel investment strategically, and keep labor unrest to a minimum in order to be competitive in the global economy. Countries that developed less, in this view, had governments that were unable to resist pressure from interest groups and thus implemented policies that served the short-term interests of those groups but undermined the economies' long-term prospects for development.[21] More recently, efforts to introduce free markets to Russia and other formerly communist countries have led to a similar focus on "state capacity." Although early advice to these governments focused on getting the state out of the economy, experience showed that state involvement, at least in some key areas (such as combating corruption), was essential, and that where such state activity was ineffective, development was undermined.[22]

U.S. troops intervened in Haiti in 1994 in Operation "Uphold Democracy." Although U.S. forces were able to restore basic order in Haiti, little subsequent progress was made in building a stable economy.

Andrew Lichtenstein/The Image Works

The global economic crisis that emerged in 2008 caused further focus on how different state–society arrangements affect policy. After three decades in which most states had taken an ever-smaller role in the economy, the crisis seemed to show the weakness of that model. The crisis hit hardest in the most market-oriented economies, including the United States, the United Kingdom, and much of Europe. China, with its state-managed capitalism, fared well. Similarly, in Russia, the increased involvement of the state in the economy after 1999 accompanied rapid growth. Moreover, both Russia and China adopted foreign policies making extensive use of economic power. State–society relations therefore remain an important influence on foreign policy.

## WHAT IS THE NATIONAL INTEREST, AND WHO SAYS SO?

Theories that link foreign policy to citizen and societal influence typically explore the roles of organized interest groups, public opinion, and the media in determining foreign policy. They ask, how is the *purpose* of the state's foreign policies determined, and what is the *power* of different actors (including governmental actors) in formulating these goals? Put differently, when the phrase "national interest" is used to justify a policy, the questions become, *who* defines the national interest this way, and *how* is that definition of national interest chosen over others?

The national interest is a central topic in many discussions of foreign policy. Realist theory in particular assumes that each state has a single set of interests, and that policy makers ought to recognize those interests and pursue them. Much everyday debate concerning foreign policies around the world concerns what a state's national interest is and how it ought to be pursued. Typically, elements of the national interest are viewed as wealth, power, and prestige. However, there are two important objections to the concept of "national interest," as well as to its application. First, even if we assume that there is a single national interest, it seems that people never agree on what it is. Even experts who share a commitment to advancing the interests of a particular country often disagree on what those interests are, and these disagreements are the fodder of political conflict.

Second, and more fundamental, many would argue that the concept of "national interest" is in fact a myth, or a concept that a variety of special interests invoke to promote their goals. This view sees establishment of a "national interest" as an example of structural power. This view is evident in complex interdependence theory, with its emphasis on multiple actors with multiple interests, and in economic structuralism, which sees different corporations and classes pursuing their interests and trying to use the state to promote them. It is also visible in theories of interest group politics that are widely applied to the study of domestic politics. In this view, societies are made up of multiple interests that are not easily reconciled. Different groups may genuinely see their interest as the national interest, or they may cynically try to use the label "national interest" or "vital national interest" to gain particular benefits. For this reason, it is essential to consider the role of interest groups in foreign policy making.

## INTEREST GROUPS IN FOREIGN POLICY

The role of interest groups is consistently emphasized in analyses of politics and policy making. Generally speaking, however, the role of interest groups has received less attention in the study of foreign policy than in the study of domestic politics. In fact, interest groups have a powerful stake in various aspects of foreign policy. Because many interest groups are primarily motivated by business and are centered on particular industries, we see interest groups most clearly in the making of foreign economic policy. Given the vast sums of money spent on defense in most countries, we see a great deal of interest group involvement on security issues as well. However, the kinds of foreign policy issues that are the subject of interest group activities vary from country to country. In some countries, immigration is a major concern of industrial and labor groups. In other countries, the pervasive influence of cultural products (such as films, television shows, music, and fashion) from abroad drives organized groups to try to change policies. In most countries, interest groups contest their state's relationship with the world economy.

To understand the role of interest groups, we must focus on three questions, each of which is very broad. First, what do interest groups want? Second, how do they go about getting what they want? Third, how successful are they at getting it?

**What Do Interest Groups Want from Foreign Policy?**    The goals of interest groups are as diverse as the interest groups themselves, so it is difficult to generalize. However, interest groups can be divided into three broad categories, based on their motivations. The first category consists of interest groups that support foreign policies that have very predictable economic benefits for the group. A typical example is an interest group of automobile producers lobbying for increased tariffs on foreign automobiles. Such tariffs decrease competition and allow domestic producers to sell more cars at higher prices.

Worldwide, two economic interest groups that have most consistently, and most successfully, lobbied governments for protection from foreign competition are the steel industry and agricultural interests. In both these industries, there has tended to be a consistent surplus of production in the world, which drives prices down. Although lower prices are good for consumers, they are bad for producers, who consequently band together to pressure governments for protection.

A second category of interest groups consists of those seeking revenue directly *from* the government. Most prominent here are groups hoping to sell their goods or services to the government. In many countries, the most significant actors within this group are military contractors. Military budgets generally dwarf all other foreign policy spending (such as foreign aid), and a significant portion is spent on every kind of good used by the military, from air mattresses to aircraft carriers. Military contracts are often highly lucrative, and foreign policy choices or military strategy can significantly influence the level of a government's demand for a particular product. Recognizing the influence of outsiders on procurement decisions, in 2006, India prohibited agents of arms manufacturers from visiting its defense ministry in an effort to reduce their influence on procurement, but the ban seems to have had little effect as firms find ways around it.[23]

A third category of interest groups is not interested primarily in money, although this may be one of their goals. These groups are formed by people and organizations with particular concerns about some aspect of foreign policy. Some of these groups would probably rather be labeled NGOs, but for our purposes they are not fundamentally different from interest groups (see the discussion of NGOs in Chapter 7). Some focus on policy toward a particular country; others are concerned with policy on a particular issue, such as immigration or global warming.

**How Do Interest Groups Influence Foreign Policy?**    Interest groups pursue their goals in a number of ways, depending on the resources available to them and on the governmental system in the country in which they are operating. Interest groups that have a large number of members, for example, can seek to convince politicians that supporting the group's goals will be rewarded at the next election. Thus, labor unions have sometimes

Russian President Vladimir Putin meets ExxonMobil Chairman and CEO Rex Tillerson. What influence do corporate leaders have on foreign policies?

MIKHAIL KLIMENTYEV/RIA NOVOSTI/KREMLIN POOL/EPA/Newscom

been effective in lobbying for greater barriers to trade because their large membership and effectiveness in getting their members to vote make them valuable to politicians. In South Africa, for example, the ruling African National Congress (ANC) has been forced to resist calls by business leaders for greater economic liberalization because of the ANC's significant dependence on trade union members, who oppose liberalization.[24]

Another resource available to interest groups in varying amounts is money. Sometimes decision makers can simply be bribed. Money can obtain influence in at least three other ways. First, although politicians routinely deny that campaign contributions influence the decisions they make, interest groups make significant contributions to political campaigns on the assumption that contributions do indeed create influence. If campaign contributions do not influence policies, then many of the smartest business leaders around the world are wasting a great deal of money.

Money can also be influential when used indirectly. Interest groups can influence policies by shaping public opinion—by going directly to the people through advertising. The opinion and editorial pages of leading newspapers and news/talk shows on television are preferred locations for advertising aimed at the politically active portion of the public. They may also conduct research on a specific issue and share the results with politicians, bureaucrats, and the public.

Finally, interest groups influence foreign policy by hiring lobbyists. Lobbyists are individuals who make a profession out of their connections with policy makers. Their access to policy makers can, in effect, be sold to their clients. For this reason, individuals who have recently served in influential positions in government are especially sought after as lobbyists, and such individuals command high fees for their work. In the United States, many former high-ranking government officials, including secretaries of state and defense, directors of the Central Intelligence Agency, generals, and members of Congress, have left office and moved into lobbying for interest groups, which are willing to pay them hefty fees to return to where they worked in the public interest and work instead for the private interest. A similar process takes place in many other countries.

In Germany in 2005, for example, Chancellor Gerhard Schröder ardently supported an important agreement with the Russian gas monopoly Gazprom to build a new pipeline to bring Russian gas to Germany. Two months later, after leaving office, Schröder took a lucrative position as chairman of the board of the consortium formed to build the pipeline.[25] Observers wondered whether Schröder's access to the top levels of the German government, rather than his ability as a businessman, was his main job qualification. The role of prominent former public servants in lobbying firms raises some interesting questions. Such officials often appear on television or in newspapers promoting one policy or another. When a former government official recommends a particular policy, is he or she speaking as a private citizen, as a former government official, or as a spokesperson who gets paid to disseminate a particular point of view in the press?

**To What Extent Do Interest Groups Drive Foreign Policy?**   It is difficult to generalize about the success of interest groups in determining foreign policy, especially given all the other factors that might influence policy. Moreover, there is likely to be significant variance across states. Whereas the United States has a political system that is especially open to influence by interest groups, many other states have fewer channels through which interest groups can operate. Moreover, interest groups' influence can vary over time. For example, China's increasing international trade has led its firms to play a more assertive role in lobbying on foreign policy.[26] That said, interest groups do not always have as much influence as they would like.

Governments have sought to devise ways to resist pressure from groups seeking protection. Many see the World Trade Organization (WTO) as a broad effort to shift trade policy to an organization that is less subject to lobbying. Similarly, many see the formation of the EU's "single European market" as a means of shifting trade policy decisions from national capitals to EU bureaucrats, presumed to be less subject to interest group pressures. However, an immense lobbying establishment has now built up in Brussels (administrative home of the EU), so that any respite from the influence of lobbying will likely be temporary.

# PUBLIC OPINION

Public opinion is an important consideration in almost all policy decisions, even in nondemocratic societies, and foreign policy is no exception. Unfortunately, despite the global spread of public opinion polling, most analysis of the influence of public opinion on foreign policy has concerned one country, the United States.[27] Research on public opinion and foreign policy has focused on four separate issues:

- **What effect *should* public opinion have on policy?** This is a normative question. Should public opinion play an important part in leaders' considerations, either because of democratic values or because "the people know best"? Or should foreign policy be the domain of experts, who have more knowledge and better judgment than the average citizen?

- **What does public opinion "look like"?** Are people well informed or not? Are their attitudes stable or unstable? Is foreign policy important to them or not?

- **What influences public opinion on foreign policy?** Where does the public get its information, and who or what is influential in shaping and changing public attitudes? Can leaders actively shape public opinion? What about the news media?[28]

- **What effect *does* public opinion have on foreign policy?** This question is central in understanding the sources of foreign policy. Do decision makers limit their policies to what they think will be popular? Can public opinion force leaders to adopt new policies or change unpopular ones?

**Should Public Opinion Matter?**    Some people argue that the public should have extensive influence over foreign policy. The point of democracy is to give the governed control of the government, and foreign policy should be no exception. Moreover, some hope that public opinion will have a positive effect on foreign policy.

In general, our view of the desirability of a strong public influence on foreign policy is partly related to our level of trust in the government to do the right thing by itself. Which is more dangerous, an irresponsible government or an uninformed public? For those who mistrust leaders, the public check on foreign policy is crucial. For those worried about the influence of interest groups on foreign policy, an involved public provides a necessary counterweight. However, for those concerned that the public is uninformed or subject to irrational passions, leaving foreign policy to the experts is more desirable.

**What Does Public Opinion Look Like?**    A great deal of research has focused on the relatively simple question: What do people think about foreign policy? Researchers have tried to measure popular support for various actual or potential foreign policies. They also assess the extent to which people disagree with each other or the government. For example, during much of the Cold War, many scholars wrote of a "Cold War consensus" that referred to agreement across most of the U.S. political spectrum on the need to contain communism and on the best ways to do it. A similar consensus exists today in Pakistan regarding relations with India.[29]

In all the research on public opinion and foreign policy, a few facts consistently emerge. First, most citizens do not pay much attention to foreign policy except in times of crisis. Most of the time, only 20 to 30 percent of citizens in democracies are interested in foreign affairs.[30]

Second, and related, most citizens know very little about foreign affairs. Surveys show repeatedly that citizens (especially in the United States) know little about the geography, history, or current leadership of other countries. Moreover, sometimes what citizens "know" is manifestly wrong. A majority of U.S. citizens vastly overestimates the amount of foreign aid the United States gives to poor countries. The public can be misinformed even on issues to which it is paying close attention. A study of multiple polls taken before and after the U.S.-led invasion of Iraq in 2003 showed that 20 to 25 percent of Americans incorrectly believed that Iraq had been directly responsible for the 2001 terrorist attacks on the United States (see Figure 5.1).[31]

These basic facts—citizens care little, know little, and sometimes harbor significant misperceptions—have led many to wonder how states can develop wise foreign policies if the voters are apathetic and uninformed? Private foundations and the government (not to mention college professors) thus expend considerable resources trying to get people more engaged.

**FIGURE 5.1**    In 2002, only 4 percent of the U.S. public believed Iraq had anything to do with the terrorist attacks on September 11. As President Bush began mentioning Iraq more often when speaking about the "global war on terrorism," more people began to associate Iraq with 9/11. By January 2003, 44 percent believed that most or some of the 9/11 terrorists were from Iraq. In fact, none of the terrorists were Iraqi. This is an example of the ability of a popular leader to sway the public's beliefs.

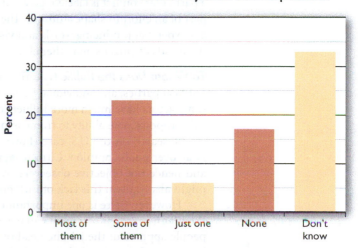

Survey Results: As far as you know, how many of the September 11th terrorist hijackers were Iraqi citizens?

Source: Knight Ridder poll conducted by Princeton Survey Research Associates. Jan. 3–6, 2003, http://www.pollingreport.com/iraq17.htm. Reprinted by permission of The Polling Report.

Some scholars find public ignorance "rational." They argue that because citizens have many issues to focus on, it makes sense that they pay little attention to foreign policy. They can always learn more when a situation merits it.[32]

Contrary to earlier studies that found public opinion to be highly volatile, changing quickly based on events or on attempts at persuasion, more recent research has found that individuals tend to have a structured set of beliefs about foreign policy that are linked to one another, are mostly consistent with one another, and are relatively stable over time.[33]

### What Determines the Content of Public Opinion?

The study of the effect of public opinion on foreign policy has been informed by broader research on the sources of political attitudes in general. The predominant school of thought today sees public opinion as being structured and consistent, if not deeply informed. But to the extent that the public does have views, where do they come from?

Much of the content of public opinion seems to be determined by elite views, because these are generally views to which the public is exposed. In other words, rather than public opinion influencing political leaders, often the opposite occurs. As Seymour Martin Lipset, a prominent scholar of public opinion, put it, "The president makes public opinion, he does not follow it."[34] Citizens hear opinions on foreign policy issues primarily from government officials, publicly recognized "experts," and leading journalists. It makes sense that the range of public opinion would therefore reflect the range of elite opinion. However, much depends on the degree of elite consensus. Consensus among elites creates a **mainstream effect**, whereby only one view is expressed by leaders and people get only one view from the media. In such an atmosphere, people are likely to adopt this "mainstream" view.[35] The ability of Vladimir Putin to shape Russian public opinion in recent years has shaped Russians' opinions of Russia's relations with its neighbors.

**mainstream effect**

The tendency for the public to follow political leaders and the media when those actors have consensus on an issue.

### *Competition over Public Opinion*

When there is a lack of consensus among elites, however, there is likely to be a battle over public opinion.[36] This battle often takes the form of an effort to frame the issue in a way that will lead people toward a particular conclusion. For example, a political party that opposes immigration will try to frame the issue in terms of lawbreaking or diminished security, whereas a party that favors immigration will try to frame the issue in terms of the gains to society from the increased labor supply. Whether a particular conflict is labeled "genocide" or a particular practice is called "torture" is often part of an effort to shape attitudes. The people who specialize in political communication are experts at producing words and visual images that establish their preferred frames in the minds of citizens and other elites.

### *To Whom Does the Public Listen?*

Many actors—including interest groups and NGOs, political parties, and individual leaders—seek to frame issues, but research indicates that some actors have much more influence over public opinion than others and, hence, have a disproportionate ability to frame issues and sway public opinion.

Research on the U.S. case shows that elected officials do not generally have much sway over public opinion. Citizens appear to recognize that these officials are partisan and hence not objective observers. A low level of trust for elected officials in general might also explain this lack of influence.

However, there is one important exception to the weak influence of public officials: Popular heads of government can have a significant effect on public opinion.[37] The more people approve of the job the head of government is doing, the more likely people will be to trust his or her judgment on foreign policy issues. Thus, although many people see Vladimir Putin's popularity as being dependent on his control of Russian media, the converse is likely true as well. Putin has immense influence on public opinion because he is so popular, and if his popularity were to decline, so would his influence.

Popularly recognized "experts" are also shown by research to have influence over public opinion. These experts are sometimes former government officials, such as former ministers of defense or foreign affairs. On military matters, former senior officers are often viewed as experts. Occasionally, even college professors are accorded this status. These experts' opinions are transmitted to the public through a variety of avenues. Experts are sought out for interviews by journalists, and they are often guests for longer discussions on television talk shows. These experts are influential for two related reasons. First, they are introduced as experts, which gives them credibility. Second, they are viewed (often incorrectly) as being nonpartisan and unbiased. In reality, many of these experts are paid by special interest groups or even foreign governments to promote specific policies.

Finally, prominent journalists may also influence public opinion. They are widely recognized, and people often trust these journalists to give them most of their information about the world. Whereas most of the news they report is presented as "objective," journalists have a great deal of latitude concerning which stories get covered and how they are framed.

**Does Public Opinion Influence Foreign Policy?**   This question is difficult to answer because it is hard to detect influence. If a change in public opinion is followed by a change in policy, can we conclude that the change in public opinion caused the change in policy? Not necessarily. It might be that some third factor (a crucial event or a campaign by some group) caused both public opinion and policy to change. Or it may be that leaders first decided to change policy and then promoted a change in public opinion. Even if public opinion does have an effect, it might not be possible to detect. If policy makers consider a change in policy but reject it because they are afraid of the public's reaction, then public opinion has had an influence—but unless we can listen in on discussions at the highest levels of government, we will never see evidence of that influence.

Historically, public opinion has undoubtedly played a role in some foreign policies. A frequently cited case in the United States is opposition to the Vietnam War. The U.S. Congress voted overwhelmingly to give President Lyndon Johnson authority to send ground forces into Vietnam in 1964. That congressional vote reflected public opinion, which supported the troop deployment to halt the spread of communism in Southeast Asia. By 1967, large demonstrations against the war erupted, primarily on college campuses. By 1968, public opinion had shifted dramatically, and support for the war within Johnson's Democratic Party eroded. Johnson chose not to run for re-election, recognizing that he probably could not even win his own party's nomination. Almost every account of that conflict finds that public opinion played a decisive role in altering government policy. A similar process seemed to be under way in 2006, when many voters cited dissatisfaction over the U.S. war in Iraq in an election that saw significant reversals for the ruling Republican Party. Olympia Snowe, a Republican senator from Maine, commented immediately after the election that policy on the war "absolutely has to change."[38] Public opinion can get a country into a war as well as out of it, as the case of the Spanish-American war shows (see "The History Connection: Press and Public Opinion in the Spanish-American War" later in the chapter).[39]

Public opinion can be equally important in motivating change in economic policy. In Mexico, for example, shifting public opinion, which increasingly came to view Mexico as a "developed" rather than "developing" country, enabled President Vicente Fox to pursue

# THE HISTORY CONNECTION

## PRESS AND PUBLIC OPINION IN THE SPANISH-AMERICAN WAR

In perhaps no episode in history has the role of the press and public opinion been more controversial than in the run-up to the Spanish-American War (1898), in which the United States seized from Spain territories including Cuba, Puerto Rico, and the Philippines.

The push toward war was strongly supported in the United States by two competing New York newspapers, the *New York World*, owned by Joseph Pulitzer, and the *New York Journal*, owned by William Randolph Hearst. The two papers, competing to be the first to reach a circulation of 1 million, ran increasingly sensationalist stories throughout the 1890s about Cubans' struggle for independence from Spain, riots in Havana, and Spanish repression of the populace.

As Cuba slid toward conflict, Hearst in particular saw the opportunity to increase circulation. He sent reporters and artists, including author Stephen Crane and sculptor Frederick Remington, to capture the scene in Cuba for his readers. When Remington wrote to Hearst that there was no war in Cuba to report on, Hearst responded, "Please remain. You furnish the pictures. I'll furnish the war." Pulitzer and Hearst competed to print the most gripping stories of the mistreatment of Cubans by the Spanish. Coverage of the situation in Cuba occupied as many as eight pages in some issues of the *Journal*, and competing papers sought to avoid being outdone. Overall, the effect was that the U.S. news media saturated readers with calls for war.

When the U.S. battleship *Maine* exploded in Havana harbor in February 1898, the *Journal* blamed the explosion on Spain (a claim for which there was little evidence) and openly called for war against Spain. On April 4, 1898, a special issue of the *Journal* dedicated to war with Spain was published in 1 million copies, a huge number at that time.

U.S. President William McKinley initially opposed going to war to seize Cuba, preferring

Hearst's New York Journal left little doubt that the Maine had been sunk by Spain.

instead that Cuba gain autonomy from Spain. However, pressure from public opinion and Congress constrained his choices. On April 11, 1898, McKinley sought permission from Congress to intervene in Cuba, and Congress quickly passed what was effectively a declaration of war. By all accounts, the attention given to the events by the New York newspapers was indispensable in convincing Americans to support war with Spain and in convincing McKinley that it would be politically devastating for him to oppose it.

Hearst and Pulitzer were memorialized in different ways. Ironically, Pulitzer, who was credited with inventing "yellow journalism," became the namesake of a prestigious prize for journalism. Hearst, who sought to surpass Pulitzer, was the model for the title character in *Citizen Kane*, regarded as one of the finest films ever made.

## Critical Thinking Questions

1. Can you think of recent events in which sensationalist press helped drive a particular foreign policy?

2. How does the shift to online journalism change the influence of the press?

3. Can citizens take some role in making the press more responsible? How?

a free trade policy after his election in 2000. In addition, scholars have perceived shifts in Mexican attitudes toward the United States, with closer ties to the United States seen as a way of improving the lot of average Mexicans.[40] At the same time, however, outcry against the war in Iraq forced Fox's government to oppose the war.

**The Case against the Importance of Public Opinion**   Do these examples from U.S. and Mexican policy demonstrate that public opinion has a powerful effect on foreign policy? Most scholars and policy makers are skeptical, seeing these cases as notable exceptions. Because most people take little interest in foreign policy and know little about it, they are disinclined to take an active role in shaping it. The vast majority of foreign policy is carried out in relative obscurity. On most issues, most of the time, therefore, leaders can ignore public opinion.

**Latent Public Opinion**   Although the public may be passive and apathetic about most foreign policy questions most of the time, the knowledge that the public can become very active at any time does influence foreign policy decision making.[41] Thus, public opinion might have a *latent* effect. Leaders try to anticipate which issues or policies are likely to turn public.

If public opinion is usually latent (inactive), what determines when and for which issues it becomes active? One finding in research is that public opinion becomes more important when leaders disagree. When there is debate within a government or among the broader "foreign policy elite" that includes experts and nongovernmental research institutions, the opposing sides are likely to turn to the public to gain support for their positions. This can occur even in authoritarian societies. In Iran, for example, there has been public disagreement between "hardliners" and "liberals" concerning, among other things, the country's policies toward nuclear weapons and toward the West. In the Soviet Union, foreign policy debates, including debates over the possibility of winning a nuclear war, emerged in public on several occasions.

Another factor that increases public interest is military casualties. In many military conflicts, public support erodes when casualties rise (see Figure 5.2). This phenomenon has had an important constraining effect on planning military operations. Whether force will be used—and how operations are planned—is strongly influenced by leaders' desire to avoid casualties.

Such considerations influenced the first Bush administration's decision not to push on toward Baghdad to eject Saddam Hussein during the first U.S.-Iraq war in 1991 and prompted the Clinton administration's determination to rely only on bombing, and not on ground troops, to force Serbian troops out of Kosovo in 1999. So worried was Clinton about public opposition to U.S. casualties, which would have been inevitable in a ground invasion, that he did not even want to threaten an invasion or prepare for it as a way of pressuring the Serbian government. More recently, the increased use of drone strikes by the United States in Afghanistan and Pakistan was driven in large part by the goal of achieving military results with minimal risk to U.S. forces.

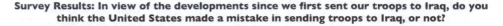

**FIGURE 5.2** Looking at the graph, what hypotheses might one advance about the influence of public opinion in this case?

Survey Results: In view of the developments since we first sent our troops to Iraq, do you think the United States made a mistake in sending troops to Iraq, or not?

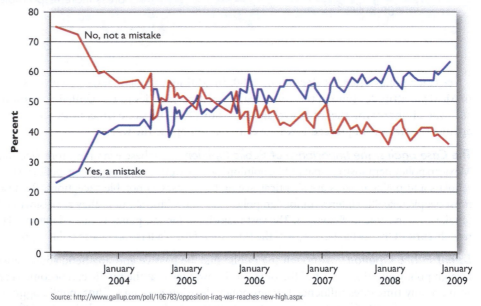

Source: http://www.gallup.com/poll/106783/opposition-iraq-war-reaches-new-high.aspx

## THE MEDIA IN FOREIGN POLICY

**media**

The different means through which news and entertainment are conveyed.

For decades, scholars have studied how the news **media** influence public opinion and politics, and with the news media in upheaval due to the disruptions brought on by the rise of social media, the topic is more interesting than ever. This is a rapidly changing aspect of public affairs, international politics included. Therefore, our discussion examines traditional media, but also asks how new media, and new practices of accessing news, change the picture.

**What Determines Which Issues the Media Cover and How They Are Covered?** Even if news sources do not always tell people what they should think, they do influence, simply by what they choose to cover, what issues people will think *about*. When a network news program decides to do its one international story on a particular issue, or when that issue is the only international story on the front page of a newspaper, this suggests to the viewer or the reader that the issue is an important one. Thus, it is important to understand how this agenda is formed.

How do editors and journalists decide what the public needs to know, and what other pressures do the media face? Media companies seek to make money through subscriptions and advertising. Therefore, journalists and editors have strong incentives to give their audience not just what they *need*, but what they *want*. Journalists and editors might believe that citizens need a deeper understanding of the sources of terrorism, the problems of poverty in Africa, or the foreign policy views of the Japanese government. But do viewers *want* to read about those issues or see them covered on a television program? Or would people rather watch an exclusive interview in which a movie star discusses her battle with substance abuse? In an environment in which profits are driven by the ability to sell advertising, and advertising revenue is driven by the number of viewers, there are strong incentives to assume that what viewers will watch or read is what they need. In the online news world, this has led to "clickbait," sensational headlines designed to get the viewer to click on them, thus driving advertising revenues up.

In 2009, only two international stories (the war in Afghanistan and election protests in Iran) were among the top ten stories (in terms of minutes of coverage) on U.S. television network news. The death of pop star Michael Jackson earned more coverage than any international story except Afghanistan. The war in Iraq, where the United States was still heavily involved, was not among the top twenty stories.[42]

"After a hard day at the office, all Barry wants to do is put his feet up and listen to somebody tell him what to think."

David Sipress/The New Yorker Collection/The Cartoon Bank

Increasingly, people get their news not directly from mass media in which the stories are chosen for them, but from social network sites such as Facebook or Twitter. In some cases, what we see is driven by what our "friends" like, in others by an algorithm that uses our previous "clicks" to predict what we are likely to select. Another development is that more and more people are viewing news on handheld devices. Among other effects, it appears that this causes people to visit a site more briefly than if they were using a computer.[43] We do not know yet what effect this might have on how people think about international affairs.

**Efforts to Influence Media Coverage** Politicians and other interested parties have always sought to influence media coverage, and the rise of new media allows them, in many cases, to bypass the media and go straight to individual viewer. For example, just as lobbyists seek to persuade legislators to address certain issues, they also try to get journalists to cover certain issues. Now, they can bypass media outlets altogether and wage a social media campaign to promote particular views. Similarly, politicians use their websites and YouTube to spread carefully targeted messages, without the media as an intermediary, and they use Twitter to draw attention to themselves and to drive traffic to their own messages or those they view as sympathetic.

One result of the proliferation of news sources is the intense competition for people's attention. Those seeking to get their stories into the news, therefore, compete to devise events that are worthy of news coverage and provide exciting footage for television. An NGO might sponsor a particularly spectacular rally or public display. Legislators may schedule hearings and require well-known people or executive branch officials to testify at those hearings in order to create good video or photo opportunities. Such events are timed carefully so that they are less likely to coincide with other events that might compete with them for attention.

In getting a particular issue on the agenda, the executive branch of the government has powerful advantages over other groups. First, because foreign policy is chiefly the responsibility of the executive branch, the activities of a head of government, the secretary of state or foreign minister, and the defense minister are inherently newsworthy.

If the head of government simply gives a speech expressing concern about an issue, it is immediately important news. High-ranking government officials thus have immense power to shape the news agenda.

In many countries, leaders have more direct means of controlling traditional media. In Mexico, prior to political reform in the 1990s, most media outlets were controlled by or allied with the ruling party, the PRI (Institutional Revolutionary Party). Moreover, most newspaper advertising revenue came from the government, so newspapers had powerful incentives to keep the leaders happy. This allowed leaders to shape news coverage and to avoid coverage of difficult issues. As the political process in Mexico became more democratic, media became more independent. This independence led to a period of "high politicization," in which the media were controlled by political and economic elites.[44] More recently, Russia and Venezuela have seen successful efforts by governments to increase control over media.

The relationship between private media companies and democratic governments is also increasingly close. In Italy, longtime Prime Minister Silvio Berlusconi was also the country's biggest media mogul, and he used his control over both private and state media to advance his political interests. In the United Kingdom, investigations in 2011 and 2012 revealed that NewsCorp, the country's biggest media company, had hacked into officials' cell phones and sought to use its immense influence with the public to pressure politicians to adopt policies favored by its owners. An official's diary revealed that Rupert Murdoch, head of NewsCorp, had pressured British Prime Minister Tony Blair to go to war against Iraq in 2003, promising that his media outlets would support the policy.[45] In the United States, conservatives routinely complain about a liberal bias in Hollywood, and one of the leading news outlets, Fox News, is directed by a former head of the Republican National Committee. Increasingly, governments are striving to control new media the way they have sometimes tried to control old media. The Chinese government has for years tightly censored the Internet, so that topics or opinions to which it objects disappear immediately or are unavailable through search engines. The state of the art in 2015 was represented by the Russian government's extensive and carefully choreographed effort to shape how Russians and others saw its invasion of Ukraine. This included not only the presence of the government's view on media it controlled, but also a global effort to spread certain images of the conflict, and even to use the "comment" section on news websites to counter views it saw as damaging.

Actors including governments, NGOs, companies, and individual politicians are using new media, including websites, videos posted on sites like YouTube, and social media like Twitter, to craft campaigns that reach media consumers without the filter of media companies. For example, in 2012 a small NGO was able to place the Lord's Resistance Army (LRA) on the international agenda by posting on YouTube the video *Kony 2012*, which publicized the violence committed by the LRA and its leader, Joseph Kony. The video quickly went viral, and within two weeks, the U.S. Senate issued a resolution calling for the demobilization of the LRA.

The rise of new media, and the changes in people's habits in accessing information regarding politics, raises many questions that we cannot answer. We are aware, for example, that our ability to "choose" the news we read means that we are increasingly unlikely to encounter opinions with which we disagree or topics that we aren't already familiar with. It is less clear what the implications are for how this will shape our attitudes, our votes, or the way politicians respond.

Reuters photographer Mohammed Salem is assisted by a colleague after being injured at the Erez border crossing in Gaza, 2007.

Gaza Press/REX/Newscom

## THE MEDIA, PUBLIC OPINION, AND THE STATE

It is difficult to state conclusively which actor among the state, media, and public opinion is "driving" the other two, especially as "the media" become more and more diffuse. There are three traditional models of influence, as shown in Figure 5.3. In the real world, all of these processes may be happening simultaneously, with interest groups, lobbyists, and public relations firms competing to shape the outcome of the process.

**FIGURE 5.3**   Three models of influence.

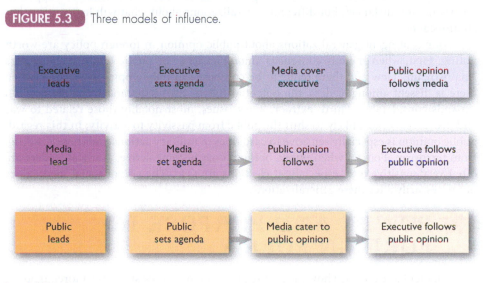

Source: Paul D'Anieri.

The first model focuses on the ability of the executive branch of government to shape the public agenda through the media. By getting the media to focus on particular issues and by using its access to media to frame those issues, the executive can create public demand for the very policies it favors. In this model, the public is a "captive" of the executive branch (and the media). In fact, some proponents of this model argue that government responsiveness to public opinion is a myth created by the government itself. The executive branch has the ability to bring an issue to the public's attention not only through rhetoric but also through action. Deploying military force, signing a new agreement, or attending a "summit meeting" with foreign leaders can focus attention on a particular issue.

In the second model, the media lead. This model assumes that the media have an independent notion of what ought to be on the agenda, and perhaps even what ought to be done about it. In this view, media coverage of an event raises public concern, and the public demands that the government "do something" about the problem in question. Alternatively, the government, anticipating the concern being generated by media attention, may take steps even before the public demands them.

In both of these models, the public is largely passive, which reflects much of the research on public opinion. In the third model, the public may be passive, but its role as consumers of advertising forces the media to cater to it. News providers figure out what kinds of stories the public will pay attention to—which ones will prompt them to buy a newspaper, tune in to a television program, or click on a link—and then provide those kinds of stories. Political leaders then seek to show that they are doing something about the issues the public cares about. For example, knowing that the public is very willing to consume news reports about death and violence, the media give prominent coverage to the deaths of soldiers in war. This coverage puts considerable pressure on governments, given public sensitivity to casualties. It would seem likely that people's increasing ability to choose which stories they see would increase the salience of this third model.

There is some truth in all of these models. Different forces seem stronger at different times and on different issues. Rather than creating simple models relating public opinion, the media, and foreign policy makers, it may be more helpful to devise *contingent generalizations*, in which we make one generalization about what tends to happen in one set of circumstances, but different generalizations about what will happen in other circumstances.

Four contingent generalizations about public opinion in foreign policy are worth noting. First, when there is consensus among leaders, the public tends to follow this "mainstream" view and there tends to be consensus in public opinion. Second, when there is dissent among leaders, the potential role of the media and of public opinion expands considerably. Third, extraordinary issues, most notably those related to war and peace, seem most likely to shift the public from passivity to activity; in this regard, public opinion is especially sensitive to casualties in military actions and those resulting from terrorism. Fourth, when public opinion does become active, political leaders are often very sensitive to it, especially if elections are near. The rise of social media does not necessarily alter these generalizations.

# ★ POWER AND PURPOSE IN FOREIGN POLICY

This chapter has examined how the nature and structure of the state affect foreign policy and the influence of different societal actors. Both topics connect closely to our themes of power and purpose. Democracy is above all a normative commitment to a particular form of government, one that empowers citizens over rulers. The democratic peace approach connects this state-level commitment to the international level, making the promotion of democracy a central purpose of some states' foreign policies. However, some governments consider the promotion of democracy itself to be a tool of power politics intended to undermine one's adversaries.

The discussions of national interest, interest groups, and the media all focus on the tight connection between power and purpose. Who gets to define the purpose of a state's foreign policy, and what kind of power does that yield? Government officials, competing interest groups and advocates, and the media all vie for control of the agenda, and new media are changing the playing field for this battle. The ability to get an entire society and government to pursue the goal that one supports—whether that is a particular economic, military, or humanitarian policy—is in some respects the ultimate power.

# RECONSIDER THE CASE

## WAR, REVOLUTION, AND DEMOCRATIZATION IN THE MIDDLE EAST

On December 17, 2010, a Tunisian street vendor named Mohamed Bouazizi set himself on fire to protest harassment and humiliation by local police. Bouazizi's dramatic suicide triggered widespread unrest that precipitated the fall of authoritarian regimes across the Middle East. In Tunisia, President Zine El Abidine Ben Ali resigned after twenty-three years in power. In Egypt, President Hosni Mubarak stepped down after thirty-two years. In Libya, rebels ejected Muammar Gaddafi after forty-two years in power. In Yemen, Ali Abdullah Saleh was forced out after twenty-two years of rule. In Saudi Arabia and Bahrain, governments successfully quashed calls for change, and in Syria, protests aimed at ousting Bashar al-Assad descended into civil war. This unexpected Arab Spring opened up dramatic new possibilities.

Western governments supported democratization in the region, but not without reservation. When protestors in Egypt called for President Hosni Mubarak to step down, Western leaders hesitated. Mubarak had pursued a secular agenda and repressed the Muslim Brotherhood, an Islamist movement and Egypt's largest opposition group. Western leaders refrained from supporting protesters in Saudi Arabia, which is both a theocratic Islamic dictatorship and a staunch Western ally. In the case of Libya, NATO warplanes attacked government forces to keep them from targeting civilians. In Syria, the United States considered direct military intervention, then decided against it.

Barack Obama backed away from democracy promotion, saying: "It [democracy] is one of our best exports, if it is not exported simply down the barrel of a gun.... [I]n a lot of countries ... the first question is freedom from want and freedom from fear. If people aren't secure, if people are starving, then elections may or may not be able to address those issues."*

Democracy advocates in both major parties were dismayed by Obama's turn toward realism. They emphasized that although George W. Bush had taken a particularly militant approach to promoting democracy, the policy had deep roots in U.S. foreign policy under Democratic as well as Republican presidents. Jennifer Windsor, executive director of Freedom House, stated: "To see democracy as a particularly Republican or Bush policy is to misunderstand our country's foreign policy history."[†]

By 2015, the Arab Spring had degenerated into widespread conflict rather than democracy. Libya, Syria, and Yemen were engulfed in civil war; Iraq remained unstable; and in all those states, the Islamic State found fertile ground to grow. Only in Tunisia does democratization still appear to be moving forward.

### Critical Thinking Questions

1. How confident are you that the democratic peace theory is essentially correct? What limits might you place on it?

*(Continued)*

2. How has the debate on democracy promotion shifted in recent years?

3. How would you weigh the relative importance of democracy promotion compared with other foreign policy goals?

*"Barack Obama: 'Elections Aren't Democracy,'" Washington Post, January 19, 2009. For a discussion and critique of Obama's position on democracy promotion, see Fred Hiatt, "Obama's Lack of Passion for Supporting Freedom," Washington Post, April 8, 2012.

†Peter Baker, "Quieter Approach to Spreading Democracy Abroad," New York Times, February 22, 2009.

## SUMMARY

- This chapter has considered two related questions about the role of state and society in foreign policy making. First, how does the nature of the state influence the substance of foreign policy? Second, what are the societal influences on foreign policy?

- Democratic peace theory, in its individual form, asserts that it matters profoundly what kind of states are involved in any interaction. Democratic states, it is contended, behave very differently than nondemocratic, or autocratic, states do. A second, "dyadic" model holds that toward autocracies, democracies are just as warlike as autocracies, but that democracies do not resort to war when dealing with each other.

- At a general level, the state structure argument asserts that the form of state institutions influences the kinds of tools a government is most likely to employ. Moreover, the focus on "state strength" finds that some states are more open to societal influence than others.

- Both interest groups and public opinion play important roles at times, but no simple generalization can capture the complexity of these relationships. Because most people take little interest in foreign policy and know little about it, they are disinclined to take an active role in shaping it. The vast majority of foreign policy is carried out in relative obscurity, beyond the front pages (or even the inside pages) of the newspapers. Ultimately, many analysts believe it is less important to focus on society and more important to focus on the government officials who are closest to actual policy making. We turn our attention to them in the next chapter.

## KEY CONCEPTS

1. The state
2. Democratic peace theory
3. "Individual" versus "dyadic" models of democratic peace theory
4. Structural, normative, and institutional explanations of the democratic peace
5. State structure
6. State strength
7. Interest groups
8. Lobbying
9. Public relations
10. Latent public opinion
11. Mainstream effect

## STUDY QUESTIONS

1. Many studies have shown that democracies
   a. never go to war.
   b. go to war less often than other countries.
   c. go to war just as often as other countries.
   d. go to war more often than other countries.

2. What theory postulates that democracies rarely, if ever, fight with each other?
   a. The individual model of democratic peace theory
   b. The dyadic model of democratic peace theory
   c. Economic structuralism
   d. Rational choice theory

3. What areas do scholars point to as providing evidence that a zone of peace already exists?
   a. North America and Western Europe
   b. Southeast Asia
   c. South America
   d. The Middle East

4. Which interest groups play the most visible role in public policy?
   a. Economic interest groups
   b. Ideological interest groups
   c. Government employee unions
   d. All of the above.

5. The public's tendency to follow political leaders and the media when those actors have consensus on an issue is called the
   a. mainstream effect.
   b. latent effect.
   c. politics of compromise.
   d. rally around the flag effect.

6. How do different theoretical approaches view the role of the state in foreign policy?

7. What are the hypothesized links between democracy and peace in democratic peace theory?

8. How strong is the evidence supporting democratic peace theory? What are the major criticisms of democratic peace theory?

9. What are the policy implications of democratic peace theory?

10. How does state structure influence foreign policy? Why do people disagree about how much influence public opinion should have on foreign policy?

11. In what ways might public opinion influence foreign policy, and what are the limits on such influence?

[Correct answers: 1. c; 2. b; 3. a; 4. a; 5. a]

## END NOTES

1. Robert Jervis, *Perception and Misperception in International Politics* (Princeton, NJ: Princeton University Press, 1976), pp. 14–15.

2. Bruce Russett, *Grasping the Democratic Peace* (Princeton, NJ: Princeton University Press, 1993), pp. 3–40.

3. James Fearon, "Domestic Political Audiences and the Escalation of International Disputes," *American Political Science Review*, Vol. 88, No. 3 (September 1994): 577–592.

4. Russett, *Grasping the Democratic Peace*, pp. 30–38; Zeev Maoz and Bruce Russett, "Normative and Structural Causes of Democratic Peace, 1946–1986," *American Political Science Review*, Vol. 87, No. 3 (September 1993): 624–639.

5. Bruce Bueno de Mesquita, James D. Morrow, Randolph M. Siverson, and Alastair Smith, "An Institutional Explanation of the Democratic Peace," *American Political Science Review*, Vol. 93, No. 4 (December 1999): 791–807.

6. David A. Lake, "Powerful Pacifists: Democratic States and War," *American Political Science Review*, Vol. 86, No. 1 (March 1992): 24–37; Dan Reiter and Allan C.

Stam III, "Democracy, War Initiation, and Victory," *American Political Science Review*, Vol. 92, No. 2 (June 1998): 259–277.

7. Bueno de Mesquita et al., "An Institutional Explanation," p. 801.

8. John M. Owen, "How Liberalism Produces Democratic Peace," *International Security*, Vol. 19, No. 2 (Fall 1994): 87–125.

9. In "An Institutional Explanation," Bueno de Mesquita et al. list eight "empirical regularities" that they associate with the democratic peace.

10. Zeev Maoz and Nasrin Abdolali, "Regime Types and International Conflict, 1816–1976," *Journal of Conflict Resolution*, Vol. 33, No. 1 (March 1989): 3–35.

11. Michael Doyle, "Kant, Liberal Legacies, and Foreign Affairs," *Philosophy and Public Affairs*, Vol. 12, No. 3 and No. 4 (Summer and Fall 1983): 205–235, 323–353; Maoz and Abdolali, "Regime Types and International Conflict," pp. 4–6.

12. Jack S. Levy, "The Causes of War: A Review of Theories and Evidence," in Philip Tetlock, Jo L. Husbands, Robert Jervis, Paul C. Stern, and Charles Tilly, eds., *Behavior, Society, and Nuclear War*, Vol. I (New York: Oxford University Press, 1989), p. 270.

13. See the critique of Doyle's categorization of World War I in David Spiro, "The Insignificance of the Liberal Peace," *International Security*, Vol. 19, No. 2 (Fall 1984): 50–86. Doyle's justification is in "Kant, Liberal Legacies, and Foreign Affairs," footnote 8.

14. Ido Oren, "The Subjectivity of the 'Democratic' Peace," *International Security*, Vol. 20, No. 2 (Fall 1995): 147–184.

15. Spiro, "The Insignificance of the Liberal Peace," p. 51.

16. Address of the President of the United States to the Senate, January 22, 1917, http://www.lib.byu.edu/~rdh/wwi/1917/senate.html.

17. The process of expansion of the zone of peace in Europe is discussed in detail in Jan Zielonka and Alex Pravda, eds., *Democratic Consolidation in Eastern Europe, Volume II: International and Transnational Factors* (Oxford, UK: Oxford University Press, 2001).

18. Peter Katzenstein, ed., *Between Power and Plenty: Foreign Economic Policies of Advanced Industrial States* (Madison: University of Wisconsin Press, 1978).

19. T. J. Pempel, "Japanese Foreign Economic Policy: The Domestic Bases for International Policy," in Katzenstein, ed., *Between Power and Plenty*, pp. 139–190.

20. Peter Katzenstein, "Conclusion: State Structure and Strategies of Foreign Economic Policy," in Katzenstein, ed., *Between Power and Plenty*, pp. 295–336.

21. Joel Migdal, *Strong Societies, Weak States: State-Society Relations and State Capabilities in the Third World* (Princeton, NJ: Princeton University Press, 1988).

22. See, for example, Nils Boesen, *Enhancing State Capacity—What Works, What Doesn't, and Why?* (Washington, DC: World Bank, 2004).

23. *The Economist*, October 21, 2006, p. 54.

24. Ian Taylor, *Stuck in Middle GEAR: South Africa's Post-Apartheid Foreign Relations* (Westport, CT: Praeger, 2001).

25. *Washington Post*, December 10, 2005.

26. Erica S. Downs, "New Interest Groups in Chinese Foreign Policy," testimony at U.S.-China Economic & Security Review Commission, April 13, 2011, www.brookings.edu/research/testimony/2011/04/13-china-companies-downs.

27. Douglas Foyle, "Foreign Policy Analysis and Globalization: Public Opinion, World Opinion, and the Individual," *International Studies Review*, Vol. 5, No. 2 (June 2003): 165. For one exception, see Thomas Risse-Kappen, "Public Opinion, Domestic Structure, and Foreign Policy in Liberal Democracies," *World Politics*, Vol. 43, No. 4 (July 1991): 479–512.

28. For an excellent review of the literature on public opinion in U.S. foreign policy, see Philip J. Powlick and Andrew Katz, "Defining the American Public Opinion/Foreign Policy Nexus," *Mershon International Studies Review*, Vol. 42 (1998): 29–61.

29. Mohammad Waseem, "The Dialectic between Domestic Politics and Foreign Policy," in Christophe Jaffrelot, ed., *Pakistan: Nationalism without a Nation?* (London: Zed Books, 2002), p. 264.

30. Risse-Kappen, "Public Opinion, Domestic Structure, and Foreign Policy in Liberal Democracies," p. 481.

31. Program on International Policy Attitudes, "Misperceptions, the Media and the Iraq War," October 2, 2003, www.worldpublicopinion.org/pipa/articles/

international_security_bt/102.php?nid=&id=&pnt=102&lb=brus.

32. Robert Shapiro and Benjamin Page, "Foreign Policy and the Rational Public," *Journal of Conflict Resolution*, Vol. 32, No. 2 (1988): 211–247; John Aldrich, John L. Sullivan, and Eugene Borgida, "Foreign Affairs and Issue Voting: Do Presidential Candidates 'Waltz Before a Blind Audience'?" *American Political Science Review*, Vol. 83 (1989): 123–142.

33. Ole R. Holsti, "Public Opinion and Foreign Policy: Challenges to the Almond-Lippman Consensus," *International Studies Quarterly*, Vol. 36, No. 4 (December 1992): 448–449.

34. Seymour Martin Lipset," The President, the Polls, and Vietnam," *Transactions*, Vol. 3 (1966): 20, quoted in Powlick and Katz, "Defining the American Public Opinion/Foreign Policy Nexus," p. 29.

35. Powlick and Katz, "Defining the American Public Opinion/Foreign Policy Nexus," p. 35; John Zaller, *The Nature and Origins of Mass Opinion* (Cambridge, UK: Cambridge University Press, 1992).

36. Powlick and Katz, "Defining the American Public Opinion/Foreign Policy Nexus," pp. 34–35; Benjamin I. Page, *Who Deliberates? Mass Media in American Society* (Chicago: University of Chicago Press, 1996).

37. Benjamin I. Page and Robert Y. Shapiro, "Presidents as Opinion Leaders: Some New Evidence," *Policy Studies Journal*, Vol. 12 (1984): 649–661.

38. Robert Toner, "A Loud Message for Bush," *New York Times*, November 8, 2006.

39. Luis Carlos Ugalde, "U.S.-Mexican Relations: A View from Mexico," in Luis Rubio and Susan Kaufman Purcell, eds., *Mexico under Fox* (Boulder, CO: Lynne Rienner, 2004), pp. 123, 132.

40. Andrés Rozental, "Fox's Foreign Policy Agenda: Global and Regional Priorities," in Rubio and Purcell, *Mexico under Fox*, pp. 96, 109.

41. Powlick and Katz, "Defining the American Public Opinion/Foreign Policy Nexus," pp. 33–35.

42. These statistics are from the Tyndall Report, "Top 20 Stories of 2009," http://tyndallreport.com/yearinreview2009/. The analyses cover weeknight newscasts. Up-to-date weekly analyses of network coverage can be found at http://www.tyndallreport.com.

43. Amy Mitchell, "State of the News Media 2015," Pew Research Center, http://www.journalism.org/2015/04/29/state-of-the-news-media-2015/.

44. Daniel C. Hallin, "Media, Political Power, and Democratization in Mexico," in Myung-Jin Park and James Curran, eds., *De-Westernizing Media Studies* (New York: Routledge, 2000), pp. 97, 99, 108.

45. *The Guardian*, June 15, 2012, www.guardian.co.uk/media/2012/jun/15/rupert-murdoch-tony-blair-iraq-alastair-campbell.

# 6

North Korean President Kim Jong-un, May 2015. How do individual leaders influence foreign policy?

Xinhua/Alamy

# BUREAUCRACIES, GROUPS, AND INDIVIDUALS IN THE FOREIGN POLICY PROCESS

## Learning Objectives

**6-1** Identify the major points of the rational action, bureaucratic politics, and organizational process models of foreign policy making.

**6-2** Understand the arguments for and against the importance of individual decision makers in foreign policy making.

**6-3** Weigh the influence of group dynamics on decision making.

**6-4** Identify the range of sources of misperception in foreign policy making.

**6-5** Understand prospect theory and its implications for decision making in international politics.

# CONSIDER THE CASE

## KILLING OSAMA BIN LADEN

Shortly after the terrorist attacks of 9/11, Al Qaeda leader Osama bin Laden disappeared into the mountains near Tora Bora, Afghanistan. Finding and killing him was a major priority for the United States. Bin Laden eluded pursuers until August 2010, when American intelligence discovered what they believed could be bin Laden's compound in the Pakistani city of Abbottabad. President Obama and his advisers had two difficult choices: when to attack and how.

Attacking too soon risked attacking the wrong target, needlessly killing innocent people, provoking a major incident with Pakistan, and making the U.S. government look inept. However, waiting for more evidence of bin Laden's presence carried huge risks too. Bin Laden might be tipped off, either by intelligence gathering on the ground in Pakistan or by a leak in Washington. Or he might just move on to a new safe house. The Obama administration deferred planning an attack until February 2011, when there was more evidence that bin Laden was there.

How to attack also proved a difficult choice, with different options involving different kinds of risk. According to interviews conducted after the raid by the scholar Graham Allison, Obama quickly discarded the idea of a joint operation with Pakistan, for fear that someone in the Pakistani government would tip off bin Laden.* Several of Obama's closest advisers, including Joint Chiefs of Staff Vice Chairman James Cartwright, advocated using B-2 bombers to drop thirty-two 2000-pound bombs on the compound, killing everyone inside (including roughly twenty women and children). Others backed a plan to attack the compound with Hellfire missiles fired from drones. It was not certain, however, that the missiles had the firepower to guarantee killing bin Laden.

A raid by U.S. Navy SEALs offered the highest rewards, but also the highest risks. The United States would know for sure whether or not bin Laden had been killed, bystander deaths would be minimized, and vital intelligence might be collected at the site. But the risks were huge; any number of unforeseen circumstances might cause the mission to fail catastrophically. In 1979,

public confidence in President Jimmy Carter was harmed irreparably when a bold raid to free U.S. hostages in Iran failed because helicopters crashed during a dust storm. This operation could be even worse: If Pakistani forces discovered the raid, they might capture U.S. soldiers and put them on trial, as they had a CIA operative earlier in 2011. This possibility prompted Obama to include two more helicopters with more SEALs, so that the team could fight its way out of Pakistan if it were detected. As it turned out, one helicopter crash-landed in bin Laden's compound, and one of the extras was needed to complete the mission.

The day before the raid, Obama took a vote among the advisers working on the plan. A CIA reevaluation of the intelligence yielded an estimated 40–60 percent chance that bin Laden was in the compound.[†] Vice President Joe Biden and Defense Secretary Robert Gates voted against the raid. Gen. Cartwright continued to support the bombing option. Only a minority, including CIA director Leon Panetta, backed the SEAL team raid.

The case highlights several general problems with foreign policy decision making. First, information is often at a premium—for more than a decade, the United States had no idea where bin Laden was, and even after he was found, confirming his presence was difficult and risky. Second, some things cannot be known in advance, such as what random events might cause the raid to fail. Third, even a group of like-minded people trying desperately to solve the same problem can disagree on the best course. Fourth, people make foreign policy decisions in conditions of incredible stress. How do these and other factors affect the decision-making process? How can political leaders overcome these obstacles to arrive at better decisions?

---

*Graham Allison, "How It Went Down," Time, May 7, 2012, pp. 34–41. This discussion relies heavily on Allison's article.

†David Corn, "How Obama Got Bin Laden," The Daily Beast, April 29, 2012, www.thedailybeast.com/articles/2012/04/29/how-obama-got-bin-laden-a-detailed-account-from-showdown-by-david-corn.html.

In Chapter 5, we focused on the nature of the state as a source of foreign policy behavior. In this chapter, we make two related shifts. First, we are again changing our level of analysis. The theories discussed in Chapters 3 and 4 tend to focus on the system level, and those discussed in Chapter 5 focus on the state level. In this chapter, we look inside the state for sources of foreign policy, beginning with several levels that might be labeled "substate" and working all the way down to the level of the individual. In contrast to the approaches we have examined so far, the understanding of international relations discussed in this chapter assumes that foreign policies "bubble up" from within a government, and so are not "made" at the top or imposed by circumstances.

Second, we change our focus from *structure* to *process*. In the previous chapter, we focused on the *structure* of the state, and in Chapters 3 and 4, we emphasized the *structure* of the system. Structural approaches see outcomes as determined by a set of unchanging constraints (structures), such as the distribution of power or the type of government. The approaches discussed in this chapter stress process as a distinct source of variation in state behavior.

# FOREIGN POLICY ANALYSIS

In Chapter 5, "foreign policy" replaced "international politics" as the subject of analysis. In considering the influence of factors *within* the state and society, we are shifting from the question "How does international politics work?" to the question "What determines foreign policies?" Obviously, there is a great deal of overlap in these two questions, but they contain different emphases and are likely to yield different answers.

Since the early 1960s, the field of **foreign policy analysis** has grown rapidly. It includes scholarly research as well as much of the analysis undertaken by government intelligence agencies and foreign ministries around the world. In seeking to predict what other governments do, these actors put a lot of effort into understanding how different governments make foreign policies and what might influence a change in these policies.

**foreign policy analysis**

Analysis that attempts to understand states' behavior in terms of actors and processes at the domestic (state and substate) level.

Barack Obama and advisers watch the attack on Osama bin Laden in the White House situation room, May 2011. How did the decision-making process affect the choice of tactics in the attack?

White House Photo / Alamy

Foreign policy analysis can be divided into three areas of study. The first concerns the workings of *bureaucracies.* Based largely in the disciplines of management and organizational behavior, the study of bureaucracies gives important insight into why leaders feel constrained and frustrated by them. The second approach examines the process of *decision making,* not only in large bureaucracies, but also in small groups, such as a leader's immediate advisers. A third school of thought considers the *psychological* characteristics of leaders themselves and draws on insights from the field of psychology to help explain the many ways in which the idea of rationality seems to provide a poor explanation of behavior. You will notice, however, that all three of these schools of thought focus on the executive branch of government. Why do we not consider the judicial branch or, especially in democracies, the legislative branch? This question must be answered before considering the bureaucratic, decision-making, and psychological approaches in detail.

# BRANCHES OF GOVERNMENT

The role of the different branches of government varies across countries, and across time and issues within countries. Most foreign policy analysis, however, focuses on the executive branch for three reasons. First, in many countries, the constitution or legislation specifies that the head of government shall be responsible for making foreign policy. In the U.S. Constitution, for example, Article II, Section 2, stipulates that the president has the right to sign treaties and appoint ambassadors (subject to Senate confirmation).

Second, there is often (although not always) agreement within a country that the country needs to have a single voice abroad and that the head of government should be that voice. Thus, international "summit meetings," such as those held by the G-7 countries, are attended by heads of government, not groups of legislators. There is a perceived need to speak with a single, united voice on the international stage and to play down internal disagreements on policy. There are certainly exceptions to this general rule, such as when legislators, citizen groups, or opposition politicians seek to make foreign policy themselves or to undermine the authority of the head of government, but these cases are relatively rare. Most of the time, the head of government leads foreign policy making.

Third, heads of government tend to control the making of foreign policy because they control the executive branch of government. Most foreign policy is made not through legislation but through negotiation, implementation of laws, and sometimes war. The conduct of diplomacy, the gathering of intelligence, and the waging of war are functions carried out by agencies of the executive branch.

In the United States, the Constitution makes the president commander-in-chief of the armed forces, and these forces can be sent into combat on the president's orders. Congress has the constitutional authority to declare war but has not used it since the outbreak of World War II. In practice, the president can initiate war whether Congress approves or not. After the Vietnam War, Congress passed the **War Powers Resolution** to reassert congressional control over decisions to go to war, but it is not clear that the resolution has had much effect. If the president puts U.S. troops into a combat situation, the resolution requires that the troops must be removed after sixty days unless Congress passes legislation allowing the operation to continue. This leaves the president with a great deal of latitude, especially as Congress is often reluctant to appear not to support troops in the field.

In the United Kingdom, the power to declare war formally lies with the monarch but in practice rests with the prime minister. Parliamentary consultation or approval is

**War Powers Resolution**

A 1973 law that limits the U.S. president's ability to go to war without permission of Congress.

not required. These traditional arrangements spurred debate in 2011 when the UK joined others in intervening in Libya. At that time, the foreign minister stated the government's intention to change the law to require parliamentary consultation prior to deploying force. But reformers have found it difficult to resolve the tension between giving the prime minister latitude to act quickly in crises and giving Parliament some real authority in such matters.[1] In Germany, in contrast, the chancellor has much less authority: troops cannot be deployed without the prior approval of the parliament.

## LEGISLATURES IN FOREIGN POLICY

Although foreign policy is largely the domain of the executive branch, legislatures do influence policy. The most significant source of legislative influence is control over budgets. In most democracies, all government expenditures must be approved by the legislature. This enables the legislature to block measures it opposes. Although the U.S. Congress found it difficult to persuade presidents Johnson and Nixon to negotiate a settlement in Vietnam, it found that the "power of the purse" was an effective means to enforce its will: Congress passed a resolution forbidding the expenditure of public money on the war. Essentially, this resolution said, "As commander-in-chief, you can do what you wish with the military, but you cannot pay for it with public funds." The cutoff of funding effectively forced the withdrawal of U.S. troops from Vietnam. A similar move was attempted in 2006 to force withdrawal from Iraq, but the measure did not pass.

However, the power of the legislature varies across countries. Steven Philip Kramer contrasts the French system sharply with that of the United States, arguing that the French National Assembly "has little say in foreign policy" and that the French Senate "has even less."[2]

In parliamentary systems, the parliamentary majority chooses the prime minister (and the rest of the ministers). Thus, a situation in which the executive branch is controlled by one party and the legislature by another is impossible. Instead, when a majority coalition is made up of multiple parties, there may be difficult bargaining over foreign policy within the coalition.[3] In some cases, disagreement over foreign policy may prompt a governing coalition to collapse, forcing new elections. In Israel, for example, the need to keep a coalition intact has been a significant constraint on nearly every government's foreign policy. In 2011, German involvement in the coalition effort to assist Libyan rebels was limited because a small party within the ruling coalition, the Free Democratic Party, opposed German participation.

## COURTS IN FOREIGN POLICY

Traditionally, domestic courts have been involved in foreign policy only in isolated instances. Courts' jurisdiction generally has been limited to domestic affairs, and foreign policy is rarely the subject of lawsuits. A classic example to the contrary is the **Pentagon Papers**, a series of secret Defense Department reports on the origins of the Vietnam War that raised serious questions about U.S. involvement in that war. In 1971, they were leaked to the *New York Times* by a Defense Department employee. The administration of President Richard Nixon sued to prevent publication of the documents, arguing that they were secret, but the U.S. Supreme Court ruled that the constitutional guarantee of a free press outweighed the government's interest in secrecy. The subsequent publication of the papers played an important role in undermining public support for the war. More recently, when a large trove of secret U.S. government documents was released to

**Pentagon Papers**

A series of secret Defense Department reports on the origins of the Vietnam War that raised serious questions about U.S. involvement in the war.

WikiLeaks, the soldier who leaked the documents, Chelsea Manning, was arrested and sentenced to a lengthy prison term.

The courts' role in foreign policy may be growing as they take on issues of civil liberties and human rights. Antiterrorism efforts have raised several issues that courts have been asked to resolve, especially concerning the detention of suspects without trial. In *Hamdan v. Rumsfeld* (2004), the U.S. Supreme Court was asked to clarify the legal rights of Salim Ahmed Hamdan, who has dual U.S. and Saudi Arabian citizenship, was captured in Afghanistan, and was alleged by the U.S. government to be an "unlawful combatant." The Court ruled that Hamdan did indeed have legal rights as a U.S. citizen that needed to be protected, and that the war powers of the executive branch did not limit the jurisdiction of the courts in the matter. The ruling was seen as placing limits on how terrorism suspects could be treated by the government. In 2009, an Italian court found twenty-five people, including twenty-one CIA agents, guilty of kidnapping a terrorism suspect and transporting him to Egypt, where he was allegedly tortured. The Americans were tried in absentia because the United States refused to extradite them, so they did not go to jail.

Increasingly, domestic courts are being asked to try foreign government officials for various misdeeds. In 1998, Spanish Judge Balthazar Garzón issued an arrest warrant for former Chilean dictator Augusto Pinochet for the alleged murder by Pinochet's government of Spanish citizens. Pinochet was vacationing in Britain at the time, and Garzón issued a Europe-wide arrest warrant, which obligated the British to arrest Pinochet and hand him over. The British courts then had to rule on whether the extradition was legal. Thus, the Spanish and British courts got involved in a major diplomatic tussle that primarily concerned the conduct of Chilean politics. Ultimately, the diplomatic crisis was avoided by a British court's ruling that Pinochet was too ill to stand trial. This allowed him to be released without setting any precedent about putting former dictators on trial abroad.

Since the Pinochet case, prosecutors and judges have appeared increasingly willing to seek to bring to trial former state leaders who have committed abuses and then traveled outside their own countries. Garzón later caused another diplomatic panic when he sought to investigate the role of former U.S. Secretary of State Henry Kissinger in political violence in Latin America. In 2004, former Ukrainian Prime Minister Pavlo Lazarenko was tried and convicted in the United States on money laundering charges stemming from allegations of corruption when he was prime minister. The increasing use of international, as opposed to domestic, courts to try government officials is discussed in Chapter 13.

## THE EXECUTIVE BRANCH IN FOREIGN POLICY

Both courts and legislatures play an important role from time to time in the making of foreign policy. This is truer in democratic political systems, in which legislatures and courts generally have more independence than they do in nondemocratic systems. Nonetheless, the vast majority of foreign policy decisions are made and implemented within the executive branch, so the remainder of this chapter focuses on the executive.

# THE RATIONAL ACTION MODEL

Discussions of how governments make foreign policy decisions almost always compare actual decisions to some ideal abstraction of how decisions should be made. This ideal is often referred to as the **rational action model**.

In trying to explain any decision, people implicitly assume that it is based on some underlying rationality. We equate the question "Why did they do that?" with the question

**rational action model**

A model that bases explanations of decisions on the assumption that decision makers have clear goals, calculate the costs and benefits of various courses of action, and choose the action that will best serve their goals.

**FIGURE 6.1** Rational Action model.

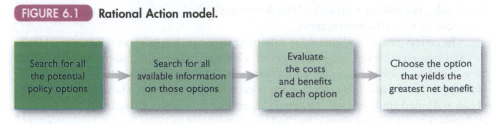

Source: Paul D'Anieri.

"What did they hope to gain by that?" In framing the question that way, we presume that any action is a logical attempt to achieve an identifiable goal. We do not ask whether the actor is trying to achieve some goal; we simply assume it. Once we make this assumption, we find the explanation by working backward: What goal would this policy most obviously serve? The pursuit of that goal must explain the policy. The alternative is to assume that actors do things for no reason—an assumption that defies reason and would make explanation impossible.

To say that a decision was arrived at rationally does not mean that it turns out well. Sometimes there are no good options, and sometimes carefully calculated risks turn out badly. But arriving at a rational decision does require making a conscious attempt to calculate the best choice. Figure 6.1 illustrates the four-step process of the rational action model.

Economists and some international relations scholars have refined the general rational action assumption into **expected utility theory**. This theory is especially useful in thinking about decision making under uncertainty, when not all conditions are known and the results of a particular policy cannot be perfectly predicted. Expected utility theory focuses on two factors: payoffs and probability. *Payoffs* are the benefits (economists refer to these as the *utility*) of various outcomes. *Probability* is the chance that a particular outcome will result from a certain policy. Thus, expected utility theory views rational decision making not as choosing the policy with the highest payoff but as choosing the one with the highest expected utility—the value when both payoffs and the probabilities of obtaining them are taken into account.

In mathematical terms, expected utility is equal to the value of an outcome times the probability of obtaining it. For example, when playing the lottery, the expected utility is the payoff times the odds of winning. If there is a one-in-a-thousand chance of winning $900, the expected utility is the chance of winning (.001) times the payoff ($900), or $0.90. Using the expected utility approach, it is rational to buy a ticket for such a lottery only if the ticket costs less than the expected utility of $0.90.

The lottery example points to a problem for expected utility theory: Millions of people play lotteries in which their expected utility is less than the cost of playing, meaning that people are either unable to calculate expected utility or are irrational in other ways. The theory cannot explain these decisions without stretching the definition of rationality considerably (by assuming that there is "utility" in playing the game itself). Likewise, many scholars and practitioners contend that in foreign policy, decision making deviates considerably from the ideal of rationality. Various approaches have been used to account for this.

Alternatives to the rational action model do not assert that policy making is *irrational*, but rather that it deviates from strict rationality in significant, and sometimes predictable, ways. In a highly influential work published in 1969, political scientist Graham Allison applied two alternative approaches to the 1962 Cuban Missile Crisis to

**expected utility theory**

A variant of the rational action model. The theory asserts that leaders evaluate policies by combining their estimation of the utility of potential outcomes with the likelihood that different outcomes will result from the policy in question.

show how and why policies deviate from what would normally be regarded as "rational."[4] Allison's "bureaucratic politics" model focused on how the struggle for influence among bureaucracies affects the policies they create and prevents them from arriving at the ideal policy. His "organizational process" model looks at how the routines that bureaucracies follow produce policies based on the implementation of procedures, rather than on the search for the ideal policy.

# BUREAUCRACIES IN FOREIGN POLICY

Most foreign policies are conceived of and carried out by bureaucracies, and this has led scholars to ask how the workings of bureaucracies affect the policies they produce. Governments cannot work without bureaucracies. Legislatures and heads of state can make decisions, but they cannot implement policies by themselves. Nor are they able to collect the information needed to make policies or to closely monitor implementation. These tasks are delegated to the bureaucracies of the executive branch. Even in China, a country with a highly centralized political system, the expanding range and complexity of foreign policy issues require that specialized bureaucracies be given an expanded role in foreign policy development and implementation.[5]

Every country has a roughly similar set of executive branch institutions (bureaucracies). In most countries, these are called **ministries** (in the United States, they are called *departments*). The two most important bureaucracies with respect to foreign affairs are the ministry of foreign affairs and the ministry of defense (or the Department of State and the Department of Defense, respectively, in the United States). A third key organization is one that collects and analyzes information, or *intelligence*, on other countries. In the United States, this mission is divided among several organizations, including the Central Intelligence Agency (CIA) and the National Security Agency (NSA). In Britain, this mission is given to the Secret Intelligence Service (MI6) and General Communication Headquarters (GCHQ). Russia's intelligence service is known as the Foreign Intelligence Service. China's is called the Ministry of State Security.

In addition to these organizations that are primarily concerned with foreign and security affairs, other ministries and agencies have important foreign affairs concerns as part of broader missions. Ministries of economics and finance (in the United States, the Departments of Commerce and the Treasury) oversee foreign economic policy. Some countries have separate ministries of foreign trade. Thus, the question of who makes foreign policy in the executive branch becomes complicated very quickly. Depending on the issue, almost any ministry or agency can have a role in foreign policy. Coordination and competition among these different agencies and within them is an important challenge for every government in the world.

Those who focus on bureaucracies in foreign policy agree on one central point: The ways in which bureaucracies work deviate substantially from the notion of the unified rational state assumed by many theories and by popular news accounts. Although a

**ministries**

The main institutions of the executive branch of government. In the United States, these institutions are called "departments."

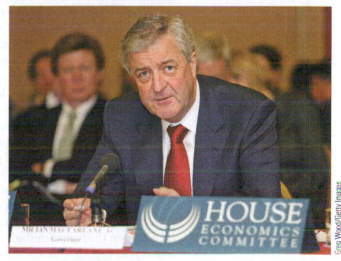

Australian Reserve Bank Governor Ian Macfarlane testifies to Parliament, 2004. What role do legislators play in foreign policy?

news account or a realist analysis may say that "Russia" took an action or "Germany" enacted a new policy, those actions are usually implemented by agencies within those governments, and the decisions to enact those policies are heavily influenced by those agencies.

# THE BUREAUCRATIC POLITICS MODEL

The bureaucratic politics model of foreign policy asserts that different bureaucracies have distinct, and often competing, interests. Policy often results from the messy process by which these bureaucracies fight for their interests, rather than from a search for the most "rational" policy for the country. Put differently, this perspective sees foreign policy making as influenced by a giant case of "office politics," in which policies may be chosen according to how bureaucrats and organizations pursue their own political agendas rather than foreign policy needs. Thus, a study of China finds that "competition for turf and influence by rival bureaucracies appears to pervade the Chinese foreign policy system."[6]

**Bureaucratic Interests**   Why do different bureaucracies have different interests? Are they not all concerned with serving the national interest? Bureaucracies may promote different policies for two reasons: role and budget. First, because each agency has a particular notion of its "mission," it will tend to promote solutions that fit with that role. For example, the role of foreign ministries is to conduct diplomacy, solving problems through negotiation; defense ministries' role is to wage war, solving problems through the use of force. It is to be expected, then, that because these two bureaucracies have different roles and different tools at their disposal, they are likely to propose different solutions to foreign policy problems.

A second reason bureaucracies conflict over policy is that they are in competition over budgets, which will in turn affect the scope of their mission. Bureaucracies tend to seek larger budgets; to justify them, they need to show that what they do is more important than what other bureaucracies do. Hence, any bureaucracy will tend to support the policies that put it in charge, use its solutions, and place a premium on its resources. This increases the importance of the organization, justifies a larger budget and more missions in the future, and increases the prestige of the organization.

These role and budgetary concerns of bureaucracies lead many analysts to assert that in discussions over policy making, "where you stand depends on where you sit." In other words, top bureaucrats' positions on policy issues are determined by the interests of the organization they head, not just the government they serve. In many respects, the bureaucratic politics model looks like the realist balance of power theory applied to relations between bureaucracies rather than to those between states.

A good historical illustration is found in the career of Winston Churchill, who is most famous for having been prime minister of Britain during World War II. Before that, Churchill served in several positions in the British government. As president of the Board of Trade prior to World War I, he argued against greater spending on the navy. Just a few years later, as First Lord of the Admiralty, in charge of the navy, he ardently asserted the need to substantially increase the budget in order to build more ships. Later, as Chancellor of the Exchequer (finance minister) in the 1920s, he again advocated reduced spending on the navy. Similarly, as Minister of Colonies in France in the late nineteenth century, Théophile Delcassé advocated that France send an expedition to the Nile River to challenge Britain's position in that region. Later, as Foreign Secretary (in charge of diplomacy), Delcassé sought to recall the expedition.[7] Examples like these are cited as evidence that bureaucratic politics strongly influence policy positions.

**Competing Priorities**  In the United States, much is written about the struggle over foreign policy between the Department of State, which is viewed as tending to advocate diplomatic solutions, and the Department of Defense, which is seen as putting a greater emphasis on military solutions to problems. In his study of the Cuban Missile Crisis, Allison shows that military leaders advocated a surprise attack on Cuba from the very outset and continued to advocate that position. The State Department, in contrast, feared that a military response might spiral out of control and advocated holding off on military action until efforts at negotiation had been exhausted.

The bureaucratic politics model does not imply that all military leaders are "warmongers." Rather, these leaders see their primary mission as prevailing in a military conflict, should one occur. In the Cuban Missile Crisis, military leaders viewed the crisis in those terms, and from a military perspective, it appeared that an early strike, before the Soviet missiles could be made operational, was safer. Delaying a strike would make it less likely that such a strike would succeed.

Before the U.S. invasion of Iraq in 2003, the State Department and the Defense Department disagreed profoundly concerning the best way to deal with Iraq. The State Department sought to continue the diplomatic process as long as possible and to work within the United Nations Security Council where possible. The State Department was concerned about the diplomatic consequences of going to war and the difficulties involved in occupying Iraq afterward. The Defense Department believed that war was necessary and that diplomatic wrangling was making it harder to time the attack. In a recent study, Rajiv Chandrasekaran shows how a bureaucratic battle disrupted the Obama administration policy on Afghanistan. The State Department advocated peace talks with the Taliban rebels, and the National Security Council pushed for the 2009 troop surge intended to defeat the rebels.[8]

**Effects of Bureaucratic Politics**  A crucial conclusion of the bureaucratic politics model is that the policies that emerge from bureaucratic conflict are often policies that *nobody* intended. When two or more organizations fight it out, the result is often unpredictable. In the case of the Cuban Missile Crisis, the Air Force and the CIA both sought the mission of flying U-2 spy planes over Cuba to monitor the situation. The eventual result was a compromise: Air Force pilots flew CIA planes. However, while this dispute was being resolved, neither organization made any flights for several days. Neither side advocated delaying flights, but that was the result. The consequence was that the missiles were discovered much later, and much closer to operational readiness, than would otherwise have been the case. This intensified the crisis by reducing the amount of time that Kennedy and his advisers had to find a solution.

To summarize, the bureaucratic politics approach sees foreign policy as the result of a battle, not as a decision carefully arrived at. The result may be a decision preferred by one of the bureaucratic actors, it may be a compromise between competing bureaucratic parties, or it might be something that none of them intended.

**Critique of the Bureaucratic Politics Model**  Critics of the bureaucratic politics approach assert that this portrait of "where you stand depends on where you sit" is a gross oversimplification. There are many examples of bureaucracies' advocating positions opposite to what this approach would have predicted. In the United States during the administration of Ronald Reagan in the 1980s, the State Department was widely seen as advocating the use of the military to counter leftist insurgents in Latin America; the Defense Department resisted this approach. During the first Bush administration and the Clinton administration, the State Department advocated that the United States take an

# THE POLICY CONNECTION

## ORGANIZING TO FIGHT TERRORISM

Many governments have reorganized their intelligence and law enforcement agencies to deal with the rise of transnational terrorism. In the United States, review of the September 11, 2001, attacks revealed that various U.S. government agencies had had evidence that Al Qaeda was planning a major attack involving hijacked airplanes.* However, the information was scattered among different organizations and was never put together in such a way as to present a clear picture of the danger. Prior to 2001, the organizational mission of the FBI included catching criminals after the fact, but not preventing crime. The CIA and other intelligence agencies were not tasked with threats on U.S. soil. Following the attacks, there was a far-reaching overhaul of security and intelligence services that created more than 250 new organizations, including the Department of Homeland Security, and established the Director of National Intelligence, to coordinate the sixteen major intelligence organizations.[†] These changes in structure were intended to create changes in *process*.

In practice, the benefits of the changes are uncertain. In December 2009, a Nigerian man boarded a flight from Amsterdam to Detroit with a bomb that failed to detonate. Afterward, it emerged that there had been considerable evidence that the man was a danger, but again, it had not been brought together. Moreover, bureaucratic infighting continuously undermined the newly created position of Director of National Intelligence, who was never able to gain budgetary or operational control over the CIA, which continued to report directly to the White House. Turnover was high, with four directors in five years. Moreover, some argued that the organizational apparatus developed to combat Al Qaeda was less well suited to fighting the Islamic State.[‡] Could the United States continue to adapt organizationally?

Germany faced a different problem. In its federal system, there is no national police or intelligence service akin to the FBI or Britain's MI5. Instead, each of the *Länder* (states) has its own police force. Coordination among these sixteen separate forces on terrorism and other national and international problems is difficult. For example, efforts to create a single nationwide database on terrorism are hindered by the fact that each state collects different data and organizes it differently.[§]

Pakistan encountered a different problem still. Its counterterrorism policy was largely handled by its intelligence organization, the Inter-Services Intelligence (ISI). Before September 11, 2001, the Pakistani government had actually supported the Taliban movement in Afghanistan because that movement was seen as extending Pakistani influence. However, the Taliban's sheltering of Al Qaeda, and Al Qaeda's attacks on the United States, meant that Pakistan now had an interest in helping the United States combat those organizations. Simply changing the internal practices of the ISI and the sympathies of ISI personnel has not been easy, and many observers continue to assert that ISI pursuit of Al Qaeda and Taliban forces in Pakistan is halfhearted.[¶] As Taliban

---

*See *The 9/11 Commission Report, Final Report of the National Commission on Terrorist Attacks upon the United States, Official Government Edition* (Washington, DC: U.S. Government Printing Office, 2004), Chapters 3, 8, and 11 (pp. 71–107, 254–277, 339–360). The report is available online at www.gpoaccess.gov/911/index.html.

[†]Audrey Kurth Cronin, "Don't Use Counterterrorism to Fight ISIS," *Foreign Affairs*, (March/April 2015).

[‡]Cronin, "Don't Use Counterterrorism."

[§]"Immune No More," *The Economist*, August 26, 2006, p. 43.

[¶]"The Trouble with Pakistan," *The Economist*, July 6, 2006.

*(Continued)*

insurgents began attacking Pakistani government installations as well as U.S. targets in Afghanistan, Pakistani forces attacked them more directly, but the issue remained tense, both within Pakistan and between Pakistan and the United States.

## Critical Thinking Questions

1. To what extent were U.S. intelligence failures prior to September 11, 2001, and prior to the Iraq war the result of organizational structure and process, as opposed to other factors?

2. Why has it been difficult to address the problems through reorganization?

3. What other kinds of decision-making problems are likely to complicate efforts to combat terrorism?

active role in stopping "ethnic cleansing" in the former Yugoslavia, using military force if necessary. The military opposed armed intervention, fearing that it would be bogged down in a conflict whose goals were unclear and from which there was no easy way out. In Mexico, prior to the U.S. invasion of Iraq in 2003, there was profound disagreement *within* the Foreign Ministry between UN ambassador Adolfo Zinser and foreign minister Jorge Castañeda. Zinser refused to discuss policy with Castañeda and instead dealt only with President Vicente Fox.[9]

Further, some analysts are skeptical about the power of bureaucracies to escape the control of the head of government, who generally has a large staff dedicated to managing policy. Although President John F. Kennedy and Secretary of Defense Robert McNamara quarreled with military leaders during the Cuban Missile Crisis, Kennedy prevailed.[10] A more notorious case was the disagreement between President Harry S Truman and General Douglas MacArthur during the Korean War (1950–1953). When MacArthur, a charismatic and popular World War II hero, advocated extending the war to China, Truman simply fired him. Similarly, in June 2010, Barack Obama fired General Stanley McChrystal, the top commander in Afghanistan, after McChrystal and his staff expressed their lack of confidence in the civilian leadership.

## THE ORGANIZATIONAL PROCESS MODEL

The organizational process model stresses how the *procedures* by which bureaucracies make decisions influence the *content* of those decisions. This approach stresses the fact that bureaucracies make policies not by weighing the costs and benefits of all alternatives, but rather by applying similar procedures to the wide variety of questions that arise.[11]

Bureaucracies are created in large part to deal with an immense number of essentially similar situations. They create **standard operating procedures** to organize their work. These can range from the process used at a department of motor vehicles for issuing drivers' licenses to that used at a ministry of foreign affairs to manage new information coming in from its embassies abroad. These procedures can be thought of as the bureaucratic equivalent of a computer program, which always performs the same function in response to the same input. If every time a foreign citizen wanted to enter Mexico, the Foreign Ministry had to figure out from scratch whether to issue a visa, the process would be incredibly inefficient. Instead, standard procedures are put in place to indicate what documents are required, what questions are asked, and

**standard operating procedures**

Procedures that bureaucracies adopt to deal efficiently with a large number of similar tasks.

**FIGURE 6.2**   **Diagram of the intelligence process.** Intelligence agencies around the world follow a standard process in gathering, analyzing, and disseminating information. Especially important is the feedback by which current findings inform planning for future information gathering. What kinds of problems might surface when this process breaks down?

Diagram of the Intelligence Process

Source: http://thediagram.com/7_2/theintelligenceprocess.html.

what rules are applied in making the decision. Similarly, intelligence agencies collect an immense amount of data and cannot manage all of it unless there are established practices for categorizing the data, filing it for later retrieval, synthesizing it into reports, and deciding which findings are important enough to be brought to the attention of higher authorities (see Figure 6.2). In the military realm, armed forces cannot wait until they are at war to decide how they will fight a battle. Instead, they develop standard procedures, known as *doctrine*, that cover everything from how to wage tank warfare in the desert to how to cook the soldiers' dinner. In sum, procedures allow large organizations to function.

But just as a computer cannot do something it is not programmed to do, organizations have difficulty performing tasks that are outside their typical responsibilities or that require departing from standard operating procedures. Almost everyone has had the frustrating experience of dealing with a bureaucracy that invokes a set of predetermined rules and procedures in response to a unique situation. Standard operating procedures work well at handling large numbers of similar problems, but by their nature, they are not tailored to unusual situations. Foreign policy often involves atypical situations, and applying standard procedures to these nonstandard situations can lead to undesirable outcomes that deviate from the rationality assumption. Good examples of this problem include German war plans prior to World War I (see "The History Connection: The Schlieffen Plan and World War I") and the organization of counterterrorism (see "The Policy Connection: Organizing to Fight Terrorism"). Collecting and sifting through vast amounts of data require standard operating procedures, but the threats that one is seeking to identify are by their nature unique, not standard. U.S. intelligence agencies failed to detect the 9/11 plot in part because flying planes into buildings had not been done before, and the agencies therefore were not looking for data on that threat.

# THE HISTORY CONNECTION

## THE SCHLIEFFEN PLAN AND WORLD WAR I

Among the best known cases in which the implementation of predetermined plans led to unintended (and disastrous) results was the German army's war plan prior to World War I. The strategy was to avoid having to fight simultaneously on two fronts: against France to the west and Russia to the east. To prevent this, Chief of the Imperial German General Staff Alfred von Schlieffen developed a plan whereby at the outset of war, the bulk of German forces would strike rapidly at France by marching through Belgium and Holland (thus bypassing the strongest French defenses). In the meantime, a much smaller force would keep Russia in check. Because Russia was a huge country with a somewhat underdeveloped military and transportation infrastructure, it would take several weeks for Russia to prepare to attack. The idea was to defeat France while Russia was still mobilizing. Then, as Russia became stronger, forces could be shifted to the east.

The military merits of the plan are debatable, but the diplomatic effects were profound. Germany's war plans depended on moving to war as rapidly as possible once a crisis occurred. To the extent that Belgium and Holland prepared to slow the German advance or Russia began mobilizing its forces sooner than anticipated, the plan's success was imperiled.

Map of the Schlieffen Plan

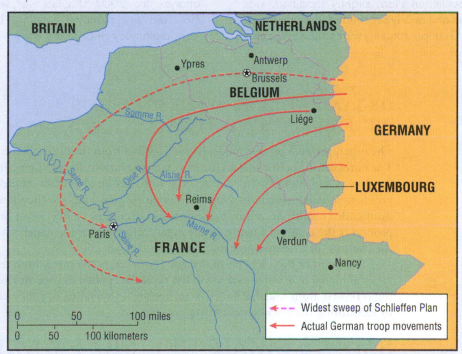

Source: http://encarta.msn.com/media_681500236_761569981_-1_1/schlieffen_plan_and_actual_troop_movements.html. Reprinted with permission from Microsoft Corporation.

*(Continued)*

Thus, during the July Crisis in 1914, the German army put immense pressure on German civilian leaders and diplomats to begin the war before its enemies could prepare. In particular, once Russia began its mobilization, the clock was ticking. Unless France could be defeated by the time Russia was ready to fight, Germany would be doomed. The existence of a standard, pre-determined plan for war removed any potential diplomatic flexibility Germany might have sought.

The situation in 1914 was exacerbated by the nature of military transportation. Mobilization was carried out primarily by rail, and extremely precise schedules had been worked out to move troops to the front and return railcars to the rear. These precise schedules did not allow for a "lull" or a halt in mobilization once it had begun. Such a halt would have led to logistical chaos and severely delayed further mobilization. Hence, the train schedules themselves made it extremely risky, in military terms, for diplomats to agree on a halt in mobilization.

The Schlieffen Plan, slightly modified, was carried out and nearly succeeded. Belgian troops delayed German forces longer than expected and were reinforced surprisingly quickly by British forces, allowing France to regroup. The Russian army was able to mount an initial attack on the eastern front much more quickly than expected. The tragedy was not in the plan's failure, but in the fact that implementing the plan made it almost impossible to let diplomacy run its course before the initiation of war.

## Critical Thinking Questions

1. Given what you know about the outbreak of World War I, what other strategic options might Germany have devised? How much blame for the war should be placed on the Schlieffen Plan versus other factors?

2. Contrast diplomacy efforts during the July Crisis that led to World War I with those made during the Cuban Missile Crisis. How was diplomacy related to military strategy in the Cuban case?

3. Can the models in this chapter be used to analyze the 2003 U.S.-led war with Iraq? How did war planning influence U.S. and Iraqi diplomacy prior to the war?

## ORGANIZATIONAL PROCESS VERSUS BUREAUCRATIC POLITICS

The organizational process model is quite distinct from the bureaucratic politics model. The bureaucratic politics model focuses on organizations struggling against one another for power and budgets. In contrast, the organizational process model examines the problem-solving procedures adopted by organizations and how they sometimes lead to unintended results. According to the bureaucratic politics model, what emerges from the process is the result of a battle. In the organizational process model, what comes out is the "output" of a defined process.

The point of both schools of thought, however, is the same. Both indicate that the rational model of decision making that is typically applied to governmental policy making is flawed. Both find that a significant amount of variation in policy can be explained by examining the workings of bureaucracies.

# SMALL GROUP DECISION MAKING

Although foreign policy is informed and executed by bureaucracies, many observers remain convinced that on important issues, key decisions are made by the head of government and his or her closest advisers. Therefore, much attention has been focused on the small groups of advisers that help heads of state make their decisions. The goal of such research is both to explain foreign policy and to offer advice on how to improve that process.[12]

Several pathologies of small group decision making may have particularly profound effects on foreign policy, leading policy to deviate significantly from "rational" decision making. Most important among these pathologies is a phenomenon, dubbed *groupthink* by one prominent analyst, whereby a group very quickly arrives at a single solution and closes off debate. In crucial situations, groups of decision makers are often under a great deal of pressure to reach a consensus on policy. This need for consensus can lead decision makers to agree quickly on the first option that seems optimal, rather than examining a wide range of options, as rational decision making requires.[13]

*"All those in favor say 'Aye.'"*
*"Aye."*    *"Aye."*    *"Aye."*    *"Aye."*
*"Aye."*    *"Aye."*

There are two reasons a group may dismiss certain options before they have been thoroughly assessed. First, in many groups, teamwork is highly valued, which often leads a group member to fall in with the preferences of the team even when he or she disagrees. Because all the members are expected to support the group's decision, members hesitate to criticize an option that appears to be favored by the rest of the team. Hence, when one option begins to emerge as a favorite, there tends to be a rush to support it rather than to scrutinize it. Getting along with colleagues often requires refraining from subjecting their proposals to serious criticism, yet such criticism is exactly what the rational action model assumes will take place. These tendencies exist in a wide variety of groups, and those making foreign policy are no exception.

In foreign policy, however, another factor may lead to even greater restriction of debate. A single individual (the head of government) is in charge of making the decision and is also responsible for the career success of everyone else in the room. Once it appears that the leader favors a particular choice, there are strong disincentives to criticize that policy. Criticism may be regarded as disrespectful at best, and at worst as disloyal. Access to the leader and influence are at stake. In some cases, dissent can cost an individual his or her job in the inner circle. In the most extreme cases, such as in the Soviet Union under Joseph Stalin (who ruled from 1922 to 1953) or in North Korea today, such disagreement could result in the adviser's imprisonment, exile, or execution.

For these reasons, advisers tend to try very hard to figure out ahead of time what policy the leader will support and then to advocate that view. Once a policy is favored, there are strong incentives to support it rather than to question it or to advocate a different option. In this way, one of the most important requirements of rational decision making—an evenhanded evaluation of all the options—may be very unlikely in the real world of small group decision making.

Many analysts of the decision making that led to the U.S. invasion of Iraq in 2003 have pointed to groupthink in the U.S. intelligence community. A bipartisan report by the U.S. Senate Select Committee on Intelligence, published in 2004, found that "IC [intelligence community] personnel involved in the Iraq [weapons of mass destruction] issue demonstrated several aspects of groupthink examining few alternatives, selective gathering of information, pressure to conform within the group or withhold criticism, and collective rationalization."[14] The report went on to point out that several standard procedures specifically intended to avoid groupthink, such as "'red teams,' 'devil's advocacy,' and other types of alternative or competitive analysis," were neglected.[15]

# INDIVIDUAL DECISION MAKING

So far, we have "unpeeled" the layers of decision making from the level of the state down to bureaucracies and then to small groups. Ultimately, some scholars point out, many of the most important policy decisions are made by a single decision maker, the head of state. If this individual has some latitude for action and if different leaders do not all behave identically, then it follows that the particular characteristics of the individual leader will have a substantial effect on what kind of policies are made. This is why the media spends so much effort analyzing a new leader who has come to power in an important country. At the level of the government, it explains why intelligence agencies spend so much effort collecting clues to the psychology or leadership style of foreign leaders.

In several important historical cases, the characteristics of individual leaders appear to have played a crucial role in determining policy. Germany under Adolph Hitler is one such example. Many people believe that under a different leader Germany would not have pursued the policies that it did. Ironically, many also believe that if not for Hitler's leadership, Germany might have won World War II, or at least been able to fight much longer. Most people, when considering elections for new leaders, believe that different leaders will have very different foreign policies. In the case of the United States, people in the United States and around the world believe that different individuals would pursue dramatically different foreign policies, whether the choice is between Bush and Gore or Obama and Romney. In all of these cases, and more generally, individual leadership seems to matter. But how? How is the "personality" or "style" of one leader different from that of another, and how do individual traits guide leaders to different responses to the same situation or challenge?

Skeptics wonder whether individual leaders really make that much difference. Leaders may be subject to so many international and domestic political constraints that they often feel they have little freedom of action. For example, Barack Obama came to power in the United States committed to getting U.S. troops out of Afghanistan and to closing the U.S. detention facility at Guantanamo Bay, Cuba. When he took office and had to face the options and their consequences, however, he pursued policies nearly identical to those of his predecessor. He initiated a "surge" in Afghanistan similar to the buildup George W. Bush had pursued in Iraq, and he decided to keep holding prisoners at Guantanamo Bay, largely because there were no palatable alternatives for dealing with the detainees held there. The point is not that politicians may be hypocrites, but that circumstance may tightly constrain their options, so that two individuals with vastly different styles and preferences might end up choosing similar policies. To the extent this is true, their individual preferences and personality traits have less influence.

## PERCEPTION AND MISPERCEPTION

Ambiguity and uncertainty are inherent characteristics of international politics. How leaders resolve such uncertainty can help explain policy choices, and different ways of resolving ambiguity may explain why different leaders might respond differently to the same situation. A great deal of research, marrying psychological experiments on cognition to historical evidence gathered from case studies, has been conducted on the sources of perception and misperception in international politics. This extensive body of research encompasses a vast number of theoretical approaches; what follows is a summary of some of the more prominent approaches and their key concepts.

One important distinction is between "unmotivated" and "motivated" bias. **Unmotivated bias** is bias that results from the simplifications and categories that every decision maker uses to make sense of a complicated world. **Motivated bias**, discussed later in this section, is bias that is driven by some psychological or emotional need.

Unmotivated bias naturally creeps into the way that people grapple with large amounts of information and simplify highly complex problems. Central to the idea of unmotivated bias is the notion that decision making is characterized by "bounded rationality." The theory of **bounded rationality** posits that decision makers try to be rational but that they face inherent limits on their ability to do so. People are limited in how much information they have access to and in their ability to effectively process all the information. Time limits further reduce the ability to acquire and process information. People, therefore, take a number of "shortcuts" to make timely decisions in a world of bewildering complexity and limited information. In this view, decision making is not *irrational* but rather is *imperfectly rational*. Several approaches from the cognitive psychology literature have been applied to the study of international politics to show how unmotivated bias is a product of humans' cognitive limits.

**Attribution Theory**    Attribution theory focuses on how decision makers' theories about how the world works are shaped and how they change. The theory sees decision makers as "naïve scientists," actively working to understand the world accurately.[16] In this view, the key process is **attribution**, whereby individuals attribute the behavior of others to one cause or another. Of particular interest are generalized findings in the field of psychology about how preexisting beliefs shape the interpretation of new information. Rather than going through a full scientific process, as implied by the rational decision making model, individuals with limited time instead look around until they come up with an explanation that is fairly plausible, and they often stop there. Thus, those explanations that we already have are likely to be used first to explain new events.

One particular finding of psychological research is especially relevant to the study of international politics: the **fundamental attribution bias**, in which people apply different attributions to their adversaries than to themselves. When an adversary does something we do not like, we tend to attribute it to their "bad" or aggressive intentions; when they do something positive, we tend to attribute it to circumstances beyond their control. We tend to apply the opposite set of biases to ourselves, attributing negative behaviors to circumstances and positive behaviors to our own goodwill.

The fundamental attribution bias lends important insight to the workings of the security dilemma. In an anarchic world, each actor is faced with uncertainty about others' intentions. Actors are, therefore, concerned about the abilities of others to hurt them. If one state makes a move to expand its influence, does the act arise from aggression or from a desire to protect itself? The fundamental attribution bias indicates that actors are more likely to mistake a peaceful state for an aggressive one than vice versa. Other things being equal, this tendency will make it more likely that a security dilemma will spiral toward higher levels of armament, mistrust, and conflict. At the same time, actors tend to believe strongly that their own moves are unthreatening to others and that others can easily see this. Hence, if others respond negatively to their policies, actors tend to conclude that others are hostile, not that they genuinely feel threatened.[17]

**unmotivated bias**

Bias that occurs as a result of the simplifications inherent in the process of perceiving an ambiguous world.

**motivated bias**

Bias that occurs as a result of some psychological need, such as the need for all of one's beliefs to be consistent with one another or the need to believe that a good solution to a problem is available.

**bounded rationality**

A theory that decision makers try to be rational but face several inherent limits on their ability to do so.

**attribution**

The process whereby individuals attribute the behavior of others to one cause or another. Attribution can create unmotivated bias in decision makers.

**fundamental attribution bias**

The tendency to believe that if adversaries make a concession, they were forced to, but if they make an unwelcome move, they did so freely with bad intentions; and the tendency to have the opposite bias about ourselves.

What is in this photo? The US defense department released these pictures on November 8, 1962, to support its claim that the Soviet Union was installing missiles in Cuba. Interpretation of surveillance photos can have a major impact on decision making.

This problem may have played an important role in the early years of the Cold War.[18] U.S. leaders interpreted a variety of Soviet actions as proof of the Soviet Union's aggressive designs to expand as far as possible into central Europe. Installing pro-Soviet governments in Poland, Czechoslovakia, and East Germany was seen as strong evidence of Soviet expansionism. Much less attention was given to the Soviet withdrawal from Austria, which it had also occupied at the end of World War II. It is difficult to build trust in situations in which concessions are not noticed.

Today, the same phenomenon may be occurring in a variety of conflicts around the world. For example, states that have possessed nuclear weapons for a long time consider it obvious that their own weapons are not threatening to others, whereas they perceive efforts by other states to gain nuclear weapons as a sign of aggression. The states seeking nuclear weapons probably see their own efforts not as acts of aggression but as acts of deterrence, preventing others from attacking them. A similar phenomenon takes place in international trade negotiations. Countries tend to regard their own barriers to trade as necessary and justifiable economic, environmental, or safety policies. At the same time, they tend to view other states' trade barriers as deliberate efforts to "cheat" in international trade. Thus, the United States sees EU loans to Airbus as illegal subsidies but does not see U.S. military contracts to Boeing as subsidies. The EU sees it the other way around, and there have been a series of conflicts over the two companies' competition in the market for commercial airliners.

**Historical Lessons and Analogies**   Another example of unmotivated bias that results from bounded rationality is the use of lessons or analogies from the past to interpret present circumstances. Psychologists note that people tend to develop mental categories over time and to try to fit new people or events into these already familiar categories. Historians point out that leaders repeatedly use decisive events from early in their adult lives as the basis for categories with which to interpret later phenomena.

An example of fitting people into standard categories was illustrated by James F. Byrnes, who was U.S. Secretary of State in the early Cold War period (1945–1947). He had to deal with the Soviet leader Joseph Stalin, whose motivations were unclear. Having served in the U.S. Senate, however, Byrnes believed he knew how to deal with the Soviets: "It's just like the U.S. Senate. You build a post office in their state, and they'll build a post office in our state."[19]

**lesson of Munich**

The lesson learned from British attempts to appease Hitler at the 1938 Munich peace conference—namely, that costly wars can be avoided by confronting hostile leaders promptly.

***The Lesson of Munich***   More often noted is how leaders compare new crises with old ones. One of the most common scenarios over the past sixty years has been to assume that authoritarian leaders whose countries are aggressive are just like Hitler. The **lesson of Munich**, referring to British attempts to appease Hitler at the 1938 Munich peace conference, has influenced policies repeatedly since World War II. The decision to confront the Soviet Union after World War II was motivated in large part by the belief that, had Hitler been confronted sooner, World War II could have been avoided. The British prime minister at the time, Neville Chamberlain, has been criticized since for "appeasement," but he himself was acting on the basis of the lesson of a previous war: The horrors of World War I, it was believed, could have been avoided if the July 1914 crisis had been resolved through concessions rather than confrontation. In responding to the North Korean invasion of South Korea in 1950, U.S. President Harry Truman explicitly compared the situation to events prior to World War II: "Communism was acting in Korea just as Hitler, Mussolini, and the Japanese had acted ten, fifteen, twenty years earlier. . . . If this was allowed to go unchallenged, it would mean a third world war, just as similar incidents had brought on the second world war."[20] When communism was gaining popularity in Vietnam in the late 1950s, U.S. leaders believed that it must be stopped or it would gain in momentum and power, just as Hitler had.[21] The lesson was invoked again by President George H. W. Bush in 1990 when Iraq invaded Kuwait. Bush explicitly compared Saddam Hussein to Hitler.

After September 11, 2001, comparisons of current events with those before World War II again became popular. During the debate over invading Iraq in 2003, British Foreign Secretary Jack Straw warned that hesitating in the conflict with Iraq would be equivalent to the reluctance to confront Hitler in the late 1930s. The cover of an issue of *Time* magazine showed Saddam Hussein with a red X painted over his face, directly mimicking the cover the magazine had run after the fall of Hitler in 1945.[22] In 2006, George W. Bush compared Osama bin Laden to Hitler, referred to Islamic terrorists as "fascists," a term widely applied to Nazi Germany, and equated criticism of his policy in Iraq with "appeasement"[23] Bush stated further that today's terrorists are "the successors to fascists, to Nazis, to communists and other totalitarians."[24] Secretary of Defense Donald Rumsfeld asserted that terrorism presents the same kind of threat as Nazi Germany's invasion of Poland in 1939: "I recount this history because once again we face the same kind of challenges in efforts to confront the rising threat of a new type of fascism."[25] It is debatable whether the equating of today's issues with those of 1939 was actually influencing the Bush administration's policy or whether this rhetoric was merely a way of justifying that policy. Even if the latter is true, it shows the leaders' belief that the analogy would be compelling to listeners. Most recently, in 2014, Russia's invasion and annexation of the Ukrainian territory of Crimea was compared to Germany's invasion of Czechoslovakia in 1938, and Putin was repeatedly compared to Hitler.[26]

***The Lessons of Vietnam***   Although the lesson of Munich has been widely influential, the Vietnam War also taught "lessons" to subsequent generations, although not everyone learned the same lessons from that conflict. To those who came of age during the Vietnam conflict, that war provides a point of view from which to evaluate every subsequent military conflict. The lessons taken from that war by many, especially those in the military, are that starting wars is much easier than ending them, and that what starts as a small intervention can grow into a conflict of massive proportions if the alternative is to admit defeat.

Thus, U.S. National Security Adviser (and later secretary of state) Colin Powell, who experienced Vietnam firsthand as a young officer, developed a set of criteria collectively known as the **Powell Doctrine** to guide the use of force. The criteria included being clear about goals and using "overwhelming" force rather than starting small and then raising force levels. When asked in 1992 about the possible use of "surgical" bombing to compel Serbian forces to refrain from attacks against Bosnians, Powell replied, "As soon as they tell me it is 'limited,' it means they do not care whether you achieve a result or not. As soon as they me tell me 'surgical,' I head for the bunker."[27]

In a similar vein, U.S. military leaders sought to gain approval for as large a force as possible for the 2003 invasion and occupation of Iraq, hoping to crush opposition quickly. When resistance to U.S. occupation increased after the war, newspapers and

**Powell Doctrine**

A set of criteria guiding military engagement, including establishing clear goals and using overwhelming force.

leaders alike raised the question of whether the United States was again getting into a Vietnam-like "quagmire."

A more recent example concerns the disastrous "Blackhawk down" incident, in which a helicopter carrying U.S. special forces was shot down in Somalia in 1993, killing eighteen soldiers and causing the United States to retreat from its mission there. In 2009, the U.S. government identified an important Al Qaeda suspect in Somalia and, as in the case of Osama bin Laden, needed to decide whether to kill him with a missile attack, risking bystander deaths and foregoing intelligence, or send in special forces to apprehend him. In the key meeting to choose a strategy, a State Department official referred back to the 1993 incident: "Somalia, helicopters, capture. I just don't like the sound of this." A later analysis argued that although the policy worked (the suspect was killed by a missile strike), the analogy with the earlier Somalia case was highly misleading.[28]

*Generational Change*  Working from the lessons of history does not always or necessarily lead to bad decisions. Indeed, almost everyone would agree that being informed by history is essential to good decision making in foreign policy. Research has shown, however, that decision makers are very uneven in their use of history. Most individuals view current problems in light of only a few historical events and are unable to conduct a broad, open-minded search for the historical lessons that apply best to any particular circumstance. Thus, Munich and Vietnam come up over and over again.

One possible result of the simplistic use of history is that there may be generational change in foreign policy attitudes. When an entire generation is seared by a particularly traumatic or triumphant foreign policy experience, such as a war, there is some tendency for people whose political attitudes were formed at that time to see future problems in light of that formative experience. That does not mean that everyone in the same generation will see the same thing. In the United States, for example, many people of a certain age tend to look at current events in light of the Vietnam experience that shook a generation, but now, as then, there are deep and bitter divisions over the lessons of that experience. Some view that conflict as a mistake from the beginning, which was halted through the commitment of domestic protestors. Others regard it as an honorable war that was abandoned because of the treachery of domestic protestors. As that war recedes, so will its central role in how we view foreign policy. In 2011, Susan Rice, United States Ambassador to the United Nations, said that the Obama administration's foreign policy team has moved beyond Vietnam: "We just don't have that Vietnam hangover. It is not the framework for every decision—or any decision. I'm sick and tired of reprising all the battles and dramas of the 1960s."[29] An earlier generation was influenced primarily by World War II, and an even earlier generation was influenced by World War I. Today's college students, with few exceptions, remember none of those conflicts but came of age during the wars in Afghanistan and Iraq that followed the terrorist attacks of 2001. It remains to be seen what lessons will be taken from those conflicts or if they will spawn as much disagreement as Vietnam has.

**prospect theory**

A theory that contends that how individuals weigh options is heavily influenced by whether a particular outcome is seen as a gain or a loss.

**Prospect Theory**  One of the more exciting developments in decision-making theory in recent years has been "prospect theory," for which Daniel Kahneman won the Nobel Prize in economics in 2002.[30] **Prospect theory** contends that how individuals weigh options is heavily influenced by how the choices are framed. To anyone who has seen politicians attempt to "spin" a discussion in their favor, this point may seem obvious. But prospect theory is more precise, is supported by experimental evidence, and leads to some very important generalizations that are relevant to international politics.[31]

Among prospect theory's most important findings is that individuals are much more willing to take risks to avoid a loss than to achieve a gain (see Figure 6.3). For example, research subjects are willing to take a greater risk to avoid the loss of a dollar than to gain a dollar. In terms of expected utility, there is no difference between losing a dollar and failing to win one, but prospect theory shows that psychologically the difference is significant and that it has a measurable impact on people's behavior.

In international politics, one important lesson is that leaders will take considerable risks to protect what they have (to avoid a perceived loss). In other words, there is a strong **status quo bias** in international affairs. Intuitively, this makes sense: We expect that the inhabitants of an invaded territory would fight harder to defend their land than the invaders would fight to conquer new territory. The U.S. experience in the Vietnam War or the Russian experience in invading Afghanistan in 1979 illustrate this phenomenon.

Prospect theory may help explain why smaller, weaker states sometimes refuse to bow to threats from larger, more powerful actors. If it is protecting something it believes already belongs to it, the small state may have a high sensitivity to loss and may therefore be willing to accept higher-than-normal risks of going to war. This tendency is something that decision makers could learn to take into account.[32]

For example, when the United States and its NATO allies sought to coerce Serbia into withdrawing from Kosovo in 1999, there seemed to be good reason to believe that the threat of force, or the application of moderate force, would be enough to do the job. Only a few years earlier, when the territories in question were Bosnia and Herzegovina, a limited bombing campaign was sufficient to induce concessions from Serbia. In the Kosovo case, however, an extensive and highly destructive bombing campaign was necessary. Why were the two cases different, and could the resistance in the Kosovo case have been predicted?

Prospect theory might help us understand why Serbia behaved differently in the two situations and might have helped anticipate the problems in Kosovo. Derek Chollett and James Goldgeier point out that whereas Bosnia and Herzegovina had not traditionally been controlled by Serbia, Kosovo had been controlled by Serbia for many years. It was predictable, these analysts therefore contend, that Serbian President Slobodan Milosevic would pay higher costs to avoid the loss of Kosovo than to achieve the gain of Bosnia.[33]

A particular problem arises when both sides perceive the status quo to be on their side. If both sides see giving in as a loss of an existing territory (or principle), both might be quite willing to accept risks to avoid the loss. This may be what occurred in 1914, when both Austria and Russia believed that the status of Serbia could not be maintained and that losing influence there would do substantial damage to their position. Austria saw Serbia's support of separatists within Austria as a threatening departure from the status quo, whereas Russia saw Austria's efforts to limit Serbian autonomy as an equally threatening departure. Because both sides feared a loss if they did not prevail, diplomacy, rather than war, was seen as especially risky. A similar danger presented itself in the Cuban Missile Crisis. From the U.S. perspective, a Cuba without nuclear weapons was

**FIGURE 6.3** According to standard rational choice theories, each increment of change in payoff is worth the same amount. If that were true, the line in the graph would be straight. Prospect theory finds that whether a change in payoff matters a lot or a little depends on whether one is on the "loss" or the "gain" side of the status quo. Note that the "gain" side is not a mirror image of the "loss" side: on the loss side, value goes down more steeply and further than on the gain side.

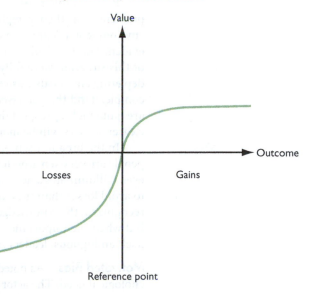

**Prospect Theory Value Function**

**status quo bias**

The tendency of leaders to take considerable risks to avoid a perceived loss.

the status quo, and any change from that was a loss. But with the missiles already partly installed, would the Soviet Union view this as a *new* status quo and be equally ready to take risks to defend it? Apparently not, or at least not so much that Khrushchev was willing to risk nuclear war.

Prospect theory applies to issues other than security concerns as well. In negotiations over trade liberalization, actors (not only states, but interest groups as well) often react much more negatively to the specific losses that some economic sectors might endure from a reduction in trade barriers than to the likely overall gains that occur from such agreements. Prospect theory finds that it is easier to agree on how to divide up gains than to agree on how to divide up losses.[34] Therefore, even states that can agree on how to distribute the benefits from a trade deal may find it much harder to agree on how to share the losses, because they are much more sensitive to the losses.

Prospect theory also has interesting implications for cooperation on environmental problems. The theory implies that once actors clearly perceive a tangible loss from further environmental degradation, they will take risks to avoid those losses. Thus, when scientific evidence on the depletion of the ozone layer became clear and the health consequences of this situation were fully understood, an international agreement on limiting ozone-depleting chemicals was reached fairly quickly. Although the issue of global warming is complex (and the perceived economic costs of limiting production of greenhouse gases are quite high), prospect theory implies that if the high costs of global warming become clearer, leaders will be more likely to take risks to avoid them.

In the broadest sense, prospect theory confirms something we already knew—that people are very sensitive to how a particular issue is "framed." In a narrower sense, however, it illuminates a new and useful principle: Leaders are likely to take much bigger risks to avoid losses than they are to achieve gains. When the importance of the status quo is recognized, this knowledge can induce caution in those who would revise the status quo. But when the importance of the status quo is not recognized or when the status quo is itself ambiguous, leaders can make important miscalculations.

**Motivated Bias**    As noted previously, motivated bias is bias that is driven by some psychological need. The actor subject to motivated bias tends to see what she or he *wants* to see. There is a range of potential sources of motivated bias, from personal insecurities that may result from childhood issues to the fear created by the prospect of war. The distinction between motivated and unmotivated bias is useful not just for categorizing psychological theories but also for thinking about how to reduce misperceptions.

**cognitive dissonance**

A theory that holds that individuals tend to construct internally consistent views of the world and that psychological discomfort, or "cognitive dissonance," results when some new piece of information does not fit with an individual's existing beliefs.

*Cognitive Dissonance*    Much early research on misperception among leaders focused on **cognitive dissonance** theory, which addresses a classic type of motivated bias.[35] The theory holds that individuals tend to construct internally consistent views of the world and that psychological discomfort results when some new piece of information does not fit with an individual's existing beliefs. This discomfort is known as *cognitive dissonance*. The theory holds that because cognitive dissonance is uncomfortable, new information that contradicts existing views will either be discredited or will be interpreted to confirm rather than challenge existing beliefs. (We often refer to this as "being in denial.") Similarly, new information that reaffirms existing beliefs tends to be more readily believed and more heavily emphasized than information that calls those beliefs into question. This argument has led to a great deal of research on "belief systems," based on the view that leaders have consistently structured beliefs and that if analysts understand these belief systems, they can understand and predict how the leaders will react to new information.

In international relations, cognitive dissonance seems to be especially prominent in antagonistic relationships, in which evidence that an adversary is making a concession is

# THE GEOGRAPHY CONNECTION

## MAPS AND THE FRAMING OF PROBLEMS

This chapter explores how perceptions of issues can influence decisions. Consider these maps of the Middle East conflict, which show boundaries at different points in time.

### Critical Thinking Questions

1. Which map might a Palestinian be likely to see as the "normal" situation that a peace

agreement should achieve? Which map might an Israeli see as "normal?"

2. Now consider these maps in light of prospect theory. Considering Palestinians' and Israelis' different perspectives on the "baseline" for assessing a division of territory, what difficulties arise for negotiators?

Palestinian and Israeli Land

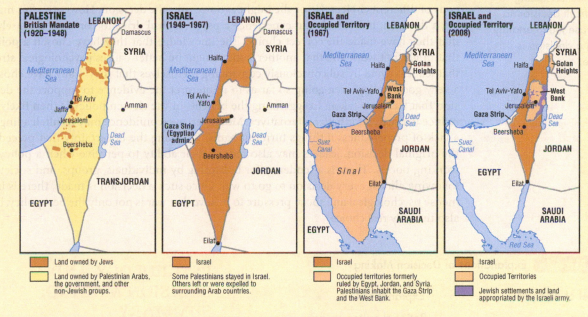

Source: http://www.lib.utexas.edu/maps/middle_east_and_asia/jewish_land_use.gif. Courtesy of the University Libraries, The University of Texas at Austin.

likely to be rejected and evidence of an unfriendly move is likely to be readily accepted. In the Cold War, both Soviet and U.S. leaders adopted views of each other that were wholly negative, and both sides therefore had a very difficult time perceiving when the other side had made a concession or perhaps become less belligerent.

Thus, when Mikhail Gorbachev initiated a much more conciliatory line in Soviet foreign policy in the late 1980s, many people in the United States warned that Gorbachev's goal was not really to improve relations with the United States but to lull the West into complacency in order to achieve a long-term Soviet victory. Evidence that the Soviet Union was changing from within and was seeking international stability did not fit with the views of many Americans that the Soviet Union was implacably hostile and could not change. As cognitive dissonance theory indicates, new evidence did not change the existing view; rather, it was reinterpreted to support it. Even after the opening of the Berlin Wall in 1989, which effectively ended communism in Eastern Europe, prominent American leaders cautioned against assuming that a fundamental change in Soviet foreign policy was under way.

Today, some people label leaders who reject the need for international collaboration on global warming as suffering from cognitive dissonance. These leaders, critics argue, find ways to dismiss increasingly compelling evidence of global warming while exaggerating the significance of data that cast doubt on the existence of the problem.

Cognitive dissonance theory is especially useful in explaining why foreign policies do not change in light of changed circumstances or new evidence. Because it only explains continuity, however, it is less useful at explaining how foreign policy changes. Nor does it explain where a particular belief system came from in the first place.

**bolstering**

The tendency of decision makers facing a difficult decision to increase their certainty once a decision is made.

*Bolstering*    A concept related to cognitive dissonance is **bolstering**, whereby decision makers facing a difficult decision tend to increase their certainty once a decision is made.[36] Before making a close call, a decision maker might keenly perceive the pros and cons of different choices. He or she might agonize over the decision. However, after making a decision, individuals can experience a psychological drive to convince themselves that they have made the correct choice. The knowledge that they have chosen a policy that might not work and that another policy might be better causes psychological stress that leaders avoid by subconsciously convincing themselves that they really have chosen a very good policy, even going so far as to reinterpret the evidence to support the decision that has been taken. Exaggerating the benefits of the chosen policy is then likely to reduce the search for better alternatives. Moreover, overconfidence may result, leading to a lack of preparedness if things turn out badly. By losing the uncertainty that preceded the original decision, leaders may also reduce their ability to perceive when a policy is working poorly. There is a tendency for bolstering by individuals, groups, and societies following almost every decision to go to war. Once such a decision is made, there is immense psychological and social pressure to believe that war is not only the best policy, but also the only real choice.

| TABLE 6.1    Explanations of Decision Making | |
| --- | --- |
| **Level of Analysis** | **Explanations** |
| State/system | Rational action model<br>Expected utility theory |
| Bureaucracies | Bureaucratic politics model<br>Organizational process model |
| Small groups | Groupthink |
| Individual: Unmotivated bias | Attribution theory<br>Bounded rationality (example: use of historical lessons and analogies)<br>Prospect theory |
| Individual: Motivated bias | Cognitive dissonance theory<br>Bolstering |

## PSYCHOLOGY AND DECISION MAKING: SUMMARY

The study of psychology has added immensely to our understanding of foreign policy decision making, as Table 6.1 illustrates. It has helped explain why foreign policy makers often seem to deviate from the standard tenets of rational decision making. However, although psychological theories can predict the results of laboratory experiments, they generally do not provide clear predictions in the real world of foreign policy, where it is impossible to

# THE CONNECTION TO YOU

## WHAT ARE YOUR BIASES?

Political leaders are not the only individuals subject to bias. We all are. In fact, much of the basic psychological research on bias and decision making was conducted on university students. Bias is not unique to foreign policy but is endemic in all decision making, whether as political participants or in everyday life.

Begin with something trivial. How do we choose the clothes we wear? Is this a "rational" process? To some extent it probably is—we are likely to put on a sweater or a coat in the winter, to wear cleats when we go to play soccer, and to put on something waterproof if it is raining. But to what extent do nonrational considerations play a role? For example, it often seems that there is some degree of groupthink in what people wear—we ask our friends what they are wearing, or we just look and copy.

Take a more momentous decision, such as where to go to college. Many young people experience immense stress over this decision. It is not hard to imagine some of the biases discussed in this chapter influencing the decision. For example, having friends or parents state early in the process that a particular college or type of college is inappropriate might cause one to exclude it without much thought (groupthink). We may visit a university that we have long admired, find it uninspiring, and feel confused afterward (cognitive dissonance). After agonizing between two possibilities, once we have chosen one, do we

then convince ourselves, and tell those around us, that this was clearly the best option (bolstering)?

What factors, then, shape our views on political issues? When we make a decision—to speak out for or against a policy, to vote for one candidate over another, or to contribute to an NGO—to what extent do we follow the dictates of rational decision making, weighing all the options and the expected utility of each before deciding? Do we conduct a thorough search for information, or do we rely on what we already know? Which historical examples or theories come most quickly to mind? Do we seek to go along with those around us, or are we willing to contradict the group? When we encounter contradictions between our deeply held views and new evidence, do we reject the new evidence or question our deeply held views? Do we advocate taking larger risks to defend the status quo than to change it?

### Critical Thinking Questions:

1. What political issues are most important to you and why? What events or circumstances in your own life may have contributed to your view of these issues?

2. What foreign policy events have been most salient to you? What enduring lessons have you learned?

3. If someone were to examine your views on foreign policy, what biases might they find?

control for a variety of other influences.[37] In particular, although all of the phenomena addressed here sometimes occur, we cannot predict when one kind of deviation from rationality rather than another will occur. None arises in a constant or predictable way.

Despite these limitations, psychology offers lessons for analysts as well as practitioners of foreign policy. For students and scholars, one lesson is that the rationality assumption cannot perfectly describe or explain what happens in the real world. For those who make foreign policy, a lesson is that they should not base their policies on the expectation that others will behave perfectly rationally. For example, if a policy maker's strategy for resolving a crisis depends on an adversary's ability to correctly perceive the message sent and to weigh costs and benefits in a rational way, then the policy maker had better come up with an alternative strategy. A second, perhaps equally important, lesson is that our *own* perceptions, understandings, and policy choices are not "rational" in any objective sense but rather are influenced by our experiences, our beliefs, and our personalities.

# ★ POWER, PURPOSE, AND DECISION MAKING BY BUREAUCRACIES, GROUPS, AND INDIVIDUALS

This chapter highlights how the substance of policy—including the purpose of policy—is influenced by the process by which policy is made. Substate actors such as ministries and different branches of the armed forces have their own goals, related to budget and mission, and their own sources of power to pursue those purposes. Bureaucratic struggles and organizational process can create unintended policies that diverge from shared notions of national purpose. Psychological insights on decision making further put into question the way that the purpose of policy is defined. Thus, the effort to explain all policies as reflections of clearly defined rational purposes is sometimes misleading.

## RECONSIDER THE CASE

### KILLING OSAMA BIN LADEN

In retrospect, the Obama administration's ability to maintain secrecy throughout the planning process was one of the most remarkable aspects of this case. The discussion remained secret for more than six months in an era in which leaks of allegedly "top secret" affairs are routine. During this time, the website WikiLeaks published a huge trove of classified U.S. government documents, many relating to efforts to combat Al Qaeda. This secrecy was crucial to the operation's success, but it was not without negative effects.

The government of Pakistan was outraged at the violation of its sovereignty. It was embarrassed that bin Laden was living peacefully in one of its cities, that the United States did not trust Pakistan enough to share intelligence on the matter, and that U.S. forces were

able to fly undetected deep into Pakistan and carry out the raid without Pakistani forces being aware. The damage to the already shaky U.S.-Pakistan relationship was enormous. Graham Allison suggested that some of this damage could have been avoided had some key U.S. leaders not been excluded from the initial planning because of secrecy. He argued that Joint Chiefs of Staff Chairman Mike Mullen and Defense Secretary Robert Gates might have been able to develop a plan to make the raid less humiliating to Pakistan.*

*Graham Allison, "How It Went Down," Time, May 7, 2012, pp. 34–41.

*(Continued)*

Following the raid, however, there was little secrecy. Much publicity was given to the supposedly top secret SEAL Team Six, and government officials leaked extensive details of the operation to reporters. The revelation that a bogus vaccination program had been used to collect DNA from those in the compound enraged public health advocates around the world, who feared that important vaccination efforts would now be rejected as fronts for the CIA. A Pakistani doctor who helped run the vaccination program was arrested for treason and sentenced to a lengthy prison term, and several vaccination workers were later murdered.

It appears that the desire to bask in the glory of a successful operation, and to stress President Obama's role in the triumph, motivated many of the leaks of operational details. Critics of the Obama administration lambasted the extent of leaks from the administration. Opponents also charged that Obama should receive no special credit because the decision to initiate the raid was an easy one that any president would have made. This spurred additional revelations from within the administration to emphasize that Obama had made a tough choice that others would not have made. Leaving this intense politicization aside, the question of whether a different leader would have done the same thing is the crucial one for political scientists, because it focuses on a much bigger question about explaining international politics: Do individual leaders make a difference?

## Critical Thinking Questions

1. Which aspects of the decision to raid the Abbottabad compound would have been taken by any leader? Which decisions might someone else have taken differently?

2. What elements of group or individual psychology played a role in the decision to carry out the raid?

3. What aspects of the decision-making process used in this case were exemplary? What shortcomings were in evidence?

## SUMMARY

- The theories examined in previous chapters held that understanding the details of the internal workings of a government is not necessary to explain its decisions in the international arena. The approaches covered in this chapter contend that what goes on *inside* the government can have a great impact on what kinds of foreign policy come *out* of the government.

- Both courts and legislatures play an important role in foreign policy from time to time, but the executive branch makes and implements the vast majority of decisions.

- Analysis of foreign policy often examines deviations from an ideal rational action model.

- Bureaucratic agencies within a state may have conflicting interests and competing priorities. According to the bureaucratic politics model, foreign policy is the outcome of a battle within the bureaucracy. The organizational process model examines how standard operating procedures limit the policy options available.

- Groupthink may lead a group to arrive at a single solution without thoroughly considering the alternatives.

- Psychological research helps explain how individual political leaders can deviate from the rational action model. Some bias results from psychological need (motivated bias), but even people striving for objectivity experience bias (unmotivated bias).

- Bounded rationality posits that decision makers try to be rational but have inherent limits on their ability to exhaustively examine all possible policies.

- The use of historical analogies often introduces bias because individual decision makers have access to a very narrow range of historical experience.

- According to prospect theory, individuals are much more willing to take risks to avoid a loss than to achieve a gain.

## KEY CONCEPTS

1. Foreign policy analysis
2. Expected utility
3. Bureaucracy
4. Standard operating procedures
5. Groupthink
6. Motivated versus unmotivated bias
7. Bounded rationality
8. Prospect theory

## STUDY QUESTIONS

1. Which branch of government makes the vast majority of foreign policy decisions?
   a. The legislature
   b. The judiciary
   c. The executive branch
   d. All of the above.

2. What factors lead bureaucracies to disagree about the best policies?
   a. Conflicting roles and budgets
   b. Standard operating procedures
   c. Fundamental attribution bias
   d. Generational change

3. Which approach explains how rational decisions are made?
   a. Expected utility theory
   b. Bounded rationality theory
   c. Fundamental attribution bias
   d. Prospect theory

4. What approach best explains why a decision maker might incorrectly ascribe bad intentions to an act committed by a hostile state?
   a. Expected utility theory
   b. Bounded rationality theory
   c. Fundamental attribution bias
   d. Prospect theory

5. Which approach asserts that limited time and information may prevent individuals from arriving at the most rational decision?
   a. The rational choice model
   b. Bounded rationality theory
   c. Prospect theory
   d. Cognitive dissonance theory

6. Under what circumstances would two states be most likely to go to war according to prospect theory?
   a. When both states want to gain territory or influence
   b. When one state wants to gain territory and one state does not want to lose territory
   c. When one state wants to gain influence and one state does not want to lose influence
   d. When both states fear the loss of influence or territory

7. How does the expected utility approach explain foreign policy?

8. Why are bureaucracies necessary for policy making?

9. In what kinds of situations do standard operating procedures appear to be especially inappropriate?

10. What potential hazards arise in small group decision making?

11. What does prospect theory imply about foreign policy decision making?

12. What policies might improve the content of foreign policy by improving the process by which it is made?

[Correct answers: 1. c; 2. a; 3. a; 4. c; 5. b; 6. d]

## END NOTES

1. BBC, "Parliament 'War Powers' Must Be Law by 2015, Say MPs," December 6, 2011, www.bbc.co.uk/news/uk-politics-16050574.

2. Steven Philip Kramer, "French Foreign Policy: The Wager on Europe," in Ryan K. Beasley, Juliet Kaarbo, Jeffrey S. Lantis, and Michael T. Snarr, eds., *Foreign Policy in Comparative Perspective* (Washington, DC: Congressional Quarterly, 2002), p. 60.

3. See Juliet Kaarbo, "Power Politics in Foreign Policy: The Influence of Bureaucratic Minorities," *European Journal of International Relations*, Vol. 4 (March 1998): 67–97.

4. Graham T. Allison, "Conceptual Models and the Cuban Missile Crisis," *The American Political Science Review* 63, No. 3 (September 1969): 689–718.

5. Brian Ripley, "China: Defining Its Role in the Global Community," in Beasley et al., *Foreign Policy in Comparative Perspective*, p. 132.

6. Ripley, "China: Defining Its Role in the Global Community," p. 132.

7. Both of these examples are from Robert Jervis, *Perception and Misperception in International Politics* (Princeton, NJ: Princeton University Press, 1976), p. 26.

8. Rajiv Chandrasekaran, "'Little America': Infighting on Obama Team Squandered Chance for Peace in Afghanistan," *Washington Post*, June 24, 2012.

9. Andrés Rozental, "Fox's Foreign Policy Agenda: Global and Regional Priorities," in Luis Rubio and Susan Kaufman Purcell, eds., *Mexico under Fox* (Boulder, CO: Lynne Rienner Publishers, 2004), p. 105.

10. Stephen D. Krasner, "Are Democracies Important? (Or Allison Wonderland)," *Foreign Policy*. Vol. 7 (Summer 1972): 159–172.

11. See John D. Steinbrunner, *The Cybernetic Theory of Decision* (Princeton, NJ: Princeton University Press, 1974).

12. See, for example, Alexander L. George, *Presidential Decisionmaking in Foreign Policy: The Effective Use of Information and Advice* (Boulder, CO: Westview Press, 1980).

13. Irving L. Janis, *Groupthink: Psychological Studies of Policy Issues and Fiascoes* (Boston: Houghton Mifflin, 1982).

14. United States Senate, Select Committee on Intelligence, "Report on the U.S. Intelligence Community's Prewar Intelligence Assessments on Iraq," July 7, 2004, p. 28.

15. "Report on the U.S. Intelligence Community's Prewar Intelligence Assessments on Iraq," p. 35.

16. See Richard E. Nisbett and Lee Ross, *Human Inference: Strategies and Shortcomings in Social Judgment* (Englewood Cliffs, NJ: Prentice Hall, 1980).

17. Jervis, *Perception and Misperception in International Politics*, pp. 354–355.

18. Deborah Welch Larson, *Origins of Containment: A Psychological Approach* (Princeton, NJ: Princeton University Press, 1985), p. 38.

19. Larson, *Origins of Containment: A Psychological Approach*, p. 194.

20. Harry S. Truman, *Memoirs Volume 2: Years of Trial and Hope* (Garden City, NY: Doubleday, 1956), pp. 332–333.

21. See Yuen Foong Khong, *Analogies at War: Korea, Munich, Dien Bien Phu, and the Vietnam Decisions of 1965* (Princeton, NJ: Princeton University Press, 1982).

22. The two covers can be viewed at www.time.com/time/covers/0,16641,19450507,00.html (Hitler) and www.time.com/time/covers/0,16641,20030421,00.html (Saddam).

23. "Bush Compares Bin Laden to Hitler," British Broadcasting Company, September 5, 2006, news.bbc.co.uk/2/hi/americas/5318204.stm; Janadas Devan, "How Appeasement Became a Bad Word," *The Straits Times*, September 3, 2006. For a defense of the term "Islamic fascism," see Victor Davis Hanson, "It's Fascism—and It's Islamic," *Baltimore Sun*, September 8, 2006, A13.

24. Bush speech at the 2006 American Legion convention, reprinted in "The President's Speech," *New York Times*, August 31, 2006, www.nytimes.com/2006/08/31/washington/31text-bush.html.

25. CBS News, "Rumsfeld: World Faces New 'Fascism,'" August 30, 2006, at http://www.cbsnews.com/news/rumsfeld-world-faces-new-fascism/.

26. Simona Kralova, "Crimea Seen as 'Hitler-style' Land Grab," BBC News, March 7, 2014.

27. *The Guardian*, September 29, 1992, p. 7.

28. Daniel W. Drezner, "Analogical Reasoning Strikes Again," ForeignPolicy.com, drezner.foreignpolicy .com/posts/2012/02/21/analogical_reasoning_strikes_again.

29. James Mann, "How Obama's Foreign Policy Team Relates to the Vietnam War—or Doesn't," *Washington Post*, June 24, 2012.

30. The classic work in this field is Daniel Kahneman and Amos Tversky, "Prospect Theory: An Analysis of Decision Under Risk," *Econometrica*, Vol. 47 (1979): 263–291.

31. See Jack S. Levy, "An Introduction to Prospect Theory," *Political Psychology*, Vol. 13 (1992): 171–186; and Levy, "Prospect Theory, Rational Choice, and International Relations," *International Studies Quarterly*, Vol. 41, No. 1 (March 1997): 87–112.

32. See Jeffrey D. Berejikian, "A Cognitive Theory of Deterrence," *Journal of Peace Research*, Vol. 39 (2002): 165–183.

33. Derek H. Chollett and James M. Goldgeier, "The Scholarship of Decision Making: Do We Know How We Decide?" in Richard C. Snyder, H. W. Bruck, and Burton Sapin, with Valerie M. Hudson, Derek H. Chollett, and James M. Goldgeier, *Foreign Policy Decision-Making (Revisited)* (New York: Palgrave MacMillan, 2002), p. 160.

34. Levy, "Prospect Theory, Rational Choice, and International Relations," p. 93.

35. On cognitive bias in international affairs, see Jervis, *Perception and Misperception in International Politics*, Chapter 11 (pp. 382–408). The classic work in psychology on cognitive bias is Leon Festinger, *A Theory of Cognitive Dissonance* (Stanford, CA: Stanford University Press, 1957).

36. See Richard Ned Lebow, *Between Peace and War: The Nature of International Crisis* (Baltimore, MD: Johns Hopkins University Press, 1981), p. 110; and Irving L. Janis and Leon Mann, *Decisionmaking: A Psychological Study of Conflict, Choice, and Commitment* (New York: The Free Press, 1977), pp. 74–95.

37. These problems of "external validity" are summarized in Levy, "Prospect Theory, Rational Choice, and International Relations," pp. 98–100.

United Nations Peacekeepers in Goma, Congo, November 2008.
YASUYOSHI CHIBA/AFP/Getty Images

# INTERNATIONAL ORGANIZATIONS AND TRANSNATIONAL ACTORS

## Learning Objectives

**7-1** Define international governmental organization, international nongovernmental organization, transnational corporation, and transnational advocacy network.

**7-2** Understand the distinction between intergovernmentalism and supranationalism.

**7-3** Describe the structure of the United Nations and the functions of its various agencies, programs, funds, and commissions.

**7-4** Evaluate different arguments concerning the significance of the United Nations.

**7-5** Describe the structure of the European Union and the functions of its various branches and institutions.

**7-6** Analyze the challenges facing the European Union.

**7-7** Assess the influence of transnational corporations on governments.

**7-8** Identify the ways in which international nongovernmental organizations and transnational advocacy networks influence international politics.

## CONSIDER THE CASE

# INTERNATIONAL AND TRANSNATIONAL ACTORS IN LIBYA'S CIVIL WAR

In February 2011, the Libyan government arrested an outspoken critic in Benghazi, sparking protests. Motivated by long-simmering resentment at Muammar Gaddafi's government and spurred by the example of the Arab Spring in Tunisia and Egypt, the unrest spread across the country. The government sought to crush the protests violently, and when protest groups armed, the result was civil war. Human rights organization Amnesty International publicized the arrest globally and then provided detailed reporting throughout the crisis, providing much of the information on which international media and governments relied. Amnesty also reported cases in which rebel forces fabricated or exaggerated government atrocities.

The civil war sparked a humanitarian crisis. In late February, the International Committee of the Red Cross and its local affiliate, the Libyan Red Crescent, began providing food and supplies to people displaced by the fighting. As the crisis went on, the World Food Program, among others, joined in providing aid. Several governments provided ships to deliver aid, and Turkey provided a hospital ship to treat the injured. However, aid organizations were reluctant to accept military offers to facilitate humanitarian assistance, for fear of jeopardizing their neutrality. The International Organization for Migration was dealing with more than 30,000 people a day crossing from Libya into Tunisia and Egypt.*

Transnational advocacy networks such as the International Crisis Group and the Genocide Intervention Network provided additional information and advocated international action to stop the violence. Governments around the world hesitated to intervene. For some, the desire to see Gaddafi go was tempered by the fear that some rebels were linked to the transnational terrorist group Al Qaeda, a claim that opposition leaders denied. Others simply opposed interfering in Libya's domestic politics. Throughout the conflict, the African Union tried to negotiate a cessation of hostilities, but rebels rejected agreements that did not require Gaddafi to leave office, and Gaddafi violated cease-fires to which he had agreed.

On February 26, 2011, the UN Security Council passed a resolution that froze the assets of Gaddafi and his closest supporters and referred the case to the International Criminal Court, which subsequently issued an arrest warrant for Gaddafi. In March 2011, when Gaddafi was on the verge of capturing the rebel stronghold Benghazi, the Arab League urged the UN to establish a "no-fly" zone to prevent Gaddafi from using its superior air force against the opposition and civilians. On March 17, the Security Council voted to create a no-fly zone. Two days later, U.S., British, and French forces fired more than one hundred cruise missiles at Libyan targets, beginning an international military mission that included seventeen states and was led by the North Atlantic Treaty Organization (NATO).

As Gaddafi's government teetered, international oil companies vied to gain favorable positions to exploit Libya's considerable oil wealth. Britain's BP, France's Total, and Italy's ENI had been doing business in Libya before the uprising, and some people believed that their interests explained their governments' willingness to participate in overthrowing Gaddafi. Firms that did not have a foothold in Libya saw a possible chance to gain one if the economy opened up. On August 24, the Libyan capital Tripoli fell to rebel forces, though pro-Gaddafi forces held out for weeks longer in some regional towns.

International efforts to deal with the civil war in Libya raise important questions about who the key actors will be in the future. Individual nation-states (beyond Libya) played a limited role by themselves. Rather, states pursued their goals largely through international organizations such as the African Union, the UN, the Arab League, and the International Criminal Court. Moreover, states relied on international organizations and nongovernmental organizations (NGOs) to do things they could not do by themselves, while NGOs and transnational corporations pressured states and worked independently of them.

*"Libya: International Aid Groups Scrambling to Help Refugees from Libya," Los Angeles Times, February 25, 2011, latimesblogs. latimes.com/babylonbeyond/2011/02/libya-protests-13.html.

The case of Libya epitomizes both the hopes and the frustrations that international organizations (IOs) elicit. Many people express skepticism about the ability of individual states and traditional, established international institutions, such as the UN and the World Bank, to solve difficult international crises. Where these older institutions are failing, regional IOs and new international NGOs are intervening to provide solutions.

This trend raises several important questions. In what ways can international governmental organizations (IGOs) solve problems that states, or temporary alliances between states, cannot? What is the function and future of transnational NGOs? How are these organizations infringing on state sovereignty, and is their rise an indication of the end of the Westphalian system? This chapter addresses these questions by examining the structure and function of the UN, the EU, and other IGOs, and by exploring the rise of NGOs and other transnational actors and their impact on the state.

# TYPES OF INTERNATIONAL ORGANIZATIONS

**International governmental organizations (IGOs)** are generally defined as organizations whose membership consists of three or more nation-states.[1] In such organizations, representatives of states gather to discuss issues that are of mutual interest to the member states. IGOs are also generally defined as having permanent secretariats or bureaucracies (so the UN and World Trade Organization [WTO] are IGOs, but the G-7 is not). Today, there are thousands of IGOs (see Table 7.1). Some, like the UN, have universal or nearly universal membership, meaning that every state is a member. Others have some subset of states as members, based on either a particular interest or a particular region. The Association of Southeast Asian Nations (ASEAN), as its name implies, consists of member states located in Southeast Asia and concerns itself with regional issues. The Organization of Petroleum Exporting Countries (OPEC) has members around the world and is concerned with promoting the interests of oil exporters. Some IGOs are more obscure and are concerned with more mundane issues. The mission of the International Postal Union, for example, is to coordinate the delivery of mail across state borders. All of these organizations, however, share a common characteristic: They are formed by states and have states, rather than individual citizens, firms, or other actors, as their members.

Transnational actors, in contrast, are organizations that work across national boundaries but whose members are not states. These, too, are proliferating today. One of the most prevalent categories of transnational actors is **transnational corporations (TNCs)**—corporations that have operations in more than one country (also known as multinational corporations, or MNCs). A second broad category of transnational actors is transnational **nongovernmental organizations (NGOs)**. NGOs are so diverse that characterizing them simply is difficult. The category includes groups, such as Greenpeace, which are similar to domestic interest groups but have concerns and organizational structures that are transnational in scope. It also includes groups that focus not on influencing governments but on conducting activities in different countries. Examples include many humanitarian organizations, such as the International Committee of the Red Cross, prodemocracy groups such as the International Renaissance Foundation, and health care providers such as the International Planned Parenthood Federation. Most large organized churches conduct activities in many

**International governmental organizations (IGOs)**

Organizations whose membership consists of three or more nation-states.

**transnational corporations (TNCs)**

Corporations with operations in more than one country; also called multinational corporations (MNCs).

**nongovernmental organizations (NGOs)**

A broad category of diverse organizations, including groups similar to domestic interest groups but with transnational concerns and organizational structures, and groups that focus not on influencing governments but on conducting activities in different countries.

**TABLE 7.1** Types and Examples of International Organizations[2]

| International Governmental Organizations (IGOs) | | |
|---|---|---|
| Global IGOs | Security | UN Security Council |
| | Trade | World Trade Organization |
| | Finance | International Monetary Fund<br>Bank for International Settlements |
| | Development | World Bank<br>UN Conference on Trade and Development |
| | Human rights | UN High Commission for Refugees |
| | Humanitarian aid | UN Relief and Works Agency |
| | Environment | UN Environment Program |
| Regional IGOs | Security | North Atlantic Treaty Organization<br>African Union |
| | Trade | Economic Community of West African States (ECOWAS)<br>Association of Southeast Asian Nations (ASEAN) |
| | Finance | European Central Bank |
| | Development | Asian Development Bank<br>African Development Bank |
| | Human rights/Humanitarian aid | European Human Rights Commission |
| | Environment | International Commission for Protection of the Danube River<br>Mediterranean Commission for Sustainable Development |
| Transnational Actors | | |
| TNCs | | Coca-Cola, Mitsubishi, Royal Dutch Shell, Novartis, many others |
| INGOs | Security | International Committee of the Red Cross<br>Campaign to Ban Landmines |
| | Trade | International Trade Union Confederation<br>Global Exchange |
| | Finance | Jubilee Debt Campaign |
| | Development | OxFam<br>Save the Children |
| | Human rights | Human Rights Watch |
| | Humanitarian aid | Amnesty International<br>Médecins Sans Frontières |
| | Environment | Greenpeace World<br>Wildlife Fund |

countries and can also be thought of as transnational actors. The key characteristic of all these organizations is that their members may be individuals or national-level organizations but are not states.

# WHY FORM INTERNATIONAL ORGANIZATIONS?

Why do states form IGOs, and why do they work through them? Liberal institutionalism provides the standard explanation: States form IGOs because it is in their interest to do so. Some problems can be solved more easily and less expensively with IGOs than without them. In particular, liberal institutionalism focuses on collective action problems (prisoners' dilemmas), such as the security dilemma, the temptation to enact competitive tariffs, and the difficulty in agreeing to protect the environment.

In liberal theory, international organizations address three crucial problems for states trying to solve collective action problems: transaction costs, information, and monitoring.[3] *Transaction costs* refer to the efforts needed to negotiate and organize collaboration. By providing forums for negotiation, frameworks for agreement, and bureaucratic capacity to help implement agreements, international organizations make it easier and less costly for states to cooperate. *Information* refers to data that international organizations can collect and provide to states to create fruitful bases for negotiations. Having each state collect its own data is wasteful and leads to competing claims. *Monitoring* refers to the need to ensure that other states are fulfilling their obligations. International organizations can do this more cheaply and with greater neutrality than can the parties to agreements.

For example, the WTO reduces transaction costs by providing an ongoing procedure for more than one hundred countries to coordinate their tariffs. The Intergovernmental Panel on Climate Change collects data and conducts scientific analysis to provide an unbiased assessment of global climate change. The International Atomic Energy Agency (IAEA) monitors the nuclear programs of member states to assure everyone that other members are not cheating on the agreement. Some of these tasks might be vastly more complicated and expensive to implement without the mechanism of IGOs. Others would be impossible. For example, without the reliable information on various countries' nuclear programs provided by the IAEA, the security dilemma, combined with uncertainty about other countries' programs, would likely compel far more countries to pursue nuclear weapons.

IGOs are sometimes created not to solve specific collective action problems but to provide a forum for discussion (reducing transaction costs). This is the primary function of the UN General Assembly. It has no predetermined agenda, but it provides a forum in which states can discuss and debate issues that arise. The UN Security Council has a narrower agenda but is also primarily a forum. Similarly, one primary goal of the WTO is simply to organize meetings at which states negotiate to solve trade problems.

There are thousands of IOs less prominent than the UN, each playing some role in linking governmental decision making in one particular area. There remains considerable disagreement about the significance of states' growing reliance on IOs. To some, the result is an increasingly important web of "global governance." The word *governance*, rather than *government*, emphasizes that norms are being established and affairs regulated in the absence of an overarching government. A single government need not be established to achieve global governance.

**Intergovernmentalism**

Making international decisions by negotiation and agreement between state representatives.

**supranationalism**

Delegating international decisions to an international organization.

It is useful to distinguish between two different principles of international organization, intergovernmentalism and supranationalism. **Intergovernmentalism** refers to a process through which decisions are reached directly between the representatives of governments. In **supranationalism**, governments delegate decision making to the international organization, and the people making the decision are, at least in principle, acting for the benefit of the group, not of one individual member. The difference is evident in the composition of two components of the European Union. The Council of the European Union is based on intergovernmentalism: Members of the council are appointed by their governments, take instructions from them, and represent their interests, even as they try to solve joint problems. The European Commission is based on supranationalism: Its members are pledged to working for the benefit of the EU, not any particular member. Traditionally, international organizations have been based on the principle of intergovernmentalism, but as IOs deal with increasingly complex matters, supranationalism has increased.

The European Union, in particular, has seen a significant shift toward supranationalism. To determine which issues should be dealt with at the EU level and which should be left to the member states, the EU has developed the principle of *subsidiarity*: Any issue that can be dealt with adequately at the national level should be left to that level. Only issues that require an EU-wide policy should be dealt with at the EU level.

In the years following World War II, many IOs were formed, including the UN (1945) and the EU (originally formed as the European Coal and Steel Community [ECSC] in 1951). The UN was born fully formed with a wide range of institutions, and many had great hopes that it would foster peace and economic development. In contrast, the ECSC was formed around a relatively narrow issue and had a similarly limited institutional apparatus. The UN, in the eyes of many, has failed to fulfill the high hopes of 1945, whereas the EU has achieved broader and deeper collaboration than anyone thought possible. Although the UN has sometimes struggled to limit conflict, the EU has helped to make war among European states seem inconceivable after centuries in which it was considered normal. And whereas the importance of the UN is often questioned, the EU has come to be seen as the standard for a regional IGO. A discussion of these two IGOs, therefore, reveals the potential and the limitations of IGOs.

# THE UNITED NATIONS SYSTEM

The UN was formed after World War II to provide a means by which the great powers of the day could join forces to promote peace and development. It is the most visible IGO and the one with the broadest scope. Its membership is universal. Indeed, membership in the UN is generally seen as the main criterion by which a state can be said to be a recognized sovereign state in the modern system. The UN General Assembly has a mandate that allows it to address nearly any area of international relations, and its vast array of specialized organizations addresses a great number of issues, as Figure 7.1 indicates.

The UN is important symbolically because it is the nearest thing there is to a body that represents the international community. Some people see the UN as the hope of mankind, as providing a way to solve global problems effectively and without force. Others see it as a potential threat to national sovereignty and as interfering with states' domestic matters. Most, however, recognize that the UN is unlikely to play either of these roles. States are too jealous of their sovereignty, and too diverse in their interests,

**FIGURE 7.1** The Principal organs of the United Nations system.

## Security Council

Peacekeeping Operations
UN Peace-Building Commission
Counter-Terrorism Committee
International Atomic Energy Agency

## General Assembly

### Subsidiary Bodies

Main Committees
Standing Committees
Human Rights Council

### Programs and Funds

UNCTAD (UN Conference on Trade and Development)
UNDCP (UN Drug Control Program)
UNEP (UN Environmental Program)
UNDP (UN Development Program)
UNIFEM (UN Development Fund for Women)
UNICEF (UN Children's Fund)
UNFPA (UN Population Fund)
UNHCR (UN High Commissioner for Refugees)

## Economic and Social Council

### Specialized Agencies

ILO (International Labor Organization)
FAO (Food and Agricultural Organization)
UNESCO (UN Education, Cultural, and Scientific Organization)
WHO (World Health Organization)
World Bank (WB)
IMF (International Monetary Fund)
ICAO (International Civil Aviation Organization)
IMO (International Maritime Organization)
ITU (International Telecommunication Union)
IPU (International Postal Union)

### Functional Commissions

Narcotic Drugs
Crime Prevention and Criminal Justice
Science and Technology for Development
Sustainable Development
Status of Women
Population and Development
Statistical Commission

### Regional Commissions

Africa
Europe
Latin American and the Caribbean
Asia and the Pacific
Western Asia

## International Court of Justice

## Secretariat

### Departments and Offices

Office of the Secretary-General
Office of Internal Oversight Services
Office of Legal Affairs
Department of Political Affairs
Department of Peacekeeping Operations
Office for the Coordination of Humanitarian Affairs
Office of the High Commissioner for Human Rights
Department for General Assembly and Conference Management
Department of Public Information
Department of Management

to allow the UN to become a dominating global government, either for good or for ill. It does, however, play some very important roles in world politics.

## PURPOSES AND PRINCIPLES OF THE UN

The UN Charter embodied a set of principles (purposes) and created a set of institutions, and both were controversial. In terms of principles, the goal of effective international action competed with the goal of preserving state sovereignty. Nearly every state insisted that no statement in the UN Charter could be interpreted as undermining or taking priority over the individual states. Thus, Article 2 of the UN Charter states, "The Organization is based on the principle of the sovereign equality of all its Members." As international security problems have increasingly emerged from instability within states rather than conflict between them, the tension between promoting international security and respecting state sovereignty has increased.

A second area of tension, both in principle and in terms of the UN organization, was the relative rights of large and small states. U.S. President Franklin Roosevelt, who played a major role in setting up the UN, recognized that the organization would never work if the "great powers" could be outvoted by the small ones, so five countries deemed to be **great powers** (Britain, China, France, the Soviet Union, and the United States) were given permanent seats on the Security Council and the right to veto any Security Council measure. Giving these states special status contradicted the principle of sovereign equality. In some measure, this arrangement was compensated for by the **one state, one vote** voting scheme in the General Assembly, where the smallest state has the same rights as the most powerful.

## ORGANIZATION OF THE UN

**The General Assembly**   Today, the UN General Assembly has 193 members, from the largest states in the world to microstates like Nauru. In the General Assembly, all states, regardless of size, have equal rights, and each has a single vote. Superficially, the UN General Assembly looks like a legislature in that representatives from the states of the world gather to debate and pass resolutions on the issues of the day. However, the main purpose of the General Assembly is not to pass laws but to provide a forum for debate on global issues and to express, when possible, international consensus.

The General Assembly differs fundamentally from national-level legislatures in two significant ways. First, although the General Assembly has the right to consider almost any issue it chooses, its resolutions are not considered law and therefore no state is compelled to comply. The UN Charter gives the General Assembly the power to "discuss any questions or any matters within the scope of the present charter," but the General Assembly's only clear power is over the UN budget.[4] In part, the power of the General Assembly was limited out of respect for the doctrine of sovereignty. It was also limited in response to the interests of the most powerful states, which refuse to be bound by an organization they do not control.

Second, the budget authority ("power of the purse") that makes domestic legislatures so powerful is not available to the General Assembly. The UN budget is small (the regular budget was just over $5 billion in 2012) because it depends on dues payments from members, who are unwilling to make large payments. During the 1980s, the ability of the UN to carry out its basic tasks was hampered when the United States, the largest contributor

**great powers**

The UN Charter ascribed this status to Britain, China, France, the Soviet Union (Russia), and the United States.

**one state, one vote**

A voting system in which each state has one vote, regardless of its size, population, or other characteristics. Used in the UN General Assembly and many other international organizations.

to the budget, withheld payments because it had various complaints. Today, more than 80 percent of UN members fail to pay their dues in full and on time.[5]

This does not mean, however, that the General Assembly is irrelevant. On the contrary, it is quite important as an arena in which issues are debated and discussed, and its resolutions, although not binding in a legal sense, have a great deal of influence in terms of agenda setting—in expressing the shared purpose of the international community. The General Assembly has the ability to put issues at the top of the international agenda. By defining certain standards for dealing with problems, the General Assembly often shapes subsequent agreements that are reached within other organizations. The Millennium Development Goals discussed in Chapter 12 are a case in point. When some group sits down to work out international standards on some problem, an existing General Assembly resolution setting out a standard is likely to have a significant influence because symbolically, if not legally, the General Assembly is seen as expressing world opinion.

**The Secretariat**  The various UN agencies are supported by a Secretariat with roughly 8900 employees, which performs organizational, budgetary, translation, research, and other support services and administers decisions. Unlike delegates to the General Assembly and the Security Council, personnel of the Secretariat are employed by the UN, not by their home governments, and they take an oath not to take instructions from their home governments. Nonetheless, governments engage in considerable political maneuvering to have their candidates chosen for particular posts. The Secretariat has been a target in recent years of accusations of inefficiency and even corruption.

The UN Secretariat is headed by a **secretary-general**. The power of the secretary-general stems less from his or her role as head of the UN bureaucracy than from his or her role as the personification of the UN. To the extent that any individual can presume to speak for the international community, it is the UN secretary-general. The position of secretary-general thus carries immense prestige. UN secretaries-general have, over the years, played an important role in mediating conflicts as well as in promoting new

**secretary-general**
The head of the UN bureaucracy and the personification and public face of the UN.

Ellen Johnson Sirleaf of Liberia accepting the Nobel Peace Prize in part for her support of women's participation in peace-building work. What role do international actors and non-state actors play in conflict resolution?

norms and publicizing neglected problems. Since its founding, the UN has had eight secretaries-general:

- Trygve Lie (Norway), 1946–1952
- Dag Hammarskjöld (Sweden), 1953–1961
- U Thant (Burma), 1961–1971
- Kurt Waldheim (Austria), 1972–1981
- Javier Pérez de Cuéllar (Peru), 1982–1991
- Boutros Boutros-Ghali (Egypt), 1992–1996
- Kofi Annan (Ghana), 1997–2006
- Ban Ki-moon (South Korea), 2007–present

**Security Council**

The fifteen-member council within the UN in charge of dealing with threats to international security.

**The Security Council** In questions of war and peace, the **Security Council** is the most important component of the UN, but it has rarely been able to fulfill the hope placed in it. According to Article 24 of the Charter, the members of the UN "confer on the Security Council primary responsibility for the maintenance of international peace and security, and agree that in carrying out its duties under this responsibility the Security Council acts on their behalf." The Security Council has fifteen members, including the "permanent five" with veto powers. The ten nonpermanent members are elected to two-year terms by the General Assembly. The council is chaired by a president; the presidency rotates among the members, in alphabetical order, from month to month. The Security Council's purpose is to help to avoid conflict in the international arena by performing deterrent, peacekeeping, and negotiating functions.

*Deterring and Countering Aggression* The UN Charter provides two statements on the use of force that are in constant tension with each other. Article 2 provides that "all members shall refrain in their international relations from the threat or use of force against the territorial integrity or political independence of any state, or in any other manner inconsistent with the purposes of the United Nations." Article 51, however, states that "nothing in the present Charter shall impair the inherent right of individual or collective self-defense if an armed attack occurs against a member of the United Nations, until the Security Council has taken measures necessary to maintain international peace and security." This exception for self-defense is routinely invoked by those using force to justify their actions. For example, when the United States attacked Iraq in 2003, the U.S. government invoked the right of self-defense as a legal basis for the attack. Many have since argued that because Iraq had not actually attacked the United States there was no legal basis to claim self-defense.

The deterrent function of the Security Council is based on the model of collective security established in the League of Nations. The idea is that all states agree to join forces against any state that commits an act of aggression. Presumably, any state would be deterred from using force if it could expect retaliation by all or most other states. If this deterrent is credible, collective force should rarely have to be used. In practice, collective security has rarely worked as envisioned.

There are three barriers to the simple application of UN-sponsored force to retaliate against aggression. First, it is rarely very clear which state in a conflict is the aggressor. In many cases, all states involved can plausibly claim that they were responding to another's aggression (thus justifying their use of force). Second, states will rarely condemn their friends and allies or come to the aid of their rivals. Third, even when all agree on what the problem is and what ought to be done, states are often unwilling to commit their forces to action in a conflict that might be of only limited interest to them. In every country, there are often strong domestic constituencies opposed to war, especially when the issue at stake does not appear to be a vital interest.

*Peacekeeping*  One of the most important contributions made by the UN over the years has been in peacekeeping, which is discussed in detail in Chapter 8. Peacekeeping helps solve the security dilemmas that can prevent warring parties from agreeing to stop fighting even when they want to stop. More recently, "second-generation" peacekeeping has given UN forces a more active role, including providing humanitarian relief, protecting civilians, and running elections.

The UN has sponsored many peacekeeping missions around the world. Some of these have been relatively brief; others (see Table 8.2 [Chapter 8] and "The Geography Connection: UN Peacekeeping Missions") are now more than fifty years old. Although the long durations of these deployments indicate that peacekeepers are not solving the underlying conflicts, they also show that peacekeepers are still needed to prevent conflict (and are succeeding). Most recent deployments have been responses not to conflict between countries, which was the trend through the 1980s, but to civil wars within collapsing states.

Peacekeeping forces are lightly armed, and therefore, they cannot repel a determined effort to break the peace. These Dutch peacekeepers were captured and held hostage by Serb forces in Bosnia in 1995.

In some cases, UN peacekeepers have been seen as ineffective or worse. In the former Yugoslavia, UN forces were lightly armed and had very constraining rules of engagement, but they were put in a situation in which they might be confronted by a large and well-armed hostile force. In several key cases, peacekeepers had to stand aside as Serbian forces with superior capability did exactly what the peacekeepers were supposed to prevent, invading "safe zones" for refugees. By providing a false sense of security, the peacekeepers may have done more harm than good. In 2012, the UN sent 300 observers to Syria to monitor the civil war there. They were not intended to fight or to stop others from fighting, and when violence continued unabated, they were withdrawn to protect their safety.

However, the fact that UN peacekeeping efforts sometimes fail does not indicate that peacekeeping is not an important tool. Peacekeeping cannot succeed when states or groups are determined to go to war. Rather, it succeeds when states or groups hope to avoid conflict but might be afraid that others will take advantage of them.

Even when states are willing to contribute forces to peacekeeping missions, the question remains of how to pay for them. When a mission is sponsored by the UN, it would seem reasonable that the cost should come out of the UN budget. However, states have resisted the formation of a separate UN peacekeeping budget that would require an ongoing contribution from each country. Therefore, UN peacekeeping operations are almost always underfunded. The countries that provide the troops (which are usually smaller states perceived as neutral, rather than the permanent Security Council members) often have to provide a disproportionate share of the funding as well, decreasing the willingness of countries to participate.

**The Specialized Agencies**  When it was founded in 1945, the UN included an **Economic and Social Council (ECOSOC)** to oversee work on development and related issues. Today, this council has been supplemented by a wide array of related programs, funds,

**Economic and Social Council (ECOSOC)**

The UN council that oversees work on economic and social issues.

# THE GEOGRAPHY CONNECTION

## UN PEACEKEEPING MISSIONS

Examine the distribution of UN peacekeeping missions in this map, noting the dates.

### Critical Thinking Questions

1. What patterns do you notice in the location of the missions? How has the pattern shifted over time?

2. What might explain the geographic distribution of missions? Why do conflicts in some areas receive peacekeeping missions, whereas those in other areas do not?

Un Peacekeeping Missions

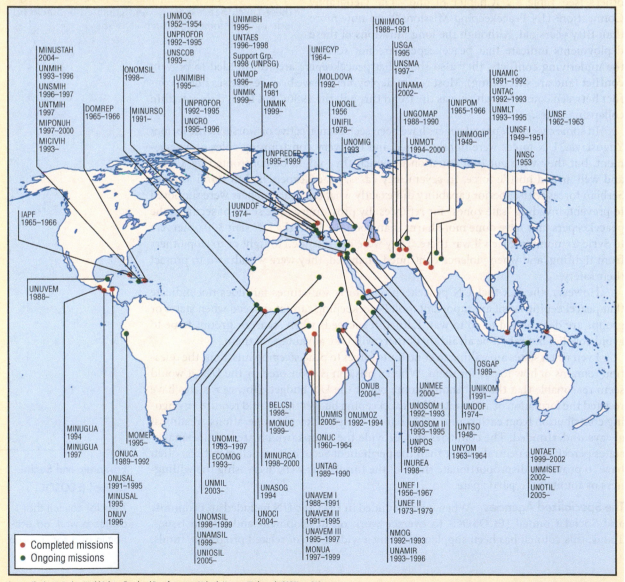

Source: Charles W. Kegley, *World Politics: Trend and Transformation*, 11th ed. (Boston: Wadsworth, 2007), p. 560.

commissions, and specialized agencies. Some of these are well known, such as UNICEF (the United Nations Children's Fund[6]); the IAEA, charged with monitoring compliance with the Nuclear Non-Proliferation Treaty; the World Bank Group, which plays a central role in economic development (see Chapter 12); and the WHO, which coordinates policies on disease prevention. Other agencies are more obscure, such as the World Meteorological Organization and the UN Statistical Commission. UN organizations are essential to international collaboration on some matters of great importance to the states of the world. In some respects, it is the work of the specialized agencies, rather than the General Assembly or the Security Council, that has concrete daily effects around the world.

**The International Court of Justice**    The International Court of Justice (ICJ), also known as the World Court, adjudicates disputes that arise over treaty obligations. Many treaties stipulate that if there is disagreement over the terms of the treaty or over what constitutes a violation, the dispute will be resolved by the ICJ. More generally, the ICJ is also acknowledged as the authority on what the body of international law says and how it should be interpreted. This agency is discussed in more detail in Chapter 13.

**International Court of Justice (ICJ)**

Also known as the World Court, the body that adjudicates disputes that arise over treaty obligations.

## FOUR VIEWS OF THE UN

There are many different ways of evaluating the role of the UN. These depend in large part on which purposes of the organization are singled out, what measures are applied, and especially, which theoretical perspective is adopted. This section summarizes four views.

**The UN as World Government**    The notion of the UN as an embryonic world government provokes two opposite reactions. Some place great hope in the idea that the UN may become a genuine world government because they believe that only through world government can fundamental issues of security and prosperity be resolved. At the theoretical level, this view follows the realist analysis that derives international insecurity from international anarchy. Optimists see the UN as potentially ending anarchy by becoming a single, democratic, global sovereign. Few people involved with the UN take the idea of the UN as a world government seriously; rather, they focus on much more limited roles.

Others fear the idea that the UN might be a nascent world government. Those who put a premium on state sovereignty are concerned that a stronger UN might undermine local sovereignty and democracy. An even more anxious view sees the UN as a potentially totalitarian world government, eroding individual freedom everywhere. The *Left Behind* series of novels, immensely popular for a time in the United States, portrayed the anti-Christ as coming from the United Nations.

**The UN as Irrelevant**    In contrast to those who hope or fear that the UN will form a genuine world government, many see the UN as essentially irrelevant to international politics. The UN has little legal or military power to compel other actors. It does not even have enough financial resources to substantially influence most actors. In those rare cases when the great powers do agree, skeptics point out, they do not need the UN to help them coerce smaller states. Some of those who see the UN as irrelevant see this irrelevance as a good thing; others see it as unfortunate.

**The UN as a Tool for States**    According to liberal institutionalism, the UN is neither good nor bad in itself; nor does it have any commanding authority over states. Rather, the UN is a tool that states can use, when they want to, to achieve various goals. When states seek to collaborate, the UN provides an organization that facilitates such collaboration. When states disagree, as they often do, these disagreements can be voiced in the UN.

In some cases, states may use the UN to help resolve disagreements and facilitate collaboration. In others, they may use the UN as an arena in which they can compete against their opponents.

**The UN as a Source of Norms**   From the perspective of constructivism, the United Nations and its related organizations have a powerful role, because much of their work focuses on defining internationally shared understandings of various problems. This view of the UN was advanced by Secretary-General Ban Ki-moon in 2007: "Despite its universal outreach, the United Nations cannot be in all places, nor provide a solution to every challenge. But we can, and should, serve as a forum to set a global agenda and consensus."[7] By adopting one view on an issue, such as indigenous people's rights, ways of measuring poverty, or ideal standards for air quality, UN agencies legitimize that position. This is not power in the coercive sense on which realism focuses, but rather in the sense of soft power on which constructivists and some liberals focus. The prestige of the UN means that positions agreed upon there inherently carry weight around the world.

# THE EUROPEAN UNION

The UN is significant because it claims a broader mandate than any other IGO and claims to speak for the "community of states." The EU is significant for the *depth* of its integration. It has extended cooperation further than any other IGO, such that the boundary between international and domestic authority is now blurred. The EU appears to be achieving on a regional scale what some dream of on the global scale: a supranational level of government that, at least in some spheres, authoritatively governs relations between states. The defining attributes of the nation-state, such as a single foreign policy and military force, have been elusive, but in many economic areas the EU functions like a single state.

## HISTORICAL EVOLUTION OF THE EU

**The ECSC and the Treaty of Rome**   The EU originated in the European Coal and Steel Community (ECSC), which was formed in 1951 to coordinate the national markets for coal and steel in Europe in the aftermath of World War II. The economic purpose of the ECSC was to manage these key industries to promote industrial recovery from the war. The political purpose was to promote peace by binding the countries together in the economic sectors that were central to preparing for war. Those two motivations continue to be relevant today. European integration has provided substantial economic benefits as a result of decreased barriers to trade and a larger market and has helped bind together politically countries that had been almost constantly at war with each other in previous centuries.

Two of the early advocates of the EU, Robert Schumann of Germany and Jean Monnet of France, were instrumental in establishing a wide-ranging vision of European integration, declaring the goal of building an "ever-closer union." They recognized that this union could not be established in a single step. Instead, the strategy was to do as much as was politically feasible at any given time and to assume that each step would validate collaboration and lead to demands for further steps, in a self-reinforcing process. This process, known as **spillover**, has indeed characterized the development of the EU since the 1950s. Even those who were skeptical about more idealistic notions of a "United States of Europe" were often willing to support small, incremental increases in integration for their concrete political and economic benefits. Spillover was vividly illustrated in 2012, when many argued that the only way out of the debt crises plaguing several members of

**spillover**

A process by which small, incremental steps toward cooperation create the impetus for even further integration.

**FIGURE 7.2**    **European Union expansion at a glance.**

**Belgium** (1); **France** (2); **Germany** (3);
**Italy** (4); **Luxembourg** (5); **Netherlands** (6)

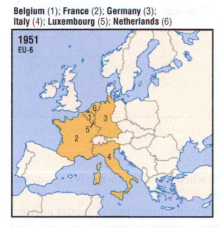

**Denmark** (7); **Ireland** (8); **U.K.** (9)

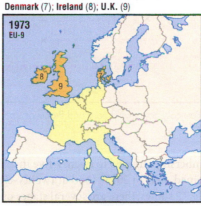

**Greece** (10); **Portugal** (11); **Spain** (12)

**Austria** (13); **Finland** (14); **Sweden** (15)

**Cyprus** (16); **Czech Republic** (17); **Estonia** (18);
**Hungary** (19); **Latvia** (20); **Lithuania** (21); **Malta** (22);
**Poland** (23); **Slovakia** (24); **Slovenia** (25);
**Bulgaria** (26); **Romania** (27)

**Croatia** (28)

the euro zone was to create joint debt, and that the only way to do that was to create a common fiscal (government spending) policy for all members of the euro.

In 1957, the **Treaty of Rome**, widely regarded as the founding document of today's EU, was signed by six states: Belgium, France, West Germany, Italy, Luxembourg, and the Netherlands. To the ECSC were added Euratom, covering nuclear power, and the European Economic Community, which covered trade liberalization.

In the subsequent decades, European integration moved forward intermittently, both in terms of "widening" (adding new members) and "deepening" (extending cooperation between existing members). Widening occurred slowly until the 1990s (Figure 7.2). After being rejected by France in the 1960s, Britain became a member in 1972, adding a key economic and political power, along with Ireland and Denmark. When Greece joined in 1981 and then Spain and Portugal in 1986, the power of the EU in helping transform postauthoritarian societies was demonstrated. Austria, Sweden, and Finland, previously neutral, joined following the end of the Cold War, bringing membership in 1995 to

**Treaty of Rome**

The 1957 treaty that established the European Economic Community, the predecessor of the European Union.

**TABLE 7.2** Stages of Economic Integration

|  | Free Trade Area | Customs Union | Common Market | Economic Union |
|---|:---:|:---:|:---:|:---:|
| Removal of tariffs among members | × | × | × | × |
| Common external tariff |  | × | × | × |
| Free movement of labor and capital |  |  | × | × |
| Harmonization of regulations |  |  |  | × |

Source: Adapted from Theodore Cohn, Global Political Economy: Theory and Practice, 2nd ed. (New York: Pearson Longman, 2005).

fifteen. Membership jumped to twenty-five in 2004, when ten of the formerly communist countries joined, and in 2015 stood at twenty-eight.

As Table 7.2 shows, there are several stages of economic integration. As states pursued deeper economic integration, which provided for freer movement of goods, services, and labor, they had to agree to joint decision making in these areas. The European Union today is an economic union, and has gone beyond it in some respects (Figure 7.3).

The 1992 Maastricht Treaty set into motion the most important development in European structures since the Treaty of Rome. It officially changed the organization's name to the European Union and amended the Treaty of Rome. Most significantly, it added the creation of a common security and foreign policy to the agenda of the union and stated as a goal the establishment of a single currency. These two changes were significant steps toward establishing a single political entity, because a distinct foreign policy and a separate currency and monetary policy are two central characteristics of

**FIGURE 7.3** Evolution of the structure of the European Union.

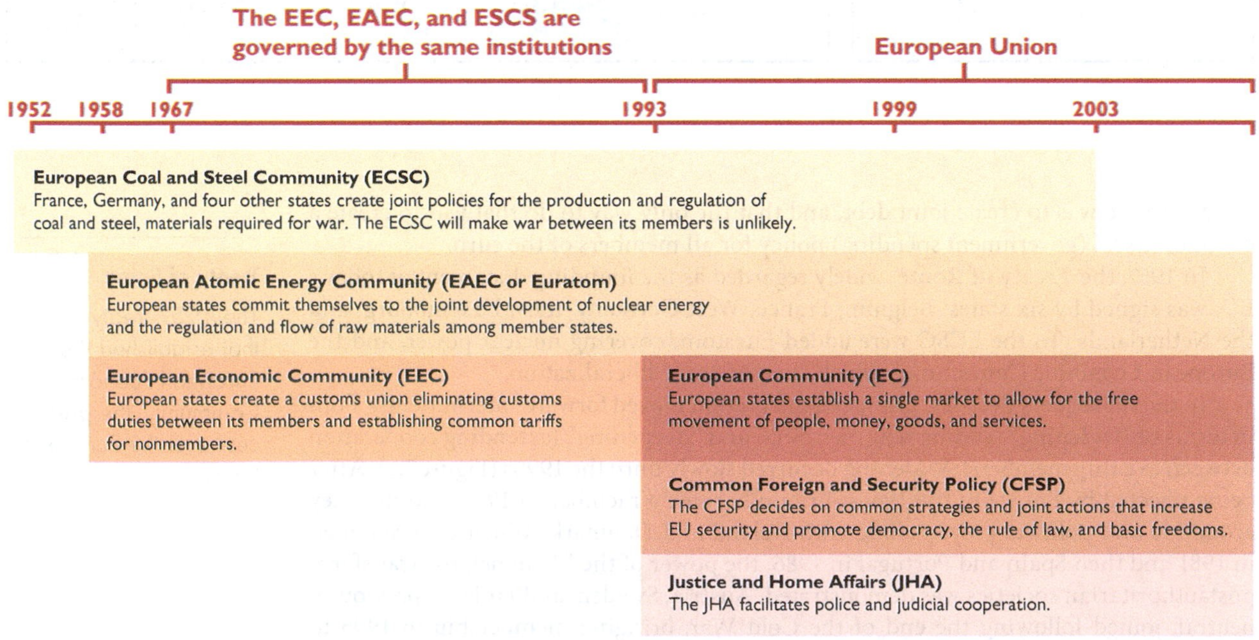

**The EEC, EAEC, and ESCS are governed by the same institutions**

**European Union**

1952   1958   1967                                    1993          1999          2003

**European Coal and Steel Community (ECSC)**
France, Germany, and four other states create joint policies for the production and regulation of coal and steel, materials required for war. The ECSC will make war between its members is unlikely.

**European Atomic Energy Community (EAEC or Euratom)**
European states commit themselves to the joint development of nuclear energy and the regulation and flow of raw materials among member states.

**European Economic Community (EEC)**
European states create a customs union eliminating customs duties between its members and establishing common tariffs for nonmembers.

**European Community (EC)**
European states establish a single market to allow for the free movement of people, money, goods, and services.

**Common Foreign and Security Policy (CFSP)**
The CFSP decides on common strategies and joint actions that increase EU security and promote democracy, the rule of law, and basic freedoms.

**Justice and Home Affairs (JHA)**
The JHA facilitates police and judicial cooperation.

# THE POLICY CONNECTION

## SHOULD BRITAIN LEAVE THE EU?

In 2015, the British government announced plans to hold a referendum on withdrawing from the European Union. Why would Britain want to withdraw from an organization that is so widely regarded as a success? What would be the consequences for the EU, and what might the EU do to keep Britain in the EU?

Prime Minister David Cameron stressed that his hope was not that the UK would leave the EU but that the EU would modify its workings so that the UK could tolerate staying. He hoped that the threat of a "Brexit," as a British exit from the EU came to be known, would prompt other members to take Britain's concerns more seriously. "The changes we need are the changes that are good for Britain and good for Europe," Cameron said.*

Cameron's demands of the EU focus on employment law and welfare benefits for people who migrate within the EU. As part of the EU's single market, EU citizens can work in any country and have similar rights wherever they go. The EU adopted the stronger labor protections and welfare provisions that prevail in much of continental Europe. Britain, with a historically more free market approach, perceived that these arrangements led to many migrants coming to the UK and then claiming British welfare and employment benefits. Cameron also insisted that the historic EU goal of "ever closer union" be abandoned.

Other British politicians, generally in Cameron's Conservative Party and in the UK Independence Party (UKIP), want the UK to leave the EU regardless of any changes in the EU. They express deeper fear about the loss of British sovereignty and about preserving what they perceive as Britain's unique culture and historical position apart from Europe.

Many in Britain appear to support remaining in the EU. Business groups have been especially prominent in warning of the economic consequences of a Brexit. Their fear is that if the UK were not in the EU, many firms would move their operations out of the UK in order to remain within the EU.

Leaders in other EU capitals expressed frustration at Britain's position. The UK has already secured an "opt-out" on many key pieces of EU policy. Moreover, many of the changes sought by Cameron could not be enacted without changing the EU treaties, which would require referenda in many of the other member states. Implementing change would be complicated and politically hazardous for other leaders.

In Germany, Chancellor Angela Merkel (like Cameron, a conservative) supported some of the changes Cameron hoped to make. Others, including Poland's Donald Tusk, president of the European Council, and Jean-Claude Juncker, head of the European Commission, indicated their openness to limits on the benefits available to internal migrants. However, they strongly opposed eroding the basic freedom of movement that underpins the single market in labor.[†]

The dynamics of the situation are difficult to predict. Cameron's victory in the 2015 general election puts him in a strong position to negotiate with other EU members—but it may also have strengthened those in Britain who are more hostile to the EU. It seems possible that Cameron may struggle to convince voters to remain in the EU after receiving some of the concessions he has sought.

### Critical Thinking Questions

1. Is the UK better or worse off outside the EU? In what respects?

2. Is the EU better or worse off without the UK? In what respects?

3. What does this case tell us about the limits on European integration?

---

*"When is the EU Referendum," The Telegraph, May 25, 2015.

†"EU referendum: Merkel will work with Cameron on EU—but will Tories let him?" The Guardian, May 9, 2015.

a sovereign state. The Maastricht Treaty also established a common Justice and Home Affairs division, which further eroded differences among state policies.

Since 1992, the common foreign and security policy and the single currency have become much more of a reality than skeptics predicted, but perhaps less than optimists hoped. In the area of foreign and security policy, the EU now participates as a single entity in some significant international forums, such as the WTO and Middle East peace talks. This arrangement appears to give the states more influence together than they would have separately. Moreover, they have formed an EU rapid reaction force of 60,000 soldiers for use in peacekeeping and related missions. This is the first European military force ever fielded.

However, deep divisions emerged over the U.S.-led invasion of Iraq in 2003. Several key states, including Britain, Italy, Spain, and Poland, supported the invasion and supplied troops. The majority, however, including France and Germany, were adamantly opposed. It was difficult to see how a common policy could emerge from such divergent positions. Similar divisions have emerged over other major foreign policy issues, including relations with Russia and policy toward the global financial crisis.

**Single Currency**   In 1992, twelve of the then fifteen EU members adopted a single currency, and in 2002, euro coins and notes replaced traditional currencies such as the French franc, the Italian lira, and the German mark. Today, nineteen of the EU's twenty-eight members are members of the euro zone. A single currency reduces transaction costs and problems with instability, but it requires the states to agree on a single monetary policy and to live with it. Not all members of the EU have adopted the single currency: Britain, Denmark, and Sweden chose not to join, and many of the newer members have yet to meet the requirements for joining the single currency.

Monetary policy for the euro is now made by the European Central Bank, which is analogous to the U.S. Federal Reserve and is based in Frankfurt, Germany. The member states that adopted the euro have ceded their right to have an independent monetary policy. Initially, the single currency operated quite successfully, increasing its value relative to the dollar dramatically and to some extent displacing the dollar as the standard currency for international transactions. But it was based on the optimistic assumption that the states could maintain a single monetary policy with divergent fiscal policies (and in divergent economic conditions). These assumptions turned out disastrously, and beginning in 2010 the euro zone was in nearly continual crisis (see Chapter 11). In 2015, Greece's inability to deal with its economic problems within the rules of the single currency nearly led to its exit from the Euro zone. One of the questions facing the EU today is whether the euro zone members will need to harmonize their spending policies in order to maintain the single currency, and if so, whether this will open a gap between EU members that belong to the euro zone and those that do not.

**The Lisbon Treaty**   As the EU expanded to twenty-seven members in 2007, it became apparent that its existing decision-making structures would have to be modified. The new states would have to be assigned voting weights, and this would naturally dilute the influence of the older members. Moreover, with more than twenty-five members, if the use of the single-state veto were not minimized, EU decision making, already considered cumbersome, might be completely immobilized. To address these problems, the members signed the Treaty of Lisbon, which came into force in 2009. Most important, the Treaty of Lisbon created a genuine president of the EU Council, chosen by member states for a two-and-a-half-year term, rather than rotating the presidency from country to country every six months. It created a new High Representative for Foreign Affairs to give the EU more weight in foreign affairs by combining the previously separate heads of External Affairs and Foreign and Security Affairs. Essentially, these changes created a stronger and more coherent EU executive branch. To make it easier for the enlarged EU to make decisions, the voting system was modified and the use of the veto was more narrowly circumscribed. Finally, the weight of the European Parliament (representatives of voters) was increased relative to that of the European Council (representatives of governments).

## ORGANIZATION OF THE EU

Like many nation-states, the EU has executive, legislative, and judicial branches. The organization of the EU engenders tensions among several competing goals, including efficiency of decision making, effectiveness of implementation, the sovereignty of the member states, and the rights of EU citizens.

**The European Commission**   The European Commission is analogous to the cabinet in a domestic government. Each commissioner heads a ministry (such as Justice, Freedom and Security, or Economic and Monetary Affairs). Although the commissioners come from the member states, their explicit mission is to govern for the benefit of the entire community, and they are not allowed to take instructions from their home governments. In this respect, the EU is a supranational organization, not merely an international organization of member-states. In addition to overseeing implementation of policy, the commission is also charged with drafting new legislation, either on its own initiative or at the request of the Parliament or council. In most areas of policy, only the commission has the power to initiate legislation.

**European Commission**
The body within the EU that carries out many executive branch functions.

**The Council**   In contrast to the commission, the members of the Council of the European Union explicitly represent the governments of the member states. The explicitly intergovernmental formulation of the council tempers the supranational identity of the commission. Once proposed by the commission, legislation is acted on by the council and the Parliament. In a process known as "co-decision," both the council and the Parliament must approve a bill in order for it to become law. Some issues require a unanimous vote in the council, but for many issues a qualified majority is sufficient, meaning that the vote need not be unanimous but more than a simple majority is required for passage. Under the Treaty of Lisbon, a "double" majority is required for many measures; that is, the measure must be supported by 55 percent of member states (fifteen out of the current twenty-eight); and states representing at least 65 percent of the EU population. The practical effect of these rules is that either a few large states or a large number of small ones can block legislation.

**Council of the European Union**
The body within the EU that represents the governments of the member states and, along with the European Parliament, acts on legislation.

**The European Parliament**   The European Parliament is the only EU institution whose members are elected directly by the citizens, and this independence from member governments makes it strongly supranational. It is also, in terms of its authority, the weakest of the major EU institutions. It has some authority to amend legislation and to veto it on some issues, but in other areas it only has the right of consultation. This arrangement has led to what some critics have called a "democratic deficit" in the EU: Members of the institutions with the most power are not elected, and the one institution whose membership is elected has the least. Under the Treaty of Lisbon, the European Parliament is put on a par with the council, so that they may be thought of as a lower and upper house of a bicameral parliament.

**The European Court of Justice**   Almost all judicial functions in Europe continue to be handled by the courts of the member states. The European Court of Justice (ECJ) functions roughly analogously to the U.S. Supreme Court, handling disputes over the meaning of a particular EU law. It also hears charges that a member state is not fulfilling its obligations or that the European Commission has exceeded its authority. Thus, it is the arbiter of disputes among EU institutions.

## PROBLEMS AND PROSPECTS FOR THE EU

The EU has undergone a remarkable transformation in the past two decades, from an organization with twelve members concerned primarily with implementing a customs union, to something approaching a European superstate, with twenty-eight members, 450 million citizens, and economic power to rival that of the United States. The attractiveness of the EU is shown by the extraordinary efforts that the formerly communist states have undertaken to join. Indeed, perhaps its greatest accomplishment in the past two decades has been its success in promoting and supporting democracy in those states.

Yet several challenges appear on the horizon. First, it remains uncertain how effective the twenty-eight-member union will be at decision making. The EU today is not only larger but much more diverse than it was two decades ago. Moreover, widening and deepening were based on some optimistic assumptions about common conditions and common interests. The economic crisis caused major second thoughts about some of these steps. Second, the question of expansion continues to arise. The EU has successfully brought in much of postcommunist Europe, but there is intense disagreement regarding further expansion, especially with regard to Turkey. Third, agricultural subsidies continue to hinder the move to free markets in Europe. Throughout all the liberalization of trade that has taken place in Europe in recent decades, agriculture has been sheltered and remains heavily subsidized. These subsidies, mandated by the Common Agriculture Policy, eat up nearly half of the EU budget and are therefore a barrier to pursuing other spending priorities. Moreover, they substantially undermine the economic position of agricultural producers in the developing world. Yet it is not clear that there is a politically acceptable strategy for dealing with this issue. Above all, after decades of intermittent progress, the EU now faces the prospect of regression on several fronts, including the potential departure of Britain and the reversal of democratization in Hungary, one of the early victories for the EU effort to advance democracy in postcommunist Europe.

Despite the problems it faces, the process of European integration is almost universally regarded as a great success story. Countries that were once constantly preparing for war with each other now consider such conflict unimaginable. Economic integration has helped bring prosperity. The chance to join the EU has helped transform postcommunist Europe. For these reasons, the EU has been seen as a model for other regions of the world.

## OTHER REGIONAL IGOs

The success of the European Union has helped increase enthusiasm around the world for similar regional groupings (Table 7.3). Can the EU model be replicated? Most of these projects have focused on economic, rather than political, integration—but that is how the EU started as well. It is unclear whether the common vision and spillover that

**TABLE 7.3**  Major Regional Economic Organizations, 2010

| Name | Acronym | Year Founded | Number of Member Nations | Status |
|------|---------|--------------|--------------------------|--------|
| Association of Southeast Asian Nations | ASEAN | 1967 | 10 | Free trade area |
| North American Free Trade Agreement | NAFTA | 1994 | 3 | Free trade area |
| Economic Community of West African States | ECOWAS | 1975 | 15 | Various minor agreements |
| West African Economic and Monetary Union | UEMOA | 1994 | 8 | Monetary and customs union |
| Commonwealth of Independent States (former Soviet Union) | CIS | 1991 | 10 | Negotiations toward single economic space stalled |
| Mercado Común del Sur (South America) | Mercosur | 1991 | 5 | Free trade area |
| Free Trade Area of the Americas (North/South America) | FTAA | Proposed | 34 | Negotiations stalled |

pushed integration forward in Europe will take place elsewhere or whether Europe will turn out to be a unique case.

# TRANSNATIONAL ACTORS

Transnational (nongovernmental) actors are changing the face of international politics today by being involved in almost every important issue in the world. In terms of numbers, transnational organizations may be increasing their numbers even more rapidly than international organizations. As in the case of international organizations, the rise of transnational actors raises the question of whether the nature of international politics is fundamentally changing.

## WHAT ARE TRANSNATIONAL ACTORS?

**Transnational actors** are actors whose activities cut across state boundaries. This simple definition applies to an incredible variety of actors and organizations. Whereas there are roughly 200 states in the world and about 250 IGOs, there are roughly 60,000 transnational corporations and nearly 16,000 transnational nongovernmental organizations.[8] This section focuses on two major kinds of transnational actors. (Others include transnational terrorist groups, discussed in Chapter 9, and transnational criminal organizations.)

- Transnational (or multinational) corporations (TNCs or MNCs) are companies whose production and sales operations span more than a single country. In an era of globalization, the numbers are increasing rapidly, as even relatively small firms seek international suppliers and markets.

**Transnational actors**
Actors whose activities cut across state boundaries.

- International nongovernmental organizations (INGOs) include a wide range of nongovernmental, nonbusiness organizations that operate across state boundaries. They are distinguished from IGOs in that their members are individuals, not states. Included in this category are groups such as the International Olympic Committee and the International Committee of the Red Cross. An important subset of INGOs are transnational advocacy networks (TANs). These are groups that work on specific issues, which can range from helping to solve some world problem to spreading a particular belief system to promoting the study of a particular subject. Examples are Human Rights Watch and Greenpeace.

A distinction should also be made between firms and organizations that are primarily national, with a small part of their operations abroad, and those that are fully transnational, with only a small part of their scope of operations in any one country. For example, the Labour and Conservative parties in the United Kingdom are both transnational actors in the sense that they collaborate with kindred parties in other states, but they are essentially British national organizations. By contrast, Human Rights Watch, although headquartered in the United States, has offices in eleven other countries and conducts activities in many more.

What effect do transnational actors have on international politics? To some extent, this depends on how "international politics" is defined. The traditional state-centric view is that transnational actors need to be taken into account only to the extent that they influence states and the relations between states. A broader view holds that the activities of transnational actors are important in themselves and deserve to be studied as a major component of international affairs. Some transnational actors are powerful economically; others shape international norms, monitor governments, or provide humanitarian services.

## TRANSNATIONAL CORPORATIONS

The transnational corporation is not a new invention. Companies such as the British East India Company and the Hudson's Bay Company were formed in the seventeenth century to profit from economic opportunities opening up in regions newly discovered by Europeans. Until after World War II, however, there were few such companies, and they tended to be based in one country, going abroad only for sales or to purchase raw materials. After World War II, large corporations became increasingly international in their production operations.

Major corporations today pursue global strategies for production, sales, research, and investment. Energy firms such as Shell and Exxon/Mobil are present in nearly every country in the world, to pump oil, to refine it, or to sell the products made from it. Similarly, consumer products firms such as Coca-Cola, Unilever, and McDonalds are nearly everywhere. A single automobile may contain parts produced in several countries, and many information technology firms use programmers and engineers in multiple countries and market their products globally.

The role of transnational corporations in world politics has been a source of constant debate. The positive and negative effects of TNCs on the countries in which they operate and their power vis-à-vis governments are hotly debated. A central question for developing states has been whether TNCs tend to promote or to inhibit economic growth, a discussion closely tied to debates about globalization and development strategies. One view is that TNCs operating in developing countries seek only to extract raw materials and to take advantage of low labor costs, and therefore tend to contribute little to economic development. Opponents of TNCs further charge that TNCs use their economic influence to maintain low standards for labor and environmental protection (as in the sweatshop problem described in Chapter 12). The competing view is that the capital that TNCs invest helps boost productivity and that the local workers and managers trained by TNCs add to the local skill pool, promoting further development. Moreover, supporters of TNCs point out that their presence expands the tax base in the host country. In recent years, the latter view has gained ground among governments, and many countries welcome the arrival of TNCs for the economic benefits they bring, even while being wary of their influence. Indeed, governments sometimes compete intensely to lure global firms. For example, the state of Alabama offered Mercedes Benz $250 million in aid to build a car factory near Tuscaloosa in 1993.

To many observers, the competition to lure TNCs has troubling implications. What effects do TNCs have in shaping local laws and local government decisions? Because some large firms are located in many countries, they can sometimes shift resources from one country to another to escape government policies they do not like, or to try to extract concessions from governments. This, it is argued, gives TNCs more leverage over governments. Some see this leverage as undesirable because it undermines the ability of governments to promote higher social and environmental standards. Others see it as achieving some of the same benefits of the EU, by forcing states to adopt policies more compatible with one another.

However, not all economic assets are equally easy to move. Portfolio investment (investment in stocks) can be sold off and moved fairly easily, and cash can be moved quickly, but bricks-and-mortar investments, such as factories, cannot. Once a company invests significantly in immobile assets, power shifts from the company to the host government. In recent years, for example, after investing billions of dollars in the development of energy infrastructure, foreign energy firms in countries as diverse as Bolivia, Russia, and Venezuela have been forced by the host governments to sell their investments for less than they were worth (a process known as *expropriation*).

Indigenous protestors block a highway in Guachala, Ecuador, May 2009. The protestors opposed government policy on exploitation of mineral and oil rights. How are the rights and interests of local populations weighed against those of international corporations?

Dolores Ochoa/AP Images

# THE HISTORY CONNECTION

## EARLY TRANSNATIONAL CORPORATIONS: THE BRITISH EAST INDIA COMPANY AND THE HUDSON'S BAY COMPANY

The transnational corporation is considered a recent development, and in its modern form, it is. But today's TNC had predecessors in the joint stock companies that were set up to finance shipping and trade between European states and their colonies in North America, India, and Southeast Asia during the age of exploration.

The British East India Company was founded in 1600 with 125 investors, £72,000, and most important, a charter from the government granting it a monopoly on British trade with the East Indies (modern-day Indonesia). The company made its mark in India, and over the next few centuries became synonymous with the British colony there. The company thrived by controlling the British trade with India and exploiting India's economic resources. It was later central in establishing the British colonial presence in China that provoked the Opium Wars. By the mid-nineteenth century, the company effectively controlled most of India, Burma, Singapore, and Hong Kong.*

The British East India Company was much admired, and analogous companies were set up by the Dutch, whose firm displaced the British and others in Indonesia. Not everyone was impressed with it, however. Adam Smith wrote, "The difference between the genius of the British constitution which protects and governs North America, and that of the mercantile company which oppresses and domineers in the East Indies, cannot perhaps be better illustrated than by the different states of those countries."[†]

The Hudson's Bay Company was formed in 1670, along a similar model, to exploit the growing demand for North American beaver pelts for the European hat industry. It too had the benefit of a state-granted monopoly over a massive territory, encompassing most of present-day Canada. As the fur trade died out, the Hudson's Bay Company was able to branch out into a wide variety of other ventures because it owned most of western Canada. After Canadian independence in 1867, most of the company's land was ceded to the Canadian government, but it remained a force to be reckoned with. In World War I, it provided more than 300 ships to the British war effort. The company still exists today, its trading post network having evolved into one of the largest department store chains in Canada.

### Critical Thinking Questions

1. How has the political role of TNCs changed since the heyday of the British East India Company and the Hudson's Bay Company?

2. Do governments today have more or less power relative to TNCs than the British government had relative to the British East India Company and the Hudson's Bay Company? How has the power of governments changed in this regard?

*See Philip Lawson, The East India Company: A History (New York: Longman, 1993).

†Adam Smith, The Wealth of Nations, Book I, Chapter VIII (Chicago: University of Chicago Press, 1976).

A company with interests in two countries might lobby the government of one to pressure the government of the second on its behalf. This approach could open up a completely separate channel of corporate influence. It is precisely this concern that was raised through the post–World War II decades in Latin America, where U.S. government pressure on behalf of U.S. companies sometimes extended to the dispatching of troops to depose governments unfriendly to U.S. business. The United Fruit Company, which owned much of the land in Guatemala, helped convince the United States to overthrow the government in Guatemala, which was pursuing a land reform that threatened the company's holdings. The CIA helped oust President Jacobo Árbenz Guzmán in 1954, helping to spur a civil war that lasted into the 1990s. Similarly, lobbying by the U.S. firm ITT played an important role in causing the Nixon administration to have the CIA help bring the Chilean dictator Augusto Pinochet to power in 1973. In recent years, both Russia and China have pressured other governments to enact policies that support the business interests of their companies.

TNCs also try to use governments as salespeople. This is especially true of TNCs that are based in one country but sell around the world. In the aircraft business, for example, where Boeing is identified primarily with the United States and Airbus with the EU, governments frequently use foreign policy to help sell "their" companies' aircraft. U.S. government documents published by WikiLeaks indicated that the U.S. government provided a wide array of inducements to governments around the world to get their state-controlled airlines to buy aircraft from Boeing. U.S. President George W. Bush sent a personal letter to King Abdullah of Saudi Arabia urging the kingdom to buy more than fifty Boeing aircraft for Saudi Airlines and the royal family's fleet. The king responded with a request that his personal aircraft get the same security upgrades as Air Force One, a request that was apparently granted.[9] In November 2010, Saudi Airlines ordered twelve 777 aircraft worth $3.3 billion. In December 2011, an agreement was reached for Saudi Arabia to purchase eighty-four F-15 fighter jets worth $30 billion from Boeing.

Overall, many analysts believe that the various constraints placed on states by TNCs and the influence TNCs have on states are effectively eroding state sovereignty. One of the early works on TNCs was, therefore, called *Sovereignty at Bay*.[10] More recently, the increasing scope and power of TNCs is an important component in arguments that the sovereign state is rapidly losing its significance. In response to such concerns, states have worked through the United Nations to propose a "global compact" to promote agreed principles for TNC involvement. The compact includes principles such as that "businesses should…make sure they are not complicit in human rights abuses" and "businesses should work against corruption in all its forms, including extortion and bribery."[11]

## TRANSNATIONAL ADVOCACY NETWORKS

Among the many different INGOs, **transnational advocacy networks (TANs)** play a growing role in international politics. Transnational advocacy networks are groups that organize across national boundaries to pursue some political, social, or cultural goal.[12] The range of groups, and the range of issues they cover, is so broad that it is difficult to devise a more precise definition. A few examples of well-known TANs serve to illustrate this point.

- Médicins Sans Frontières (Doctors Without Borders) organizes international teams of doctors to provide medical help in areas struck by disaster or war.

- Greenpeace organizes activists across the globe to lobby governments for stronger policies to protect the environment.

- Human Rights Watch monitors human rights abuses around the world and publicizes them to put pressure on governments.

**transnational advocacy networks (TANs)**

Groups that organize across national boundaries to pursue some political, social, or cultural goal.

These TANs have complex relations with governments. At times, they appear in adversarial roles, either opposing government policies or lobbying for change; at other times, they work closely with governments to achieve common goals that governments cannot achieve by themselves, in areas such as health care, human rights, and democratization.

**Lobbying Governments**   Among the primary roles of TANs is lobbying governments across the world in favor of specific policies. Some organizations perform a watchdog function, identifying and publicizing government shortcomings so that others can promote accountability. For example, Human Rights Watch and similar organizations seek to persuade states to adhere to certain standards of human rights. They have almost no means to compel governments; instead, their main weapon is research and publication. Human Rights Watch, through its network of monitors, often gathers more reliable reporting on human rights practices than either governments or the private news media can obtain. Therefore, both governments and the news media rely on Human Rights Watch reports. Although these reports do not stop human rights violations, they provide motivation to citizen groups and are often highly embarrassing, both to the governments in question and to their allies.

In other cases, the goal of a group can be to persuade all governments to adopt a new standard of behavior. The Campaign to Ban Landmines, for example, successfully persuaded governments around the world to agree to a treaty banning the use of antipersonnel mines. Labor groups have established codes of workers' rights and have sought to convince transnational corporations to abide by these codes even in countries with lower standards.

There are perhaps two crucial differences between domestic and transnational lobbying. First, in transnational lobbying, resources raised in one country can be used in others. Therefore, especially in poorer countries, lobbying groups with transnational connections can be much more influential than they otherwise might be. This influence is not always welcome, and some governments have responded by prohibiting international financing for local NGOs. Second, transnational lobbying can seek to move many countries at once toward a common policy position. When the goal in question is some kind of international agreement (as in the landmine treaty), influencing policy in many states at once is crucial.

Liberian Red Cross workers remove the body of an Ebola virus victim in Bajor, Liberia, September 2014. The Red Cross deployed thousands of volunteers to help step the epidemic.

**Setting Agendas**   TANs play an influential role in setting international agendas, as emphasized particularly by constructivist international relations theory. It is very difficult, of course, for TANs to compel reluctant governments. But many times TANs raise an issue before it becomes one of importance to governments. On such issues, TANs can set the agenda by defining key goals, promoting norms, and setting standards. When an IGO or a group of states addresses this issue later, they may find that a set of standards and expectations already exists. Although the IGO or the states are not forced to adopt these standards, doing so is often the easiest alternative. Thus, by raising the issues first and defining agendas, norms, and standards, TANs can influence the behavior of IGOs and states.

**Providing Services**   Many transnational advocacy networks do not merely advocate; they act. Organizations such as the International Committee of the Red Cross (ICRC), Doctors Without Borders, CARE, and thousands more provide many kinds of aid directly to people around the world. Especially in poor countries, where governments are incapable of providing for certain needs, these organizations play a role complementary to that of governments and help millions of people.

In the delivery of aid around the world, transnational aid organizations can often accomplish tasks that even the most powerful governments cannot. Because they are not affiliated with governments, they can often establish relationships and go places where official government representatives cannot. For example, although the U.S. and Sudanese governments may be unwilling to collaborate with each other, the NGOs and the Sudanese government might find it easier to work together. Especially when needs arise rapidly, as in the case of natural disasters, governments often must rely on transnational aid organizations to deliver aid. The aid organizations have local knowledge and logistic networks that governments cannot easily set up quickly, and governments have the funding for which NGOs are sometimes desperate.

Similarly, in conflict-prone areas, where the presence of foreign government personnel might provoke violence, governments rely heavily on transnational aid organizations to deliver all sorts of aid. Aid organizations are often perceived as more neutral, and thus less threatening, than states or IGOs.

However, the relationship between transnational aid organizations and government is complicated and can sometimes create difficult ethical dilemmas. Even in the best of cases, there are often disputes about control. Host governments, often concerned about sovereignty and about getting the political credit for providing aid, seek to control the distribution of aid on their territory. In some cases, they try to channel aid primarily to their supporters. Aid organizations, concerned that assistance be distributed according to their own principles and priorities and wishing to avoid theft and corruption, usually like to control the process as much as possible.

In cases where a country is experiencing internal conflict (often a primary cause of the problems that aid organizations help with), the government might seek to prevent aid organizations from delivering aid to those it sees as its adversaries. In the case of Sudan, one of the local agencies employed to distribute aid from the UN-led Operation Lifeline Sudan was, in fact, linked to one of the combatant groups. This agency distributed the aid in a way that it found politically useful, but in the process it undermined the goals of minimizing death and suffering.[13] Fiona Terry shows how, in several cases, including the Rwandan genocide in 1994, the India–Pakistan war of 1971, and Palestinian refugees over many years, humanitarian groups provided food and shelter that unwittingly assisted "refugee-warriors" as they prepared to launch attacks, often on civilians.[14]

# THE END OF THE WESTPHALIAN STATE SYSTEM?

The increasing importance of international organizations and transnational actors, combined with the broader processes of globalization, has led some analysts to argue that the Westphalian state system is essentially dead. There are three components to this argument. First, the increasingly free movement of goods, ideas, finance, and people across borders means that territorially bounded entities are inherently weaker than mobile ones. This chapter showed how transnational corporations can outmaneuver states, which, by definition, are territorially bounded. Second, supranational organizations (IGOs such as the WTO, the UN, and the EU) are being given more and more of the responsibilities that were formerly reserved for states. Third, TANs can coordinate lobbying activities across countries and in many cases can accomplish tasks that states cannot.

# THE CONNECTION TO YOU

## INTERNATIONAL NGOs AND TANS ON CAMPUS

Student activities are an integral part of the university experience. They connect students to classmates, help them build real-world skills, and introduce them to international politics through the activities of NGOs, TANs, and other organizations.

Have you signed a petition advocating for human rights at a table set up by your campus's chapter of Amnesty International? Many transnational NGOs have campus chapters. Human rights NGOs such as Amnesty International seek to get university students involved in protesting human rights abuses, both locally and around the world, and often set up tables to seek signatures on petitions. Some students travel abroad on mission trips sponsored by campus religious groups for some mix of charity work and proselytizing. Others participate in an alternative spring break program or a service learning program that combines service with academic study and credit.

Student action on campuses around the world has shaped both foreign and domestic policy. In the 1960s and 1970s, protests on U.S. campuses pressured the federal government to end the Vietnam War. In the 1980s, students led efforts to get universities to sever connections with South Africa's government, based on that government's institutionalized racism, known as apartheid. These U.S. efforts were linked to an international movement to isolate South Africa and force change (apartheid was abolished in 1994). More recently, students on many campuses have joined together to protest working conditions in so-called sweatshops that produce much of the university-themed clothing licensed by universities

and worn by students. American, Canadian, and British university students formed United Students Against Sweatshops (USAS), which has worked with universities and labor activists to form the Worker Rights Consortium, which promotes standards of conduct and sends delegations to producing countries to monitor compliance.

Students often respond to humanitarian crises. After Haiti was struck by a massive earthquake in 2010, university students around the world spontaneously formed organizations and conducted events to raise funds for relief and reconstruction. These local efforts were generally linked with international aid groups and transnational advocacy networks, which could use the money raised to get food, supplies, and people where they were needed in Haiti.

In a previous chapter, we noted that voting participation is lower for students than for other segments of the population. But does that mean that this generation cares less about global issues? Anecdotally, it seems that this generation's willingness to participate in certain kinds of transnational advocacy networks might be higher. One might speculate on the sources of this difference.

### Critical Thinking Questions

1. What kinds of NGOs and TANs are operating on your campus?

2. Are students more inclined to support TANs than to vote? If so, why?

3. What are the immediate and long-term effects of student involvement in these groups?

These three processes are seen as reinforcing each other. International organizations tend to promote the harmonizing of laws and regulations that facilitate a rise in transnational activities. Transnational actors promote increasing the authority of international organizations, both directly through advocacy and indirectly through activities that give nation-states incentives to form common polices. For example, the tendency of TNCs to structure their transactions to minimize taxation gives states an incentive to coordinate tax policies. Although the size of the state sphere has stayed constant or diminished, the size of the nonstate sphere has increased dramatically. Proportionally, then, the state has become less dominant. It has gone from being the only player on the international scene to being one of many.

For advocates of this view, the EU has been the ultimate example, even if recent difficulties have tarnished its image. Many of the traditional prerogatives of the sovereign state no longer exist in the separate European capitals, but rather are located in Brussels. But this is not simply a case of several sovereign states merging into a larger sovereign state, because the EU does not have many of the characteristics of a nation-state. Rather, Europe today seems to transcend the sovereign state framework entirely. It is ironic, perhaps, that the region that "invented" the sovereign state system in the sixteenth and seventeenth centuries is dismantling it in the twenty-first century.

Those who are skeptical about the demise of the Westphalian system assert that the sovereign state is not only surviving, it is alive and well. Ultimately, they argue, sovereignty resides with the organization that, in Max Weber's terms, possesses a monopoly on the legitimate use of force. As nation-states combat organized crime and transnational terrorism, for example, they are recognized as the only actors that can legitimately use force—and therefore retain their sovereignty. The failure of international organizations—including the EU and the UN—to cope with the international security threats of recent years indicates that in the areas that matter most, states still dominate when they want to.

If transnational activities have increased, and if international organizations have gained more authority, statists argue, it is because states have found it in their interest to allow this. For example, prominent realists as well as Marxists argue that the spread of TNCs in the last half-century occurred because it served the interests of the most powerful states in the system, especially the United States, where many of these companies were based.

Similarly, some have viewed the EU not as an organization that curtails the power of states, but as one that increases states' power. Governments can get laws passed in Brussels that they could never get through their own legislatures. Thus, Europe's "democratic deficit" is seen as strengthening states over societies.

There is probably some truth in both views. It is true, as skeptics point out, that states have allowed globalization and the increase in transnational activities to occur and could probably reverse such changes if they made a concerted effort. However, there is little doubt that the costs of such a reversal, in both economic and political terms, are increasing. The state that retreated from the world economy would undergo substantial loss of income, and the government that tried to do this would likely meet powerful domestic opposition.

Perhaps it is a mistake, then, to view sovereign states as opposed to or in contradiction to international organizations. Clearly, international organizations and transnational actors are increasingly important in the world today. Much of the time, their interests and activities complement, rather than contradict, those of states. The question, therefore, is not which is more powerful, but rather how are international governmental organizations and transnational actors shaping state goals and the ways that states pursue solutions?

## RECONSIDER THE CASE

# INTERNATIONAL AND TRANSNATIONAL ACTORS IN LIBYA'S CIVIL WAR

Following the overthrow of the Gaddafi government, international organizations and transnational actors increased their involvement in Libya. In September 2011, the UN Security Council established the UN Support Mission in Libya (UNSMIL) and tasked it with "assisting the Libyan authorities in restoring public security and the rule of law, promoting inclusive political dialogue and national reconciliation, and in helping the National Transitional Council (NTC) embark on the drafting of a new constitution and laying the foundation for elections."*

The World Bank also got involved, conducting a "needs assessment" in the fall of 2011 that focused on financial management, infrastructure, basic services, and employment. These projects were aimed primarily at providing sound technical advice to the transitional government on how to begin rebuilding public finances and the economy.

The International Criminal Court, which had been charged by the Security Council to investigate possible war crimes in Libya, charged Gaddafi's son Saif al-Islam Gaddafi with war crimes. The younger Gaddafi was held by the militia group that had captured him. When the international legal team assigned by the ICC to defend Gaddafi met with him, they were arrested and held by the militia group, accused of passing secret messages to Gaddafi. The ICC was outraged, but had little ability to coerce the militia group or the transitional government.

Nor did the work of NGOs in Libya always go smoothly. In Misrata, the health NGO Médecins Sans Frontières (MSF, or Doctors Without Borders) withdrew because the new government was torturing prisoners suspected of having ties to the Gaddafi regime. An MSF representative said that "Patients were brought to us in the middle of interrogation for medical care, in order to make them fit for further interrogation. This is unacceptable."† Given MSF's global credibility, its withdrawal was seen as particularly strong evidence of abuses in post–Gaddafi Libya. The U.S. and British governments registered protests with the Libyan transitional government.

In 2012, the transitional government passed a law that banned domestic Libyan NGOs from receiving funding from foreign partners. The ban (similar to those passed in Egypt and other countries) appears to have been aimed at reducing political opposition to the transitional government, and it had the effect of weakening prodemocracy and other NGOs. Foreign NGOs were ordered out of the city of Sirte. Amnesty International's International Secretary General Salil Shetty stated that the new government was in some respects as bad as that of Gaddafi.‡

International oil companies stepped up their efforts as well. Those already operating in Libya under Gaddafi began restarting production in late 2011. They had a head start on others hoping to gain access to Libya's reserves, the largest in Africa, but they were hampered by investigations into their relationships with Gaddafi. They were suspecting of securing their contracts in Libya by bribing members of Gaddafi's circle. The Securities and Exchange Commission in the United States as well as the transitional government in Libya opened investigations.

As Libya descended into civil war, with two competing governments and multiple militias vying for control in different parts of the country, it became both more difficult and more important for international organizations and NGOs to work there. By early 2015, the Islamic State had exploited the anarchy to become active in the country. In June 2015, the UN held a conference of the major contestants for power and tried to forge a path back toward peace and a stable government. Although there was some hope that the threat from ISIS would push the many sides toward collaboration, Libya's future remained precarious.

Libya's transition was rocky and unpredictable, but international organizations and transnational actors continued to play a large, and often contested, role there.

## Critical Thinking Questions

1. Why would national or local officials want to restrict the work of international NGOs that come to their country to provide help?

2. What levers of influence are open to foreign governments, IGOs, and TANs in Libya? How do their menus of options differ?

3. How are the purposes of TANs different from those of states in this case? How do their means of effecting change differ?

*UNSMIL, "Background," unsmil.unmissions.org/Default.aspx?tabid= 3545& language=en-US.

†Mark Urban, "Libya: Is a Breakdown in Order Forcing NGOs Out?" BBC News, January 27, 2012, www.bbc.co.uk/news/ world-16761200.

‡Jamie Dettmer, "Exclusive: Libya's Crackdown Worries Democracy Advocates," The Daily Beast, May 28, 2012, www.thedailybeast. com/articles/2012/05/28/exclusive-libya-s-civil-crackdown-worries-democracy-advocates.html.

# POWER, PURPOSE, AND NONSTATE ACTORS

As complex interdependence theory stresses, international organizations and transnational actors have a wide range of purposes, broadening the agenda of international politics. Moreover, all of these actors—international organizations, transnational actors, NGOs, and transnational advocacy networks—can have an important influence on how states and groups of states define *their* purposes. In other words, these organizations have considerable soft power and in some cases institutional power as well.

But these actors have direct capabilities as well, as this chapter has stressed. NGOs can provide crucial aid on the ground where governments cannot, helping to solve a wide range of problems. They can collect and disseminate information that governments find useful or dangerous. Transnational corporations can advance state interests by contributing to economic development and employment or undermine state interests by cutting wages, lobbying for lower taxes, or polluting the environment. In sum, nonstate actors wield considerable power today to pursue their own purposes and shape the purposes of other actors in the international system.

## SUMMARY

- The UN was formed at the end of World War II to provide a means by which the great powers of the day could join forces to promote peace and development. It is the most visible IGO, the one with the broadest scope, and the nearest thing to a body that represents the international community. It has significant agenda-setting power, and its peacekeepers have helped stabilize many conflicts around the world, but it has not managed to become anything like the world government that some hope for and others fear.

- The European Union has pushed the bounds of international collaboration further than any other IGO, building supranational government in some spheres and deep intergovernmental cooperation in others. Development of the EU has been based largely on the process of spillover, in which incremental steps build the impetus for further integration. Even though the EU has encountered significant challenges, it is still seen as a model that other regions hope to emulate.

- Transnational advocacy networks (TANs), a subset of INGOs, work on specific issues, which can range from helping to solve some world problem to spreading a particular belief system to promoting the study of a particular subject. TANs set agendas, lobby governments, and provide services.

- The increasing importance of international organizations and transnational actors, combined with the broader processes of globalization, has led some analysts to argue that the Westphalian state system has eroded significantly. Others argue that states retain considerable control, and that if transnational activities have increased and if international organizations have gained more authority, it is because states have found it in their interest to allow this. Regardless of where one stands on this debate, there is little doubt that the proliferation of IOs and transnational actors has dramatically altered the context of many international issues.

## KEY CONCEPTS

1. International organizations
2. Transnational actors
3. Intergovernmentalism
4. Supranationalism
5. Spillover
6. Global governance
7. Transnational corporations (TNCs)
8. Transnational advocacy networks (TANs)

## STUDY QUESTIONS

1. Human Rights Watch is an example of a(n)
   a. transnational corporation.
   b. international governmental organization.
   c. peacekeeping agency.
   d. transnational advocacy network.

2. The European Union is an example of a(n)
   a. transnational corporation.
   b. international governmental organization.
   c. peacekeeping agency.
   d. transnational advocacy network.

3. Which of the following is an early predecessor of today's transnational corporations?
   a. McDonalds
   b. IKEA
   c. The Dutch East India Company
   d. The British Broadcasting Corporation

4. Which of the following organizations has achieved a degree of supranationalism?
   a. The EU
   b. The UN
   c. The Arab League
   d. Greenpeace

5. Which of the following organizations is based on a strategy known as spillover?
   a. The EU
   b. The UN
   c. The Arab League
   d. Greenpeace

6. Which of the following strategies do TANs use to shape the purpose of international activity?
   a. Set agendas
   b. Lobby governments
   c. Provide services
   d. All of the above.

7. What are the competing understandings and evaluations of the UN?

8. What are the key organs of the EU, and what responsibilities do they have?

9. Why are other regions seeking to emulate the EU model, and what barriers do they face?

10. How are transnational corporations influencing international politics?

11. How are transnational advocacy networks influencing international politics?

12. In what ways are international organizations and transnational actors undermining the Westphalian state system?

[Correct answers: 1. d; 2. b; 3. c; 4. a; 5. a; 6. d]

## END NOTES

1. For a more detailed definition, see Union of International Associations, ed., *The Yearbook of International Organizations 2008/2009 Volume I: Organization Descriptions and Cross-References* (Munich: Walter De Gruyter, 2008).

2. The author is grateful to Catherine Weaver for suggesting the inclusion of this table and for sharing a model.

3. See Robert O. Keohane, *After Hegemony: Cooperation and Discord in the World Political Economy* (Princeton, NJ: Princeton University Press, 1984).

4. UN Charter, Chapter IV, www.un.org/en/documents/charter/chapter4.shtml.

5. Global Policy Forum, "UN Budget: Tables and Charts," www.globalpolicy.org/finance/tables/inxbuget.htm.

6. The acronym UNICEF represents an earlier version of the organization's name, the United Nations International Children's Emergency Fund.

7. Ban Ki-moon, address at the Royal Institute of International Affairs, July 11, 2007, www.un.org/apps/news/infocus/sgspeeches/statments_full.asp?statID=100.

8. Peter Willetts, "Transnational Actors and International Organizations in Global Politics," in John Baylis and Steve Smith, eds., *The Globalization of World Politics* (Oxford, UK: Oxford University Press, 2001), pp. 356–357.

9. Eric Lipton and Nicola Clark, "Diplomats Help Push Jet Sales on Global Market," *New York Times*, January 2, 2011.

10. Raymond Vernon, *Sovereignty at Bay: The Multinational Spread of U.S. Enterprises* (New York: Basic Books, 1971).

11. United Nations, "About the Global Compact," www.unglobalcompact.org/AboutTheGC/index.html.

12. For a detailed discussion of transnational advocacy groups, see Margaret E. Keck and Kathryn Sikkink, *Activists Beyond Borders: Advocacy Networks in International Politics* (Ithaca, NY: Cornell University Press, 1998).

13. Fiona Terry, *Condemned to Repeat? The Paradox of Humanitarian Action* (Ithaca, NY: Cornell University Press, 2002), pp. 36–37.

14. Terry, *Condemned to Repeat?* pp. 36–37.

Russian soldiers in Crimea, Ukraine, 2014. Russia's use of soldiers disguised as local Ukrainian militants represented a novel use of force.
Stephen Foote/Alamy

# INTERNATIONAL INSECURITY AND THE CAUSES OF WAR AND PEACE

## Learning Objectives

**8-1** Identify the range of explanations of the causes of war and evaluate the strengths and weaknesses of each explanation.

**8-2** Articulate and defend an argument concerning the causes of war.

**8-3** Identify the major sources of contentious politics.

**8-4** Demonstrate the links between domestic and international conflict.

**8-5** Connect explanations of war to appropriate foreign policies.

**8-6** Understand the role that arms control can play in ameliorating the security dilemma.

**8-7** Evaluate the policy of collective security and its weaknesses.

**8-8** Analyze peacekeeping as a means of limiting conflict.

**8-9** Evaluate different perspectives on the causes of civil war and protest.

**8-10** Explain the international dimensions of civil war and protest.

# CONSIDER THE CASE

## MODERN WARFARE

Consider this partial list of recent international conflicts:

- 2001: India and Bangladesh skirmish over their border.
- 2001: The United States and allies invade Afghanistan.
- 2003: The United States and allies invade Iraq.
- 2006: Israel invades Lebanon.
- 2008: Russia invades Georgia.
- 2011: NATO and allies intervene in Libyan civil war.
- 2012: Sudan and South Sudan skirmish over their border.
- 2014: Russia seizes Crimea and invades eastern Ukraine.

What do all of these conflicts have in common? Not all can be considered wars because of their short duration and low number of casualties. The conflict between India and Bangladesh lasted only a few days, and resulted in only seventeen battle deaths (but displaced thousands of civilians from their homes). The Iraq war caused, according to one systematic accounting, more than 200,000 violent deaths.*

In terms of grievances, the reason for the invasion of Afghanistan was to eject a regime that was sheltering terrorists. The invasion of Iraq was intended to depose a regime that was feared to be building weapons of mass destruction. The Russia–Georgia, Israel–Lebanon, Sudan–South Sudan, and Russia–Ukraine conflicts all concerned territory and were inflamed by ethnic tensions and national self-determination. The intervention in Libya, conducted primarily through air strikes, was initially intended to protect civilians from attack by government forces but morphed into a mission to help rebel forces overthrow the government of Muammar Gaddafi.

These conflicts involve not only states but a wide range of nonstate actors. Perhaps the most dramatic change in international politics in recent years is that security and conflict are no longer problems linked only to states—nonstate actors are now parties to

international conflict and are involved in other roles as well. The United States invaded Afghanistan not simply to get rid of the Taliban government but to root out Al Qaeda, a transnational terrorist organization that had found haven there. The Taliban was expelled from Kabul within weeks, but Al Qaeda continued to fight on. When Israel invaded Lebanon in 2006, the goal was not to attack the government or army of Lebanon but rather to attack Hezbollah, a transnational militant group that controlled parts of southern Lebanon from which it attacked Israel. The conflict between Russia and Georgia was driven by secessionist nonstate groups in Georgia, and Russia's invasion of eastern Ukraine was disguised as an internal Ukrainian secessionist movement.

Only three of these conflicts led to clear victory for one side. In the Russia–Georgia war, two Georgian territories won their independence, though many in the international community did not recognize it. Georgia was defeated, and by losing those two territories shrank considerably. In Libya, Muammar Gaddafi was forced from power as part of a revolution. Russia's annexation of Crimea appears unlikely to be reversed.

Two of the conflicts led to short-term victories that became long-term burdens. In both Afghanistan and Iraq, the United States and allies easily attained their immediate military objectives, but they found their long-term political objectives unattainable. In the Israel–Lebanon case, not much changed in terms of territory or central grievances. Israel inflicted heavy damage on Hezbollah in Lebanon, but its inability to defeat them decisively boosted Hezbollah's image and damaged Israel's. South Sudan's effort to seize a key oil field was successful for only a few days before its forces were repulsed.

The costs of these conflicts were enormous. The *Lancet*, a British medical journal, estimated that the total number of deaths from the Iraq War, including battlefield casualties and indirect deaths (due to starvation, disease, and health care disruptions), was more than 600,000. By 2009, the war and occupation had cost the United States more than $800 billion, and two

*(Continued)*

prominent economists estimated the overall cost of the war, including long-term costs such as treating veterans for physical injuries and mental illness, at $3 trillion.[†] The Sudan–South Sudan conflict led to relatively few battlefield casualties, but the fighting displaced thousands of people from their homes in a country that was incapable of feeding or sheltering them.

*See Iraq Body Count at https://www.iraqbodycount.org/.
[†]James Glanz, The Economic Cost of War," New York Times, February 28, 2009, www.nytimes.com/2009/03/01/weekinreview/01glanz.html?pagewanted=all; Joseph E. Stiglitz and Linda J. Bilmes, "The True Cost of the Iraq War, $3 Trillion and Beyond," Washington Post, September 5, 2010, www.washingtonpost.com/wp-dyn /content/article/2010/09/03/AR2010090302200.html.

D espite the death, suffering, and economic devastation caused by war, states and other actors repeatedly determine, in a wide variety of circumstances, that going to war is in their interests. What is it about international politics that makes war sometimes seem the best alternative despite its high costs? Is it the anarchical nature of the system? The nature of some kinds of states? The intractability of grievances? The irrationality of groups and individuals? Is war preventable? Does the involvement of nonstate actors change the causes or effects of war?

The high cost of war makes prevention seem like a highly beneficial strategy, but to prevent war, we need to understand its causes. As the variety of conflicts discussed here demonstrates, however, explaining war is a huge intellectual challenge, and preventing it a huge political challenge.

## THE CAUSES OF WAR

On May 23, 1618, a group of Protestants, enraged at efforts to curtail their religious freedom, seized two officials of the King of Bohemia at Prague Castle and threw them out the window. The event, known as the Second Defenestration of Prague, touched off the Bohemian Revolt, the first stage of the Thirty Years' War. By 1648, central Europe had been despoiled and roughly a quarter of the population wiped out.

How could the early equivalent of a world war be caused by throwing a few bureaucrats out of a window? Most historians would argue, of course, that the Second Defenestration of Prague did not really *cause* the Thirty Years' War. Rather, the war was the inevitable result of deep conflicts. The great powers of the day—Spain, France, Sweden, and the Holy Roman Empire—were struggling to dominate Europe. Religious conflict emanating from the Protestant Reformation intensified hostility. In this view, the events in Prague were only a spark and, given the

"You see, we have to build our navy up to what the other nations said they would build theirs up to, if we built ours up."

Mary Petty The New Yorker Collection/The Cartoon Bank

underlying impetus toward war, any spark could have set it off. Put differently, absent a situation primed for war, the incident might have had little effect (or might not have occurred at all).

Similar arguments can be made about the origins of other wars, such as World War I or the 1969 "Football War" between El Salvador and Honduras. Was World War I caused by Gavrilo Princip's assassination of Archduke Francis Ferdinand or by underlying power politics or imperialism? Was the "Football War" caused by the violence surrounding the World Cup qualifying matches between Honduras and El Salvador, or was it caused by underlying tensions between the two countries that had been building for years?

It is logical that if we seek to prevent war we must understand what causes it, but this is more easily said than done. There are more theories about the causes of war than can possibly be reviewed here, and there is no consensus among scholars about which theory is best, or even where to begin. There are likely multiple causes of war, at multiple levels of analysis, and these causes interact with one another.[1]

## THE POLICY CONNECTION

### PREVENTIVE WAR

In the months following the September 2001 terrorist attacks on the United States, U.S. President George W. Bush outlined a series of foreign policy principles that came to be called the Bush Doctrine. Among those principles was the argument that the United States might wage preventive war on a country that was in the process of gaining weapons of mass destruction. In other words, it might be necessary to attack a country that was not attacking the United States if that country was seen as hostile and was gaining nuclear capability. A group of advisers known as "neoconservatives" had been advocating such a policy since the early 1990s, but the terrorist attacks of 2001 strengthened the view that such a policy was both justifiable and necessary.

Bush elaborated the argument for preemption in several speeches. In his 2002 State of the Union address, he said, "The United States of America will not permit the world's most dangerous regimes to threaten us with the world's most destructive weapons." He identified three potential targets—Iraq, Iran, and North Korea—calling them the "axis of evil." In a speech at the U.S. Military Academy at West Point later the same year, he said, "Our security will require all Americans to be forward-looking and resolute, to be ready for preemptive action when necessary to defend our liberty and to defend our lives."*

The same issue had arisen immediately after World War II, when the United States possessed nuclear weapons and the Soviet Union did not. Some U.S. military strategists advocated preventive strikes on Soviet facilities to prevent the Soviets from gaining nuclear weapons. However, such a policy was dismissed because of the perceived unacceptability of deliberately starting a war and the large number of civilian casualties that would likely result. The United States again rejected preventive war during the Cuban Missile Crisis.

The issue of preventive war was prominent again in 2011–2012 as U.S. and Israeli leaders talked openly of attacking Iran to prevent it from acquiring nuclear weapons. The attractions of the policy of prevention were clear: Dealing

*(Continued)*

Iran's nuclear reactor at Bushehr, Iran. Some have advocated attacking Iranian nuclear facilities before they have produced nuclear weapons. What is the logic behind such a strategy, and what are the risks?

with potential nuclear proliferation through military attack could avert major dangers without the delays, complications, and fallibility of the diplomatic process.

However, critics of preventive war pointed out several problems with the strategy. First was the danger that any war started for such reasons would get out of control or drag on much longer than intended. Second was the question of whether preventive war was legal under international law. Some policy analysts were concerned that if the United States were perceived as waging illegal war, it would lose the moral leadership that was so important in the war on terror. Third was the danger that the strategy might cause what it was intended to prevent—that states feeling threatened by U.S. attack might respond, not by backing down but by accelerating efforts to procure nuclear weapons and systems to deliver

them for use on the United States. This appears to have been the response of North Korea and Iran to the U.S. invasion of Iraq.

## Critical Thinking Questions

1. In what circumstances, if any, is preventive war a good policy? What criteria should be used in evaluating this question?

2. How do terrorism and weapons of mass destruction alter the security dilemma and the incentive to strike first?

3. How might states behave in a world in which preventive war was considered legal?

*Both Bush quotes are from the Public Broadcasting System, Frontline, "Chronology: The Evolution of the Bush Doctrine," www.pbs.org/wgbh/pages/frontline/shows/iraq/etc/cron.html.

# SYSTEM-LEVEL THEORIES

**Realism**   As discussed in Chapter 3, realist explanations are based on the anarchic nature of the system. Simply put, the world is a dangerous place. There is nothing other than self-interest to stop one state from attacking or threatening another. States in a self-help system arm to defend themselves, and this makes other states less secure. This is the security dilemma. The result is competition for military dominance.

War breaks out, in this view, "because there is nothing to prevent it."[2] This system-level version cannot explain why any *particular* war breaks out. Rather, it explains why wars in general break out: "The origins of hot wars lie in cold wars, and the origins of cold wars are found in the anarchic ordering of the international arena."[3] Accordingly, even states that do not have expansionist agendas will initiate war if they expect it to make them safer in the future. An example of this sort of war might be the Soviet Union's attack on Finland in 1940, which was intended to give the Soviet Union a greater territorial buffer to protect Leningrad (now St. Petersburg), which was located very close to the prewar border.

In the systemic realist view, any number of **proximate causes** can ignite a war: the assassination of the Archduke Franz Ferdinand (World War I), Germany's unquenchable desire for conquest (World War II), or the U.S. government's mistaken assessment of intelligence on Iraq in 2003. In all these cases, realists would contend, the proximate causes resulted from international anarchy and were able to set off wars because of international anarchy. Critics of this approach argue that anarchy by itself cannot cause war: If all states were satisfied with their positions, there would be no war, even under anarchy.[4] To the extent this is true, we need to look to lower levels of analysis to understand the outbreak of particular wars.

Realists debate what distribution of power (bipolar or multipolar; balanced or unbalanced) is most likely to lead to war. Statistical studies on these questions yield unclear results. One author concludes, "No particular distribution of power has exclusive claim as a predictor of peace or war either in theory or in the empirical record of the period 1816–1965."[5] Others argue that *change* in the distribution of power, especially rapid change, increases the chance of war.[6] Despite these debates, realists agree that anarchy is the underlying cause of war.

**Capitalism and War**   Economic explanations of the causes of war have been offered at the system level as well as at the state level. At the system level, the most familiar explanations of war are offered by economic structuralism, which argues that capitalism inevitably produces the need for states to expand. Declining returns on investment at home, the need for more labor and raw materials, and the quest for markets abroad all lead capitalist states to expand. Scholars have attributed the surge in European imperialism in the late nineteenth century and the outbreak of World War I to these dynamics. Later, Marxist scholars called attention to U.S. economic motivations for playing a prominent global role after World War II, including its involvement in the Vietnam War.[7] Some today fear that China's growing need for raw materials to feed its economic growth will make it more aggressive.

**Free Trade and Peace**   Since the early nineteenth century, liberal theorists have argued that free trade reduces the likelihood of war. This is a system-level theory because the amount of free trade is not a characteristic of one state but of a system of states. This view concurs with the economic structuralist perspective that war has often been fought for economic gains but finds, in contrast to structuralism, that this tendency can be overcome through free trade. Two arguments support this claim.

**proximate causes**

An event that immediately precedes an outcome and therefore provides the most direct explanation of it.

First, if wars are fought to acquire raw materials, free trade offers a better alternative. The costs of outfitting armies, sending them to war, and occupying a conquered country are extraordinary; it is much cheaper, liberals assert, to buy needed supplies on the free market than to acquire them through conquest. Therefore, they conclude, war should occur for economic reasons only in the absence of an open market.

Second, the interdependence of economies and the spread of firms around the world ought to blur the economic distinction between "them" and "us" for both populations and firms. Destroying a country that is a major market for one's exports and a major source of inputs is a losing proposition for the country. The costs might be especially high for multinational firms with factories and offices in many countries. Skeptics dispute both the theory and the evidence in this argument.[8] The French philosopher Jean-Jacques Rousseau argued that interdependence is often unequal and therefore leads to economic coercion and from there to conflict. He advised smaller states especially to become *autarchic* (economically self-sufficient) to avoid conflict.

Empirically, the same kinds of statistical studies used to test the democratic peace hypothesis have been applied to the economic interdependence hypothesis and have produced little support for this claim. The reason for this lack of support becomes evident when one considers the role of geography in trade and war. States tend to trade most with their neighbors. They also tend to go to war most frequently with their neighbors. Therefore, there is a tendency for war between trading partners, even if trade does have some benefits. World War I is a good example. Trade among the European powers was at an all-time high in 1914, but this did not prevent them from fighting the most destructive war to that point in history.

## STATE-LEVEL AND SUBSTATE-LEVEL THEORIES

**Regime Type**    As noted in Chapter 5, many people have argued that a country's form of government has a significant impact on whether the country is peaceful or not. To summarize, it is widely argued that democracies tend not to fight each other. Even those who assert the validity of the democratic peace theory, it should be noted, do not assert that authoritarian states are the *cause* of wars. Democracies have not been found to be more peaceful than nondemocratic states. Rather, they tend not to go to war *with each other*.

An intriguing argument developed more recently contends that although democracies may be more peaceful in general, *new* democracies are especially prone to waging war because they do not yet have the institutionalized tendency toward compromise that constrains the incentive to build public support through assertive foreign policies. "Using the same databases that are typically used to study the democratic peace theory, we find considerable statistical evidence that democratizing states are more likely to fight wars than are mature democracies or stable autocracies."[9]

**expected utility**

A variant of the rational action model. The theory asserts that leaders evaluate policies by combining their estimation of the utility of potential outcomes with the likelihood that different outcomes will result from the policy in question.

**Expected Utility Theory**    Expected utility theory predicts that states will choose the available course of action that has the highest **expected utility**. If war has a higher expected utility than peace for a given state, then that state will go to war. In practice, it is difficult if not impossible to measure the expected utility of different policies. Such judgments must be subjective. But conceptually, expected utility theory makes a crucial point: A state initiates war when leaders believe it is in the state's interest to do so. This logic underpins the policy of deterrence, which seeks to raise the costs of war for a potential adversary. If the other state's expected utility of war can be driven down below the expected utility of some other policy, then war might be averted.

# THE GEOGRAPHY CONNECTION

## POVERTY, WEALTH, AND WAR

This map shows relative wealth in countries around the world as well as places where conflicts have occurred in recent years.

### Critical Thinking Questions

1. Can you judge from this map whether conflict is in some way linked to wealth and poverty?

Where does the relationship seem to hold? Where doesn't it?

2. What other maps might you want to study to understand the geography of war?

Economic Development and Conflict

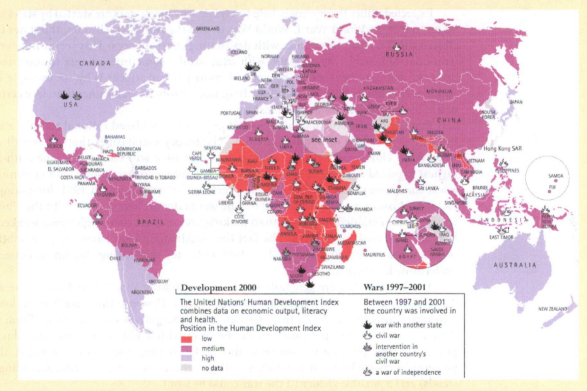

**Development 2000**

The United Nations' Human Development Index combines data on economic output, literacy and health.
Position in the Human Development Index

- low
- medium
- high
- no data

**Wars 1997–2001**

Between 1997 and 2001 the country was involved in

- war with another state
- civil war
- intervention in another country's civil war
- a war of independence

Source: "Poverty" from The Penguin Atlas of War and Peace by Dan Smith, copyright © 2003 by Dan Smith. Used by permission of Penguin, a division of Penguin Group (USA). Reproduced with permission from The Atlas of War and Peace by Dan Smith. Copyright © Myriad Editions/www.myriadeditions.com.

Was Saddam Hussein irrational in accepting war with the United States in 2003 (and 1991)? Or was going to war with the United States less certain to cause his downfall than giving into U.S. demands?

AP Photo/Iraqi TV via APTN

Expected utility theory might help to explain why many wars are started by states that go on to lose. In World War I, World War II, and the Arab–Israeli wars, the states that started the wars lost, sometimes with devastating consequences. This seems inherently irrational. Similarly, why do states with weak armies sometimes choose to resist more powerful states, rather than make concessions to avoid an attack? Why, for example, did Saddam Hussein in 1991 not withdraw Iraqi troops from Kuwait rather than face certain defeat by the U.S.-led military forces?

Expected utility theory shows why it might be considered rational to fight a war even when the odds of winning are low. The theory emphasizes that states will not necessarily choose a *successful* strategy, but that they will choose the one with the *highest expected utility*. For a weak state backed into a corner, a long shot at winning a war may have greater utility than the certainty of surrender. In 1991, for example, Saddam Hussein may have believed that he was better off losing a war with the United States, if he remained in power, than making concessions that might have weakened him and led to his overthrow. The fact that Saddam Hussein ruled Iraq for another twelve years after being defeated in 1991 indicates that losing did not necessarily undermine his interests.

The empires that are generally regarded as initiating World War I, Germany and Austria-Hungary, not only lost—they ceased to exist. How can this have been rational? Expected utility theory raises the question: What alternatives were available? From the Austrian and German perspectives, the problem with avoiding war was that during peacetime their position in Europe seemed to be slipping away. In other words, they perceived a choice between a *certain loss* (if peaceful events kept evolving according to trends) and a *possible victory* (if the war could be won).

This analysis offers an important policy lesson: If you want to avoid war, be sure that your opponent has a better alternative. Even a country in a dominant position may be attacked if its adversary cannot find a better alternative. John F. Kennedy was seen as having been uncommonly wise when, in the Cuban Missile Crisis, he insisted on giving Soviet leader Nikita Khrushchev a way to "save face." If making a concession on the Cuban missiles meant complete humiliation for Khrushchev personally and for the Soviet Union as a state, war might have seemed the better alternative for them. Kennedy promised to remove U.S. missiles from Turkey and to refrain from attacking Cuba. This concession allowed Khrushchev to claim that the Soviet Union had accomplished its goals.

Although expected utility theory holds that states go to war because they see it as being in their interest, the theory says very little about what those interests might be. What goals of states are so important that they might provide sufficient motivation to accept the inherent risks of going to war? Several other theories examine state-level motivations.

**Aggressive States**    Chapter 3 noted that some variants of realist theory have a strong state-level component. This is consistent with the view that anarchy is the *permissive* cause of war, but that some more positive cause is required to actually start a war.[10] Aggressive states provide one explanation. Revisionist states—states that reject the status quo—might see war as one means of achieving a more favorable situation. According to **power transition theory**, a state that has gained power over time might seek a reordering of affairs that recognizes its power and provides it more benefits. This is one explanation for German policy leading to both World War I and World War II. Two particular motives that might cause states to reject the status quo: imperialism and nationalism.

**Imperialist States**    State-level economic theories of war focus on how individual states pursue military conquest for economic reasons. **Economic imperialism** is the effort to improve a state's economic situation through military expansion, usually to gain better control of resources and markets. Many scholars (and not only economic structuralists) attribute the colonial conquests of the sixteenth through the nineteenth centuries to economic imperialism. The desire to gain control of important natural resources was also seen in World War II, in Japan's expansion into Southeast Asia and in Germany's attacks on Poland and then the Soviet Union through which it gained territory, or "living space" (*Lebensraum*), and oil.

In one form of this argument, a politically powerful **military-industrial complex**, linking military contractors and armed forces, lobbies governments to continuously increase defense spending. Some believe that the military-industrial complex exaggerates security threats or even helps create them in order to drive up profits. This concern was made famous by the warnings of U.S. President (and retired five-star general) Dwight Eisenhower in his farewell address in 1961. More recently, former Secretary of State Colin Powell warned of the emergence of a "terror-industrial complex."[11] A related argument contends that coalitions of domestic actors that will benefit from expansionist foreign policies propagate "myths of empire" to justify imperialism. When these coalitions are able to prevail domestically, aggression is likely to result.[12]

**Nationalism**    Nationalism and ethnic strife have often been viewed as primary sources of international conflict.[13] As noted in Chapter 2, the rise of nationalism increased the ability of governments to mobilize their populations for war. World War I, World War II, and the wars in the former Yugoslavia have all been blamed on nationalism, as have several incidents of genocide (in Rwanda in 1994 and in Armenia in 1915–1918) and terrorism (the Irish Republican Army in Britain and Basque separatists in Spain).

*Nationalism* can be defined as the doctrine that recognizes the nation as the primary unit of political allegiance. The nation, in turn, can be defined as the largest group that people define as their in-group. Traditionally, national identity was viewed as somehow linked to genetics, such that there was a fundamental identifiable difference between people of one nationality and another. Some still hold that view, but scholars view a "nation" as something that is perceived rather than based in physical reality. In other words, nations are socially constructed, or, as in the title of an influential book on the subject, *Imagined Communities*.[14]

**power transition theory**

A theory that postulates that war occurs when one state becomes powerful enough to challenge the dominant state and reorder the hierarchy of power within the international system.

**economic imperialism**

Efforts by states to improve their economic situation through military expansion, usually to gain better control of resources and markets.

**military-industrial complex**

A term made popular by President Dwight D. Eisenhower that refers to a group consisting of a nation's armed forces, weapon suppliers and manufacturers, and elements within the civil service involved in defense efforts.

Palestinian youths throw rocks at Israeli border police in Shuafat refugee camp, in Jerusalem, Israel, February 2010. Religion, nationalism, and territory all play important roles in this conflict.

AP Images/MUAMMAR AWAD

In its most virulent forms, nationalism can lead to conflict by itself. When one group of people (Nazi Germany is the best example) believes it is so superior to others that it has the right (and perhaps the duty) to rule over or even exterminate other groups, it is easy to see how violence can result. That sort of doctrine was widespread in the era before World War II.

More broadly, nationalism has led to conflict when combined with the related doctrine of national self-determination. This doctrine is based in democratic theory, which asserts that each group of people should rule itself. However, basing the notion of the body politic on ethnic and national criteria, rather than on territory, sows the seeds for innumerable conflicts. The nation-state is an abstraction; almost no state in the world is ethnically or nationally homogenous.[15] National groups are often mixed together and often cross established political boundaries.

As a result, the drive for national self-determination invariably involves giving one group control over a territory and either reducing other groups to second-class status or ejecting them from the territory altogether. It may also involve trying to conquer territory belonging to other states in order to bring an ethnic group under one government. Thus, the doctrine of national self-determination can lead directly to violence.

There can be little doubt that nationalism has been an important component in the origins of some wars. Since the end of the Cold War, ethnic conflict has played a role in civil and international wars in nearly every region of the world. However, nationalism does not appear to be the sole cause of war because some wars lack an ethnic dimension (the U.S. Civil War is one example). Moreover, although war is an age-old phenomenon, nationalism and the idea of the nation-state are relatively modern phenomena, dating roughly to the period of the French Revolution. If war is caused by nationalism, there should have been little war prior to the era of nationalism. Conversely, nationalism is nearly universal, but war is not. At best, therefore, nationalism can only provide a partial explanation of war.

**War as a Diversion** The diversionary theory of war holds that wars are sometimes initiated to distract the public from other, more troubling issues. Thus, Vyacheslav Plehve,

Russian interior minister at the time of the Russo-Japanese War (1904–1905), is reported to have advocated war, saying, "What this country needs is a short, victorious war to stem the tide of revolution."[16] The same effort to influence public opinion has been linked to other decisions to go to war, including those of Germany in 1914, Argentina in invading the Falklands/Malvinas islands in 1982, and the United States in attacking suspected terrorist bases in Afghanistan and Sudan in 1998. Indeed, historian Geoffrey Blainey claims that the argument that war is a "foreign circus staged for discontented groups at home … was invoked to explain individual wars from the Hundred Years war, which began in 1328, to the Vietnam War more than six centuries later."[17] Although diversionary wars have traditionally been viewed as a policy of autocratic leaders who had no democratic legitimacy for their rule, the theory has been applied more recently to democracies as well.[18] As with many other theories that seem plausible, it is hard to see how the diversionary theory explains why war happens in some circumstances and not in others.

## INDIVIDUAL-LEVEL THEORIES

Individual-level explanations of war find the causes of war either in human nature or in the psychology of individual leaders. An important distinction between theories at this level is whether or not they assert that the shortcomings of individuals can be overcome. For example, if genetics determines that we are all aggressive, there may not be much that can be done. But if wars are caused by the mistakes, either of people in general or of particular leaders, better education or decision making may reduce conflict.

**Human Aggression**   Some scientists argue that war is simply another form of aggression, which is "hardwired" into human beings through genetics. According to this view, some tendency toward aggression is innate in many species of animals. Researchers study the sources of violence in the animal kingdom, which include disputes over food, mates, and territory, as well as differences between groups. Scientists also study variations in patterns of violence, including those based on sex, age, and population density, among other factors. Moreover, research has shown that violence can be conditioned by experience.[19]

This research implies that human beings have the same predispositions toward violence as other animals. Humans are only narrowly removed, in evolutionary terms, from an environment that truly was anarchic and in which the weak were at the mercy of the strong. Stronger, more aggressive individuals were better able to protect and feed their young, and were preferred by mates. In this environment, the aggressive were more likely to pass on their genes. Thus, it is argued, **natural selection** favored aggression in human beings. Psychologist Sigmund Freud argued, "It is a general principle, then, that conflicts of interest between men are settled by the use of violence."[20]

Evidence against the thesis that people are inherently aggressive has been sought by anthropologists, who have scoured the world to find nonviolent primitive societies. The existence of societies with no violence would undermine the idea that violence is innate in human beings and instead support the idea that violence is learned through socialization. Several small and geographically isolated peaceful societies have been identified, but it is not clear whether conflict and violence were genuinely absent or whether these societies used powerful socialization effects (such as ostracizing those who commit acts of violence) to deter violence.[21]

The notion that people are aggressive or power-hungry has been adopted by a wide range of political and international relations theorists. As Thucydides stated: "Of gods we believe and of men we know, it is in their nature to rule whenever they can."[22] Similarly, Hans Morgenthau states, "Human nature, in which the laws of politics have their roots,

**natural selection**

The tendency for traits that increase the likelihood of an individual's surviving and producing offspring to become more common in future generations of a species.

has not changed since the classical philosophies of China, India, and Greece endeavored to discover these laws."[23] Christian theologians from Augustine of Hippo in the fifth century to Reinhold Niebuhr in the twentieth have made the same argument, as have philosophers such as Benedict de Spinoza.[24] Both religious and scientific arguments lead to the conclusion that conflict is the inevitable outcome of human nature.

The problem with the innate aggression hypothesis is that it cannot explain *variation* in the amount of conflict observed. The human genome is more or less constant, yet the level of war and peace varies greatly over time and across space. This is true whether we consider violence between states or between street gangs. The biological explanation, even to the extent that it is true, does not get to the key question of why violence happens at some times and not others.

Moreover, there is a powerful counterargument, also based on natural selection: Because individual human survival in the wild is a very uncertain proposition, humans who cooperate in groups are more likely to survive and reproduce, as are those who avoid the high fatality rates of war. Therefore, natural selection would favor those individuals who could collaborate with their fellows instead of killing them. This view resonates with the feminist critique of a masculine definition of power as the ability to coerce or injure, rather than as the ability to collaborate.

**Individual Leaders: Madmen and Megalomaniacs**   Chapter 6 devoted considerable attention to biases that can cause misperceptions on the part of state leaders. In a state where a single leader can be highly influential in the choice to go war, such misperceptions can be seen as the proximate cause of war. Thus, World War II in Europe is explained largely by the pathological aggression of Adolph Hitler, and it is difficult to explain the Napoleonic wars that ravaged Europe in the early nineteenth century without looking at the remarkable ambition and leadership of Napoleon Bonaparte. This approach seems to fit well with the democratic peace theory, which would argue that in democracies such leaders would be unable to bring their countries to war single-handedly. Many theorists, however, find this view of war unconvincing, in part because such explanations seem closely linked to the wartime propaganda that every state produces to portray its adversaries as evil aggressors, bent on conquest for its own sake. Moreover, scholars find that behind many of these "madmen" lie genuine conflicts of interest. Thus, Germany's involvement in World War II, for example, is seen as driven less by Hitler alone than by the distribution of power that developed in Europe in the 1930s.[25]

**Misperception**   The views of expected utility theory are sharply contested by those who focus on the processes of misperception. According to this perspective, war is almost always the result not of rational calculations, but of *irrational* calculations and of psychologically driven misperceptions. Such misperceptions lead states to begin wars that look crazy in retrospect.

Problems of misperception are likely to be strongest when leaders are under psychological stress, such as when they find themselves in a crisis, on the verge of war.[26] In other words, misperception is likely to be worst when accurate perception and sound judgment matter most.

Several examples of misperception and conflict were discussed in Chapter 6, including Germany's belief in 1914 that Britain would not join the war. Soviet ruler Joseph Stalin calculated in 1939 that signing a nonaggression pact with Hitler would protect the Soviet Union from attack. When Germany attacked, Stalin was so stunned that he did not speak publicly for a week while German troops routed the Soviet army. American leaders never took seriously the notion that Japan would attack Pearl Harbor, whereas the Japanese who planned the attack expected the United States to respond by withdrawing from the Pacific, not by resolving to destroy Imperial Japan. In the early 1960s, the United States believed that a few of its military advisers could easily help the South Vietnamese army defeat a poorly armed peasant communist movement in Vietnam, and in 1979, Soviet leaders believed they could quickly conquer Afghanistan (they were still there a decade later). Saddam Hussein believed in 1990 that no one would do anything about Iraq's invasion of Kuwait.

The belief that war often results from misperception has led to a search for ways to prevent such misperceptions. This was an especially important theme during the Cold War, when the stakes were particularly high. But the stakes remain high now, whether in considering a nuclear war between India and Pakistan or a brief intervention that ends up lasting a decade. Avoiding misperception is seen as an important means of avoiding war.

**The Fog of War**    Expectations about war that turn out to be wrong are not simply the result of misperceptions or stupidity. War is an immensely complex endeavor, and its path and consequences are inherently unpredictable. The inability to predict how a war will go and the difficulty in controlling it once it starts are problems that have been studied for centuries. The Prussian strategist Karl von Clausewitz coined the phrase the **fog of war** to characterize the difficulties in controlling war once it starts.

Expected utility theorists contend that misperception does not really undermine their theory, because misperception only reveals itself in hindsight. Given what they know *at the time*, expected utility theorists contend, leaders of two states will go to war when both calculate that the expected benefits of going to war exceed the benefits of making the concessions needed to avoid war. War, therefore, can be seen as being caused by disagreement over the distribution of military power and as ending when warfare clarifies the distribution of power.[27]

Why is it so difficult to predict how war will turn out? Even wars in which the winner is correctly predicted from the onset rarely turn out as expected. For example, no one doubted that the United States could prevail in the U.S.–Iraq war that began in 2003, but few predicted that the defeat of the Iraqi army and the dismantling of Saddam Hussein's state would lead to an insurgency that the United States would struggle for years to defeat. Neither the speed of the original victory nor the dragging on of the ensuing insurgency was widely anticipated.

Every war is unique, in terms of the combatants, the circumstances, the technologies, and the tactics. This makes it hard to apply findings from one war to the next. Germany's wars with France (and others) from 1870 through 1945 illustrate this point. The Franco-Prussian War of 1870 was over in six weeks. Prussia (a forerunner of Germany) was able to use a new technology, railroads, to move its troops very rapidly to outmaneuver the French forces. Because Prussia was able to win through maneuver, there were no major battles and casualties were low. Military planners in subsequent decades assumed that the next war would be the same. In 1914, the belief that a war would be quick and that casualties would be low fed the willingness of all sides to go to war. However, several technological innovations whose effects had not been anticipated changed the nature of war. Barbed wire and machine guns, among other factors, made defense very easy, and attack became nearly suicidal. As a result, the war rapidly stalemated into trench warfare, and huge numbers of soldiers were sacrificed in futile efforts to break through opposing lines.

In the years leading up to World War II, the French learned the lessons of defense from World War I and devised a series of fortresses, known as the *Maginot Line*, to repel Germany. However, another new technology had emerged: the tank. German tacticians figured out how to form separate tank forces that could move through or around enemy lines and rapidly cut them off from behind. These tactics made the French fortifications

**fog of war**
A phrase coined by Prussian strategist Karl von Clausewitz to characterize the difficulties in controlling war once it starts.

useless. Germany never attacked the Maginot Line when it invaded France in 1940. Instead, German forces went around them and were in Paris within weeks. In each of these three wars, fought on the same territory by the same combatants, the relative strengths of offense and defense were completely different. States whose leaders anticipated these strengths correctly had an advantage, but especially in World War I, the costs of learning were enormous. Germany was defeated in World War II only when Russian generals learned the German tactics and deployed them with a devastating effect against Germany's overstretched forces at the Battle of Stalingrad (1942–1943) and afterward.

To summarize, it is often difficult to anticipate how a war will proceed. Each war is different in terms of the combatants and in terms of the military objectives. At the same time, military technology changes over time, and the effects of these changes can rarely be anticipated until the technology is actually used in war.

## THE SEARCH FOR SCIENTIFIC EXPLANATIONS

Despite the massive amount of research on the subject, there remains little consensus on the causes of war. As the expected utility and misperception approaches both assert in different ways, the decision to go to war is based on the perception that war is the best alternative available. To the extent that this is true, however, the theories do not say much about the broader causes—about the roles of economics, domestic politics, nationalism, the distribution of power, and other factors that contribute to the belief that war is the best option. All of these factors can be plausible explanations when applied to one or a few cases. However, none provides a satisfying general explanation of variation in the outbreak of war—of why wars occur in some cases, but not in others.

Why, with all of the data collected on wars and all of the sophisticated methods of analysis available, are scholars unable to definitively determine the causes of war? Does the evidence not support some explanations better than others? In some cases, it does, but different paradigms conceptualize the problem differently and therefore are difficult to compare directly or to evaluate using a single body of evidence.

The lack of conclusive answers about the causes of war should not obscure the fact that several of the most plausible-sounding and widely held understandings of war do not hold up to scrutiny. Statistical analyses of data have shown that neither balance of power nor imbalance of power is closely associated with war. Economic interdependence does not reduce the likelihood of war and may increase it. A democratic form of government does not reduce the likelihood of a state's being involved in war. By eliminating these plausible explanations, scholars can focus more attention on other potential causes.

Despite the vast amount of research on the subject, there are several obstacles to a scientific explanation of the causes of war. Some of these obstacles are conceptual, and some have to do with the nature of evidence and data collection.

**Conceptual Problems**   One conceptual problem has to do with different ways of defining the "causes" of war. This discussion so far has referred to at least three different views of the causes of war.

- Permissive conditions—reasons why war is *possible*. This understanding of cause is especially prominent in realist theory.
- General sources of conflict; also known as the *underlying* causes of war. This notion of cause is found in many theories at the system and state levels.
- *Decisions* to initiate war; a definition especially prominent at the state and individual levels.

**TABLE 8.1**  **Summary of Causes of War**

|  | System Level | State Level | Individual Level |
|---|---|---|---|
| Theories that assert that war is inevitable | Realism (war is caused by anarchy) Economic structuralism (war is caused by capitalism) |  | War is caused by human aggression |
| Theories that assert that war is avoidable | Economic liberalism (free trade leads to peace) | Democratic peace theory Expected utility theory Realism (war is caused by aggressive states) Economic structuralism (war is caused by capitalism) | War depends on the psychology of individual leaders War is driven by psychological misperceptions |

One of the most difficult questions for scholars as well as policy makers is whether to focus on the underlying causes of war or the proximate causes (see Table 8.1). This is the question raised at the outset of this chapter concerning the Thirty Years' War. Underlying causes refer to the long-term buildup in tensions that lead countries to believe that they may go to war with each other and to prepare for such a war. Proximate causes are the crises that move countries from a situation of hostility to one of outright conflict.

Those who focus on underlying causes see these as more fundamental, both for explaining why wars happened in the past and for preventing them in the future. In this view, if there is a long-term buildup toward war, any number of proximate causes can set it off, and the particular incident does not really much matter. This view does not put much stock in the claim that World War I was caused by the assassination of the Archduke Franz Ferdinand, even though that statement is in some sense true. The major powers of Europe had been planning for war with each other for some time; all were expecting it to happen sooner or later, and some even welcomed war. Thus, it did not matter that the Bosnian crisis of 1912 did not lead to the war, and it would not have mattered if the 1914 July crisis had somehow been resolved. Sooner or later, the war would have occurred. In this view, it was the underlying problems in the distribution of power and the alliance system that caused the war. Or, from an economic structuralist view, it was the underlying workings of the capitalist system.

Others reject this view, arguing that war is never inevitable and that if crises can be managed successfully for long enough, the tensions underlying them might eventually diminish. Had World War III broken out over the Cuban Missile Crisis, future historians (if there had been any) could easily have argued that the war was inevitable; that if war had not occurred over the 1961 Berlin crisis or the 1962 Cuban crisis, it would have broken out later over something else. In retrospect, however, it is now clear that war between the Soviet Union and the United States was not inevitable. The Cold War ended and the Soviet Union collapsed without World War III happening. Therefore, some scholars and policy makers see the proximate causes of war as the most crucial.

For this reason, a great deal of research has gone into studying crisis resolution. Research has focused on how the stress of crisis influences individual psychology and group decision making. Research has also been directed at improving crisis decision-making procedures—covering everything from ensuring that a country's top leaders

**War: The funnel of causation.** Explanations of war operate at different levels of generality, from showing why it is possible, to hypothesizing about what makes it more likely and what causes the final decision to attack.

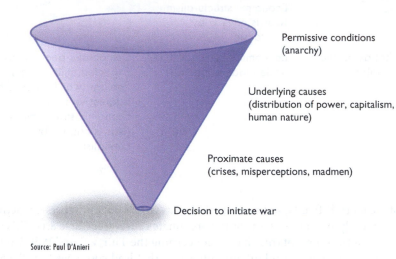

Permissive conditions
(anarchy)

Underlying causes
(distribution of power, capitalism, human nature)

Proximate causes
(crises, misperceptions, madmen)

Decision to initiate war

Source: Paul D'Anieri

can gather in one place quickly to ensuring that they can contact leaders in other countries rapidly.

Different explanations coexist because the road to war is a complex process. Many factors contribute, making explanations focusing on one or a few factors insufficient. Some causal factors occur prior to others. In other words, before the decisions of individual leaders can cause a war, other conditions (such as underlying conflicts) must exist. Thus, we can think of a "funnel of causation" in which successive factors increase the likelihood of conflict, but none of them is by itself determinative (see Figure 8.1). Even if there were agreement on the "list of ingredients" of war, figuring out how they fit together would still be problematic.

Moreover, there may be *multiple pathways* to war, meaning that no single cause will explain all wars. Some wars may concern territory; others might concern national self-determination; and still others may involve neither. We actually have a good general understanding of what makes wars more or less likely, and therefore, we are rarely surprised when one breaks out. We know the warning signs. But a broad model that predicts exactly which combinations of circumstances will lead to war and which will not is beyond our current understanding.

**Data Problems**  In addition to conceptual problems, there are data problems. It is relatively easy to obtain data on many states over many years on such basic characteristics related to war as population, national wealth, military spending, government type, and the like. But it is much harder, if not impossible, to collect data on other factors, such as the nature of the decision-making process within a government or the evaluations of risks, payoffs, and alternatives discussed in expected utility models. Most governments work hard to keep these matters secret. Finding large amounts of comparable data on a variety of conflicts is, and probably will remain, impossible. The available data are sometimes sketchy and therefore subject to multiple interpretations. For all of these reasons, a considerable amount of work needs to be done before we fully understand the causes of war.

# PROTEST, REVOLUTION, AND CIVIL WAR

So far, our discussion has focused on war between states, but conflict within states—including protest, revolution, and civil war—is often just as important. Indeed, from 1945 to 1999, about 16 million people died in civil wars, roughly five times the number that died in international wars in the same period.[28] Protest and revolution also have had an enormous role in recent years. The Arab Spring of 2011, in which the authoritarian regimes in Tunisia, Libya, and Egypt were overthrown and those in several other countries were challenged, had significant repercussions.

Traditionally, scholars have drawn a sharp distinction between domestic or civil conflict and international conflict, treating them as distinct phenomena with distinct causes. But as recent examples make clear, conflicts that start as domestic conflicts often become internationalized. As we have seen, the effort to overthrow Muammar Gaddafi in Libya in 2011 drew a political response from the United Nations and a military intervention on the part of the North Atlantic Treaty Organization (NATO). Ukraine's 2014 revolution spurred an invasion from Russia.

What is civil war? Civil war is defined as a conflict between organized groups within a nation-state. Many researchers label a conflict a civil war only when battle deaths reach the threshold of 1000. In most cases, one side in the civil war is the state. However, when multiple forces claim to rule, it may not be clear which one is the state. We refer to these countries as "failed states." Some civil wars are fought over one region's efforts to secede, so what begins as a civil war may end as an international war between two independent states. This was the case in the wars that accompanied the fragmentation of Yugoslavia in the 1990s, and in the conflict between Sudan and South Sudan that preceded and followed South Sudan's secession.

A variety of domestic conflicts that do not rise to the level of civil war can be grouped under the label contentious politics. This includes protest movements and revolutions (the rapid change of a country's form of government). Although civil wars create the most concern in international politics because of their high level of violence, protest and revolution also have far-reaching effects.

## CAUSES OF CIVIL WAR

What are the causes of civil war, and how do they differ from the causes of international war? It might seem that explanations of international war could double as explanations of civil war, but that is generally not the case. The crucial difference is that an international war is between like actors (two or more states), whereas civil wars usually pit a state against nonstate opponents who adopt insurgent or terrorist, tactics (discussed in the next chapter). Although an international war may strengthen the victor, civil war almost always weakens the state. Anarchy, which is an important aspect of many explanations of international war, is, at least in theory, not present at the domestic level. To the extent that a civil war brings about a failed state, anarchy is an effect of conflict rather than a cause of it.

Explanations of civil war focus on two sets of factors: grievances and resources. Grievance-based approaches look at the reasons people rebel. Resource-based approaches focus on economic factors as a source of conflict and as a constraint on states' ability to resist rebellion.

Rebel movements that seek either to take over a state or to secede to form a new state cite a variety of grievances as motivations and as reasons they deserve to rule. These grievances may be political, economic, territorial, ethnic, or religious.

- Political: seeking to overthrow the government or to force it to reform.
  - Spanish civil war of the 1930s, in which fascists seized the state and republican forces fought unsuccessfully to retake control.
  - Libyan civil war (2011) and Syrian civil war (2012), in which opposition groups sought to overthrow dictatorships.
- Economics: seeking to force a government to adopt different economic policies or to address some economic grievance.
  - Rebellion in Nigeria's Niger River delta region by people seeking greater local control of oil resources.
  - Guatemalan civil war, 1960–1996, over land reform and economic rights of the poor.
- Territorial autonomy or independence.
  - South Sudan's successful fight to separate from Sudan, 1990s–2011.
  - Chechen wars to separate from Russia, 1994–2000.
- Ethnicity and religion.
  - Rebellions that led to the breakup of Yugoslavia and the formation of several new nation-states.
  - "The Troubles" in Northern Ireland, a conflict between Catholics and Protestants and over British control of the territory.

In many cases, these grievances overlap. For example, the civil wars that destroyed Yugoslavia combined ethnic and religious conflict with demands for regional autonomy. The civil war that led to the creation of South Sudan had ethnic, religious, and economic elements that combined in the eventual demand for independence. The strife between the Arab Muslims in the north and the animists and Christians in the south began just as Sudan gained its independence from Egypt in 1956. In addition to these differences, there were conflicts over limited land and over control of potentially lucrative oil fields.

Grievance-based models have wide popular currency, in part because these explanations often match the explanations given by the combatants themselves—what they say they are fighting for. However, researchers increasingly argue that grievance does not, in fact, explain civil wars. Based on statistical analyses of many civil wars (just as scholars of warfare rely on data sets of international wars), several prominent studies have indicated that the presence of grievances does not explain the occurrence of civil war. The point is not that grievances are not present in cases of civil war (they are), but rather that such grievances are *always* present in nearly every polity, yet they lead to civil war in only a small number of cases. In this view, then, the source of violence is not the grievances, but the inability of states and societies to resolve or contain them peacefully.

For example, it seems intuitively obvious that states with prominent ethnic cleavages will be more prone to insurgency and civil war. Yet a prominent study by James Fearon and David Laitin shows that, after controlling for wealth, there is no correlation between ethnic cleavage and civil war.[29] At the same time, their research shows a connection between wealth (per capita GNP) and civil war. In other words, many societies have ethnic differences, but the risk of violent conflict goes up in poorer countries and goes down in wealthier ones. Why? Fearon and Laitin identify two ways in which economic resources

Members of the Southern People's Liberation Army in Sudan. Their secessionist movement, which was based on a range of grievances, succeeded in 2011. But the civil war, which had lasted more than two decades, caused over 2 million deaths.

Jack Picone/Alamy

account for the variation. First, poorer societies have poorer states—governments with less ability to solve people's problems and less ability to combat violent movements. Second, poorer individuals are more likely to join insurgent movements because they have less to lose economically. People with good jobs might not want to risk losing them. Thus, we see ethnic divisions leading to violent conflict in Sudan, Rwanda, and Yugoslavia, but not in Belgium (divided between Flemish and Walloon), Canada (where Quebec has considered secession for decades), or Spain (where strong regionalism has led to sporadic terrorist violence but not civil war). A variant on the poverty argument focuses on relative deprivation. The argument here is that people are most likely to rebel when their level of wealth departs significantly from their expectations, as when a developing economy hits an economic crisis and people fall back into poverty when their expectation was for further growth.[30]

Other factors may contribute to the ability of rebel groups to initiate and sustain a violent challenge to the state. Countries with more mountainous terrain are more likely to experience civil war, because such terrain offers better protection for insurgents. Thus, numerous invaders over the past century have been unable to subdue local forces in Afghanistan. Areas with easily extractable natural resources are also more likely to experience civil war. The resources provide both a motive to secede and a means of funding an insurgency. The phenomenon of conflict diamonds—diamonds that are both a target of civil war and a means of funding it—is a prime example, but oil and mineral resources can play the same role.

## CONTENTIOUS POLITICS AND ITS IMPACT ON INTERNATIONAL RELATIONS

Domestic unrest does not need to reach the level of civil war to have an important impact on international politics. The Arab Spring of 2011 transformed the international politics of the Middle East. Similarly, a string of revolutions, involving very little violence, led to the demise of communism in Europe in 1989–1991 and thereby ended the Cold War.

# THE HISTORY CONNECTION

## RELIGION, HISTORY, AND OIL IN IRAQ'S INSURGENCY

After the defeat of the Iraqi army in 2003, conflict broke out between militias in Iraq and between those militias and the U.S. forces occupying the country (see Figure 8.2). With Saddam Hussein gone, the question was who would rule Iraq. For the United States, the intention was to set up a multiparty democracy, as had been done successfully in Germany, Italy, and Japan after World War II. But for many Iraqis, the key question was whether the country would be run by people from the Sunni or the Shia branch of Islam and whether the ethnic Kurds (a non-Arab Sunni group) would rule their traditional territory in the north of the country. In contrast to the simplistic view of Islam as a single unified force, the warring factions in Iraq were all composed of Muslims.

Hostility among the three main groups, Shia, Sunni, and Kurds, is based in large part on collective "memory" of events that happened generations, or even centuries, ago. The basic split between Shia and Sunni Muslims dates from the seventh century, when the death of the Prophet Mohammed was followed by a split between those who thought that religious and political authority should pass to caliphs (elders chosen by elite consensus) and those who thought it should pass to imams (descendants of Mohammed). These two groups became known as Sunni and Shia, respectively. In 680, Mohammed's grandson Hussein was slain in Karbala by Sunnis on the day now commemorated by Shia as Ashura, and that day has come to be marked by violence in post–Saddam Iraq (and elsewhere). A series of attacks during Ashura in 2004 killed 170 Shia and wounded 500. Similarly, attacks in 2006 and in 2007 on the Shia Al-Askariya mosque, where the eleventh and twelfth imams were buried in 944, were calculated to stir up violence between Shia and Sunni.* A central question for those seeking to overcome these divisions is: How can hostilities that have been 1300 years in the making be overcome in a short period of time?

Religion, ethnicity, and self-determination were not the only issues at stake. Also at question is who would control and benefit from Iraq's vast oil wealth, including reserves, refineries, and pipelines. Particularly controversial was control of the city of Kirkuk, which lay astride a major oil field and had a population divided between Kurds and Sunnis.

Saddam Hussein had managed to suppress these conflicts. Saddam was a Sunni Muslim, and his government actively repressed both the Shia concentrated in the south of the country and the Kurds in the north. His authoritarianism was largely successful in crushing resistance. When he was weakened by outside forces in 1991, both groups rose up. The Kurds were protected by a UN mandated "no-fly zone," but the Shia received no similar protection and were ruthlessly crushed after U.S. troops left. After 2003, the Kurds saw the opportunity to gain full independence, and the Shia were determined to avoid their previous fate. This left the Sunnis, who had dominated the country under Saddam, fearing for their position, and they were the groups who fought most actively against U.S. troops.

After most of the U.S. troops were removed, the battle for control of Iraq continued. Some of this was carried out through Iraq's new democratic institutions—elections and parliament—but much violence remained, both between different Sunni and Shia militias and between the Kurdish region and the central government. In 2013–2014, the conflict in Iraq partly merged with the civil war in neighboring Syria, as the "Islamic State in Syria and Iraq," an extremist Sunni group, participated in both conflicts.

### Critical Thinking Questions

1. Are authoritarian governments better able than democracies to manage religious and ethnic conflicts?

*(Continued)*

2. Are there latent social cleavages or economic conflicts that could lead to violence in your country? What kinds of factors might trigger protest or violence?

3. What other factors besides religion and ethnicity might become the basis for conflict between nonstate actors?

*"Al-Askariya Shrine: 'Not Just a Major Temple'," *Times Online*, February 22, 2006, www.timesonline.co.uk/tol/news/world/iraq/article733713.ece.

**FIGURE 8.2** **Ethnic division in Iraq.** If nationalism requires that each distinct group have its own state, what are the prospects for peace in Iraq? How did the country stay together for most of the twentieth century?

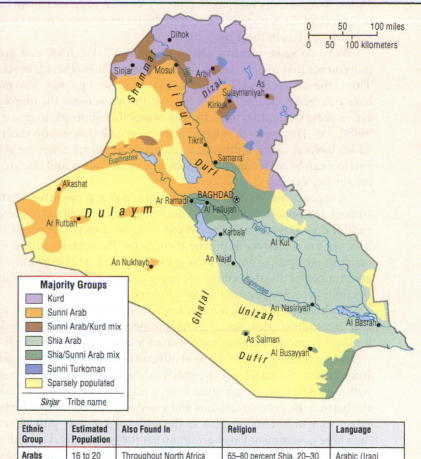

| Ethnic Group | Estimated Population | Also Found In | Religion | Language |
|---|---|---|---|---|
| Arabs | 16 to 20 million | Throughout North Africa and the Middle East, Iran | 65–80 percent Shia, 20–30 percent Sunni, less than 5 percent Christian | Arabic (Iraqi dialect) |
| Kurds | 3.6 to 4.8 million | Turkey, Iran, Syria, Armenia, Georgia, Azerbaijan | Mostly Sunni, Shia, and Yazidi minority | Kurdish |
| Turkomans | 300,000 to 800,000 | Related to other Turkic peoples in Turkey, Azerbaijan, Iran, and Turkmenistan | Primarily Sunni | South Azeri Turkish |
| Others | As many as 1 million | Mostly Christians, Iranians, and other groups found in the Middle East | At least 50 percent Christian; Shias, Sunnis, and members of other religions account for the balance | Mostly Arabic, some Persian and other languages |

Contentious politics can have significant international dimensions. Protest can lead to political revolutions that fundamentally change the character of state governments, with profound international repercussions. The French Revolution led to the Napoleonic wars. The overthrow of Germany's democracy in the 1930s spurred World War II. The Iranian revolution of 1979 brought a fundamentalist Islamic government to power, and protests in 2007 nearly brought that government down. Protests in the 1960s played an important role in ending the Vietnam War.

Protest is often aimed not at overturning a government but at changing specific policies, and in many instances the grievances of protestors are closely linked to international politics. The protests that led to the overthrow of Ukraine's government in 2014 were prompted by the government's decision not to sign an agreement with the European Union. The austerity measures adopted in Greece, Italy, and Spain in recent years at the insistence of the European Union and the International Monetary Fund (IMF) spurred massive protests in those countries.

Why do some protests, after starting small, catch on and grow into irresistible movements that force states to change course, while others lose steam and disappear? This is the subject of a vast literature in comparative politics. Two main foci of research have emerged. One line of work looks at the movements themselves. Resource mobilization theory examines the difficulty of mobilizing people to action and keeping them mobilized. This research is based heavily on collective action theory (see Chapter 14), which looks at why it is difficult to get actors to pursue collective action and how those barriers can be overcome. In this view, the organization and resources of the movement are the key variables.

A second line of research explores the "political opportunity structure"—the constraints and opportunities that the movement faces. Political opportunity structure can include divisions among elites and reduced government repression, both of which make it easier for protestors to pursue their goals. Particularly salient events that make it easier to rally people around a cause can also increase opportunity. For example, major environmental disasters constitute opportunities for environmental groups, and stolen elections provide opportunities for prodemocracy activists.

Technology is having a major impact on the ability of groups to mobilize activists and to coordinate their activity. The Internet, cellular phone networks, and applications for these networks have made it possible for large numbers of people to communicate in real time, reducing some of the most difficult organizational challenges for protest leaders. Information can travel quickly, widely, and efficiently, both bottom-up and top-down, within movements. At any given time, a huge number of individual citizens can, from the bottom up, provide accounts and video of government misdeeds that help mobilize others to action. They can also, in the midst of a protest, provide real-time intelligence on where government forces are and what they are doing. Using this information, protest leaders can, from the top down, let protestors know where they should gather, what slogans to chant, and so on. These tactics have helped shift the balance of power between governments and protest movements and have made it much easier to internationalize protest. News about protests and about government misdeeds now flows around the world instantly, and expertise, political support, and finance can flow into countries from outside very quickly.

Technology cuts both ways, however, and governments too are using new technology, from Internet surveillance to unmanned aircraft (drones), to keep track of potential adversaries. The government of China, for example, controls access to the Internet in ways that block certain topics from access by most Chinese citizens. Although Chinese dissidents have been ingenious in developing "work arounds," much of the ease and fluidity of Internet organization has been removed. Similarly, when protests are under way, movements' reliance on the Internet and cell phone networks can become a huge vulnerability, as local cellular networks and access to the Internet can easily be shut down.

## DOMESTIC–INTERNATIONAL LINKAGES IN CONTENTIOUS POLITICS

The Arab Spring of 2011 illustrates how three different mechanisms—diffusion, intervention, and spillover—can transform a domestic protest or conflict into an international conflict. The series of protests that wracked the region began in Tunisia. **Diffusion** is the spread of protest and tactics through the process of observation and copying. Tunisia's protests *diffused* to other countries when activists in those countries, emboldened and inspired by the Tunisian example, began protesting against their own authoritarian regimes. **Intervention** is the active involvement of outside actors in contentious politics or civil war. Libya's protests became internationalized when NATO *intervened*, using military force to tip what had become a civil war in favor of anti-Gaddafi forces. **Conflict spillover** is the spread of a domestic conflict across state borders. The conflict in Libya subsequently *spilled over* into Mali when thousands of refugees and Gaddafi loyalists fled across the border, putting stress on the Malian government that contributed to a military coup there in 2012.

While domestic conflict can spread into the international realm, the opposite is also true: International conflict can be a source of domestic conflict. The US.-led invasion of Iraq in 2003 ejected Saddam Hussein from power, but also led to a violent internal conflict as different groups battled for control of the country. Much the same result occurred when the United States forced the Taliban from power in Afghanistan in 2001. World War I also led to significant domestic turmoil in the combatant states: The Russian Revolution brought communism to Russia, and the ensuing civil war led to millions of deaths. A less violent revolution overturned the government of Germany.

Civil wars and other domestic conflicts have important effects on other dimensions of international politics. As noted previously, it seems that poverty has some role in causing civil war. At the same time, civil war is undoubtedly a cause of poverty. One of the main reasons the poorest countries are poor is that they have a high incidence of conflict, which drains government resources and destroys economic value. Civil conflict is also a major source of migration, both within states and across international boundaries. This puts the human rights of refugees at risk and imposes difficulties on the receiving states.

## THE RISE OF THE ISLAMIC STATE

The lines between domestic and international conflict, and between terrorism, insurgency, and conventional warfare, have been blurred more than ever by the rise of the "Islamic State," also known as "ISIS" and "ISIL," which in 2014–2015 took control of significant parts of Iraq. The Islamic State declared itself to be a new Caliphate, that is, an Islamic theocracy, with aspirations to create a single, global Islamic government.

The Islamic State owes its rise to a mixture of domestic, international, and transnational causes that appears to be emblematic of contemporary conflict. It rose in a vacuum left by state collapse in Iraq, which was caused by the U.S. invasion in 2003. The Islamic State then grew to take part in the civil war in Syria, which originated domestically but was inspired and fed transnationally by the Arab Spring and was supported internationally by a variety of states with an interest in supporting one side or another.

**diffusion**

The spread of protest and tactics through the process of observation and copying.

**intervention**

The involvement of outside actors in contentious politics or civil war.

**conflict spillover**

The spread of a domestic conflict across state borders.

Tactically, the Islamic State succeeded in doing something generally considered very difficult, which is to use the tactics of terrorism and insurgency to take territory and hold it. The exceeding brutality of the Islamic State appears to have either eliminated or intimidated potential opposition within the territory it controls. A wide variety of actors have sought to push it out of the territory it occupied. These actors included local groups opposed to the politics of the Islamic State and global powers (notably the United States) worried about the regional threat posed to the Iraqi government and the global threat of terrorism from the implacable group.

Despite its use of terror, not only against its enemies but against those it claims to rule, one strength of the Islamic State has been its ability to attract followers from around the world to travel to the region to join it. This indicates that at least some people consider this form of rule legitimate, which analysts struggle to explain. In late 2014, fighters in Libya declared their allegiance to the Islamic State, raising the possibility that the group's influence might spread far from Iraq and Syria. The impact of the Islamic State and efforts to combat it are major problems facing policy makers and analysts today.

# MANAGING THE SECURITY DILEMMA AND PREVENTING INTERNATIONAL CONFLICT

States often pursue security not by trying to win the competition for power, but by seeking to escape or manage the security dilemma. As discussed in Chapter 3, the liberal school of thought considers this both desirable and possible. Considerable effort has gone into identifying techniques to resolve international disagreements without resorting to violence, and such efforts have succeeded in many cases.

## ARMS CONTROL

Arms control aims to make war less likely and less destructive. Arms control agreements can help prevent the outbreak of war by reducing uncertainty about states' capabilities and intentions. Thus, arms control is of particular use in situations in which states do not have a powerful desire for expansion but might initiate war out of the fear of what will happen if their enemy strikes first. Historically, a substantial number of wars seem to have started this way. World War I is an example. As the 2015 Iran nuclear agreement shows, arms control agreements can be reached even between deeply antagonistic countries.

An early arms control agreement was the 1922 Washington Naval Agreement, which limited the size of the fleets of the five signatories (France, Italy, Japan, the United Kingdom, and the United States) in order to maintain the prevailing distribution of power in the Pacific. The goal was not to undo the logic of deterrence or to equalize the size of the states' forces, but rather to make the existing deterrence more robust and stable.

**Arms Control and Crisis Stability in the Cold War** The great danger during the Cold War was that during a crisis both states would be tempted to strike first, to try to destroy as many of the opponent's weapons as possible before they were launched. The strategist Thomas Schelling pointed out that not only would each country have a strong incentive to go first, but that each would know that the other side had the same incentive. Schelling envisioned a U.S. or Soviet leader thinking, "'He thinks we think he thinks we think … he thinks we think he'll attack; so he thinks we shall; so he will; so we must.'"[31] To put it more generally, when offensive weapons are perceived to have a large advantage, the knowledge that war is possible can become a self-fulfilling prophecy.[32] Arms control is intended to reduce this danger by reducing the advantage from a first strike and by reducing uncertainty about other states' armaments.

In the 1972 SALT-I treaty, the United States and the Soviet Union agreed to limit the number of nuclear weapons. Maintaining a rough balance reduced the chance that one side could attack first and win a war. Moreover, the two sides agreed not to interfere with each other's spy satellites. Only through mutual surveillance could each side be satisfied that the other was complying with the agreements.

European Union foreign policy chief Federica Mogherini and Iranian Foreign Minister Mohammad Javad Zarif attend the announcement of an agreement on Iran's nuclear program on April 2, 2015, in Lausanne, Switzerland.

### The Nuclear Non-Proliferation Treaty

One of the most difficult challenges today is the spread of nuclear weapons. Many countries have the economic and technological ability to build nuclear weapons but do not want to. However, these countries can only refrain from building nuclear weapons as long as most other countries do the same. Without very detailed and intrusive inspections, it is impossible to tell a peaceful nuclear energy program from a nuclear weapons program. The danger is that some countries will build nuclear weapons not because they really want them, but because they fear that others might be getting them and therefore believe that they need some deterrent. Thus, following North Korea's nuclear test in 2006, there was considerable speculation that South Korea and Japan might decide they needed nuclear weapons as well. Similarly, if Iran obtains nuclear weapons, others in the region, such as Turkey and Saudi Arabia, may respond in kind.

This problem has been addressed through the **Treaty on the Non-Proliferation of Nuclear Weapons (NPT)**. Signed in 1968, the NPT is an agreement that states without nuclear weapons will refrain from obtaining them and will allow detailed inspections so that other states can be certain they are fulfilling their obligations. To make this work, the International Atomic Energy Agency (IAEA) maintains a large staff of expert scientists who travel around the world conducting inspections and notifying the world of violations. The NPT is far from foolproof. It does not prevent proliferation by states that are determined to obtain nuclear weapons. It only provides reassurance that states are meeting their commitments.

### The 2015 Iran Nuclear Agreement

Perhaps the most important arms control agreement since the Cold War was reached in 2015, when Iran and six other states (China, France, Germany, Russia, the UK, and the United States) agreed to a "Joint Comprehensive Plan of Action" to limit Iran's nuclear weapons capabilities in return for an end to economic sanctions that the United States, the EU, and the UN had enacted against Iran. The agreement was especially difficult to reach, as trust among the negotiating parties was very low. Iran wanted a commitment that sanctions would be removed before it took steps to destroy capabilities and allow inspectors in, whereas the United States and others wanted the exact opposite. Both sides feared a trick, but ultimately both came to believe that an imperfect agreement offered more security than ongoing stalemate. Commitments were specified in such minute detail that the document ran to 109 pages.

**Treaty on the Non-Proliferation of Nuclear Weapons (NPT)**

An agreement that states without nuclear weapons will refrain from obtaining them and will allow detailed inspections so that other states can be certain they are fulfilling their obligations.

Fabrice Coffrini/AFP/Getty Images

Critics of the agreement feared that it would empower Iran to "go nuclear" and to increase support for Syria and for terrorist groups. Supporters argued that the agreement would delay Iran's progress toward a nuclear weapon; that the verification provisions would provide warning; and that without the agreement, Iran would have no reason to refrain from building nuclear weapons.

**The Campaign to Ban Land Mines**   The 1997 Ottawa Treaty prohibits the deployment of antipersonnel mines and requires destruction of existing stockpiles. Unlike previous arms control efforts, this one was primarily promoted not by states, but by nongovernmental organizations (NGOs). Land mines are very effective and cost-effective military weapons, providing a cheap, easy, and long-lasting way to deny a particular territory to an enemy's troops. But land mines are viewed as especially inhumane weapons because they kill indiscriminately. Once land mines are laid, they are rarely removed, and long after a war is over, civilians are still killed and maimed by land mines. Despite the military utility of land mines, 156 countries have agreed to the treaty.

**Limits to Arms Control**   Skeptics argue that arms control works only when it is not needed—that only states that are peaceful are willing to reach agreements, and that states only agree not to do things they did not intend to do anyway. In 1934, as Japan grew more assertive, it simply renounced the Washington Naval Treaty. Critics of the SALT treaties point out that they did not really slow the arms race. The SALT-I treaty, for example, limited the number of missiles, but both sides were allowed to add as many warheads as they could to each missile. As a result, the treaty actually ushered in a large growth in the number of warheads. Similarly, those countries most interested in acquiring nuclear weapons either refuse to sign the NPT (Israel, India, Pakistan, North Korea) or violate it (Iran).

A more basic problem is that the two goals of arms control sometimes conflict. Some weapons may help prevent wars but increase destructiveness. There is no doubting the horrendous effects of land mines on civilians around the world. But because they are stationary weapons, mines can only be used to defend territory and not to attack. They are one of a few weapons that do not exacerbate the security dilemma. They also reduce the mutual first-strike dilemma that many arms control agreements are intended to address. The United States, for example, relies heavily on land mines to help defend South Korea from a possible invasion by North Korea. Using land mines reduces the number of troops or other weapons that would need to be deployed, thus decreasing North Korea's fear of an impending attack (and saving a lot of money). As a result, the United States has been unwilling to sign the international land mine ban, a policy for which it has been criticized. Unfortunately, the destructiveness of war is still one of the main deterrents to initiating war, so agreements that lower the cost of war might accidentally increase the likelihood of war.

## COLLECTIVE SECURITY

For generations, people have held the hope that war would be prevented not only by the actions of the potential combatants, but by the intervention of other disinterested states whose primary goal would simply be to prevent war. The goal of the League of Nations, formed after World War I, was to reduce international aggression: If one state committed aggression, all other states would join together to attack it. This doctrine, discussed in Chapter 2, is known as **collective security**. The threat of collective retaliation, it was reasoned, would make it irrational for any state to initiate an attack. In the 1930s, however, disinterested states generally put the goal of avoiding war ahead of the principle of collective security. When Japan invaded Manchuria in 1931 and Italy invaded Ethiopia in 1935, the targeted states appealed to the League of Nations to implement collective

**collective security**

A doctrine nominally adopted by states after World War I that specified that when one state committed aggression, all other states would join to attack it.

security, but other states chose not to go to war to punish the attackers. Thus, some argue that collective security works worst when it is needed most.[33]

The principle of collective security reemerged after the Cold War. When Iraq invaded Kuwait in 1990, many countries agreed that the invasion was an act of aggression that must be reversed. More significantly, as the Cold War was ending, the United States and the Soviet Union could agree to authorize, through the UN, the use of force to eject Iraq from Kuwait. The United States provided most of the force for the subsequent attack, but the war had the support of a very wide range of states and was sanctioned by the UN Security Council.

However, hope for a new world order based on collective security did not survive the decade. When war broke out in the former Yugoslavia, the powerful states of western Europe were determined not to get involved. Instead, they initially tried to insulate themselves from the conflict by tightening policies preventing refugees from entering their countries. Later, when several states resolved to intervene to stop aggression by Serbian forces, they did not receive unanimous support from the UN Security Council. NATO-led interventions in 1995 and again in 1999 can perhaps qualify as successful applications of the doctrine of collective security, but they proved divisive.

## PEACEKEEPING AND PEACE ENFORCEMENT

*Peacekeeping* and *peace enforcement* are based on very different logics. Peacekeeping works much like the arms control agreements that are aimed at preventing war. Traditional **peacekeeping**, also known as *first-generation peacekeeping*, entails the deployment of foreign troops or observers into a region to reassure the parties to a conflict that they will be safe from attack. Peacekeepers can be deployed in either international or civil conflicts (the current range of missions is listed in Table 8.2). Peacekeepers are typically deployed before hostilities have broken out or when a cease-fire has taken place. Such missions require the consent of the conflicting parties and are usually authorized under Chapter VI of the Charter of the United Nations, which concerns "Pacific Settlement of Disputes."

Peacekeeping can begin only when two sides have agreed that they want to stop fighting (or avoid going to war). States or groups at war sometimes want to stop fighting but believe they cannot do so for fear that their adversaries will take advantage of a truce by rearming and then starting the war from a stronger position, by launching a surprise attack, or by continuing attacks covertly while claiming to have stopped. Arriving at an agreement to verify a truce can be impossible when the two sides do not trust each other.

Peacekeeping provides outside forces to monitor a truce or peace agreement. The role of peacekeeping is not to physically prevent two sides' forces from attacking each other (which would fall under *peace enforcement*). In fact, peacekeeping missions are usually lightly armed, and if one side does decide to attack, the peacekeepers may be incapable of stopping the attack (or even of protecting themselves). For this reason, a UN peacekeeping force was withdrawn from Syria in 2012 when continued violence made it impossible to carry out its mission. Instead, the role of the peacekeepers is to provide two kinds of reassurance to the two sides in the conflict. First, peacekeepers monitor the agreement and provide each side with reliable, unbiased reports on whether the other side is meeting its commitments. Second, peacekeepers are often placed physically in a territory between the two sides or in a territory that the two sides are fighting over. This positioning creates a situation in which each side knows that to attack the other side, it must first attack an international peacekeeping force (often containing soldiers from countries with a powerful capacity to respond). The incentive to attack is thus reduced considerably.

**peacekeeping**
The introduction of foreign troops or observers into a region to increase confidence that states will refrain from the use of force.

**TABLE 8.2**   Active UN Peacekeeping Missions, March 31, 2015

| Mission | Countries | Year of Origin | Uniformed Personnel |
|---|---|---|---|
| UNTSO | Egypt, Israel, Jordan, Lebanon, Syria | 1948 | 147 |
| UNMOGIP | India/Pakistan | 1949 | 42 |
| UNFICYP | Cyprus | 1964 | 921 |
| UNDOF | Israel, Syria | 1974 | 788 |
| UNIFIL | Lebanon | 1978 | 10,440 |
| MINURSO | Western Sahara | 1991 | 197 |
| UNMIK | Kosovo | 1999 | 15 |
| MONUSCO | Congo | 1999 | 21,023 |
| UNMIL | Liberia | 2003 | 5,871 |
| UNOCI | Cote d'Ivoire | 2004 | 7,137 |
| MINUSTAH | Haiti | 2004 | 6,850 |
| UNAMID | Sudan (Darfur) | 2007 | 17,155 |
| UNISFA | Abyei (Sudan/South Sudan) | 2011 | 4,094 |
| UNMISS | South Sudan | 2011 | 12,350 |
| MINUSCA | Central African Republic | 2014 | 10,198 |
| MINUSMA | Mali | 2013 | 10,337 |

Source: www.un.org/en/peacekeeping/resources/statistics/factsheet.shtml. Reprinted by permission of United Nations.

## THE CONNECTION TO YOU

### WHO SHOULD FIGHT?

Should military service be determined by conscription (forcing people to serve and choosing them by lottery), should it be required of everyone, or should it rely on volunteers? Historically, states have relied on conscription, especially in times of war, when huge numbers of soldiers are needed and people hesitate to volunteer. In many countries, however, compulsory military service has been required even in peacetime. Advocates believe that universal service promotes civic responsibility and promotes national cohesion. Additional debates in recent years have surrounded whether women should serve, and if so, in what roles, and whether openly gay soldiers should be allowed to serve in the military.

In the United States, conscription goes back to colonial times, when the militia system required men to enroll in local militias. National conscription was used during the Civil War, World

*(Continued)*

War I, and World War II, but was discontinued between conflicts. After World War II, however, the Cold War spurred authorities to institute a peacetime draft, requiring all men ages 18–26 to register for possible selection. The Vietnam War brought a huge increase in selection, but university students could defer their service, the result of which was that those serving in Vietnam came disproportionately from the lower classes. The Vietnam draft was hugely unpopular, and as the war wound down in 1973, the United States went to an all-volunteer force, recruiting soldiers with the promise of adventure and higher education. However, men ages 18–25 are still required to register with the Selective Service in case the draft is reinstated.

Since the 1970s, controversy has shifted from the draft to the service of women and gays. The role of women in the military has slowly expanded since the 1970s, especially in Iraq and Afghanistan, where the distinction between combat and noncombat roles has been blurred. Gays have always served in the military; the controversy over whether they could do so openly appeared to have ended in 2012, when the policy was officially changed to allow gays to serve openly.

The U.S. move to an all-volunteer army reflects a broad trend in the post–World War II world. The United Kingdom slowly phased out conscription between 1945 and 1960. Several European countries had universal military service, in which all (male) citizens were required to serve for a period. Germany suspended universal service in 2011. Prior to the suspension, the required term of service had been gradually reduced to six months, with provision for conscientious objectors to be assigned to nonmilitary public service roles, such as in civil defense. In France, which originated modern national conscription under Napoleon, it continued until 1996. In Italy,

conscription continued from unification in 1861 until 2000. Conscription has a long history in China and is still technically in force, but China's huge population yields enough volunteers that conscription has not been needed recently. Most of these countries have also expanded the role of women over time, and all but China allow gays to serve openly. Bans against gays in the military are still widespread in the Middle East and Africa.

Among the countries that retain active conscription are Israel and Russia, though in neither country is service universal. In Israel, citizens over age 18 are required to serve (making Israel one of few countries to conscript women), but there are exemptions for religious Jews and most Arabs. Conscription is still in effect in Russia, where the term of service was reduced to one year in 2008. Widespread and brutal hazing of conscripts in Russia has led to high rates of avoidance and undermined the quality of those conscripted. One of the major arguments for going to a volunteer force is that volunteer professional soldiers can be trained to a much higher level than conscripts.

Technological changes have reduced the importance of the sheer number of soldiers as an aspect of military power. This may make the issue of compulsory service recede in importance. But in the kinds of conflicts that require significant "boots on the ground," people may continue to ask about whose boots they should be, and who gets to stay home.

## Critical Thinking Questions

1. What is the fairest way to staff the military?

2. Is compulsory service beneficial for building national cohesion? If so, should it be adopted on those grounds?

3. Should military veterans be given preference in competing for jobs? For political office?

Peacekeeping is not meant as a permanent solution (although, in fact, some peacekeeping missions have gone on for decades). Rather, it is intended to end the fighting on relatively neutral terms and to provide enough stability for peace negotiations to take place. Eventually, in theory, an agreement should end the dispute and allow the peacekeepers to be withdrawn.

**peace enforcement**

The application of force (or the threat of force) to compel states to stop fighting.

**Peace enforcement** can be defined as the application of force (or the threat of force) to compel states or groups to stop fighting. The logic is simple: Military intervention by an external actor (usually a powerful state or group of states) can force warring parties to stop fighting. The U.S.-led attack in Iraq in 1991 was seen by some as a peace enforcement move: Iraq attacked Kuwait, and the U.S.-led coalition then attacked Iraq to reverse its aggression. The international interventions in the former Yugoslavia (in Bosnia in 1995 and over Kosovo in 1999) are other prominent cases. In contrast to peacekeeping, peace enforcement operations do not require the consent of the conflicting parties. They are generally authorized by Chapter VII of the UN Charter, which allows the UN to "take such action by air, sea, or land forces as may be necessary to maintain or restore international peace and security."[34]

In the 1990s, *second-generation peacekeeping* emerged to deal with crises in places such as Somalia, Cambodia, and the former Yugoslavia. Second-generation peacekeeping goes beyond monitoring missions and may provide humanitarian assistance, help countries carry out elections, and protect civilians, with armed force if necessary. Like peace enforcement missions, second-generation peacekeeping missions do not require the consent of all parties. To capture the idea that these missions blur the distinction between traditional peacekeeping and peace enforcement, they are sometimes called "Chapter VI½ missions."

## RECONSIDER THE CASE

## MODERN WARFARE

Even an abbreviated list of the international and civil conflicts around the world in recent years creates the impression that violent conflict is an ever-present dimension of world politics. Yet most countries, most of the time, are at peace. Both for policy makers and scholars, understanding the differences is essential. We seek reliable explanations of war in part because we hope they will yield more reliable prescriptions for peace.

In developing generalized explanations of war, we look for factors that occur in many cases of war but that are not present when war does not occur. The Defenestration of Prague may have been unique, but a triggering event or proximate cause is present in many cases. Is a triggering event necessary? Similarly, the specific distribution of power present in Europe in 1618 may not be replicated in other cases, but an intense concern over the distribution of power seems to recur in many cases.

A central question in all kinds of social science explanations is whether a particular cause is a *necessary* condition for an effect (meaning that the effect cannot occur without that cause) or a *sufficient*

condition (meaning that this cause, by itself, can cause the effect in question). The simplest explanations are those with a single cause that is both necessary and sufficient. War, it appears, is so complex that no single cause is either necessary or sufficient, and a complex mix of factors leads actors to choose violence. The understanding that a wide range of underlying causes can lead to war leads to an emphasis on preventing disagreements from becoming violent in the first place. That has been the role of arms control, peacekeeping, and peace enforcement, and these policies have had considerable success.

### Critical Thinking Questions

1. Can we identify any factors that, by themselves, are sufficient to cause war?

2. What factors or combination of factors are necessary to cause war? Is there some necessary ingredient such that if people could control that factor, they could limit war?

# POWER, PURPOSE, AND INTERNATIONAL CONFLICT

In this chapter we confront power and purpose at their most elemental level. The rawest form of power is the ability to kill and destroy, and the threat of this power undermines security, the most basic purpose in international (and domestic) politics. Although there is little agreement on what causes war, it is clear that states initiate war when their most crucial goals are at stake—either some irresistible opportunity exists, or some daunting danger looms. The pursuit of military power—the acquisition of more and better weapons—becomes a major goal of states, but often the ultimate goal of acquiring weapons is not to use them but to deter others from using them. Thus, finding ways to avoid and to mitigate conflict are as important as preparing to fight.

## SUMMARY

- There is no consensus among scholars about what causes war. There are multiple causes of war, at multiple levels of analysis, and these causes interact with one another. Explanations for war differ according their level of analysis and their focus on permissive, underlying, or proximate causes of war.

- In the realist view, states in a self-help system arm to defend themselves, and this makes other states less secure. The result is competition for military dominance. In this view, any number of proximate causes can ignite a war.

- Economic structuralists find that capitalism inevitably produces the need for states to expand.

- Democracies have not been found to be more peaceful than nondemocratic states, but they tend not to go to war with each other.

- Expected utility theory can explain why many wars are started by states that then go on to lose. This theory emphasizes that states will not necessarily choose a successful strategy but will choose the one with the highest expected utility.

- Individual-level theories see war as a result of human aggression and misperception.

- The Prussian strategist Karl von Clausewitz coined the phrase "the fog of war" to characterize the difficulties in controlling war once it starts.

- Civil war is defined as a conflict between organized groups within a nation-state.

- Explanations of civil war focus on two sets of factors: grievances and resources.

- Recent research finds that grievances exist everywhere, but that resource differences explain variation in the outbreak of civil war.

- Diffusion, intervention, and spillover can transform a domestic protest or conflict into an international conflict.

- Arms control agreements can help prevent the outbreak of war by reducing uncertainty about states' capabilities and intentions.

- Traditional peacekeeping, also known as first-generation peacekeeping, entails the introduction of foreign troops or observers into a region to reassure the parties to a conflict that they will be safe from attack.

- Peace enforcement, defined as the application or threat of force to compel states or groups to stop fighting, has become more common in recent years.

## KEY CONCEPTS

1. Security dilemma
2. Human aggression
3. Imperialism
4. Nationalism
5. Fog of war
6. Permissive conditions

7. Underlying causes
8. Resource mobilization theory
9. Political opportunity structure
10. Collective security
11. Peacekeeping
12. Peace enforcement

## STUDY QUESTIONS

1. The Second Defenestration of Prague was _____ of the Thirty Years' War.

   a. a proximate cause

   b. a permissive cause

   c. an underlying cause

   d. All of the above.

2. The predominant realist explanation of the causes of war focuses on the

   a. system level.

   b. state level.

   c. substate level.

   d. individual level.

3. Realists view anarchy as _____ of war.

   a. a proximate cause

   b. a permissive cause

   c. an underlying cause

   d. All of the above.

4. What do economic structuralists tend to see as the cause of war?

   a. The need of capitalist states to expand economically

   b. The anarchical nature of international politics

   c. The aggressive nature of individual leaders

   d. The decline of free trade among states

5. The difficulty in controlling war once it starts is known as

   a. the security dilemma.

   b. anarchy.

   c. natural selection.

   d. the fog of war.

6. Empirical research shows a connection between civil war and

   a. ethnic cleavage.

   b. democracy.

   c. wealth (per capita GNP).

   d. crisis stability.

7. How can the realist paradigm explain a country's decision to strike first?

8. How does expected utility theory explain a country's decision to go to war?

9. What are the major factors causing civil war?

10. What obstacles are there to a definitive explanation of war?

11. How do arms control agreements seek to overcome the security dilemma?

12. How is collective security intended to preserve peace? What obstacles does it face?

[Correct answers: 1. a; 2. a; 3. b; 4. a; 5. d; 6. c]

## END NOTES

1. Greg Cashman and Leonard C. Washington, *An Introduction to the Causes of War: Patterns of Interstate Conflict from World War I to Iraq* (Lanham, MD: Rowman and Littlefield, 2007), p. 3.

2. Kenneth N. Waltz, *Man, the State, and War: A Theoretical Analysis* (New York: Columbia University Press, 1954), p. 188.

3. Kenneth N. Waltz, "The Origins of War in Neorealist Theory," *Journal of Interdisciplinary History*, Vol. 83, No. 4 (Spring 1988): 620.

4. Randall Schweller, "Realism's Status Quo Bias: What Security Dilemma?" *Security Studies*, Vol. 5, No. 3 (1995/1996): 90–121.

5. Bruce Bueno de Mesquita, "Risk, Power Distributions, and the Likelihood of War," *International Studies Quarterly*, Vol. 25, No. 4 (December 1981): 541–568.

6. Daniel S. Geller, "The Stability of the Military Balance and War among Great Power Rivals," in Paul F. Diehl, ed., *The Dynamics of Enduring Rivalries* (Urbana: University of Illinois Press, 1998), pp. 165–190.

7. See, for example, Harry Magdoff, *The Age of Imperialism* (New York: Monthly Review Press, 1969).

8. A historical overview and critique of the view that free trade leads to peace can be found in Geoffrey Blainey, *The Causes of War*, 3rd ed. (New York: The Free Press, 1988), Chapter 2, pp. 18–32, "Paradise Is a Bazaar."

9. Edward D. Mansfield and Jack Snyder, "Democratization and the Danger of War," *International Security*, Vol. 20, No. 1 (Summer 1995): 302.

10. See Schweller, "Realism's Status Quo Bias," pp. 90–121.

11. Walter Isaacson, "GQ Icon: Colin Powell," *GQ* (October 2007): 2, www.gq.com/news-politics / newsmakers/200709/colin-powell-walter-isaacson-war-iraq-george-bush.

12. Jack Snyder, *Myths of Empire: Domestic Politics and International Ambition* (Ithaca, NY: Cornell University Press, 1991).

13. See John L. Comaroff and Paul C. Stern, eds., *Perspectives on Nationalism and War* (Amsterdam: Gordon and Breach, 1995).

14. Benjamin Anderson, *Imagined Communities: Reflections on the Origins and Spread of Nationalism*, rev. ed. (London: Verso, 1991).

15. Walker Connor, "Nation-Building or Nation-Destroying?" *World Politics*, Vol. 24, No. 3 (April 1972): 319–355.

16. See David Walder, *The Short Victorious War: The Russo-Japanese War, 1904–1905* (New York: Harper & Row, 1974).

17. Blainey, *The Causes of War*, pp. 72–73. Blainey, it should be noted, is quite critical of this view (pp. 74–84).

18. See Alistair Smith, "Diversionary Foreign Policy in Democratic Systems," *International Studies Quarterly*, Vol. 40 (March 1996): 133–153.

19. Konrad Lorenz, *On Aggression* (New York: Harcourt Brace Jovanovich, 1966). See also Raymond Aron, "Biological and Psychological Roots," in Lawrence Freedman, ed., *War* (Oxford: Oxford University Press, 1994), pp. 77–81.

20. Sigmund Freud, "Why War?" in Melvin Small and J. David Singer, eds., *International War: An Anthology*, 2nd ed. (Chicago: The Dorsey Press, 1989), pp. 176–181. Freud's essay was part of a correspondence with Albert Einstein on the causes of war.

21. David Fabbro, "Peaceful Societies: An Introduction," *Journal of Peace Research*, Vol. 15, No. 1 (1978): 67–83.

22. Thucydides, *History of the Peloponnesian War*, Book V, section 105.

23. Hans Morgenthau, *Politics among Nations: The Struggle for Power and Peace*, 5th ed. (New York: Knopf, 1978), p. 3.

24. Waltz, *Man, the State, and War*, pp. 20–22.

25. See Randall Schweller, *Deadly Imbalances: Tripolarity and Hitler's Strategy of World Conquest* (New York: Columbia University Press, 1998).

26. Richard Ned Lebow, *Between Peace and War* (Baltimore, MD: Johns Hopkins University Press, 1981).

27. This view is expressed through a historical argument in Blainey, *The Causes of War*, Chapter 8, and in formal rational choice terms by James D. Fearon,

"Rationalist Explanations of War," *International Organization*, Vol. 49, No. 3 (Summer 1995): 379–414.

28. James D. Fearon and David D. Laitin, "Ethnicity, Insurgency, and Civil War," *American Political Science Review*, Vol. 97, No. 1 (February 2003): 75.

29. Fearon and Laitin, "Ethnicity, Insurgency, and Civil War."

30. Ted Robert Gurr, *Why Men Rebel* (Princeton, NJ: Princeton University Press, 1970).

31. Thomas Schelling, *Strategy of Conflict* (Cambridge, MA: Harvard University Press, 1960), p. 207.

32. Stephen van Evera, "Offense, Defense, and the Causes of War," *International Security*, Vol. 22, No. 4 (1988): 5–43.

33. Richard K. Betts, "Systems of Peace or Causes of War: Collective Security, Arms Control, and the New Europe," *International Security*, Vol. 17, No. 1 (Summer 1992): 5–43.

34. Charter of the United Nations, Chapter VII, Article 42.

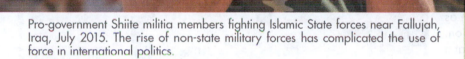

Pro-government Shiite militia members fighting Islamic State forces near Fallujah, Iraq, July 2015. The rise of non-state military forces has complicated the use of force in international politics.

Ahmad al-Rubaye/Getty Images

# THE USE OF FORCE

## Learning Objectives

**9-1** Define *force* and understand the link between the threat of violence and the actual use of violence.

**9-2** Distinguish the policy of defense from that of deterrence.

**9-3** Explain the effects of WMD on deterrence, defense, and crisis stability.

**9-4** Define terrorism.

**9-5** Summarize and evaluate the competing explanations of the causes of terrorism.

**9-6** Link different explanations of terrorism to possible policy responses.

# CONSIDER THE CASE

## THE ATTACK OF THE DRONES

In June 2014, Nasser al-Wuhayshi was killed in Yemen by a missile fired from an unmanned aerial vehicle, or drone. Al-Wuhayshi was the leader of Al Qaeda in the Arabian Peninsula, the Yemeni branch of Al Qaeda, and had formed an offshoot called Ansar al-Sharia, which became popular across the Middle East after the 2011 Arab Spring. Al-Wuhayshi was regarded as one of the top leaders of Al Qaeda, and his death was seen as a significant blow to the organization. The same month, it was reported that a strike in Libya had killed Mokhtar Belmokhtar, a commander of Al Qaeda in the Maghreb, but that killing was unconfirmed. These attacks were part of a broader campaign, which in 2011 included seventy-five attacks that killed approximately 650 people. In early 2012, the U.S. Department of Defense announced plans to substantially increase its arsenal of unmanned aircraft.

U.S. Air Force Predator Unmanned Aerial Vehicle (UAV) at Tallil Air Base in Iraq. How might the advent of UAVs change the strategies of military forces that possess them and those that do not?

Why have drones become such a popular weapon for the United States, which has a larger and more diverse arsenal than any other country? Drones carry no crew, so they are less costly in two respects. First, the absence of a pilot eliminates the risk to military personnel, should the aircraft be shot down. This, in turn, reduces the political costs for countries that are extremely sensitive to military casualties. Second, pilotless aircraft are much cheaper to build and operate, because they do not require space and protection for a pilot. Moreover, without a pilot's weight and tendency to fatigue, drones can patrol over a target area for hours, either collecting intelligence or waiting for a target to appear.

The strategic implications of drones are especially important in counterinsurgency, where placing troops on the ground can play into the hands of an insurgent force by providing easy targets. Air strikes deny insurgents targets, and instead make the insurgents targets. Beginning in the 1990s, the United States and its allies increasingly used attacks by aircraft or missiles in Iraq, in the former Yugoslavia, and against terrorists. Speaking in 2012, U.S. Counterterrorism Coordinator John Brennan summarized the strategic case for drone use: "Large, intrusive military deployments risk playing into al-Qaeda's strategy of trying to draw us into long, costly wars that drain us financially, inflame anti-American resentment and inspire the next generation of terrorists."* Drones reduce these problems, and so have become central to U.S. counterterrorism efforts.

---

*"Yemeni al-Qaeda Leader 'Killed in Drone Strike,'" BBC, May 7, 2012, www.bbc.co.uk/news/world-middle-east-17979424.

There are many forms of power in international politics, including economic, cultural, and military power, but military power is commonly viewed as the most fundamental. Different theoretical perspectives disagree on just how important military power is, but all agree that it plays a central role, and many see military power as the last resort available to actors seeking to prevail in a disagreement. Many analysts, therefore, identify the contest to accumulate military power, and the ability to use it effectively, as the central problem in international politics. Because of the expense of acquiring military power and its destructiveness, the question of purpose is central in considering the political use of military power. That is true whether we are considering conventional weapons, weapons of mass destruction (WMD), cyber warfare, insurgency, or terrorism. All are employed as means to achieve particular ends. Each operates according to a different logic. Each incurs different costs. But each is intended to achieve purposes that cannot be achieved using other methods. This point is captured in the oft-cited assertion that "war is the continuation of policy by other means."[1] The implication is that to be useful the deployment of force must have a purpose, and that purpose must be achievable through force and valuable enough to offset the incredible costs of war. Carl von Clausewitz, the Prussian strategist responsible for that famous assertion, further stressed that state purposes are often best served by *avoiding* battle.[2]

For what purposes do states and others employ violence? Only the most important goals are worth the costs of acquiring and using military force. The terms *international security* and *national security* identify a primary purpose: security. The goal of most actors who acquire and use military force, most of the time, is to *prevent* the use of military force by others. The definition of "security" has been broadened in recent years to include security from environmental, health, and economic threats, but the traditional notion of security—safety from the threat of attack—remains at the top of the agenda of international politics. Simply scanning the headlines of a newspaper shows that the use of military force and the desire for protection against it remain constant concerns for states and citizens around the world. When states, groups, or individuals are threatened with physical violence, other issues become secondary.

Not only states but many other actors consider the use of force and the threat of force to be useful tools of policy. Violence and the threat of it are used not only to prevent others from using violence but to pursue a range of other goals, such as the removal of a regime considered especially odious, a revision of territorial boundaries, or a change in rights for a group of people. This chapter analyzes how state and nonstate actors use force to achieve their goals in international politics.

## MILITARY FORCE AND ITS PURPOSES

What does it mean to say that someone used *force* rather than *persuasion*? Force can be defined as the use of violence or the threat of violence to achieve a political goal. There are two things to notice about this deceptively simple definition.

First, the word *force* is a euphemism for the word *violence*. Whether employed by a small gang or a large army, the use of force involves violence: killing, wounding, and starving people and destroying property. Thus, how much force a state has at its disposal is equivalent to how much capacity it has to kill and destroy and how much capacity it has to defend its own citizens and property.

Second, the *threat* of violence can also be considered the use of force. The ability to commit an act of violence often has an effect by itself, even if actual violence is not committed. States often seek to acquire sufficient military capability that others can be frightened into making concessions. Gaining concessions without ever going to battle

**force**

The use of violence or the threat of violence to achieve a political goal.

has been a major theme in strategic writings at least since the sixth century BCE, when the Chinese military strategist Sun Tzu wrote his *Art of War*.[3]

## COERCIVE DIPLOMACY

**coercion**

The use of a threat to change another actor's behavior.

**Coercion** occurs when an explicit or implicit threat is used to persuade another actor to change its behavior. In some cases, threats are explicit and readily apparent. In other cases, threats may remain implicit. Simply possessing the means to destroy creates a threat that others are aware of, whether a threat is intended or not. Negotiation and threats are closely connected, even if they appear to be contradictory. Every negotiation entails an implied threat in the form of a question: "What happens if we do not arrive at an agreement?" Depending on the answer to this question, one side may have a much greater incentive than the other to reach a deal, and either side may want to use threats of some type to coax its counterpart into an agreement.

It is equally true that every threat is an offer to negotiate. Even a coercive threat ("If you do not do what we say, we will attack") is an attempt to bargain. Sometimes, a threat may be necessary to begin a bargaining process because without it an actor that regards the status quo as beneficial may have no incentive to negotiate. A threat is only convincing, of course, to the extent that it would be rational to carry it out.

**credibility**

The ability and will to carry out a threat.

**Credibility** is an essential concern in applying threats of force to gain concessions. Credibility can be defined as the extent to which an actor making a threat has both the *capability* and the *will* to carry out the threat. Thus, military capability helps make the threat of force credible and therefore provides benefits even if it is never employed on the battlefield. In general, states with larger military capabilities are likely to be in a better bargaining position. Capability is relatively easy to measure, such as by counting weapons systems, but will is notoriously hard to gauge. In particular, the actors in a conflict can be hugely unequal in their willingness to suffer casualties. This difference in will can sometimes undermine the threats of actors with huge advantages in capabilities.

## DEFENSE VERSUS DETERRENCE

If some actors seek to use the threat of force to coerce others, all use the threat of force to avoid being the victims of such coercion. If a state can convince others that an attack would be unwise, it can reduce the credibility of the threat of such an attack and therefore reduce its vulnerability to coercion. There are two ways in which the potential use of force is leveraged to prevent another country from attacking: defense and deterrence. The distinction is essential. States shift their reliance on defense versus deterrence depending on the technology and tactics available to them and their perceived power relative to states they see as potential adversaries.

The simplest way to provide security is to be able to repel an attack. This has been the traditional means of defense, and it involves building fortifications, buying weapons, and training soldiers to fight off a potential attack. Around the world, the signs of such preparations are visible almost everywhere. The Great Wall of China, Moscow's Kremlin, the castles of medieval Europe, and the "battery" (now

Tim Hall/Photodisc/Getty Images

The Great Wall of China is an example of a purely defensive structure. It was powerful in defense but nearly useless in attack.

| TABLE 9.1 | Defense–Deterrence Continuum |

| Pure Defense | Mixed | Pure Deterrence |
| --- | --- | --- |
| Walls, fortifications | Most conventional weapons, including ground troops, aircraft, navies, tanks | Strategic nuclear weapons, most insurgent strategies |

Battery Park) at the southern tip of Manhattan were all built to protect against attacks. A second goal of these preparations, equally important, is to convince an opponent that an attack will fail and therefore should not be attempted. This has the additional effect of rendering coercive threats less effective.

However, in some cases, it may either be difficult or exceedingly expensive to actually defend a territory. How can a country then protect itself from attack? An alternative to defense is **deterrence**, which entails convincing a potential opponent not to attack by raising the costs of attack so that they exceed the perceived benefits. Even if it is impossible to defeat a very powerful enemy on the battlefield, it may be possible to cause enough destruction in the course of the war to convince the potential attacker that it is simply not worth it. In its purest form, deterrence does not focus on actually defeating the attack. U.S. and Soviet strategies in the Cold War exemplified a pure deterrent strategy. Neither side could hope to repel an attack by nuclear-armed missiles. Both sides sought, instead, to convince the other that such an attack would be met with a devastating response. The nuclear strategies of other countries are based on the same logic. Similarly, insurgent strategies, discussed later, do not aim to defeat an army in battle, but to raise the costs of an occupation unbearably high.

Historically, defense and deterrence strategies have often overlapped (see Table 9.1). From early history to World War II, the measures taken to defeat an attack also served to raise the cost of an attack. However, the advent of the airplane in the early twentieth century raised the possibility of a pure deterrence strategy based on aerial bombing of an enemy's cities. The emergence of WMD further increased the possibility of "pure" deterrence. These weapons are very difficult to use in offensive operations but can be used to raise the costs of an attack.

**deterrence**

A policy aimed at convincing a potential opponent not to attack by raising the costs of attack so that they are higher than the perceived benefits.

## THE SECURITY DILEMMA

The discussion so far has given the impression that states should expend considerable resources to acquire as much military capability as possible. Indeed, through much of history, this is what many states have done. However, obtaining the capacity for violence is not without its problems. If nothing else, it is expensive. But the **security dilemma** creates an even bigger challenge to a policy of unrestrained procurement of military capabilities. Military capability is seen by others as a threat even if no threat is ever stated. The more powerful a state becomes, the more other states will perceive it as a threat and begin to treat it accordingly. This behavior is sometimes not readily apparent, but it is, in fact, pervasive. When one country gains new capabilities, those around it consider adding to their own arsenals, or even attacking preemptively. In 1981, Israel attacked Iraq to destroy a facility that Israel feared would be used to produce nuclear weapons. One justification for the U.S. attack on Iraq in 2003 was to prevent it from gaining WMD. Iran's nuclear program, which itself might be seen as a response to perceived threat from others, has provoked speculation that a similar preemptive attack would be forthcoming. The decision to arm or not arm can be viewed as another version of the prisoner's dilemma discussed in Chapter 3 and is illustrated in Table 9.2.

**security dilemma**

The difficult choice faced by states in anarchy between arming, which risks provoking a response from others, and not arming, which risks remaining vulnerable.

**TABLE 9.2**    **Potential Arms Race as a Prisoner's Dilemma**

| | | State A | |
|---|---|---|---|
| | | **Cooperate (refrain from further arming)** | **Defect (build more weapons)** |
| **State B** | **Cooperate** | (3, 3) Neither state arms further, so they continue to deter each other with their existing armaments, but the costs of preparing for war and fighting it stay level. | (1, 4) State A has more weapons, is more secure, and can threaten State B. |
| | **Defect** | (4, 1) State B has more weapons, is more secure, and can threaten State A. | (2, 2) Both states arm, so they continue to deter each other, but they have spent money and war will be more costly if it occurs. |

Actors compete not only in the quantity of weapons they amass, but in the technological sophistication of those weapons and the ways they are used. New developments in technology and strategy create new challenges for international security. How is the nature of military power changing? How can states defend themselves against both old and new threats? In an attempt to answer these questions, this chapter analyzes how defense, deterrence, and coercive diplomacy are influenced today by modern military strategies and weaponry. In particular, this chapter examines the use of WMD, high- and low-tech weaponry, and terrorism and considers how effective policies can be pursued given the current level of understanding of these phenomena. Weapons of mass destruction shifted the focus from defense to deterrence, but low-tech weapons and terrorism are shifting the focus back toward defense.

# CONTEMPORARY COMPETITION FOR MILITARY ADVANTAGE

The contemporary competition for military advantage is characterized by the military preponderance of the United States, the acquisition by a few states of high-tech weaponry that reduces the cost of war, and the proliferation of low-tech weapons that are used as deterrents. In addition, a recent increase in sensitivity to casualties plays a considerable role in the ability of many states to leverage their military strength to their advantage.

## MILITARY PREPONDERANCE

A few states, first and foremost the United States, have advantages in conventional weaponry rarely seen in history. U.S. weaponry is the most advanced in the world, and the United States has more weaponry in almost every category than any other country (although several other countries have more soldiers). Included in that weaponry is the air and naval capacity to put troops on the ground and sustain them in almost any part of the world. Only a few states possess advanced weapons, and only the United States possesses the ability to deploy them around the world for prolonged periods. Not surprisingly, the United States spends vastly more money on the military than any other country (see Figure 9.1).

**FIGURE 9.1** Measured by how much different countries spend on their militaries, power in the world today is grossly imbalanced, probably more so than at any other time in history.

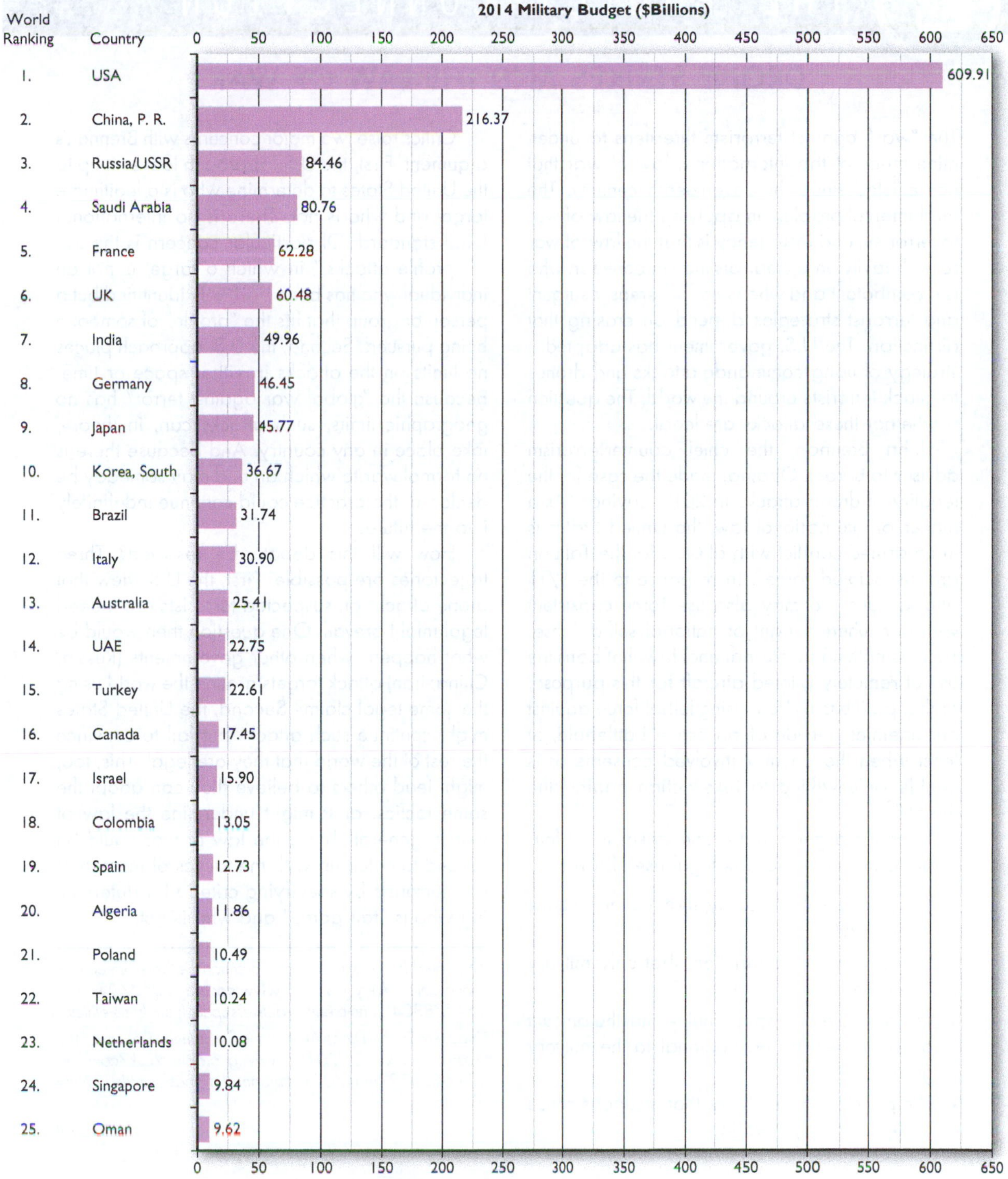

| World Ranking | Country | 2014 Military Budget ($Billions) |
|---|---|---|
| 1. | USA | 609.91 |
| 2. | China, P. R. | 216.37 |
| 3. | Russia/USSR | 84.46 |
| 4. | Saudi Arabia | 80.76 |
| 5. | France | 62.28 |
| 6. | UK | 60.48 |
| 7. | India | 49.96 |
| 8. | Germany | 46.45 |
| 9. | Japan | 45.77 |
| 10. | Korea, South | 36.67 |
| 11. | Brazil | 31.74 |
| 12. | Italy | 30.90 |
| 13. | Australia | 25.41 |
| 14. | UAE | 22.75 |
| 15. | Turkey | 22.61 |
| 16. | Canada | 17.45 |
| 17. | Israel | 15.90 |
| 18. | Colombia | 13.05 |
| 19. | Spain | 12.73 |
| 20. | Algeria | 11.86 |
| 21. | Poland | 10.49 |
| 22. | Taiwan | 10.24 |
| 23. | Netherlands | 10.08 |
| 24. | Singapore | 9.84 |
| 25. | Oman | 9.62 |

Source: Based on the Stockholm International Peace Research Institute (SIPRI) Military Expenditure Database 2014.

# THE POLICY CONNECTION

## DRONE STRIKES AND THE LAW OF WAR

The "war" against terrorism threatens to undermine much of the international law of war that has existed since the seventeenth century. The fundamental problem in applying the law of war to terrorism and insurgency is that the law of war relies heavily on a clear distinction between who is a combatant and who is not, whereas insurgent and terrorist strategies depend on erasing that distinction. The U.S. government has adopted a strategy of using commando attacks and drones to attack terrorists around the world. The question is whether these attacks are legal.

John Brennan, the chief counterterrorism adviser to Barack Obama, made the case for the legality of drone attacks in 2012, saying, "As a matter of international law, the United States is in an armed conflict with al Qaeda, the Taliban and associated forces, in response to the 9/11 attacks, and we may also use force consistent with our inherent right of national self-defense. There is nothing in international law that bans the use of remotely piloted aircraft for this purpose, or that prohibits us from using lethal force against our enemies outside of an active battlefield, at least when the country involved consents or is unable or unwilling to take action against the threat."

Brennan argued that drone strikes meet four basic requirements for the legal use of force:

- The principle of necessity, that the target have military value
- The principle of distinction, that only military objectives be targeted
- The principle of proportionality, that the amount of force used be proportional to the military gain
- The principle of humanity, that weapons cause no unnecessary suffering*

Critics raise two major concerns with Brennan's argument. First, the U.S. approach leaves it up to the United States to determine who is a legitimate target and who is not. There is no international legal standard. Of particular concern is the use of "profile attacks," in which a target is not an individual who has been positively identified but a person or group that fits the "profile" of someone being pursued. Second, the U.S. approach places no limits on the attacks in either space or time. Because the "global war against terror" has no geographic limits, such attacks can, in theory, take place in any country. And because there is no formal war to which an end may someday be declared, the practice could continue indefinitely into the future.[†]

How will this debate be resolved? Three trajectories are possible. First, the U.S. view that drone attacks on suspected terrorists are indeed legal might prevail. One question then would be what happens when other governments (Russia, China, Iran) attack targets around the world using the same legal claim? Second, the United States might continue such attacks but fail to convince the rest of the world that they are legal. This, too, might lead others to believe they can adopt the same tactics, or it might undermine the law of war in general. Third, the law of war could be revised to catch up with the tactics of insurgents and terrorists by specifying criteria for determining who is "fair game" and who is not.

---

*National Public Radio, "John Brennan Delivers Speech on Drone Ethics," May 1, 2012, www.npr.org/2012/05/01/151778804/john-brennan-delivers-speech-on-drone-ethics.

†Naureen Shah, "Drone Attacks and the Brennan Doctrine," The Guardian, May 2, 2012, www.guardian.co.uk/commentisfree/2012/may/02/unmanned-drones-usa?INTCMP=SRCH.

*(Continued)*

## Critical Thinking Questions

1. What is the best way to balance the need to combat terrorism with the desire to maintain clear limits on who can be attacked and where attacks can take place?

2. How would our views on the legality of drone strikes change if such strikes were carried out by Canada, Norway, Iran, or Russia?

3. How should states balance the desire to follow international law with the goal of protecting themselves from attacks?

However, as conflicts in Afghanistan and Iraq (and in Vietnam earlier) have shown, having a preponderance of force does not guarantee the ability to achieve one's objectives. The overwhelming superiority of U.S. conventional forces has led many states and other actors to conclude that it is hopeless to compete with the United States in terms of conventional weapons. As a consequence, the incentive to build up nonconventional capabilities has increased; the spread of WMD, insurgency, and terrorism is a direct result of the fact that most other states and groups have no hope of competing with the United States in terms of conventional weapons. Therefore, these unconventional strategies will likely become increasingly popular options.

## THE ROLE OF HIGH-TECH WEAPONS

Recent decades have witnessed a technological revolution in conventional weaponry. Most widely known, because of their visibility in recent conflicts, are unmanned aircraft (drones) and **precision-guided munitions**, which include bombs and missiles with a variety of guidance systems providing a high degree of accuracy (many such systems can deliver weapons within ten feet of a target). Militarily, the significance of such weapons is their ability to destroy a given target with a high degree of reliability. Politically, precision-guided munitions have been important not only for what they hit, but for what they generally do not hit: unintended targets, including civilians. This potential has allowed military planners to contemplate "surgical" use of these weapons to destroy certain targets yet incur low "collateral damage," or civilian deaths. This reduction of collateral damage makes it easier to contemplate using these weapons for coercion. This is exactly what happened in 1999 in Kosovo, where U.S. forces were able to strike at targets important to Yugoslavia's government and military while causing relatively few civilian casualties (although the Chinese embassy in Belgrade was accidentally bombed). Paradoxically, this capability also increases expectations that civilian casualties will be avoided, thus increasing resentment when they occur. There has been considerable outrage about civilian casualties from U.S. air strikes, and this outrage has undoubtedly undermined the effort to win "hearts and minds." New weapons such as drones and precision-guided weapons also hold out the hope that meaningful military results can be achieved with very low risk of casualties in the attacking force. The ability to minimize the risk to soldiers and to innocent bystanders makes war much more politically palatable. Whether this is a good thing is, of course, debatable.

**precision-guided munitions**
Weapons with guidance systems and maneuvering capability that allow them to strike individual targets with a high degree of accuracy. Also known as "smart bombs."

## CYBER WARFARE

The use of computers to attack other computers is among the newest applications of technology to warfare. From the distribution of electrical power to the control of fancy

A software demonstration shows how a global problem (intrusion) can spread from a single employee's work station.

refrigerators, nearly every aspect of modern life has become mediated by computer networks. The same openness that has allowed the Internet to transform our lives makes it highly vulnerable to disruption or to being used for malicious purposes.

Cyber warfare has evolved quickly from stealing secrets to attacking computer systems to damaging myriad devices that rely on computer processors. The Stuxnet worm, discovered in 2010, spread widely but was programmed for a very narrow task: disrupting the control software in centrifuges made by Siemens, a German firm. Such centrifuges had been illicitly acquired by Iran for use in its nuclear program, and by damaging the centrifuges, Stuxnet delayed Iran's progress. It appears almost certain that the Stuxnet worm was produced and disseminated by a government, and the most likely suspects were the United States and Israel, but its origin could not be traced definitively. Stuxnet caused immense concern in the cybersecurity community because the worm could be modified to disrupt a wide range of industrial systems and public utilities.

In contrast to weapons such as drones and precision-guided munitions, cyber weapons are available to the whole range of actors, including terrorist groups, criminal organizations, and other nonstate actors. Cyber warfare has some of the characteristics of terrorism and insurgency, in which states (as well as firms) offer large and visible targets, whereas terrorist, insurgent, or criminal groups may be hard to find. Because cyber attacks are often launched from computers that have been taken over by viruses, it can be extremely difficult to figure out who is behind a particular attack. This can provide states with an opportunity to attack an adversary secretly. The ability to disguise the source of an attack can make retaliation very difficult, which in turn makes deterrence very difficult.

Cyber warfare, therefore, is not just another weapon. It potentially impinges on nearly every aspect of our lives. Governments have struggled to devise "rules of engagement" for cyber warfare, just as they have rules of engagement for kinetic operations. Such rules of engagement would state when (and with whose approval) governments could undertake steps ranging from monitoring Internet traffic to shutting down vulnerable networks to attacking networks and computers to cause havoc. However, because cyber warfare overlaps heavily with intelligence gathering, it is not easy to have a completely open discussion about it without giving away important secrets. Thus, the primary focus initially has been on defense, and institutions of all kinds are spending increasing resources on IT security. Governments, however, are also investing money in cyber warfare units within their militaries. Both the United States and China have developed dedicated cyber warfare units. It appears that this could be the ground for a new "arms" race.

## THE PROLIFERATION OF LOW-TECH WEAPONS

Although high-technology weapons have changed the capabilities of the most powerful states in the system, lower-technology weapons have proliferated in vast numbers around the world. Low-tech weapons include everything from assault rifles and grenade launchers to antiaircraft missiles. The ultimate low-tech weapon in recent years, the improvised explosive device (IED), has played a prominent role in the conflicts in Iraq and Afghanistan. These weapons make use of widely available and inexpensive materials to create huge tactical problems for their makers' adversaries. Intense competition in the global arms industry has increased supply and driven down the price of low-tech weapons (see Figure 9.2).

**FIGURE 9.2** Arms proliferation around the world is driven by the sales of a few large suppliers.

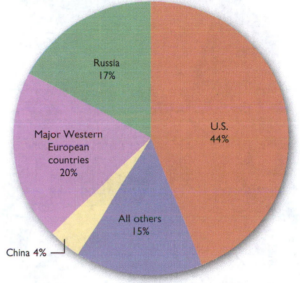

**Major Global Arms Sellers, 2004–2011**

Russia 17% · Major Western European countries 20% · U.S. 44% · All others 15% · China 4%

Source: Congressional Research Service, Conventional Arms Transfers to Developing Nations, 2004–2011.

Although none of these weapons kill immense numbers of people at once, the huge numbers of them means that they can kill many thousands of people, just as nuclear weapons can. In the most lethal conflict of the 1990s, approximately 800,000 Rwandans were killed with little more than rifles, machetes, and improvised weapons. In Sudan, roughly 2 million people were killed with low-tech weapons in the civil war from 1983 to 2005. Low-tech weapons are readily available to various nonstate actors, such as terrorist groups, separatist movements, and criminal organizations. The insurgencies that have bedeviled the United States and its allies in Iraq and Afghanistan are armed almost exclusively with such weapons. The result is that security threats no longer come only from states and are no longer aimed only at states.

## THE EMERGENCE OF HYBRID WARFARE

Russia's invasion of Crimea and eastern Ukraine in 2014 combined covert operations, sponsorship of rebels within Ukraine, and a media disinformation campaign in a novel way that became known as "hybrid warfare." When armed men seized key positions in the Ukrainian territory of Crimea, it appeared that they were locally based separatists. It later became clear that many of them were Russian soldiers and intelligence agents. By disguising their invasion as a domestic rebellion, Russia hoped to bolster the claim that Crimeans sought to leave Ukraine and join Russia, and to avoid the domestic and international ramifications of openly invading a neighbor. A massive effort by state-controlled Russian media sought to counter claims that Russian forces were involved, with the result that even Western media outlets hesitated to use the word "invasion."

The involvement of domestic Ukrainian separatists bolstered the claim that this was an internal rebellion, not an invasion, but the separatists were few in numbers, politically

*"World War III? Hmm. O.K., but, remember, nobody gets hurt."*

Robert Weber/The New Yorker Collection/Cartoonbank.com

divided, and poorly armed. The insertion of regular Russian military units ensured that they could seize a significant swath of Ukrainian territory. It appeared, then, that a new method of warfare had been developed, which combined external covert forces with support for domestic rebels. Whether this effort was truly unprecedented was debatable, but the broader point is that military innovation is constant.

## SENSITIVITY TO CASUALTIES

Sensitivity to casualties has been on the rise in many countries since World War II. Although most societies still have a high tolerance for casualties suffered to defend their homeland, their willingness to endure soldiers dying abroad has decreased considerably. Research on the United States finds evidence of this trend as far back as the Korean War (1950–1953), and by 1965, Undersecretary of State George Ball predicted that public support for the Vietnam War would decline as casualties increased.[4]

In many countries, the public will support military intervention abroad only as long as deaths remain very low. As casualties mount, policy makers and citizens alike question the use of force. For military and political planners, such a loss of support can be devastating. As a result, which fights get fought and how they get fought are heavily influenced by the need to minimize battle deaths. The advent of precision-guided weapons has made reducing battle deaths easier for the few states that possess them, but it has also increased expectations that war can be fought at a low cost. However, the proliferation of low-tech weapons and the spread of insurgency techniques have made it possible in some cases to raise casualty rates even for powerful armies.

Different levels of sensitivity to casualties can dramatically influence power relations between countries. Deterrence and coercion rely on being able to raise the costs of a given course of action higher than the benefits. Some countries may be comparatively weak in their ability to inflict such costs on others, but comparatively strong in their ability to withstand such pain. Other countries may be the opposite. This was the case in the Vietnam War:

AP Photo/Steve Miller

Sensitivity to casualties was so high that after 2003, the U.S. government refused to allow the press to photograph the return of the bodies of soldiers killed in combat.

North Vietnam lost at least 1 million people in that war, and the United States lost roughly 58,000. Yet the United States found the cost intolerable before North Vietnam did. This does not mean that the Vietnamese did not value human life, but rather that they valued what they were fighting for much more than the United States did. Ultimately, Vietnam's advantage in sensitivity to casualties outweighed the U.S. advantage in the ability to inflict casualties. The essence of insurgent and terrorist strategies today is to inflict casualties on societies that are highly sensitive to them.

To summarize, the post–Cold War era has been defined, in military terms, by a set of unprecedented developments whose interacting effects are not often appreciated. Oddly, the effects of different developments may counteract each other in some ways. More than at any time in history, one country is vastly predominant in the means of waging war. However, this imbalance has prompted some states to seek WMD, while other actors have turned to terrorism and still others to insurgency. Similarly, high-tech weaponry has created the ability to wage war in a more precise and less destructive way. Yet this advantage has been eroded by a corresponding increase in sensitivity to casualties. And although the great fear has been and continues to be the employment of WMD, proliferation of low-tech weapons has made mass death possible without WMD.

# WEAPONS OF MASS DESTRUCTION (WMD)

In many respects, the advent of nuclear weapons changed the fundamental rationale governing the use of force. Among the nuclear-armed states and their allies, the emphasis shifted from defense to deterrence. Defeating an adversary on the battlefield made less sense when a nuclear war might kill everyone in the warring states. Instead, the goal of policy was to create fear of *any* war on the grounds that it might lead to a nuclear response.

The shift from defense to deterrence began almost immediately with the annihilation of Hiroshima and Nagasaki. Those attacks did not contribute meaningfully to defeating the Japanese military. Instead, the Japanese government, seeing the terrible destruction that could be wrought by nuclear weapons, quickly surrendered; in other words, they were deterred from further resistance. The apparent lesson was that nuclear weapons could be used to coerce adversaries, especially if they did not have nuclear weapons of their own. It quickly became evident, however, that nuclear coercion would not be so simple, as the United States found that its monopoly on nuclear weapons did not make the Soviet Union bend to its will.

## TYPES OF WMD

There are five categories of WMD, though only two (nuclear and chemical weapons) have been used in modern warfare:

- Nuclear weapons, which create an explosion from nuclear fission or fusion. They can be thousands of times as powerful as those dropped on Japan in World War II. In addition to blast effects, they create extreme heat, blinding light, radiation, and radioactive fallout.
- Chemical weapons, which include
  - Choking agents: These primarily attack the lungs, causing them to fill with fluid. Important examples include the chlorine and phosgene gases that were used in World War I.

- Blistering agents: These cause chemical burns on the skin, in the eyes, and in the lungs, as well as various secondary effects. A prominent example is mustard gas, which was used in World War I.
  - Nerve agents: These chemicals, often absorbed through skin, interfere with the transmission of nerve signals that control breathing. One of these, sarin gas, was used by the Syrian government against rebels in 2013.
- Biological weapons, which use various infectious agents, including anthrax, botulism, pneumonic plague, and smallpox.[5]
- **Radiological weapons**, which use various radioactive materials, some of which are highly poisonous. Radiological weapons can be based on a broader range of materials than can nuclear weapons, and can use smaller amounts. They rely on a conventional explosion (creating a so-called dirty bomb). For these reasons, they are much easier to build than nuclear weapons.
- **Electromagnetic pulse (EMP) weapons**, which use a powerful burst of energy to damage electronic circuits. The most powerful EMP weapons are driven by nuclear explosions, but nonnuclear variants also exist.

The attractiveness of nonnuclear WMD (and of chemical and biological weapons in particular) is that they are much easier and cheaper to produce than nuclear weapons. Therefore, states or groups that do not have the resources to acquire nuclear weapons can pursue other WMD. Chemical weapons are especially easy to produce. On the other hand, these weapons are not very easy to deploy with a massive effect. Chemical and biological weapons have to be delivered in mass quantities to have mass effects. Moreover, distribution of these weapons is a challenging task. Chemical weapons were of limited use in World War I in part because shifts in winds sometimes brought them back on the forces that discharged them. Anthrax, although deadly, is very difficult to produce in a form that hangs in the air and is therefore likely to be inhaled.

Moreover, for any of these weapons to be useful as a deterrent (or as an offensive weapon), the deterring country must be able to deliver the weapon to the homeland of the potential adversary. Therefore, the quest for WMD has been accompanied by a quest for long-range delivery systems (generally long-range missiles). Consequently, along with efforts to reduce the proliferation of WMD, states are also trying to reduce the proliferation of long-range missiles.

Even if chemical, biological, and radiological weapons do not automatically have a massive destructive effect, they would likely have a massive *disruptive* effect—for example, by causing large population groups to avoid going outside, to seek preventive medicines, or simply to live in great fear. When small amounts of anthrax were mailed to the U.S. Capitol in 2001, only a few people died, but much of Washington, D.C., was disrupted. To capture this distinction, the U.S. Department of Homeland Security now refers to "weapons of mass destruction, disruption, and effect."

## NUCLEAR DETERRENCE IN THE COLD WAR

The nuclear relationship that developed between the United States and the Soviet Union was driven by two strategic puzzles that remain relevant today. First was the problem of **crisis stability**, discussed in the previous chapter. Both sides feared a surprise attack that would destroy their weapons before they could be launched. Therefore, even from a defensive perspective, there was an incentive to strike first—to "use 'em or lose 'em," as the saying goes.[6] As the number of weapons grew into the thousands, it became much

**radiological weapons**

Weapons that use conventional explosives to distribute radioactive material, which has long-lasting poisonous effects. Also known as "dirty bombs."

**electromagnetic pulse (EMP) weapons**

Weapons that use a powerful burst of energy to damage electronic circuits.

**crisis stability**

The likelihood that a crisis, once it begins, will have dynamics that tend to lead toward war.

less likely that one side could execute a first strike that wiped out all of the other side's weapons. Even after a massive attack, each side would retain a "second-strike" capability. This situation came to be known as mutual assured destruction (MAD). Stability stemmed from the assurance that there was little advantage in going first.

The second puzzle was how to make nuclear weapons politically useful. Contrary to early expectations, nuclear coercion did not prove very easy, largely because the threat was not perceived as credible. A paradox of nuclear weapons is that even if their use might be irrational, the *threat* of using them appears to have substantial deterrent value. Even if escalating a conventional war to a nuclear war would be irrational, the fear that it could happen probably helped deter conventional war. One strategist of the Cold War era thus referred to "the threat that leaves something to chance."[7] In sum, nuclear weapons are much more useful in deterrence than in coercion or actual use.

## PROLIFERATION

While the focus in the Cold War was on the weapons of the most powerful states, today smaller states are seeking the perceived benefits of WMD, as Tables 9.3 and 9.4 show. As the United States gets further ahead of other countries in terms of conventional weapons, deterrence through defense becomes increasingly impossible for weaker states. U.S.-led campaigns against Iraq (1991, 2003) and in the former Yugoslavia (1995, 1999) demonstrated that the United States could use high-tech weapons to soundly defeat an adversary at little cost in U.S. lives. Many states, such as North Korea and Iran facing the United States, Pakistan facing India, and Israel facing the Arab states, fear that they may not be able to defend themselves against a conventional attack. Instead of (or in addition to) increasing their defense capabilities, therefore, these states are focusing increasingly on deterrence, which is accomplished most effectively and cheaply through WMD. At the same time, terrorist groups seeking to maximize the effects of their attacks are naturally interested in developing WMD.

## WMD AND CRISIS STABILITY

Does nuclear proliferation really undermine security? A prominent realist theorist of international politics, Kenneth Waltz, argued that proliferation of nuclear weapons will likely make the world more, rather than less, safe. Waltz's argument, simply put, is that by making it easier to deter an attack than to wage an attack successfully, nuclear weapons increase stability. "If countries with nuclear weapons go to war, they do so knowing that their suffering may be unlimited. Of course, it also may not be, but that is not the kind of uncertainty that encourages anyone to use force."[9]

Others dispute this view on several grounds.[10] First, the argument that nuclear weapons contribute to deterrence relies on the assumption that leaders are rational, a view that many analysts find questionable. Second, it assumes that civilian leaders, even if rational, have effective control over militaries. As weapons spread to less stable countries, some believe, it is more likely that weapons will be controlled by military organizations not fully in tune with their countries' national interest. There is also fear, especially concerning Pakistan, that a government might be toppled by radical groups with connections to terrorists or with extreme ideologies

**TABLE 9.3**  **Estimated Total Nuclear Warheads Worldwide, 2015**[8]

| Country | Warheads |
|---|---|
| Russia | 7500 |
| United States | 7260 |
| France | 300 |
| China | 260 |
| United Kingdom | 215 |
| Pakistan | 100–120 |
| India | 90–100 |
| Israel | 80 |

**TABLE 9.4** Chemical and Biological Weapons Programs Worldwide, as of 2012[11]

| Country | Chemical Weapons | Biological Weapons |
|---|---|---|
| Algeria | Possible | Research effort |
| Myanmar | Probable | |
| Canada | Former program | Former program |
| China | Probable | Likely maintains an offensive capability |
| Cuba | Possible | Probable research program |
| Egypt | Probable | Likely maintains an offensive program |
| Ethiopia | Probable | |
| France | Former program | Former program |
| Germany | Former program | Former program |
| India | Discontinued | Research program |
| Iran | Known | Likely maintains an offensive program |
| Iraq | Former program | Former program |
| Israel | Probable | Research program |
| Italy | Former program | |
| Japan | Former program | Former program |
| Libya | Former program | Former program |
| North Korea | Known | Research, possible production of agents |
| Pakistan | Probable | Possible |
| Russia | Probable | Research program |
| South Africa | Former program | Former program |
| Sudan | Possible | Possible research interest |
| Syria | Known | Research, possible production of agents |
| Taiwan | Possible | Possible research program |
| United Kingdom | Former program | Former program |
| United States | Former program | Former program |
| Vietnam | Possible | |

that might motivate the use of nuclear weapons. Similarly, some governments might be less able to protect nuclear weapons or materials from theft.

Even if leaders are rational and in control, crisis stability will continue to depend on mutual confidence in a secure second-strike capability. This is especially problematic for new nuclear powers, which are likely to have small arsenals deployed in a limited geographic area and a single means of delivering the weapons. These states, and their weapons, may be tempting targets for a first strike, not only by another nuclear power, but

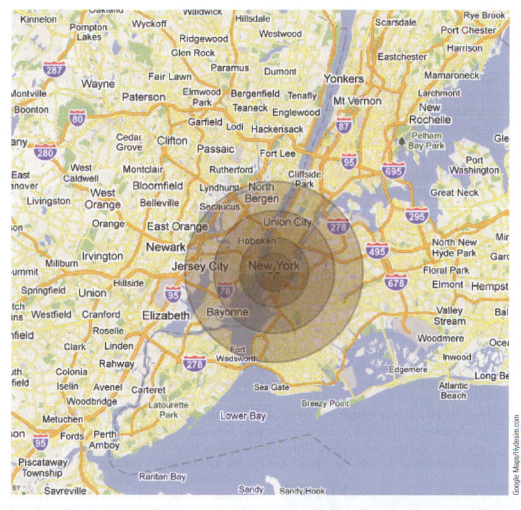

Estimated radius of a nuclear blast in New York City. The concentric circles show various levels of blast damage.

Google Maps/Hydesim.com

also by a well-armed conventional power. A potential attacker might believe that it could completely eliminate a small arsenal with a first strike, and that doing so might be safer than enduring the chance that the arsenal will grow or become more securely defended. The state with the small arsenal of WMD faces the "use 'em or lose 'em" dilemma. The result, therefore, is that as WMD proliferate, the temptation to wage preventive war and the challenges of maintaining crisis stability will increase in importance.

## WMD AND THE SECURITY DILEMMA

In sum, the dynamics of the proliferation of WMD are not fundamentally different from those of conventional weapons. States that perceive a security threat can be expected to respond by increasing their own military capabilities. When it is easier to prevent an attack by threatening retaliation than by building the capacity to win on the battlefield, states can be expected to do this. Those states that build powerful military capabilities can anticipate that others will arm against them, with WMD if necessary. This is the classic security dilemma.

WMD more clearly separate the defensive and deterrent functions of weapons, and are particularly effective at strengthening deterrence by increasing the damage that can be inflicted on an attacker. The deterrent power of WMD explains why states make such costly efforts to gain them, and why the states that have them wish to keep them. States seeking to gain WMD capabilities are generally experiencing intense security threats. In particular, those that face nuclear-armed rivals, or rivals with whom they cannot compete in conventional terms, have a strong incentive to obtain WMD. And although the spread of WMD may induce some states to be more cautious in their policies, it also creates the potential for a high level of crisis instability. Moreover, in recent years, the problem of WMD proliferation has meant that states must prepare not only for the possibility that other states will acquire WMD, but also for the possibility that terrorists will gain access to these weapons.

# TERRORISM, INSURGENCY, AND COUNTERINSURGENCY

**insurgency**

An effort to overthrow the political power in a territory through violence.

**guerilla warfare**

Warfare in which tactics of harassment and ambush are favored over direct battle.

In terms of the scale of destruction, insurgency and guerilla warfare seem quite different from the deployment of WMD, but they share the same logic. Like deterrence, **insurgency** and **guerilla warfare** focus not on defeating the enemy on the field of battle, but on raising the costs of conflict so that they are higher than any possible benefit to the attacker.[12]

Weak actors use insurgent tactics to minimize their weakness while exploiting the weaknesses of their adversaries. As the gaps between powerful militaries and weaker ones have grown, and as more armed conflicts have involved nonstate actors incapable of conventional defense, insurgency has become a more widely used tactic.

Gunman attack a wounded policemen after killing 12 employees of the French satirical magazine Charlie Hebdo, Paris, January 2015.

Examples of insurgent warfare in recent decades include wars in Vietnam, Iraq, and Afghanistan (where the Soviet Union faced this strategy in the 1980s and the United States has confronted it since 2001). Earlier cases that have been widely studied include the case of Malaya, where local insurgents sought independence from Britain; China, where communists led by Mao Zedong opposed Chinese nationalist forces and the Japanese military from the 1920s through the 1940s; and Saudi Arabia, where Britain instigated a local insurgency against Ottoman rule during World War I.

A general set of lessons has emerged about the successes of insurgency and counterinsurgency. Insurgency is chosen by forces too weak to defeat an opponent's army in open battle. Rather than wage open warfare, insurgents seek to strike quickly through ambushes and then disengage before a larger battle ensues.

Similarly, they seek to avoid standard lines of battle, instead, crossing into territory ostensibly held by the enemy to attack areas that should be safe. Thus, Mao Zedong stated that "the guerrilla must move amongst the people as a fish swims in the sea." When insurgents try to hold a territory, the opposing army can bring its superior forces to that area and force the insurgents either to fight a battle they will likely lose or to abandon the territory. Thus, insurgency is less well suited to holding territory than to raising the enemy's costs. The insurgent force does not try to match the strength of an established power, but rather seeks to take advantage of its own weaknesses, such as controlling no territory and having no large force concentrations that can be attacked. For this reason, insurgency is often labeled as an **asymmetric conflict**.

Most analysts agree that winning the "hearts and minds" of noncombatants is crucial to the outcome of an insurgency/counterinsurgency conflict.[13] Only when the general public supports the insurgents can they move freely behind enemy lines and prepare attacks without being discovered. When the public opposes the insurgency, people are more likely to provide intelligence that helps counterinsurgent forces avoid traps and ambushes. For example, a key goal of the United States in Iraq was to persuade local Iraqis to provide warning of IEDs. If the counterinsurgent forces cannot win the support of the population, they will likely be forced either to give up or to wage war on the population itself, as the United States did in attacking villages that supported insurgents in Vietnam, or as Russia did in depopulating areas of Chechnya in the 1990s.

The challenge for both insurgents and counterinsurgents is determining how to carry out day-to-day operations in a way that does not undermine support from the population. As an insurgent leader, Mao Zedong instituted a set of rules (such as not stealing from people, being courteous to them, and returning borrowed items) intended to ensure that his forces did not alienate the population among whom they operated. For the United States in Vietnam, Iraq, and Afghanistan, short-term efforts to eliminate insurgents (arresting suspects and taking them away for interrogation, for example) had the long-term effect of angering local populations and increasing support for the insurgents. The fact that foreign troops fighting an insurgency often do not speak the language or understand the culture in which they are operating puts them at a huge disadvantage relative to locally based insurgents. Many analysts looking back on the Vietnam War have pointed out that U.S. forces rarely, if ever, lost a battle. But in fighting an insurgency, winning battles is insufficient, and sometimes irrelevant, to strategic victory because insurgents can raise costs intolerably high without ever winning head-to-head battles.

The war in Afghanistan provides a good illustration of the challenges of insurgency. The United States and its allies possess immense capability to find and destroy insurgent forces, but that is not enough. General Stanley McChrystal, commander of NATO forces in Afghanistan in 2009–2010, stated: "The Russians killed 1 million Afghans, and that didn't work."[14] He recognized that every civilian casualty caused several more people to join the insurgency. Therefore, he implemented very strict rules of engagement to prevent civilian casualties and other offenses that set back the battle for hearts and minds. Afghan insurgents did not face the same constraints. They had an enemy that was easily located and attacked, they did not face the same criticism for killing noncombatants, and they were not limited by restrictive rules of engagement. U.S. soldiers feared that the restrictions placed on them prevented them from winning battles with Taliban forces, but using too much force might win the battle while losing the war. "Right now we're losing the tactical-level fight in the chase for a strategic victory," one officer pointed out. "How long can that be sustained?"[15] The increased use of drones and special forces in Afghanistan and elsewhere is intended to deprive insurgents of their primary targets—ground troops—while minimizing the civilian casualties that boost insurgents' recruiting efforts.

**asymmetric conflict**
A conflict between actors with very different strengths, vulnerabilities, and tactics.

## THE POWER AND PURPOSE OF TERRORISM

The advent of cross-border terrorism by well-funded and well-organized nonstate organizations causes scholars and policy makers alike to rethink the fundamental questions of power and purpose. The ability of these nonstate actors to drive the global security agenda has called into question traditional conceptions of international power, which have been based on size of territory, economic resources, and arsenals.

Because these actors are pursuing goals that have little to do with state interests, a great deal of debate has focused on understanding the purposes of terrorists. Historically, terrorists have had a variety of objectives. Some appear to have far-reaching messianic goals, such as bringing down the capitalist economic system or waging a holy war. Others appear to have very limited local goals, such as driving an unwelcome political power out of a particular territory.

Terrorism has become a central focus of international politics today. Terrorist attacks in the United States in 2001, in Madrid in 2004, in London in 2005, in Bombay in 2008, in Paris in 2015, and in Moscow repeatedly, have brought to major cities a level of violence and fear from which they had previously been immune. As a result, in many societies, fear of attack by terrorists has replaced fear of attack by other states as the primary external security threat. Although terrorism is not new, the role it is now playing in the politics of international security is new. Consequently, scholars and policy makers are struggling to assess the impact of terrorism on international politics and to gauge how radical a change it actually represents. A central point emerges: Terrorism is difficult for states to deal with because the two traditional approaches to security—defense and deterrence—are less effective against terrorists than against states.

## DEFINING TERRORISM

**terrorism**

Use or threat of violence by nongovernmental actors to change government policies by creating fear of further violence.

Because the words *terrorism* and *terrorist* are so laden with emotion (they have become nearly synonymous with "evil"), it is difficult to use the words analytically in a way that makes it clear what terrorism is (and is not) and who is (and is not) a terrorist. **Terrorism** is the use or threat of violence by nongovernmental actors in an effort to change government policies by creating fear of further violence. This definition—and it is not the only one possible—stresses three key points.

First, terrorism is a method, not a goal. Although some may perceive terrorism as senseless violence, most experts agree that terrorism is almost always a means to achieve particular goals. Walter Laqueur, a leading scholar on terrorism, emphasizes that terrorism "is not an ideology or a political doctrine, but rather a method—the substate application of violence or the threat of violence to sow panic and bring about political change."[16] Similarly, Robert Jervis defines terrorism as "the use of violence for political or social purposes that is not publicly authorized by leaders of recognized political units, including acts that are sponsored and supported by states, but not publicly avowed."[17] In contrast, violence that is committed only for monetary gain or for the sake of killing is generally not defined as terrorism. Hence, there is a difference between terrorism and organized crime or psychopathic violence.

As a tactic or method, terrorism works quite similarly to any kind of coercive diplomacy or deterrence. The goal is to raise the costs of certain policies so that states will choose other policies. For example, the Irish Republican Army (IRA) bombed innocent civilians in British cities to raise the cost of British control of Northern Ireland. Al Qaeda commits its attacks in order to raise the cost of various policies it opposes, including U.S. support for Israel and the stationing of U.S. troops in Saudi Arabia.

Despite the fear it creates, terrorism is a weapon of the weak. Like insurgency, terrorism is adopted by actors who do not stand a chance of competing with a government in conventional terms. A group adopts terrorism only when its cause is not popular enough to prevail through normal political channels. Terrorism presents a weapon with which the weak can "sting" the powerful, but it is important to recognize what terrorism cannot do: It cannot, by itself, take control of a territory or govern a society. Thus, terrorist groups that accomplish the goal of rising to power have to adopt different strategies in order to govern. The distinction between terrorism and governing was blurred in 2014 with the rise of ISIS, or the Islamic State, which moved from a terrorist and insurgent force to take control of parts of Syria and Iraq. The Islamic State continued to deploy terror against the residents of the area it controlled, but to succeed it had to do much more than that, including running an economy.

Second, violence committed by a government is generally not labeled "terrorism."[18] By this definition, a government that bombs another country's population, even with WMD, is not a terrorist, regardless of how evil it might be. During the Cold War, a prominent nuclear strategist described the mutual threats against the populations of the United States and the Soviet Union as a "delicate balance of terror." Yet few people called the United States or the Soviet Union terrorists for employing this threat. Similarly, today, when a state's military force uses bombs to kill people or to coerce a government, its actions are not generally called terrorism. When a nonstate group uses bombs to kill people, this behavior *is* called terrorism. This difference makes clear that in deciding what terrorism is, it is important not only what is done and to whom, but *by whom* it is done. Some people see this distinction as hypocritical, but there may in fact be a good reason to distinguish violence used by states from violence used by nonstate groups (just as both of these are distinguished from the violence committed by ordinary criminal gangs).

Finally, the target of terrorism is usually not the immediate victims (those killed or maimed), or even their close relatives, but rather the broader society and the government.[19] Most of the time, terrorists are not concerned with exactly whom they kill. Rather, the dramatic way in which people are killed conveys the desired message. Especially when targeting democracies, the mechanism of influence seems to be to kill innocent people, either to get the broader population to pressure governments for change in policy or to undermine government credibility. There are exceptions; in some cases, terrorists seek to directly attack state leaders or military forces. By killing innocents, or particularly visible individuals, terrorists seek to achieve political effects that are disproportionate to the amount of violence used.

The "terror" of terrorism comes only in part from the number of people killed, which is often quite small. In 1996, for example, a person was 33 times more likely to die from meningitis than from terrorism, 822 times more likely to die by murder, 1200 times more likely to die by suicide, and 1833 times more likely to die in a car accident.[20] Yet none of these inspire the fear that results from terrorism. Rather, the terror and the political effect are a result of the *way* people are killed, which is violent, sudden, public, and seemingly random.

**States, Nonstate Actors, and Terrorism**   As the preceding discussion shows, the concept of terrorism is based on the belief that certain acts are acceptable if undertaken by states, but unacceptable if undertaken by others. This raises the question of who is regarded as a legitimate actor in international politics, a question of the sort pursued by the constructivist approaches. To put this idea in different language, terrorists are *private* actors who use violence for *public* goals. Thus, terrorism can be contrasted with state violence, which is public violence for public goals, and common crime, which is private violence for private goals.[21]

Since the Treaty of Westphalia, a norm shared by states internationally has been that the use of armed force is reserved for sovereign states. That norm is enforced internally by states on their own citizens, but it has also generally been observed internationally. Most definitions of the state, therefore, focus on its monopoly over the legitimate use of force. Although other actors (bank robbers, street gangs, or terrorists) might use force, only states can use force *legitimately*, in the generally accepted view. This explains why threats of violence against civilians by nonstate actors are seen as less legitimate, and having less moral standing, than those by states. Some people see this conception of terrorism as hypocritical, but these distinctions are widely accepted.

**Terrorism as Asymmetric Conflict**   Terrorism, like insurgency, is a form of *asymmetric conflict*, a term that emphasizes that terrorism involves a conflict between different kinds of actors with very different strengths, vulnerabilities, and tactics. This view of terrorism contrasts starkly with the traditional conception of war, in which combat takes place between similar actors (states).

It is essential in any analysis to acknowledge two differences between states and terrorist groups.

- States control territories and populations, among other things. Therefore, they can potentially be deterred. Terrorists, because they do not control territory and are not responsible for populations, have nothing of value against which to make deterrent threats.

- Terrorists can choose when and where to strike states, whereas states often cannot locate and engage terrorists. If states cannot locate terrorists, then conflict takes place on terms determined by the terrorists.

The first point shows why states have a difficult time deterring terrorists. The second explains why states have a difficult time defending against them. Neither of the two strategies on which states rely to prevent attacks from other states works effectively against terrorists. For this reason, many advocate addressing terrorism not with acts of war, but through law enforcement.

## CAUSES OF TERRORISM

In recent years, combating terrorism has become one of the most important policy challenges for many governments. However, the task of designing effective counterterrorism policy is hampered by our limited understanding of the causes of terrorism.

Why does terrorism emerge in some cases but not in others? Why do some individuals become terrorists while others, in seemingly similar circumstances, do not? As in the literature on the sources of war, that on terrorism varies from system-level approaches (such as the argument that terrorism is an inherent result of globalization) to individual-level approaches, which seek to identify the specific psychological characteristics of the individuals who carry out attacks. In between are societal-level explanations, which ask why some societies seem willing to give terrorists the cover they need to avoid capture. As in the literature on war, some approaches to terrorism view it as inherently irrational and try to explain the pathologies behind it. Other approaches view terrorism as rational and seek to explore the goals being pursued by terrorists and the choice of terrorism rather than some other method. Power and purpose remain at the center of the discussion. So far, no explanation of terrorism has gained wide support among scholars. This subject will likely be one of the main lines of research in international relations in coming years.

# THE HISTORY CONNECTION

## A BRIEF HISTORY OF TERRORISM

The term *terrorism* is at least 200 years old, and the phenomenon is much older than that. The words *zealot*, *thug*, and *assassin* all come from the names of premodern terrorist groups. During the Roman Empire, a group of Jewish people known as the Zealots fought an armed struggle against Roman rule in Israel. A subset of that group, the *Sicarii* ("Daggers"), carried out a campaign of murder against other Jews who did not support the Zealot movement.* From the eleventh through the thirteenth centuries in Persia, a group known as the *Assassins* developed a secret force of trained killers who murdered their victims, usually prominent political figures, in public. This practice of killing in public to maximize publicity, and of accepting certain death, has echoes in today's terrorism.[†]

In nineteenth-century Russia, terrorism took on what might be called its first "modern" incarnation, as an act of the weak against the state. A group known as *Narodnaya Volya* ("The People's Will") conducted a series of attacks on leading tsarist government officials, including the assassination of Tsar Alexander II in 1881. This movement is relevant not only because of its political influence but because it developed the "cell" organization— in which no member knows the identity of more than a few others—that is still used by terrorist organizations today. The successors to *Narodnaya Volya* popularized the use of terrorist tactics among politically extreme groups in the late nineteenth and early twentieth centuries. These groups tended to target major political figures. In the United States, anarchist Leon Czolgosz assassinated President McKinley in 1901. In 1914, a Serbian nationalist group assassinated the heir to the Austro-Hungarian throne, Archduke Franz Ferdinand, touching off World War I.[‡]

In recent decades the conflict between Palestinians and Israel has been a source of much terrorist activity. In 1972, Palestinian terrorists invaded the athletes' village at the Olympic games in Munich, Germany, killing several Israeli athletes and taking several others hostage. As a result of satellite television transmissions, which were new at the time, events in Munich could be seen around the world as they happened. Since the goal of terrorism is to make an impression on as many people as possible, the advent of live television coverage has dramatically increased terrorism's power. This process reached its zenith in 2001, when images of the World Trade Center burning and then collapsing were shown repeatedly on television around the world.

Leftist or anarchist movements instigated terrorist attacks in the 1970s and 1980s. These echoed the Russian leftist terrorist movements of the nineteenth and early twentieth centuries. Germany, Italy, Greece, and Japan all had homegrown movements that carried out substantial violence in protest against their own governments' policies. These groups were largely crushed in the 1980s, through infiltration by law enforcement and because they never had many members to begin with. However, by collaborating transnationally in training and operations, they foreshadowed the loose transnational alliance of Al Qaeda affiliates that emerged in the 1990s. Leftist and anarchist movements in the United States, including the Weather Underground and the Symbionese Liberation Army, quickly faded on their own.

A third set of terrorist campaigns has occurred during conflicts over national self-determination. The IRA sought to end British control over Northern Ireland and set off bombs around Britain for several years before agreeing to a truce in 1998. In Spain, the Basque separatist group ETA has engaged in a campaign of bombings and intimidation in an effort to gain an independent Basque territory. Similarly, in Turkey, the Kurdish Workers' Party (PKK), a group fighting for Kurdish

*(Continued)*

independence, was responsible for a series of bombings for many years before the arrest of its leader led to a decrease in attacks. In Sri Lanka, the Tamil Tigers, fighting for an independent homeland for the Tamil ethnic group, pioneered the use of suicide bombers in their struggle with the Sri Lankan government.

## Critical Thinking Questions

1. Throughout history terrorism has been used by a wide range of groups and has been invoked to support a wide array of causes. Is there anything fundamentally new about the terrorism of recent years?

2. Does examining the long history of terrorism offer significant insight into its causes, or would it be better to focus on recent years?

3. Are there useful lessons to be learned from terrorist movements in history that either were defeated or simply faded away?

---

*David C. Rapaport, "Messianic Sanctions for Terror," Comparative Politics, Vol. 20, No. 2 (January 1988): 195.

†Rapaport, "Messianic Sanctions for Terror," p. 195.

‡Anna Geifman, Thou Shalt Kill: Revolutionary Terrorism in Russia, 1894–1917 (Princeton, NJ: Princeton University Press, 1993).

**Rational Choice Explanations** From the rational choice perspective, the problem of explaining terrorism becomes an attempt to answer the question, "To what set of circumstances is terrorism a rational response?" The key, from this perspective, is to understand the options open to very weak actors in combat with powerful governments. For a group that considers itself to be at war with a vastly more powerful adversary, engaging in conventional war would guarantee defeat.

This point is perhaps more easily understood if we return to our distinction between defense and deterrence by (actual or threatened) retaliation. When an actor believes that it cannot muster enough force to defeat an adversary on the battlefield, it can instead adopt a policy of retaliation: raising the cost of a particular policy in an effort to force the adversary to adopt a different policy. At one end of the military spectrum, this results in efforts by states to obtain WMD. At the opposite end, this results in a shift to "low-intensity" tactics, such as insurgency and terrorism.

For the IRA, for example, terrorism against the British government was intended to raise the cost of British control of Northern Ireland. Palestinian attacks against Israelis are similarly seen as aimed at raising the cost of Israeli occupation of territory claimed by Palestinians. Attacks by Chechens against civilians in Russia are aimed at forcing the Russian government to grant the territory of Chechnya autonomy or independence.

To the extent that terrorism is a tool, how can we explain groups such as Al Qaeda, which seem focused on wreaking havoc on societies they oppose? Al Qaeda, at least originally, had a clearly announced goal of its terrorism: to force the United States to remove forces stationed in Saudi Arabia. More broadly, members of the group share a sense of grievance against American policies in the Middle East, including U.S. support for Israel against Palestinians and support for authoritarian allies such as Saudi Arabia. Al Qaeda has also sought to deter other states from collaborating with the United States in Iraq and Afghanistan.

Terrorism can also be a means of communicating outrage to the general public as well as to governments. Many interpret much of the anticapitalist terrorism in western Europe during the 1970s as an attempt to call attention to the injustice of the prevailing system. The Oklahoma City bombing of 1995 can also be seen as a protest against the U.S. government's treatment of far-right groups. In both cases, there is no sign that the terrorists had any notion that their actions would lead to a change in the system of government or even a change in policy. Rather, the actions were meant to attract global attention to the terrorists' cause.

**Poverty**    Some see poverty as an underlying cause of terrorism. In this view, the poverty that is endemic in so much of the world creates a sense of desperation and alienation that makes people willing to tolerate or even to participate in terrorism against the wealthy and powerful societies that control the world economy. A cursory look at the areas from which terrorism is emerging today appears to support the plausibility of this approach. The Palestinians who commit suicide bombings against Israelis live in grinding poverty. The young Afghanis who support the Taliban and Al Qaeda live in one of the poorest countries in the world. The influential author and *New York Times* columnist Thomas Friedman contends that although poverty does not directly cause terrorism, "poverty is great for the terrorism business because poverty creates humiliation and stifled aspirations and forces many people to leave their traditional farms to join the alienated urban poor in the cities—all conditions that spawn terrorists."[22]

Obviously, not all poor people are terrorists. Very few are. Therefore, if there is a connection between poverty and terrorism, it must be an indirect one. Many have argued that poverty in some parts of the world contributes to terrorism by creating a large number of young men with no hope of advancement through education or good jobs. Such hopelessness might have several effects that contribute to terrorism. First, it might make people more susceptible to radical political or religious doctrines. Those who see no hope on earth might be more likely to subscribe to extreme religious beliefs that promise rewards in the afterlife. Second, it might make individuals more hostile toward the existing political and economic system and therefore more interested in overthrowing it. To the extent that poverty occurs in societies with corrupt and authoritarian governments, that tendency may be strengthened. Third, hopelessness gives individuals less to lose. People with good prospects of advancing economically are less likely to want to sacrifice that to terrorism.

These arguments make intuitive sense, but there is little evidence showing a link between poverty and terrorism.[23] Although many terrorists come from poor backgrounds, many others come from relatively wealthy backgrounds. Most notable in this regard is Osama bin Laden, who came from a family of multimillionaires to lead the Al Qaeda organization. Many of his initial supporters also came from well-to-do Saudi families. The individuals who conducted the attacks of September 11, 2001, all had university educations, and by entering the United States, they had gained access to an economy in which any of them could have thrived.

Similarly, the anticapitalist terrorists who plagued Europe in the 1970s and 1980s generally came from upper-middle-class backgrounds and were reacting, to some extent, against that background. In the United States, the few homegrown terrorist movements (such as the Weather Underground and the Symbionese Liberation Army of the early 1970s) sprang from the educated and wealthy, not the masses of urban poor. More broadly, there is relatively little organized terrorism in many of the poorest countries of the world. If poverty leads directly to terrorism, terrorism should predominate in sub-Saharan Africa, where it is largely absent. In sum, there seems to be little identifiable relationship between poverty and terrorism.

**Religion**    The obvious religious agenda of much recent terrorism has led some to argue that religious extremism is itself the cause of terrorism.[24] Some argue that any religion, if it is adhered to strongly enough, can produce the kinds of beliefs that seem to justify terrorism. Religion may contribute to extremism by fostering the belief that God's will justifies whatever measures are taken to achieve it. This notion justified the torture to which Catholics and Protestants subjected each other throughout history, and it appears in the rhetoric of some Muslim terrorist groups today. The notion that God's will provides an absolute commandment to action helps undermine any tendency toward compromise that might otherwise emerge in a situation. These arguments are quite controversial and are difficult to discuss because they engage powerful emotions.

Particularly widespread in the world today is the contention that followers of Islam are especially prone toward religious violence and terrorism because of various concepts in the Qu'ran (such as jihad, or holy war), which can be used to justify such violence. Because many Islamic terrorist groups assert that the Qu'ran commands them to undertake holy war, it is easy to reach the conclusion that the Qu'ran indeed does so. Scholars and students should be careful, however, about reaching such a conclusion for several reasons.

First, although some of the most violent terrorists have claimed Qu'ranic sanction for their actions, many more Muslim scholars and practitioners recognize no such commandment. In fact, many scholars point to sections of the Qu'ran that offer clear statements against such violence. Fundamentalist Islam "represents only a small niche in the spectrum of Islamic views of political theology. Its beliefs and its actions fly in the face of doctrines of warfare that run widely and deeply in the Islamic tradition: a prohibition of the direct intentional killing of innocents; the requirement of justly constituted authority; a restrictive understanding of who is an aggressor that would thoroughly reject Osama bin Laden's assessment of the United States."[25]

Second, the tendency for religious extremists to claim divine or scriptural support for their actions is not unique to Islam. Hindu hardliners in India and Jewish extremists in Israel make similar claims, as did Christian Crusaders for centuries. These extremists may be no more representative of anything inherent in their faiths than Islamic fundamentalists are of theirs. Until recently, the conflict between Catholics and Protestants in Northern Ireland, which constituted terrorism by Christians against Christians for essentially religious reasons, was by far the greatest terrorist threat to the United Kingdom. Speaking in New York in 2002, Malaysian Prime Minister Mahathir Mohamad complained that "only Muslim terrorists are linked to their religion.... When Muslims in Bosnia-Herzegovina were being slaughtered by the Serbs, there was no mention of Christian Orthodox terrorists. These Christian Orthodox terrorists killed far more people than were killed on September 11. The world did not mobilise to fight Christian Orthodox terrorists even when they terrorized the Kosovars."[26]

Similarly, there is no clear connection between religion or religious intensity and suicide attacks. Suicide bombing was developed as a technique by the Tamil Tigers in Sri Lanka, whose members were neither Muslim nor highly religious. Tamils in general are Hindu, but the Tamil Tigers were a communist group and hence tended toward atheism, giving them no hope of religious salvation for their acts.

Third, the religious sources of terrorism warrant skepticism for the same reason that simple explanations based on poverty do: Religion is widespread, but terrorism is rare. Moreover, much terrorism throughout history has not been religiously motivated. Only in the past two decades does religion appear to have become the major motivation for terrorism. Prior to that time, nationalism and ideology (anarchism, socialism, and the like) were the most common motivators of terrorism. Even today, a good deal of terrorist activity is not wrapped up in religious conflict, as shown by the Basque terrorist group ETA (Euskadi Ta Askatasuna, or "Homeland and Freedom") and the Kurdish PKK (Kurdish Workers' Party), both of which share the religion of those whom they attack.

Just as it is an oversimplification to equate poverty with terrorism because terrorism seems to occur in poor countries, it is an oversimplification to equate terrorism with Islam, simply because much terrorism in recent years has emanated from Islamic societies. There is no doubt that religion and poverty can be powerful sources of grievance, as can

"Shoe Bomber" Richard Reid, who tried to detonate explosives smuggled in his shoe aboard a flight from Paris to Miami in December 2001. Reid was a British citizen who traveled to Pakistan and Afghanistan, where he was trained by Al Qaeda.

## SECURITY AND LIBERTY IN THE AGE OF TERRORISM

Protection of physical security and of liberty are two basic functions of democratic government that have always been in tension. Historically, governments have tended to impinge more on civil liberties during times of war and domestic conflict. Around the world, governments have adopted a range of tactics to combat terrorism that inevitably limit people's civil liberties in ways that were unthinkable before 2001.

You may have noticed this if you have traveled by airplane. Security procedures now ban everyday products that were routinely carried a few years ago—scissors, nail files, and normally sized containers of shampoo, toothpaste, and the like. Since a terrorist unsuccessfully tried to blow up a plane with a bomb in his shoe, passengers have had to remove their shoes for scanning. In the United States, the use of millimeter wave radar at security checkpoints reveals a fuzzy nude image of the traveler to an observer in another room. The U.S. Transportation Security Administration, which implements airport security, maintains that images are not saved and that passengers' privacy is protected. Passengers whose scans reveal some anomaly are subject to intrusive physical examinations. Most passengers have simply acquiesced to the new measures, and no impact on demand for air travel has been noted.

One important tension is between the desire to "profile" terrorists and the desire to avoid racial profiling. With security personnel trained to spot potential terrorists and citizens encouraged by slogans like "if you see something, say something," people who appear to be of Middle Eastern descent are subject to increased scrutiny. In different countries, other groups may be targeted. In Russia, hostility toward people from the Caucasus region has been dramatic and sometimes violent.

For those who are seriously suspected of involvement in terrorism, the consequences can be much harsher. Since 2001, debate has raged over the rights of suspected terrorists, with traditional notions of civil liberties and due process pitted against the urgency of preventing attacks. Until 2001, torture was not a matter of debate in the Western world. It had been outlawed, and evidence gained by torture was not admissible in court. Since 2001, many have advocated using "advanced interrogation" techniques such as waterboarding, and the U.S. government asserted that unless an interrogation technique endangered someone's life, it should not be considered torture. Advocates of torturing suspects argued that doing so saved innocent lives and that the people tortured were clearly involved in terrorism, even if they had not been tried or found guilty. Although many of these arguments were advanced by the Bush administration, the Obama administration adopted most of the same procedures and tactics, as have other governments.

The difficulty in apprehending suspects in other countries and gathering enough evidence to convict them has led to the adoption of policies that involve either imprisoning people indefinitely or simply assassinating them (as in a drone attack).

Not long ago, it was unthinkable that democratic governments would do these things. Yet alongside the demand to protect civil liberties, governments are responsible for protecting people against terrorism. The worst of these new measures—racial/ethnic profiling, arbitrary detention, imprisonment or killing without trial—are applied only to a very small group of people who are mainly Muslim or are seen as sympathetic to radical causes. This may explain why these policies enjoy support among the vast majority of citizens.

*(Continued)*

## Critical Thinking Questions

1. Where would you draw the line between protecting individual civil liberties and protecting citizens in general from terrorism?

2. What dangers do you foresee in these new policies being abused? Do you believe that you might become a victim of their abuse?

3. Is forcing democracies to restrict civil liberties a conscious goal of terrorists?

the desire for national self-determination or the desire to change a form of government. But although all of these factors can be motivations for terrorism, all are dealt with by most people most of the time without recourse to terrorism. So none of them, by itself, provides a sufficient explanation for terrorism.

**The Individual Level**    What makes a person a terrorist? There appears to be a range of motives for terrorism and a range of historical and economic conditions that give rise to terrorism. The best conclusion, then, is that terrorism results when powerfully felt agendas cannot be advanced through other means. That is only a partial explanation, however, because for the vast majority of individuals, such grievances do *not* lead to a decision to murder innocent civilians. Why, given a situation in which their agendas cannot be met through political channels, do some people continue to work nonviolently, others give up, and yet others resort to terrorism?

From this perspective, the question shifts from people's grievances, which may be shared by many, to the decision to adopt violence, which occurs only among a tiny subset of the aggrieved. A great deal of research is currently being conducted on the psychological sources of terrorism. Here the question is not "Why is there terrorism?" but "Why are there terrorists?" or rather "Who becomes a terrorist?"

This type of research may have important implications for combating terrorism. Just as domestic law enforcement officials attempt to develop "profiles" of serial killers, an ability to profile potential terrorists could be very useful. So far, there have been few conclusive findings in this area. But just as the adoption of psychological models has enhanced our understanding of foreign policy making, it promises to add a great deal to our understanding of terrorism.

Sociological studies have indicated that terrorists tend to be young (in their twenties), male (more than 80 percent), college-educated, and from upper-class or middle-class backgrounds.[27] However, there are important exceptions to these findings. In Northern Ireland, terrorists on both the Catholic and the Protestant sides were overwhelmingly from working-class backgrounds. The same is true for the PKK in Turkey.

More recently, research has focused on identifying a profile for suicide bombers. Because the identities of these individuals are usually discovered after the attacks, it may be possible to research their backgrounds and to draw some conclusions about what they may have in common. The hope is that building such a profile may enable law enforcement agencies to more effectively prevent suicide attacks. However, findings so far are insufficient to yield straightforward lessons. One of the most thorough reviews of research on profiling terrorists concludes: "People who have joined terrorist groups have come from a wide range of cultures, nationalities, and ideological causes, all strata of society, and diverse professions. Their personalities and characteristics are as diverse as those of people in the general population. There seems to be general agreement among psychologists that there is no particular psychological attribute that can be used to describe the terrorist or any 'personality' that is distinctive of terrorists."[28]

One study found that the poverty rate among suicide bombers in Palestine was lower than the rate in the overall Palestinian population (13 percent versus 32 percent), and their education level was higher. Although suicide bombers are obviously willing to take their own lives, psychologists have found evidence that they do not exhibit the standard risk factors for suicide, such as mood disorders or other mental illness.[29]

The most famous group of suicide bombers, those who carried out the attacks of September 11, 2001, seem not to fit any identifiable profile of a terrorist or suicide bomber. These men were older, well-off financially, well educated, and not obviously loners. Some of them had little difficulty integrating into American life. They traveled around Europe and the world, meeting each other and a wider network of operatives, and patiently prepared for years, learning to fly commercial airliners and devising a plot of astonishing ingenuity.

**Group Dynamics and Terrorism**   The inability—so far—to identify a psychological profile of a suicide bomber has led some researchers to argue that the key factor is not the individual, but the organization. In this view, some organizations are both willing to promote the tactic and are able to motivate individuals with different psychological backgrounds to carry out the attacks. In some respects, this is a frightening finding; it implies that a wide range of people are potential suicide bombers, given the right circumstances.

To the extent that this is true, a far different conclusion concerning prevention emerges: The mission is not to profile individuals, but to profile groups. Why do some groups use this tactic, whereas others do not? Does the reason have to do with the strength of their grievance or the level of desperation perceived by the group? Or is the decision tactical, based on what kind of effect suicide bombing is expected to have on the population being targeted for influence?

A key factor in the utility of suicide bombing may be whether the population from which the bombers emerge is sympathetic to the tactic. From this perspective, the question shifts from the individual and group levels to the societal level. Why do some societies condone suicide bombings, whereas others do not? In a society sufficiently angered or aggrieved, suicide bombing may come to be seen as more legitimate. Moreover, suicide bombers might be viewed as heroes, which should make recruiting much easier. One researcher argues that the tactics used to recruit suicide bombers and to get them to carry through with their missions are not fundamentally different from standard military recruitment and training around the world, which focus on the value of the unit over the individual and on the virtues of sacrifice.[30]

Sociological and psychological approaches to explaining terrorism may yield significant fruit, but for now we must admit that we have a lot of questions and very few reliable answers. Thus, this discussion cannot reach a firm conclusion. We can elaborate a set of grievances that might lead to terrorism, but the set of grievances is very broad, and most people cope with such dissatisfactions through means other than terrorism. Terrorism can be viewed in rational terms as a means of promoting change undertaken when all other means seem to fail. This prompts us to explore the range of grievances that groups around the world feel and the varying capacities of different countries for peaceful resolution of political conflict. But terrorism, in some cases, seems aimed more at expressing frustration and outrage than at actually changing anything. To the extent that this is true, psychological explanations may help us better understand terrorism.

Our limited understanding of terrorism has important implications for efforts to combat it. Because the underlying sources of terrorism have not been clearly identified, it is difficult to design reliable policies to address it. As a result, there is intense disagreement as to how to think about combating terrorism, with some seeing the task as falling within the realm of law enforcement and others viewing it as falling within the realm of warfare.

# THE GEOGRAPHY CONNECTION

## COMBATING TERRORISM THROUGH SOCIAL NETWORK ANALYSIS

This "map" shows the links among terrorist organizations active in India, as generated through a technique known as *social network analysis*. The idea is to gather data on interactions among members of a group of people in an effort to understand the nature of a network. Important data might include phone calls, email messages, or electronic transfers of funds. Even if the messages are encrypted, the amount of traffic can establish a pattern. The pattern of communications might indicate who the key actors in a network are and how the network functions. The thickness of the lines represents the density of

connections between two actors. The size of the circle represents the extent to which that actor plays a brokerage role between many otherwise unrelated actors. "Inter Service Intelligence," the largest circle, is the name of Pakistan's intelligence agency.

### Critical Thinking Questions

1. What does this analysis tell us about the sources of terrorism in India?

2. How might information such as this be used to render a group less effective?

Social Networks Analysis Map

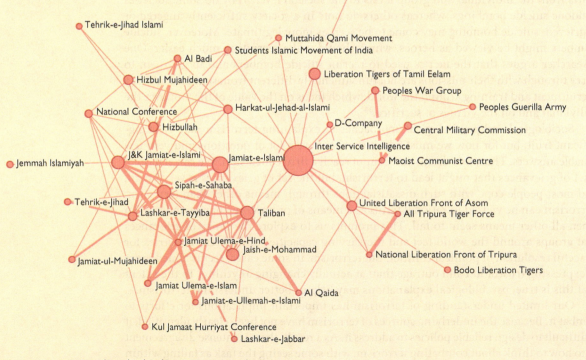

Source: Basu, Aparna (2005) Social Network Analysis of Terrorist Organizations in India.

# MILITARY POWER AND ITS PURPOSES

The use of force entails the exercise of military power to achieve a particular purpose. That basic relationship captures political violence ranging from terrorism to nuclear war. Different actors acquire the ability to harm others both to protect themselves and to coerce others. In the past few decades, two major trends have emerged. First, the range of actors on which we focus has broadened to include nonstate groups. Second, the tools of military power have shifted, as they have throughout history, to change the options open to state and nonstate actors. The proliferation of small arms and the tactics of IEDs and terrorism have empowered insurgents and terrorists. Drones and precision-guided munitions empower the states that possess them and make it easier to avoid getting bogged down in insurgencies. There is underlying continuity, however, in the competition to force higher costs onto one's potential adversaries while limiting one's own vulnerability. That remains the goal of all military strategy.

While we typically think of military power in coercive terms, other dimensions of power are highly relevant to the deployment of military power. Sensitivity to casualties strongly conditions the outcomes of military conflicts. Aspects of structural power, including which actors are considered legitimate to deploy lethal force, and which are not, also influence how military force is deployed and what political effects it has. This dimension of military power appears to be changing as fast as technology is changing, as terrorism and insurgency become more widely accepted, and as formerly "off the table" tactics such as torture and invasive surveillance become more widely accepted as responses.

## RECONSIDER THE CASE

## THE ATTACK OF THE DRONES

Military technology is constantly evolving, and revolutionary change sometimes occurs. Although the rise of drones changes the calculus of force in the short term, no weapons system delivers a permanent advantage. Drone strikes may reduce the cost of attack, but they do not eliminate it. Nor do they eliminate the risk of killing innocent bystanders, and such "collateral damage" continues to provoke outrage from the communities that are targeted, from national governments, and from observers around the world.

Taliban havens in Pakistan along the border with Afghanistan have been an important target, but the government of Pakistan has not given permission for attacks there. Thus, they are often seen as violations of Pakistani sovereignty. More broadly, the use of drones

to kill terrorism suspects—who are not members of any military and have not been tried or found guilty of a crime—raises concerns around the world about whether such killings are legal.

Despite the objections, the use of drones is spreading because of the economic and strategic advantages they provide. More than thirty countries now have drones in service, and the numbers of drones and of countries deploying them seem likely to increase. The spread of drones raises several questions. What are the effects of making it easier and cheaper to use force? What happens when other states acquire the kind of drone capability the United States now has? Will authoritarian governments be able to use their surveillance and attacking capabilities to more easily crush protest movements?

*(Continued)*

## Critical Thinking Questions

1. What means might the targets of drone strikes adopt to reduce or offset their impact?

2. Does the use of drones fundamentally shift the technological balance in favor of the states that possess them?

3. What are the strategic implications of the proliferation of drones around the world?

## SUMMARY

- Force can be defined as the use of violence or the threat of violence to achieve a political goal.

- Coercion occurs when an explicit or implicit threat is used to persuade another actor to change its behavior.

- Defense is the act of repelling an attack by building fortifications, buying weapons, and training soldiers to fight off a potential attacker.

- Deterrence entails convincing a potential opponent not to attack by raising the costs of attack so that they are higher than the perceived benefits.

- The security dilemma creates a challenge to a policy of unrestrained procurement of military capabilities. When one country gains new capabilities, those around it consider adding to their own arsenals, or even attacking preemptively.

- The contemporary competition for military advantage is characterized by the military preponderance of the United States, development of high-tech weaponry, the proliferation of low-tech weapons, and the emergence of cyber warfare.

- Most societies still have a greater tolerance for casualties suffered to defend their homeland than for those suffered to conquer or occupy other countries.

- Nonnuclear WMD are much easier and cheaper to produce than nuclear weapons. Therefore, states or groups that do not have the resources or materials to acquire nuclear weapons can pursue other WMD.

- Like deterrence, insurgency and terrorism focus not on defeating the enemy in battle, but on raising the costs of conflict (or of implementing a policy) so that they are higher than any possible benefit to the attacker.

- Insurgency is chosen by forces too weak to defeat an opponent's army in open battle. The insurgent force seeks to take advantage of its own weaknesses, such as controlling no territory and having no large force concentrations that can be attacked.

- Rational choice, poverty, and group dynamics have all been used to explain terrorism, but a compelling explanation remains beyond our grasp.

- Terrorism has shifted the security strategy away from deterrence, which prevailed during the Cold War, back toward defense.

- Understanding the nature of this asymmetric conflict and understanding the sources of terrorism are two of the main tasks that will face today's generation of students.

## KEY CONCEPTS

1. Security dilemma
2. Coercive diplomacy
3. Defense versus deterrence
4. Sensitivity to casualties
5. Weapons of mass destruction (WMD)

6. WMD proliferation
7. Preventive war
8. Crisis stability
9. Terrorism
10. Asymmetric conflict

## STUDY QUESTIONS

1. Recent weapons used to attack insurgents and terrorists include
   a. drones and precision-guided munitions.
   b. improvised explosive devices.
   c. weapons of mass destruction.
   d. denial-of-service attacks.

2. Cyber warfare has made use of
   a. drones and precision-guided munitions.
   b. improvised explosive devices.
   c. weapons of mass destruction.
   d. denial-of-service attacks.

3. _____ can be defined as the extent to which an actor making a threat has both the will and the capability to carry out the threat.
   a. The application of force
   b. Coercive diplomacy
   c. Credibility
   d. A security dilemma

4. _____ is the use of a threat to change another actor's behavior.
   a. The application of force
   b. Coercive diplomacy
   c. Credibility
   d. A security dilemma

5. The unrestrained procurement of military capabilities often leads to
   a. asymmetric warfare.
   b. cyber warfare.
   c. insurgency.
   d. a security dilemma.

6. Which of the following strategies entails raising the costs of attack so that they are higher than the perceived benefits?
   a. Defense
   b. Deterrence
   c. Coercion
   d. All of the above.

7. What did von Clausewitz mean when he wrote, "War is merely the continuation of policy by other means"?

11. In what sense are India and Pakistan, or the United States and Iran, involved in security dilemmas?

12. Why do some countries seek WMD? Why do other countries not do so?

13. What factors have increased the potential for nuclear proliferation in recent years?

14. What are the hypothesized causes of terrorism? What problems arise with the various explanations?

15. How does terrorism undermine the traditional strategies of defense and deterrence?

[Correct answers: 1. a; 2. d; 3. c; 4. b; 5. d; 6. b.]

## END NOTES

1. Carl von Clausewitz, *On War*, edited and translated by Michael Howard and Peter Paret (Princeton, NJ: Princeton University Press, 1984), p. 87.

2. von Clausewitz, *On War*, p. 96.

3. Many translations of Sun Tzu's *Art of War* are available, including those with applications to business and other fields.

4. For evidence on public opinion and casualties in Korea and Vietnam, see John E. Mueller, *War, Presidents, and Public Opinion* (New York: Wiley, 1973); George Ball's views are cited in Ole R. Holsti,

"Public Opinion and Foreign Policy: Challenges to the Almond-Lippman Consensus," *International Studies Quarterly*, Vol. 36, No. 4 (December 1992): 446.

5. U.S. Centers for Disease Control, "Bioterrorism Agents/ Diseases," www.bt.cdc.gov/agent/agentlist-category.asp.

6. See Thomas Schelling, *Strategy of Conflict* (Cambridge, MA: Harvard University Press, 1960), Chapter 9, pp. 207–229.

7. Thomas Schelling, "The Threat That Leaves Something to Chance," in *Strategy of Conflict*, Chapter 8, pp. 187–206.

8. Stockholm International Peace Research Institute, "World Nuclear Forces Table," www.sipri.org/contents/expcon/worldnuclearforces.html.

9. Kenneth N. Waltz, "More May Be Better," in Kenneth N. Waltz and Scott D. Sagan, *The Spread of Nuclear Weapons: A Debate* (New York: W. W. Norton, 1995), p. 7.

10. For a good summary, see Scott D. Sagan, "More Will Be Worse," in Waltz and Sagan, *The Spread of Nuclear Weapons*, pp. 47–91.

11. Data from the Center for Nonproliferation Studies (CNS), "Chemical and Biological Weapons: Possession and Programs Past and Present," at http://cns.miis.edu/cbw/possess.htm. States listed by the CNS as having "possible" programs or as "likely" to have programs are listed here as "suspected." Precise status of many countries is unknown.

12. See T. X. Hammes, "Fourth Generation Warfare Evolves, Fifth Emerges," *Military Review* (May–June 2007): 14–23.

13. Growth in the literature on insurgency and counterinsurgency has been spurred by the current conflicts in Afghanistan and Iraq. See John A. Nagl, *Counterinsurgency Lessons from Malaya and Vietnam: Eating Soup with a Knife* (Westport, CT: Praeger, 2002); and *FM 3-24: Counterinsurgency* (the latest U.S. Army/Marine Corps counterinsurgency manual), www.fas.org/irp/doddir/army/fm3-24.pdf.

14. Quoted in C. J. Chivers, "General Faces Unease among His Own Troops, Too," *New York Times*, June 23, 2010, p. A11.

15. Quoted in Chivers, "General Faces Unease," p. A11.

16. Walter Laqueur, "Left, Right and Beyond: The Changing Face of Terror," in James F. Hoge Jr. and Gideon Rose, eds., *How Did This Happen? Terrorism and the New War* (New York: Public Affairs, 2001), p. 71, quoted in Lisa Anderson, "Shock and Awe: Interpretations of the Events of September 11," *World Politics*, Vol. 56 (January 2004): 312.

17. Robert Jervis, "An Interim Assessment of September 11: What Has Changed and What Has Not?" in Demetrios James Caraley, ed., *September 11, Terrorist Attacks, and U.S. Foreign Policy* (New York: Academy of Political Science, 2002), p. 180.

18. Beginning with the origin of the term in revolutionary France, all the way through the Soviet Union under Joseph Stalin, the word *terrorism* was generally applied to states that used terror to control their population. Only more recently has the meaning of the word been reversed, so that it refers to attacks by nonstate actors or individual citizens on states or on other citizens.

19. Audrey Kurth Cronin, "Behind the Curve: Globalization and International Terrorism," *International Security*, Vol. 27, No. 3 (Winter 2002/2003): 32.

20. Richard Falkenrath, "Analytical Models and Policy Prescriptions: Understanding Recent Innovation in U.S. Counterterrorism," *Studies in Conflict and Terrorism*, Vol. 24, No. 3 (2001): 170, cited in Peter J. Katzenstein, "Same War—Different Views: Germany, Japan, and Counterterrorism," *International Organization*, Vol. 57 (Fall 2003): 734.

21. Jervis, "An Interim Assessment," pp. 182–183.

22. Thomas L. Friedman, "Connect the Dots," *New York Times*, September 25, 2003, www.nytimes.com/2003/09/25/opinion/25FRIE.html.

23. See Michael Mousseau, "Market Civilization and Its Clash with Terror," *International Security*, Vol. 27, No. 3 (Winter 2002/2003): 6.

24. A good example of a religious explanation for terrorism is Daniel Philpott, "The Challenge of September 11 to Secularism in International Relations," *World Politics*, Vol. 55 (October 2002): 66–95.

25. Philpott, "The Challenge of September 11 to Secularism in International Relations," p. 84.

26. "Islam, Terrorism and Malaysia's Response," Remarks by Mahathir Mohamad, the Asia Society, New York, February 4, 2002, http://asiasociety.org/policy/governance/national/islam-terrorism-and-malaysias-response.

27. Congressional Research Service, "Sociological Characteristics of Terrorists in the Cold War Period," www.fas.org/irp/threat/frd.html.

28. Rex A. Hudson, *The Sociology and Psychology of Terrorism: Who Becomes a Terrorist and Why?* (Washington, DC: Library of Congress, 1999).

29. Michael Bond, "The Making of a Suicide Bomber," *New Scientist* (May 15, 2004): 34.

30. See Bond, "The Making of a Suicide Bomber," p. 34.

Employees at a smartphone application firm in Mumbai, India, 2015. Indian companies play a major role in the globalization of the information technology industry.
Dhiraj Singh/Bloomberg/Getty Images

# FUNDAMENTALS OF INTERNATIONAL POLITICAL ECONOMY

## Learning Objectives

**10-1** Explain the benefits of trade in terms of the theory of comparative advantage.

**10-2** Define "exchange rates" and the "balance of trade" and explain how the two interact.

**10-3** Define "protectionism" and identify different barriers to trade.

**10-4** Show how economic structuralists and realists evaluate the gains from trade differently than liberals.

**10-5** Describe constructivist and feminist approaches to international political economy and show how they depart from other approaches.

**10-6** Connect theoretical arguments about international political economy to contemporary policy discussions.

**10-7** Articulate and defend an argument concerning the relative merits of different approaches to international political economy.

## CONSIDER THE CASE

## CHINA'S RISE TO ECONOMIC POWER

In 2008, Beijing hosted the summer Olympic Games in brand new facilities designed by famous architects. The event was not merely an athletic and commercial extravaganza, but a symbol of China's meteoric rise to economic and political power. China is now the second largest economy in the world, after the United States. Since 1980, its economy has grown by an average of 10 percent per year.

For most of the twentieth century, China was among the poorest countries in the world. Long dominated by foreign powers, China reasserted its independence in the first half of the century, and in 1949 the Communist Party, led by Mao Zedong, consolidated power in the country and adopted communism and central economic planning. These policies were intended to modernize and industrialize China, but they isolated China from the international economy. Poverty persisted and even worsened. From 1958 to 1961, a new economic policy known as the Great Leap Forward led to a famine in which at least 15 million people starved.

After Mao's death in 1976, Deng Xiaoping, Mao's successor, recognized that market forces were needed to foster economic growth in China. On the move away from communist orthodoxy, he said, "Who cares if a cat is black or white, as long as it catches the mice?" The government gradually opened the country to foreign investment, which brought badly needed capital and technology to designated economic development zones on the coast, and these regions boomed. In 2002, China joined the World Trade Organization, further opening its economy.

The Chinese government was determined to avoid the exploitation it had experienced under the unequal treaties of the nineteenth century. It insisted that foreign firms invest through Chinese companies and that they share their technology, so that China could move up the value chain. Global firms might have rejected such demands from another country, but they were extremely eager to gain access to China's astonishingly cheap labor force and its potentially enormous market. With 1.2 billion people moving from poverty to the middle- and upper-income ranges, China provided a huge untapped market. Transnational firms were willing to make concessions to get into China, and Chinese firms have come to compete with their partners.

China's macroeconomic policies have also contributed to its boom. By keeping the value of China's currency low, the Chinese central bank ensures that Chinese goods are inexpensive in foreign markets. This has led to charges that China is competing unfairly, but it is not easy for foreign governments to pressure China to change. China has accumulated massive holdings of foreign currencies, including more than 2 trillion U.S. dollars. The Chinese central bank buys U.S. government bonds that fund the U.S. budget deficit. Thus, in any trade conflict with China, the United States has much to lose if China stops buying U.S. bonds. Moreover, firms from Apple to Walmart make huge profits on goods made cheaply in China and have no interest in a trade war. China's increased economic power was evident when economic crisis hit the United States and Europe in 2008. The world looked to the Chinese government to stimulate China's economy so that increased demand there could offset the fall in demand in the United States and Europe—China is now big enough to play the role that others once looked to the United States to play.

China's booming economy has probably brought more people out of poverty than any global development scheme, but that development also contributes to the economic and military might of a government that many fear. Although China's rise in power is undeniable, the purposes to which that power will be put, both domestically and globally, remain in question. That makes China's rise one of the most important changes in contemporary global politics.

The effects of international trade and finance are so widespread that it is easy to take them for granted. If we stop to examine our clothes, our computers, our cars, and our food, we recognize that international trade is responsible for much of the way we live our lives. In news reports, international trade and financial disputes arise so frequently that they no longer seem novel. International trade is becoming so commonplace that it may seem unimportant, but the opposite is true—as rising and falling oil prices, trade protests, and immigration debates indicate. The increasing flow of goods, services, money, people, and ideas across state borders brings both immense opportunity for mutual benefit and the potential for mutual damage and conflict. This mixture of opportunity and hazard makes the international political economy an increasingly important part of the field of international politics.

# THE IMPORTANCE OF INTERNATIONAL ECONOMICS

**International political economy (IPE)** is the two-way relationship between international politics and international economics. The links between politics and economics run in both directions. Events in the international economy often have political consequences. When importing goods from Asia causes job losses at U.S. manufacturers, for example, U.S. citizens appeal to politicians to address the problem. The reverse is also true: Policies made by individual states often affect the international economy. For example, when the U.S. government increases subsidies for ethanol production to reduce dependence on petroleum and enrich farmers, it has the effect of reducing the amount of crops available for food, which drives up prices around the world. Similarly, a debt crisis in one country can cause economic havoc in many others. The links between economies mean that even policies that are intended solely for domestic purposes (such as farm subsidies) have international repercussions.

The study of IPE encompasses a variety of economic and political questions concerning the movement of goods, money, people, and ideas across borders. States are only partly able to control economic processes that occur entirely within their borders; they are even less able to influence the activities that cross borders. Trade creates the potential for conflict, but because it is so lucrative, there are also powerful incentives to work out differences through compromise and negotiation. **Globalization**—the rapid increase in the cross-border movement of goods, money, people, and ideas—is increasing both the conflict inherent in international commerce and the need to find negotiated solutions.

International trade confronts states with an array of issues to which they must respond. To what extent should free trade be the state's primary economic policy? What are the benefits and dangers of such a policy? How does increasing exposure to the international economy affect the state's ability to govern its own domestic economy? If economies are mutually dependent, to what extent do states need to coordinate their domestic economic policies? Most troubling, perhaps, how can interdependence be managed when states disagree either on the goals or on the best policies? Can economic sanctions provide an alternative to the use of military force?

Beneath all these questions lies one certainty: Economics has become central to contemporary politics. U.S. President Bill Clinton captured this notion famously when, running for the presidency in 1992, he made a mantra of the line, "It's the economy, stupid." Despite the popular notion that the economy functions best without interference from the government, Clinton understood clearly that in contemporary democracies,

**International political economy (IPE)**

The two-way relationship between international politics and international economics.

**globalization**

A process in which international trade increases relative to domestic trade; in which the time it takes for goods, people, information, and money to flow across borders and the cost of moving them are decreasing; and in which the world is increasingly defined by single markets rather than by many separate markets.

# THE GEOGRAPHY CONNECTION

## THE WEALTH OF THE WORLD

This map shows the movement over time of the earth's economic "center of gravity." In the year 1 CE, at the height of the Roman Empire, the center of gravity was in today's Afghanistan because economic activity to the east (India and China) offset that in western Europe. By 1500, it had barely moved, but it then began a steady march north and west as Europe's economies outpaced others.

### Critical Thinking Questions

1. How useful is the center of gravity as a descriptor of the world economy?

2. In what periods did the center of gravity move the fastest? Why?

3. Why did the path of the center of gravity reverse course around 1950?

Evolution of the Earth's Economic Center of Gravity, 1 CE to 2025.

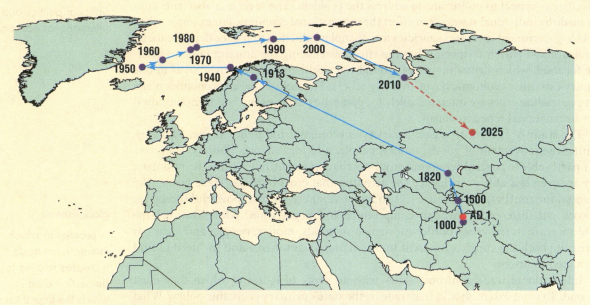

Source: *The Economist*, June 28, 2012, www.economist.com/blogs/graphicdetail/2012/06/daily-chart-19?zid=306&ah=1b164dbd43b0cb27ba0d4c3b12a5e227.

people hold governments accountable for the workings of economies. When times are bad, governments are expected to take measures to remedy the situation or risk being voted out (or, in less stable countries, overthrown). When the economy is strong, voters seem content to return incumbents to power.

This notion that the government is responsible for the economy is relatively recent, dating in the United States to the New Deal of President Franklin Roosevelt. Prior to that time, economic difficulties were seen as natural calamities, no more within the government's ability to prevent or fix than a drought. Since that time, economists as well as politicians have accepted that certain government **fiscal and monetary policies** can influence the economy. As economies become more closely linked, however, one government's economic policies have increasingly significant effects in other countries, which may provoke a response from adversely affected countries. Political leaders face the challenge of trying to govern economies that are increasingly out of their control. Welfare now rivals warfare as the main foreign policy concern for many states.

# KEY ECONOMIC CONCEPTS AND THEORIES

For the student or scholar of international politics, there are three basic economic questions: Why do states trade? What are the benefits of trade? Who gets the benefits of trade? These fundamental questions must be answered in order to understand contemporary debates about international trade, finance, and globalization. This chapter examines the concepts and theories developed to address these questions.

Why do states trade? The answer seems obvious: People buy things from abroad because they are cheaper, and people sell things abroad to make more profits. This answer is basically true, but it obscures several issues that go to the heart of IPE. It is essential to understand the benefits of trade in order to understand states' motives for preserving trade despite the trouble it often causes. Therefore, a brief economics lesson is in order. Although they may seem a bit technical, a few key concepts from economics capture the essence of political debates about international economy. First, this chapter explores economists' answers to the question "Why do states trade?" Later, the chapter examines the concepts of the balance of trade, exchange rates, and protectionism, which are frequently discussed but rarely understood.

## THE THEORY OF COMPARATIVE ADVANTAGE

Developed by the English economist David Ricardo in the early nineteenth century, the **theory of comparative advantage** goes beyond intuitive understandings of trade to show logically how and why trade is beneficial to both partners. The theory has crucial implications for our understanding of international trade and the political debates that surround it. The basic point is that by specializing and trading, states and individuals can increase overall consumption and efficiency.

Like most economic models, the theory of comparative advantage uses a few simple assumptions to derive more profound conclusions and sets aside many real-world complexities for the sake of clarity and simplicity. A simple example will illustrate the theory: Imagine a world with two countries, China and the United States; and two goods, wheat and textiles. Imagine also that the only factor in the production of these two products is labor. Imagine, finally, that labor can move between production of wheat and production of textiles (but not between countries) and that the cost of transportation is negligible.

Suppose that in the two countries, the amount of wheat and textiles that can be produced by one person working for one day is as shown in Table 10.1. In this example, labor is more productive in China than in the United States—both wheat and textiles are made with less labor in China than in the United States. Why would China import anything

**fiscal and monetary policies**

The two major ways in which governments can influence their economies. In fiscal policy, a government uses a budget deficit or surplus to stimulate or slow economic growth. In monetary policy, a central bank raises or lowers interest rates to stimulate or slow economic growth.

**theory of comparative advantage**

A theory developed by the English economist David Ricardo to show logically how and why trade is beneficial to both partners.

**TABLE 10.1** Production Conditions

|  | Wheat (Bushels per Day of Labor) | Textiles (Yards per Day of Labor) |
|---|---|---|
| China | 300 | 1200 |
| United States | 100 | 200 |

from the United States when both products can be made with less labor in China? The answer lies not simply in comparing China's productivity to that of the United States, but in comparing productivity *across* sectors *within* the two countries. The key question is, "How much labor must be diverted from one sector to produce more in the other?" In China, wheat and textiles are produced at a rate of 300:1200, or 1:4. For every extra bushel of wheat the Chinese wish to produce, they must forgo 4 yards of textiles. In the United States, wheat and textiles are produced at a ratio of 100:200, or 1:2. In the United States, producing an additional bushel of wheat requires surrendering only 2 yards of textiles. In effect, wheat is more expensive in terms of textiles in China than in the United States. Similarly, the Chinese must give up only one-quarter of a bushel of wheat to get a yard of textiles, whereas those in the United States must give up one-half of a bushel. Textiles are twice as expensive in terms of wheat in the United States as in China.

It is this *difference in relative prices* that creates the basis for profitable trade. Consider what is possible in trading 1 bushel of American wheat for 3 yards of Chinese textiles (note that this price of 1:3 falls between the domestic prices of 1:2 in the United States and 1:4 in China). For the Chinese, trade with the United States makes it possible to get a bushel of wheat for only 3 yards of textiles, rather than 4 as in the domestic economy. For the Americans, trade makes it possible to receive 3 yards of textiles for each bushel of wheat, rather than only the 2 yards obtained by shifting labor from wheat to textiles in the domestic economy. Both countries receive more goods for the same cost.

To illustrate the overall effects of such trade, we can calculate the consumption possible in each country with trade and without it. Suppose that each state has 20 workers and that labor is initially divided evenly between sectors (10 workers producing wheat and 10 producing textiles). Part A of Table 10.2 shows the overall outputs, based on the labor productivity specified in Table 10.1. Part B of Table 10.2 shows the overall production that can be achieved through specializing (the United States totally, China partially). In the

**TABLE 10.2** Overall Output with and without Specialization and International Trade

|  |  | Wheat (Bushels per Day) | Textiles (Yards per Day) |
|---|---|---|---|
| A No specialization and no trade | China | 3000 | 12,000 |
|  | United States | 1000 | 2000 |
|  | Total | 4000 | 14,000 |
| B Specialization but no trade | China | 2000 | 16,000 |
|  | United States | 2000 | 0 |
|  | Total | 4000 | 16,000 |
| C Specialization and trade | China | 3000 | 13,000 |
|  | United States | 1000 | 3000 |
|  | Total | 4000 | 16,000 |

United States, all 20 workers are now working in wheat production; in China, one-third of the workers are working in wheat and two-thirds are working in textile production. *Overall production increases by 2000 yards of textiles with no additional labor and with no reduction in wheat production!* Part C of Table 10.2 shows the overall production that can be achieved by both specializing and trading, exchanging 1000 bushels of U.S. wheat for 3000 yards of Chinese textiles (at the price of 1:3). By specializing and trading, both states are able to increase their consumption of textiles without using additional labor or reducing their consumption of wheat.

Two important conclusions can be drawn. First, with specialization, the overall amount of production and consumption increases *without* any increase in inputs. In this example, total textile production has increased from 14,000 to 16,000 yards, with no reduction in wheat production. Second, specialization and trade lead to increased consumption in *both* countries. Each country can increase its consumption of textiles by 1000 yards (or shift more workers back into wheat) through trade. Trade increases overall consumption without any cost. This example shows in technical terms what people experience practically every day. By buying shoes made in China and televisions made in Taiwan (and selling U.S. music there), Americans can consume more than they otherwise would be able to afford.

The answer to the original question, therefore, is that states trade because trading allows them to produce and consume more and because it leads to greater overall efficiency. Both states can benefit simultaneously. As long as the two states have different ratios of productivity from one sector to the next, this result holds. Adding real-world factors, such as the cost of transportation, the large number of countries that engage in trade, and the large number of goods traded, complicates the analysis but does not undermine this fundamental logic.

## THE CONNECTION TO YOU

### WHERE DOES YOUR STUFF COME FROM?

Where do your clothes come from? Ninety-eight percent of the clothing sold in the United States is manufactured overseas. The world's leading clothing exporter is China, with 29 percent of the world market, followed by Mexico, India, Indonesia, and Bangladesh. One-third of all the socks in the world are manufactured in Datang, China, by workers making $270 per month.*

How do you connect to your friends? Via a smartphone, tablet computer, or laptop? Nearly all of these are manufactured in Asia.

How do you get to school or work? If you drive a car, at least part of it was made overseas.

The market share of domestic U.S. auto brands, known as the "big three" fell below 50 percent in 2007. However, that statistic itself is misleading, because many of the cars sold by "foreign" manufacturers are in fact manufactured in the United States. Toyota's popular Camry is assembled in Georgetown, Kentucky; Honda's Accord is made in Marysville, Ohio (and in England, New Zealand, China, and Thailand). Even the cars made in the United States, however, contain components sourced from suppliers around the world. Automobile production is thus thoroughly globalized.

*(Continued)*

To fuel that car (or bus), one needs fossil fuels of some type, and these too come from an industry that is thoroughly globalized. The world's largest oil exporters are Saudi Arabia, Russia, Iran (before sanctions took effect), the United Arab Emirates, and Norway. The largest importers are the United States, China, India, Japan, and Germany.

Finally, consider what we eat. Free trade agreements and decreased transportation costs have globalized the food trade, allowing food to be produced where the geographic conditions (soil, climate, etc.) are most beneficial. The search for tastier foodstuffs has driven much of colonialism and globalization over the past 500 years, which is why Indonesia was originally known as the Spice Islands and why Ricardo's original formulation of the theory of comparative advantage used the example of Portuguese wine (and British textiles).

The food trade allows people in mountainous Japan to consume wheat and beef grown in wide-open Kansas, people in landlocked Kansas to consume salmon, and people all over the northern hemisphere to consume fresh fruits and vegetables in the middle of winter. Our favorite indulgences, such as chocolate, tea, and coffee, are grown in a relatively small number of countries and exported around the world. In recent years, a "local food" movement has emerged in opposition to the expense and pollution involved in transporting so much food around the world, but it has had only a limited impact so far.

If you live in the United States, Canada, or Europe, you might reasonably wonder "What do we still make here?" In part, the answer is "A lot less than we used to." Manufacturing plays a much smaller role in advanced economies today than in the past. Agriculture is still important in many developed economies, as is natural resource extraction (oil in Canada and the United Kingdom, natural gas in the United States, minerals in Australia). In part, however, the question "What do we make here?" misses a larger point. Developed economies are based less on manufacturing and more on services and technology. Thus, although the iPad is made in China, it is designed almost entirely in California. Smartphones are built in Asia but are designed mostly in the United States and Europe, where most of the apps are written. Facebook does not "make" anything, but has made many of its employees very wealthy. While governments in traditional manufacturing zones are wondering how to get their factories back, those in the developing world are wondering how to move beyond manufacturing into the technology sector that yields huge profits.

## Critical Thinking Questions

1. What are the advantages and disadvantages of getting so much of our stuff from abroad?

2. What are the advantages and disadvantages of focusing one's economy on manufacturing or on technology and services?

3. How much attention do you pay to where something comes from when you make a purchase?

*"Clothing 'Made in America': Should U.S. Manufacture More Clothes?" ABCNews.com, March 11, 2011, abcnews.go.com/Business/MadeInAmerica/made-america-clothes-clothing-made-usa/story?id=13108258.

## COMPARATIVE ADVANTAGE AND LIBERALISM

The finding that trade makes both partners better off and increases overall efficiency underpins liberal trade theory and liberal international relations theory more broadly. Indeed, the liberal international theory introduced in Chapter 3 was inspired in large part by economists such as Ricardo and Adam Smith. The theory of comparative advantage establishes in the economic realm what liberals claim more broadly—that when states cooperate, both can benefit simultaneously. The theory proves mathematically that both sides can gain simultaneously through trade. In this way, the theory powerfully contradicts the realist view that international affairs is a **zero-sum game** in which one side can gain only at the expense of another.

In contemporary international politics, the theory of comparative advantage is still used, implicitly or explicitly, to justify increased international trade, decreased barriers to trade, and international economic integration. The growing integration of the European Union (EU), the development of the North American Free Trade Agreement (NAFTA), and the lowering of tariffs through the World Trade Organization (WTO) all make sense in terms of comparative advantage. By making trade easier, these institutions allow states to specialize in the areas in which they are most efficient, leading to greater overall production and consumption.

However, realists and economic structuralists do not simply accept the logic of comparative advantage. They criticize the goals implied by the liberal model and focus on other potential effects of trade. Much of the political discussion of free trade—for example, between those who support and those who oppose the **Trans Pacific Partnership**—pits followers of the liberal economic model against those who reject that model in favor of realism or economic structuralism (although proponents of these views rarely use those labels). These critiques are discussed next.

## THE BALANCE OF TRADE

Every month, governments around the world release statistics on their countries' balance of trade. These statistics are reported in major newspapers and are announced on most newscasts. In recent years, the statistics have usually shown that the U.S. trade deficit is increasing (Figure 10.1). So what? What is the "balance of trade," and what about it is important enough to make the news month after month?

First, it is important to recognize that the balance of trade often is not balanced at all. In economic terms, the **balance of trade** is simply exports minus imports (measured in dollars or another currency). In other words, it is a net accounting of how much in the way of goods and services is exported from a country compared to how much is imported. When the trade balance is zero, the economy is importing exactly as much as it exports. When the balance is negative (a *trade deficit*), the economy is importing more than it exports, so that exports minus imports is a negative number. The balance is positive (a *trade surplus*) when the country is exporting more than it imports. News reports give the distinct impression that a surplus is good and a deficit is bad. Why is this so?

Trade deficits are viewed not in isolation but with reference to their implications for the rest of the economy, and especially for employment. A trade deficit implies that goods that otherwise might be produced domestically are being produced abroad. If that is true, then the shift of production from the home economy to other countries decreases the demand for labor at home, which, other things being equal, implies that wages and employment will decrease. In a modern democratic country, these are two of the most sensitive political issues. In contrast, a surplus is seen as being beneficial because it implies that the country, by selling goods abroad, can employ more workers at higher wages than if production and sales were limited to the domestic market.

Trade surpluses are seen as beneficial for other reasons too. When an economy is exporting more than it imports, the demand to buy that state's currency will be higher than the need to sell, and the value of the currency will increase, which many believe is beneficial to the economy. Overall, however, the key point is that the balance of trade

**zero-sum game**

A situation in which any gains by one side are offset by losses for another.

**Trans Pacific Partnership**

A proposed agreement to reduce barriers to trade among twelve countries in North and South America, Asia, and the Pacific, including Australia, Canada, Chile, Japan, Mexico, Singapore, and the United States.

**balance of trade**

Exports minus imports (measured in dollar value); a net accounting of how much in the way of goods and services is exported from a country compared to how much is imported.

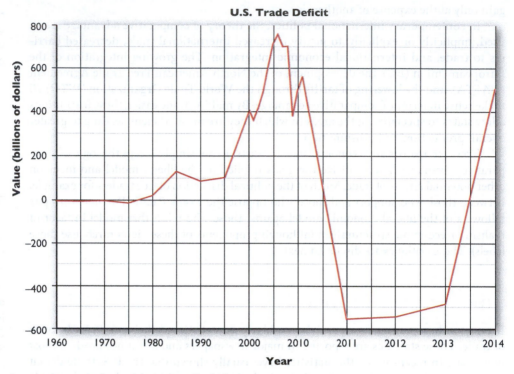

**FIGURE 10.1** The graph shows the emergence of the U.S. trade deficit and its growth. What are the sources of the deficit, and how much of a policy concern should it be?

Sources: http://www.census.gov/foreign-trade/statistics/historical/gands.pdf.

crucially affects key state goals: economic prosperity in general and the level of employment in particular.

The concern over trade deficits has led some people to advocate "fair trade" rather than simply "free trade." The distinction, advocates of fair trade claim, is that under **fair trade**, action would be taken against states that pursued a trade surplus as a means of stimulating their economies. This view sees trade imbalances as the result of cheating on free trade rules, which, in fact, is only one possible source of imbalance.

It is important to recognize that a focus on balance of trade turns trade into a zero-sum game. It is mathematically impossible for two states both to have a surplus relative to each other. One state can obtain a greater benefit (trade surplus) only if its partner suffers a corresponding loss (trade deficit). For this reason, the balance of trade becomes the cornerstone of the modern realist analysis of trade. For the same reason, liberals tend to reject its importance, arguing that trade imbalances are usually offset by surpluses in financial transactions or that trade imbalances will remedy themselves if the market is left to work on its own. Some argue that a trade deficit is simply a result of being wealthy and is not to be feared. It is natural, in this view, that the wealthy United States buys more from Vietnam than relatively poor Vietnam buys from the United States; therefore, trade deficits are not anything to worry about. However, states often work intensively at maximizing their exports and reducing their imports, which leads inevitably to conflict. To the extent that states focus on the balance of trade, conflict rather than cooperation will define international economic relations.

**fair trade**

A narrower approach to free trade that advocates retaliation against states that are perceived as "cheating" on free trade.

# EXCHANGE RATES

Currencies are often labeled "strong" or "weak," and they are said to "rise" or "fall." These vague terms all relate to the price of a currency. Like potato chips or computers, currencies can be bought and sold. And like the price of anything else, the price of a currency depends on supply and demand. So, when the dollar is "strong," it is relatively expensive for others to buy, and other currencies are relatively cheap in terms of dollars. For example, between July 2007 and July 2008, the value of the U.S. dollar dropped by about 15 percent, from 0.74 to 0.63 euros. That may seem a trivial decline, but it would add $3400 to the U.S. price of a $20,000 Volkswagen imported from Germany (Table 10.3).

Why do these prices change? There are many reasons, but a simplified explanation is that **exchange rates** change because supply and demand change. One reason people buy and sell currencies is to use them in importing and exporting. If importers outside Europe want to buy goods made in Germany, they need to pay the German sellers in euros. If all they have is dollars, they must trade dollars for euros. As demand for European goods increases, the number of people wishing to sell dollars and buy euros will increase. The supply of dollars for sale will go up, the supply of euros for sale will go down, and the price of euros (in terms of dollars) will increase. The value of the dollar thus declines.

Differences in interest rates also influence the demand for currency, and hence exchange rates. If interest rates are higher in Europe than in the United States, investors can make more money investing in Europe and will convert some of their dollars into euros to do that, again raising the price of euros. Similarly, if a government issues more currency to stimulate its economy, the supply of that currency increases relative to other currencies, and its value decreases. Billions of dollars' worth of currencies are traded on world markets every day as investors speculate on future currency fluctuations and try to hedge other risks.

Why do exchange rates matter? Exchange rates affect trade just as trade affects exchange rates. If the dollar decreases in value against the euro, it will take more dollars to buy the same number of euros. This means that goods whose prices are determined in terms of euros will become more expensive for Americans paying in dollars. If one dollar buys one euro, then a Volkswagen that costs €20,000 can be bought in the United States for $20,000. If the value of the dollar falls by 20 percent, so that $1 = €0.80, the German supplier must increase the U.S. price of that Volkswagen to $25,000 to make the same profit (in euros) as before.

This price fluctuation will likely have two effects. First, to the extent that the imported goods have no domestic substitutes, the increased prices paid for them cause inflation in the domestic economy and divert purchasing power away from other goods. If a consumer spends an extra $5000 to buy an automobile, she will spend $5000 less on other things. Second, domestically produced goods will become more competitive. A car manufactured in the United States that costs $22,000 would be more expensive than the $20,000 Volkswagen, but cheaper than the Volkswagen after the exchange rate change caused its price to rise to $25,000. This is bad for the foreign exporters, who lose business, and good for the U.S. manufacturer, who will see demand for its cars rise (and may even be able to raise prices slightly). Because exchange rates have powerful effects on the prices of goods, and therefore on the success of different countries' manufacturers, they are the subject of intense political attention. In sum, for those who compete with imported products, a weak currency can be helpful and a strong currency destructive.

**TABLE 10.3** Effect of Exchange Rates on Import Prices: Hypothetical Cost of a Volkswagen

| Price in Euros | Price in Dollars July 2007 ($1 = €0.74) | Price in Dollars July 2008 ($1 = €0.63) | Price Increase |
|---|---|---|---|
| €14,800 | $20,000 | $23,400 | $3400 |

**exchange rates**
The price of one currency in terms of another.

# THE INTERACTION OF EXCHANGE RATES AND THE BALANCE OF TRADE

Combining the discussions of exchange rates and the balance of trade raises two key points. First, in theory, these factors should balance each other. If the United States has a trade deficit with Germany, there will be more demand for euros than for dollars. The price of the euro will go up, leading to an increase in the prices of German goods in the United States and a decrease in the prices of U.S. goods in Germany. In theory, this self-regulating process will continue until a new equilibrium is reached with balanced trade at a different exchange rate. This process is illustrated in Figure 10.2. In practice, this rarely happens completely because so many other factors affect exchange rates and trade flows. For example, for many years, a falling U.S. dollar was accompanied by rising, rather than falling, U.S. imports. The willingness of other countries to lend the U.S. government and consumers vast sums of money meant that normal constraints on purchasing were loosened.

The second key point about exchange rates and the balance of trade is that if states put a high priority on achieving a trade surplus, they can manipulate their currency price to boost trade. By lowering interest rates, printing more money, or selling reserves of its own currency, a government can deliberately reduce the value of its currency (or *devalue* the currency) relative to others. Imports become more expensive, and hence decrease. At the same time, the devaluing country's products become comparatively cheaper, and exports increase. This has been a major issue of contention between the United States and China. China has maintained a policy of keeping the value of its currency, the yuan, low compared to the dollar. In mid-2015, China surprised the world by devaluing its currency by about 3 percent in an effort to stimulate its economy. Members of the euro zone have given up their ability to manipulate their exchange rate, and this

**FIGURE 10.2** The interaction of exchange rates and the balance of trade.

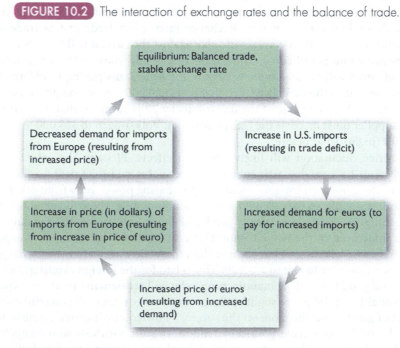

Source: Paul D'Anieri.

has caused a huge problem for economies such as Greece. Facing a massive recession, one option normally would be to devalue the currency. This would make Greek goods more competitive internationally. But without its own currency, Greece lost this option and suffered massive recession as a result.

States have considerable temptation to compete to have the lowest-valued currency in order to boost their domestic employment. This behavior is called **competitive devaluation**. Competitive devaluation, which took place during the Great Depression, leaves everyone worse off by undermining the stability needed for trade to take place. Exchange rates, therefore, are not as abstract as they seem; nor are they merely financial indicators. Their ability to affect world trade and employment levels makes them a tempting but dangerous tool for governments trying to improve their trade position.

## PROTECTIONISM

States that want to protect domestic producers against competition from foreign firms can do so through a variety of measures, collectively known as **protectionism**. Protection can be aimed at specific industries or at the entire economy. In some cases, an industry is protected because it employs so many people that unemployment would rise considerably were the industry to fail. In many countries, agriculture and steel fit this description. In other cases, an industry is protected because it is seen as essential for broader economic growth. In the twentieth century, the auto industry was regarded as such an industry; today, the computer and programming sector is viewed that way. The United States, for example, has shown concern over becoming too dependent on foreign supplies of microchips. Other industries might be seen as essential for national defense. For this reason, many countries protect arms manufacturers and their suppliers.

Protection of a specific industry can be accomplished through a variety of means (see Table 10.4). Perhaps the simplest is the **quota**, a numerical limit placed on the amount of

**competitive devaluation**

Competition between states to have the lowest-valued currency in order to boost domestic employment.

**protectionism**

Measures taken by states to limit their imports.

**quota**

A numerical limit on the amount of a certain item that can be imported.

**TABLE 10.4**  Protectionist Measures: Who Pays and Who Benefits?

|  | Who Pays? | Who Gets the Money? | Who Wins? | Who Loses? |
|---|---|---|---|---|
| **Quotas** | No payment | No payment | Domestic producers, who can charge higher prices and innovate less | Consumers, who must pay higher prices for less innovative goods; producers in other countries |
| **Tariffs** | Exporting firms | Government | Domestic producers, who can charge higher prices and innovate less | Consumers, who must pay higher prices for less innovative goods; producers in other countries |
| **Subsidies** | Governments (taxpayers) | Domestic producers | Domestic producers, who can make the same profit charging a lower price | Producers in other countries, who have to charge full price |
| **Regulations that discriminate against imports** | Governments (pay for enforcement) | Bureaucrats (especially if they can take bribes to help firms avoid regulations) | Domestic producers, who face reduced competition and so can charge more | Consumers, who must pay higher prices; producers in other countries, whose costs are higher |

**tariff**

A tax on imports, used to protect domestic producers from foreign competition.

**subsidies**

Direct payments to producers to help them remain profitable.

a certain item that can be imported. In the 1980s, a quota was placed on Japanese automobiles imported into the United States in order to protect U.S. auto firms. One of the most widely used protectionist measures is the **tariff**, which is simply a tax on imports. By adding to the cost of imported goods, the tariff makes it easier for domestic producers to compete. Also widely used are **subsidies**, which are direct payments to producers to help them remain profitable. Subsidies are often implemented for other policy reasons, but they reduce foreign competition, whether they are intended to or not. The extensive subsidies to farmers in the United States and Europe are often cited by developing countries as barriers preventing them from competing more successfully in the global marketplace.

Finally, almost any type of regulation (such as environmental or health regulation) can serve as a protectionist measure if, in practice, it creates more difficulty for importers than for domestic producers. European Union restrictions on genetically modified crops, viewed in Europe as a health measure, are viewed as trade barriers by U.S. farmers and agribusinesses because U.S. firms produce more genetically modified crops and seed than EU firms do and are therefore disproportionately hindered by the restrictions. Argentine beef ranchers make the same complaint about U.S. health regulations.

In addition to measures aimed at individual industries, protectionism can target the overall economy. In this case, the goal of the measure is generally to create a favorable balance of trade by providing some level of protection to every domestic producer. Two measures can be used to protect an entire economy: a general tariff that applies to every good, and a currency devaluation.

# FIVE APPROACHES TO INTERNATIONAL POLITICAL ECONOMY

Realist, liberal, economic structuralist, constructivist, and feminist theories seek to explain the IPE as much as they do other aspects of international relations. Indeed, in important respects, the economic theories of liberals and economic structuralists predate their theories of international relations. Examining these five approaches to IPE serves two purposes. First, it extends our understanding of the theories. Second, and more important, it helps us understand the fundamental debates about economic policy that we hear every day. Policy disagreements are often debated in terms of economics. In many cases, however, policy disagreements are actually rooted in different normative assumptions (different values about what goals are most important).

## LIBERALISM

The liberal approach to IPE has already been discussed in some detail in the section on comparative advantage. The theory of comparative advantage shows that through trade various states can all increase their welfare at the same time. Because welfare is an essential goal of contemporary states, states will (and *should*, liberals argue) pursue more free trade. Liberals argue that protectionism, although tempting for certain actors within states, leads to overall inefficiency and loss for almost everyone. The main challenge of international trade politics, in the liberal view, is to resist the temptation to seek selfish advantage through protectionism and instead to seek mutual advantage through trade. "Probably the most important insight in all of international economics is the idea that there are *gains from trade*—that is, that when countries sell goods and services to one another, this is almost always to their mutual benefit.… The single most consistent mission of international economics has been to analyze the effects of … protectionist policies—and usually, though not always, to criticize protectionism and show the advantages of freer trade."[1]

For example, economists predicted that the institution of the WTO, a new free trade agreement in 1995, would lead to efficiency gains of $270 billion per year.[2] The gains of protection, liberals hold, are an illusion: protectionism diverts resources from efficient uses and impedes economic growth. Liberals attribute the duration and depth of the Great Depression to the policies states adopted to shield themselves from trade, and they credit the emergence of a free trading system after World War II with the incredible increases in wealth seen throughout the developed world.

Anticipating the criticisms from economic structuralists, liberals assert that the extreme poverty present in much of the world is not a result of free trade but the result of *not enough* free trade. When Third World countries try to protect their domestic economies through tariffs, quotas, and the like, liberals argue, they shut themselves off from an important engine of efficiency and growth: the international market. Especially in terms of wages, liberals find that free trade helps the poorest nations. In countries where poverty makes people willing to work cheaply, goods produced with a lot of labor can be produced relatively cheaply. As more firms move their manufacturing facilities to such countries, the demand for these workers will rise, and so will wages. Theoretically, this will continue until Third World wages equal those of the First World. China is seen as a case in point. China's opening to world trade has led to hundreds of millions of people being lifted out of poverty.

**The Realist and Economic Structuralist Critique**   Realists and economic structuralists do not completely reject liberal analysis, but by exploring several questions that liberalism neglects, they arrive at very different conclusions about the nature of IPE. Rather than focusing on the overall benefits of trade, they ask about the distribution of those gains. Economic structuralists argue that the increased wealth created by trade tends to accrue to the wealthier side, so that trade widens the gap between the rich and poor. Realists agree, and examine how power allows some states to exploit others economically. Realists are also concerned with how economic power can lead to political and military power. Realism and economic structuralism reject one of liberalism's underlying assumptions. Liberalism assumes that economic exchange, whether between individuals or states, is essentially a voluntary exchange between free actors. Realism and economic structuralism see exchange as inevitably involving some degree of coercion of the weaker actor by the stronger.

The example of wheat and textile trade between the United States and China can be used to illustrate the problems that both economic structuralists and realists have with liberalism. By specializing and trading, the United States and China could increase overall textile production by 2000 yards. The liberal analysis stops here, concluding that since trade increases production at no extra cost, it is good for everyone. Realists and economic structuralists, however, ask, "How are these gains from trade divided?" The question is impossible to answer without making further assumptions, but for many the answer is crucial. If China and the United States trade textiles for wheat, at what price do they trade? In our example, the benefits from trade were split evenly: The price of 1 bushel of wheat for 3 yards of textiles falls neatly halfway between the Chinese domestic price and the American domestic price, and as a result, each side gains the same 1000 yards of textiles. But how was this price established? It was chosen arbitrarily to simplify the math in the example.

Vietnamese workers transporting goods at the border crossing in Hekou, China. Trading goods brings profit to both sides, but who gets more?

dave stamboulis/Alamy

Suppose China says to the United States, "We will trade with you, but not at the price of 1 bushel for 3 yards. We will only trade at the price of 1 bushel for 2.1 yards." What will happen? At that price, the international price of wheat is substantially less than the Chinese domestic price (4:1), but only slightly lower than the American domestic price (1 bushel gets 2.1 yards in trade, versus 2 yards domestically). China gains a lot (1.9 yards of textile per bushel of wheat), and the United States gains little (0.1 yard of textile per bushel of wheat). Why would the United States agree to such a deal? Because it would still be marginally better off trading internationally at 1:2.1 than trading domestically at 1:2. The United States could refuse to trade unless China agreed to pay more. Would China give in? That would presumably depend on who needed the trade more. This, economic structuralists and realists emphasize, is a question of *power*. As long as one country needs trade more than the other, the gains from trade will be distributed unequally. Or if one side can use other means (such as military threats or colonial control) to influence trade, then the benefits of trade are likely to be distributed unequally. The question of the distribution of the gains of trade becomes the focus of economic structuralist and realist analyses. It is a question not emphasized by liberal analysis. In this respect, the theories do not directly conflict, but rather ask different questions.

## REALISM

Realist analysis of IPE, like realist analysis more broadly, deals with the interests of the state, not with the interests of individuals within the state or with economic efficiency. This emphasis on state economic interests underlies variants of realism such as **mercantilism** (prominent in the sixteenth through the nineteenth centuries), economic nationalism (nineteenth and twentieth centuries), and protectionism, or neomercantilism (twentieth and twenty-first centuries). All of these doctrines share a focus on state goals, a concern with the distribution of the gains from trade, and an emphasis on the conflictual nature of international trade.

**mercantilism**

A trading doctrine that focused on state power in a conflictual world. It was based on the idea that the overall amount of wealth in the world was fixed by the amount of precious metals. Therefore, international trade was a zero-sum game, and the goal of every state was to run a trade surplus in order to accumulate more money.

To see why a focus on distributive questions leads inevitably to a conflictual view of IPE, examine again the comparative advantage example. When liberals consider the overall gains from trade, they see that the level of production goes up, so both states can gain simultaneously. But when realists examine how the gains from trade are divided, they see that one side can gain only if the other loses. The situation is now a zero-sum game. In our U.S.-China example, the gains from trade consist of 2000 additional yards of textiles. For China to increase its share of the gains (say, to 1200 yards of textiles), the U.S. share must correspondingly decline (to 800).

Why do realists take this particular perspective rather than the liberal view? Traditionally, the answer returns to realists' central focus on state survival, four aspects of which emphasize distribution rather than overall wealth.

First, in the realist view, even seemingly mundane trade relations have important power consequences. "The interdependence of national economies creates economic power, defined as the capacity of one state to damage another through the interruption of commercial and financial relations. The attempts to create and to escape from such dependency relationships constitute an important aspect of international relations in the modern era."[3] When countries enact economic sanctions on others, they are using their ability to sever existing trade relationships to coerce another country. The more one is benefiting from trade, the more one loses from a cutoff, and the more power one's partners have. Russia's threats to cut natural gas deliveries to Ukraine are one recent example. Economic sanctions against Iran to force cessation of its nuclear weapons program are another.

Second, economic wealth can be converted into political and military power (most directly by paying soldiers and purchasing bombs and bullets). If one state gains more wealth from a given transaction, it can potentially increase its military power vis-à-vis the other state. This problem of **relative gains** implies that even if both sides gain, the side that gains more may increase its power over the side that gains less.

Third, realist theory of IPE has more recently focused on prosperity and employment. Contemporary citizens expect their governments to ensure some degree of economic security. To the extent that prosperity and high employment become state goals, realists assert that these goals, too, will be placed above the pursuit of overall economic efficiency. The establishment of prosperity and high employment as state goals makes the balance of trade a primary concern of contemporary realist analysis. The doctrine of focusing trade policy on the balance of trade is known as **neomercantilism**. If the United States runs a large trade deficit with Japan, for example, the implication is that employment, wages, and profits are higher in Japan and lower in the United States than they would be without such an imbalance. In the realist view, the U.S. government can be expected to try to change that balance of trade, even if it emerged in the free market and even if the efforts to change it reduce overall economic efficiency. In this way, the realist view of IPE has moved well beyond traditional concerns with military power and survival to the issue of domestic prosperity.

Fourth, states seek self-sufficiency, especially in the industries critical to war efforts. If a state becomes too dependent on other states for key military inputs such as steel, it faces the prospect of being cut off in a time of need. In the contemporary world, many states expend considerable resources to maintain a high degree of self-sufficiency in food, oil, and most defense industries. Thus, economic efficiency does not always contribute to the state's ability to survive. In such cases, realists argue, states will put survival first and endure economic inefficiency to maintain self-sufficiency.

**relative gains**

A problem with free trade arising from the fact that if one state can gain more wealth from a given transaction, it can potentially increase its military power vis-à-vis the other state. This implies that even if both sides gain, the side that gains more may increase its power over the side that gains less.

**neomercantilism**

The belief that states should seek a trade surplus. This focus on the balance of trade makes trade a zero-sum game, as it was for traditional mercantilists.

# THE POLICY CONNECTION

## ECONOMIC SANCTIONS

When Russia invaded Ukraine in 2014, the European Union and the United States responded by imposing economic sanctions on Russia. These measures restricted loans to Russian state banks, sales of oil industry technology, and sales of weapons. Sanctions also targeted dozens of Russian officials who were held responsible for the invasion. But the gas industry, which is Russia's largest exporter, was exempted from EU sanctions because the EU is heavily dependent on Russian gas.

Economic sanctions are an attractive tool of policy because they are a visible and significant measure that avoids the danger, cost, and destruction of war. Relevant examples include sanctions against Cuba, North Korea, and Iran. The deployment of sanctions against Russia rekindled a long-term debate over the effectiveness of economic sanctions. Do they work, and if so, under what conditions? Debate about the overall effectiveness of sanctions continues, but most scholars agree that their effectiveness is limited to a very small set of circumstances, and much research is concerned with identifying what those circumstances are.

The United States enacted a trade embargo against Cuba in 1960. The goal was to undermine the regime of Fidel Castro. Cuba responded by establishing a partnership with the Soviet Union. Although Cuba struggled economically, Castro remained in power until 2008 before handing power to his brother. Many argued that by providing an external excuse for the regime's failures, sanctions actually bolstered Castro's power. In 2014, the Obama administration began cautiously seeking to reestablish diplomatic ties with Cuba, but many were firmly opposed to loosening sanctions while Cuba remained unfree.

In 2006, the United Nations enacted sanctions against Iran in response to Iran's nuclear weapons activities. Initially focused on imports related to nuclear weapons, the sanctions were extended to cover Iran's access to the international banking system, which made it nearly impossible for Iran to trade internationally. This proved more effective in harming Iran's economy, and Iran's subsequent interest in negotiating a deal on nuclear weapons appeared to be motivated by the damage to its economy caused by sanctions. Similar sanctions were enacted against North Korea, though with less effect.

Although the coercive effects of economic sanctions are debatable, sanctions also exert soft power, and they may be more influential in that respect. Because sanctions are costly to the states that enact them, they convey a certain level of commitment to their position. States and governments that are subject of sanctions are identified internationally as outcasts, and they may be as interested in overcoming that stigma as in regaining trade ties.

## Critical Thinking Questions

1. In what circumstances are sanctions likely to be most effective?

2. In what circumstances might sanctions strengthen a government, and engagement weaken it?

3. Should the effect of economic sanctions on the poor be a major factor in deciding when to adopt them?

Whereas in previous centuries many realists focused on self-sufficiency and found trade beneficial only in a very limited range of circumstances, contemporary realists agree with liberals that trade provides benefits for all states involved. But because realists emphasize distribution, they support trade only to the extent that the terms are favorable (or at least not *un*favorable). When two states that share this viewpoint trade with each other, bargaining will likely be intense. Recent disputes among the United States, the EU, and China, among others, support the argument that conflict over the gains from trade is the dominant characteristic of IPE.

## ECONOMIC STRUCTURALISM

Economic structuralism shares realism's concern with distribution, but takes it in a different direction. For economic structuralists, the fundamental actors in politics are not states, but classes. Economic structuralism therefore asks about the effects of the international economy on different classes, spotlighting its effects on the poor. For this reason, much of the practical agenda of economic structuralist international political economics has involved issues of underdevelopment and poverty in the Third World.

Economic structuralists, like realists, ask, "What determines how the gains from trade are divided?" Like realists, economic structuralists emphasize that power determines how the gains from trade are divided, and in this sense, their international argument replicates their domestic argument. When rich and poor countries trade or when transnational corporations hire impoverished workers in the Third World, the poorer actor is always more desperate than the richer one. The richer actor is able, therefore, to bargain for a disproportionate share of the gains. As the Russian revolutionary V. I. Lenin put it, "The uneven and spasmodic character of the development of … individual countries, is inevitable under the capitalist system."[4]

In recent years, this perspective has gained much visibility in the movement to improve working conditions in Third World factories that manufacture goods for First World consumers. Activists have been successful in showing, for example, how little of the price paid for a pair of name-brand athletic shoes accrues to the workers who made them, and how those workers often work long hours in difficult and unhealthy conditions to earn these meager wages. Although not presented in Marxist terms, such analyses are good examples of economic structuralist thought. Slogans about the distribution of wealth between the "99 percent" and the "1 percent" get at the same idea—that the benefits of economic exchange are being distributed unfairly.

A second practical focus of economic structuralism has been the issue of child labor. For example, the use of children in Pakistan to assemble many of the soccer balls used throughout Europe and North America has received

Banana plantation in Guatemala. Nearly all the bananas are exported. Is this an example of mutually beneficial trade, or of economic exploitation?

James Heil/Redux

much attention. Liberals tend to view this employment pragmatically, pointing out that if children could not work these jobs, their families would be even poorer and more desperate than they are now and that denying children jobs would not put them in school. Economic structuralists respond that this is precisely the point: The economic desperation of such people makes it rational for them to take any work offered at any wage. The response, they say, should be to alter the balance of power between workers and employers so that employers have greater incentive (or are required by law) to pay a reasonable wage and children have enough economic security that they do not feel compelled to pass up school for work. In the developed world, economic structuralists contend, this balance is provided through the bargaining power of labor unions and through the establishment of minimum wage laws, which do not exist in many developing countries.

Economic structuralism stresses how these dynamics function over time. If one actor starts out wealthier than another, then the wealthy actor, being less desperate, will be able to bargain for a greater part of the gains from trade. Because the rich actor gains more, the gap between the two actors' wealth is larger after the transaction than before. When the same two actors meet again, the increased disparity in wealth makes the bargaining position of the wealthy actor even stronger, and it bargains for a still bigger share of the gains from trade. Over time, therefore, economic structuralist analysis predicts that the gap between the wealthy and the poor will widen, rather than narrow (see Figure 10.3).

Two important points emerge from this analysis. First, the assertion that gaps in wealth increase over time puts economic structuralist analysis in direct opposition to liberal analysis. Whereas liberal analysis shows how economic disparities tend toward equilibrium in a free market, economic structuralist analysis predicts that disparities will widen. Second, in the economic structuralist view, once a disparity is established, it tends to be self-perpetuating. From this perspective, even where colonialism ended

**FIGURE 10.3** The liberal view differs from the realist and economic structuralist views on the effects of free trade on preexisting inequalities. Following neoclassical economic theory, liberals see a trend toward equilibrium, in which gaps in wealth shrink while everyone gets richer. Realists and economic structuralists see gaps in wealth growing as a result of free trade.

**Effect of Free Trade on the Wealth Gap**

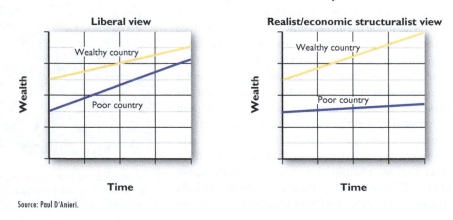

Source: Paul D'Anieri.

decades or centuries ago, the effects of colonialism are still being felt and will not go away by themselves over time.

## CONSTRUCTIVISM

Constructivist approaches to IPE address the profound disagreements among the three views discussed previously. A key determinant of international economic policies, constructivists find, is the understanding of the nature of IPE held by citizens, state leaders, and global policy makers. Whereas the three schools of thought that have been outlined assume that states have certain goals, constructivists hold that actors' goals vary, and therefore those goals must be a central subject of research. Some actors might subscribe to liberal views; others might hold economic structuralist views. Moreover, actors may have strong interests in promoting one view over the others. Over time, the views of various actors can change, so that shared understandings emerge and dissipate. As these understandings of interests change, policies can be expected to change as well. In other words, rather than adopting one or another of these broad approaches, constructivists ask which approach to a problem was adopted by the actors in a given situation. In particular, constructivists explore the extent of normative agreement on key issues. As normative agreement develops between states, it becomes much more likely that the states will agree on policy coordination. Several examples will help illustrate how constructivist theory is applied to IPE.

In one of the earliest and most influential constructivist studies, John Ruggie showed that the international trading system that encompassed the Western world after World War II was the result, above all, of a normative commitment (value judgment) that came to be shared by the key countries. This commitment, which Ruggie labeled **embedded liberalism**, was essentially liberal in its recognition of the benefits of free trade, so the major focus of the postwar trading system was on the reduction of tariffs. However, leaders also recognized that free trade would be politically unsustainable if it caused excessive disruption or hardship to domestic economies (interests of concern largely to realists and economic structuralists). As a result, the postwar system included important exceptions to a pure free trade approach. In this view, it was an idea—the compromise between free trade and protection—rather than a concrete factor, such as money or power, that led to agreement.[5]

This approach can be applied to a wide variety of issues in IPE. For example, in trying to explain why a certain "recipe" for economic stability was attempted in a wide variety of developing and postcommunist countries in the 1990s, constructivists would show how a set of prescriptions known as the "Washington consensus" came to dominate thinking on economic policy.

Today, one the most potentially far-reaching developments is a widespread shift in thinking about the role of governments in the economy. The notion that economies function best when governments are least involved was never fully accepted globally, but the post-2008 economic crisis has contributed to the view that state intervention is important and that markets left to themselves will induce crises.

The constructivist approach makes no sweeping statements about the nature of the IPE, focusing instead on the argument that what we collectively think about the international economy goes a long way toward explaining policies. Nor does constructivism make any predictions about how the world is likely to develop. Rather, this approach finds prediction difficult because of the complexity of anticipating how actors' understandings of their interests will evolve. In fact, it should be noted that all of the perspectives discussed have had limited success in clearly and correctly predicting future developments.

**embedded liberalism**
According to John Ruggie, the normative consensus that guided international economic arrangements after World War II. It combined a commitment to expansion of free trade with acceptance that states would have to intervene domestically to protect themselves from some of the effects of free trade.

# THE HISTORY CONNECTION

## THE GREAT DEPRESSION

On October 28, 1929, U.S. stocks lost 13 percent of their value. They fell another 12 percent the following day, which came to be called "Black Tuesday." Thus began the Great Depression, which impoverished much of the United States, and spread around the world. Within a few years, roughly a quarter of American workers were unemployed and the GDP had fallen by nearly 30 percent. (For comparison, in the "great recession" that began in 2008, U.S. GDP declined by just over 2 percent, and unemployment peaked at about 10 percent.)

How did a stock market crisis in New York lead to a global depression? Because many individuals and financial institutions had borrowed heavily in order to invest in the growing stock market, the collapse of 1929 left many people and firms unable to repay loans. As a result, banks came under severe financial stress. A bank panic ensued, in which people withdrew their money from banks, out of fear that the banks would collapse and take people's savings with them. With cash in extremely short supply, banks sharply curtailed lending activity. Because both businesses and consumers depended on credit for purchases, the collapse in credit led to a collapse in consumption. As demand fell, so did prices—a condition known as *deflation*.

Although deflation of prices might seem like a good thing, it can start a devastating cycle. Once potential buyers anticipate that prices will fall, they have an incentive to delay purchases until prices go lower. As a result, consumption drops further. As producers were unable to find buyers, they laid off workers. Unemployed workers were unable to buy, so overall demand in the economy fell even further.

The depression spread around the world in part because of protectionism. In 1930, the U.S. Congress passed the Smoot-Hawley Tariff Act, a huge increase in tariffs intended to let fewer imports into the United States, thereby increasing demand for U.S. goods and labor. This led to a collapse in demand in countries that supplied the United States. They responded with tariffs against the United States. The collapse in trade, a sort of deglobalization, exacerbated the depression around the world.

In financial terms, the fact that most countries still fixed the price of their currency to gold (the "gold standard") meant that the supply of money contracted. As banks and individuals hoarded money, taking money out of the financial system, there was no way for governments to inject more money into the economy to maintain the supply of credit. This contributed to deflation and to the credit crisis.

Governments responded in different ways. In the United States and United Kingdom, politics turned to the left. Franklin Roosevelt, elected in 1932, introduced the New Deal, which substantially increased government involvement in the economy. By borrowing vast sums of money and spending it on public works projects, the government sought to put people back to work and, by putting money in workers' pockets, to increase demand for consumer goods. The United States also passed legislation strengthening the power of labor unions and introducing the Social Security system, among other things. Other countries, however, turned to the right. In Germany, the depression made the Communist Party more popular, but fear of the communists led many to support the right wing Nazi Party, led by Adolf Hitler.

Economist Ben Bernanke, writing seventy years later, stated, "To understand the Great Depression is the Holy Grail of macroeconomics."* By 2008, Bernanke was Chairman of the Federal Reserve Board, and the depression was no longer just an academic subject. The United States was again surprised by a collapse of credit and of

*(Continued)*

asset prices (including stocks and housing). Again the crisis quickly spread around the world. The threat of a new deflationary spiral and a long-term depression led many to look back to the Great Depression for lessons. In contrast to 1930, however, there was no illusion that disaster might be averted without intervention, and governments leapt into action to avoid economic collapse, debating all the way what causes depressions to start and to spread.

### Critical Thinking Questions

1. In what respects do the events of 1929–1930 resemble those of 2008–2009?

2. What changes since the Great Depression might make it easier or harder to avoid a repetition today or in the future?

*Ben S. Bernanke, Essays on the Great Depression (Princeton, NJ: Princeton University Press, 2000), p. 5.

## FEMINISM

The basic feminist critique of the four IPE approaches described previously is that by ignoring women and issues of gender, these approaches fail to fully understand how the IPE works, and they cause harm to women by ignoring their role in it. Understanding the role of women in IPE, feminists contend, is essential to understanding the dynamics of the global economy. Conventional analyses fail to see how the IPE contributes to the economic and political oppression of women, especially the poorest and most vulnerable women. Moreover, many development economists as well as feminists assert that women play an underappreciated role in the economic growth of developing nations.

**Differential Effects of the Economy on Women**    Feminist scholars argue that the international economy has particular effects on women, because women often are assigned specific (disadvantageous) roles in the economy. In addition, feminists assert, women often play multiple roles, some of which are excluded from analysis because of an artificial analytical distinction between "public" and "private." "Women's and girls' ability to participate in educational, productive, and civic activities and thus to empower themselves economically and politically is often limited by a household division of labor that assigns to women and girls the bulk of the responsibility for everyday household maintenance tasks."[6] In the developing world, some of these household tasks impose enormous burdens: Collecting firewood takes the average woman more than an hour per day in some countries, and collecting and managing water is a further burden. Under-developed public transport systems increase the time these chores require and therefore are particularly burdensome on women.[7]

Whereas liberal economists propose that free trade will make everyone better off, once adjustment to new conditions takes place, feminists ask how costs and benefits will be distributed across genders (just as economic structuralists ask how the costs and benefits will be distributed across classes). The work that women do in factories in return for wages is included in standard economic analysis, but the "domestic" work they do—raising children, finding and preparing food, and maintaining a household, and the fact that these tasks prevent women from seeking wage labor—is often ignored. Similarly, informal production by women, whether in maintaining household gardens or doing piecework in the home for the international market, is often not accounted for. Thus, feminists claim, women's work is systematically undervalued.

Feminists also find that the costs of globalization are unevenly distributed, in part because the costs to women are not visible in standard analyses based on macro-level statistics. Measures of gross domestic product (GDP) per capita and income inequality are calculated without regard to differences between women and men, and this approach can obscure significant gender inequities. For example, in the wealthiest industrialized countries, where men and women have roughly equal access to education, there is a remarkable disparity in the estimated earned income of women and men. In the United States, for example, women in 2004 on average earned $30,581, while men earned $49,075—38 percent more. In Ireland, men on average earn 49 percent more than women, and in Japan, they earn 66 percent more.[8] In many countries, education, which is demonstrated to have an important influence on earning power, is less available to girls than to boys.[9] In the poorest countries, the effects of economic discrimination can be dramatic: "In India alone, among children aged one to five, girls are 50 percent more likely to die than boys—meaning that 130,000 Indian girls are mortally discriminated against every year."[10]

Aspects of globalization that are generally viewed as beneficial can have very negative effects on women. For example, cheap international travel and the Internet facilitate "sex tourism," the practice of traveling to other places primarily to engage in sexual exploitation without fear of punishment. The Internet makes it easy for those who offer such services to make themselves known to potential customers around the world. Cheap international travel makes it economically viable for people in developed countries to participate. The phenomenon is widespread in various countries in Southeast Asia and Latin America, and in some countries sex tourism plays a major role in the economy.[11] Women, and especially girls under age eighteen, are the predominant targets. The U.S. State Department estimates that more than 1 million children are victimized every year.[12] By vastly increasing the demand for such "services," and therefore the profits to be made by those organizing them, cheap travel and the Internet have increased the incentive to exploit girls and women.

**Women as Agents of Development**   Whereas some view women as victims of international economic processes, others point out the crucial role that women can play in solving broader problems. Indeed, some feminists reject the idea of women as "victims," stressing instead the ways in which women actively work to transform their economic circumstances and, by extension, the international economy.

The argument that women have a special role to play in international development is the feminist argument that has perhaps had the widest influence beyond the feminist movement. Because women play a disproportionate role in child rearing, for instance, they play a crucial role in reducing children's poverty. Studies have shown that women tend to use a much higher proportion of their earned income on household expenditures, including higher-quality food, home maintenance (including sanitation), and clothing and school fees for children, whereas men are somewhat more likely to spend money on entertainment, drugs, and prostitution.[13] Likewise, the human development indicators monitored by the United Nations Development Programme indicate that the children of women who receive higher levels of education and earned income in turn attain higher levels of literacy and life expectancy. Women's overall development is strongly correlated with overall human development, particularly for children.

Based on such findings, development aid programs since the 1970s have increasingly targeted women. One of the most significant innovations was the development of microlending programs for women. Mohammed Yunus and other microlending pioneers

Women weaving products for sale at a local cooperative in Rwanda. Development advocates have been trying to gain leverage from women's roles as producers, which have tended to be ignored if they take place in the "informal" economy.

Wayne HUTCHINSON/Alamy

recognized that the key obstacle to women's economic development was their lack of access to credit that could be used to invest in entrepreneurial activities. Social customs that deny women property rights (necessary for collateral for loans) effectively choked off an important path to increased earning. Even a very small loan can make a significant difference in a woman's earning power.

For example, women sewing garments by hand can realize a huge increase in productivity if they can purchase a sewing machine with funds from a microloan. A woman can pay off the loan and then continue to be much more productive, and therefore earn more, well into the future. Similarly, a woman who cooks and sells food in her neighborhood can vastly increase her productivity with a small investment in equipment. Women, therefore, represent an untapped source of economic development.

Moreover, although some people reject the notion that women behave differently than men, women's behavior is seen as one of the reasons that microlending has been so successful. Women, it appears, repay loans at a much higher rate than do men. This is important because microlending organizations can only make new loans as old ones are repaid. Women's higher repayment rate is thought to be based not on individual differences between women and men, but rather on the nature of the cooperative groups formed by women to manage the loans; such groups exert a strong normative pressure to repay the loan so that the next woman can benefit.

# COMPARISON OF THE APPROACHES

The key characteristics of each approach to IPE are summarized in Table 10.5. Note that there is some overlap as well as some degree of contradiction among the approaches. Realists and economic structuralists agree on the vital importance of distributive issues.

But while realism looks at national interests, economic structuralism focuses on class interests, which in many analyses means the interests of the capitalist class, which is assumed to be dominant both economically and politically. When economic structuralist analyses equate rich and poor states with rich and poor classes, or when realism takes up the issue of underdevelopment, the two schools become nearly indistinguishable analytically, but they still differ on their normative commitments. Economic structuralism and liberalism disagree on the key issue of whether, left to themselves, free markets reduce or increase inequality. The two approaches agree, however, that substate actors such as firms and classes, rather than states (the focus of realism), are the key actors and that arguments about "national interest" usually disguise the interest of some powerful actor seeking government protection. Finally, realism and liberalism also disagree about whether international trade is a positive-sum or a zero-sum game. On much of the basic economics, they agree: Neither realists nor economic structuralists contradict most of liberal economic theory, and they accept the theory of comparative advantage. But they have a very different notion of who the important actors are and of whether free trade is beneficial to all or only to some.

**TABLE 10.5**    Summary of Major Approaches to International Political Economy

| | Key Actors | Key Processes | Key Questions | Value Commitment |
|---|---|---|---|---|
| **Liberalism** | Individuals and firms | Trade, which increases wealth | What factors lead to more open international trade? | Economic efficiency, overall wealth, free trade |
| **Realism** | States | Conflict over the gains from trade | How does power affect the distribution of gains from trade? How does trade affect the distribution of power? | State power, domestic employment, self-sufficiency |
| **Economic structuralism** | Classes, transnational corporations | Unequal distribution of the gains from trade | How does international trade contribute to poverty? How can that be changed? | Equality (both domestic and international) |
| **Constructivism** | States, state leaders, intellectual leaders | Diffusion of new ideas, development of new values | What understandings of international political economy are dominant? | Varies |
| **Feminism** | Individuals (especially women), NGOs | Gender-based exploitation, gender-based development programs | How does international political economy affect women? How can gender-based programs promote development? | Recognition of influence of gender, equality for women |

Source: *Paul D'Anieri.*

## RECONSIDER THE CASE

## CHINA'S RISE TO ECONOMIC POWER

It is often pointed out that if current trends continue, China's GDP could pass that of the United States as early as 2020. Many look to an era in which China, not the United States, is the world's leading economic power, and in which the world looks to Beijing rather than to Washington for economic leadership. Yet the key question is whether current trends will continue. Skeptics point to several challenges that face China now and will arise in the future.

Despite its growing economic might, China is still in many respects a developing country. In 2014 its per capita GDP ranked seventy-ninth in the world and was roughly one-seventh that of the United States. Development ranges widely from the global cities of the east coast to the underdeveloped villages of the interior. This disparity has led to massive migration to the coastal cities, creating challenges both for those cities and for villages that are losing many of their young people.

The enormous role of the state in the economy continues to create challenges as well. A great deal of investment and lending policy is driven by the goal of maintaining political stability, rather than sound investment. Some analysts predict that many loans in China will never be repaid and that China will face a banking crisis. Corruption is also a major concern because it undermines the business climate and misallocates investment. Inflation is also a danger: as China's economy booms, demand for nearly everything has increased. Finally, China has a demographic problem.

The "one child" policy has been successful in limiting China's population explosion. With so few births, however, the ratio of working-age population to retirees will eventually shrink, meaning that each worker will have to support more retirees.

All of these problems are made potentially more explosive by China's authoritarian form of government. The government actively and ruthlessly stifles the dissent that arises from these and other problems. So far, this has maintained order, but without elections or other democratic means of channeling grievances, the potential exists for more serious unrest.

With regard to many of these economic issues, China has become a "normal" country rather than the isolated autocratic state it was forty years ago. China faces the same policy debates and dilemmas that other countries face. The difference, however, is that China's enormous economic size means that it has a huge influence on everyone else's economy as well. That is true both when it deliberately seeks to have an influence and when it does not.

### Critical Thinking Questions

1. Does it matter to anyone outside of China and the United States if China surpasses the United States as the world's biggest economy? How?

2. What does the case of China tell us about the links between democracy and economic growth?

# ★ POWER AND PURPOSE IN INTERNATIONAL POLITICAL ECONOMY

The last column of Table 10.5 is of crucial importance. The analytical disagreements among the various schools often reflect different goals. Debate over purpose underlies much theoretical and empirical debate about international political economy. For example, two analysts might agree that NAFTA increases overall efficiency and will make Canada,

Mexico, and the United States all wealthier, and that many workers in each country will have to find new jobs as tasks are moved to more efficient producers. One analyst might argue that the overall efficiency gains are worth the disruption caused to workers needing to readjust and that NAFTA is therefore beneficial. Without disagreeing about the facts, the other could argue that the costs imposed on workers who must find new jobs are too high a price to pay and that NAFTA therefore was a bad idea. The disagreement here is not explanatory—it does not stem from disagreement over how the world works. The disagreement is normative, concerning values; each gives a different answer to the question "How much inequality is acceptable in the effort to gain greater overall wealth?"

In contemporary international politics, actors are concerned with both efficiency and distribution of gains. There is relatively little disagreement with Ricardo's finding that trade leads to economic gains. But the distribution of those gains is a sensitive political issue, whether to those concerned with power or to those concerned with welfare and equity. In this sense, international trade can be characterized as a **mixed-motive game** (similar to the prisoner's dilemma), in which actors have incentives that partially overlap with and partially contradict those of their partners. There can be no general statement concerning how sensitive actors are to the distributive issues—this varies across actors and over time. However, the more sensitive actors are to distributive issues, the more difficult it will be to achieve the mutual gain of free trade. For realists and economic structuralists, international economics is still about gaining and exercising power, whereas for liberals, it is largely about cooperating to pursue prosperity.

Moving from theory to the real world, these mixed motives are visible in operation every day. The United States uses its considerable power to attempt to decrease its trade deficit with China, and China uses its power to maintain its surplus, while at the same time both states take care not to let the dispute completely ruin the relationship, which remains profitable. The same story can be told about the United States and the EU, the EU and China, and many other relationships.

**mixed-motive game**

A situation in which actors have incentives that partially overlap with and partially contradict those of their partners. The prisoner's dilemma is one representation of a mixed-motive game.

## SUMMARY

- Because domestic economic prosperity has become one of the most salient political issues in most countries and because international trade has increased, the effects of international economics on domestic economics are becoming more central to international politics and foreign policy.

- The ability of one state's domestic policies or problems to harm or benefit other states transforms the domestic economy of each state into an international concern. Governments that seek to promote domestic prosperity, therefore, need to be concerned with the policies of other states.

- Some analysts predict that this interdependence will lead to greater cooperation; others see it leading to greater conflict. Either way, these trends put international political economy (IPE) at the center of contemporary international politics.

- The theory of comparative advantage has crucial implications for our understanding of IPE. It proposes that by specializing and trading, states and individuals can increase overall consumption and efficiency.

- The theory of comparative advantage powerfully contradicts the realist view that international affairs is a zero-sum game.

- Focusing on the balance of trade shifts international trade back to a zero-sum game.

- In theory, exchange rates and the balance of trade should balance each other. In practice, if states put a high priority on achieving a trade surplus, they can manipulate their currency price to boost trade. This behavior is called competitive devaluation.

- Tariffs and subsidies are two of the most common protectionist measures used to protect domestic industry.

- The same approaches that are used to understand international politics in general, or to explain international conflict, can also be applied to the problem of IPE. The focus of Western nations on free market economics makes the liberal view the most widely held view of IPE, but crises in the Western economies has led to more focus on state control domestically, and on economic realism internationally.

- Economic structuralist and feminist analyses also often work their way into policy debates as well as academic discussions.

- Disagreements over particular economic policies such as tariffs, free trade, and development are often traceable either to the different analyses based on these theories or to the different normative goals of the theories.

## KEY CONCEPTS

1. Liberalization
2. Barriers to trade
3. Fiscal policy
4. Monetary policy
5. Zero-sum game versus positive-sum game
6. Balance of trade
7. Exchange rates
8. Distribution of gains from trade
9. Protectionism
10. Neomercantilism
11. Embedded liberalism
12. Gendered economic roles

## STUDY QUESTIONS

1. Which approach proposes that by specializing and trading, states and individuals can increase overall consumption and efficiency?

   a. Constructivism

   b. Realism

   c. The theory of competitive advantage

   d. Game theory

2. What term is used to define exports minus imports?

   a. Fiscal policy

   b. Competitive advantage

   c. Competitive devaluation

   d. Balance of trade

3. If the United States has a trade deficit with Germany, there will be greater demand for euros and the price of the euro will go up. What is this an example of?

   a. The theory of competitive advantage

   b. The ideal interaction between exchange rates and the balance of trade

   c. Mercantilism and neomercantilism

   d. The use of fiscal policy to stabilize domestic economies

4. Which of the following strategies do states use to try to stabilize their domestic economics?

   a. Tariffs and subsidies

   b. Quotas and exchange rates

   c. Fiscal and monetary policies

   d. The theory of competitive advantage

5. How can a state deliberately devalue its currency?

   a. By lowering interest rates

   b. By printing more money

   c. By selling reserves of its own currency

   d. All of the above.

6. Which of the following are common protectionist measures?

   a. Tariffs and subsidies

   b. Quotas and exchange rates

   c. Fiscal and monetary policies

   d. All of the above.

7. What are the benefits of free trade, and who gets them? What are the costs of free trade, and who pays them?

8. In what respect does liberal trade theory see trade as a positive-sum game?

9. In what respect do realist and economic structuralist theories see trade as a zero-sum game?

10. What is the perceived importance of the balance of trade?

11. How do people's views of international trade depend on whether they focus on overall efficiency or on the distribution of gains?

12. What differences exist in male and female economic roles, and how do these differences influence global development?

[Correct answers: 1. c; 2. d; 3. b; 4. c; 5. d; 6. a]

## END NOTES

1. Paul R. Krugman and Maurice Obstfeld, *International Economics: Theory and Policy*, 6th ed. (Boston: Addison Wesley, 2003), p. 3.

2. *Sunday Times* [London], July 24, 1994.

3. Robert Gilpin, *U.S. Power and the Multinational Corporation: The Political Economy of Direct Foreign Investment* (New York: Basic Books, 1975), p. 38.

4. V. I. Lenin, *Imperialism: The Highest Stage of Capitalism* (New York: International Publishers, 1939), p. 62.

5. John G. Ruggie, "International Regimes, Transaction, and Change: Embedded Liberalism in the Postwar Economic Order," *International Organization*, Vol. 36, No. 2 (Spring 1983): 379–415.

6. UN Millennium Project, *Taking Action: Achieving Gender Equality and Empowering Women* (London: Earthscan, 2005), p. 7.

7. UN Millennium Project, *Taking Action*, pp. 7–8.

8. United Nations Development Programme, *Human Development Report 2006* (New York: United Nations, 2006), p. 367.

9. UN Millennium Project, *Taking Action*, pp. 4–6.

10. Nicholas Kristof, "Wretched of the Earth," *New York Review of Books* (May 31, 2007): 34.

11. U.S. Department of Justice, "Child Sex Tourism," www.usdoj.gov/criminal/ceos/sextour.html.

12. U.S. Department of State, Office to Monitor and Combat Trafficking in Persons, "The Facts About Child Sex Tourism," August 19, 2005, www.state.gov/g/tip/rls/fs/2005/51351.htm.

13. UN Millennium Project, *Taking Action*, pp. 88–89. See also L. Haddad, J. Hoddinott, and H. Alderman, *Intrahousehold Resource Allocation in Developing Countries: Methods, Models and Policy* (Baltimore, MD: Johns Hopkins University Press, 1997); and Kristof, "Wretched of the Earth," p. 35.

Ships transit the Panama Canal. The boom in global trade has created delays in transiting the canal. An expansion scheduled for completion in 2016 is intended to double the canal's capacity.

BlackMac/Shutterstock.com

# THE GLOBALIZATION OF TRADE AND FINANCE

## Learning Objectives

**11-1** Distinguish between quantitative and qualitative changes in global interactions.

**11-2** Describe the historical evolution of the post–World War II trading system.

**11-3** Identify the major issues surrounding the World Trade Organization.

**11-4** Analyze the competing goals of international monetary arrangements and the tensions between these goals.

**11-5** Describe the evolution of the international financial system since the nineteenth century.

**11-6** Analyze the sources and mechanisms of crisis in the contemporary international financial system.

**11-7** Evaluate competing arguments about the benefits and problems of globalization.

# CONSIDER THE CASE

## GREECE'S DEBT CRISIS AND THE THREAT TO THE EUROPEAN UNION

In 2015, it appeared that the government of Greece might default on its debt and be forced to exit the euro zone and readopt a national currency. The crisis echoed an earlier one from 2010 that had been alleviated by a bailout from the EU and the IMF. Why was Greece unable to pay its debt, and how did that threaten the rest of Europe?

After Greece joined the single European currency in 2001, its borrowing costs dropped because the euro was seen as much more stable than the drachma. The Greek government took advantage of this, borrowing extensively to fund generous pensions and public services. As long as borrowing remained within limits and the Greek economy grew, lenders were confident that Greece could meet its obligations. However, beginning in 2008, when the economy shrank because of the global recession and tax revenues decreased correspondingly, the gap between government income and spending widened to the point where lenders feared that the government would not be able to pay its debt. Lenders compensate for increased risk by charging higher interest rates. The higher interest rates made it even harder for Greece to repay its debts, in a vicious cycle characteristic of debt crises.

Normally, a country in such a situation might address the problems through monetary policy: Printing more money would help pay debts and would devalue the currency (leading to higher exports). But as a member of the euro zone, Greece had no independent control of monetary policy. Critics of the EU pointed out that this inflexibility was devastating, and some predicted that Greece would be forced to leave the euro zone.

The Greek crisis threatened to spread to the rest of Europe through two mechanisms. First, the banks and investors that had lent money to Greece were based in many other countries and often owed money to others. If Greece failed to pay its debts, the banks that lent

them the money would be unable to pay *their* debts, and so on, in a chain reaction of default. Second, the crisis spread through fear. As Greek default loomed, investors began looking more critically at other states' ability to repay their debts. Attention focused initially on Spain, which had problems comparable to those of Greece. Spain, as a much larger economy, presented a much larger danger to the system.

Greece's partners in the euro zone had to choose between two potential contagions. On one hand, if Greece defaulted, the crisis might quickly spread around Europe. On the other hand, if Greece were bailed out, what incentive would others have to be more responsible?

A debate raged over who was to blame for the disaster and what should be done about it. Many European leaders, led by Germany's Angela Merkel, blamed the problem on Greece's high government spending and lax tax collection. The answer was to reform government, raise taxes, and cut spending. The Greek government, and many economists, argued that cutting spending while raising taxes would shrink the Greek economy further, making it even harder to pay the debt and impoverishing the Greek people. They argued that some of the debt had to be forgiven.

The crisis in 2015 resembled a game of "chicken." With disaster looming for both Greece and the euro zone, it was unclear which side would cave in first, or whether neither side would relent and the disaster would occur. Greek's socialist government held a referendum to win support for its refusal to agree to the EU's austerity demands. Voters supported the government's position, but the government then accepted many of the demands of international creditors.

The 2015 crisis was widely seen as the greatest in the history of the EU. Can crises such as this one lead to a reversal of globalization, or can states learn to handle such international crises more effectively?

The global financial crisis that began in 2008 had its roots in the globalization of trade and finance systems in the preceding decades. Increasing freedom to move money across borders has led to a vastly increased scope for investment in foreign countries, which can be a boon both to investors and to the economies in which they are investing. But because this money can move very quickly, and because the amounts of money in the global marketplace dwarf those in any one domestic market, domestic markets can quickly be overwhelmed by currency movements. Governments now have less ability to control domestic and international finance than at any time in history. A defining question today is whether it is possible to gain the benefits of financial globalization while avoiding the dangers.

# THREE CHARACTERISTICS OF GLOBALIZATION

People use the term *globalization* to mean many different (and sometimes contradictory) things. **Globalization** refers to a process in which the time and cost required to move goods, people, information, and money across borders are decreasing; in which international trade increases relative to domestic trade; and in which the world is increasingly defined by a single market rather than by many separate markets.

First, the cost and the time it takes to move almost anything around the world are falling. Lower transportation costs mean that price differentials in distant places can be exploited more easily than in the past. This is especially true of differential labor costs. Fifty years ago, it was difficult to take advantage of cheap labor located overseas because much of the savings in labor costs would be eaten up in the costs of transporting finished goods to markets. As transport costs fall relative to labor costs, it becomes easier to produce even low-profit-margin goods wherever labor is cheapest. This accounts for the massive consumption by Americans of goods manufactured in Asia. In some cases, electronics components are manufactured with high-wage, high-skill labor in one country, shipped across the ocean for assembly in low-wage areas, and then shipped back across the ocean for consumption.

Second, perhaps the most basic aspect of globalization is the growing importance of international trade relative to local and domestic economies. For almost every country in the world, foreign trade is growing much faster than the domestic economy. The logical result is that, over time, the portion of each country's economy that either is sold as exports or is bought as imports is growing. Figure 11.1 shows that trade makes up an increasing share of many countries' economies.

The third and most far-reaching aspect of globalization in the past two decades has been in financial flows. Not only goods and people, but money and investment also flow across borders in sums vastly larger than only a few years ago. As recently as 1980, the amounts of currency being traded by private actors (banks and investment firms) were relatively small compared with those controlled by governments. As a result, governments had considerable influence over exchange rates. By the 1990s, trading by private actors exceeded the total currency reserves of governments (Figure 11.2). Currency trading now dwarfs foreign trade: In 2001, global exports were $5.7 trillion for the *year*, whereas currency trading averaged $1.25 trillion per *day*.[1] In this area, a change in amount (quantitative change) led to a change in the nature of the system (qualitative change). The role of states in setting foreign exchange rates was significantly weakened, and that of markets was strengthened.

**globalization**

A process in which the time it takes for goods, people, information, and money to flow across borders and the cost of moving them are decreasing; in which international trade increases relative to domestic trade; and in which the world is increasingly defined by single markets rather than by many separate markets.

**FIGURE 11.1**   For most countries, foreign trade comprises an ever-increasing share of the overall economy.

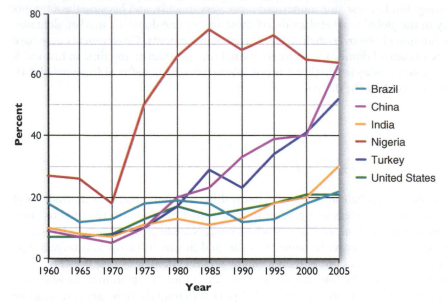

**Trade as a Share of GDP in Selected Countries over Time**

Source: World Bank, http://ddp-ext.worldbank.org/ext/DDPQQ/member.do?method=getMembers&userid=1&queryId=135. Data collected into document.

**FIGURE 11.2**   The flow of money across borders is rapidly increasing. The amount of money moved dwarfs the amount of goods and services, and the amount of money moved by private actors surpasses that controlled by governments.

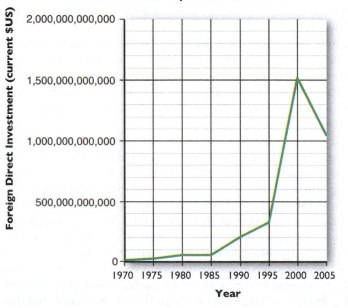

**Increase in Global Capital Movements**

Source: World Bank, http://ddp-ext.worldbank.org/ext/DDPQQ/member.do?method=getMembers&userid.

Those who view globalization as qualitatively new point to several developments as evidence:

- Private international financial transactions now dwarf the financial resources controlled by states, displacing most states' ability to influence financial markets.
- States have much less ability to limit the movement of money and goods in and out of their territories, decreasing states' influence over their own economies.
- Firms can move resources and production around the world to find the most favorable conditions, maximizing their leverage over less mobile actors, such as states, local governments, and workers.
- Comparative advantage today is increasingly based not on natural resource endowments but on factors such as technology, education, and network effects that can shift from one country to another, and on regulatory environments.

Together, these trends indicate that states have lost control over globalization. In previous eras, states could choose whether to decrease barriers to commerce. Today, the elimination of such barriers is a fact states must deal with, whether they like it or not.

# GLOBALIZATION OF TRADE

## THE HISTORICAL CONTEXT

International trade increased steadily in the decades leading up to World War I. However, there was no agreed-on international framework to facilitate international trade. Much international trade was carried out through the colonial system: European countries imported raw materials from their colonies in the south and exported finished products. Trade agreements among the wealthy states were made on a bilateral basis. World War I destroyed many of these trading relationships, as trading partners became military adversaries.

Efforts to rebuild international trade after World War I were hampered by a variety of factors, but most prominent was the **Great Depression**, which began just a decade after the war's end, in 1929, and was spurred in part by the policies adopted to cope with the aftermath of the war. Most states responded to the decline in their economies by enacting protectionist measures, such as tariffs. The goal of these measures was to get consumers to purchase domestically produced goods rather than imports, thus providing business for domestic firms and workers. However, when every country followed this same policy, any gain in domestic consumption was outweighed by losses in export sales. Moreover, the overall efficiency of each economy suffered, as the gains from trade were forgone. As a result, the measures taken to combat the depression made matters worse. It was difficult to see what any individual state could do to solve this problem. If one state chose to keep its markets open to foreign products while others did not, the open state would face the worst of both worlds: loss of overseas markets without an increase in shares of the domestic market. Thus, the prisoner's dilemma applies to trade policy. Prior to World War I, Great Britain was so powerful that it could use its influence to prod others to lower trade barriers, but its financial and trading position was so weakened by the war that this was no longer possible. In addition, the rise of nationalist doctrines tended to emphasize the competitive side of international trade at the expense of mutual gain.

**Great Depression**

The global depression that lasted from 1929 until World War II, during which the economies of the United States and Europe declined by as much as 25 percent. In economics, a decline in output of less than 10 percent is referred to as a *recession*; a deeper contraction is called a *depression*.

**Origins of the Bretton Woods System**    Following World War II, conditions changed in important ways. The leading economic powers broadly agreed on the *purpose* of improving trade cooperation, and the United States had the *power* to push toward that end. First, leaders in many states perceived that rebuilding free trade was critical. Second, World War II had enormously shifted world economic power in favor of the United States. At the same time, U.S. attitudes toward international leadership had changed. The policy of isolationism, which had led the United States to shun the League of Nations and to stay out of World War II until the Pearl Harbor attack, had been discredited. Pearl Harbor had shown that isolationism would not protect the United States from attack, and the perceived menace of the Soviet Union convinced most Americans that a strong global actor was needed and that only the United States could play that role.

For these reasons, the United States and its allies met in 1944 to set up a new trading and financial system. The **Bretton Woods system** consisted of both trade and financial provisions, which were intended to promote free trade and increase wealth around the world. These were seen not only as worthwhile goals in general, but also as a way of defeating communism and promoting peace. The main trade provision was known as the **General Agreement on Tariffs and Trade (GATT)**. Initiated in 1946, the GATT lasted until 1995, when it was replaced by a stronger version embodied in the World Trade Organization (WTO).

The economic power of the United States played an important role in formation of the Bretton Woods system. Not every country agreed to all the provisions the United States had proposed. Realists argued that free trade was not in the interest of everyone, but was supported by the United States because it served U.S. interests. The United States was in a favorable competitive position and would gain economically and politically from greater free trade. Because the United States controlled half the world economy, it could provide strong incentives to do things its way. Any country that was excluded from the system or that chose not to participate would find itself disadvantaged in U.S. markets and investment.

**The Principle of Nondiscrimination**    The mechanism of the GATT was simple. First, members agreed that they would use tariffs rather than other methods (such as quotas) as their primary means of protection. Second, they would work over time to slowly decrease the level of those tariffs. These reductions were carried out in nine "rounds" held over the succeeding decades.

The revolutionary aspect of the GATT was that it produced an entirely new principle guiding tariff levels. Prior to World War II, trade agreements were conducted bilaterally (between two states) and were based on the principle of **reciprocity**. Reciprocity meant that two states would agree to have the same tariffs on each other's goods. That seemed fair enough. However, it meant that any country might have many different tariffs for the same good, depending on where that good came from. This was economically inefficient because it meant that firms seeking to sell a particular good in a particular country were not all competing on the same terms. This undermined competition, removing an important impetus to increased efficiency.

The GATT was based on the principle of **nondiscrimination** rather than reciprocity. Nondiscrimination meant that a given state's tariff on a particular good would be the same for all GATT members. Giving one state a better deal than others in return for some reciprocal concession was no longer permitted. If a state lowered a tariff for one GATT member, it was obliged to lower the tariff for all members. This principle was also known as the *most favored nation* principle, meaning that every GATT member would be treated as well as the most favored nation. The key achievement of the GATT was that

---

**Bretton Woods system**

The system that guided economic arrangements among the advanced industrial states in the post–World War II era. It included the GATT, the fixed exchange rate system, the IMF, and the World Bank. Bretton Woods was a resort in New Hampshire where the negotiations took place.

**General Agreement on Tariffs and Trade (GATT)**

The main trade provision of the Bretton Woods system.

**reciprocity**

An arrangement whereby two states agree to have the same tariffs on each other's goods.

**nondiscrimination**

A principle guiding tariff policy that requires a country to apply equal tariffs on all of its trading partners; also referred to as the *most favored nation* principle.

**FIGURE 11.3** Overall, tariffs have steadily been eliminated since World War II. Many see this decline in tariffs as largely responsible for increases in global trade and overall wealth.

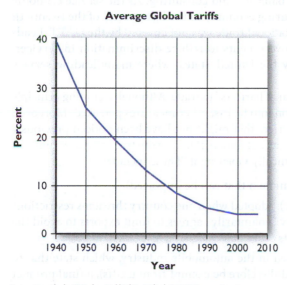

Average Global Tariffs

Source: From Charles W. Kegley, *World Politics*, 11th ed. © 2008 Cengage Learning.

it put all foreign producers on an equal footing. This facilitated competition according to comparative advantage and hence improved overall efficiency. Moreover, it tended to produce, over time, a decline in tariff levels, slowly bringing foreign and domestic producers ever closer to an equal footing (see Figure 11.3).

**"Embedded Liberalism"** Why were tariffs not eliminated completely, if this was the ultimate goal? Why were some states (notably the United States) willing to allow nonreciprocity, which meant that their markets were more open to others than others' markets were to them? The short answer is that the deviations from free trade were viewed as politically necessary in order to cushion its effects.

To open up all markets in the GATT countries to unlimited international competition was seen as being too disruptive for domestic economies, and in particular for those who would lose their jobs to competition from overseas producers. Today we see a similar issue in debates concerning the "offshoring" of jobs and the movement of industries from rich countries to poorer ones.

Especially in the aftermath of the Great Depression, and in an era in which socialist and communist political parties were quite popular in Britain, France, and Italy, the responsibility of the government to ensure that workers had jobs was taken much more seriously than it is today. One lesson of the Great Depression was that the market will not always fix itself if left alone. The modern welfare state represents a new social contract in which government is expected to intervene in the economy to ensure prosperity. Thus, the arrangements of the Bretton Woods system, including the GATT, were a compromise between economic liberalism (letting the market work to increase wealth) and state intervention to soften the impact that the market might have on domestic economies. This compromise came to be labeled *embedded liberalism* because it placed liberalism within the broader goals of governments.[2] Expanding trade and fostering economic efficiency were never the sole purposes of the Bretton Woods system.

**From the GATT to the WTO**   A central problem with the GATT was that it only covered certain classes of products. Agriculture was left entirely out of the original agreement and was treated only in a limited way in subsequent rounds. Nor did the GATT cover trade in services, such as insurance, banking, and consulting. As the service economy increasingly displaced the manufacturing economy in the last quarter of the twentieth century, an ever-larger part of international trade was not covered by the GATT. Leading service firms put pressure on governments to reduce discrimination in services. This issue was pushed primarily by the United States, where many leading service firms were located.

States increasingly enacted "nontariff barriers" to trade. Although a guiding principle of the GATT was to channel protection into tariffs, other measures persisted. Moreover, as tariff levels dropped, nontariff barriers that might not have been noticed previously became relatively more intrusive. A variety of nontariff barriers to trade could circumvent the intent of the GATT without technically violating it. These include:

- Quotas (limits on the number of an item that can be imported)
- Voluntary export restraints (VERs), adopted when one country threatens restrictions on trade and an exporting country "voluntarily" agrees to limit exports to avoid the imposition of more stringent limits
- Domestic content laws, widely used in the automobile industry, which state that to be sold as a domestic product (and therefore be exempt from tariffs), a final product must have a certain percentage of its components assembled domestically
- Health and environmental regulations, which can easily be written in ways that give an advantage to domestically produced products over imports

What could be done when one country enacted a nontariff barrier that others claimed violated the agreement? The dispute resolution mechanism under the GATT was slow, and enforcement measures were weak. This frustrated smaller countries, which found

Traditional procession with cattle, Switzerland. The Swiss government is one of many that heavily subsidizes agriculture to support rural villages. Agriculture has been highly resistant to trade liberalization.

R Puppett/Blickwinkel/Age Fotostock

that the United States had much more leverage in making them accept its position on various matters. But it also frustrated the United States because, as a leading exporter, it found itself the main target of nontariff barriers around the world. Some of these disputes could be resolved through political pressure, but doing so took considerable time and effort. As disputes over nontariff barriers increased, so did frustration with the weakness of enforcement mechanisms.

**The WTO**    To address the problems inherent in the GATT, 117 states signed a new agreement in 1994 founding the WTO. The main provisions of the GATT were incorporated into the WTO, and a General Agreement on Trade in Services (GATS) was added. In return for greater protection of intellectual property rights in the developing world, the advanced economies agreed to eliminate protection for their textile industries by 2005. Agriculture was the main sticking point in the negotiations, with the United States, the EU, and Japan reluctant to open their markets to international competition.

The main change in moving to the WTO was the development of an enforcement mechanism that allows states to challenge each other's laws. If the laws are found to be barriers to trade that violate the agreement, then the WTO can assign penalties against the offending states. These penalties consist of countertariffs that the injured state can enact to offset the damage. To supporters of free trade, this was an essential development, providing a means to fight back against the increasing use of various domestic regulations as nontariff barriers. However, many people were concerned that the new measures would undermine state sovereignty and could be used to overturn important environmental, health, and labor legislation.

**Dispute Resolution in the WTO**    The WTO dispute settlement process is intended not simply to judge right and wrong, but to mediate conflict. The first step, therefore, is consultation, to see if the parties can reach an agreement. If they cannot, the case is then referred to a panel, the members of which are chosen with the approval of the parties (or, if they cannot agree, by the larger Dispute Resolution Body). The findings of the panel are then provided to the parties and to the Dispute Resolution Body, where they can be overturned only by a unanimous vote. This is the most important contrast with the GATT, where a single vote, even from the accused party, could reject the panel's findings. The expectation is that once a panel finding has been accepted, the offending state will change its behavior. If it doesn't, however, there are provisions for the aggrieved party to levy trade sanctions, both to compensate it for its losses and to encourage the offender to comply with the ruling. This process does not work quickly, and cases sometimes take years, but the same is true of many lawsuits in domestic courts.

A major case concerning competition between the airline firms Boeing (based in the United States) and Airbus (based in Europe) pitted the EU against the United States. The United States brought a complaint against Europe, arguing that low-interest loans and other subsidies to Airbus constituted an unfair barrier to free trade. The EU brought a case in return, claiming that U.S. tax breaks and military contracts with Boeing provided an unfair subsidy. In 2010, WTO dispute resolution panels found both sides' accusations valid, and the dispute has dragged on, with the EU bringing new charges in late 2014.

The United States is both the most common filer of complaints and the most common target of complaints by others. In late 2009, Brazil won a ruling that U.S. subsidies to cotton farmers unfairly hurt Brazilian exports. The ruling allowed Brazil to retaliate by imposing tariffs against U.S. exports proportional to the U.S. cotton subsidies. Brazil targeted not only U.S. cotton exports, the source of its complaint, but also U.S. automobiles, and threatened to target software as well in an effort to increase domestic pressure on the U.S. government to change its policies.[3] In 2015, China removed a quota on the

# THE HISTORY CONNECTION

## THE HISTORY OF GLOBALIZATION

Skeptics about globalization point out that in historical context, much of this phenomenon is not new. If globalization is viewed as a process in which the costs of transport and communication decrease and the division of labor widens geographically, then the process has been in place for centuries. "Essentially, the basic motivations that propelled humans to connect with others—the urge to profit by trading, the drive to spread religious belief, the desire to exploit new lands, and the ambition to dominate others through armed might—all had been assembled by 6000 bce to start the process we now call globalization."* From this perspective, the "global" economy has been spreading for centuries. Several examples help illustrate this perspective.

- **Migration** *Homo sapiens* originated in Africa and spent the next 50,000 years spreading out to inhabit almost the entire globe. The waves of migration that brought the Huns, Magyars, Mongols, and Goths out of the plains of Asia into Europe in the first millennium CE wrought extraordinary political, economic, and cultural changes. The history of the Western Hemisphere is, in many respects, a story of successive waves of migration from Asia, Europe, and Africa.

- **Trade** Much early interaction was driven by the desire to trade profitably, just as it is today. The Silk Road, connecting Europe to China via Central Asia, was an important commercial route from the eleventh through the fourteenth centuries. Made famous in particular by the Venetian Marco Polo (1254–1324), the Silk Road first brought Chinese noodles to Italy, where they would be called spaghetti. A primary impetus of the Age of Exploration was the desire to find a quicker, cheaper trade route from Europe to East Asia. Trade continued to grow nearly constantly up until World War I.

Some scholars, therefore, see the most recent boom in international trade not as a new development but as a return to the normal course of affairs that was interrupted by the great conflicts of the twentieth century.

- **The food economy** Genetically modified crops and shopping mall Chinese food are only the most recent in a long line of agricultural transplants with far-reaching consequences. Some argue that a key source of the industrial revolution in Europe was that labor was freed up by the importation from South America of the potato, which could provide more calories per unit of land than existing crops. The transplant of the rubber plant from Brazil to Southeast Asia made possible the automobile boom of the twentieth century (by providing rubber for tires). The importation of strains of wheat from Central Europe enabled the Great Plains of the United States and Canada (previously known as the Great American Desert) to become the world's breadbasket.

- **Speed of communication** The most far-reaching shift in communication in history may not have been the emergence of the Internet but the invention of the telegraph, which introduced nearly instant communication in the mid-nineteenth century. From that point on, the price of stocks in the New York market could be monitored around the country, leading to the rapidly moving financial markets we are familiar with today. In 1858, New York and London were connected by telegraph, spurring a celebration that nearly burned down City Hall in New York. The increase in speed of communication that occurred with the move from the hand-delivered letter to the telegraph was as dramatic as the increases later provided by the emergence of the Internet.

## Critical Thinking Questions

1. Do you agree with the argument that globalization is not really new?

2. What key factors make globalization today fundamentally different from what occurred in the past?

3. Which component of globalization (trade, migration, culture, and so on) do you see as being most important in the coming decade?

---

*Nayan Chanda, as quoted in William Grimes, "The Rise of Globalization, A Story of Human Desires," New York Times, May 30, 2007, p. B6. The quotation is from Chanda's book Bound Together: How Traders, Preachers, Adventurers and Warriors Shaped Globalization (New Haven, CT: Yale University Press, 2007).*

export of rare earth metals (essential in producing touch-screens) after the United States brought a complaint to the WTO.

## CONTEMPORARY CHALLENGES

The WTO agreement has achieved many of the major goals advanced by its supporters. Global trade has continued to grow, and nontariff barriers have come under attack. States have eagerly sought membership in the WTO, and no state has ever left the group. As of 2015, the WTO had 161 members, and many other states were seeking to join. The largest (in terms of GDP) nonmembers are Iran and Algeria.

However, a great deal of dissatisfaction remains concerning the international trading system, leading some people to question whether the agreement will continue to play an influential role in the future. A round of negotiations begun at Doha, Qatar, in 2001 remained incomplete in 2015. Agricultural protectionism has been the major stumbling block. Having given advanced industrial economies access to their markets for manufactured goods and services, developing countries are increasingly unwilling to tolerate what they see as an unequal arrangement in which North American and European governments subsidize their agricultural producers, undermining the competitiveness of developing countries' agricultural exports. Twenty-two developing states walked out of a meeting at Cancun in 2003 over the issue. A meeting at Bali, Indonesia, in 2013 appeared to put negotiations back on track, but by 2015 no agreement had been finalized.

**Diffusion of Economic and Political Power**   As the preceding discussion indicates, poorer countries are now playing a prominent role in negotiations over world trading arrangements, largely due to the diffusion of economic power. The U.S. share of global GDP has declined from nearly 50 percent when the GATT was formed in 1947 to roughly 20 percent today. Many scholars invoke hegemonic stability theory to explain the growth in free trade after World War II. In this view, barriers to increased free trade can only be overcome when a single state is powerful enough to persuade (through threats and incentives) other states to go along.[4] Since the 1980s, adherents of this view have fretted about what would happen in an era of declining U.S. power.[5] Today, the United States is still the largest economy in the world, but it now controls only a fifth of global GDP and only one vote of more than 150 in the WTO. Meanwhile, China's share of global GDP has risen to roughly 15 percent. To the extent that economic power matters, there is no doubt that it is more evenly distributed than in the past.

Critics of hegemonic stability theory point out that many of those advocating this theory happen to be Americans. From the perspective of developing countries, the diffusion of power is good in that they may now be able to force the leading economic states to make some concessions, specifically in regard to agriculture. Whether or not this situation will inhibit further collaboration remains to be seen.

**Regionalization: Free Trade Areas**   Regional trading agreements have proliferated in recent years, in part because the global liberalization process at the WTO has bogged down. The model for all such agreements is the enormously successful European Union, although most regions do not envision such extensive political integration. The North American Free Trade Agreement (NAFTA) between the United States, Canada, and Mexico, which took effect in 1994, is a significant example. Within a free trade area (FTA), there are no tariffs at all, and efforts are made to limit other barriers to trade. As a result, members of the FTA have an advantage over those outside, even if those outside are members of the WTO. In other words, barriers may be low for WTO members, but they are even lower or nonexistent for partners in an FTA.

The United States sought to build on the success of NAFTA by bringing in Latin America to form a Free Trade Area of the Americas. Those efforts stalled and were supplanted by negotiations for the Trans Pacific Partnership. In Asia, there have been proposals to expand the Asian-Pacific Economic Cooperation (APEC) group into some sort of regional FTA. However, the fact that at least two states in the region (China and Japan) are regarded as potential security threats inhibits willingness to collaborate, as does the wide range of forms of government. In the former Soviet Union, Russia has sought to build an FTA around the Commonwealth of Independent States, but the hesitation of key states (most notably Ukraine) has hampered that effort.

Supporters of free trade have mixed opinions on the virtues of regional FTAs. To some, regional trade agreements are a step in the right direction and may be a stepping-stone to increased global trade cooperation. Others see regional FTAs as fragmenting the global trading system. Some fear the rise of a series of regional trade blocs, each dominated by a large wealthy country that has privileged access to the less developed countries in that region and a strong bargaining position relative to them. This might resemble the system two centuries ago, when the leading economic powers in Europe carried on much of their trade not with each other but within their separate colonial empires.

**Competing Interest Groups**   Theoretically, the debate over the WTO, free trade, and globalization pits those who follow liberal trade theory, as described in Chapter 10, against those who support economic structuralist and realist views. Practically, the debate takes place within interest group politics, pitting those who stand to gain from freer trade against those who stand to lose. As discussed in Chapter 5, interest groups are often involved in lobbying on foreign policy, and especially on foreign economic policy. Decisions on tariff levels and FTAs can mean billions of dollars in gains or losses for different economic actors, whether they are firms, industries, workers, or even localities.

It is misleading, therefore, to think about trade politics only in terms of what national governments want, for every government is subject to competing domestic interests, pushing and pulling it in different directions. For example, a wide range of actors lobbied the governments of WTO signatories at several stages. First, as the agreement was being negotiated, they tried to get governments to insist on terms the firms found favorable. Second, once an agreement was finalized, they lobbied for or against approval, depending on whether it served their interests. Third, firms and industries lobby their governments to bring charges against other countries they see as competing unfairly. Fourth, many groups lobby for and against provisions under consideration in each round of negotiations.

Finally, decisions to admit new members are subject to considerable political pressure, particularly in the case of China (2001) and Russia (2012). Because their economies are so large, firms and industries had much to gain (in terms of markets) or to lose (in terms of competition). Moreover, some opposed granting membership because both governments are considered major violators of human rights. Interest group politics are also prominent in EU discussions about changing rules or admitting new members.

Economists have developed a general theory to explain which economic actors tend to seek protectionism and which tend to support free trade. Actors who control inputs that are plentiful locally (such as labor, land, or capital) tend to support free trade. Because their inputs are plentiful locally, they are likely to be cheap, and free trade will open markets where they can compete successfully on price. Actors who control inputs that are locally scarce tend to oppose free trade. The local scarcity of these inputs allows those who control them to charge premium prices, and competition from abroad would reduce those prices. In the United States, where capital is plentiful but cheap labor is relatively scarce, financial interests support free trade, as do manufacturers who can move production overseas. Labor and industries that cannot easily move production tend to oppose free trade. In contrast, in countries where land is scarce, such as Japan, agricultural interests oppose free trade. In much of the Third World, where labor is plentiful, labor and industries that rely on abundant labor support free trade. Although this simple rule does not explain all trade preferences, it provides a general idea about how free trade can affect different economic actors within the same country differently.

One group of actors is rarely mentioned in discussions of free trade: consumers. This group plays an insignificant role in the politics of trade, despite the fact that

Argentinian farmers protest in Buenos Aires in 2013, seeking a greater share of the retail price that consumers pay for fruit.

David Fernández/EPA/Newscom

consumers benefit massively from the lower prices that free trade brings. Because consumers are a diffuse group, they are not as well organized as "special" interests. Protectionism preserves the jobs of a relatively small number of workers (and the profits made by their companies) at the expense of an increase in cost to a vast number of consumers. Each threatened worker or firm has a huge incentive to lobby for protection, whereas each consumer has a smaller interest, even if the total damage done to consumers is great.

Free trade advocates cite statistics indicating that every job saved by protectionism costs consumers far more in lost savings. For example, protection for U.S. sugar farmers triples the price of U.S. sugar. This costs consumers $1.9 billion per year, while saving an estimated 3600 jobs—or $600,000 per job year.[6] A much more efficient policy is to remove the protection and then use taxing and social policy to compensate and retrain displaced workers.

How much harm should be done to consumers and taxpayers in order to protect workers and firms? This was the central question in debates over protecting U.S. car companies as they faced bankruptcy in early 2009. The Obama administration was concerned that the demise of U.S. car firms would cause the failure of many other firms, such as suppliers, driving unemployment up permanently. The fact that auto workers provide a historically strong Democratic voting bloc in pivotal states also likely played a role in the administration's thinking. This is the kind of challenge that comes between the theory and practice of free trade.

**Trade Policy as a Two-Level Game**  For state-level policy makers considering trade agreements, therefore, two sets of negotiations take place simultaneously, one with other countries and one with domestic constituents. A popular metaphor for this process is the two-level game, in which a solution must be found that works at both levels simultaneously.[7] This is often difficult—and sometimes impossible. Leaders cannot always find a solution that satisfies both international partners and domestic constituents. In such cases, domestic constituents nearly always win out because they will determine whether the politicians in question remain in office. In many cases, domestic interests themselves are in conflict. The cagey negotiator can try to convince trade partners that he or she cannot make further concessions because domestic actors (such as the legislature) will not permit them.

# GLOBALIZATION OF FINANCE

Compared with changes in the international trading system, changes in the international financial system have been much more far-reaching. The international financial system has experienced two revolutions in recent decades. First, in 1971, the United States single-handedly ended the system of fixed exchange rates that had prevailed since 1946. Second, in the 1980s and 1990s, governments lifted limits on capital movements, paving the way for the massive international flows of capital today. In quantitative terms, the growth in the movement of money around the world has reached astonishing levels, with nearly 5 *trillion* dollars' worth of currency traded *every day* in foreign exchange markets in 2015. It is easy for firms and individuals to buy stock in foreign countries and to sell it just as quickly. Thus, the amount of cross-border **portfolio investment**—investing by purchasing stocks rather than physical assets—has skyrocketed. These changes bring the risk of financial crises, such as the one that occurred in Asia in 1997, that can spread quickly from one country to another.

**portfolio investment**
Investments made by purchasing stocks rather than physical assets.

# THE CONNECTION TO YOU

## THE GLOBAL INDIVIDUAL

The effects of globalization are felt at the local and individual levels as well as at the international level. Global market forces can bring new factories to a town or close existing ones; they can cause employment to increase or decrease; they can bring new immigrants or cause people to go elsewhere in search of work.

Individuals, in many cases, are becoming globalized as well. One major driver is migration. People migrate for a variety of reasons. They are forced out by violent conflict, seek to escape oppressive governments, or try to reunite with family. In some poor countries, the money sent home by migrants is a major source of revenue for their families back home. Moreover, migrants to developed states often return to their countries of origin to begin businesses there.

Global air travel is cheaper and faster, and reaches more destinations. In much of the world, even small cities have airports with connections to global hubs like New York's JFK, London's Heathrow, or Dubai International. This is allowing more and more people to travel abroad for work or vacation, seeing conditions in other parts of the world, dealing with the feeling of being a foreigner, and perhaps learning a foreign language.

Nearly 3.7 million students around the world were enrolled outside their home countries in 2009. The largest sending countries are China, India, and Korea. In the United States, 270,000 university students studied abroad during the 2009–2010 academic year—which sounds like a lot, but is only 1 percent of all students enrolled in higher education. More than 56 percent of those study abroad experiences were of a short-term nature—eight weeks or less. Only 3.9 percent remained for a full academic year. The United Kingdom was the most popular destination, and Europe accounted for more than half of all trips. Despite its proximity, Latin America received only 15 percent of U.S. students.*

Many students who do not study abroad meet people from around the world on their own campuses. The United States, Canada, the United Kingdom, and Australia are major destinations for students from around the world. In Australia, which leads the world, more than 20 percent of university students are international students (compared with 15 percent in the United Kingdom, 6.5 percent in Canada, and 3.5 percent in the United States). During the 2010–2011 academic year, there were more than 700,000 international students at U.S. universities. The leading senders are, not surprisingly, the world's two most populous countries, China and India, with South Korea, Canada, and Taiwan following in that order.

Globalization is having an impact on many people far beyond universities. As more and more industries are globalized, more and more employees travel internationally as part of their jobs or work for a company headquartered abroad or as part of an international team. Thus, many have predicted that being crossculturally competent will be a major career asset in the future.

### Critical Thinking Questions

1. How does traveling abroad or making friends with individuals from other countries change one's perspective on international affairs?

2. To what extent are students you know deliberately preparing for international work by studying foreign languages or traveling overseas?

3. How much variation do you see in individuals' access to global work, travel, and study?

*Statistics in this box are from the Institute of International Education, Opendoors 2011 "Fast Facts," www.iie.org/en/Who-We-Are/News-and-Events/Press-Center/Press-Releases/2011/2011-11-14-Open-Doors-Fall-Survey-Study-Abroad; and from OECD iLibrary, "Education at a Glance 2011: Highlights," http://dx.doi.org/10.1787/eag_highlights-2011-en.

## THE MONETARY "TRILEMMA"

In deciding how to approach international monetary policy, states historically have had three goals:

- *Predictable exchange rates:* Fixed exchange rates facilitate free trade and investment by eliminating the risk that fluctuations in exchange rates will destroy anticipated profits. Stability and predictability are accomplished by fixing exchange rates.

- *Free movement of capital:* Free capital movement allows investors to invest where returns are greatest and provides poor economies access to much-needed foreign investment.

- *Autonomous monetary policy:* Governments use monetary policy to respond to changes in their domestic economies (raising and lowering interest rates to regulate growth and inflation), without regard for policy choices in other countries or international markets.

It is a fundamental rule in international finance that it is impossible to attain all three goals simultaneously. This inability to attain all three goals is sometimes referred to as a *trilemma*, because states, and groups of states, must decide which one of the goals to forsake when they devise different exchange rate mechanisms and international financial practices.[8]

It is possible, for example, for states to fix their exchange rates and to have complete capital mobility. But the only way to maintain fixed exchange rates, if currencies can move freely, is to alter domestic monetary policy according to the dictates of the international market, rather than according to domestic policy goals. As demand for currencies varies, states must raise and lower interest rates or buy and sell currency in order to maintain the fixed exchange rate. In such a system, interest rates cannot be used to control domestic economic growth and inflation, as they generally are today. Such a system existed prior to World War I and was known as the gold standard. Today, countries such as China "peg" their currencies. They do not formally dictate the currency's price, but intervene in markets, buying and selling their currency so that the market price stays near the target. China keeps the value of its currency low by selling yuan to buy U.S. dollars, which it invests in government bonds. It also uses currency controls to limit the market pressure on the exchange rate. But raising the value of one's currency requires buying it with dollars or some other international currency, and if markets are continuously pushing a currency's value down, a country can eventually run out of the dollars needed to prop it up. This can lead to a currency crisis as the value of the currency collapses, as occurred in Thailand in 1997.

Alternatively, it is possible to maintain free international flows of capital and domestic monetary autonomy if exchange rates are allowed to float. Essentially, that is the system in use today in most of the world. To do so, however, exchange rates must float, and fluctuations in exchange rates can seriously disrupt international trade and cause other problems as well.

## WHO PAYS THE COSTS OF ADJUSTMENT?

In every system, the central question is how imbalances in currency flows are addressed. What happens when, in response to imbalances in imports or differences in investment opportunities, the demand for one country's currency rises relative to others? In a floating exchange rate system with free capital flow, imbalances are corrected through changes in the currency exchange rates. Some countries will see their currencies rise or fall in

Then Greek Prime Minister Antonis Samaras and German Chancellor Angela Merkel address the press after a discussion of the European financial crisis, August 2012. The single European currency facilitated free trade and capital movement, but made it very difficult to adjust to different rates of economic growth.

value, with predictable effects on importers and exporters. In a system in which capital movement is limited, the inability to move huge sums of capital helps limit instability, but currency imbalances continue to occur as a consequence of trade, so that states must alter domestic policies and limit trade to achieve balance. In a system without domestic policy autonomy, domestic economies are forced to absorb the changes emanating from the international system. Each system puts the burdens of adjustment on different actors. Much of the politics of international finance concerns states' desire to force the **costs of adjustment** onto others.

**costs of adjustment**
Financial burdens that are imposed on a country as a result of changes in the international economic system.

## EVOLUTION OF THE INTERNATIONAL FINANCIAL SYSTEM

Since the late nineteenth century, three different international financial systems have existed, separated by two long intervening periods in which states struggled to create a new system after the previous one had collapsed.[9] These five periods are summarized in Table 11.1 on the next page.

**The Classical Gold Standard, 1870–1914**   In the system that prevailed until World War I, every major currency was valued in terms of a certain weight of gold. Because currencies were fixed to gold, exchange rates were highly stable. This stability facilitated the steady increase in trade and international investment prior to World War I. In terms of the trilemma of policy choices, the **gold standard** prioritized fixed exchange rates and the free flow of capital at the expense of domestic monetary autonomy.

The strength of this system was its stability and predictability. Because each country's currency was linked to gold, there was no capacity at all for monetary policy, apart from buying or selling gold. Most economists see the inability to expand the monetary supply as a major brake on economic growth. The gold standard functioned as well as it did, most agree, because of the leading role played by the British government and

**gold standard**
A system in which each currency represents a specific weight of gold. This facilitates stability but is highly inflexible.

**TABLE 11.1** Systems of International Financial Arrangements

| System | Goals Emphasized | Goals Sacrificed | Who Maintained the System, and How? | Who Adjusted? |
|---|---|---|---|---|
| System I: Classical Gold Standard (1870–1914) | Fixed exchange rates to facilitate trade | Domestic autonomy | Great Britain, through trade and financial dominance | States whose currencies deviated from established rates; all adjusted to Great Britain |
| Intervening Period: Interwar Era (1914–1944) | Domestic economic autonomy | Exchange rate stability, capital mobility | No one; system crashed in Great Depression | States and firms; states dominated markets |
| System II: Bretton Woods (1946–1971) | Stable exchange rates to facilitate trade; domestic autonomy (embedded liberalism) | Capital mobility | Bretton Woods institutions, especially the IMF backed by U.S., power | States whose currencies deviated from established rates; all adjusted to the United States |
| Intervening Period: Post–Bretton Woods (1971–1980s) | Maintain some exchange stability with greater domestic autonomy; increasing capital mobility | Pursuit of all goals simultaneously meant none was fully achieved | Negotiations among major trading states (G-7); maintenance depended on agreement | States sought to force each other to adjust; the United States could no longer avoid adjustment; states dominated markets |
| System III: Global Capital Mobility (1980s–) | Capital mobility | Domestic autonomy | No one; markets are expected to provide equilibrium | States and firms; markets dominate states |

British banks. Britain was willing to lend money to governments that were experiencing short-term imbalances in their payments, ensuring that small crises did not spread and become big ones.

**The Interwar Era, 1914–1944** The economic demands of World War I caused all the major countries to abandon the gold standard and instead to print large amounts of currency to finance the war effort. Moreover, the war severely weakened Britain's financial position. Both of these factors undermined the gold standard system. The solution, in the eyes of many, was for the United States, which had become the dominant financial player, to take over Britain's role in financing the world economy.

The United States, however, embraced isolationism instead. When Germany's inability to pay debts associated with World War I threatened other countries' financial systems, the United States refused to finance a new loan to avoid crisis. Moreover, citizens and governments were no longer willing to endure economic recession and depression as the price for international financial stability. Shared purpose no longer existed. The major economic powers sought to force the costs of economic adjustment onto one another. The result was financial instability, which exacerbated the Great Depression.

# THE GEOGRAPHY CONNECTION

## THE WORLD IS FLAT. OR IS IT SPIKY?

Many maps (including almost all of those in this book) use state-level statistics because these are easiest to find and to map. However, this perspective misses a great deal of variation that is evident when statistics are presented using other scales. Consider these maps, which measure different aspects of economic and scientific activity.*

### Critical Thinking Questions

1. What issues arise when you look at data aggregated by square kilometer rather than by country?

2. How does "globalization" look different from this perspective?

3. How concerned should people be about the vast differences in conditions displayed in these maps?

---

*The argument that the world is "flat" can be found in Thomas Friedman, The World Is Flat: A Brief History of the Twenty-First Century (New York: Farrar Straus and Giroux, 2005). For a competing analysis, see Pankaj Ghemawat, "Why the World Isn't Flat," Foreign Policy, No. 159 (March/April 2007), pp. 54–60.

Population

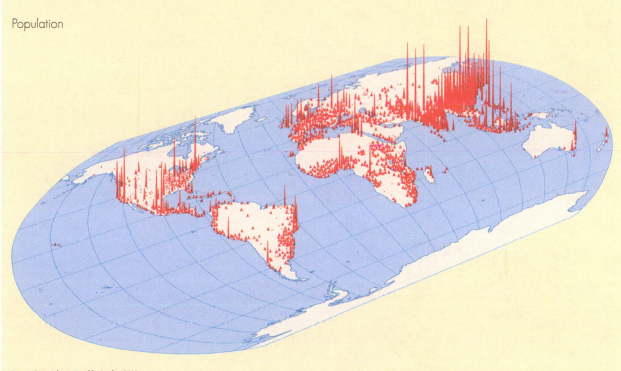

Source: From *Atlantic Monthly*, October 2005.

(continued)

Light Emissions

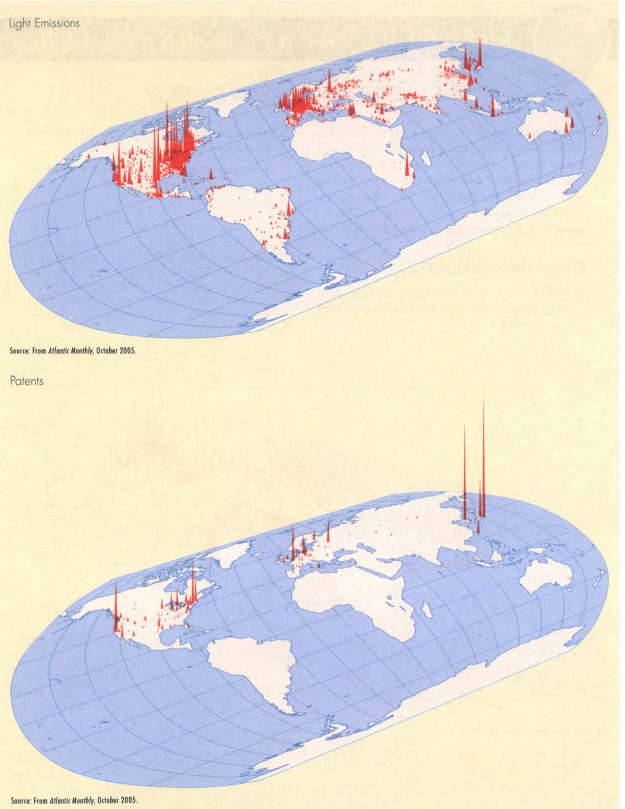

Source: From *Atlantic Monthly*, October 2005.

Patents

Source: From *Atlantic Monthly*, October 2005.

**The Bretton Woods System, 1946–1971**   Following World War II, the United States had the power and the will to lead a new international financial system. It embraced internationalism, aimed both at avoiding the mistakes that had led to World War II and at heading off competition from the Soviet Union. However, the purpose of economic policy had changed in favor of state intervention in the economy for the purposes of maintaining economic stability and guaranteeing welfare. There would be no return to the gold standard. Instead, the United States and its partners pursued embedded liberalism, a compromise between the desire to facilitate international trade and the need to give domestic governments latitude to govern their economies.

In terms of the trilemma of policy choices, the Bretton Woods system opted for fixed exchange rates and domestic monetary autonomy at the expense of the free flow of capital across borders. The system had several key components:

- The price of the U.S. dollar was fixed to gold at $35 per ounce. In some respects, this was a return to the gold standard, but there was a key difference: The United States continued to issue more dollars in order to facilitate economic expansion.

- The prices of other currencies were fixed to the U.S. dollar. This provided the stability of fixed exchange rates. It also meant that other states had to adjust to changes in the world economy (for example, some economies' growing faster than others), while the United States, as the standard setter, never had to adjust.

- All countries placed limits on the import and export of capital. Imbalances in financial flows would occur primarily as a result of trade imbalances, which limited the size of the potential problem.

The International Monetary Fund (IMF) was created to help the system overcome imbalances. Shorter-term imbalances—when a state had more currency flowing out than in—were handled with loans. IMF aid for longer-term imbalances required states running a deficit to cut imports in order to restore the currency balance. These conditions were widely resented because the austerity they required could throw a domestic economy into recession, and because all of the cost of adjustment fell onto states running a current account deficit. The virtue of the Bretton Woods system was that it found a compromise that allowed for the expansion of international trade (facilitated by stable exchange rates) while allowing an extensive degree of domestic autonomy (facilitated by limited capital movement, IMF adjustment assistance, and periodic adjustments in exchange rates). However, strains inherent in the system eventually led to its demise.

In the Bretton Woods system, adjustment to imbalances was forced largely onto states running trade and current account deficits. As long as the states in question were willing to adjust, and the amount of adjustment needed was limited, the system worked. But by the 1960s, the biggest problem in the system was the United States. U.S. spending on fighting the Cold War sent large amounts of U.S. currency flowing out of the country. The number of dollars held in foreign hands grew much faster than the supply of gold backing them. In return for the U.S. military and political role in facing off against the Soviet Union, key U.S. allies agreed to hold those dollars, rather than redeeming them and diminishing U.S. gold reserves. As this "dollar overhang" increased, it became clear that all dollars could never be redeemed at $35 per ounce of gold. Implicitly, then,

Children play with blocks made from German currency, 1923. Hyperinflation made the currency nearly worthless.

those holding dollars abroad were subsidizing the U.S. economy and foreign policy. In other words, the costs of adjustment, which were typically forced onto the deficit country, were not forced onto the United States when it was the deficit country.

In the late 1960s, three developments brought the problem to a crisis. First, the combination of the Vietnam War and the Great Society antipoverty programs increased the U.S. budget deficit substantially and pushed the current account deficit even higher. Second, as the "dollar overhang" grew, investors and governments abroad became less willing to finance it. Finally, international objections to the Vietnam War undermined U.S. moral authority, and other states saw less reason to hold dollars as "payoff" for the U.S. role in combating the Soviet Union. By the early 1970s, redemptions of dollars from abroad for U.S. gold increased, as others sought to force adjustment back onto the United States.

In 1971, U.S. President Richard Nixon announced that the United States would no longer redeem dollars for gold and that henceforth the dollar would be allowed to float against other currencies. The Bretton Woods era was over. Without the U.S. commitment to the price of the dollar in terms of gold, the fixed exchange regime was dead. Since that time, currency prices have fluctuated according to the supply and demand for each currency.

**The Post–Bretton Woods System, 1971–1980s** With no agreed-on mechanism to determine who would bear the costs of adjustment, there was a danger in the post–Bretton Woods era that each state would try to force the costs onto others and that the result would be the sort of mutually defeating policies that had existed in the 1930s. Moreover, the ability of the various states to conduct independent domestic economic policies was now threatened. One country's decisions on interest rates and monetary policy could now substantially affect exchange rates, which in turn could create negative economic effects in other countries.

# THE POLICY CONNECTION

## STIMULUS VERSUS DEBT REDUCTION: DOMESTIC POLICY AND INTERNATIONAL POLITICS

Globalization has made it increasingly difficult for states to maintain completely independent economic policies. Policy changes in one country cause economic effects that spill over into others. These connections become particularly worrisome in economic crises, when disaster can spread from one economy to the next and one state's anticrisis measure can undermine others' economies. In 2010, a dispute emerged among major Western countries concerning the relative importance of stimulating their economies out of recession and containing the growth of their debt. Economic stimulus packages, like those enacted in the United States and many other countries in 2009, are based on fiscal policy: If the government spends more than it takes in through taxes, the net effect is to inject money into the economy, helping end recession. But to spend more than it takes in, the government must borrow. In 2009, many leading industrial states (Japan, the United Kingdom, the United States) agreed that a fiscal stimulus was necessary, while Germany, historically more fiscally conservative, was less convinced. Those favoring stimulus argued that for it to work, governments needed to join together. Globalization meant that the effects of any state's stimulus would "spill" outside its borders, diluting the effects on the home economy. Thus, if only one or a few states adopted stimulus packages, the effect might be insufficient.

In 2010, however, the tension sharpened as the Greek debt crisis made two things clear. First, financial markets were beginning to doubt the ability of governments to pay back their debts. This could undermine recovery, increase borrowing costs, and lead to debt crisis, as Greece experienced. Second, such a crisis could severely damage the economies even in countries that did not overborrow, because their banks held many of the loans.

In the United States, there was a fierce debate, with President Barack Obama and many liberals worrying that insufficient economic stimulus would prolong the recession, while fiscal conservatives worried more about growing debt. In contrast to past debates, the United States also found itself under considerable international pressure to limit deficit spending. In Germany, the conservative government of Angela Merkel sided with those who saw debt as the major danger. In the United Kingdom, an election shifted power from the Labour Party to a coalition of Conservatives and Liberal Democrats, which also focused on debt and quickly adopted a massive budget cutting program. Both the United Kingdom and Germany urged the United States to bring its deficit under control.

Why did Germany and the United Kingdom care about U.S. fiscal policy? As the largest economy in the world, any crisis in the United States would have a powerful effect on almost everyone else, and especially on major trading partners like the United Kingdom and Germany. Moreover, increased borrowing by the United States was likely to drive up interest rates even if it did not lead to crisis. With a fundamental disagreement about which threat to the U.S. and global economies was greater—debt crisis or recession—it was impossible to agree on a coordinated policy.

The danger emerged that the different policies would cancel each other out. If the United Kingdom and Germany took demand out of their economies through austerity packages, it could offset U.S. efforts to increase demand in its economy. Similarly, the sacrifices that UK citizens were going to make through reduced government services might achieve less effect if U.S. borrowing created a debt problem anyway.

Globalization has brought an increased need for policy coordination, especially in times of crisis, but no way of achieving it. Economies with contradictory policy needs, and societies with contradictory policy preferences, have much less freedom to behave independently of one another.

## Critical Thinking Questions

1. Why were different governments able to reach some consensus in 2009, but not in 2010, over the merits of further economic stimulus?

2. Can new international rules or institutions facilitate greater coordination of domestic economic policies?

3. Is the case discussed here exceptional, or will this problem be inherent in a globalized economy?

As a result, the leaders of the biggest economies tried to agree on what exchange rates they would aim for and what measures they would take to achieve them. These discussions became institutionalized in the form of the Group of Seven leading economies, called the G-7. Augmented now by the G-20, the group still meets to coordinate economic policies.

The post–Bretton Woods international monetary system was a mixture of coordinated government interventions, unilateral government policies, and market forces. In terms of the trilemma of policy choices, it included partly floating exchange rates, limits on capital movements, and a moderate degree of domestic policy autonomy. Exchange rates were "partly fixed" because they were only partly controlled by markets. When exchange rates were within ranges that governments found acceptable, they were left alone. But when a particular currency was viewed as too weak or too strong, governments sometimes intervened in markets (buying and selling currencies) to alter the price.

**Global Capital Mobility**   In the 1980s and 1990s, an increasing number of states removed the restrictions on capital flows that had been part of every state's policies since World War II. These shifts in policy to allow capital to flow freely were not made as part of any international agreement. Rather, they have occurred as individual states have decided, one by one, to drop their capital controls. Why have states removed capital controls?

First, in terms of interest group politics, actors who controlled a lot of capital (investment banks and corporations hoping to invest abroad) put pressure on governments to allow freer capital movement. For states in which finance was an important business, liberalization was seen as an economic opportunity (think of the economic benefits to New York and London of being leading financial centers). The export of financial services, and of money itself, can be highly lucrative, so countries with leading financial sectors, such as the United States and Great Britain, were among the first to drop restrictions on capital movement.

Second, a new shared purpose emerged, an ideology of liberalization. The post–World War II emphasis on state intervention in economies eroded, beginning with the Thatcher government in Great Britain (1980–1990) and the Reagan administration in the United States (1981–1989). The belief that markets were better than governments at allocating economic resources gained influence and made these two governments willing to surrender control. Thus, the earliest liberalizers were motivated by a combination of ideology and economic interest. Other countries then followed in order to avoid losing investment and to participate in the growth in the global financial services industry.

Finally, for countries that sought to bring in investment to promote economic development, allowing capital mobility provided access to massive amounts of international capital. Global investors were much more willing to invest in economies where they had the freedom to move money in and out at will. For countries in Asia, this was a particularly important motivation. Opening up to global capital made it possible for developing states to bring much more money into their stock markets, providing investment that they badly needed and could not accumulate domestically.

For investors, the ability to invest in stock markets around the world was a great opportunity, allowing them to spread their risk and to invest their money wherever rates of return were highest. Developing countries that had been starved of investment in the past were now seen as offering important opportunities—to the benefit of both investors and the receiving countries. In contrast to the traditional form of overseas investment—building or buying bricks-and-mortar assets—investing in the stock market (portfolio investment) allowed foreign investors to sell their assets quickly and move the money elsewhere as economic opportunities changed.

**Toward a Post-Dollar Era?**   Even after the decline of the Bretton Woods system, the global financial system revolved around the dollar. The dollar was the largest currency in the world in total value, and it was widely viewed as the most solid because it had the power and credibility of the U.S. government and the U.S. economy behind it. Therefore, most international transactions were carried out in dollars, and many governments maintained large reserves of dollars.

In recent years, however, various factors have undermined the role of the dollar as the main currency of international commerce and as a reserve currency. The founding of the euro created another highly stable currency, backed by an economy larger than that of the United States. Many governments and firms shifted some reserves into euros to spread their risk. The steady strengthening of the euro relative to the dollar in the euro's early years provided an advantage to those holding euros and furthered the notion that the dollar was receding as the dominant currency. Concerns over U.S. government debt, which many thought implied a future devaluation of the dollar, contributed to flight from the dollar. Throughout Europe, it made increasing sense to conduct international trade in euros rather than dollars. Even though the dollar remains the dominant global currency today, that position looks less certain than in the past.

What are the alternatives to a dominant dollar? One possibility is a world of multiple major reserve currencies. The dollar might be joined by the euro and the Chinese yuan, if it were made freely convertible. An advantage might be that the issuing governments would compete to have the most stable, freely accessible currency and transparent markets and policies. A disadvantage would be that without policy coordination among the reserve currencies, changes in values could cause serious disruptions in the global economy. A different option would be to create a new global currency, managed by an international organization. It seems unlikely that there will be sufficient will (and common purpose) to establish such a common currency anytime soon, but in fact a prototype already exists. The IMF has a quasicurrency called the Special Drawing Right (SDR), which is based on a "basket" of leading currencies (dollar, euro, yen, pound). The SDR, then, is already a stable multicurrency system, but it is limited to use as an accounting mechanism within the IMF. Thus, although it seems likely that the dominant position of the dollar will erode, there is no good alternative yet available.

## THE PERILS OF FINANCIAL GLOBALIZATION

Flows of capital around the world are now so large that not even the biggest governments can control them. As long as markets work well, there is no problem. But markets do not always work well; they can sometimes spiral out of control, with dire consequences for governments, investors, and average citizens alike. Within domestic economies, governments use a large range of regulatory mechanisms to prevent the kind of economic crises that occurred at the beginning of the Great Depression and in the housing and banking sectors in 2008–2009. As bad as those crises were, governments had some tools at their disposal to minimize the damage. At the international level, no such regulatory apparatus exists. Therefore, when domestic crises become international crises, as they often do in a highly globalized economy, there are few policy levers readily available. The current wide-open international financial system has been subject to both debt crises and exchange rate crises. Currently, the ability of governments to solve these, either individually or together, is limited.

**Debt Crises**   Debt crises have repeatedly threatened the stability of individual countries and of the international financial system since the 1980s. The most significant crises, such as those that took place in Latin America in the early 1980s, in Mexico in 1994, and in Asia in 1997, have essentially similar roots. The crisis that struck the United States and Europe beginning in 2008 had slightly different sources.

Developing countries often do not have enough extra money in their economies to finance investment along with current consumption. Yet without such investment, they cannot increase their efficiency to catch up with advanced economies. So, they borrow internationally. If the investment is successful, the increased earnings will allow the borrower to pay off the debt with interest and still make a profit. At the same time, those who have excess capital are often looking for places to invest it profitably. The more excess capital there is in the system, the more desperate investors are in their search for investment targets. This factor was especially prominent in the 1970s: Increases in oil prices left Middle Eastern oil exporters with enormous supplies of capital, and they were looking for places to invest it. Much of this money was lent to Latin American economies through U.S. banks.

In the United States, and in several European countries in the past decade, the debt crisis began not primarily with government borrowing, but with debt in the housing and investment markets. In these countries, borrowing was driven not by the needs of economic development, but by a combination of factors. On the demand side, consumers incurred debt to buy goods and homes, especially given the perception that home values were certain to increase. On the supply side, loose monetary policies kept interest rates low, enticing actors to borrow. In contrast to earlier crises, the initial inability to pay came from firms and individuals, not states, but by 2010, states such as Greece were in danger of default as recession decreased tax revenues and increased spending on unemployment benefits and stimulus measures.

A **debt crisis** occurs when the debtor is no longer willing or able to make the scheduled payments on its debts (see Figure 11.4). Sometimes a debtor is able to continue payment but sees the costs of defaulting on the loans as lower than the cost of sacrificing domestic goals in order to continue making payments. If a government fears domestic unrest, it may default, causing a debt crisis. The Latin American debt crisis arose in 1982 when Mexico announced that it could no longer make payments on certain loans. Two rapid increases in oil prices in the 1970s inhibited economic growth both within Mexico and around the world, decreasing demand for Mexican imports. So while obligations to repay debts remained constant, the supply of income with which to repay them declined.

Most international loans are denominated in dollars. Borrowers borrow dollars, not their local currency, and must pay back dollars. Therefore, any debt crisis can be exacerbated by a loss in the value of the debtor's currency relative to the dollar. If that occurs, the borrower must raise even more of its own currency to make the fixed payment (in dollars) on the loan. This problem hit homeowners in Hungary especially hard in 2009–2010. Many had borrowed money in euros because interest rates were lower, but the fall in the value of the Hungarian forint meant that debt payment in forints increased as the value of the currency dropped. It took IMF intervention to stabilize the forint and head off the crisis.

There are two ways in which debt crises can fall into a spiral that makes them much harder to solve. First, uncertainty over a country's ability to repay its loans will lead

**debt crisis**

A crisis that occurs when a debtor country is no longer willing or able to make the scheduled payments on its debts.

**FIGURE 11.4** International debt crisis.

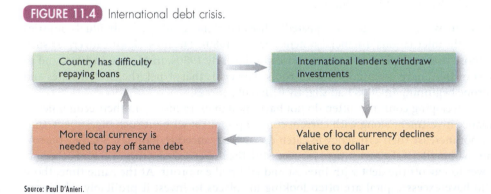

Source: Paul D'Anieri.

investors to withdraw their investments. That causes them to sell the currency of the country in question, reducing its value. It then becomes even harder to repay debts, so that more investors leave, continuing the downward spiral.

A second mechanism that exacerbates debt crises is the need to "roll over" debt—to replace old loans with new ones. If interest rates increase for any reason, the new debt will require more money to repay than the old debt. When confidence in a country's ability to repay its debts decreases, lenders require a higher interest rate to compensate for the increased risk. As old debt is rolled over into new debt at a higher interest rate, the crisis deepens.

Who is to blame for debt crises? This question arises not only internationally, but also in domestic debt crises such as the one that emerged in 2008 in the United States. Lenders sometimes use bad judgment in making loans; borrowers sometimes use bad judgment in borrowing. Sometimes loans are not bad in principle, but economic mismanagement can undercut a state's ability to repay. Sometimes changes in the global financial situation undermine even loans that were originally sensible. Typically, international lenders and organizations such as the IMF, which is often called in to help resolve crises, put the responsibility on the borrower rather than on the lender, a practice that has engendered considerable resentment.

**Monetary Crises**  Monetary crises can arise independently of debt problems, although the two problems are sometimes connected. A **monetary crisis** emerges when investors anticipate that the value of a particular currency is likely to fall. In ideal circumstances, the markets will simply adjust as people sell the currency, and a new, lower price for the currency will be established. However, in an era with a great deal of cross-border stock investment and instant movement of capital, there may be a panic, sending the value of the currency crashing downward and the entire economy with it. Most often this happens when a government is trying to hold the value of its currency at a particular price and currency traders doubt its ability to do so.

When the value of a currency drops, the value of stocks priced in that currency drops as well. This may prompt investors to sell stocks, and thus the currency. This drives the value of the currency down further, prompting even more investors to sell, and so on, until the value of both the currency and the stocks valued in that currency is greatly reduced. Because investors with other kinds of debts (for example, building loans) might be relying on their stock assets to pay off those other loans, the crash of the stock market can cause repercussions throughout the economy (as it did in the United States in 1929). This cycle is represented in Figure 11.5.

**monetary crisis**

A crisis that emerges when rapid sales of a particular currency cause its value to collapse.

**FIGURE 11.5** International monetary crisis.

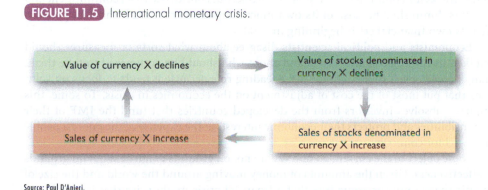

Source: Paul D'Anieri.

**Confidence and Contagion**   In both debt crises and monetary crises, a manageable downturn turns into an unmanageable panic when investors lose confidence in the ability of the markets to right themselves. The belief that the value of a currency or asset will decrease prompts people to sell, creating a self-fulfilling prophecy. Worse still, the ability of investors to move capital so quickly leads to a contagion effect—a spreading of the crisis from one country to another. When Thailand's economy began to spiral downward in 1997, investors began withdrawing their money from other Asian economies. When Greece threatened to default in 2015, confidence in Spain and Portugal decreased as a result. The central policy question of the contemporary international financial system is whether some mechanism can be developed to halt international financial crises before they turn into panics and spread around the world.

In domestic economies, there is a relatively simple solution: The government acts as a lender of last resort. A **lender of last resort** is an actor that is committed to continuing to lend money to stressed economic actors when market institutions would refuse to do so. Because investors know the government will back up banks rather than letting them fail, they maintain confidence that a crisis will not spread, and panic is averted. In the United States, for example, a government agency, the Federal Deposit Insurance Corporation (FDIC), guarantees people that they will receive their savings back even if their bank goes bankrupt. In the EU, the European Central Bank played a similar role in 2007, injecting more than $100 billion into the financial system when problems with mortgage-backed securities threatened several investment firms.[10] The U.S. government similarly headed off a collapse of the domestic banking system in 2008–2009. The EU (primarily Germany) played that role for Greece in 2010, but balked in 2015.

Previous international monetary systems had a mechanism to provide a lender of last resort. Under the classical gold standard, the Bank of England played that role. Under the Bretton Woods system, the United States and the IMF played the same role. The IMF negotiated terms and devised austerity programs that recipients were required to follow, while the United States provided most of the money to finance bailouts. That arrangement continued informally in the post–Bretton Woods system. The 1980s Latin American debt crisis and the 1994 Mexican crisis were managed largely through solutions organized and funded by the U.S. government and implemented by the IMF.

In the current system of capital mobility, it is not clear how the role of lender of last resort will be fulfilled. In the 1997 Asian financial crisis, the IMF negotiated a set of measures to stem the panic and stabilize the situation, but it was much harder than in previous crises to get member countries to contribute the money needed to fund the bailout. This history leaves much uncertainty about solving future crises. The United States still seems committed to playing some role, but confidence in its commitment and ability is diminished because of its own much weaker international financial position after its own financial crisis beginning in 2008.

Economists and political scientists disagree about what sorts of measures should be taken in future economic crises and about who should be authorized to take them. Many people object to giving the IMF a leading role because it tends to focus on solutions that put most of the cost of adjustment on the economies in crisis. To some, this emphasis absolves investors from the developed countries that fund the IMF of their responsibilities and protects their economic interests at the expense of the poorest people in the debtor countries.

Some object to the current ad hoc system not on grounds of fairness but on grounds of effectiveness. Given the amounts of money moving around the world and the size of a panic that can occur, some fear that a financial crisis might arise that is simply too

---

**lender of last resort**

An actor that is committed to continuing to lend money to stressed economic actors when market institutions would refuse to do so.

big and fast-moving for the IMF to solve "on the fly." The fear is that a global financial crash, worse than any ever seen, is now possible.[11]

# THE DEBATE OVER GLOBALIZATION

The rhetoric we hear today concerning globalization tends to be rather strident in one direction or another. Some see globalization as wholly positive, bringing the economic benefits of markets to rich and poor alike. Others see it as mostly negative.

## DOES GLOBALIZATION AID THE POOR OR THE RICH?

Those who support globalization in trade and finance argue that the biggest beneficiaries are poor workers in poor countries. This view is rooted in standard liberal economics: The market produces wealth, and interfering in the market makes everyone poorer. Liberals argue that when governments or other forces intervene in the economy, it is usually politically motivated and does not serve the interests of the poor. By opening up opportunity, especially for, unskilled labor, globalization allows the poor to participate economically in ways they could not do before. Moreover, globalization, by making poor countries wealthier, allows them to spend more money on education, health care, and other services that are essential to further reducing poverty. Liberals argue that protectionism has a poor track record of aiding economic development. A great deal of evidence supports this view. Poor countries that participate in the global economy tend to grow more quickly than those that remain isolated. Thus, supporters of globalization argue that if countries remain poor, it is because they have too little exposure to international markets, not too much. China's experience exemplifies the arguments of the liberal view of globalization. Within three decades of abandoning economic isolation, China has seen more than 600 million people lifted out of poverty and has increased spending on many public services.

Critics of globalization argue that it puts more power in the hands of those who are already the wealthiest and most powerful. By reducing barriers to the movement of capital, it allows those who control capital (wealthy corporations and investors in the developed states) to have more power over workers and governments. This, critics claim, empowers them to coerce workers to accept lower wages and governments to weaken regulation. Clearly, those in advanced economies who have their jobs "offshored" pay the costs of adjusting. But opponents of globalization do not believe that poor workers in developing countries benefit as a result. Focusing on the work conditions in "sweatshops" (see Chapter 12), they do not see workers in these places rising into the middle class. Rather, these critics believe that workers' economic desperation is being exploited: Because they are desperate to feed their families, they work long hours, with dangerous chemicals and machinery, with no ability to unionize, and for a pitiful wage that shows no promise of increasing.[12] In sum, opponents contend that the money that is saved when First World workers are fired and Third World workers are hired goes not to Third World workers but rather to First World corporations and to their executives and shareholders, who are already the wealthiest people in the world.[13]

There may be some truth in both views. Whether workers benefit or lose from globalization probably depends on how much education they have. Whether they are in the United States or Sri Lanka, workers with little education or skill tend to be relatively poorly paid. However, disagreement remains on whether globalization increases opportunity for these workers or decreases it, or whether that still depends on what country they are in.

*"I totally agree with you about capitalism, neo-colonialism, and globalization, but you really come down too hard on shopping."*

## DOES GLOBALIZATION CAUSE A REGULATORY "RACE TO THE BOTTOM"?

Critics of globalization also focus on the pressure that globalization puts on governments, and on the ways that it increases the power of global corporations at the expense of governments. Critics are particularly concerned that globalization helps corporations pressure governments to reduce protections for health, environment, workers, and so on. According to this view, countries must now compete for investment more than before, and the only way to win it is by making more and more concessions to corporations. This means not only reducing health, labor, and environmental standards, but also lowering taxes on corporate profits. Neither local workers nor small businesses have the ability to make the same threats, because they have less freedom to move elsewhere. As a result, tax burdens are likely to be shifted from corporations to citizens. For example, in order to attract a Mercedes-Benz car factory to Tuscaloosa Alabama, local governments bought and developed a site worth $30 million and then sold it to Mercedes for $100. The Alabama legislature gave the company tax abatements, as well as allowing the company to withhold 5 percent of workers' wages to pay for the factory, with the employees then receiving a tax credit from the state. The absence of strong labor unions in the region also influenced the decision. Workers in the new plant were promised minimum wages of $8–$10 per hour, compared to the prevailing wage of $30 per hour in Mercedes' German factories.[14]

Some researchers have questioned whether the race to the bottom actually occurs. Foreign investment is still highest not in poor countries with very few regulations, but in wealthy countries that are the most heavily regulated in the world.[15] Moreover, supporters of free trade argue that since governments and interest groups are so good at inventing nontariff barriers to trade disguised as labor, environmental, and health regulations, some limits on these barriers are not bad. Nonetheless, even supporters of globalization recognize that the perception of the "race to the bottom" must be dealt with if the benefits of globalization are to be maintained.

# RECONSIDER THE CASE

## EUROPE'S DEBT CRISIS

When the Greek debt crisis unfolded in 2010, it raised some very big questions for policy makers around the world on at least three levels. At the level of individual countries, policy makers had to weigh two competing threats: If governments borrowed more money to stimulate their economies, they might in the future be more likely to run into a debt crisis like that experienced by Greece. But if governments moved quickly to deal with debt by reducing spending, they might push their own fragile economies back into recession. Doing so would not only be wildly unpopular, but would reduce the tax revenues needed to make debt payments. Because the boom years had left these economies with high costs, and therefore uncompetitive, it remains unclear whether economic growth can stay ahead of the growth in debt or whether default, with all its consequences, is eventually inevitable.

At the level of supranational organizations, the EU faced something of an existential crisis. Countries cannot easily share a single currency if they do not face similar economic circumstances. Otherwise, the monetary policies appropriate for one economy might be the opposite of those needed by another. Greece's inability to use monetary policy made a bad situation worse. Although some speculated that Greece might be forced to leave the euro zone, others speculated that Germany might do so to escape the tight connection to the policies of less frugal governments. Dismantling the euro zone would be exceedingly disruptive, and many pointed in the opposite direction. To have a single currency, they argued, Europe needed a single government, able to impose a single fiscal policy, and to effectively transfer wealth when that was needed.

For the broader international community, the European crisis helped shift attention from the short-term economic crisis to the longer-term potential for debt crisis. Meeting at Toronto in June 2010, the G-20 states agreed to halve their deficits by 2013 and to stabilize their debt/GDP ratio by 2016—targets that few are likely to meet. The statement left some wiggle room in the timetable, however, recognizing that some states might need to continue to stimulate their economies through borrowing to avert a prolonged recession. U.S. President Barack Obama pointed to the problem that deficit reduction could make debt repayment harder, not easier, if it led to economic contraction: "We must recognize that our fiscal health tomorrow will rest in no small measure on our ability to create jobs today."*

## Critical Thinking Questions

1. To what extent can a single, large state provide the financial resources to head off a developing financial crisis?

2. Does the crisis of 2008 mark a fundamental turning point in the history of international political economy? If so, what are the defining characteristics of the new era?

3. Is it possible for one state to insulate itself from bad economic decisions in other states, or does globalization make that impossible?

*Quoted in "G-20 Leaders Agree to Halve Budget Deficits," New York Times, June 28, 2010, p. B7.

# POWER, PURPOSE, AND GLOBALIZATION

The purpose of globalization is constantly debated. Some see globalization as synonymous with "progress"; others see it as a threat to economic interests and traditional cultural values. Reality is far more complicated. Almost everyone sees globalization as bringing both significant opportunities (such as cheaper and better goods, more customers, or better vacations) and dangers (economic competition, disruption, and unemployment). Exactly which manifestations of globalization are welcome and which are viewed as threats varies widely according to actors' interests and values.

Coercive power is both a cause and an effect of globalization. Power is seen as a cause of globalization to the extent that particular actors—states or corporations—that anticipate benefits from globalization use their influence to promote it. Others oppose globalization—by opposing new free trade measures or lobbying for tariffs, for example—because they anticipate a negative impact on their interests. Power is also seen as an effect of globalization—some actors may find themselves empowered by the free movement of goods and service, and others may see their power reduced. Structural power is also a cause and an effect of globalization. Prevailing understandings of economics and the proper role of states and markets, which are often unquestioned, drive debates on globalization, and as globalization proceeds, structural power shifts.

The United States was for decades both a driver of globalization and a beneficiary of it, but today appears to be less enthusiastic as China, Brazil, and others compete more successfully. Thus, perceptions about the effect of globalization on national power can have a feedback effect on countries' support for globalization. For many observers, however, the question of purpose is irrelevant to globalization because states do not have the power to stop it. In this view, globalization is driven not by the policies of states, firms, and other actors, but rather by technological and economic factors beyond anyone's control.

## SUMMARY

- The globalization of trade and finance is among the most important developments in international politics today.

- After World War II, the United States and its allies created the GATT, which shifted trade agreements from a bilateral basis to a multilateral basis and replaced the principle of reciprocity with the principle of nondiscrimination.

- Members of the GATT agreed to use tariffs as their primary means of protection and to work over time to slowly decrease the level of those tariffs.

- Although successful, the GATT was plagued by states' use of nontariff barriers to trade.

- The WTO was established with an enforcement mechanism that allows states to challenge each other's laws and the WTO to assign penalties.

- Regional trading agreements have proliferated in recent years.

- Compared with changes in the international trading system, changes in the international financial system have been much more far-reaching—ending fixed exchange rates and lifting limits on capital movements. Globalization has created financial markets that dwarf the markets for goods and services.

- In deciding how to approach international monetary policy, states historically have had three goals: predictable exchange rates, free movement of capital, and autonomous monetary policy. The inability to attain all three goals simultaneously is sometimes referred to as a trilemma.

- Since the late nineteenth century, three different international financial systems have existed (the classical gold standard, the Bretton Woods system, and global capital mobility) separated by two long intervening periods.

- Financial globalization creates huge opportunities and threats. The perils of financial globalization include debt crises and monetary crises.

- A lender of last resort is an actor that is committed to continuing to lend money to stressed economic actors when market institutions would refuse to do so. It is unclear who will play the role of lender of last resort in future economic crises.

- States are still learning to cope with the effects of globalized finance, and international mechanisms to manage the dangers inherent in such an arrangement have not developed as fast as financial movements have grown.

## KEY CONCEPTS

1. Globalization
2. Bretton Woods system
3. General Agreement on Tariffs and Trade (GATT)
4. World Trade Organization (WTO)
5. Most favored nation principle, or nondiscrimination
6. Nontariff barriers to trade
7. Regionalization
8. Two-level games
9. Internationalization of finance
10. Costs of adjustment
11. Gold standard
12. Debt and monetary crises

## STUDY QUESTIONS

1. Which economic goals did the classical gold standard prioritize?
   a. Fixed exchange rates
   b. Domestic monetary autonomy
   c. The free flow of capital
   d. Both fixed exchange rates and the free flow of capital

2. Which economic goals did the Breton Woods system prioritize?
   a. Fixed exchange rates
   b. Domestic monetary autonomy
   c. Both fixed exchange rates and domestic monetary autonomy
   d. Both fixed exchange rates and the free flow of capital

3. Who has recently served as a lender of last resort during global economic crises?
   a. The European Union
   b. Brazil
   c. China and Russia
   d. The United States and the IMF

4. What type of crisis occurs when a debtor is no longer willing or able to make the scheduled payments on its debts?
   a. A debt crisis
   b. A monetary crisis
   c. A stability crisis
   d. A currency crisis

5. What was the chief innovation of the WTO?

    a. It established bilateral trade agreements.

    b. It established an enforcement mechanism to challenge laws that establish barriers to trade.

    c. It forced members to lower tariffs.

    d. It forced members to use tariffs rather than other means of protection.

6. What barriers to trade did states establish prior to Bretton Woods?

    a. Tariffs

    b. Quotas

    c. Subsidies

    d. All of the above.

7. What makes globalization today different from past expansions in international trade?

8. How was the formation of the Bretton Woods system motivated by the "lessons" of the interwar period?

9. How does the principle of nondiscrimination differ from the principle of reciprocity?

10. How did nontariff barriers undermine the GATT?

11. What is the "trilemma" of international monetary policy?

12. Why have controls on capital movements been reduced over time?

[Correct Answers: 1. D; 2. C; 3. D; 4. A; 5. B; 6. D]

## END NOTES

1. Thomas D. Lairson and David Skidmore, *International Political Economy*, 3rd ed. (Belmont, CA: Thomson Wadsworth, 2003), p. 109.

2. John G. Ruggie, "International Regimes, Transactions, and Change: Embedded Liberalism in the Postwar Economic Order," *International Organization*, Vol. 36, No. 2 (Spring 1983): 379–415.

3. "Picking a Fight," *The Economist*, March 9, 2010.

4. A seminal work in this field was Charles Kindleberger, *The World in Depression 1929–1939* (Berkeley: University of California Press, 1973).

5. Robert Keohane, *After Hegemony: Cooperation and Discord in the World Economy* (Princeton, NJ: Princeton University Press, 1984).

6. Aaron Goone, "U.S. Sugar Protectionism," *Dartmouth Business Journal* (May 11, 2011), http://dartmouthbusinessjournal.com/2011/05/u-s-sugar-protectionism/.

7. Robert Putnam, "Diplomacy and Domestic Politics: The Logic of Two-Level Games," *International Organization*, Vol. 42, No. 3 (1988): 427–460.

8. See Benjamin Cohen, *The Geography of Money* (Ithaca, NY: Cornell University Press, 1998); and Barry Eichengreen, *Globalizing Capital: A History of the International Monetary System* (Princeton, NJ: Princeton University Press, 1996).

9. On the evolution of the international monetary system, see Eichengreen, *Globalizing Capital*.

10. *International Herald Tribune*, August 14, 2007.

11. See Paul Krugman, *The Return of Depression Economics* (New York: W. W. Norton, 1999).

12. Peter S. Goodman and Philip P. Pan, "Chinese Workers Pay for Wal-Mart's Low Prices," *The Washington Post*, February 8, 2004, p. A1, www.washingtonpost.com/ac2/wp-dyn/A22507-2004Feb7?language=printer.

13. Mark Rupert and M. Scott Solomon, *Globalization and International Political Economy* (Lanham, MD: Rowman & Littlefield, 2006).

14. "Mercedes to Build Plant in Alabama," *Los Angeles Times*, September 30, 1993, articles.latimes.com/1993-09-30/business/fi-40474_1_rural-alabama.

15. Geoffrey Garrett, "Global Markets and National Politics: Collision Course or Virtuous Circle?" *International Organization*, Vol. 52, No. 4 (Autumn 1998): 787–824.

The Mangueira slum *"favela"* overlooks the Rio de Janeiro's famed Maracana Stadium prior to the start of the 2014 World Cup football (soccer) tournament in Brazil.

Mario Tama/Getty Images

# THE PROBLEM OF GLOBAL INEQUALITY

## *Learning Objectives*

**12-1** Identify different ways of defining and measuring poverty, and articulate the implications of using different definitions and measurements.

**12-2** Discuss the UN Millennium Development Goals.

**12-3** Explain the problem of late development and the challenges faced by late developers.

**12-4** Identify strategies for late development, and analyze the strengths and weaknesses of these strategies.

**12-5** Contrast competing explanations of the success of the "Asian Tigers."

**12-6** Evaluate the role of foreign aid in economic development.

# CONSIDER THE CASE

## THE RISE OF BRAZIL

In 2014, Brazil hosted the World Cup, the world's most popular sporting event, and in 2016, it will host the summer Olympic Games. As with China, which hosted the summer Olympics in 2008, these events are viewed as signs that Brazil has reached the status of one of the world's major economic and political powers. In 2012, Brazil passed the United Kingdom to become the world's sixth biggest economy. How has it risen so fast in recent years, and what are its prospects?

Brazil was colonized by Portugal beginning in 1500, and millions of African slaves were brought to the territory to exploit its natural resources. Brazil became independent from Portugal and instituted a republic in the 1820s, at the same time that most of Latin America became independent of Spain. Following a bloody war with Paraguay in the 1860s, Brazil adopted a policy of isolation, which it has abandoned only in recent decades. Like other countries in the Western Hemisphere, Brazil experienced a huge influx of migrants from the 1880s through the 1920s. In the twentieth century, Brazil alternated between democratic and authoritarian rule, with the military ruling from 1965 to 1985, when democracy was re-established. Throughout Brazilian history, economic disparity has been a major political issue. Much of the population is impoverished, but a relatively small number are extremely wealthy.

In the early 1980s, Brazil was at the center of the Latin American debt crisis. The International Monetary Fund (IMF) and the World Bank helped restructure loans to avoid default, but put strong pressure on countries in crisis to reduce domestic spending and to open their economies internationally. Partly as a result of this experience, Brazil has focused on being less reliant on energy imports and on doing more of its borrowing in the local currency, the real, to avoid a situation in which a decrease in exchange rates makes it harder to pay off dollar-denominated debt. This episode, along with a return to democracy in 1984, helped push Brazil toward a more market-oriented approach to economic development.

In 1989, the newly elected President Fernando Collor de Mello introduced a program of economic liberalization that included both domestic privatization and increased free trade. In 1994, Fernando Henrique Cardoso was elected President. Cardoso had been an enormously influential sociologist who helped develop dependency theory, a contemporary version of economic structuralism. As president, however, Cardoso continued and extended liberal economic policies.

Many companies based in Brazil have become internationally competitive. Among the firms privatized in the 1990s was the aircraft company Embraer, which makes many of the regional jets in commercial service around the world. Agriculture, traditionally a large part of the economy, has extended into processed food products, with higher value added. The boom in global commodity prices also helped Brazil, especially as major offshore oil discoveries have opened up new export possibilities. Petrobras, Brazil's state-controlled petroleum company, was the fourth largest company in the world in 2011. Despite the growth in Brazil's oil and gas sector, the government has made energy independence a major goal, and has relied heavily on hydroelectric power and on ethanol fuel made from the abundant sugarcane crop to achieve this. This has made Brazil a global leader in alternative fuels.

O verall world wealth has increased dramatically since World War II, and in the past two decades, hundreds of millions of people have escaped poverty in countries such as China, India, and Brazil. Between 2000 and 2010, the proportion of people living below the poverty line (defined as $1.25 per day at 2005 prices) fell by more than half. In 2012, the World Bank reported that despite the global economic crisis in 2008, poverty declined that year in every region of the world. In Africa, where the number of people in poverty nearly doubled between 1981 and 2008, the poverty rate seems to have peaked, and actually fell by about 5 percent in 2008.[1]

At the same time, however, poverty remains high in many places, and by some measures inequality is increasing. Most of the good news comes from China; the number of people living in poverty outside of China was stable between 1981 and 2008.[2] Moreover, increases in food prices offset some of the increase in incomes, so that adequate nutrition remains beyond the means of many people around the world.[3] And although the number of people living on less than $1.25 per day has declined, that is a fairly low standard, and billions still live on incomes that by any Western standard constitute poverty. The grinding poverty of the world's poorest countries stands in stark contrast not only to the vast wealth of the wealthy countries, but also to the progress made in many other formerly poor countries that are now closing the gap with the wealthiest (see Figure 12.1). These glaring statistics raise three fundamental questions: Why is poverty so persistent? Why has poverty declined markedly in some countries in recent decades while persisting in others? What can be done to reduce poverty and inequality? There are no simple answers, as this chapter will demonstrate.

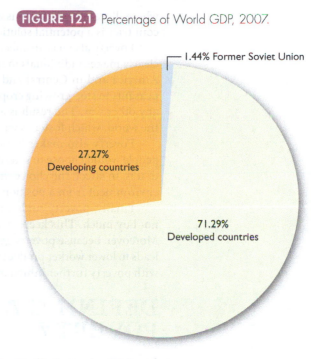

**FIGURE 12.1** Percentage of World GDP, 2007.

1.44% Former Soviet Union

27.27% Developing countries

71.29% Developed countries

Source: http://www.ers.usda.gov/Data/Macroeconomics.

# ETHICS AND SELF-INTEREST IN COMBATING POVERTY

Why should we address poverty in the world? The answer seems self-evident, but different actors—states, international organizations, NGOs, individuals—have a range of motives with regard to this issue. The way different actors think about poverty and inequality influences the priority they attach to the problem and the strategies they adopt.

Perhaps the most obvious reason to seek to reduce poverty is normative—it seems immoral or unethical not to try to do something. Nearly every religious credo places considerable value on the willingness of the wealthy to aid the poor. On a less doctrinal level, nearly everybody who sees pictures of starving children with bloated bellies feels that something ought to be done to help. Professional ethicists also provide detailed philosophical arguments showing that the wealthy have an ethical duty to help alleviate poverty.[4]

Self-interest also motivates efforts to stem poverty. Poverty has global effects that the governments of rich countries perceive as an interest in fighting. First, poverty is viewed as an underlying factor in a broad range of political problems that affect wealthy countries. Despite considerable doubt about any direct link between poverty and terrorism, it is still widely believed that reducing poverty would decrease the supply of recruits to terrorist groups and would reduce the willingness of societies to support or tolerate terrorism. More broadly, the hostility toward the West that seems to grip some societies is linked at least in part to resentment over gaps in wealth and might be moderated by economic development.

Second, poverty is seen as a source of a wide range of problems that spill over from poor to rich countries, including immigration, crime, and health threats. Much migration, historically and today, has been driven by the desire of immigrants to escape poverty and find the opportunity to get ahead economically. In North America and Western Europe, where illegal immigration is a major policy problem, reducing poverty in the "sending" countries is a potential solution.

Poverty also has an effect on the level of transnational crime. Economic desperation clearly makes individuals more willing to break the law to get by. For example, in South America and in Central and South Asia, it is very difficult to convince impoverished peasants to stop growing crops for drug production when they cannot feed their families any other way. The result is a ready supply of drugs for customers in wealthier parts in the world, which fosters social problems there.

Poverty also makes it much harder to combat environmental problems.[5] Very few people would choose to starve to save an acre of rainforest or an endangered species, but that is, in effect, the choice that many people face every day. It is much easier to save the environment from a position of wealth.

Finally, poverty undermines economic growth in rich countries. Poor people do not buy much. This keeps overall consumer demand lower than it otherwise might be. Moreover, because poverty generally prevents people from becoming highly educated, it leads to lower worker productivity. The health problems and political instability that come with poverty further inhibit overall productivity. In sum, poverty is bad for the economy.

# DEFINING AND MEASURING POVERTY

In response to very simple questions, such as whether poverty or inequality is increasing or decreasing, statistics on global poverty paint a complex and sometimes contradictory picture. To make sense of the barrage of statistics, it is necessary to understand differences in what is being measured.

## POVERTY VERSUS INEQUALITY

**poverty**

The lack of sufficient income, often accompanied by insufficient nutrition, housing, and other necessities. Poverty can be defined in absolute terms as "income poverty" or in relative terms, with a focus on the range of choices open to individuals.

Traditionally, **poverty** was defined in absolute terms, as a condition characterized by comparatively low income, a definition referred to as "income poverty." However, many economists, such as the Nobel Prize–winning poverty scholar Amartya Sen, reject that definition in favor of one that focuses on relative capabilities—on the range of choices open to an individual.[6] Thus, the UN Commission on Human Rights defines poverty as "a human condition characterized by the sustained or chronic deprivation of the resources, capabilities, choices, security and power necessary for the enjoyment of an adequate standard of living and other civil, cultural, economic, political and social rights."[7]

In this view, poverty is defined in relative terms. However, poverty is often measured in *absolute* terms, such as income, in part because such data are more readily available. In contrast to poverty, *inequality* is inherently comparative; in measuring inequality, the question becomes, "How much wealth or income does one person have compared to someone else?" It is very possible that a person's income is growing, but more slowly than that of others. As a result, income is increasing but so is inequality. Does this mean poverty is increasing or decreasing? Questions like these make it essential to be clear about definitions.

When examining individual welfare, analysts and policy makers are often concerned with absolute poverty: Do individuals have enough income to avoid malnutrition, to get basic health care, housing, and education? Politics, however, is also deeply concerned with issues of equality (both within and between countries). In many discussions, therefore, simply preventing people from starving or freezing to death is rarely considered the goal of economic policies. Reducing inequality in the population and keeping people moving upward economically are also important goals.

# MEASURES AND STATISTICS

Several different methods of measuring poverty and inequality are in widespread use.

- *Average income:* **Per capita GDP** refers to the *average* income of the people in a country. It is calculated by dividing the overall annual income of the country by the population. It is probably the most widely used statistic because it is among the easiest to determine. However, it is also one of the most misleading, especially in societies where there is considerable inequality. In such a society, for every millionaire whose income is far above the average, there must be thousands of others whose income is far below the average. Thus, to the extent that a country has a small number of wealthy people who make a disproportionate share of income, per capita GDP tends to underestimate poverty.

- *Average income adjusted for cost of living:* One problem with traditional GDP figures is that they do not take into account that goods cost different amounts in different countries. Thus, it is difficult to imagine how anyone survives in a country with a per capita GDP of $500. However, $500 goes further in many poor countries than it does in rich countries. Calculating GDP at **purchasing power parity (PPP)** takes this difference into account by figuring in the relative cost of goods. The difference can be significant: In 2014, for example, China's per capita GDP was measured at $7,380 using normal methods, but $13,130 using the PPP method.[8] Purchasing power parity is widely considered a better statistic by economists but is less frequently used because calculating it requires a great deal of data on comparative prices.

- *Poverty level:* The poverty level establishes an income standard below which a person is said to be in poverty and then counts the number of people below the "poverty line." The World Bank uses a global standard of $1.25 per day in 2005 dollars, measured at PPP. Many governments use a much higher number. By the World Bank standard, for example, almost no one in the United States would be in poverty. When China readjusted the figure it uses domestically to bring it closer to the World Bank standard, the number of people said to be in poverty there increased by 100 million.

- *Basic human needs approaches:* Some measurements have tried to get away from reliance on income figures and to focus on what actually matters—people's living conditions. This change in measurement approach accompanies shifts to policies that aim at providing for these basic human needs. One widely used measure is the **Human Development Index (HDI)**. Produced by the United Nations Development Programme, the HDI supplements calculations of per capita GDP (at purchasing power parity) with measures of life expectancy, literacy rates, and average years of schooling.

- *Inequality:* Some analysts focus on the question of inequality within a society. They often use a statistic known as the **Gini coefficient**, which compares the incomes of the top and bottom fractions of society. The coefficient ranges from 0 to 1, with 1 representing a situation in which one person has all the income and everyone else has none, and 0 representing a situation in which everyone has equal income (see Table 12.1).

- *Gender equality:* The **Gender Development Index**, published by the United Nations Development Programme, measures the economic equality of men and women. It is similar to the Gini coefficient, but it compares men and women rather than the poorest and richest. High-ranking (most equal) countries include Norway, Iceland, Sweden, Australia, and the United States (at .94). Low-ranking countries include most of the countries of sub-Saharan Africa, such as Niger (.28), Burkina Faso (.32), Mali (.33), and Burundi (.33). Women are especially disadvantaged in countries where poverty is harshest.

**Per capita GDP**

The average income of the people in a country.

**purchasing power parity (PPP)**

A measure used to calculate GDP that takes into account that goods cost different amounts in different countries.

**Human Development Index (HDI)**

A measure of poverty produced by the United Nations Development Programme that supplements per capita GDP (at purchasing power parity) with measures of life expectancy, literacy rates, and average years of schooling.

**Gini coefficient**

A statistic developed by Italian statistician Corrado Gini to compare the incomes of the top and bottom fractions of a society.

**Gender Development Index**

A measure, published by the UN, of the economic equality of men and women.

**TABLE 12.1** Gini Coefficients of Selected Countries (Most Recent Available)

| Highest (Most Inequality) | Lowest (Least Inequality) | Selected Other Countries |
| --- | --- | --- |
| Seychelles, 0.657 | Slovenia, 0.248 | China, 0.420 |
| Comoros, 0.643 | Ukraine, 0.248 | Mexico, 0.480 |
| South Africa, 0.631 | Sweden, 0.260 | United States, 0.408 |
| Namibia, 0.613 | Czech Republic, 0.263 | Russia, 0.396 |
| Botswana, 0.604 | Belarus, 0.264 | India, 0.339 |
| Haiti, 0.592 | Slovak Republic, 0.265 | United Kingdom, 0.380 |
| Zambia, 0.574 | Denmark, 0.268 | Australia, 0.340 |
| Honduras, 0.574 | Norway, 0.268 | Canada, 0.336 |

Source: https://www.quandl.com/collections/demography/gini-index-by-country.

# THE CONNECTION TO YOU

## FAIR TRADE AND POVERTY REDUCTION

States and international organizations are not the only actors leading development efforts. NGOs and transnational advocacy networks play a role as well. One example is the fair trade movement, which seeks to engage people in wealthy countries in ensuring that workers in poor countries are paid a fair wage for their role in producing goods. The goal is to combat the inequities that economic structuralists see as inherent in trade between wealthy and poor.

The idea of the movement is to identify which products are produced under fair trade guidelines and to encourage consumers to buy these products, even if they are more expensive. Fairtrade International, based in Bonn, Germany, certifies that products are produced in a way that "provides [producers] with a better deal and improved terms of trade. This allows them the opportunity to improve their lives and plan for their future. Fairtrade offers consumers a powerful way to reduce poverty through their everyday shopping."* Assuming that the market is not accomplishing this on its own, the effect of fair trade is to shift some of the value added in producing a good from firms and their owners to workers. To the extent that increased payment to producers is passed on to consumers, the effect is less on the firms than on the consumers.

The fair trade movement is especially prominent in the coffee industry, one of the industries in which the plight of workers in Latin America was originally brought to the attention of consumers in the First World. Many companies seek to gain the benefits of fair trade without participating in the formal Fairtrade system. Starbucks, for example, devotes considerable attention on its website to discussing "responsibly grown coffee." It works with Conservation International, an NGO based in Virginia. Similarly, advocates for Fairtrade chocolate point to reports that non-Fairtrade chocolate is sometimes produced through "child slavery."[†]

*(Continued)*

Picking coffee in Costa Rica. To what extent can international trade be modified to be of greater benefit to the poorest people in the supply chain?

Some economists, however, question the necessity and effectiveness of the fair trade movement. From a free market perspective, interference in the natural pricing mechanism of the market can only lead to inefficiency. From this perspective, producers whose product's price is artificially increased by fair trade practices are likely to see demand for their products decrease.

Skeptics have also seen fair trade as nothing more than a cynical marketing ploy by corporations eager to get consumers to pay more for their product. Consumers often pay substantially higher prices for "fair trade" products, with the understanding that the increased cost is going to poor producers. Skeptics question how much of this higher price actually goes to workers and small farmers. One study that traced the relationship between coffee produced in Latin America and consumed in Finland found that farmers and workers did benefit, especially when the market price was very low, but that most of the extra price paid by consumers stayed in the consuming country (in the form of increased profits for roasters, wholesalers, and retailers). The fees that organizations such as Fairtrade charge firms to carry their certification also absorbs some of the increased price.[‡]

## Critical Thinking Questions

1. How important is the notion of "fairness" in the purchase decisions that you and other people you know make?

2. What alternatives to helping producers exist besides "ethical consumption" and reliance on the market?

3. If we are concerned with the wages and working conditions of those who produce chocolate and coffee, what is the most effective way to help?

---

[‡]*Joni Valkila, Pertti Haaparanta, and Niina Niemi, "Empower Coffee Traders? The Coffee Value Chain from Nicaraguan Fair Trade Farmers to Finnish Consumers," Journal of Business Ethics, Vol. 97 (December 2010): 257–270.*

[*]*Fairtrade International: "What Is Fairtrade?" www.fairtrade.net/what_is_fairtrade.html.*

[†]*Fairtrade USA, "Products: Cocoa," www.fairtradeusa.org/products-partners/ cocoa.*

Given all these different ways of measuring poverty and inequality and the trends in the world today, it is possible to reach very different conclusions about the overall state of affairs.

- Many countries in Asia and in Central Europe that were formerly poor are now reducing the gap with the wealthiest countries. These countries provide evidence that both overall poverty and inequality are decreasing.

- Another group of countries, mostly in Africa, have made much less progress, and in some cases are worse off than they were in 1980, even in absolute terms. This group of countries suggests that there has been no improvement in the worst cases of poverty and that overall inequality (defined as the gap between the richest and poorest) has increased.

- Between countries, inequality is decreasing, as developing economies are growing faster than developed economies.

- Within countries, gaps between the wealthiest and the poorest are generally growing, after a century in which they tended to narrow.

- There are major gender gaps in wealth, especially in the poorest countries. Many economists now believe that the economically disadvantaged status of women harms not only the women but also the overall economy.

## THE UN MILLENNIUM DEVELOPMENT GOALS

**UN Millennium Develop-
ment Goals**

A set of goals and accompanying targets set by the UN, aimed at addressing poverty and inequality.

In 2000, the United Nations established the **UN Millennium Development Goals**, a set of goals with accompanying targets to achieve by 2015. One aim of establishing these goals was to create a greater sense of urgency and a greater claim on resources. In other words, one goal was to get wealthy states to acknowledge that addressing poverty and inequality is important for development. The specific targets were intended to provide some concrete standard against which to measure change in the coming years. Consider a few examples.

- Goal 1: Eradicate Poverty and Extreme Hunger
  - Target 1. "Halve, between 1990 and 2015, the proportion of people whose income is less than $1 a day."
  - Target 2. "Reduce by half the proportion of people who suffer from hunger."
- Goal 8: Develop a Global Partnership for Development
  - Target 2. "Develop further an open trading and financial system that is rule-based, predictable, and nondiscriminatory and includes a commitment to good governance, development, and poverty reduction—nationally and internationally."
  - Target 5. "In cooperation with the private sector, make available the benefits of new technologies—especially information and communications technologies."[9]

Some targets are more easily measured than others. Progress on daily income levels can be assessed by statistical analysis, as shown in Figure 12.2, but it is much harder to determine whether the international trading system has been reordered according to the stated goals. Still, there have been important successes. As noted above, the headline goal of halving the number of people living in poverty appears to have been met. Similarly, the goal of halving the number of people without access to safe drinking water has also been met. Other targets have not been met, even if there has been some improvement. For example, 800 million people still live in poverty (defined as living on less than $1.25 per day); 160 million children under the age of five have stunted growth due to malnutrition; very little progress has been made on environmental threats.[10] Perhaps this should not be surprising; after all inequality has been centuries in the making. Whether the targets are met is only part of the point. The targets were also intended to raise expectations and to solidify the commitment of wealthy states to address global poverty. In 2015, as the

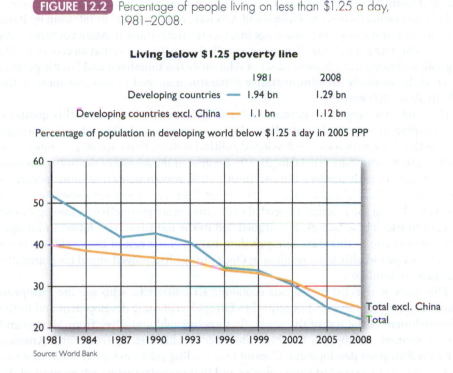

**FIGURE 12.2** Percentage of people living on less than $1.25 a day, 1981–2008.

**Living below $1.25 poverty line**

| | 1981 | 2008 |
|---|---|---|
| Developing countries | 1.94 bn | 1.29 bn |
| Developing countries excl. China | 1.1 bn | 1.12 bn |

Percentage of population in developing world below $1.25 a day in 2005 PPP

Total excl. China
Total

Source: World Bank

Source: http://www.bbc.co.uk/news/magazine-17312819; data from World Bank, http://data.worldbank.org/topic/poverty.

deadline for the original Millennium Development Goals passed, an effort was under way to develop a new list, which ballooned from the original eight goals to seventeen goals and 169 subgoals.[11]

# THE HISTORICAL ROOTS OF INEQUALITY

Global poverty and inequality are not recent developments. Rather, they have emerged over centuries. In their search for solutions, different schools of thought place different emphasis on the significance of poverty's historical roots. Economic structuralists tend to argue that inequality was produced by colonialism and will persist unless specific steps are taken to reverse the effects of colonization. Many others believe that, whatever the roots of poverty, the solutions lie simply in the adoption of sound economic policies today.

Economic inequality has not always been as pronounced as it is today. At different points in history, civilizations around the world flourished and outperformed other regions. The fantastic tombs of the Egyptian pharaohs were built at a time when Europe and North America had rather primitive societies. The Muslim world achieved great advances in mathematics while Europe was mired in the Dark Ages. Until the middle of the last millennium, there was a relatively low level of inequality across states.

In 1750, the countries that are today considered the developing world produced 73 percent of global manufacturing output, while the United States and Europe together produced only 23.3 percent. By 1900, the figures were practically reversed: The United

States and Europe produced 85.6 percent and the developing countries only 11 percent.[12] Similarly, per capita incomes in Europe and Asia were roughly equal in 1800, but by 1900, the wealthier European states had average incomes ten times those in Asian countries.[13] As Herman Schwartz put it, "One of the great peculiarities of history is that an economically marginal, technologically backward set of religiously fractionalized and fanatic peoples 'governed' by virtually no administrative apparatus managed to conquer most of the world in about 300 years."[14]

How did this happen? Generations of scholars have tried to answer this question. Several explanations, not all mutually exclusive, have emerged. One school of thought contends that European societies developed political systems that encouraged innovation and investment, which are crucial to growth. Because of the advent of the sovereign state and capitalism in early modern Europe, in this view, governments had some incentives to let commerce flourish rather than controlling it. Moreover, the development of capital markets facilitated the investment needed to discover more productive technologies and put them to use. These factors, it is argued, led to the industrial revolution in Europe, and not elsewhere. In this view, Europe's domination of the rest of the world was not a cause of Europe's wealth, but a result of it: Once Europe had moved ahead economically, it was easy to dominate.

This view is rejected by various economic structuralists, who see the European colonial conquest of the world as central to Europe's economic development and to the impoverishment of the rest of the world. By shipping gold and silver from Mexico and Peru, for example, Europeans forcibly transferred wealth directly from Latin America to finance European development. Control over trading relationships ensured that raw materials would be extracted from colonies and that manufacturing, where most of the money was made, would be carried out in Europe. The U.S. colonies broke out of this relationship through the American Revolution, but by the time most other colonies gained their independence, they were in a position of poverty and political weakness relative to Europe. In other words, decolonization provided political independence but not economic independence.

There are other views as well, but these two broad perspectives underline the key debate today. Did Europeans discover the secrets of wealth generation and surpass other countries, or did Europeans conquer and exploit others to achieve development at the expense of the underdevelopment of their colonies? The answers to these questions are linked not only to notions of responsibility for global poverty but also to proposed solutions. Those who believe that Europeans simply discovered the best economic system tend to believe that the key to development today is for others to develop the same kinds of systems—democratic and market-oriented—that prevail in the developed economies. Those who see development and underdevelopment as essentially linked tend to believe that some restructuring of economic relations between rich and poor is required.

## THE PROBLEM OF LATE DEVELOPMENT

Even if Europe got ahead of the rest of the world simply by developing better economic and political institutions, it does not necessarily follow that other states can follow the same path. The **problem of late development** is that those states that are developing later have to contend with something that the first developers did not: economic competition from more advanced states.[15]

Early developers enjoy what economists call **first-mover advantages**, three of which are especially relevant.

**problem of late development**

The economic challenge faced by developing states because of economic competition from more advanced states.

**first-mover advantages**

Advantages enjoyed by firms or countries that first enter a new industry, including advantages gained from economies of scale, network effects, and access to investment funds.

# THE HISTORY CONNECTION

## THE OPIUM WARS

In the early nineteenth century, British merchants were buying increasing amounts of goods (much of it tea) in China for resale in Britain. To achieve a balance of trade, the British hoped to sell goods in China as well. Then, as today, China was seen as a potentially lucrative market. (There were more than 400 million people in China in the mid-nineteenth century.)

Although many British goods did not sell well in China, the British did succeed in selling opium. The British produced opium in their colony in India, and its sale in China became an increasingly important source of revenue. The Chinese sought to limit the trade in part because of the negative influence on their balance of trade and in part because of the social havoc created by widespread drug addiction. By 1839, Britain was selling more than 4.5 million pounds of opium extract in China.

In 1840, the authorities in the city of Guangzhou (formerly Canton) seized and destroyed British opium shipments. In response, the British Navy attacked Guangzhou and several other cities. British military superiority was decisive, and in 1842, the Chinese were compelled to sign the treaty of Nanjing, which handed control of Hong Kong to Britain (which controlled it until 1997) and opened Guangzhou and other port cities to unlimited British imports of opium and other goods. Other powers such as France and the United States were then able to force identical concessions from China. The Chinese again sought to end the opium trade in 1856, and a second opium war led to another Chinese defeat and to further concessions to European states.

The great care China has taken in opening itself to trade in recent years and the resentment that sometimes seems to characterize Chinese attitudes toward the West have their roots in the humiliation China suffered in the Opium Wars.[*]

## Critical Thinking Questions

1. To what extent is force used today to promote international trade?

2. How might memories of the colonial era lead to different perspectives on free trade in countries that were colonized and in colonizing countries?

---

[*]See Timothy Brook and Bob Tadashi Wakabayashi, eds., Opium Regimes: China, Britain, and Japan, 1839–1952 (Berkeley: University of California Press, 2000).

---

- *Economies of scale:* In almost every industry, goods and services can be produced more cheaply when they are produced in bulk. Those who enter an industry first can be first to produce a good on a large scale. Later developers have to start small, just as the first developers did. Producing on a smaller scale and therefore at a higher cost, they struggle to compete with the early developers.

- *Network effects:* When a particular industry begins to succeed in a certain location, other firms related to that business tend to locate in the same area to reduce costs. Having related firms nearby gives established businesses two advantages over new entrants. First, transportation costs are decreased. Second, the concentration of many people and firms in a particular area leads to greater innovation, by existing firms and new ones. Detroit (in automobiles) and Hollywood and Bombay (in film) are prominent examples. More recently, the location of a few early firms in the area around Palo Alto, California, led that region, known as Silicon Valley, to dominate the global market for computers and software. Many other cities around the world have sought to emulate Silicon Valley's success, but building a second such center is inherently difficult because of competition from the first. Aspiring entrepreneurs from around the world often head to Silicon Valley rather than try to replicate its advantages where they are.

- *Investment funds:* In both direct and indirect ways, investment is crucial to economic development. Directly, the ability of firms to invest in new technology or to build more efficient plants will determine their success. Indirectly, those societies that invest in public goods such as education, infrastructure, and efficient administration will provide a more favorable environment for business. But where do the funds for such investment come from? They come from the profits of earlier economic activity. Therefore, those who succeed early on will have more money to invest and hence will be more likely to succeed later on.

Access to investment funds may be more available to late developers today than in past decades, because globalization of financial markets (see Chapter 11) has made it much easier for profits earned in one country to be invested in another country. Therefore, investment capital is increasingly available to developing countries that can provide promising opportunities. However, although foreign direct investment in developing countries has increased, it tends to focus on a few of the most promising countries and to ignore the neediest.

## DECLINING TERMS OF TRADE

**declining terms of trade**

Conditions of international trade that force countries that primarily produce raw materials to export ever-increasing amounts of raw materials to earn the revenue needed to buy the manufactured goods they require.

A problem related to late development is **declining terms of trade**. The terms of trade refer to the relative prices of the goods a country imports and exports. Many developing countries have relied on exports of commodities, including agricultural products, fuels, and minerals. However, as a result of technological advances, raw materials (especially agricultural products) tend to take up an ever-smaller portion of the cost of manufactured goods. Raw materials were the costliest portion of key nineteenth-century manufactured goods such as locomotives. Today, however, the raw materials in a computer or a cell phone make up only a tiny part of the overall cost. Some lucrative businesses, such as software, insurance, and banking, involve no raw materials at all. For states whose economies rely primarily on exports of raw materials (including agricultural products), this fact of modern life creates a losing battle. They must export ever-increasing amounts of raw materials to earn the revenue needed to buy the manufactured goods and the services they require. In the first decade of this century, commodities, and oil in particular, increased in price, creating economic booms in exporting states, but recently they have fallen back in price, with negative consequences for the producing countries. Moreover, the overall historical trend is downward. Because colonial policies often forced colonies to abandon manufacturing and concentrate on raw materials production, many poor countries came to rely primarily on raw materials exports.

To avoid declining terms of trade, countries (as well as firms) strive to move from exporting raw materials and goods produced by unskilled labor to exporting manufactured goods and goods created by skilled labor, for which profit margins are highest. This transition is sometimes difficult. For example, whereas businesses in the United States and Europe now have access to cloud computing through ultra-fast Internet connections, aspiring competitors in Africa are still hoping to get reliable electricity twenty-four hours per day to keep their computers operating. If the Internet is the key to the future, then the rich look poised to extend their lead (see Table 12.2).

## HISTORICAL STRATEGIES FOR OVERCOMING LATE DEVELOPMENT

Ever since Britain began industrializing in the eighteenth century, those states that have followed have been seeking strategies to overcome late development. Important successes in the nineteenth century were the United States and Germany. In the twentieth century, Japan and the "Asian Tigers" managed to achieve development. Today, Brazil and China are among those on the move. Are there lessons to be learned from these cases that can help those that are still struggling?

The United States' strategy toward competing with Britain was developed in Alexander Hamilton's 1791 "Report on Manufactures," in which Hamilton advocated protectionism against imports as a means to development. By creating steep barriers to imports from other countries, the United States gave its firms the opportunity to develop without competition from established firms in other countries. The United States also had at least two advantages that others could not easily match. The first was an enormous amount of cheap capital in the form of land that was taken from Native Americans. The second was a close historical connection with Britain, which provided much of the investment that financed the growth of U.S. industry, and of railroads in particular.

Like the United States, Germany used protectionism to help protect its "infant industries." Unlike the United States, Germany did not rely primarily on private capital markets but rather used taxation to accumulate capital, which it then invested in the economy. Germany's efforts were bolstered by a first-rate education system focused on science and technology, which directly contributed to industrialization. Japan also combined protectionism against imports with government-driven accumulation of capital for investment. After World War II, the Japanese government identified key economic sectors for investment, such as electronics, which Japan came to dominate in the late twentieth century.

These three success stories all relied heavily on protectionism in the early stages; the countries opened up markets to international competition only after their firms could compete successfully against others. The later cases, including Germany and Japan, also relied heavily on state direction of the economy. This model, therefore, became the dominant model in the decades after World War II. By the 1990s, however, it was seen as a failure and was largely abandoned. The policies that succeeded for the "late developers" may not succeed for the "late, late developers." The debate over development strategies therefore continues.

| TABLE 12.2 | **Internet Users:** Percentage of Population, 2013 | |
|---|---|---|
| **Highest** | **Lowest** | **Other Countries of Interest** |
| Iceland, 96.5 | Eritrea, 0.9 | Canada, 85.8 |
| Bermuda, 95.3 | Timor-Leste, 1.1 | Germany, 84.0 |
| Norway, 95.1 | Myanmar, 1.2 | United States, 84.2 |
| Sweden, 94.8 | Burundi, 1.3 | Brazil, 51.6 |
| Denmark, 94.6 | Somalia, 1.5 | China, 45.8 |

Source: http://data.worldbank.org/indicator/IT.NET.USER.P2.

# STRATEGIES FOR DEVELOPMENT TODAY

Different development strategies are linked to the different interpretations of the historical roots of inequality and to broader views of international political economy and economic theory.[16] Realists and economic structuralists tend to believe that Europe (especially Britain) developed at the expense of its colonies, and those who hold this view are more skeptical of free trade as a solution. They see the keys to Germany's and Japan's success in protectionism and in the role of the state. Liberals tend to see U.S., German, and Japanese success resulting from their focus on exports and embrace of free markets.

Views on development today are also conditioned by the lessons learned from the successes and failures of recent decades. In the second half of the twentieth century, three broad strategies of development dominated: import substitution (which predominated in Latin America, India, and parts of Africa), state socialism (which dominated the Soviet bloc in eastern Europe but was tried on other continents as well), and export-led growth (which predominated in East Asia). Of the three, only export-led growth retains a wide degree of credibility today, simply because the other strategies did not succeed. However, it has been difficult to figure out exactly *how* export-led growth succeeded and whether it can be replicated for "late, late, late developers."

## IMPORT SUBSTITUTION

**import substitution**

The strategy of producing domestically those goods that a country has been importing.

The term **import substitution** refers to the strategy of producing domestically those goods that a country has been importing. It is based on the model that succeeded for the first round of late developers, including the United States, Germany, and Japan (although it also appealed to followers of Marx). This model was adopted widely in Latin America during and after World War II, as well as in India. In many countries, the strategy was aimed at breaking disadvantageous relationships with former colonial powers.

The central strategy was to shift from the production of raw materials to manufactured goods. Initially, this would be done by replacing goods that were being imported from developed countries with substitutes produced domestically. Because these goods were already being consumed in the country, the market was established. By limiting imports, domestic producers could capture these markets. The hope was that their technology would catch up with international producers and that over time barriers to trade could be lowered. This was known as "infant industry" protection. A second perceived advantage of import substitution was an improvement in the balance of payments. By producing goods domestically that were formerly imported, states could import more technology without creating a current account deficit.

Despite this model's success in earlier cases, it did not fare well in the late twentieth century for several reasons. First, the timing was unfortunate. Just as these countries shifted out of agricultural production into manufacturing, a substantial increase in global agricultural prices in the 1970s put food importers at a disadvantage. In addition, a dramatic increase in world oil prices penalized countries where industrialization was based on cheap energy.

Second, despite protection from international markets, domestic production in most import substitution countries did not become competitive in international markets. In the small consumer markets of a relatively poor country, production of important goods (such as automobiles) could never reach the economies of scale needed to make them competitive with those produced for much larger domestic markets or for international markets.

Third, reducing competition from foreign firms reduced the incentives for domestic firms to innovate and become more efficient. Instead of preparing firms for the international market, protection allowed them to remain inefficient. Poor-quality or obsolete goods might succeed in a protected domestic market, but they could not compete internationally.

Fourth, because protected firms became powerful politically, politicians were hesitant to reduce their protection. As a result, protection from competition tended to become permanent instead of temporary. In many cases, protectionism became a source of cronyism and corruption, enriching elites at the expense of economic development. For example, by maintaining protection against a particular import, a corrupt politician could provide an opportunity for a local business controlled by supporters or relatives. Or the politician could build the basis for a lucrative smuggling enterprise.

As time went on, these less efficient producers did not become more ready for the global market. Instead, protectionism allowed them to remain less efficient and led to higher prices domestically than in the world market. This took money out of consumers' hands, which, if saved, might have yielded more funds for investment.

Import substitution: When India started making automobiles, it based the Hindustan Ambassador on the 1950s British Morris Oxford model, which was already sold in India. Although the Morris Oxford was phased out in the 1960s, manufacture of the Ambassador continued until 2014.

## STATE SOCIALISM

**State socialism**, an alternative strategy for development, emerged with the establishment of the Soviet Union in 1917 and spread after World War II to eastern Europe, China, and Cuba. State socialism was a mix of two kinds of ideologies. Most prominent was economic structuralism: the notion that market capitalism and private property led inexorably to the exploitation of one class by another. Less prominent ideologically, but perhaps more prominent in practice, was state economic planning, which provided an alternative to market-based distribution.

The Soviet Union, beginning in the late 1920s, developed a series of five-year plans that outlined detailed economic goals, including the quantities of different kinds of inputs and final products to be produced. These plans led to a substantial transformation of a largely peasant society into the industrial juggernaut that defeated Germany in World War II. If one looks only at the increases in industrial production, state socialism provided remarkable results in the Soviet Union. However, a high human cost was paid: To coerce people into making the changes dictated by state planners, the government executed millions and imprisoned millions more in wretched conditions in Siberia. Millions more starved to death in the early 1930s during the collectivization of agriculture, moving people from small independent farms to huge "factory" farms.

Eventually, the Soviet model failed on economic as well as human grounds. As long as the central task was shifting resources from agriculture into industry, state planning was reasonably effective, if brutal. As more resources were put into industry, production increased. However, state planners could not plan innovation. Economic gains in the Soviet system generally came from using more resources, not from devising innovative ways to use resources more efficiently. By the 1970s, with no additional pool of unused labor or untapped natural resources to bring into production, the Soviet economy began to stagnate. The story in the other state socialist economies was the same. Over time, these economies grew much more slowly than those in the West, leaving their citizens much poorer. The Soviet Union abandoned this model suddenly when it collapsed in 1991. China abandoned it gradually, beginning in 1979. Cuba is only now modifying the model slightly.

**state socialism**

A strategy for development in which the state rather than the market allocates resources.

## EXPORT-LED GROWTH

In part as a response to the failures of import substitution, a group of countries in East Asia developed a strategy known as **export-led growth**. The leader in this strategy was Japan, which shifted from import substitution after World War II. But the countries

**export-led growth**

A development strategy that focuses on exporting to the global market.

that made it a model to study and to emulate were the so-called Asian Tigers. These countries—South Korea, Taiwan, Singapore, and Hong Kong—used this strategy to move from being among the world's poorest countries to being among the world's richest in about a half century. This different strategy was feasible in part because the Asian states conceived of the *purpose* of development differently. They placed less emphasis on self-reliance and on severing ties with former colonial masters and saw integration with international markets as acceptable and even desirable.

The central insight in the strategy of export-led growth is to "go where the money is." Rather than building industries to serve domestic markets, which for most poor countries are relatively small, this strategy focused on the markets in developed countries with larger and wealthier populations. In the second half of the twentieth century, going where the money was meant exporting primarily to the U.S., European, and Japanese markets.

Initially, the strategy was not to outcompete firms in the leading technological sectors of these economies, but rather to produce mass market goods better and more cheaply. Because workers in the Asian Tigers were, at the beginning of this process, much poorer than workers in the countries with whom they were competing, wages were much lower. Initially, then, much of the focus was on low-cost production based on abundant cheap labor, the strategy pursued by China today. Japanese and other Asian manufacturers recognized that the huge U.S. market could yield more sales and profits than an import substitution strategy would allow.

Export-led growth used the profits generated and expertise gained in producing such low-end goods to move up the value chain. Like Germany and Japan before them, the Asian Tigers had very high domestic savings rates, which provided the investment needed for technological advancement. In the 1960s and 1970s, the primary virtue of Japanese cars was that they were *cheaper* than American brands. By the 1990s, Americans were willing to pay more for Japanese cars because they were *better*. In the 1970s, Taiwan was associated in the United States with cheap radios and televisions, but by 2000, it was the world's leading producer of laptop computers, computer motherboards, and scanners.[17]

Planners in export-led economies adopted an attitude toward the world market opposite to that of import substitution and state socialism, and this attitude apparently yielded opposite results. In the 1980s and 1990s, other Southeast Asian countries, including Malaysia, Thailand, and the Philippines, began following the Asian Tiger model, with various levels of success. In postcommunist Europe, many states also adopted the position that free trade is preferable to closed markets as a development strategy.

## PRESCRIPTIONS FOR SUCCESS

The astounding economic success of the Asian Tigers led scholars and politicians alike to seek to understand their approach better, in the hope that those countries' success could be replicated elsewhere. After three decades of debate, there has been some movement toward consensus on the key determinants of the Tigers' success and the relevant lessons for other economies. Unfortunately, it is not clear that the conditions that led to their success still exist for those coming behind them.

**The Washington Consensus**    Liberals have argued that the success of the Asian Tigers is evidence that a free market approach—both domestically and internationally—is optimal. In particular, their success is seen as real-world evidence that even poor countries benefit when they follow the laws of comparative advantage and of market economics. The Asian Tigers embraced the global market, rather than retreating from it. They acknowledged that they could not compete in every sector, but rather let the market determine the niches they targeted. They were willing to import the necessary inputs and technology. By producing where they could succeed, these countries had sufficient income to import what they needed. The World Bank produced a well-known analysis of the Asian Tigers, praising these cases as a triumph of the liberal model. It stressed that state intervention in those economies was tangential to their success.[18]

This interpretation became part of what was known as the **Washington consensus** on development strategy. By the late 1980s, leaders in donor countries and in donor organizations, most importantly the IMF and the World Bank, agreed on what was required for successful development. Internationally, the Washington consensus embraced the virtues of open economies and free trade. Domestically, it focused on minimizing the state role in the economy, inspired by the policies of the Thatcher administration in Britain and the Reagan administration in the United States in the 1980s. This view dominated the advice given to developing states, and implementing free market policies became a central condition of receiving aid and loans in the subsequent decades.

**The Role of the "Developmental State"**   Others, however, strongly dispute the view that the East Asian states were textbook examples of a liberal development strategy. Doubters emphasize three key deviations from that model. First, in the early years of their development, none of these states was a democracy. South Korea, Taiwan, and Singapore were essentially authoritarian; Hong Kong was still a British colony. The authoritarian governments in these countries suppressed labor unions, sometimes violently, which kept wages much lower than they otherwise would have been. Low wages were an essential ingredient in the industrial competitiveness of these states. Only in the 1990s, when their economic success was already established, did Taiwan and South Korea become genuine democracies. In Singapore, democracy remains limited, and Hong Kong has been transferred from colonial British control to authoritarian Chinese control.

Second, in each country, the government took an active role in accumulating capital for investment and in directing that investment into particular industries. Governments picked industries in which they believed their firms could compete, such as shipbuilding in South Korea and microprocessors in Taiwan, and channeled investment into those sectors, rather than letting the market determine investment decisions. Close connections between governments and leading firms helped favored firms get access to cheap, state-subsidized loans for investment. Domestic competition was squelched so firms could concentrate on the international market. Moreover, through various mechanisms, the East Asian states provided infant industry protection to those industries identified as priorities for development.

Third, the state did not merely stand aside from the economy, but helped build the legal and bureaucratic infrastructure needed for capitalism to thrive. Financial markets will not automatically lead to development if insider trading and fraud are rampant, as Russia found in the 1990s. The state must do certain jobs, and do them very well. Among these jobs is investing in public education, which has been a hallmark of success in each of the Asian Tiger countries. Math and science education is a high priority in these countries, and the steady supply of engineers and scientists produced by state-run universities has been essential to the continuation of earlier successes.

This more statist interpretation of the East Asian economic miracle gained adherents after the Asian financial crisis of 1997–1998. That crisis helped expose the close connections between firms and the government, which in some cases were corrupt. The phrase "crony capitalism" suddenly replaced "Asian Tigers" in discussions of the region.

An alternative model of East Asian development emerged, emphasizing the positive role played by the **developmental state**. Those who focused on the developmental state

**Washington consensus**

A development strategy favored by leading donor countries and organizations that advocates open economies, free trade, and minimal interference by the state in the economy.

**developmental state**

A state that takes an active role in economic development by fostering the accumulation of capital to invest in particular industries and building the legal and bureaucratic infrastructure necessary for capitalism to thrive.

# THE POLICY CONNECTION

## CHILD LABOR AND THE SWEATSHOP DILEMMA

Much of the clothing and other consumer goods that we buy are manufactured in developing countries under conditions that many consider unacceptable. Hours are long, wages low, and workers' rights limited. Moreover, in some countries, children as young as five years old work in these factories. Worldwide, 120 million children under the age of 14 work, including 13 percent of children in the developing world.*

A number of organizations have taken up the task of combating child labor and sweatshop conditions. One, the Fair Labor Association (FLA), has nearly 200 U.S. universities and colleges as members. These institutions became involved when students protested the fact that much of the clothing bearing their school's names was made in sweatshop conditions.

The FLA Workplace Code of Conduct states: "No person shall be employed under the age of 15 or under the age for completion of compulsory education, whichever is higher"[†] The code also contains less specific provisions on wages, safety, and workers' rights. Members of the FLA commit to using contractors who are certified by the FLA as following the Code of Conduct.

However, there is another perspective on the problem, a view that might be called "economic realism." This view argues that in conditions of

Children making athletic shoes in Dhaka, Bangladesh. Would ending child labor get these children in school, or leave their families even more impoverished?

Des Willie/Alamy

*(Continued)*

poverty that are unlikely to end anytime soon, child labor and sweatshop conditions might be better than the alternatives. Columnist Nicholas Kristof of the *New York Times* traveled to Cambodia to report on the large number of people who work in the city garbage dump. People brave the filth and stink to collect things such as plastic bags and scraps of metal that they can then sell, earning roughly 75 cents per day.[‡] Working conditions are undoubtedly bad in many factories, he says, "but the primary problem in places like this is not that there are too many people being exploited in sweatshops, it's that there are not enough."[§]

The International Labor Organization (ILO) disputes the idea that child labor is economically efficient. The ILO produced a study showing that although it would take $760 billion over twenty years to put all children in school and to replace the income that they would make working, the payoff would be as much as seven times that figure.[¶]

## Critical Thinking Questions

1. What kinds of sacrifices should people in wealthy countries be forced to make in order to end child labor in the poorest countries?

2. Should child labor be banned, even if that labor provides an important source of income for families? If it should be allowed in poor countries, why not for poor people in wealthy countries?

---

[*]UNICEF, "Child Protection," at http://www.unicef.org/protection/57929_child_labour.html.

[†]Fair Labor Association, "Workplace Code of Conduct," http://www.fairlabor.org/our-work/code-of-conduct.

[‡]Nicholas D. Kristof, "Inviting All Democrats," New York Times, January 14, 2004.

[§]Nicholas D. Kristof, "Realities of Labor," Op-Ed Audio Slide Show, NYTimes.com, January 14, 2004.

[¶]"Economics Focus: Sickness or Symptom," The Economist, February 5, 2004.

---

did not reject the importance of export-led growth or the role of the market domestically. However, they believed that the state plays an essential role in accumulating capital, directing investment, and providing legal, administrative, and educational infrastructure. In recent years, the success of China has increased the credibility of the notion that a strong state is as important as the free market, and is more important than democracy. The economic crisis in the United States and Europe beginning in 2008 further undermined the influence of the Washington consensus.

## THE POSTCOMMUNIST EXPERIENCE

The importance of the state gained renewed attention in the 1990s in light of the experiences of the formerly communist states, and Russia in particular. The postcommunist states were not as poor as many other developing states, but their economies were stagnating, largely because of state control. Therefore, most of the aid and advice given to postcommunist governments focused on getting the government out of the economy and introducing the "invisible hand" of the market. A particular emphasis was on privatizing state-owned businesses. In the spirit of the free market, many advisers asserted that it did not matter how privatization was achieved or who bought the firms; what mattered was getting the firms out of the hands of the state as quickly as possible. Exposing the firms to the competitive pressures of the market would achieve several objectives: align supply and demand, weed out weak and inefficient firms, direct investment and labor toward the most productive sectors, and attract foreign investment.

However, because state apparatuses were weak and corrupt, privatizing state companies worth billions of dollars became a bonanza for those able to rig the

Reuters/SRT/London

Assassination of Andrei Kozlov, deputy director of the Russian Central Bank, in 2006. Days earlier, Kozlov had advocated harsher penalties for financial crimes.

privatization process. As a result, governments lost billions of dollars' worth of revenue, much of the economy came under the control of a small number of oligarchs, and bribery became a way of life in the government, especially in the post-Soviet states. Democracy and the free market, greeted with enthusiasm throughout the former Soviet Union in 1991, were viewed much more skeptically a decade later. By 2000, Russia and several other states had adopted a version of capitalism that preserved a major role for the state in determining economic priorities.

The central problem in the post-Soviet cases was the absence of a state authority strong enough, competent enough, and honest enough to ensure that people and firms competed fairly in the free market. The New York Stock Exchange works so well in large part because of the effective regulation of the Securities and Exchange Commission (SEC), the government agency charged with preventing fraud, insider trading, and manipulation of the market. The SEC closely monitors the financial industry, looks for illegal practices such as insider trading, and files charges against those it finds to be in violation. Without such regulation, the market could not be expected to work—yet this is essentially what was attempted in most of the post-Soviet economies.

## EMERGING CONSENSUS?

Today, much scholarship and many international organizations, such as the World Bank, are arriving at a view of development strategy that embraces both the market and the state. Although important differences of emphasis remain, most specialists acknowledge that both a competent and honest state and a willingness to embrace the market are necessary to produce economic development.

The World Bank, for example, continues to advise states to increase their openness to the global economy and to minimize market-distorting policies such as protectionism, but it is also giving increasing attention to issues of "good governance" and corruption. **Good governance** refers to government that is transparent, controlled by the rule of law, accountable, and effective. Interestingly, it now seems much easier to achieve economic openness than good governance. Once a state decides to open itself to free trade, the changes are relatively easy to implement from above. However, rooting out governmental overregulation, corruption, and incompetence requires thorough transformation, and government officials who profit from corruption may have little interest in such change.

**good governance**

Governance that is transparent, controlled by the rule of law, accountable, and effective.

## THE CHANGING INTERNATIONAL ENVIRONMENT

Even if there is an increasing consensus on the best strategies for development, two significant barriers remain. The first is that domestic transformation is very difficult to accomplish. In much of Africa, for example, it is impossible to think about serious governmental reforms in countries that are plagued by civil wars, health crises, corruption, and authoritarian regimes with little interest in such reforms.

However, even for those states that adopt sound strategies, it is not clear that the path followed by the East Asian states is still open. The East Asian economies developed during the Cold War, and this timing substantially influenced their access to markets.

# THE GEOGRAPHY CONNECTION

## WOMEN AND DEVELOPMENT

Examine these maps of GDP per capita and women's educational levels.

### Critical Thinking Questions

1. Where are the greatest disparities in educational level between men and women?

2. Do you see a correlation between overall levels of wealth and women's education?

3. If so, which of these factors is causing the other? Is it possible to tell this from the maps?

Gender Differences in Education

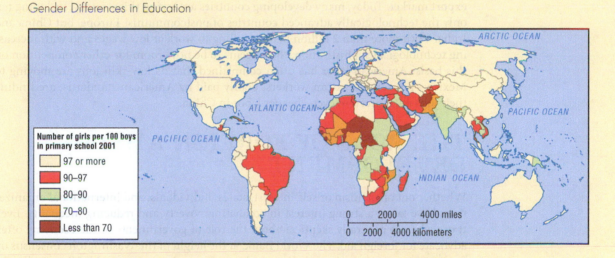

Number of girls per 100 boys in primary school 2001

- 97 or more
- 90–97
- 80–90
- 70–80
- Less than 70

0     2000     4000 miles
0   2000   4000 kilometers

GNP per Capita Growth Rates

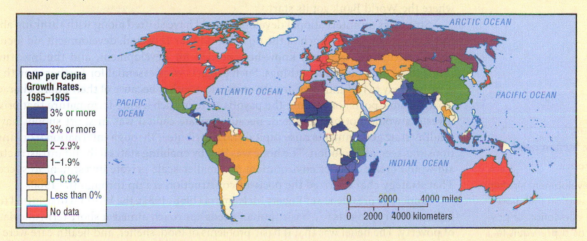

GNP per Capita Growth Rates, 1985–1995

- 3% or more
- 3% or more
- 2–2.9%
- 1–1.9%
- 0–0.9%
- Less than 0%
- No data

0     2000     4000 miles
0   2000   4000 kilometers

For Korea and Japan especially, the strategic importance of the region made the United States willing to tolerate significant trade deficits because the United States had a security interest in helping them develop. Today, there is no such strategic impetus, and every country has become much more sensitive to trade deficits. Although the WTO agreement has lowered many barriers to trade, many of the poorest states are not eligible for these benefits because they are not WTO members. Moreover, the WTO is weakest in the area in which developing countries are most competitive: agricultural exports. For example, some of the poorest countries in the world, including Benin, Burkina Faso, Chad, and Mali, rely heavily on cotton for export earnings. They must compete not only with producers in developing countries such as China and India, but with firms in wealthy countries such as the United States, which receive large subsidies from their governments.[19] This protectionism is the source of considerable resentment in the developing world, but interest group politics in the wealthy countries make it difficult to abolish.

A separate, and perhaps more daunting, challenge is the increasingly competitive nature of the world economy. When the Asian Tigers were thriving in the 1970s, there were few countries using their strategy of low-wage, high-technology production for the export market. Today, many developing countries are trying this strategy, including not only the technologically advanced countries of postcommunist Europe, but China and India. With more than 2 billion people willing to work at low wages and with increasing technological sophistication, there seems to be little room for other competition on this basis. American labor has often complained that its low-skill jobs are moving to Mexico—but some Mexican workers, poorly paid by American standards, are finding their jobs outsourced to even cheaper labor in China.

# THE ROLE OF FOREIGN AID IN DEVELOPMENT

Whether out of altruism or self-interest, states, individuals, and international organizations have taken a strong interest in combating poverty and reducing inequality. Even those who are generally skeptical about the role of governments in the economy often advocate for foreign aid. The World Bank, at the height of the Washington consensus on free markets, continued to advocate and coordinate development aid. Historically, the potential of aid was demonstrated by the reconstruction of Europe after World War II, where the World Bank got its start.

Strategies for international development aid have shifted along with thinking about the purposes of aid. In much of the post–World War II period, development aid focused on infrastructure, technical know-how needed for development, and the investment funds that could build these things. Such projects were essential for further growth but were unlikely to be funded by private investment, either because of their public character (roads, dams, ports) or because the payoffs were of such a long-term nature that private investors would not be interested. Because private capital was in short supply, having wealthy state governments raise capital and distribute it through international organizations was seen as a solution. The hope was that by enabling states to build infrastructure, aid would create a better environment for smaller-scale private investment to succeed. That strategy characterized the postwar construction era up through the 1960s.

Under the presidency of Robert McNamara (1968–1981), the World Bank shifted from infrastructure projects to a **basic human needs approach** aimed at short-term alleviation of poverty. The belief was that if basic problems of food, shelter, and health care were not addressed, individuals and societies could not make longer-term decisions and investments.

**basic human needs approach**

A development strategy focusing on the short-term alleviation of poverty as a prerequisite for further progress.

Doctor with mother and children at an HIV/AIDS community program in Nairobi, Kenya. Providing medical help has been an important economic development strategy because illness undermines economic productivity both directly (by disabling workers) and indirectly, when the early death of a parent leaves children with no one to raise them.

In the 1980s and 1990s, the goal of aid shifted again, to structural adjustment. **Structural adjustment** refers to efforts to strengthen the financial basis of a country's economy. This strategy was inspired by the focus on the free market and the role of monetary policy then ascendant in Western states (the Washington consensus). The strategy was to improve the investment climate by reducing government budget deficits and by stabilizing the value of currencies. The lead international organization was the International Monetary Fund, which channeled money from donors to recipients in exchange for the recipients' following structural adjustment programs. Participating in an IMF adjustment program was often a prerequisite for receiving other international support. The power of the IMF over recipient countries and the austerity required by structural adjustment programs led to intense resentment of the IMF.

Most recently, aid has focused on good governance. The current wisdom is that markets cannot function in the absence of a competent and honest government and that corruption plays a major role in undermining investment in particular and economic growth in general. The UN Millennium Development Goals, with their emphasis on human development, signals a partial return to the basic human needs approach.

International aid has also played an important role in addressing emergencies and humanitarian crises around the world. Food aid has repeatedly been used to reduce starvation when food supplies have fallen short for one reason or another. International aid to refugees displaced by war or natural disasters has been important, as has immediate help to countries in times of natural disaster, such as after the Haitian earthquake of January 2010.

**structural adjustment**

A strategy adopted by the World Bank in the 1980s and 1990s aimed at strengthening the financial basis of a country's economy.

## SHORTCOMINGS OF INTERNATIONAL AID

There is considerable debate on whether and how aid actually contributes to development. One problem with most international aid is that it goes primarily to governments. In general, this makes sense because it is governments that are generally charged with getting economies to function better. For example, the central goal of structural adjustment aid is to shore up weaknesses in a government's financial position. However, the government may be a central part of the problem, through some combination of corruption and incompetence, and even when a government is competent in general, it may be ill suited to carrying out the tasks envisioned by the aid.

If governments cannot or will not spend aid effectively, the aid may be wasted, which is especially harmful when money is lent rather than donated. International organizations and governments have been criticized for lending money to corrupt Third World governments, which sometimes simply funnel the money into offshore bank accounts or into the hands of their supporters. Regardless of what happens to the money, the citizens of that country are left to pay it back through tax payments, sometimes long after the corrupt government in question is gone (along with the money). For countries that have a difficult time earning enough hard currency to fund investment, having to spend that money to pay back debts incurred by previous governments for projects that yielded no benefits is especially frustrating.

Another problem is that aid sometimes flows out of a country as quickly as it flows in. What economists call the "multiplier effect" of aid then may accrue to the donor rather than to the recipient. The **multiplier effect** refers to the fact that when money is spent (for example, on goods), the person or firm receiving the money often spends all or part of it on something else, the recipient of those purchases does the same, and so on. Thus, a single donation has its effect multiplied as it flows through an economy, yielding profit to a succession of firms or individuals. If the money flows immediately out of the country, the multiplier effect goes with it.

This is especially true of so-called **tied aid**, which must be spent on goods or services from the donor country. Especially when tied aid comes in the form of loans, the receiving country may get little of the benefit of the aid but be responsible for paying back the entire loan. For example, the Freedom Support Act, through which the United States provided aid to the post-Soviet states after 1991, required that much of the money be spent on U.S. grain and farm equipment, both of which were available more cheaply in Russia. The benefit to U.S. firms was obvious, but it is not clear that this provision of the act provided a substantial benefit to the Russian economy. In a similar vein, the World Bank has been faulted for requiring that significant portions of its aid be spent on technical assistance, which generally comes in the form of costly consultants from developed states.

Some analysts support the idea of aid but believe that the shortcomings of aid are so common and so difficult to combat that, in practice, aid does more harm than good. Economist William Easterly charges that "one of the best economic ideas of our time, the genius of free markets, was presented in one of the worst possible ways, with unelected outsiders imposing rigid doctrines on the xenophobic unwilling."[20] If it is true that aid can only be implemented wisely by competent governments, it is also true that countries with competent governments are among the least likely to need aid. Many would take exception to this view, arguing that substantial aid packages make it much easier for competent governments to pursue economic reforms.

A more strident school of thought disagrees with aid in principle, based on a belief in the primacy of markets. To those who believe that any interference with the market inhibits reform, aid makes the problem worse, not better. It is hard to test this theory for two reasons. First, to withhold aid altogether would be considered inhumane by many. Second, interference with market forces is practiced by every government in the world and is provided for in international agreements such as the WTO, and it is unlikely that the "pure" market would be adopted in this one area.

---

**multiplier effect**

An economic effect whereby an increase in spending (for example, of funds provided to a country by a donor) produces an increase in national income and consumption greater than the initial amount spent. When aid flows out of a country, the benefit of aid may accrue to the donor rather than to the recipient.

**tied aid**

Aid that must be spent on goods or services from the donor country.

# MULTILATERAL AID AND THE WORLD BANK

Multilateral aid pools donations by multiple states and then distributes the aid through international organizations. There are a number of international organizations engaged in providing multilateral aid, including the World Bank, the IMF, and the UN Development Programme.

Of these organizations, the World Bank, based in Washington, D.C., is widely considered the most important because it is the primary vehicle for multilateral aid in terms of the amount of money disbursed. It also influences other donors. Individual governments and private lenders routinely rely on the World Bank's evaluations in making their own decisions about aid and lending. Moreover, it has widely recognized expertise in the area of development (although many disagree with its views). As a result, the World Bank has played a leading role in defining the "best practices" in development aid for the past six decades. More fundamentally, the World Bank has shaped the very definition of "development," which is often taken for granted but which shapes the purpose of all aid activities.[21] Because it plays this central role, the World Bank has been a primary target for criticism by those who question the dominant practices.

**Structure of the Bank**   The World Bank consists of two main structures and several smaller ones. The two main structures are the International Bank for Reconstruction and Development (IBRD) and the International Development Association (IDA).

The IBRD lends money—it does not grant it—to middle-income countries and poorer countries considered to be a good risk in terms of repayment. South Asia and Africa each receive about a quarter of the bank's loans, with Latin America, eastern Europe, and Asia receiving between 15 and 20 percent each. The two largest targets of investment are public administration and law enforcement (22 percent) and transportation (20 percent). Other targets include water and sanitation, health, and education. IBRD lending is financed by borrowing on world financial markets. The World Bank can borrow money cheaply because of its credibility and can then lend to states on terms much more favorable than they would get from private markets.[22]

The IDA was founded because the poorest countries could not meet the repayment requirements for loans from the IBRD. In 2015, eligibility for IDA loans was capped at $1215 in per capita income, a level at which seventy-seven countries with 2.8 billion people were eligible. It averages roughly $20 billion per year in new loans, more than half of which is spent in sub-Saharan Africa and almost another third in South Asia. In 2014, the top five borrowers were India, Pakistan, Bangladesh, Nigeria, and Ethiopia. Its loans have a ten-year grace period on repayment of the principal; in 2014, however, 12 percent of its aid was in the form of grants, which do not need to be repaid. The main program areas are infrastructure (47 percent), public administration (18 percent), and the social sector such as education and health services (18 percent). This funding reflects a mix of development strategies: infrastructure development, basic human needs, and improved governance. In contrast to the IBRD, the IDA obtains money to lend through contributions from governments.[23]

Whereas voting in most international organizations is based on one state, one vote, voting in the World Bank (and in the IMF) is based on the financial contributions each member makes to the bank's lending resources (see Table 12.3). In 2015, the United States had 16.1 percent of the votes, followed by Japan with 7.5 percent, China with 4.8 percent, Germany with 4.4 percent, and France and Britain with 3.9 percent each. Most World Bank member states each have less than 1 percent of the vote. Moreover, the president of the World Bank is, by tradition, always an American, and the managing director of

**TABLE 12.3** Voting Shares at the World Bank, 2015

| Country | Percent of Votes |
|---|---|
| United States | 16.14 |
| Japan | 7.48 |
| China | 4.83 |
| Germany | 4.38 |
| France | 3.93 |
| United Kingdom | 3.93 |
| India | 3.05 |
| Saudi Arabia | 3.02 |
| Russia | 2.83 |
| Canada | 2.66 |
| Italy | 2.47 |
| Spain | 2.02 |
| Brazil | 1.92 |
| Netherlands | 1.91 |
| South Korea | 1.65 |
| Belgium | 1.64 |
| Iran | 1.60 |
| Switzerland | 1.59 |
| Australia | 1.45 |
| Turkey | 1.18 |

*The rest of the World Bank's 188 members have less than 1 percent of the vote.*

*Source: World Bank, "International Bank for Reconstruction and Development Subscriptions and Voting Power of Member Countries," http://www.worldbank.org/en/about/leadership/VotingPowers.*

**conditionality**

The requirement that an aid recipient agree to a set of conditions that the donor believes will help promote development in the country.

the IMF comes from Europe. Controversy over this practice was intense in 2011 when a new director, Jim Yong Kim, an American and former president of Dartmouth College, was selected for the position in 2012 over Ngozi Okonjo-Iweala, a development economist and former finance minister of Nigeria. Okonjo-Iweala's candidacy was viewed as a challenge to the U.S. lock on the position.

The voting structure of the World Bank is based on pragmatism. It would be impossible to get the wealthy countries to put significant resources into an organization they did not control. However, this structure is one source of dissatisfaction with the World Bank, where the developing countries have little influence. This leads to accusations that the bank remains a semicolonial organization, in which the wealthy countries decide what will happen to the poor ones.

**Activities of the Bank** The World Bank has three important functions:

- Conducting research on development issues
- Making policy recommendations to specific governments
- Lending money

In practice, these three activities are closely linked (see Figure 12.3).

Policy recommendations are often linked directly to loans provided by the IBRD and IDA. In a practice known as **conditionality**, states wishing to receive loans from the World Bank must agree to certain conditions, which generally take the form of a set of policies that the World Bank believes will help promote development. Countries often resent these conditions—but when they are desperate for a loan, they feel they have little choice but to accept them. In many cases, the terms of those loans are *concessionary*, meaning that the interest rates and repayment schedules are more generous than could be obtained in private financial markets—but in all cases the loans must be repaid, whether the recipient's economy improves or not. A developing country that defaulted on loans from the World Bank would find virtually every other source of credit cut off as well. Therefore, it is important that loans are made wisely and programs implemented effectively, but that has not always been the case.

**Critiques of the World Bank** The World Bank has been the target of sustained criticism, from policy experts and social activists alike. The joint meetings of the World Bank and the IMF, held every year in Washington, D.C., are routinely the target of protests by thousands of people, and much of central Washington is shut down to keep protestors from gathering at the bank's headquarters.

Some of the criticisms of the World Bank echo the general criticisms of development aid. Others are specific to the World Bank, which has its own version of the rational action model of decision making and has been widely criticized for deviating from the model in various ways. The following are among the most significant criticisms of the World Bank:

- The voting procedure disenfranchises the poor countries that have the most at stake.
- Lending, unless it is highly effective, may leave recipients with debt but without much benefit.
- Conditionality undermines the sovereignty of recipient governments.

FIGURE 12.3 World Bank project cycle.

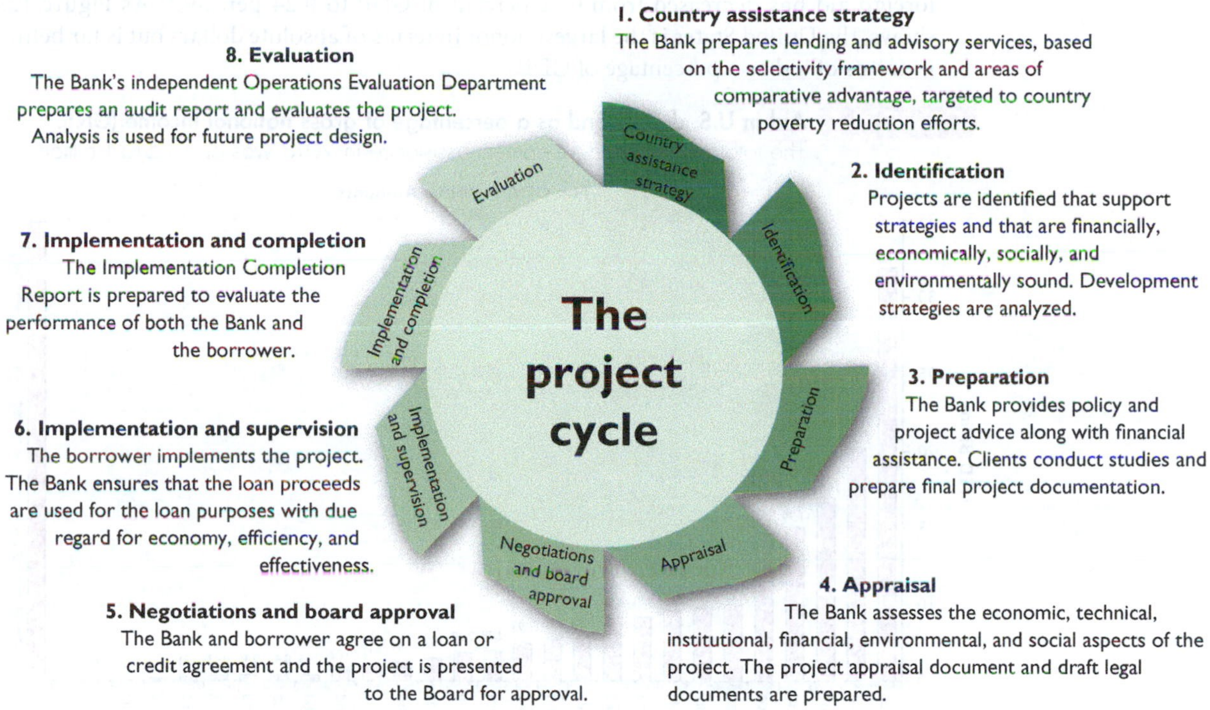
1. Country assistance strategy
The Bank prepares lending and advisory services, based on the selectivity framework and areas of comparative advantage, targeted to country poverty reduction efforts.
2. Identification
Projects are identified that support strategies and that are financially, economically, socially, and environmentally sound. Development strategies are analyzed.
3. Preparation
The Bank provides policy and project advice along with financial assistance. Clients conduct studies and prepare final project documentation.
4. Appraisal
The Bank assesses the economic, technical, institutional, financial, environmental, and social aspects of the project. The project appraisal document and draft legal documents are prepared.
5. Negotiations and board approval
The Bank and borrower agree on a loan or credit agreement and the project is presented to the Board for approval.
6. Implementation and supervision
The borrower implements the project. The Bank ensures that the loan proceeds are used for the loan purposes with due regard for economy, efficiency, and effectiveness.
7. Implementation and completion
The Implementation Completion Report is prepared to evaluate the performance of both the Bank and the borrower.
8. Evaluation
The Bank's independent Operations Evaluation Department prepares an audit report and evaluates the project. Analysis is used for future project design.
The project cycle
Country assistance strategy
Identification
Preparation
Appraisal
Negotiations and board approval
Implementation and supervision
Implementation and completion
Evaluation

- Conditionality often requires harsh economic policies, which hurt the poorest people in the recipient countries most.
- Conditions that produce hardship can lead to unrest, destabilizing the very government the bank is trying to help and undermining the basis for reform.
- Development projects supported by the World Bank have been focused only on narrow economic performance and in some cases have had severe environmental consequences.
- The bank's analysis and its conditionality policies seem to be driven by an ideology, economic liberalism, that many believe is too simplistic for the problems it addresses.

Despite the frequently bitter criticisms leveled at the World Bank, it remains one of the few available sources of investment, advice, and credibility for the development efforts of poor states. Despite the dissatisfaction with it, therefore, the rich states continue to support it financially, and poor states continue to look to it for aid.

## BILATERAL FOREIGN AID

Bilateral foreign aid, defined as aid given by one government directly to another, is almost as controversial as World Bank aid. Although there are important historical successes, bilateral foreign aid is criticized both within the donor countries and internationally.

In the United States, many politicians have criticized the amount of funding spent on foreign aid projects. Others, however, believe that U.S. aid levels are too low. Respondents to a 2013 public opinion survey estimated, on average, that U.S. foreign aid was 28 percent of the national budget. In fact, aid makes up about 1 percent of the U.S. budget.[24]

The gross overestimation of how much is being spent may have some effect on how unpopular that aid is and, therefore, on political support for such aid. Since 1960, U.S. foreign aid has decreased from 0.52 percent of GDP to 0.24 percent.[25] As Figure 12.4 shows, the United States is the largest donor in terms of absolute dollars but is far behind in terms of aid as a percentage of GDP.

**FIGURE 12.4**   Aid in U.S. dollars and as a percentage of gross national income (GNI).
The total net official development assistance in 2013 was about $134 billion.

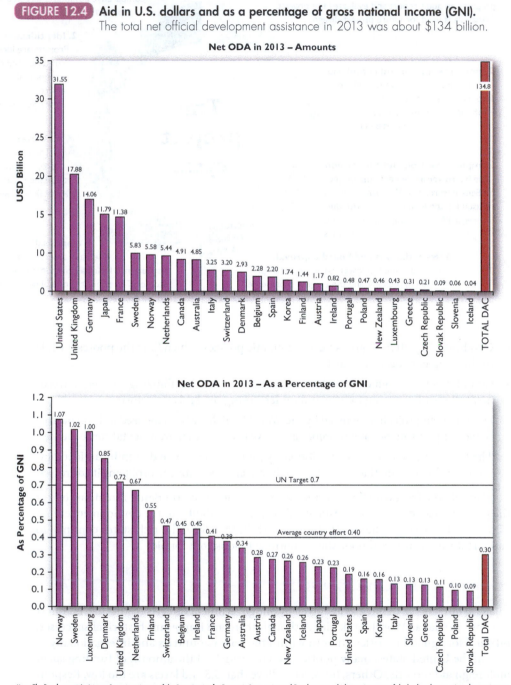

Net ODA in 2013 – Amounts

Net ODA in 2013 – As a Percentage of GNI

Note: The Development Assistance Committee is part of the Organization for Economic Cooperation and Development, which contains many of the leading donor nations, but not increasingly important donors such as China and the United Arab Emirates.

Source: OECD, 8 April 2014. http://www.oecd.org/dac/stats/documentupload/ODA%202013%20Tables%20and%20Charts%20En.pdf

There are two main arguments against bilateral aid. First, bilateral aid is often seen as serving the geopolitical needs of the donors more than the development needs of the recipients. Thus, the single largest recipient of U.S. foreign aid in recent years has been Afghanistan. For the past few decades, the top recipient was not a developing country at all, but rather Israel, a key ally in the Middle East. Following Israel, the second biggest U.S. aid recipient was Egypt, in return for its role in the Middle East peace process. Table 12.4, showing U.S. aid in 2000, 2010 and 2015, gives some indication as to how priorities have shifted.

Second, a great deal of bilateral aid is tied aid, which must be spent on goods and services from the donor country, so that much of the economic benefit accrues to firms in the donor states. In particular, critics point out that much bilateral aid is in the form of loans to buy military equipment from the donor. Such purchases contribute nothing to the economy of the aid recipient and may make the region in question less secure.

Nonetheless, foreign aid remains an important foreign policy tool, even if it is not a significant development tool for the poor countries of the world. Shifting patterns of aid programs show that countries tend to contribute where they have the most immediate foreign policy aims. In the 1990s, for example, the EU concentrated its aid efforts on the formerly communist states of eastern Europe, the stability and prosperity of which were considered essential to the security and economic interests of the EU. In the past

**TABLE 12.4** Recipients of U.S. Foreign Assistance, FY2000, and FY2010, and FY2015 (in millions of current US$)

| FY2000 | FY2010* | FY2015 |
|---|---|---|
| Israel 4,069 | Afghanistan 4,102 | Israel 3,100 |
| Egypt 2,053 | Israel 2,220 | Afghanistan 1,595 |
| Colombia 899 | Pakistan 1,807 | Egypt 1,506 |
| West Bank/Gaza 485 | Egypt 1,296 | Pakistan 882 |
| Jordan 429 | Haiti 1,271 | Nigeria 721 |
| Russia 195 | Iraq 1,117 | Jordan 671 |
| Bolivia 194 | Jordan 693 | Tanzania 590 |
| Ukraine 183 | Kenya 688 | Kenya 553 |
| Kosovo 165 | Nigeria 614 | Ethiopia 482 |
| Peru 120 | South Africa 578 | Uganda 475 |
| Georgia 112 | Ethiopia 533 | West Bank 441 |
| Armenia 104 | Colombia 507 | South Africa 438 |
| Bosnia 101 | West Bank/Gaza 496 | Mozambique 389 |
| Indonesia 94 | Tanzania 464 | Zambia 381 |
| Nigeria 68 | Uganda 457 | Colombia 381 |

*Includes supplementals and Millennium Challenge Corporation Compact disbursements in FY2010.
Source: Department of State, "Foreign Operations CBJ FY2002, FY2011" ForeignAssistance.gov, http://beta.foreignassistance.gov/explore.

# RECONSIDER THE CASE

## THE RISE OF BRAZIL

The global economic crisis in 2008 hit Brazil hard. Global recession decreased demand for Brazil's raw materials, which had driven the boom. Moreover, its currency appreciated, making its exports less competitive. With slow growth but high inflation, the central bank faced a tension between lowering interest rates to stimulate the economy and raising them to control inflation. Brazil's government predicted a 1.2 percent contraction in the economy in 2015, the worst performance since 1990. In terms of GDP, Brazil fell from sixth in the world to eighth in 2015, having been passed by the UK and India.

Poverty and inequality remain major problems in Brazil. A quarter of Brazil's people live below the poverty line. Inequality remains stark: Brazil's Gini coefficient is the sixteenth highest in the world. Programs to address poverty are expensive, and a high rate of economic growth will be required to sustain them. Although much attention has been given to Brazil's growing role in world economics and politics, its continued prosperity will have consequences at the individual level as well.

To continue its recent success, Brazil will need to confront several weaknesses. The economy is heavily dependent on raw materials exports, making it vulnerable to a decrease in commodities prices. Government welfare commitments, intended to reduce poverty and inequality, are viewed as unsustainable. Wages have gone up considerably, which is good news for workers in the short term but further undermines the competitiveness of Brazil's exports. Corruption remains widespread and has been especially visible in the construction of facilities related to the World Cup and Olympics. A huge corruption scandal at the oil firm Petrobras further damaged confidence. In August 2015, thousands of protestors angered by persistent corruption and economic recession demanded the impeachment of President Dilma Rousseff. The push for economic development has led to increased exploitation of land in the Amazon River basin, both for natural resource extraction and for conversion to farmland. This has led to widespread concern about the effects on the global climate, on biodiversity, and on the indigenous groups who live in the area.

Despite those problems, Brazil has managed to increase overall wealth while decreasing inequality, a very desirable but elusive combination. What has led to this dual success in Brazil? Good economic policies, or the good fortune of a booming global commodities market? Can this be replicated elsewhere? Will it even persist in Brazil? These are important questions both for international economics and for policy makers around the world.

### Critical Thinking Questions

1. How has Brazil's recent economic strategy compared to that of the Asian Tigers?

2. What does Brazil's success tell us about the sources of economic growth?

3. Why is it so difficult to devise policies that lift people out of poverty while also closing the gaps between rich and poor?

---

decade, China has taken on a larger foreign aid role, especially in countries in Africa with important natural resource supplies.

After the attacks of September 11, 2001, aid from various governments shifted to the states of Central Asia, which were viewed as crucial in dislodging the Taliban movement in Afghanistan and in preventing the spread of militant Islamic fundamentalism. That the governments were neither democratic nor following accepted economic development strategies was less important than that they were willing to ally themselves with the West in the "global war on terror." From the perspective of economic development, this may not make much sense, but from the perspective of national security, it makes a great deal of sense. Thus, bilateral aid is best thought of as a foreign policy tool, not as a development tool.

# ★ POWER, PURPOSE, AND GLOBAL INEQUALITY

Global inequality is one of the few international issues on which there is considerable consensus on purpose. People and governments around the world agree that poverty alleviation and the reduction of inequality are important goals. Beyond that shared purpose, there are intense debates about the causes of poverty, the best policies to alleviate it, and the relative importance of increasing wealth versus decreasing inequality.

In actual policies, we see power playing an important role. Internationally, within the governance structures of the World Bank and the IMF, the wealthiest and most powerful countries maintain a dominant role in determining which development strategies receive international support. However, the development of previously impoverished countries—especially big ones like China, India, and Brazil—has the potential to significantly alter the distribution of global economic and political power.

## SUMMARY

- The number of people living in extreme poverty has decreased in recent decades, largely due to economic growth in China. In many of the poorest countries, especially in Africa, poverty has barely declined.

- There remains considerable debate about the causes and potential cures of global inequality and of the poverty that pervades much of the world.

- Over time, consensus has grown that free trade promotes economic growth and therefore reduces poverty, but it is not clear that free trade reduces inequality.

- Import substitution as an economic strategy has largely been discredited.

- Recent experience indicates that good governance domestically has a crucial impact on economic development.

- There remains considerable debate about the appropriate role of the government in economic growth and the reduction of poverty. Some see the state as doing more harm than good; others see the developmental state as a key actor in creating and maintaining a strong market and in building internationally competitive business.

- Despite consensus that free trade increases overall wealth, many continue to argue that trade is fundamentally unfair and will lead to increasing gaps between rich and poor.

- Governments and international organizations continue to support the use of foreign aid to promote development, but there is little agreement on how well it works or on what works best.

- Foreign aid accounts for a tiny part of donor states' GDP, and much bilateral foreign aid is aimed at political goals rather than economic development.

- Global poverty and inequality will likely remain serious problems for decades to come.

## KEY CONCEPTS

1. Human Development Index (HDI)
2. Gini coefficient
3. Late development
4. Economies of scale
5. Network effects
6. Import substitution

7. Export-led growth
8. Washington consensus
9. Developmental state
10. World Bank
11. Tied aid
12. Good governance

## STUDY QUESTIONS

1. Which method of measuring poverty takes into account differences in the cost of living?
   a. Gross domestic product (GDP)
   b. Per capita GDP
   c. GDP at purchasing power parity (PPP)
   d. The Gini coefficient

2. Which method of measuring poverty measures whether basic human needs are being met?
   a. GDP at PPP
   b. The Human Development Index (HDI)
   c. The Gini coefficient
   d. The Gender Development Index

3. Which state will have the highest Gini coefficient?
   a. A state with a high GDP
   b. A state with a low GDP
   c. A state with a large income gap
   d. A state with a small income gap

4. Which of the following is a first-mover advantage?
   a. Economies of scale
   b. Network effects
   c. Investment funds
   d. All of the above.

5. Which country adopted import substitution as a development model?
   a. India
   b. Singapore
   c. Japan
   d. All of the above.

6. Which country adopted export-led growth as a development model?
   a. India
   b. Cuba
   c. Japan
   d. All of the above.

7. What are some different ways of defining and measuring poverty?

8. What challenges do late developers face that early developers did not?

9. What have been the major strategies adopted by late developers?

10. What contrasting explanations are there for the success of the Asian Tigers?

11. What are the main arguments for and against foreign aid?

[Correct Answers: 1. C; 2. B; 3. C; 4. D; 5. A; 6. C]

## END NOTES

1. "A Fall to Cheer," *The Economist*, May 3, 2012, www.economist.com/node/21548963.

2. "A Fall to Cheer."

3. "Why Nutrition Matters," *The Economist*, April 24, 2012, www.economist.com/blogs/feastandfamine/2012/04/development.

4. Henry Shue, *Basic Rights: Subsistence, Affluence, and Foreign Policy*, 2nd ed. (Princeton, NJ: Princeton University Press, 1996).

5. See UNDP, *Human Development Report 2007/2008: Fighting Climate Change: Human Solidarity in a Divided World* (New York: UNDP, 2007).

6. See Amartya Sen, *On Economic Inequality*, expanded ed. (Oxford, UK: Clarendon Press, 1997 [1973]), p. 164ff.

7. World Health Organization, "Human Rights, Health and Poverty Reduction Strategies," 2008, p. 6.

8. World Bank, "GNI per capita, Atlas method (current US$)," http://data.worldbank.org/indicator/NY.GNP.PCAP.CD; and "GNI per capita, PPP (current international $)," http://data.worldbank.org/indicator/NY.GNP.PCAP.PP.CD.

9. See www.un.org/millenniumgoals. In the text, the wording of some of the goals has been edited for the sake of brevity.

10. United Nations, "Millennium Development Goals 2015," p. 8, http://www.un.org/millenniumgoals/.

11. Nurith Aizerman, "How to Eliminate Extreme Poverty in 169 Not-So-Easy Steps," National Public Radio, July 7, 2015, at http://www.npr.org/sections/goatsandsoda/2015/07/07/420549986/how-to-eliminate-extreme-poverty-in-169-not-so-easy-steps.

12. Thomas D. Lairson and David Skidmore, *International Political Economy: The Struggle for Power and Wealth*, 3rd ed. (Belmont, CA: Wadsworth, 2003), p. 246.

13. Herman Schwartz, *States versus Markets: History, Geography, and the Development of the International Political Economy* (New York: St. Martin's Press, 1994), p. 10.

14. Schwartz, *States versus Markets*, p. 10.

15. The classic exposition of the theory of late development is Alexander Gerschenkron, *Economic Backwardness in Historical Perspective* (Cambridge, MA: Belknap Press, 1962).

16. "Sensex Nicks 9000, But What about Gini Coefficient?" *The Indian Express*, December 4, 2005, http://archive.indianexpress.com/res/web/pIe/columnists/ie_index.php..

17. Lairson and Skidmore, *International Political Economy*, p. 268.

18. The World Bank, *The East Asian Economic Miracle: Economic Growth and Public Policy* (New York: Oxford University Press, 1993).

19. See Kym Anderson and Ernesto Valenzuela, "The World Trade Organization's Doha Initiative: A Tale of Two Issues," *The World Economy*, Vol. 30, No. 8 (2007): 1282.

20. William Easterly, "The Ideology of Development," *Foreign Policy* (July/August 2007): 31.

21. For a short critique of the World Bank, see Easterly, "The Ideology of Development"; for a longer and more radical critique, see Arturo Escobar, *Encountering Development: The Making and Unmaking of the Third World* (Princeton, NJ: Princeton University Press, 1995).

22. Data in this paragraph are from the IBRD web page, go.worldbank.org/SH36X77BF0.

23. Data in this paragraph are from the IDA website, http://www.worldbank.org/ida/financing.html.

24. Ezra Klein, "The Budget Myth That Just Won't Die: Americans Still Think 28 Percent of the Budget Goes to Foreign Aid," *Washington Post*, November 7, 2013.

25. Theodore Cohn, *Global Political Economy: Theory and Practice*, 2nd ed. (New York: Longman, 2002), p. 405.

# 13

The International Court of Justice, also known as the World Court, opens a session in February, 2015, on whether Croatia and Serbia committed genocide during the wars sparked by the breakup off the former Yugoslavia in the 1990s. What role does law play in international relations?

Peter Dejong/AP Images

# INTERNATIONAL LAW, NORMS, AND HUMAN RIGHTS

## Learning Objectives

**13-1** Define "international law."

**13-2** Identify the sources of international law and rank their importance.

**13-3** Analyze the problem of enforcing international law.

**13-4** Articulate and defend an argument concerning the significance of international law.

**13-5** Define "international norms."

**13-6** Explain the evolution of international norms and their influence on international politics.

**13-7** Describe international law concerning human rights and its relationship with state sovereignty.

**13-8** Describe the structure and process of the International Criminal Court.

CONSIDER THE CASE

# CONSIDER THE CASE

## THE SECURITY COUNCIL AND INTERVENTION FROM IRAQ TO SYRIA

After Iraq invaded Kuwait in August 1990, the United States and other nations resolved that, as U.S. President George H. W. Bush put it, "this will not stand." The United States and Kuwait immediately went to the UN Security Council, which approved a series of resolutions. The first, Security Council Resolution 660, passed within twenty-four hours of the invasion, condemned the Iraqi invasion and mandated a withdrawal of Iraqi forces from Kuwait.* Resolution 678, passed in November 1990, authorized UN member states to "use all necessary means to uphold and implement Resolution 660 and all subsequent relevant resolutions and to restore international peace and security."† The words "all necessary means," it was agreed, authorized the United States and others to attack Iraq to force it out of Kuwait. In January 1991, a force led by the United States but including contingents from thirty-three countries invaded Kuwait and forced Iraq to withdraw.

In 2002, the United States again prepared to invade Iraq and again sought authority from the UN Security Council. Resolution 1441, adopted on November 8, declared Iraq to be in violation of previous Security Council resolutions and stated that there would be "serious consequences" if Iraq did not comply.‡ Several members of the Security Council, including France, China, and Russia, stated that Resolution 1441 did not authorize war, because it did not contain the clear authorization provided in Resolution 678 of 1990.

The United States and Great Britain, understanding that the Security Council would not pass a clear authorization for military attack, asserted that Resolution 1441 and previous resolutions provided the legal basis to attack. Their case that the war was legal relied on two arguments: self-defense and the upholding of Security Council resolutions. First, they claimed that they were acting in self-defense, based on Article 51 of the UN charter, which states, in part, "Nothing in the present Charter shall impair the inherent right of individual or collective self-defense if an armed attack occurs." The Bush administration contended that the right of self-defense included the right to preempt the

use of weapons of mass destruction. More broadly, the **Bush doctrine** held that preventive war against potential nuclear proliferators was legal.

Second, they claimed that existing resolutions provided authorization for the use of force and that no new resolution was needed. U.S. Secretary of State Colin Powell, speaking before the Security Council in February 2003, stated, "Iraq has now placed itself in danger of the serious consequences called for in UN Resolution 1441. And this body places itself in danger of irrelevance if it allows Iraq to continue to defy its will without responding effectively and immediately."§ They focused particularly on the words "serious consequences." Jack Straw, the British Foreign Minister, stated, "As far as the legal base is concerned, 1441 does not require a second resolution."¶ The governments also asserted that the resolutions surrounding the first invasion of Iraq in 1991, including Resolution 678, were still in effect. The failure of Iraq to fully comply with the cease-fire reached in 1991, it was argued, meant that states were still authorized under Resolution 678 to resume hostilities.

Those who viewed the war as illegal were particularly critical of the argument that the attack was justified as self-defense under Article 51 of the UN Charter. Article 51 specifically allows self-defense "if an armed attack occurs." Moreover, Article 51 allows states to use force without prior Security Council approval only "until the Security Council has taken measures necessary to maintain international peace and security." Because the Security Council had taken, through its various resolutions, the steps it believed were necessary, opponents argued, any attack was disallowed. Critics also disagreed with the argument that Council Resolution 1441 authorized war with its threat of "serious consequences." Not only did the resolution not say anything about military force as a possible consequence, it did not authorize any actor to carry out those consequences.

In contrast to the 1991 invasion, there was widespread disagreement as to whether the 2003 invasion was legal and therefore legitimate. Global indignation

*(Continued)*

was captured by UN Secretary General Kofi Annan, who stated in 2004, "From our point of view and the Charter point of view, it [the invasion] was illegal."** In subsequent years, U.S. prestige declined around the world, in part as a consequence of the perception that it should not have invaded Iraq (and in part because of the difficulties it encountered after the initial defeat of Iraq's army).

The question of Security Council authorization for military action arose again in the cases of Libya (2011) and Syria (2012). In both cases, the United States and others sought Security Council authorization to use force or to apply pressure, but the Security Council was able to agree only in the Libya case.

These cases raise several questions. First, why did the United States and its allies even bother seeking UN approval for their actions? What were the perceived benefits of gaining UN authorization and the costs of not receiving it? Second, why did it matter to other states whether the United States and its allies did or did not have UN approval for their military plans? Third, was the invasion legal? Who decides legality

in international affairs, and how does international law differ from domestic law? Fourth, in what ways did international law constrain the various actors in these cases? In what ways did it empower them? How would theorists from different schools of thought explain these cases?

---

*For the text of Security Council Resolution 660, see daccess-dds-ny.un.org/doc/RESOLUTION/GEN/NR0/575/10/IMG/NR057510.pdf?OpenElemnt.

†For the text of Resolution 678, see daccess-dds-ny.un.org/doc/RESOLUTION/GEN/NR0/575/28/IMG/NR057528.pdf?OpenElement..

‡For the text of Resolution 1441, see daccess-dds-ny.un.org/doc/UNDOC/GEN/N02/682/26/PDF/N0268226.pdf?OpenElement.

§Rachel S. Taylor, "The United Nations, International Law, and the World in Iraq," World Press Review Online, www.worldpress.org/specials/iraq.

¶Channel 4 News (UK), March 11, 2003, www.channel4.com/news/2003/02 /week_2/11_warlegal.html.

**"Annan Says Iraq War Was 'Illegal'," New York Times, September 16, 2004.

---

**Bush doctrine**

A set of principles, formed during the administration of U.S. President George W. Bush, asserting the necessity of waging preventive war against potential aggressors possessing weapons of mass destruction.

I nternational law is a very old idea that has attained renewed importance in recent decades. The more states interact with one another, the more they need to develop formal and informal rules to manage their relations. Yet the status of international law and the role that such rules can and should play are hotly debated. Since there is no recognized international government, who has the authority to make the laws? How can they be enforced? Some people argue that without a reliable enforcement mechanism, international law is not really "law." Yet there is no doubt that international law, in the form of international treaties, courts, regimes, and norms, is expanding.

Around the world, the violation of human rights is drawing increased attention. The traditional notion that what goes on within a country is not the business of anyone outside that country is eroding. How is international law evolving to deal with this trend? This chapter explores these issues by examining both concrete cases and the concepts and arguments put forward by realists, liberals, constructivists, and advocates of the other approaches to international relations.

# WHAT IS INTERNATIONAL LAW?

**international law**

The set of rules and obligations that states recognize as binding on each other.

**International law** can be defined as the set of rules and obligations that states recognize as binding on each other.[1] Three points are worth emphasizing. First, international law has traditionally been regarded as law among *states*. However, in recent decades, the increased importance of international organizations and transnational actors has led to pressure to give them an explicit role in international law. Second, only those rules that states *recognize* as binding are considered international law. Third, there is no presumption that all relations between states are regulated by international law. Only matters on which states recognize obligations are covered.

International law addresses a vast range of issues that arise between states. Treaty obligations between states, for example, deal with trade (the World Trade Organization), the environment (the Kyoto Protocol), and the conduct of war. The coverage of international law is very broad, but patchy. Some agreements cover one part of an issue but leave related matters unregulated. In other cases, some countries have signed treaties regulating conduct, and others, equally involved in the matter, have not.

# INTERNATIONAL LAW AND INTERNATIONAL RELATIONS THEORY

In early 2003, U.S. Secretary of State Colin Powell presents a vial that could contain anthrax as he tries to convince the UN Security Council that Iraq is developing weapons of mass destruction.

International law is an area of central dispute among theories of international politics, especially between realism and liberalism. At the time of World War II, realists charged that reliance on international law, rather than on power politics, had been an important factor contributing to Hitler's rise to power. More broadly, realism finds that self-interest and power politics will always trump international law. Powerful states either ensure that international law suits their interests, or they ignore it when it contradicts their interests.

Liberals see international law as an essential part of international politics and charge that realists fundamentally mistake the nature of international law. Liberals find that international law helps states regulate their relations in ways that they find mutually beneficial. International law tends to enforce itself, they say, because states that routinely violate international law suffer a loss of prestige and reputation that harms their interests.

Economic structuralists agree with realists that international law is heavily biased in favor of the powerful. The powerful states largely write the laws, and they determine when they are enforced. Normatively, however, economic structuralists tend to agree with liberals. They see international law as a possible tool to level the economic and political playing field between the strong and weak.

Constructivists build on the normative and reputational aspects of the liberal argument. International law, in this view, represents a codification of shared norms and an expression of shared purpose. It interacts deeply with state interest, because every state perceives an interest in being known as a law-abiding member of the community. From this perspective, the violation of international law is no different from violations of domestic law, which individuals sometimes get away with. Those individuals still often find themselves shunned, and most members of the community try to avoid the perception that they have broken the rules.

Feminists in general see international law as a possible means to redress much of the injustice they see in the world. Like human rights activists more broadly, they seek to establish high international standards in human rights in the hope that these standards can be used to lift the status of women around the world. Some feminists, like economic structuralists, remain leery of what they see as the imperialist nature of this project—human rights standards often seem to be promoted by wealthy Western states and enforced on poorer states in the Southern Hemisphere.

# THE HISTORY OF INTERNATIONAL LAW

International law goes back as far as recorded history.[2] Early agreements dealt with relatively simple matters, such as territorial boundaries and rules for exchanging ambassadors.

The modern history of international law, like the nation-state system, has its roots in medieval Europe. The early European states considered themselves part of a single Christian political and religious space, the heir to the Roman Empire, and believed that their relations should be governed by rules rooted in church doctrine. Because medieval European states were constantly at war with one another (or waging crusades in the Middle East), the appropriate reasons for going to war, and acceptable means of fighting war, were important issues.

## GROTIUS AND THE THEORY OF JUST WAR

Efforts to forge a European international law based on the guidance of the Catholic Church persisted into the sixteenth century. However, the Protestant Reformation had destroyed the notion of a single Christian community, and increasingly violent religious conflicts in Europe culminated in the Thirty Years' War. In 1625, in the midst of that conflict, the Dutch lawyer Hugo Grotius published *The Law of War and Peace*.

Grotius sought to produce a systematic **just war theory**, and he defined the problem in ways that are still familiar to us today. He asked two basic questions. First, in what circumstances is it permissible to go to war? Second, what kinds of practices are acceptable in the prosecution of war? Grotius based his answers on Christian theology, including the work of earlier theorists such as Augustine of Hippo and Thomas Aquinas. But he also revolutionized the study and practice of international law by advancing the concept of *natural law*—the idea that rational inquiry could reveal to people what behaviors should be legal.[3] He argued that war was just only if the reasons for going to war were just and the means used to prosecute the war were just. These principles are often known by their Latin names, *jus ad bellum* (just cause for war) and *jus in bello* (just conduct in war).

Included in Grotius's approach are several familiar ideas:

- There must be just cause to go to war.
- War must be declared by legitimate authorities.
- The means used in war must not be inhumane.
- The means used in war must be proportional to the ends obtained.

## INTERNATIONAL LAW IN THE TWENTIETH CENTURY

It is not coincidental that the most violent century in history was also the century in which states and people renewed efforts to strengthen international law.

The horrors of World War I motivated the formation of the League of Nations. The goal was to prevent war by getting states to join forces against aggression. Other treaties of the post–World War I period went further. The Kellogg-Briand Pact of 1928, signed by all of the major states, renounced war as an instrument of state policy. This treaty was quickly ignored and later mocked, but other treaties of the same era fared better, including the 1925 Geneva Protocol banning biological and chemical weapons.

**just war theory**
The theory of the circumstances in which it is ethical to go to war and the kinds of practices that are ethical in the prosecution of war.

# THE HISTORY CONNECTION

## THE GENEVA CONVENTIONS

Much of contemporary international law on the conduct of war is codified in the Geneva Conventions. The first Geneva Convention was signed in 1864; the fourth was signed in 1949 and amended in 1977. The importance of these rules was demonstrated recently when the United States was accused of violating them at prisons in Iraq and Cuba.

Although limits on the conduct of war had been discussed for centuries, in the mid-nineteenth century, as the scale of warfare increased, there were few internationally agreed limits. In June 1859, a Swiss merchant named Henri Dunant witnessed the Battle of Solferino, in what is today northern Italy. He was shocked to see soldiers dying slow, agonizing deaths, sometimes succumbing to thirst because they could not be retrieved from the battlefield and treated.

Dunant returned to Geneva and began to campaign for injured soldiers. He called for a volunteer group of nurses and doctors to treat the wounded and for international recognition that these workers were neutrals and would not be harmed by warring armies. This led to the establishment of an International Committee for Relief to the Wounded, which later became the International Committee of the Red Cross. This committee then lobbied for international recognition. In 1864, the Swiss government sponsored a diplomatic conference that established provisions for the care of the wounded and recognized the International Committee of the Red Cross.* The first Geneva Convention is known officially as the Convention for the Amelioration of the Condition of the Wounded in Armies in the Field, 1864. It protects medical workers, ambulances, and military hospitals, identified by the familiar red cross on a white background.

In 1906, the second Geneva Convention extended the provisions of the first convention to warfare at sea. The third convention, negotiated in 1925, introduced provisions for the treatment of prisoners of war. Article 17 states, "No physical or mental torture, nor any other form of coercion, may be inflicted on prisoners of war to secure from them information of any kind whatever. Prisoners of war who refuse to answer may not be threatened, insulted, or exposed to unpleasant or disadvantageous treatment of any kind."

The third convention goes into considerable detail on the rights of prisoners and on definitions of who is a "lawful combatant" and thus covered by the convention. These definitional issues seemed fairly noncontroversial until the war in Afghanistan in 2001, when there was considerable disagreement concerning which people captured by the United States and its allies were protected by the third convention and which were not.

The fourth Geneva Convention was adopted in 1949 in reaction to the unprecedented level of attacks on civilians in World War II, from the bombing of cities, practiced by all sides, to the Holocaust. This convention, which deals with the protection of civilians during war, has been invoked in recent years to indict leaders for war crimes in places such as Yugoslavia, Rwanda, and Sudan.

## Critical Thinking Questions

1. How strong a limit do the Geneva Conventions create in practice? Do states obey the conventions only when it is convenient, or do they act as though violating them carries a high cost?

2. How do you anticipate that the "war on terror," with its debates about the utility of torture and the status of "enemy combatants," will affect the role of the Geneva Conventions?

*"International Humanitarian Law," www.redcross.lv/en/conventions.htm

Children at Auschwitz Concentration Camp in Poland, 1945. The atrocities of World War II spurred development of the Genocide Convention, which stated, "Persons committing genocide ... shall be punished, whether they are constitutionally responsible rulers, public officials, or private individuals."

AP Photo/CAF pap

The outbreak of World War II and the atrocities committed in that war convinced many people, realists in particular, that international law was pointless—and convinced others that it was more necessary than ever. Following the war, the international community adopted a convention against genocide and a Universal Declaration of Human Rights, both of which continue to be relevant today.

The new danger, however, was nuclear war between the United States and the Soviet Union. In the 1960s and 1970s, the two superpowers reached a series of bilateral treaties to limit the number of nuclear weapons produced. More important, perhaps, they collaborated in getting many other countries to sign the 1968 Treaty on the Non-Proliferation of Nuclear Weapons.

International law flourished in other areas. As the EU emerged and grew, it developed an expanding body of international law applying to its members. Similarly, the General Agreement on Tariffs and Trade, and then the WTO, detailed agreements regulating the conduct of trade between states. In 1987, the first major international environmental agreement, the Montreal Protocol, banned the use of aerosol propellants that deplete the ozone layer. The twentieth century did not see sovereign states subjected to the rule of law from above—which would mean the end of the sovereign state system—but it did see the emergence of an increasingly thick web of agreements among states to govern their relations.

# SOURCES OF INTERNATIONAL LAW

The origins of international law differ fundamentally from those of domestic law. Within nation-states, laws are made by sovereign governments. In international politics, there is no sovereign above the "subjects"—the states—and there is no international legislature. So where does international law come from? Who makes it?

Article 38 of the Charter of the International Court of Justice (ICJ)—the most authoritative international judicial body—lists three major sources of international law:

- International conventions [treaties], whether general or particular, establishing rules expressly recognized by the consenting states

- International custom, as evidence of a general practice accepted as law

- The general principles of law recognized by civilized nations

Article 38 of the ICJ Charter identifies judiciary rulings and the opinions of experts as "subsidiary" sources of law. Moreover, states have delegated some legislative authority in specific areas to international organizations. A primary example is the EU's Council and Parliament.

It is worth noting as well what is *not* considered a source of international law: the United Nations General Assembly. Although General Assembly (GA) resolutions can be important in forming new norms, the GA does not have the law-writing role of a domestic legislature. The role of the Security Council is stronger: Security Council resolutions are considered binding law, but the council deals only with those particular conflicts that are brought before it. It has no authority to pass general laws that are binding on states.

In one way or another, the source of all international law is states' agreement to accept certain obligations and be bound by them. The best domestic analogy is not the laws passed by legislatures, but the private agreements and contracts entered into by firms and individuals. At the international level, such agreements and contracts can be made formally, through treaties, or they can arise informally, as an outgrowth of international customs, general practices, or general principles of law. However, neither international custom nor general principles of "civilized nations" can come to exist without states' agreeing to them and recognizing them.

Over time, formal treaties have become increasingly important relative to other sources. There has been a steady effort since World War II, carried out by the International Law Commission of the UN, to codify essential aspects of custom and general principles into formal agreements. Codification helps remove ambiguity regarding what is meant and what is not.

# ENFORCEMENT OF INTERNATIONAL LAW

Enforcement, in many people's view, is the central problem of international law. Law is only meaningful to the extent that the same rules apply to everyone. What happens when a state, an organization, or an individual violates the law? Domestic law relies on a process of determining guilt or innocence, assigning a penalty, and applying the penalty. Enforcement is a major issue in international law as well, but the process works quite differently. There are two potential mechanisms for enforcement of international law. One is enforcement by international organizations, such as the UN. The other is self-enforcement by states. Neither is perfectly reliable, and neither is fair.

## JUDGMENT

In order for enforcement to occur, there has to be some finding that international law has been violated. How does this occur in the international system? Essentially, there are two ways to make such a determination. The first is through a ruling of an international court or another international organization. The second is through a unilateral determination by a country. Both methods are problematic.

**International Court of Justice (ICJ)**

Also known as the World Court, the body that adjudicates disputes over treaty obligations.

**The International Court of Justice**    The primary international court, empowered to determine when states have violated international law, is the **International Court of Justice (ICJ)**, also referred to unofficially as the World Court, based in The Hague in the Netherlands. It is the descendent of earlier courts, including the Permanent Court of International Justice that existed under the League of Nations. The ICJ is part of the UN system.

The court consists of fifteen judges, including one each from the five permanent members of the UN Security Council. The ICJ adjudicates disputes between states on matters over which they have previously agreed that the court will have jurisdiction (see Figure 13.1). Many international treaties include provisions that disputes over the treaty shall be resolved by the ICJ. Much more broadly, many states have signed agreements that they will submit their international conduct in general to the jurisdiction of the ICJ. In cases over which the court has jurisdiction, its rulings are considered final; there is no higher court to which the losing party can appeal. However, when states have not previously agreed to the court's jurisdiction, the court has none.

With those obvious limitations, the court is generally believed to function well. States do not like to be brought before the court or to lose a case there, so they tend to avoid behavior that would likely lead to such an outcome. In that sense, the court may be influential even when cases are not brought to it. Some examples of cases considered by the court in 2009–2010 illustrate its role.

- The ICJ ruled in 2004 that U.S. courts must reconsider the cases of fifty-one Mexican citizens awaiting death sentences in the United States because the accused had not been granted all the rights required by an international consular treaty. The United States responded by withdrawing its consent for ICJ jurisdiction on that treaty, but the court asserted that it continued to have jurisdiction and found that the United States was in breach of its obligations.

- The ICJ ruled on a case brought by Argentina against Uruguay in 2006, arguing that Uruguay had violated the 1975 Statute on the River Uruguay by building two pulp mills on the river. The court ruled that Uruguay had violated the procedural requirements of the treaty, but not the substance. Argentina had asked the court to order Uruguay to dismantle the mills or pay compensation and to provide guarantees concerning future behavior under the treaty, but the court did neither.

- At the request of the General Assembly, the ICJ issued an advisory opinion on the legality of Kosovo's 2008 declaration of independence. Various actors had asserted that the declaration of independence violated general principles of international law or UN Security Council Resolution 1244, which had been adopted in 1999 to end fighting in Kosovo. In finding the declaration of independence legal, the court found specifically that Resolution 1244 was not binding on the Kosovo authorities who declared independence.

- The ICJ began considering a case in which Burkina Faso and Niger jointly submitted a border dispute for resolution. The two countries had agreed in a 2009 treaty to many of the details of their border, but agreement on one section remained contested, and they agreed to ask the ICJ to resolve the matter. In this instance, the court functioned in the role of arbitrator.

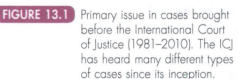

**FIGURE 13.1**  Primary issue in cases brought before the International Court of Justice (1981–2010). The ICJ has heard many different types of cases since its inception.

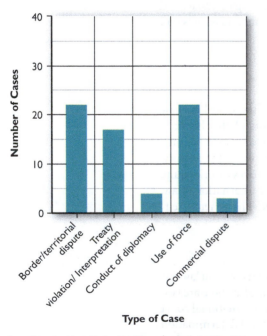

**Type of Case**

Source: International Court of Justice, "List of Cases referred to the Court Since 1946 by Date of Introduction," at http://www.icj-cij.org/docket/index.php?p1=3&p2=2; Paul D'Anieri.

As these examples indicate, the ICJ seems to play a tangential role in the dominant issues of international politics. In two of the four cases just described, the losing parties simply ignored the rulings, leaving the other parties with no further recourse.

**Unilateral Determination of Violations**   A second means of judging violations of international law is for states to decide themselves when laws or treaties have been violated. Such decisions obviously do not have the legitimacy of judgments by the ICJ or another international body. However, they may be a stronger deterrent to violations of agreements by other states. Because an aggrieved state may be more capable than an international organization of enforcing its judgment, states that contemplate violating agreements may be deterred. However, such enforcement is available only to relatively powerful states.

## ENFORCEMENT

**Enforcement by UN Organs**   In theory, enforcement of international law has been the responsibility of the UN system. The most pressing threats to international security tend to be brought to the Security Council, as do cases in which rulings by the ICJ are ignored.

The limitations of the Security Council process were discussed in depth in Chapter 7. The Security Council can enforce international law only when the five permanent members can agree to do so. Such cases have been relatively few. The most significant case in recent decades was the decision in 2011 to authorize the use of force to prevent Libyan leader Muammar Gaddafi from using military force against civilians.

**Enforcement by Specific Treaty Organizations**   Many treaties include provisions for rendering judgment on violations of those agreements. WTO members agree to accept the jurisdiction of the **WTO Dispute Settlement Body** (see Chapter 11). If a violation is found, the offending state can change its practice or can offer compensation. If it does not change its practice and does not make compensation agreeable to the plaintiff state, then the Dispute Settlement Body can authorize the plaintiff to enact retaliatory tariffs against the offending state. The system is not without flaws. In particular, developing countries may not be able, even with authorized sanctions, to meaningfully punish powerful states that violate the agreement. However, in its mandatory jurisdiction and its fairly reliable system of obtaining compliance with its rulings, the WTO mechanism is perhaps the most robust piece of international law enforcement outside the EU. It may serve as a model for future enforcement mechanisms.

**Blended Enforcement**   The WTO mechanism might be described as an instance of **blended enforcement**. In this model, the authority for penalties comes from a recognized international organization and is clearly recognized by treaty, but the actual enforcement is carried out by the aggrieved state or by others acting on its behalf. The obvious advantage of such a mechanism is that it does not rely on an international force or international sanctions, which are extremely difficult to implement in practice.

The problem with this model is that it is still likely to lead to uneven enforcement. When enforcement is left to willing states, law is likely to be enforced only when the powerful want it enforced. In the case of the Iraqi invasion of Kuwait in 1990, Kuwait would have been out of luck if the United States had not taken such a strong interest in the case. Powerful states have been considerably less willing to invest resources in enforcing international law in places where they have less at stake, including much of Africa. Moreover, to the extent that enforcement relies on Security Council authorization of the use of force, it is subject to veto by the five permanent members, who often protect their allies.

**WTO Dispute Settlement Body**

The enforcement body of the World Trade Organization, which can authorize aggrieved states to impose retaliatory tariffs against countries that violate the organization's rules.

**blended enforcement**

A model for implementing international law in which the authority for penalties comes from a recognized international organization and is clearly recognized by treaty, but the actual enforcement is carried out by the aggrieved state or by others acting on its behalf.

Residents of the Falkland Islands protest the visit of an Argentine delegation. Argentina claims sovereignty over the islands, which Britain has controlled, and over which the two fought a war in 1982. How are disputes over territory resolved?

Horacio Villalobos/Corbis

**Enforcement by Individual States**    Most international law relies on unilateral enforcement, meaning that it is up to the individual states to enforce it. Unlike citizens in the domestic arena, states in the international arena have the right to take justice into their own hands. The means open to them include diplomatic pressure, economic sanctions, and even force. The consequence of self-enforcement of international law is that enforcement is very uneven, and hence the protection of the law is very uneven. Powerful states get the most protection because others know that those states have the power to enforce the law themselves. Powerful states also can avoid being forced by weaker states to adhere to international law.

However, as supporters of international law point out, most international law is **self-enforcing** in a more basic way: Once states reach an agreement on an issue and are benefiting from that agreement, it is not in their interest to violate it. Although states that violate an agreement might get some short-term gain from doing so, they will suffer two longer-term and broader costs. First, the agreement they violate will likely be shattered, so they will be deprived of any future benefits from it. Other states are unlikely to continue honoring their obligations to a state that has violated an agreement. The repeated version of the prisoner's dilemma, discussed in Chapter 3, shows that defecting in the short term can undermine cooperation that is beneficial in the long term. Second, once a state's reputation is damaged, it will become much more difficult for that state to reach future agreements on issues that may be of considerable importance. It is, therefore, costly to damage one's reputation as a good partner.[4]

**self-enforcing**

International law is self-enforcing when states have incentives to obey, even when there is no sanction for violating the law or agreement.

# IS INTERNATIONAL LAW REALLY LAW?

The inconsistent enforcement of international law leads many to question whether international law should even be called "law." Skeptics argue that international law is an oxymoron. States, they contend, obey international law only when it suits their interest.

Supporters assert that international law is indeed law and that it has important effects on international behavior. These arguments over the status of international law arise from different theoretical approaches to international politics. Both sides have a point. International law is different from domestic law in important ways, and enforcement is a particular issue. However, international law does have important effects on state behavior, and if it did not exist, it would probably need to be created.

## THE CASE AGAINST INTERNATIONAL LAW

Realists and economic structuralists generally contend that international law is irrelevant. To the extent that it does matter, they say, international law is a tool used by the strong to control the weak. It does not, therefore, have a significant effect in constraining state behavior.

From this perspective, one problem in international law is how agreements are made in the first place. Powerful states, it is argued, force weaker states to accept laws that favor the powerful. One fundamental example is the composition of the UN Security Council, where the great powers were able to set up a system that gives them more rights than others. A second problem is enforcement. If international law is enforced by states, it will be enforced only when the powerful states benefit from it. This, realists and economic structuralists contend, contradicts the very notion of *law* as something that applies equally to all actors without exception.

## THE CASE FOR INTERNATIONAL LAW

Liberals and constructivists argue that the skeptics have missed the point. Focusing entirely on coercive enforcement ignores the ways in which international law solves problems for states and is therefore self-enforcing. The cost of destroying international treaties or ruining one's reputation is by itself often enough to ensure compliance. Enforcement, in this view, is not the key problem. As the scholar Louis Henkin wrote, "Almost all nations observe almost all…of international law…almost all of the time."[5]

International treaties and laws are established, according to this view, because states need them. If states could achieve common goals and avoid perils without international law, they would do so. International law is created because the mutual assurances and common understandings it provides enable states to avoid dangerous situations.

Those who emphasize the role of international law also point out that states that violate international law pay a price, sometimes a high one, for doing so. The U.S. invasion of Iraq in 2003 was widely perceived around the world to be a violation of international law because it was a preemptive attack not sanctioned by the UN Security Council. The opinion that it was illegal did not stop the United States from going to war, but it did cost the United States considerably in terms of global opinion. This loss of prestige was not irrelevant, as the United States subsequently ran into difficulty gaining collaboration on a variety of issues, such as tougher sanctions to stop Iran's nuclear program.

## INTERNATIONAL AND DOMESTIC LAW COMPARED

Skeptics about international law stress that international law is unlike domestic law because of the unreliability of enforcement. Advocates of international law question, however, whether enforcement is essential to compliance. Do people obey domestic laws primarily because of enforcement or primarily because their normative beliefs or self-interests lead them to comply? To those who believe enforcement is crucial to compliance, international law looks very weak. To those who believe that laws are adopted to serve actors' interests and values, most law is self-enforcing, and the distinction between international and domestic law is less significant.

These different approaches can be illustrated through an analogy with domestic traffic rules. Skeptics liken international law to the speed limit on a highway. Speed limits are often meaningless without close enforcement—we violate them all the time. Supporters of international law compare it to the rule of driving on the correct side of the road. Without such a law, the highways would be chaotic and useless. Once that rule is established, and everyone drives on the same side, only a fool will violate the law.

Ultimately, both sides have a point. Enforcement of international law is weak, so voluntary compliance plays a much bigger role. However, international law does have important effects on state behavior. States continue to create new international law, and nonstate actors advocate more (or different) international laws because international law is perceived to be at least somewhat effective. As plenty of ongoing disagreements demonstrate, not every international challenge can be solved through international agreements and international laws. However, states continue to negotiate new agreements and to form new organizations. Far from being viewed only as constraints on states, international agreements are seen as enabling states to deal with problems that cannot be solved individually.

# INTERNATIONAL REGIMES

**International regimes**

Shared understandings about how states will behave on a particular issue.

Not all agreements among states achieve the status of international law. International regimes represent an intermediate category of agreements that are not formal laws but are significant nonetheless in shaping state behavior. **International regimes** can be defined as shared understandings about how states will behave on a particular issue.[6]

In some cases, these shared understandings can be embodied in formal treaties and become international law. In other cases, they can become embodied in international organizations. Often, however, they remain unwritten and are not represented by formal organizations. The fundamental point made by scholars of international regimes is that even when they are left informal, such regimes shape behavior.

A simple example is the nuclear nonproliferation regime. States have a shared interest in preventing the proliferation of nuclear weapons. This regime is institutionalized in several ways, including in the Treaty on Non-Proliferation of Nuclear Weapons (NPT), the International Atomic Energy Agency (an international organization), and the Nuclear Suppliers Group (a group of states that export nuclear technology and have agreed to abide by guidelines for such exports). None of these agreements or organizations by themselves completely achieves the goals of the nonproliferation regime; the regime is a broader concept that helps explain what connects those formal institutions and why they exist. In 2015, two prominent scholars called for a "drone accountability regime" to "help ensure better compliance with the laws of war in the case of lethal drone use."[7]

**international norms**

Shared ethical principles and expectations about how actors should and will behave in the international arena; and social identities, indicating which actors are considered legitimate.

## INTERNATIONAL NORMS

Constructivists also point to the role played by **international norms** and to the ways in which changes in norms account for changes in behavior. These norms can take many forms:

- Ethical principles about how actors *should* behave
- Mutual expectations about how actors *will* behave in certain situations
- Social identities, indicating which actors are to be considered legitimate

Constructivist theory focuses on how normative change leads states to redefine their interests and therefore to behave differently. For example, recent decades have seen considerable change in norms concerning human rights and state sovereignty. In 1999, discussing NATO's decision to bomb Yugoslavia in response to its treatment of its Kosovar minority, Czech President Vaclav Havel asserted that "it seems that the enlightened endeavors of generations of democrats, the horrible experience of two World Wars, which contributed so substantially to the adoption of the Universal Declaration of Human Rights as well as the overall development of our civilization, are gradually bringing the human race to the realization that a human being is more important than a State … This change, among other things, should gradually antiquate the idea of noninterference, that is, the concept of saying that what happens in another state, or the measure of respect for human rights there, is none of our business."[8]

These issues remain controversial, but there has no doubt been a normative change—a change in general beliefs about what is right and wrong and about the priorities among different values. The point is not that norms *compel* states to behave in certain ways. Rather, they *motivate* states to behave in certain ways. Norms do not outweigh or compete with self-interest, but they often help redefine state interests.

**How Do Norms Spread?**    There are a great number of advocates around the world promoting a wide variety of causes with great passion. What determines which values gain the consensus necessary to motivate a large number of states to change policies? It is difficult to give a precise answer, but the ability to successfully spread the norms one supports is an element of "soft power," as defined in Chapter 1. Four channels can be identified through which norms are diffused across the international community (see Figure 13.2).

First, norms can spread through international organizations. International organizations can establish standards on issues and, using their status, present those standards or norms as having international legitimacy. For example, the expertise of the World Bank helped spread the "Washington consensus" on development strategy. Transnational advocacy networks can also be powerful in stating and promoting new norms.

Second, norms can spread from state to state. Success depends in part on the prestige and power of the governments spreading the norm. The prestige and economic power of the EU states have helped them spread many norms, including opposition to capital punishment, to the formerly communist states of eastern Europe.

Third, transnational groups of government experts, all working on the same issues, often reach agreement among themselves first and then seek to promote the agreed-on norms with their respective societies and governments. This has been the case among scientists hoping to combat various environmental and health problems.

Fourth, norms can spread across societies and then influence governments from the bottom up. **Norm entrepreneurs**—individuals who seek to promote a new norm—can sometimes begin a process that leads to the norm's eventually being widely adopted. Prior to 1994, the international norm against doing business with South Africa's apartheid government spread within the United States largely through the existing U.S. civil rights movement, which then worked to make it a national policy.[9] Transnational advocacy networks often seek to work from the bottom up, from societies to governments.

In sum, although international norms have always been a factor in international politics, people and governments around the world seem increasingly willing to explicitly take them into account in making policy. This does not mean that norms force compliance; rather, they often help change leaders' notions of what is desirable and what is acceptable.

**norm entrepreneurs**
Individuals or groups who seek to promote a new international norm.

**FIGURE 13.2** How international norms spread.

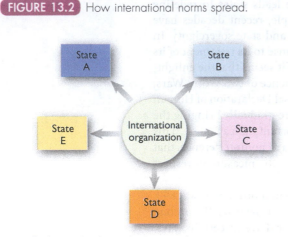

An international organization spreads a new norm.

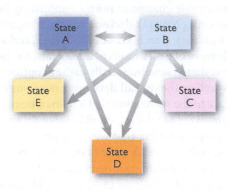

New norms spread from one state to other states.

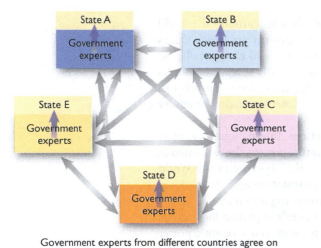

Government experts from different countries agree on norms and promote the norms within their governments.

Norms spread among societies, often through the efforts of transnational activists who attempt to persuade their governments to adopt the norms.

Source: Based on information found at http://papers.ssrn.com/sol3/papers.cfm?abstract_id=62934.

**Normative Disagreement** Although shared norms may motivate states to collaborate, normative conflict can sometimes be intense and bitter. In recent years, the norm that UN Security Council approval is required for military intervention has been supported by many states, rejected by a few, and accepted by others only within certain limits. This has led to intense resentment.

Moreover, even norms that are generally accepted do not always strengthen over time. A case in point is the norm against attacking noncombatants in war. For several centuries, this norm was generally followed throughout the world. In the first half of the twentieth century, however, it was completely abandoned, first in World War I, even more broadly in World War II, and then completely in U.S. and Soviet plans to annihilate each other's civilian populations.

Thus, there is no automatic mechanism requiring that normative consensus will increase within the international community. The rise of transnational terrorist groups

# THE GEOGRAPHY CONNECTION

## FREEDOM AROUND THE WORLD

This map shows the level of political freedom in the world, as measured by the U.S.-based group Freedom House in 2015. Freedom House bases its rankings on factors such as freedom of expression and assembly, rights of the accused, and freedom of the press.

### Critical Thinking Questions

1. What patterns or correlations can you see in the distribution of freedom around the world?

2. What other kinds of factors might be used in assessing human rights?

3. Are there countries whose rankings you would disagree with? Or countries whose rankings would change if different criteria were used?

Freedom in the World 2015

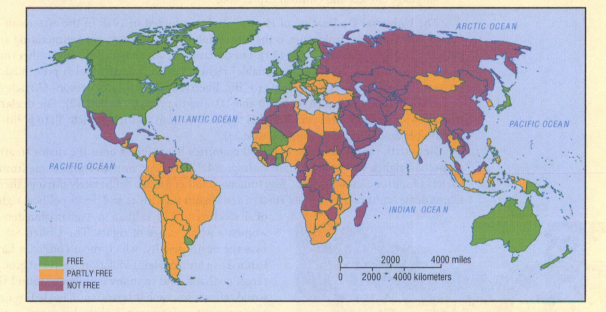

Source: https://freedomhouse.org/sites/default/files/FITW_World_Map_24x16_fa_GF2015.pdf.

indicates an undermining of a whole range of norms, including the norm that determines which actors can legitimately use force in the international system. Indeed, despite the development of international norms pointed to earlier, some would say we are living in a period of decreasing normative consensus.

# HUMAN RIGHTS

**human rights**

An array of "inalienable" individual rights, including civil liberties and political rights. Some advocates include economic rights and cultural rights as well.

**Human rights** have become an increasingly salient area of international politics in recent years. Norms concerning human rights are changing, as are norms concerning the relative weight of human rights versus state sovereignty. Concerns about human rights have been at the center of many high-profile issues in recent years. Examples include military intervention in the former Yugoslavia; tension over the rights of China's Tibetan minority; economic aid; refugees, asylum seekers, and migration; and questions about the treatment of suspected terrorists. In other words, nearly all the important issues considered in this book now have an important human rights dimension that influences how they are viewed and how policies are developed.

The scholar Charles Beitz divides human rights into five broad categories:

1. Personal rights, such as life, liberty, property, freedom of conscience, and religion.
2. Rights in law, such as equal protection, presumption of innocence, rights of the accused.
3. Political rights, such as freedom of speech, of the press, of assembly, and of association, as well as the right to choose one's government, and voting rights.
4. Economic and social rights, including the right to a job, a minimal standard of living, the right to join a union, and workplace rights.
5. Community rights, such as the rights of minority groups to self-determination, language choice, and cultural expression.[10]

The Universal Declaration of Human Rights, adopted in 1948 in the aftermath of World War II and the Holocaust, is the central international statement enumerating and defining human rights (see Table 13.1). The declaration, which is aspirational rather than binding law, lists an array of "inalienable" rights that every individual is presumed to possess. These include general rights to "life, liberty, and security of person" (Article 3), to fair trials and hearings (Articles 10 and 11), and to privacy (Article 12). The declaration also establishes more specific rights to freedom from torture (Article 5), to political asylum (Article 14), and to work (Article 23).[11]

Despite the fact that more than 150 countries have signed onto the major treaties on human rights, violations remain widespread.[12] Threats to human rights come from a variety of sources. In some cases, governments or other groups deliberately infringe them: China denies cultural rights to its Tibetan and Uighur minorities and limits political rights of all its citizens. The Taliban in Afghanistan denies women a whole range of rights. The United States uses the death penalty, which most countries have banned as a human rights violation. Terrorist groups target civilians, and in many countries around the world, efforts to combat terrorism have led to new infringements of human rights. In many cases, however, human rights are violated unintentionally, as a result of other conflicts or problems. Around the world, people are forced from their homes and become refugees as a result of wars, famines, and natural disasters. Poverty causes the violation of many social and economic rights. A competent government is a necessary condition for the protection of many basic human rights, and many governments are not up to the task.

Chinese police apprehend a pro-Tibet protester in Beijing.

Nir Elias/REUTERS

**TABLE 13.1**   **Human Rights in International Treaties**

| | Universal Declaration of Human Rights | International Covenant on Civil and Political Rights | International Covenant on Economic, Social, and Cultural Rights |
|---|:---:|:---:|:---:|
| Life | x | x | |
| Liberty and security of person | x | x | |
| Protection against slavery | x | x | |
| Protection against torture and inhumane punishment | x | x | |
| Recognition as a person before the law | x | x | |
| Equal protection of the law | x | x | |
| Access to legal remedies for rights violations | x | x | |
| Protection against arbitrary arrest or detention | x | x | |
| Hearing before an independent and impartial judiciary | x | x | |
| Presumption of innocence | x | x | |
| Protection against ex post facto laws | x | x | |
| Protection of privacy, family, and home | x | x | |
| Freedom of movement and residence | x | x | |
| Freedom of thought, conscience, and religion | x | x | |
| Freedom of opinion, expression, and the press | x | x | |
| Freedom of assembly and association | x | x | |
| Political participation | x | x | |
| Freedom to own property | x | | |
| Freedom to seek asylum from prosecution | x | | |
| Recognition of nationality | x | | |
| Protection against debtor's imprisonment | | x | |
| Protection against arbitrary expulsion as an alien | | x | |
| Protection against advocacy of racial or religious hatred | | x | |
| Protection of minority culture | | x | |
| Participation in free trade unions | x | x | x |
| Freedom to marry and found a family | x | x | x |
| Special protections for children | x | x | x |
| Self-determination | | x | x |

*(Continued)*

**TABLE 13.1** **Human Rights in International Treaties** (*Continued*)

| | Universal Declaration of Human Rights | International Covenant on Civil and Political Rights | International Covenant on Economic, Social, and Cultural Rights |
|---|---|---|---|
| Social security | x | | x |
| Work under favorable conditions | x | | x |
| Rest and leisure | x | | x |
| Food, clothing, and housing | x | | x |
| Health care and social services | x | | x |
| Education | x | | x |
| Participation in cultural life | x | | x |

Source: *Jack Donnelly, "State Sovereignty and International Intervention: The Case of Human Rights," in Gene M. Lyons and Michael Mastanduno, eds.,* Beyond Westphalia? State Sovereignty and International Intervention *(Baltimore, MD: Johns Hopkins University Press, 1995).*

Governments, international organizations, transnational advocacy networks, and NGOs are all concerned with improving protection of human rights. A variety of strategies is employed, depending on the group and the specific right being pursued. Economic and social rights are often pursued through aid and development efforts. Political rights are often pursued through public pressure campaigns, sometimes linking transnational advocacy networks with domestic NGOs. Often these overlap with government efforts.

Although many human rights are not controversial in themselves, the question of how to protect them leads to some of the thorniest international political questions today. If states have made an international treaty commitment to protect these rights and then fail to do so, does this make it a matter of concern to the international community? (See "The Policy Connection: Is Humanitarian Intervention a Duty? The Responsibility to Protect as a New Norm on p. 408") In recent years, more and more people—leaders as well as citizens—have answered this question affirmatively.

However, both the concept of human rights and the measures needed to protect them in the modern world clash with the Westphalian conception of sovereignty on which international law is based. The Westphalian system assumes that states control their own territory and citizens. Human rights assume that people have rights that states cannot deny and must protect. The Westphalian system assumes a territorial segmentation of authority. Human rights assume that rights, and the duty to protect them, are universal, regardless of boundaries. Therefore, the recent focus on human rights promotion represents a fundamental revision of the Westphalian idea that governments have sovereignty over their internal affairs, including the right to rule as they see fit.[13]

Intervention by one state in another—and military intervention in particular—is the most controversial aspect of the human rights debate today. Intervention to safeguard human rights is often advocated, and not infrequently carried out, in the contemporary system. Recent cases include Yugoslavia, Sudan, and Libya. Cases where intervention does not occur, such as Rwanda in 1994 and Syria in 2012, can be equally controversial. Even the U.S. invasion of Iraq was justified in part on the grounds that the government of Saddam Hussein consistently violated Iraqis' human rights.

# THE CONNECTION TO YOU

## HUMAN SECURITY

It sometimes seems that international politics operates at a level of abstraction far from our everyday lives, especially if we live in a country not touched by war or international economic crisis.* A focus on human rights stresses that the everyday rights of individuals are a matter of international political concern. Although we often speak of "international" or "national" security, advocates of a "human" security approach stress that the proper object of security is the individual, not the state.

In this view even the average university student has human security concerns. For instance, if your family's income falls below a certain level, you likely are eligible for financial aid to help fund your education. In most countries, education prior to college is provided free by the state (and until recently, many countries provided free college tuition). Most wealthy democracies consider basic health care to be an essential human right, and most have welfare systems and pension systems designed to ensure that people do not face the threat of starvation or homelessness that is a constant danger for many people in poorer countries. Traditional international relations sees these issues as falling outside the umbrella of security, but the human security approach sees suffering resulting from poverty as no less significant than that resulting from war.

The expanding literature on human security seeks to put individuals and their rights front and center in discussions of international politics. For most of the world's people, the biggest threat to security comes not from attack by some other country, but from the government of their own state. Moreover, civil war and economic deprivation are more of a threat to lives and welfare in many places than traditional warfare. How should international security policies take individuals into account? The human security approach is an attempt to address this question.

The focus on human security arose in part as a result of the United Nations Development Programme (UNDP), which advocated a change of focus from nuclear security and disarmament to reducing poverty around the world. Critics of the national security approach found it bizarre that U.S. and Soviet national security strategies relied on the threat of killing millions of people with nuclear weapons and depended on spending billions of dollars on weapons while many people lived in poverty. According to the UNDP, human security is defined by seven dimensions of individual welfare: economic security, food security, health security, environmental security, personal security, community security, and political security. The international relations theorist Steve Smith outlines six main threats to security defined in this way: unchecked population growth, disparities in economic opportunities, migration pressures, environmental degradation, drug trafficking, and international terrorism.[†]

Skeptics of the human security approach argue that it is difficult to solve problems if one cannot think about them clearly and that clear thinking requires analytical distinctions. In this view, confounding the problems of international security between states with those of individuals within a state makes it impossible to focus properly on either. Broadening the concept of international security to include everything from rising sea levels to homelessness to health insurance runs the risk of making the concept so broad that it is meaningless. The critics' point is not that individuals do not matter, but that the problems of local violence, individual poverty, and health care are distinct from those of international security and belong in a separate discussion.

*(Continued)*

## Critical Thinking Questions

1. What dimensions of human security are most salient to you? Are some rights more threatened for you and those around you than others?

2. How would a book like this one (or a course on international politics) look different if it adopted a human security perspective throughout?

3. In what ways does the human security perspective contribute to our understanding of human rights in world politics?

*\*Seung Lee contributed significantly to this discussion.*

*†See Steve Smith, "The Contested Concept of Security," in Ken Booth, ed., Critical Security Studies and World Politics (Boulder, CO: Lynne Rienner, 2005), pp. 51–55.*

There remain powerful arguments against military intervention. First, many people argue that such intervention is illegal under international law because it violates state sovereignty. Second, many argue that intervention happens only when it serves the interest of the interveners, and therefore is illegitimate. Third, many argue that intervening states do not have the right to put their own citizen-soldiers at risk to solve somebody else's problem. Finally, it is sometimes argued that such intervention does not work—that the institutions that protect and advance human rights, such as democracy, rule of law, and a functioning economy, cannot be established through external intervention. Supporters of intervention argue that human rights are as important an element of international law as sovereignty and that in many cases, only intervention can prevent massive suffering and genocide.[14]

**Migration and Human Rights** An inability or unwillingness of state governments to protect citizens' human rights is one major spur to migration. When migrants arrive in new states, establishing and protecting their rights is often challenging. Therefore, the questions of human rights and migration are closely connected. Migration is one international issue in which human rights questions arise even in consolidated democracies that are generally viewed as having strong guarantees of human rights.

***Sources of Migration*** A variety of hopes and fears may motivate the decision to emigrate.

• *Security:* Many people emigrate or become internally displaced unwillingly because of threats to their safety from war or famine. World War II, the Vietnam War, and the Syrian civil war are all examples of conflicts that have driven substantial migration.

Mark Eite/Aflo Co. Ltd./Alamy

Italy's Mario Balotelli. Immigration has redefined national identity in many societies. Racism in European football (soccer) is an ongoing concern.

- *Economic opportunity:* People go to places where there is economic opportunity. Historically, emigration from places such as Italy, Ireland, and Latin America was driven by economic desperation.

- *Oppression:* People flee authoritarian governments or religious persecution. Many fled the communist bloc during the Cold War. Today, people leave Cuba for both political and economic reasons.

- *Family reunification:* Once one member of a family migrates, for political or economic reasons, others often follow. Immigration policy in many countries gives preference to such cases.

- *Population growth and environmental degradation:* Environmental constraints, particularly a lack of good land in agricultural societies, motivate people to migrate to places where land is more plentiful.

- *Trafficking:* Historically, the trans-Atlantic slave trade forced many people to migrate involuntarily, leaving a profound legacy in Africa and in the Western Hemisphere. Today, trafficking for various purposes forcibly moves thousands of people each year.

**Refugees**    Many people crossing borders do so involuntarily, prompted by oppression or conflict, and become refugees under international law. The 1951 Convention Relating to the Status of Refugees defines a **refugee** as any person who "owing to a well-founded fear of being persecuted for reasons of race, religion, nationality, membership of a particular social group, or political opinion, is outside the country of his nationality, and is unable to or, owing to such fear, is unwilling to avail himself of the protection of that country."[15]

Europe faced a major humanitarian crisis in 2015, as refugees from conflict in the Middle East and Africa sought to cross the Mediterranean to enter Europe. Most of the refugees landed in Italy and Greece, which were overwhelmed, but other EU members resisted allowing refugees to relocate to their countries. In April 2015, more than 800 refugees drowned when the boat carrying them capsized between Libya and Italy. There was widespread sentiment that something must be done to prevent such tragedies, but European authorities were unwilling to allow refugees easy access and were unable either to end the conflicts in Africa that spurred the migration or to stop the smuggling networks that brought refugees to Europe.

The UN High Commissioner for Refugees (UNHCR) works with refugee populations around the world, a total of 13 million in 2014.[16] Historically, prominent examples of refugee populations have included Jews who fled persecution in many countries, huge populations moved in Europe as a result of World War II, and the "boat people" who left Vietnam after the communist victory in 1975. Today, the largest groups of refugees are in the Middle East and Southwest Asia, including large numbers of Palestinians as well as people displaced by the wars in Iraq, Afghanistan, Syria, and Libya.

The goal for many refugees, and for the states in which they become refugees, is to return to their homes. In practice, this is sometimes impossible, and refugees are able to claim **asylum,** which allows them to immigrate permanently to a new state. When refugees are not offered asylum or refuse to give up the hope of returning home, refugee status can effectively become permanent. Thus, the roughly 1 million Palestinians who left Israel as a result of the 1948 and 1967 Arab–Israeli wars continue to be refugees, as do their descendants, now numbering 5.1 million. Camps intended to be temporary have become permanent, but are often unfit for permanent settlement. Asylum seekers claim rights under international law and under many states' domestic laws, but it is not clear which countries have an obligation to help them. Generally, the biggest burden falls on the immediate neighbors of the countries from which the refugees are fleeing.

**refugee**

A person who leaves his or her country of nationality due to war, natural disaster, persecution, or the fear of persecution.

**asylum**

The granting of permission for people to enter and remain in a country to protect them from persecution in their home country.

***Undocumented Migrants*** Many people migrate without the legal protection of refugee status and without permission from the states to which they migrate. Because they do not have legal status, such immigrants generally do not have the same protections under the law as citizens. Because they are leery of appealing to authorities who might deport them, undocumented immigrants are vulnerable to exploitation by criminals and employers. Employers can pay illegal workers poorly, refuse to provide benefits, and violate safety rules because the workers have no recourse. Traffickers sometimes help people immigrate illegally in order to then use them essentially as slave labor. Even legal immigrants often encounter challenges to their human rights because immigration itself is so controversial.

***Dilemmas for Receiving Countries*** Migrants, documented or undocumented, face challenges in their adopted countries because their presence is often controversial. Economically, those who must compete for work with migrants see them as a threat to their livelihood. To the extent that migrants are poor and require social services, people also fear that they divert state resources from other missions. Cultural concerns are equally salient. Immigrants often bring their own languages, customs, traditions, and values (see Table 13.2). Some natives of receiving countries resent having people around them speaking foreign languages. Others fear that immigrants will promote values contrary to their own.

All those concerns arise for legal immigration as well. With illegal immigration, the debate becomes even more divisive. Once a person immigrates illegally, the options for the receiving state are not good. Finding illegal immigrants and sending them back home is expensive, disrupts the businesses and communities where they work, and often leads to bigger problems, such as children left in foster care when parents are deported. Moreover, many people argue that deporting immigrants is immoral or that it violates their human rights. Finally, the treatment of illegal migrants can cause significant tension with the migrants' home governments, as has happened between South Africa and Zimbabwe, between Italy and Libya, and between the United States and Mexico. On the other hand, guaranteeing the human rights of immigrants might provide an incentive for more to come because many people live in countries where human rights are not well protected. Thus, migration makes human rights an issue even in countries in North America and western Europe that are not typically seen as having human rights concerns.

### The Death Penalty, Norms, and Human Rights

The global movement against the death penalty is a case that illustrates the spread of an international norm in the area of human rights. Until a few decades ago, international pressure to eliminate the death penalty would have been unimaginable for two reasons. First, very few countries had domestic norms against the death penalty. Second, almost no one believed that what one country did in this regard was any other country's business.

More recently, however, the countries of Europe have worked to persuade or compel other countries to abolish the death penalty. In 1983, a

| TABLE 13.2 | **Top Ten Origin Countries of International Migrants, 1990 and 2013.** Why do these countries have the most outward migration? What effects might size, wealth, and stability have? How and why have patterns changed over time? |
|---|---|

| | 1990 | | | 2013 |
|---|---|---|---|---|
| Russia* | 12.7 | | India | 14.2 |
| Afghanistan | 7.3 | | Mexico | 13.2 |
| India | 6.8 | | Russia | 10.8 |
| Bangladesh | 5.6 | | China | 9.3 |
| Ukraine | 5.6 | | Bangladesh | 7.8 |
| Mexico | 5.0 | | Pakistan | 5.7 |
| China | 4.1 | | Ukraine | 5.6 |
| United Kingdom | 4.1 | | Philippines | 5.5 |
| Pakistan | 3.6 | | Afghanistan | 5.1 |
| Italy | 3.5 | | United Kingdom | 5.0 |

*Numbers for Russia include people who moved within the Soviet Union before some parts of the USSR became separate nations.

Source: United Nations; Pew Resource Center, http://www.pewsocialtrends.org/2013/12/17/chapter-3-migrant-origins/

protocol prohibiting the death penalty was added to the European Convention for the Protection of Human Rights and Fundamental Freedoms. The EU has sought to spread this norm by making membership in key European institutions, such as the EU and the Council of Europe, conditional on abolition of the death penalty. Many of the post-Soviet states outlawed the death penalty in the 1990s as part of their efforts to be admitted to European institutions.

This norm is having an effect beyond Europe. In a very controversial ruling, the U.S. Supreme Court cited the international movement against the death penalty as one reason for banning the execution of those under age eighteen. In this case, a normative change has taken place over a relatively short period of time. In 1988, the court ruled that execution of seventeen- or eighteen-year-olds was constitutional. In 2005, it reversed this ruling, citing "the overwhelming weight of international opinion against the juvenile death penalty."[17] This position remained deeply controversial, with dissenting justices strongly criticizing both the overall decision and the notion that international opinion should be taken into account. Support for the death penalty in the United States remains high.

## THE INTERNATIONAL CRIMINAL COURT

An essential part of the effort to pursue human rights in the international realm is the effort to prosecute and punish those responsible for the most heinous violations. The **International Criminal Court (ICC)** was established in 2002 to create an international forum in which to prosecute war crimes and other crimes. The ICC seeks to address genocide, crimes against humanity, and war crimes. This development is of particular interest because states are seeking to establish international law in its narrow sense—law that leads to the apprehension, prosecution, and punishment of criminals. In that sense, the implications of the court for international law and for international politics, more broadly, are far-reaching.

**War crimes** seized global attention as a result of the atrocities of World War II. Although many horrors of war are seen as unavoidable, the mass murder of Europe's Jews by Germany and the large-scale atrocities against civilian populations by Japan went beyond what could be justified by the demands of war. A central argument was that individuals could be held accountable for the actions of their countries and their armies. Twelve officials of Nazi Germany and seven officials of Imperial Japan were hanged as a result of the trials held in Nuremburg and Tokyo following World War II.

The fourth Geneva Convention, adopted in 1949, defines a range of behaviors as war crimes:

- Willful killing
- Torture or inhumane treatment, including biological experiments
- Willfully causing great suffering or serious injury to body or health
- Unlawful deportation or transfer or unlawful confinement of a protected person[18]

War crimes seemed more or less a historical matter until two events in the 1990s: the "ethnic cleansing" campaigns in the former Yugoslavia and the Rwandan genocide of 1994, in which approximately 800,000 civilians were killed.

In both cases, there were calls for the initiators of mass murder to be punished for war crimes. In neither country, however, was there a functioning judicial apparatus that could bring them to justice. Therefore, the international community, through UN Security Council resolutions, established two separate tribunals, one for Yugoslavia and one for Rwanda. The most notable prosecution of these tribunals was that of former Yugoslav leader Slobodan Milosevic (who died during the trial).

**International Criminal Court (ICC)**

International court for the prosecution of war crimes and other heinous crimes.

**war crimes**

A set of transgressions established by the fourth Geneva Convention, including willful killing, torture or inhumane treatment, willfully causing great suffering or serious injury to body or health, unlawful deportation or transfer, and unlawful confinement of a protected person.

These cases convinced many people that a permanent version was needed. One commentator lamented, "We have lived in a golden age of impunity, where a person stands a much better chance of being tried for taking a single life than for killing ten thousand or a million."[19] In 1998, by a vote of 120 to 7 with 21 abstentions, a conference in Rome approved an agreement forming the ICC.[20] In 2012, the ICC reached its first verdict, sentencing Thomas Lubanga Dyilo of the Democratic Republic of Congo to fourteen years in prison for "conscripting and enlisting children under the age of 15 years and using them to participate actively in hostilities" in the Ituri conflict in Congo in 2002–2003.

Perhaps the most innovative feature of the ICC is that individual criminals, not states, are its primary focus. Although the ICC was formed by an agreement among states, state governments are not represented at the court. In that sense, it has transcended the traditional notion of international law as the "law among nations."

The ICC can begin proceedings against an individual either when the UN Security Council or a treaty signatory brings a case to its attention or when the court's own prosecutor, based on his or her own investigations, believes an indictment is warranted.[21] The court is based on the principle of "complementarity" with domestic courts, meaning that it only pursues cases in which domestic criminal courts are either unable or unwilling to get involved. Crucially, it is left to the ICC (not individual states) to determine when it should pursue a case under these provisions. Opposition to this rule led the United States not to sign the agreement.

Of the seven countries that chose not to sign the treaty, two—China and the United States—are expected to be among the most influential states in the world in coming decades. Both feared that they might be targets of a politically motivated prosecution. For example, given the view shared by many that the attack on Iraq in 2003 was illegal, might the U.S. president be accused of war crimes and made subject to international arrest? Presumably, if judges in The Hague found the war illegal, and the United States refused to prosecute its own president, the ICC could declare its jurisdiction over the case and issue an indictment. Similarly, one might fear that civilian casualties in Afghanistan or treatment of detainees might open U.S. soldiers or officials to charges of war crimes. The U.S. government was unwilling to take the chance that the court might be used in this way. China, another nonsignatory, was apparently concerned about charges stemming from its treatment of Tibetan and Uighur minorities, and Israel was concerned about charges related to its control of the "occupied territories."

How strong a role the ICC will play in prosecuting and deterring the worst sorts of crimes remains to be seen. The process of indicting, capturing, and trying someone is sufficiently complex that it is hard to imagine it becoming a routine matter.

## THE POLICY CONNECTION

## IS HUMANITARIAN INTERVENTION A DUTY?
## THE RESPONSIBILITY TO PROTECT AS A NEW NORM

"If humanitarian intervention is, indeed, an unacceptable assault on sovereignty, how should we respond to a Rwanda, to a Srebrenica—to gross and systematic violations of human rights that affect every precept of our common humanity?" This question by UN Secretary General Kofi Annan was taken up by an ad-hoc transnational committee whose answer has helped forge a major shift in international norms on intervention.*

Decisions to intervene and decisions *not* to intervene have both been controversial. In the early 1990s, many people criticized governments in Europe and the United States for not intervening sooner to stop "ethnic cleansing" in the former Yugoslavia. In 1994 in Rwanda, 800,000 people were killed, mostly with clubs and machetes, as the international community stood by and watched. Senior officials in the U.S. government explicitly sought to avoid using the word *genocide* for fear that doing so would oblige the United States to intervene.[†] In 1999, NATO's intervention in Kosovo was widely criticized internationally.

In response to the events of the 1990s, the International Commission on Intervention and State Sovereignty issued a report promoting the concept of "responsibility to protect" (often abbreviated R2P), making the argument for a responsibility to protect people from mass crimes. In 2005, the United Nations World Summit adopted a statement on R2P that enshrined two principles[‡]: The responsibility of each individual state "to protect its population from genocide, war crimes, ethnic cleansing, and crimes against humanity."

- The responsibility of the international community to use appropriate means "should peaceful means be inadequate and national authorities manifestly fail to protect their populations from genocide."

- In follow-up discussions at the UN General Assembly in 2009, several areas of controversy arose. Should the responsibility to protect be confined to the mass crimes of genocide, war crimes, ethnic cleansing, and crimes against humanity, or should it be extended to cover threats such as natural disasters? How can the principle be applied uniformly to avoid selective intervention (especially since permanent members of the Security Council have sometimes vetoed potential interventions)? Who decides that mass crimes have been committed, and by what standard? The President of the UN General Assembly, Miguel d'Escoto Brockmann of Nicaragua, called the entire concept of R2P into question.[§]

The debate did not remain theoretical for long. When civil war erupted in Libya in 2011, the primary justification for intervention was that the targeting of civilians constituted war crimes. However, when a similar situation arose in Syria a short time later, the UN Security Council could not agree on intervention. The politics of these decisions were complicated, but a major factor in the Syria case was that Russia and China felt that NATO had overstepped its authority in the Libya case, going beyond protection of civilians to toppling Muammar Gaddafi.

Following publication of its report in 2001, the International Commission on Intervention and State Sovereignty disbanded itself, but it started a shift in shared purpose and in government policy that states by themselves would have found difficult.

## Critical Thinking Questions

1. Why might states object to R2P?

2. Who should decide whether mass crimes have taken place and whether external military intervention is justified? Should individual states have the right to make this determination?

3. What hazards might arise from making the duty to intervene clear-cut?

---

*Quoted in "The Responsibility to Report," Report of the International Commission on Intervention and State Sovereignty," 2001, http://responsibilitytoprotect.org/ICISS%20Report.pdf.

[†]See Samantha Power, "A Problem from Hell": America and the Age of Genocide (New York: HarperCollins, 2002), especially chapter 10, on Rwanda.

[‡]United Nations General Assembly, "2005 World Summit Outcome," www.who.int/hiv/universalaccess2010/worldsummit.pdf.

[§]Global Centre for the Responsibility to Protect, "Implementing the Responsibility to Protect: The 2009 General Assembly Debate: An Assessment," http://www.globalr2p.org/media/files/gcr2p_-general-assembly-debate-assessment.pdf.

# POWER AND PURPOSE IN INTERNATIONAL LAW AND HUMAN RIGHTS

International law and human rights represent some of the loftiest goals in international politics. International law holds out the prospect that relations between states can be governed by law rather than by the exercise of threats and force. The international focus on human rights holds out the hope that the global community can be a force pressing all its members to adopt higher standards of human rights and to meet the standards that they have already set. As manifestations of soft power, these ideals play an important role in shaping actors' goals. The norm that states *should* follow international law creates power, in the form of a price to be paid for violating the norm. International law also creates institutional power and facilitates collaborative power by setting out agreed rules for such cooperation.

However, these manifestations of power do not eliminate the role of coercive and structural power in international affairs. Skeptics of international law, regimes, and norms see coercion trumping law in many of the most important situations. To the extent that international law results from coercion rather than consent, it can become an element of structural power.

Defendants hear verdicts at the Nuremburg trials. These trials held at the end of World War II provided the prototype for tribunals addressing crimes committed in Yugoslavia, Cambodia, and Rwanda as well as for the International Criminal Court.

# RECONSIDER THE CASE

## THE SECURITY COUNCIL AND INTERVENTION FROM IRAQ TO SYRIA

Events in Libya and Syria in 2011 and 2012 again put the role of the UN Security Council in authorizing the use of force at the center of international politics. In 2011, as we noted in Chapter 7, the Security Council authorized the use of force to prevent Libya's government from attacking civilians. Security Council resolution 1973 established a no-fly zone and authorized states to use force to protect civilians, but specifically ruled out a "foreign occupation force."* Only ten of the fifteen members of the Security Council voted for the resolution. Five, including China and Russia, abstained. By abstaining rather than vetoing the resolution, China and Russia allowed it to go forward but signaled their uneasiness. Indeed, before long, they felt that the intervening states had overstepped the authority provided by the resolution by using force not only to protect civilians but also to help rebel forces drive Gaddafi from power. They complained, but were unable to convince the intervening states to scale back their involvement.

The Libyan case had profound aftereffects in 2012 when protests in Syria escalated into civil war there. As in Libya, the Syrian government used military force against the opposition, and in at least some cases civilians were targeted. Russia and China both vetoed multiple Security Council resolutions that would have authorized nonmilitary sanctions against the government of Bashar al-Assad. As in Libya, there were calls around the world for external intervention. Russian Foreign Minister Sergei Lavrov explicitly ruled

out the "Libyan scenario" of regime change in Syria. He objected to one resolution in particular because it justified nonmilitary sanctions by referring to Article VII of the UN Charter, which refers to threats to peace. Russia and China were motivated in part, it seems, by their alliances with Syria and in part by their general opposition to external intervention on the grounds of human rights violations.

Susan Rice, the U.S. Ambassador to the United Nations, called Russia's fear that the proposed resolution would lead to intervention "paranoid if not disingenuous," but Russia and China clearly had the Libyan case in mind. In their view, their willingness to allow intervention in Libya was taken advantage of, and they were not going to make the same mistake again.

### Critical Thinking Questions

1. How should leaders weigh the importance of getting Security Council authorization for the use of force versus the potential for vetoes to lead to immobility in the face of a humanitarian disaster?

2. If some states intervene without Security Council authorization, will others be emboldened to do so?

3. To what extent did the UN process constrain states in the Iraq, Libya, and Syria cases?

*UN Security Council Resolution 1973, www.un.org/News/Press/docs/2011/sc10200.doc.htm#Resolution.

## SUMMARY

- International law plays an important role in at least some areas of contemporary international politics.
- There are three major sources of international law: treaties, custom, and "the general principles of law recognized by civilized nations."
- International law can be enforced by international organizations such as the WTO, by states acting alone, or by a mix of these.
- The question of enforcement leads to debate about whether international law is really "law" in the same way that domestic law is.

- In the European Union and in the WTO, international law is fairly clear, strict, and enforced.

- In many other areas, states comply with international law because it would not be to their benefit to disrupt patterns of behavior that serve their interests.

- Many cases remain in which states violate international law and are not punished.

- International norms are shared ideas about how states should behave. Many actors try to promote new norms.

- International regimes are shared norms, practices, and expectations that are less formal than international law but that guide state behavior.

- By establishing the ICC, the international community placed a higher emphasis on human rights and reduced the sanctity of sovereignty.

## KEY CONCEPTS

1. Just war
2. International Court of Justice (ICJ)
3. Enforcement
4. Self-enforcement

5. International regimes
6. International norms
7. Human rights
8. International Criminal Court (ICC)

## STUDY QUESTIONS

1. ___is the set of rules and obligations that states recognize as binding on each other.

   a. International law

   b. International regimes

   c. International norms

   d. Human rights

2. Advocates of which approach to international relations argue that at the time of World War II reliance on international law, rather than on power politics, contributed to Hitler's rise to power?

   a. Realists

   b. Economic structuralists

   c. Constructivists

   d. Feminists

3. Grotius established the concept of *jus ad bellum*, or just cause for war, which asserts that

   a. war must be declared by legitimate authorities.

   b. the means used in war must not be inhumane.

   c. the means used in the war must be proportional to the ends obtained.

   d. All of the above.

4. Which of the following are sources of international law?

   a. International treaties

   b. International custom, as evidence of a general practice accepted as law

   c. The general principles of law recognized by civilized nations

   d. All of the above.

5. The International Court of Justice (ICJ) was established

   a. within the UN system.

   b. by the EU.

   c. by the United States.

   d. by the G-7 countries.

6. The actions of the WTO Dispute Settlement Body are an example of international law enforcement by

   a. the UN.

   b. the EU.

   c. blended enforcement.

   d. individual states.

7. What are the major means of enforcing international law, and what are the problems with them?

8. What are the major causes of documented and undocumented migration?

9. How is international law similar to and different from domestic law?

10. How should the imperatives of human rights and state sovereignty be weighed?

11. What are the sources and effects of changes in international norms?

[Correct answers: 1. a; 2. a; 3. a, 4. d; 5. a; 6. d]

## END NOTES

1. This definition is based on that in William R. Slomanson, *Fundamental Perspectives on International Law* (Minneapolis, MN: West, 1995), p. 3.

2. See Paul Christopher, *The Ethics of War and Peace*, 3rd ed. (Upper Saddle River, NJ: Pearson Prentice Hall, 2004), Chapter 1, pp. 8–16.

3. Christopher, *The Ethics of War and Peace*, Chapter 6, pp. 81–103.

4. A classic and readable rational choice approach to retaliation and reputation is Robert Axelrod, *The Evolution of Cooperation* (New York: Basic Books, 1984). On the importance of reputation, see John Mercer, *Reputation and International Politics* (Ithaca, NY: Cornell University Press, 1996).

5. Louis Henkin, *How Nations Behave*, 2nd ed. (New York: Columbia University Press, 1979).

6. The seminal work on international regimes is Stephen D. Krasner, ed., *International Regimes* (Ithaca, NY: Cornell University Press, 1982).

7. Allen Buchanan and Robert O. Keohane, "Toward a Drone Accountability Regime," *Ethics and International Affairs*, Vol. 29, No. 1 (2015): 15.

8. Address by President Vaclav Havel to the Senate and the House of Commons of the Parliament of Canada, April 29, 1999, http://old.hrad.cz/president/Havel/speeches/1999/2904_uk.html.

9. See Audie Klotz, "Norms Reconstituting Interests: Global Racial Equality and U.S. Sanctions Against South Africa," *International Organization*, Vol. 49, No. 3 (Summer 1995): 451–478.

10. Charles R. Beitz, "Human Rights as a Common Concern," *American Political Science Review*, Vol. 95, No. 2 (June 2001): 247.

11. See the full declaration at www.ohchr.org/EN/UDHR/Pages/Language.aspx?LangID=eng.

12. Eric Posner, "The Case against Human Rights," *The Guardian*, December 4, 2014.

13. See Martha Finnemore, *The Purpose of Intervention: Changing Beliefs about the Use of Force* (Ithaca, NY: Cornell University Press, 2003), p. 6.

14. Alex J. Bellamy and Nicholas J. Wheeler, "Humanitarian Intervention in World Politics," in John Baylis and Steve Smith, eds., *The Globalization of World Politics: An Introduction to International Relations* (New York: Oxford University Press, 2008), p. 524 ff.

15. *Convention Relating to the Status of Refugees*, Article I, http://www.unhcr.org/3b66c2aa10.html.

16. UNHCR, http://www.unhcr.org/pages/49c3646c1d.html.

17. *Roper, Superintendent, Potosi Correctional Center v. Simmons*, 543 U.S. 551 (2005), p. 578.

18. The text of the fourth Geneva Convention can be viewed at www.icrc.org/ihl.nsf/FULL/380?OpenDocument.

19. Michael P. Sharf, "Results of the Rome Conference for an International Criminal Court," *ASIL Insights*, August 1998, www.asil.org/insights/insigh23.htm.

20. The seven voting against were China, Iraq, Israel, Libya, Qatar, the United States, and Yemen.

21. International Criminal Court, "ICC at a Glance," http://www.icc-cpi.int/en_menus/icc/about%20the%20court/icc%20at%20a%20glance/Pages/icc%20at%20a%20glance.aspx.

# UN CLIMATE CHANGE CONFERENCE
# LIMA COP 20 | CMP 10

# 14

414

**COP 20 conference held in Peru.** The 20th UN Framework Convention on Climate Change (UNFCCC) Conference of the Parties, Lima, Peru, December 2014. From left: Chilean President Michelle Bachellet, Colombian President Juan Manuel Santos, Peruvian Minister of Environment and COP20 President Manuel Pulgar, Peruvian President Ollanta Humala, UN Secretary General Ban Ki-moon and UNFCCC Executive Secretary Christiana Figueres.

Anadolu Agency/Getty Images

# THE GLOBAL ENVIRONMENT AND INTERNATIONAL POLITICS

## Learning Objectives

**14-1** Evaluate the barriers to international collaboration on environmental problems.

**14-2** Identify the main issues surrounding the Kyoto Protocol process.

**14-3** Understand collective action problems and the factors that influence solving them.

**14-4** Apply the theory of collective action to international environmental problems.

**14-5** Apply realist, liberal, economic structuralist, constructivist, and feminist approaches to international politics to international environmental issues.

**14-6** Evaluate the likelihood of international conflict and cooperation on environmental problems.

# CONSIDER THE CASE

## CLIMATE CHANGE NEGOTIATIONS

In December 2011, representatives of nations from around the world met in Durban, South Africa, to negotiate a new plan to combat **global warming** and **climate change**. With the 1998 Kyoto Protocol limiting greenhouse gas emissions due to expire at the end of 2012, reaching a new agreement was necessary to prevent a lapse in global cooperation on climate change. An earlier effort to negotiate a successor to Kyoto in Copenhagen in 2009 had failed.

The European Union (EU) sought an agreement that would limit global average temperature increases to two degrees Celsius, the amount that was considered inevitable given the amount of **greenhouse gases** already in the atmosphere. The EU therefore proposed legally binding commitments to limit the emission of greenhouse gases. Many other countries rejected this approach. Because emissions increase as economies grow, developing countries worried that emission limits would undermine their economic development. This position was at odds with that of most developed countries who insisted that for limits to work and to be fair every country had to participate. Complicating the situation, the United States opposed binding limits because of domestic skepticism about global warming and concern about the economic impact of limiting greenhouse gas emissions.

In the end, the countries agreed to set binding commitments by 2015 and to implement them by 2020. It was not clear, however, that countries would actually be able to agree on binding commitments. Even if they did, another five years would go by before serious measures were implemented. The negotiators also agreed that the Kyoto Protocol would be extended beyond 2012

in a "second commitment period," but the terms of that extension were also left for future negotiations. In other words, all the important questions were deferred until the future because agreement could not be reached at Durban.

A U.S. opponent of global warming measures gloated that the Durban meeting represented "the complete collapse of the global warming movement and the failure of the Kyoto process."[*] Following the conference, Canada formally withdrew from the Kyoto Protocol, citing the high cost of complying and the fact that the United States and China, bigger polluters, had not signed on.[†] It was hard to avoid the conclusion that the effort to slow global warming had failed for the foreseeable future.

At a 2014 meeting in Lima, Peru, disagreements on a binding agreement remained intense. Poor and wealthy states struggled to overcome a basic disagreement over whether they would be held to the same expectations. The Kyoto Protocol's division of the world's countries into two groups was abandoned, but language continued to recognize the different historic contributions to greenhouse gas emissions and different current capacity to adjust. The hard questions, however, were pushed toward the 2015 meeting in Paris.

---

[*]*U.S. Senate Committee on Environment and Public Works, "Inhofe on Durban UN Climate Conference: Kyoto Process Is Dead," Press Release, December 7, 2011, epw.senate.gov/public/index.cfm?FuseAction=PressRoom.PressReleases&ContentRecord_id=18d950be-802a-23ad-463c-00218 cbecc56.*

[†]*"Canada to Withdraw from Kyoto Protocol," BBC World News, www.bbc.co.uk/news/world-us-canada-16151310.*

---

If nearly every government recognizes global warming as a danger, why can they not agree on steps to prevent it? This seems illogical. Is there something inherently difficult about global warming, or is environmental cooperation always difficult? What do theories of international politics tell us about the prospects for collaboration and conflict on environmental issues?

**global warming**

The increase in the overall temperature of the planet that results when an increase in certain gases in the atmosphere traps more heat in the atmosphere; a source of climate change.

**climate change**

Changes in long-term weather patterns that result from global warming; the overall warming of the atmosphere may have very different climactic and weather effects in different places.

**greenhouse gases**

Gases in the atmosphere that trap heat in the earth's atmosphere. As they increase in concentration, the atmospheric temperature rises, causing climate change.

**Nonrenewable resources**

Natural products whose supply is fundamentally limited, such as oil, minerals, and rare earth metals.

**Renewable resources**

Natural products that can be sustained indefinitely, as long as the rate of consumption does not exceed the natural rate of replacement.

Although many environmental problems are transnational in nature, most of the mechanisms for dealing with environmental matters lie within states. This creates a mismatch between the scale of environmental problems and the tools available to deal with them. This mismatch has led to calls for greater international collaboration to protect the environment. Although international agreements have been reached on some important issues, on many others, and most important on climate change, agreement has been elusive.

The consequences of environmental problems go well beyond narrow "environmental" effects—polluted air, extinct species, damaged beaches. Resource shortages and climate change will likely have far-reaching economic, political, and security effects. For example, the spread of pests as the climate warms is already creating significant economic damage. Increased intensity of storms will contribute to economic destruction and humanitarian disasters. Competition for natural resources, among the most important clean water, may provoke war.

The states that were represented at the 2011 Durban conference are aware of the dangers. The U.S. Defense Department, in its major policy document, states:

> Climate change and energy will play significant roles in the future security environment.... While climate change alone does not cause conflict, it may act as an accelerant of instability or conflict, placing a burden to respond on civilian institutions and militaries around the world. In addition, extreme weather events may lead to increased demands for defense support to civil authorities for humanitarian assistance or disaster response both within the United States and overseas.[1]

These issues raise a much bigger question: Is it possible that the advent of ever-greater dangers that cannot be solved by individual states will lead actors to fundamentally revise the sovereign state basis of global politics? Or will conflict over these issues cause states to reassert their dominance?

# CAUSES OF ENVIRONMENTAL PROBLEMS

As the world's population and level of economic development grow, resources tend to get scarcer and pollution tends to increase, resulting in a host of environmental problems. **Nonrenewable resources** are natural products whose supply is fundamentally limited, such as oil, minerals, and rare earth metals. **Renewable resources** are those that can be sustained indefinitely, as long as the rate of consumption does not exceed the natural rate of replacement. Examples include fisheries, forests, and many aquifers. Pollution is another basic category of environmental problem. Humans produce harmful waste products ranging from greenhouse gases that precipitate climate change to toxic chemicals that seep into water supplies to trash that jams landfills and, in the Pacific Ocean, has created a Texas-sized vortex of floating garbage. These environmental issues can be summarized in outline form:

- Nonrenewable resources
  - Oil
  - Rare earth metals
  - Species (biodiversity)

- Renewable resources
  - Fisheries
  - Forests
  - Aquifers
- Pollution
  - Water (oceans, rivers, lakes, and aquifers)
  - Air (acid rain, greenhouse gases, and other pollutants)
  - Ground (solid waste and toxic waste)

## POPULATION GROWTH

Population growth exacerbates all kinds of environmental and resource problems. In 2012, the world's population surpassed 7 billion, up from 3 billion in 1960, and was heading, according to most estimates, toward 8 billion in another twelve to fourteen years (Figure 14.1). Population growth is one of the major drivers of environmental problems, placing increased demand on scarce resources, including land, housing, food, water, and energy, while generating increased pollution.

Population is growing not because people are having more children (in many countries, they are having fewer), but because mortality has decreased dramatically. Increased agricultural productivity has made famine much rarer. Before the 1960s, food shortages placed a check on population growth in poor countries. The "green revolution," which increased the use of irrigation, fertilizer, pesticides, and improved crop breeds, dramatically increased agricultural yields. Health care has also improved. In much of the world, diseases that routinely killed many people have been wiped out or brought under control. Smallpox, which once killed millions, has been eradicated. Infant and maternal mortality have declined dramatically. The logical result, other things being equal, is population growth.

In many societies, decreasing death rates and economic development have been followed, after some lag time, by decreased birthrates. Thus, in Japan, Russia, and much of Europe, birthrates have declined dramatically and are now lower than death rates. Without immigration, population will decrease. For this reason, there is hope that the

**FIGURE 14.1** Population growth and distribution since 1000. In what ways does population growth drive environmental problems?

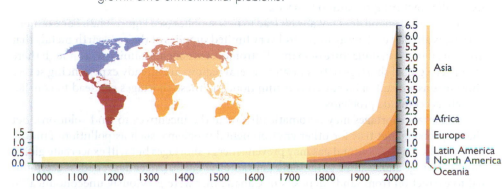

Source: www.theglobaleducationproject.org/earth/image.php?image=g-pop-growth-chart-map.gif&title=human%20population; www.theglobaleducationproject.org/earth/human-conditions.php#11.

growth in global population will eventually slow as more people move into the middle class and have fewer children. It is difficult to predict when that might happen, however, and for now global population is still increasing.

## CONSUMPTION GROWTH

Population growth is not the only driver of increased consumption and pollution. Increased consumption is leading to more dire consequences than population growth alone. Geographer Jared Diamond estimates that if everyone in the developing world were to consume as much as the average American, it would have the same effect as increasing the global population to 72 billion people.[2] As hundreds of millions move from poverty into the middle class, they will begin consuming and polluting like the middle class. One visible example is the effect of the booming Chinese automobile market on global oil prices and on pollution in Chinese cities.

## RESOURCE SUPPLY AND DEMAND

Population growth and economic development are putting pressure on the supply of many natural resources, such as food, oil, water, and land. Since 1798, when Thomas Malthus published his *Essay on the Principle of Population*, people have been predicting that population growth would outpace the capacity to feed people, leading to a massive population crash and political conflict. Historically, however, such predictions of scarcity have often proven overly pessimistic, and increases in agricultural and economic productivity have more than kept up with population growth.

The peak oil hypothesis posits that even with increased investment, the annual world production of oil will peak sometime in the coming decades and then begin to decline.[3] As with population collapse, predicted resource shortages have not always materialized. As supplies decrease, prices rise, giving consumers an incentive to use less. Higher prices also give producers incentives to discover new supplies and to extract more from existing supplies. Mines and mining techniques that are unprofitable at low commodity prices become profitable at higher prices, increasing the supply. For example, energy shortages in the 1970s brought high prices and damaged economies around the world. However, they also spurred greater efficiency and drove energy companies to invest in more exploration. The price of oil and other natural resources declined dramatically in the 1980s. Similarly, recent use of hydraulic fracturing has enormously increased the supply of exploitable natural gas and has driven prices down (though the long-term environmental effects of hydraulic fracturing remain to be seen).

However, demand does not always lead to new supplies (see Figure 14.2). For example, a battle is already under way to control very limited supplies of the rare earth metals that are crucial in the manufacture of many electronics components. Similarly, although there is not yet a global shortage of fresh water, several regions are already experiencing severe shortages as a result of increased consumption, and these shortages can lead to conflict as well as economic problems.

Materials shortages may automatically create the incentives to find solutions, but that is probably not true for other environmental problems, such as pollution. Finding new supplies of coal, oil, and gas may prevent energy shortages but will exacerbate global climate change and local air pollution. For example, high oil prices have made it economical to extract oil from sandy deposits in Canada that were previously uneconomical to exploit. These oil sands provide a huge source of oil in a politically stable country, but consuming them will contribute to global climate change.

**FIGURE 14.2**  **How long will it last?** What international political consequences might we predict from shortages of various commodities?

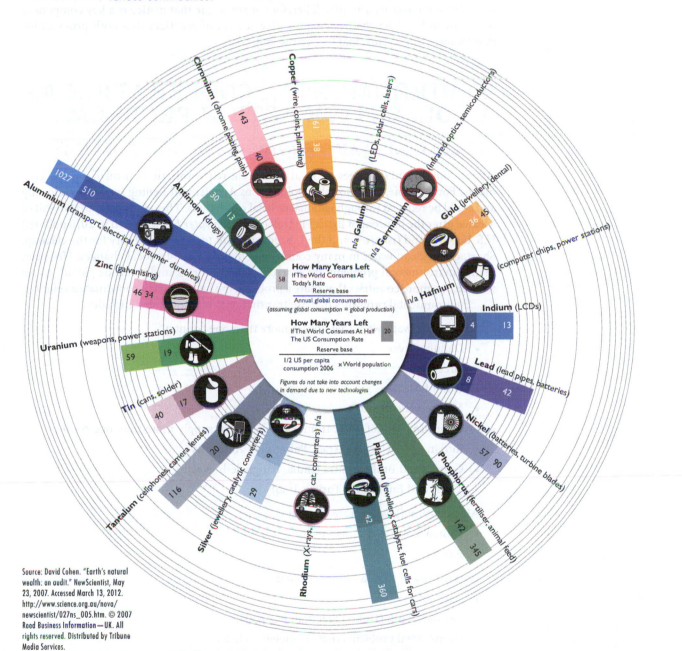

Source: David Cohen. "Earth's natural wealth: an audit." NewScientist, May 23, 2007. Accessed March 13, 2012. http://www.science.org.au/nova/newscientist/027ns_005.htm. © 2007 Reed Business Information—UK. All rights reserved. Distributed by Tribune Media Services.

## THE PROBLEM OF SUSTAINABLE DEVELOPMENT

*Sustainability* has become something of a buzzword in recent years, capturing the worry that prevailing ways of living cannot go on indefinitely. Although wealth may lead to more consumption and pollution, poverty is no solution either. Poor people consume less than wealthier people, but they are also more constrained from pursuing environmental goals.

People in extreme poverty cannot be expected to forego cutting down a forest to create farmland, to worry about where they dump their waste, or to refrain from pumping more water from an overused aquifer. Therefore, many argue that justice is a key component of sustainability. The challenge is to arrive at a set of practices that both provides for development and is sustainable over the long term.

# ENVIRONMENTAL COOPERATION AS A COLLECTIVE ACTION PROBLEM

## PUBLIC GOODS AND ENVIRONMENTAL PROBLEMS

Some pollution and shortages are local and are entirely within the control of state governments. For example, the smog that pollutes Los Angeles and Beijing is produced locally and could be reduced through national or local regulations. The oil spilled into the Gulf of Mexico after the blowout of British Petroleum's *Deepwater Horizon* well in 2010 polluted U.S. beaches and fisheries, and the U.S. government took responsibility for the cleanup. Shortages of clean water in many countries could be solved by local changes. However, many environmental problems are shared across countries, and some are global. As we will see, the more countries that share a problem, the harder it is to coordinate a solution.

Environmental problems that are transnational but not global include:

- Pollution of waterways that border more than one country
  - Danube River
  - Great Lakes
  - Gulf of Mexico
  - Mediterranean Sea
- Overconsumption of water from watersheds that supply more than one country
  - Jordan River (Jordan, Israel, Palestinian Authority)
  - Ganges and Brahmaputra (India, Bangladesh, Nepal)
  - Tigris and Euphrates (Turkey, Iraq)
- Air pollution flowing across borders
  - United States and Canada
  - Europe

**ozone layer**

A layer of ozone in the upper atmosphere that reduces transmission of ultraviolet radiation. Ozone is a form of oxygen with three atoms per molecule ($O_3$) rather than the typical two ($O_2$). At ground level, ozone is a respiratory irritant.

- Overfishing of shared bodies of water
  - Caspian Sea
  - Georges Bank (United States and Canada)
- Environmental problems that are global include:
  - Depletion of the **ozone layer**
  - Global warming
  - Biodiversity loss
  - Overpopulation
  - Oil shortages

Analyzing these problems through the lens of collective action theory helps us see why they are difficult to solve and how solutions can be facilitated. A **collective action problem** is a situation in which two or more actors have a common interest but cannot automatically collaborate to achieve it. We have examined collective action problems through the prisoner's dilemma (Chapter 3), the security dilemma, and the problem of free trade (Chapter 10). To better understand environmental issues, we delve into collective action theory in more detail.

In the economics literature, a *collective good* has two characteristics. First, it is *nonrival*, meaning that one actor's consumption of it does not reduce another actor's consumption. Clean air is a good example (as long as we are not locked in an airtight room). Second, a collective good is *nonexcludable*, meaning that if it is available to one actor, it is available to all actors. Almost any resource that is shared, such as a fishery or aquifer, has aspects of a collective good. Even goods that are generally privatized, such as oil and water, can be collective goods if they are drawn from shared reserves.

An actor can thus consume a public good without paying for it, which is known as the *free rider problem*. Similarly, many economic activities create "negative externalities," or external costs, by forcing costs (polluted air, water, or depleted resources) onto others. A central goal of environmental movements is to force actors to internalize all their costs. Externalities such as these point to the extent of *interdependence* that exists in the contemporary world. The oil or coal that one individual or state consumes is not available to another, yet the pollution one actor creates affects everyone else.

## THE TRAGEDY OF THE COMMONS

One familiar way of seeing the problem of collective action in environmental issues is through a parable known as the tragedy of the commons. Imagine a common pasture on which several farmers graze their cattle. The pasture is shared, but the cattle belong to the individual farmers. How many head of cattle will each farmer graze in the pasture? Consider the incentives of each farmer: When a farmer puts another cow on the pasture, the benefits accrue entirely to the owner of that cow. The costs (in terms of decreasing the supply of grass), however, are shared by all the farmers. Therefore, each farmer has an incentive to put another cow on the pasture, and another, and another. At some point, overgrazing depletes the pasture, and none of them can graze their cattle there. The "tragedy" is that when each farmer acts according to his or her individual interest, the result is collective catastrophe. This **tragedy of the commons** is widely used as a model of what happens with shared resources.[4] Its logic is identical to that of the prisoner's dilemma, the security dilemma, and trade wars.

The same phenomenon occurs with a fishery shared by more than one actor (the actors could be individuals, corporations, or states). For every fish one actor takes out, the benefits accrue to that actor, but the costs are shared by all the others. Each actor has the incentive to take as much as possible before the others do. This explains the widespread depletion of unregulated fisheries around the world.

The same principle applies to air pollution: The costs of polluting are widely spread, while the benefits accrue to the polluting individual company, or country. If one state reduces production of carbon dioxide ($CO_2$) while others do not, the overall level of global warming may not change much, but that state will have taken on a significant cost. Because of this collective action problem, strong international agreements are needed to solve international environmental problems.

**collective action problem**
A situation in which a group of actors has a common interest but cannot collaborate to achieve it.

**tragedy of the commons**
A version of the collective action problem in which a shared resource is overconsumed.

# FIVE APPROACHES TO INTERNATIONAL ENVIRONMENTAL ISSUES

## LIBERALISM: SOLVING THE COLLECTIVE ACTION PROBLEM

The view of international environmental problems as collective action problems fits well with liberal international relations theory. Liberalism makes two central claims: First, many environmental problems can only be solved through collaboration. Second, this reality provides incentives for self-interested actors to pursue that collaboration.

For example, the Intergovernmental Panel on Climate Change has gathered together scientists from around the world to provide data on greenhouse gas emissions and climate change that governments generally accept as fact. Because many environmental issues are not just bilateral or multilateral but global, international organizations are in many cases seen as the only mechanism through which agreements can be reached and implemented. For this reason, some people see international environmental problems as a force that will inevitably drive states toward increased global governance.

International institutions can also be essential in implementing some of the more complicated methods of solving collective action problems. For example, in preserving a shared fishery, there needs to be an agreement on how many fish can be removed each year without diminishing the number that can be harvested in the future. This amount is known as the maximum sustainable yield. Because this amount is often controversial, it is necessary to have an objective body conduct the research to establish the amount. International organizations can also play an important role in monitoring compliance, though such organizations have not been given a significant role in enforcement, which states have retained for themselves.

International environmental issues have empowered a range of actors both "above" and "below" the state, which resonates with the concept of complex interdependence. The need to agree on the science underlying environmental problems and on what activities are sustainable requires delegating considerable influence to international organizations such as the United Nations Environment Programme (UNEP). At the same time, nongovernmental organizations (NGOs) are playing an important role in shaping the norms and expectations that state actors must respond to.[5] In some cases, nongovernmental actors have succeeded in establishing new norms that have come to be widely accepted; in other cases, there is intense contestation of norms, such as the battle in the United States over the validity of climate science.

From the liberal perspective, the key factors in achieving cooperation are agreeing that the problem is indeed one that requires a joint international solution; then agreeing on what measures are required to mitigate the problem; and then devising an agreement that meets those goals, is not too difficult to implement, and is verifiable. In most cases, none of these issues is trivial. For example, even when states agree that there is a problem, there can be a lot of reasonable disagreement about how much mitigation is necessary and how much cost is acceptable.

## REALISM: ENVIRONMENTAL COMPETITION AND CONFLICT

Realists take a far more pessimistic view of the prospects for international environmental cooperation. They focus on the conflicts inherent in competing for a limited supply

**maximum sustainable yield**

The maximum amount of a renewable resource that can be harvested each year without reducing the amount that can be harvested in future years.

of natural resources and on the difficulties in forging environmental cooperation among countries that are competing politically, militarily, and economically. To be clear, realists should not be confused with skeptics about climate change or resource shortages. There is no inconsistency in being concerned about environmental issues and holding a realist view about how those issues are likely to influence international politics.

**Realism and Environmental Collective Action**   Realism is skeptical about the prospects for cooperation in environmental collective action problems, just as it is skeptical about cooperation to resolve the security dilemma. The central problem, from the realist perspective, is that states remain deeply concerned about their economic and military power and are reluctant to sign on to any agreement that might jeopardize that power. Even when states agree on the desirability of cooperation, they are concerned with relative gains—with the possibility that the agreement will allow one state to gain economically or militarily.

In the case of greenhouse gases, many countries oppose any agreement that does not constrain China as much as everyone else. Not only are they worried about the contribution of Chinese emissions to global warming, but they are concerned about Chinese economic competition. China already uses cheap production costs to outcompete firms around the world, leading to higher unemployment in other countries. If China had a further advantage because it did not bear the same costs of limiting greenhouse gas production, it would gain even further.

China, however, regards further economic growth as essential to raising its standard of living, which is still, on average, lower than in much of the rest of the world.

A farmer in India inspects his crop during a drought in the state of Punjab, July 2002. Indian farmers depend on monsoons, which do not always arrive when expected, to provide water.

It is also concerned with expanding its military capacity to match that of the United States and others, and can only do that with a larger economy. Thus, an agreement that substantially hinders Chinese economic growth is seen in China not only as costly in absolute terms, but as disadvantaging China in its competition with other great powers. This is the relative gains problem. China is concerned that limiting its emissions will disadvantage it politically and economically, while others are concerned that they will be disadvantaged if China is not limited. From the realist perspective, this conflict of interest is fundamental and very difficult to overcome.

**Realism and Resource Shortages**   When there is a fixed or limited supply of some good, such as oil, water, or some mineral, the situation is essentially a zero-sum game, and realists predict that states will respond by using what power they have to control these key resources.

Looking at history, realists see competition over resources as a major cause of war. World War I was motivated in part by an effort to redivide European colonial possessions oversees. One of the major motivations for Germany to attack the Soviet Union in World

War II was to gain access to the bountiful agricultural areas of Ukraine and the oil supplies in the Caucasus region. Similarly, Japan's quest for natural resources drove its aggression in Asia that led to the Pacific war. Some would say that the U.S. invasions of Iraq in 1991 and 2003 were motivated in large part by the goal of controlling oil supplies.[6] China's military asserting control over the South China Sea looks familiar in these historical terms.

Realists expect states to use their power to gain control of the resources they need. For example, states that control the upstream portions of rivers will capture more of the water and hydroelectric-generating capacity at the expense of downstream states. States that control deposits of natural resources and oil will limit the export of those resources. States that import raw materials will compete with each other to control supplies around the world, just as they did in the colonial era. Resource shortages can lead to civil as well as international conflict. Many analysts see the long civil war in Sudan as having been driven in large part by a water shortage that drove nomadic herders onto land already claimed by farmers. More recently, the discovery of oil in South Sudan led to conflict over control of it.[7]

## ECONOMIC STRUCTURALISM: DISTRIBUTIVE EFFECTS OF ENVIRONMENTAL AGREEMENTS

Economic structuralists focus on how environmental issues influence gaps in wealth and economic power. Concerns about how to combat environmental problems mesh nicely with broader economic structuralist arguments about the legacies of colonialism and about ongoing inequality of economic power in the world. From the structuralist point of view, the advanced industrial economies developed by exploiting the natural resources of developing countries and by polluting freely. Wealthy countries and individuals consume and pollute more, per capita, than the developing countries. In this view, the developed countries should bear a disproportionate share of the cost of solving environmental problems.

Most analysts—structuralist or not—agree that the consequences of environmental decay are felt most acutely by the most disadvantaged people. Hazardous waste dumps and polluting industries are more likely to be located near poor areas than wealthy ones; wealthy people are better able to ban such activities from their neighborhoods or simply to live in more desirable areas. Poor people and countries have much less ability to adapt to environmental disasters when they occur.

For example, sea level rise will endanger low-lying areas around the world, but will be especially devastating in places like Bangladesh, where millions of people living in flood-prone areas have little ability to relocate, and where the government is unable to bear the enormous expense of mitigating flooding. Florida will also suffer from sea level rise, but relocation and government-led abatement strategies are much more within reach economically there. Similarly, while droughts cause significant economic problems in the developed world, they can cause starvation in the developing world. For these reasons, economic structuralists tend to be advocates of strong action to remedy environmental threats around the world.

However, structuralists are equally concerned that environmental measures do not disadvantage the world's poorest people and states, a concern they share with many developing country governments. For example, many people around the world seek to prevent the loss of species, both as an end in itself and because some species may have important economic and health benefits that have yet to be discovered. No one opposes this goal, but it brings up the question of who owns the intellectual property concerning species present in developing countries. If a European company discovers something useful (a gene or chemical) in an organism found in Latin America, who gets the profits from commercialization of the product? In traditional law, the benefits accrue to the European company. Developing countries have sought a new principle that would give the countries where organisms are found rights over the resulting technology. If developing countries gain little economic benefit from the preservation of species, they are less likely to focus on that goal.

The competition for natural resources highlighted by realism fits equally well into a structuralist perspective, which sees a new colonialism in the efforts of powerful countries to gain control of natural resources in weaker countries. China, historically a victim of colonialism, is now asserting itself throughout the developing world. China's consumption of natural resources has increased dramatically over the last decade. It has become the world's leader in copper consumption and consumes more than 25 percent of the world's supply of base metals each year. In its search for oil and industrial raw materials, it has turned to Africa.

Although Chinese demand provides an important alternative market and political partner for African governments, raw materials importers elsewhere in the world worry about their access to supplies. Structuralists and realists alike both see this as part of an intensified competition for raw materials. For structuralists, a key question is whether this increased competition will lead to economic development for poor countries or only to further exploitation. For environmentalists, the key question is whether resource competition will lead to better stewardship of resources or to greater disregard for the environmental consequences of resource extraction.

## CONSTRUCTIVISM: THE EMERGENCE OF NEW NORMS AND INTERESTS?

Constructivism focuses on how ideas, such as identities, interests, and norms, shape behavior. Whereas environmental issues feature prominent material factors—weather, oil, water, and so on—constructivism directs us to look at the role of ideas in shaping behavior toward the environment and toward environmental policy.

Among the most important processes leading to international environmental cooperation is the recognition that a problem exists and that international collaboration is necessary to solve it. This formation of shared purpose is precisely the kind of process on which constructivists focus. For example, in a widely read study, Peter Haas showed that agreement to take steps to combat pollution of the Mediterranean Sea was fostered by a transnational community of government scientists that first arrived at agreement on the key issues and then worked to promote agreement within individual governments.[8]

The current dispute over climate change shows how science can become deeply politicized (Figure 14.3). Although scientists around the world have reached consensus on the basic science concerning global warming, many citizens and policy makers regard the findings as mistaken, politically motivated, or even fraudulent.

To some extent, this is an example of the role interest groups seek to play in foreign policy, as discussed in Chapter 6. Whereas environmental groups see a wide range of benefits resulting from the effort to combat global warming, industries and individuals that rely on cheap fossil fuels see danger to their interests. A major goal of environmental transnational activist networks has been to promote norms concerning the desirability of protecting the environment.

A crucial question is what factors might cause interests to shift. In the 1980s, talks on limiting production of ozone-depleting gases were stalled until new scientific data induced a relatively rapid change in perceived interests, and opposition to action disappeared rapidly. Science alone may not be enough to make the case on climate change because so

**FIGURE 14.3** **Shared understanding of a problem can help forge collaboration to solve it.** This graph shows how different groups answered the question: "Do you think that human activity is a significant contributing factor in changing mean global temperatures?"

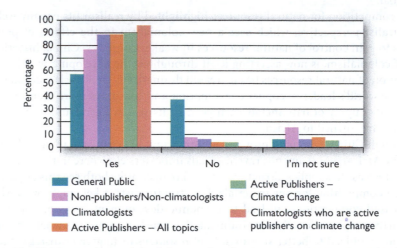

Source: Doran, P. T., and M. K. Zimmerman. "Examining the Scientific Consensus on Climate Change," Eos Trans. AGU, Vol. 90, No. 3: 22. Accessed March 13, 2012, at www.agu.org/pubs/crossref/2009/2009EO030002.shtml.

many people are so poorly educated about how science works. Ironically, unusually violent weather events, which by themselves do not constitute scientific evidence of global warming, might have more effect on public consciousness and the perceived need to take action. For example, Hurricane Katrina, which devastated New Orleans in 2005, the string of tornadoes that swept across the southern United States in 2011, and "superstorm" Sandy in 2012 were viewed by many as validation that climate change was influencing the weather. Though no single case of extreme weather can prove or disprove hypotheses about climate change, dramatic weather events can have an important effect on public support for policy change.

As is the case in other issue areas, constructivist approaches do not predict or advocate a particular outcome in the area of international environmental collaboration. They do predict that shifting norms, identities, and interests will be pivotal factors in shaping outcomes, a view with which advocates on all sides of current debates seem to agree.

## FEMINISM: GENDER, POWER, AND THE ENVIRONMENT

The central contention of feminist international relations theory is that the theory and practice of international politics is heavily influenced by gendered ideas, including traditional definitions of power, security, and the state as a distinct entity that represents national interests. Most feminists see environmental problems and the difficulties in forging environmental collaboration as fitting closely with this broader critique.

For feminist empiricists, the central questions are how environmental degradation affects women and how women might contribute to the amelioration of environmental problems. In this view, women, especially in the developing world, are among the first to experience the effects of environmental problems, and experience them most harshly. Looking at a major cyclone in Bangladesh in 1991, the UN Development Programme estimated that women were nearly five times as likely as men to perish in the storm and subsequent flooding.[9] Women are charged with provid-ing food, fuel, and water for their families; as shortages of these commodities heighten, so do the time and money expended in pursuit of them. Women look after those who are ill, so they bear the brunt of illness caused by pollution, even in advanced countries. Similarly, femi-nist empiricism finds that because women are on the front lines of many economic and social issues, they are positioned to have a disproportionate effect on solving certain kinds of environmental problems.

Many feminists also raise concerns about the effects on women of population control. In some cases, population control policies can lead to coercion of women and families that restricts reproductive rights and de-emphasizes reproductive health services.[10] The most glaring example of this is in China, where the "one child" policy has fostered coerced abortion as well as sex-selective abortion that selects against female fetuses.

Feminist standpoint theory, as applied to the environ-ment, focuses on the connections among different forms of domination. In a masculinized world, some contend, domination and control are seen as signs of strength. This domination and control can be of man over woman or of man over nature. This emphasis on control and domina-tion of nature justifies making nature serve the will of man, including extracting resources and dumping pollutants.

The feminist argument that gendered notions of power privilege "power as the ability to control" over "power as the ability to collaborate" is especially sig-nificant with regard to international environmental concerns. If collaboration on environmental issues were viewed as an exercise and validation of national power, it might be much more attractive. Similarly, the argument that the sovereign state should not be seen as autonomous and above society can be extended to the international level: If states were not defined as autonomous and distinct from one another, there would be much less basis to resist international environmental cooperation on the grounds of "national interest."

Women collecting water from a pump during a flood in Dhaka, Bangladesh, August 2002. Ironically, even when inun-dated by floods, finding sanitary drinking water is a major challenge.

# INTERNATIONAL ENVIRONMENTAL COLLABORATION: SOLUTIONS AND BARRIERS

## SOLVING INTERNATIONAL COLLECTIVE ACTION PROBLEMS

Viewing international environmental problems as collective action problems opens the discussion to a vast literature devoted to exploring solutions to collective action problems in a wide variety of circumstances. This literature points to a basic puzzle: Many collective

# THE CONNECTION TO YOU

## HOW WILL CLIMATE CHANGE AFFECT YOUR LIFE?

Climate change is still in its early phases, but the amount of greenhouse gases currently being emitted ensures that climate change will continue and worsen unless something dramatic changes. The hottest year on record was 2014. Climate change will affect the lives of today's students one way or another; either the steps we take to avert climate change or the consequences of unabated climate change will influence economics, politics, and many aspects of daily life. The choices open to societies are not easy, and the options open to any individual will be severely constrained by the choices made by societies. As the collective action problem indicates, one individual's efforts to combat climate change will have little impact by themselves. Among the choices each of us as individuals face is the extent to which we support mitigation of climate change versus adapting to the effects.

How will climate change affect your career? If steps are taken to mitigate climate change, will you be one of those who finds opportunity in developing green technology, trading emissions credits, or designing new regulations, or will you be one of those whose livelihood is hurt by rising fuel costs, increased regulation, or decreased subsidies? How will your career be influenced by climate change that does occur? Will you find your agricultural land becoming less productive or subject to much less predictable weather? Will you find opportunity selling new financial products to help hedge against natural disasters? Will you benefit from a new housing boom in places that become more desirable when weather patterns change?

Similar questions can be asked about our lifestyles. If steps are taken to mitigate climate change, will the internal combustion engine, around which much of our daily lives and culture revolve, be phased out? Will we put a premium on living not in suburbs but in communities with dense public transit networks that make transportation cheap and convenient? If global warming raises seas and intensifies hurricanes, what will happen to the beach houses that line our coasts and have driven so much economic development in places like Florida?

### Critical Thinking Questions

1. How are you involved in this problem now, as a student? Are you engaged in formal advocacy on the ongoing debate? Do you take a position in debates with your friends, family, or colleagues?

2. Are you more comfortable taking costly steps now to reduce climate change or accepting that costly effects may be forced on us in the future?

3. What is your ethical position on environmental issues? Is there a duty to do something about them, or is it simply a matter of self-interest?

action problems get solved, whereas others seem to resist solution. What accounts for the difference?

One important school of thought focuses on the design of institutions to facilitate sustainable management of common pool resources, such as shared fisheries, water supplies, oil reserves, and forests. Political scientist Elinor Ostrom won the 2009 Nobel Prize in Economics for showing how communities around the world effectively manage a wide range of common pool resources and for synthesizing from these practices a common set of principles, which include[11]:

- Excluding outside actors from access to the shared resource
- Designing rules for extracting and distributing the resource that fit local conditions
- Maximizing the number of extractors of the resource that participate in decision making
- Creating effective monitoring mechanisms and instituting increasing sanctions for violators
- Designing accessible and workable means of resolving disputes

Ostrom's research shows that collaborative institutions among independent actors can emerge to solve these problems. In theory, this finding applies to global as well as local problems, but as Ostrom acknowledges, the larger the scale of the problem, the more difficult it is to design successful arrangements.

The broader literature on collective action points to several generalizable factors that influence the difficulty of solving collective action problems.

**Number of Actors**   Other things being equal, the more actors that are part of a given collective action problem, the harder it is to solve. With a small number of actors, each actor can more clearly see its role in creating the problem, and see that it can play a major role in solving it. As the number increases, each actor becomes a smaller part of the problem and the solution, and the incentive to change behavior decreases. Moreover, maintaining an agreement is harder because as the number of actors goes up, monitoring and enforcing compliance become more difficult and more costly. Trying to break global problems into a series of regional problems might help in this respect.

**Time Horizons**   How far actors look into the future, and how they value future costs and benefits relative to the present, influences the incentive to cooperate. Liberal theory points out that if actors play the prisoner's dilemma game repeatedly, the benefits of cooperating increase over time, and the benefits from defecting (free riding) are reduced as one's partners retaliate. In environmental cooperation, the challenge is that the costs of mitigating environmental damage are immediate, whereas the benefits (avoiding future environmental damage) do not materialize until sometime in the future. The more weight given to future costs and benefits relative to the present, the easier it is to forge collaboration.

**The Free Rider Problem**   One of the central barriers to solving collective action problems is free riding. Because actors share the collective good whether they contribute to it or not, each actor has the incentive to "free ride" on the efforts of others. This problem is connected to the numbers problem: The more actors there are, the harder it is to identify and punish free riders. One essential goal of international organizations can be to monitor and provide unbiased data, the way the International Atomic Energy Agency does for the Non-Proliferation of Nuclear Weapons Treaty.

**Selective Incentives**   One way to overcome the free rider problem is to offer selective incentives (side payments, or bribes) to those who participate, while denying them to those who do not. For example, at the Durban meeting in 2011, some participants proposed offering special development aid to poor countries to get them to agree to binding limits on greenhouse gas emissions.

**Hegemony**   When one actor is disproportionately powerful, that actor can help provide the collective good either directly or indirectly. Directly, it can simply pay for the good

Landing an Atlantic Bluefin tuna off the coast of Spain. Bluefin is highly prized in Japan, and in 2012 a single 593 lb (250 kg) fish sold for $736,000. As a result, they have been heavily overfished.

William Boyce/Corbis

itself, or pay for enough of it that other actors are willing to step up. Indirectly, it can provide the incentives (side payments or threats) needed to induce cooperation by others. The hegemon has greater ability to sanction free riders. In the 1980s, the United States played this role in the environmental realm, leading efforts to limit ozone-depleting chemicals and pressuring others to agree. Since the 1990s, however, the United States has chosen not to lead on this issue, and no other potential leader has emerged.

**Privatization**   One way to change a collective good into a noncollective good is to divide it up into several privately owned pieces. This was the original solution to the tragedy of the commons in England. Each farmer received a parcel of land, so that overgrazing the land damaged only the farmer's own interests and no one else's. This is what states are doing when they declare a 300-mile "exclusive economic zone" off their shores. Bringing a wider swath of ocean and seabed under national sovereignty reduces the international collective action problem. Many problems are not amenable to this solution, however. The atmosphere cannot be divided, and the ocean can be divided only to some extent. Even if one country controls a section of ocean, if the fish move in and out of that zone, the fish stocks will still be a collective good.

**Quotas and Trading**   In many localities, overfishing has been dealt with through the assignments of individual transferrable quotas (ITQs). Fishermen are each assigned a quota (how much fish they can harvest), and they can either catch that amount or sell the right to do so to others. The overall number of fish caught is limited, but market forces determine how that catch is divided up. Similar arrangements have been used to deal with greenhouse gas emissions.

   The first step is to determine how much of a given pollutant can be tolerated. That amount is then divided up and sold or allocated to industries that already pollute. A market can then emerge for "pollution credits" that give the right to pollute. The benefit of this approach is that it allows innovation and markets to drive efficiency. Plant operators have an incentive to reduce pollution because they can sell their excess pollution credits.

## THE POLICY CONNECTION

# THE BIOFUEL DILEMMA: ENERGY SECURITY VERSUS FOOD SECURITY

Increasing demand for oil around the world has many governments worried about their dependence on imported energy. Some see biofuels (such as ethanol) as a way of reducing the use of fossil fuels and increasing energy independence. Brazil and the United States, which have abundant farmland but limited oil supplies, have relied heavily on biofuels to reduce energy imports. These two countries combined account for nearly 90 percent of global ethanol production. However, corn and other crops that go toward fuel production are not available for food, so food prices go up. This has caused concerns for the welfare of the world's poorest people.

Brazil pioneered the use of biofuels as a means of energy independence after the global energy crisis of 1973. Brazil has excellent conditions for growing sugarcane, which can be efficiently distilled to produce ethanol. The government passed laws subsidizing ethanol production and mandating that ethanol be used in automobile fuel. In Brazil today, most of the cars sold have so-called flex-fuel engines that can burn fuels ranging from 100 percent gasoline to 100 percent ethanol. This offers flexibility to consumers as the relative prices of petroleum and ethanol ebb and flow. By 2012, Brazilian demand for ethanol had outstripped the domestic supply, driving up prices.

Brazil's experience inspired U.S. biofuels policies. In the United States, the desire to increase **energy security**, the danger of global warming, and the power of the agriculture lobby prompted adoption of the Energy Security and Independence Act of 2007, which required oil refiners to mix ethanol into gasoline and paid them a subsidy of 45 cents for every gallon of ethanol they mixed into gasoline. This led the United States to surpass Brazil as the world's leading ethanol producer. The subsidy was removed

**energy security**

Protection against the threat of energy shortages either because of supply problems or because of deliberate efforts by others to inflict harm.

Harvesting sugarcane to produce ethanol in Sao Paulo state, Brazil. Brazil has developed an extensive ethanol production capacity to reduce its dependence on imported oil.

Marcele Rudini/Alamy

*(Continued)*

in 2011, but the requirement to use ethanol increased, from 12.6 billion gallons per year under the original law, to 15 billion gallons per year in 2015, and will rise to 36 billion gallons by 2022. For U.S. farmers, who comprise a very powerful interest group, the subsidies and higher prices are highly beneficial, and the role of the large farming state of Iowa in the presidential nominating process means that presidential contenders have a powerful incentive to continue to support laws promoting ethanol use.

However, diverting crops from food production drives up the price of food, which has dire consequences for millions of people already on the edge of poverty. Nearly 40 percent of U.S. corn production now goes into ethanol production rather than into the food supply, raising the price of corn by an estimated 20 percent.* This may not seem like much, but for those living in poverty, for whom food often consumes more than half their income, a 20 percent increase in a staple product can push people over the edge into hunger. In 2007, rapid increases in the price of corn led to riots in Mexico.

Moreover, the claim that biofuels reduce global warming has been met with increasing skepticism. As governments subsidize biofuels and prices rise, farmers naturally try to produce more, either by bringing more land under cultivation or by diverting crops from food production to energy production. In Brazil, bringing more land into production often means cutting down

or burning rainforests, which puts more carbon into the atmosphere than is gained by switching to cleaner fuels.

Scientists and economists have therefore stressed that biofuel production must change if negative consequences are to be avoided.[†] In the United States and in Brazil, there is now increasing focus on cellulosic ethanol—ethanol made from grasses and wood products that do not compete with the food supply and can be grown on land that is less suitable for food crops. Considerable research is dedicated to making cellulosic ethanol as cost competitive as that made from corn or sugarcane.

## Critical Thinking Questions

1. How important is energy security relative to other goals?

2. What strategies other than biofuels are available to increase energy security?

3. How effective are governments at managing multiple concerns such as energy security and food security?

---

*Scott Sendrowski, "Ethanol's Fuel Dilemma," CNNMoney, January 31, 2012, finance.fortune.cnn.com/2012/01/31/ethanol-corn-food-fuel.

[†]See David Tilman, Robert Socolow, Jonathan A. Foley, et al., "Beneficial Biofuels: The Food, Energy, and Environment Trilemma," Science, July 17, 2009, pp. 270–271.

Economically, this is efficient because it means the reductions in pollution can be channeled to where they will cause the least economic harm. This provision, widely known as *cap and trade*, has been used in various countries and localities around the world to limit different pollutants. The Kyoto Protocol provided for emissions trading, in which countries that cut emissions below required levels could sell the excess to others that were above required levels.

**Regulation** Most domestic collective action problems are solved through regulation. Environmental examples include the Federal Control of Pollution Act in Germany, the National Environmental Policy Law in Brazil, and the Clean Water and Clean Air acts in the United States. A central issue in international regulation is enforcement. Even if states agree to limit or prohibit some activity, monitoring and enforcing compliance can be difficult and costly. A major question for the future of international politics is whether states can collaborate on the kind of rigorous regulation that would be needed to deal with many global environmental problems such as climate change.

# BARRIERS TO COOPERATION

Beyond collective action problems, there is a general set of obstacles that tend to arise on many international environmental issues.

**Conflict with Free Trade Agreements**    International environmental protection often complicates the issue of free trade. Environmental regulations are sometimes viewed as barriers to trade, and some important regulations have been struck down by the WTO for that reason.

**Competing Economic Priorities**    The goal of environmental protection is a much greater priority for some countries than for others. For the poorest people of the world, environmental protection is a luxury that appears unaffordable. The same thing is true for societies as a whole. For Third World governments with debts to pay, increasing exports to pay off those debts is likely to be a higher priority than protecting the environment, especially when they are under pressure from the World Bank or the IMF. However, it is not only poor countries that put economics ahead of the environment. Countries battling an economic downturn might hesitate to increase environmental regulation. The most prominent state refusing to sign the Kyoto Protocol on climate change is the United States, which fears the economic consequences of reducing fossil fuel use.

**Complexity**    Environmental problems overlap with many other policy concerns, such as development and free trade. Environmental goals can also be at odds with each other. For example, hydroelectric and wind power are seen as energy that is "clean" and does not increase dependence on foreign sources. But hydroelectric dams have a huge impact on river systems and often force people to relocate, and wind farms spur opposition because they are unsightly, cause noise pollution, and disrupt migrating birds. Because bureaucracies tend to work within their own "silos," coordinating policies so that they do not undermine each other is very difficult.

**Equity**    From the perspective of developing countries, it seems that the developed countries, having gotten rich by exploiting natural resources and despoiling the environment, are now trying to close the door before the poorer countries can pursue the same strategies. In general, people in wealthier countries consume more resources and produce more pollution than those in poorer countries (see Figure 14.4). Europeans and Americans do not want to undergo enormous cuts in energy use as consumption grows elsewhere, but poorer countries are understandably reluctant to accept the conclusion that they should forever consume less than the wealthy countries. Either course seems unfair to a large number of countries and people.

**Economic Competitiveness**    The question of equity is closely related to economic competition. Developing countries are worried about environmental agreements that would leave them underdeveloped; advanced countries are worried about agreements that leave them at a competitive disadvantage vis-à-vis rising economic powers. Thus, China, which is still developing but is highly competitive, and the United States, which is wealthy but is losing production to China, are at an impasse: Neither will agree to terms that the other can accept. Because these are the two biggest greenhouse gas emitters, this impasse creates a major barrier to a global agreement.

**Scientific Uncertainty**    As noted previously, it is difficult to undertake economic sacrifices when it is unclear how dangerous the threat is. This problem plagues efforts to forge an agreement on greenhouse gas emissions. The role played by transnational actors and international organizations, especially transnational groups of scientists, can be crucial

**FIGURE 14.4** **Carbon dioxide emissions, 2012.** How does carbon dioxide emission vary across the developed and developing world?

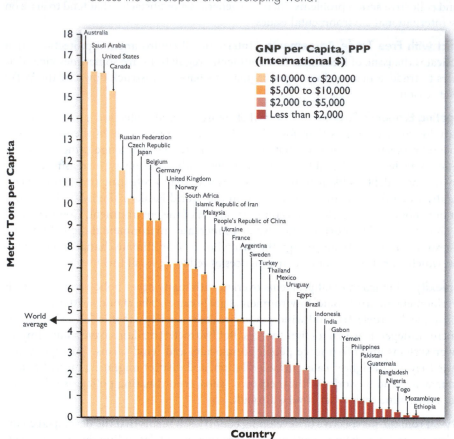

Source: IEA Statistics, "CO₂ Emissions/Population," *CO₂ Emissions from Fuel Combustion Highlights, 2014 Edition.*

**Intergovernmental Panel on Climate Change (IPCC)**

An international body that assesses scientific research on climate change for decision makers.

in causing states to redefine their interests. The **Intergovernmental Panel on Climate Change (IPCC)** has been essential in marshaling scientific evidence to remove doubts about the seriousness of global warming.

**Domestic Politics**    Finally, the domestic politics discussed in Chapter 6 play an important role in environmental collaboration. International environmental politics are an excellent example of a two-level game, in which national leaders must simultaneously negotiate with other nation-states and with domestic constituencies and can only agree to measures of which both sets of actors approve. Thus, reaching any global environmental treaty depends not only on over 170 countries around the world agreeing with each other, but on each of these governments gaining the domestic support they need to ratify the treaty. The United States signed the Kyoto Protocol in 1998, but no president has submitted it to the Senate for ratification because it is clear that it would not be ratified. Beyond the formal ratification process is a much broader political process involving all of the societal actors discussed in Chapter 6, including corporations, interest groups, NGOs, the media, and voters.

Despite the obstacles to cooperation, states have reached a large number of agreements on a wide range of issues (see Table 14.1). These agreements are reached through

**TABLE 14.1** **Major International Environmental Treaties, 1970–2008**

|  |  |
|---|---|
| 1971 | Convention on Wetlands of International Importance (RAMSAR) |
| 1972 | Stockholm Declaration by the UN Conference on the Environment |
| 1972 | London Convention on Dumping at Sea |
| 1972 | World Heritage Convention |
| 1973 | Convention on International Trade in Endangered Species |
| 1974 | International Convention for Safety of Life at Sea |
| 1978 | Convention on Prevention of Pollution from Ships (MARPOL) |
| 1979 | Convention on Long-Range Transboundary Air Pollution |
| 1979 | Convention on the Conservation of Migratory Species of Wild Animals |
| 1982 | Convention on Law of the Sea |
| 1982 | Amendments to RAMSAR Convention on Wetlands |
| 1983 | International Tropical Timber Agreement (ITTA) |
| 1985 | Vienna Convention for Protection of the Ozone Layer |
| 1987 | Montreal Protocol on Substances That Deplete the Ozone Layer |
| 1989 | Basel Convention on the Control of Transboundary Movements of Hazardous Wastes and Their Disposal |
| 1991 | Convention on Environmental Impact Assessment in a Transboundary Context |
| 1992 | Climate Change Convention |
| 1992 | Biodiversity Convention |
| 1992 | Convention on Transboundary Effects of Industrial Accidents |
| 1994 | Convention to Combat Desertification |
| 1994 | International Tropical Timber Agreement (replacement for 1983 ITTA) |
| 1997 | Kyoto Protocol on Climate Change |
| 1998 | Rotterdam Convention on Prior Informed Consent |
| 1998 | Aarhus Convention on Information, Public Participation and Access to Justice in Environmental Matters |
| 2000 | Cartagena Protocol on Biosafety |
| 2001 | Stockholm Convention on Persistent Organic Pollutants |

*Source: Daniel Keleman and David Vogel, "Trading Places: The Role of the United States and the European Union in International Environmental Politics," Comparative Political Studies, Vol. 43, No. 4 (April 2010): 429–430.*

a combination of factors that mitigate collective action problems and other barriers to cooperation. In this respect, the fact that a robust agreement on greenhouse gases has not been reached is not representative, but rather reflects the particular difficulties of that issue.

# INTERNATIONAL ENVIRONMENTAL AGREEMENTS

## THE KYOTO PROTOCOL PROCESS

**Kyoto Protocol**

An international agreement that was signed in 1997 and went into effect in 2005 that aims to reduce greenhouse gas emissions to prevent global climate change.

In December 1997, representatives of most of the world's states met in Kyoto, Japan, to finalize a treaty limiting the emission of greenhouse gases.[12] Under the **Kyoto Protocol**, 39 "Annex I" countries, the largest producers of greenhouse gases, agreed to reduce their output of such gases to below their 1990 levels by 2012. The overall reduction would be 5.2 percent, but the amount of reduction for each country varied. The EU states were committed to reducing their output by 8 percent, the United States (which did not subsequently ratify the agreement) by 7 percent, and Japan by 5 percent. Essentially, the Annex I countries are the developed countries of the world and the post-Soviet states. All other countries (non–Annex I countries) were permitted to continue increasing their production of greenhouse gases, in recognition of the fact that they produced lower amounts and needed to consume more fossil fuels to continue economic development.

Although some believed the Kyoto Protocol was too restrictive, others feared that it was too weak. Those who saw it as too restrictive were concerned about the economic effects of cutting back on the use of fossil fuels in economies that are highly dependent on them. The economic cost of the agreement is a primary reason the United States did not ratify the agreement and Canada withdrew.

Others argued that the protocol was far too weak to deal with the problem. Even if emissions by Annex I countries were reduced to below 1990 levels, overall emissions would increase because developing countries are not covered and are rapidly increasing their output (China surpassed the United States as the top emitter of greenhouse gases around 2005). Supporters of the Kyoto Protocol argued that although the agreement was imperfect, levels of greenhouse gases would rise much higher without the treaty. Most agreed further action was needed.

## POST-KYOTO NEGOTIATIONS

In the years after Kyoto, reaching an agreement got harder. At the time of Kyoto, most developing countries could be left out of Annex I because they were neither large producers of greenhouse gases nor serious economic competitors with the advanced industrial states. Since then, however, China, Brazil, India, and many other countries developed economically, and as they did, their greenhouse gases emissions grew to the point that they could no longer be ignored. At the same time, a massive effort was begun in the United States to undermine support for preventing global warming.

In December 2009, a summit was held in Copenhagen to devise a follow-up treaty to Kyoto. The summit broke down amid intense recrimination about whether developed or developing states were to blame. The different positions of these two groups created a conflict of interest that simply could not be bridged.

Most of the countries of Europe, and others such as Canada and Australia, had taken significant steps to limit greenhouse gas emissions since 1990. However, growth in the Chinese, Indian, and other developing economies made it clear that some limits on their production of greenhouse gases would eventually be needed. China had become the biggest single producer of greenhouse gases. The United States in particular resisted making any commitment unless developing states did so.

However, the developing states steadfastly resisted limits on their own emissions, which in general were still lower on a per capita basis than were those in developed states. Led by China, they even resisted a proposal under which states would choose their own legally binding limits. China and others found the idea of legally binding limits potentially dangerous to their future economic growth.

The breakdown at Copenhagen, and the bitterness that the process engendered, provoked considerable pessimism about the likelihood that catastrophic global warming (generally defined as an average increase of two degrees Celsius or more) would be averted. The 2011 Durban Summit, discussed at the outset of this chapter, reinforced this pessimism, while also providing a sliver of hope—agreement in principle on future binding limits. Whether states can actually agree to adopt such limits remains very questionable. Without serious commitments by the United States, China, and other large developing states, agreement on significant limits will be hard to reach.

# THE GEOGRAPHY CONNECTION

## WATER SHORTAGES

As this map shows, water supplies are increasingly threatened all over the world, but the danger is more intense in some areas than others.

### Critical Thinking Questions

1. Are water shortages primarily a local problem or an international problem?

2. What factors are likely to make water shortages worse? Will these factors have a greater impact in some regions than others?

3. What international political consequences are likely to result from water shortages?

Level of threat to river ecosystems.

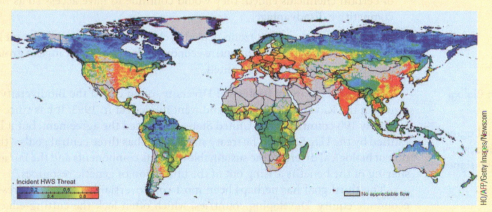

. Incident HWS Threat

No appreciable flow

HO/AFP/Getty Images/Newscom

Source: http://news.bbc.co.uk/2/hi/science/nature/5269296.stm#graphic

# OTHER ENVIRONMENTAL AGREEMENTS

**Montreal Protocol**

An international agreement, signed in 1987, that commits the signatories to reducing the production and use of gases that deplete the ozone layer.

In addition to the Kyoto Protocol, a variety of international environmental agreements—some regional, some global—address environmental problems. The **Montreal Protocol**, signed by 24 states plus the EU in 1987, now has more than 180 signatories. It commits the signatories to reducing the production and use of gases that deplete the ozone layer in the atmosphere. The Montreal Protocol was significant because it was the first major global environmental treaty and because its success convinced many skeptics that such cooperation was indeed possible. It was seen by many as a model for a treaty on greenhouse gases (the Kyoto Protocol). Cooperation to limit gases that deplete the ozone layer became possible in large part because scientific findings regarding the effect of certain chemicals on the ozone layer became indisputable. Similarly, there was wide consensus on the negative effects of increased ultraviolet radiation on human health.

The Montreal Protocol illustrates how cooperation can occur even on difficult collective action problems. Initial proposals to deal with the problem met with resistance from a wide variety of governments, industrial groups, and others. Over time, however, several factors made agreement possible.

- *Number of actors:* The chemicals that deplete atmospheric ozone were produced in a relatively small number of industrialized countries, primarily in the United States and Europe. This effectively reduced the number of states whose agreement was needed for a workable treaty.

- *Time horizon:* New scientific data made clear that the effects of ozone depletion would be felt in the foreseeable, rather than the distant, future.

- *Leadership:* The United States made dealing with the problem a high priority and used its influence to keep the issue on the agenda.

- *Shared purpose, based on scientific consensus:* New scientific findings decreased uncertainty about ozone depletion and its sources. Discovery of an enlarging "ozone hole" over Antarctica dramatically increased public concern.

- *Technology:* Chemical companies discovered new chemicals that could achieve the needed purposes without depleting the ozone layer.

- *Development and equity:* Developing countries were assured that even as production of certain chemicals ended, they would continue to have access so as not to be at a competitive disadvantage.

- *Domestic interest groups:* Ozone-depleting chemicals were very important in particular industries, but not across the entire economy. Therefore, the range of groups lobbying against the reductions was limited.

**Convention on Biological Diversity**

An international agreement aimed at conserving biodiversity, signed in 1992.

The **Convention on Biological Diversity**, often called the Biodiversity Treaty, was signed at the Rio Summit in 1992 and went into effect in 1993. It has since been signed by nearly 190 countries. The United States has signed the agreement, but it has not been ratified by the U.S. Senate. The treaty states that it has three central goals: "the conservation of biological diversity, the sustainable use of its components and the fair and equitable sharing of the benefits arising out of the utilization of genetic resources."

The third goal has perhaps been most controversial because it addresses issues of economic equity. Developing countries, which often lack the cutting-edge technology and financial resources to develop commercial applications of their biological resources, fear that the profits from exploitation of the resources will go primarily to corporations from developed countries. Thus, the treaty, rather vaguely, commits countries to a "fair and equitable sharing of benefits" from biological resources.

# THE HISTORY CONNECTION

## CRITICAL JUNCTURES IN ENVIRONMENTAL PROTECTION

The modern focus on environmental protection has deep roots. In the United States, it goes back at least to 1887, when Yellowstone National Park was established. Many other countries around the world established national parks in the following decades. In this period, the primary ethic was *conservation*—setting aside land from development so that its natural beauty could be enjoyed.

By the early twentieth century, extinction was a concern, as birds such as the dodo and the passenger pigeon had been wiped out by overhunting and global whale populations had been decimated. The United States and Canada agreed to limit the killing of migratory birds in 1918, and the International Convention for the Regulation of Whaling was signed in 1937.

Many date the modern environmental movement, especially in the United States, to the 1962 publication of *Silent Spring*, in which the biologist Rachel Carson documented the effects of pesticide use on human and animal health. The book, which not only highlighted the harmful effects of pesticides but also questioned the broader model of applying technology to solve problems, spurred a bitter debate with chemical companies and the U.S. Department of Agriculture (which sponsored pest eradication programs) on one side and environmental and health advocates on the other. Eventually, the use of popular and effective insecticides such as DDT was banned.

Britain's Clean Air Act was passed in 1956, after an episode of smog that had blanketed London for a week in 1952. The growing focus on pollution led to the passage of regulations on water and air pollution in many countries in the 1960s and 1970s. Particularly visible disasters, such as the episode in 1969 when the Cuyahoga River outside Cleveland caught fire, helped build the political will to take action.

A 1979 accident at the Three Mile Island nuclear power station near Harrisburg, Pennsylvania, essentially ended construction of new nuclear plants in the United States. An accident at Chernobyl in Ukraine (then part of the Soviet Union) in 1986 contaminated a large area and contributed to the downfall of the Soviet system. The meltdown of reactors at Fukushima in Japan in 2011 prompted several governments around the world to promise to shut down existing nuclear reactors. The result is greater reliance on other forms of electricity generation.

In 1984, a chemical leak at a plant in Bhopal, India, owned by the U.S. company Union Carbide, killed at least 3000 people (the number of victims is disputed) and injured many thousands more. Court actions over the case continue to this day. The Bhopal disaster was one of the first cases to bring environmental issues together with the questions of poverty and development. Many people in India believed that the plant was run in a negligent fashion because it was in India, not in the United States, and that they had no means of holding the corporation and its American officers accountable. Disagreements about the environmental duties of wealthy countries and their companies have continued to impede agreement on environmental measures.

One theme that emerges from these cases is that the political will to address environmental issues has often followed some particularly visible incident that prompts public opinion to press for laws that limit environmental damage.

### Critical Thinking Questions

1. What more recent events have shaped attitudes on the importance of environmental protection?

2. Does the history of environmental policy imply that protection will increase, even if slowly, or is there no inevitability about progress in this area?

3. Is it the case that it takes disaster to move policy, or can policy prevent disaster before it happens?

Critics claim that the treaty has done relatively little to protect biodiversity while making the conduct of basic scientific research much more difficult. The treaty's provisions regarding the first goal are vague and have had little observable impact on the problem. At the same time, some scientists complain that the third goal has led some countries to pass laws that make conducting basic scientific research border on criminal activity.

# POWER AND PURPOSE IN THE INTERNATIONAL ENVIRONMENT

Some theorists have speculated that environmental problems will force states to join together in new ways.[13] International security, they say, is being redefined. The new dangers to states and societies, in this perspective, come not from other states and societies, or from their armies, but from environmental degradation that threatens all states. Some see this development changing international politics in two ways. First, it makes all states allies against these common enemies. To the extent that this is true, international purpose is being fundamentally redefined.

Second, these problems cannot be solved by states working alone. Climate change can be prevented only through measures that have effects across all countries. Some fisheries will be wiped out without international agreements to limit fishing to sustainable levels. Thus, some argue that these problems will compel states to fundamentally revise the system of state sovereignty by giving real governmental authority to international organizations. In this view, states will not do so voluntarily, but through harsh necessity. Self-interest, in this view, will require surrendering state sovereignty, not defending it tenaciously. Garrett Hardin, author of the original article on the tragedy of the commons in 1968, argued then that environmental problems would require a strong international government. For this to happen, collaborative power would have to become far more salient.

Harvesting whale meat. Hunting drove several whale species to the brink of extinction, but conservation efforts have led, in several cases, to a resurgence of stocks. This has led to a resumption of hunting by several countries, but most countries still support a complete ban on whaling. What determines which species should be completely off limits to hunting?

Biophoto Associates/Photo Researchers, Inc.

Others view that perspective as hopelessly naïve.[14] From a realist perspective, environmental issues may intensify conflict between states but will not reduce the role of traditional power in international politics. Realists would cite the conflict over greenhouse gas emissions as evidence. Realists see the environment as a source of conflict, not cooperation. As resources become scarcer, states are more likely to fight over them. Oil and water in particular appear possible objects of conflict.[15] In the future, climate change may contribute to other sources of domestic and international conflict, including drought, food shortages, and migration.

The two opposing scenarios just outlined are not mutually exclusive. Elements of both scenarios could play out at the same time. It is possible, for example, that there will be further collaboration on some shared issues and conflict in others, or that resource conflicts will be managed peacefully in some places but not in others. What is beyond doubt is that the environment will be a much more significant issue in the coming decades than it has been in the past.

# RECONSIDER THE CASE

## CLIMATE CHANGE NEGOTIATIONS

By pushing off even the chance of serious action on greenhouse gas emissions until 2020, the Durban conference forced people around the world to think harder than before about the likelihood that significant global warming will occur, about the impacts it will have, and about how individuals, countries, and the international community might deal with those impacts. In this respect, one process that was solidified at Durban may take on increasing importance: the formation of an international Adaptation Committee, whose purpose is to consider how people and governments might respond to the climate change that seems increasingly inevitable.

An overall increase in the planet's temperature can be expected to have different effects in different places. These effects can be broken down into three main categories: sea level rise, which will affect the coastal areas; extreme weather, which will happen in many places, but will have a disproportionate effect in areas already made more flood-prone by sea level rise; and changes in weather patterns, which may change the amount and cycles of precipitation in ways

that have major consequences for agriculture around the world. The central question is, how will we adapt?

Adaptation may come in two broad categories. Physical adaptation envisions building infrastructure that minimizes damage, such as building sea walls that protect against sea level rise and hurricanes. Human adaptation envisions helping people deal with the consequences, such as assisting people whose homes are lost to flooding or whose farmland becomes unproductive as a result of climate change. Even if climate change is global, many of the problems it creates will fall on individuals and governments at the local and national levels. At the same time, many of these consequences will be felt internationally. Primary among these is migration: If storms, flooding, or drought drive people away from their residences, they are likely to cross national boundaries as a result. Similarly, if storms, flooding, or droughts reduce agricultural yields, supply shortages and price increases may quickly become global problems.

For the international community, the question of whether and how states, international organizations, and NGOs will work to prevent or minimize global warming

*(Continued)*

remains. However, as time passes, a second question will increase in importance: How can states work to cope with the impacts of climate change? In 2014, the U.S. Department of Defense released a "Climate Change Adaptation Road Map," which characterized climate change as a "'threat multiplier,' because it has the potential to exacerbate many of the challenges we are dealing with today—from infectious disease to terrorism."*

## Critical Thinking Questions

1. Which countries will likely be best able to manage the consequences of global warming?

2. Which kinds of mitigation will require international cooperation?

3. How will the role of transnational advocacy networks and NGOs change in a world of climate change?

*U.S. Department of Defense, "2014 Climate Change Adaptation Roadmap," www.acq.osd.mil/ie/download/CCARprint_wForeword_c.pdf.

## SUMMARY

- Environmental issues are becoming a bigger part of international politics.

- Population growth and increased individual consumption are both increasing pressure on the environment.

- Environmental issues include both resource shortages and pollution, as well as threats to biodiversity.

- Natural resources can be divided into renewable and nonrenewable resources.

- Many environmental issues can be analyzed as collective action problems. Liberal theory in particular stresses this approach.

- There are a variety of ways of addressing collective action problems, but they are difficult to solve at the international level.

- International agreements have been reached on a variety of environmental issues.

- Realists see resource shortages as a source of conflict. They argue that concerns over power make states hesitant to collaborate on environmental issues.

- Economic structuralists focus on the distributive consequences of environmental problems and solutions. They worry that environmental measures will limit the development of poor countries, and that environmental damage will fall most heavily on the poor.

- Sustainable development has become a major concern. The challenge is to make continued economic growth environmentally and economically sustainable.

- Domestic politics play an important role in international environmental politics. Firms, individuals, and NGOs lobby governments for and against various measures.

## KEY CONCEPTS

1. Energy security
2. Sustainable development
3. Collective action problem
4. Tragedy of the commons
5. Kyoto Protocol

## STUDY QUESTIONS

1. Which of the following is putting pressure on the supply of nonrenewable resources?
   a. Population growth in developing countries
   b. Economic development
   c. Advances in medicine
   d. All of the above.

2. What theory is particularly helpful in explaining environmental problems?
   a. Prospect theory
   b. Cognitive dissonance theory
   c. Power transition theory
   d. Collective action theory

3. Overfishing is an example of a(n)
   a. tragedy of the commons.
   b. externality.
   c. structural adjustment.
   d. asymmetric conflict.

4. Which approach focuses on whether increased competition for resources leads to economic development or exploitation of poor countries?
   a. Realism
   b. Liberalism
   c. Economic structuralism
   d. Constructivism

5. Which approach primarily argues that environmental problems can only be solved through collaboration, so they motivate states to cooperate?
   a. Realism
   b. Liberalism
   c. Economic structuralism
   d. Constructivism

6. Which approach forecasts future conflicts over the limited supply of natural resources?
   a. Realism
   b. Liberalism
   c. Economic structuralism
   d. Constructivism

7. What environmental issues are global rather than national or regional in scope?

8. In what way is international collaboration on environmental problems a collective action problem?

9. What are the most important factors that affect the ability of solving international collective action problems?

10. What are the major barriers to international collaboration on environmental problems?

11. What aspects of greenhouse gas emissions make this a difficult problem to address?

12. Will environmental degradation lead to more cooperation or more conflict among states?

[Correct answers: 1. d; 2. d; 3. a; 4. c; 5. b; 6. a]

## END NOTES

1. U.S. Department of Defense, Quadrennial Defense Review Report, February 2010, pp. 7, 84, www.defense.gov/qdr/images/QDR_as_of_12Feb10_1000.pdf.

2. Jared Diamond, "What's Your Consumption Factor?" *New York Times*, January 2, 2008, www.nytimes.com/2008/01/02/opinion/02diamond.html.

3. Kenneth S. Deffeyes, *Hibbert's Peak: The Impending World Oil Shortage* (Princeton, NJ: Princeton University Press, 2001).

4. Garrett Hardin, "The Tragedy of the Commons," *Science*, No. 162 (1968): 1243–1248.

5. Peter M. Haas, "Social Construction and the Evolution of Multilateral Environmental Governance," in Aseem Prakash and Jeffrey A. Hart, eds., *Globalization and Governance* (London: Routledge, 1999), pp. 303–333.

6. See, for example, Greg Palast, "Secret U.S. Plans for Iraq's Oil," *BBC Newsnight*, March 17, 2005,

http://news.bbc.co.uk/2/hi/4354269.stm; and "Guiding Principles for U.S. Post-Conflict Policy in Iraq: Report of an Independent Working Group Cosponsored by the Council on Foreign Relations and the James A. Baker III Institute for Public Policy of Rice University" (New York: Council on Foreign Relations, 2003), http://bakerinstitute.org/publications/guiding-principles-for-u-s-post-conflict-policy-in-iraq.

7. "Droughts Feed Hunger Crisis and Violence in Sudan," *PBS NewsHour*, March 5, 2010, www.pbs.org/newshour/bb/politics/jan-june10/sudan_03-05.html.

8. Haas, "Social Construction and the Evolution of Multilateral Environmental Governance."

9. UNDP, "Gender and Environment and Energy," www.beta.undp.org/content/undp/en/home /our-work/womenempowerment/focus_areas /women_and_environmentalchange.html.

10. Betsy Hartmann, "10 Reasons Why Population Control Is Not the Solution to Global Warming," *Different Takes*, No. 57 (Winter 2009), popdev.hampshire.edu/sites/popdev/files/uploads/dt/DTakes_57_final.pdf.

11. Elinor Ostrom, *Governing the Commons: The Evolution of Institutions for Collective Action* (New York: Cambridge University Press, 1990).

12. The treaty's official name is the Kyoto Protocol to the United Nations Framework Convention on Climate Change. Technically, it is an amendment to the Framework Convention on Climate Change, which was negotiated at the Rio de Janeiro Earth Summit in 1992.

13. Thomas F. Homer-Dixon labels those who believe that cooperation and ingenuity will ameliorate environmental problems "cornucopians" and those who believe that environmental issues will lead to conflict as "neo-Malthusians" (after the demographer and economist Thomas Malthus, whose 1798 *Essay on the Principle of Population* argued that population growth would inevitably lead to scarcity and conflict). See Thomas F. Homer-Dixon, "On the Threshold: Environmental Changes as the Cause of Acute Conflict," *International Security*, Vol. 16, No. 2 (1991): 76–116.

14. Robert D. Kaplan, "The Coming Anarchy," *Atlantic Monthly*, February 1994, pp. 44–76.

15. For a sobering discussion of these issues, see Michael T. Klare, *Resource Wars: The New Landscape of Global Conflict* (New York: Metropolitan Books, 2001). See also Kenneth S. Deffyes, *Hubbert's Peak: The Impending World Oil Shortage* (Princeton, NJ: Princeton University Press, 2001).

The "BRICS" Summit, Ufa, Russia, 2015. BRICS stands for Brazil, Russia, India, China and South Africa, whom some predict to be the rising powers of the coming decades. From left, Dilma Rousseff of Brazil, Narendra Modi of India, Vladimir Putin of Russia, Xi Jinping of China, and Jacob Zuma of South Africa. Does the future belong to these countries? If so, what goals will they share?

Anadolu Agency/Getty Images

# 15

# CONCLUSION: POWER AND PURPOSE IN A CHANGING WORLD

## Learning Objectives

**15-1** Identify potential sources of change in international politics in the coming decades.

**15-2** Link claims about sources and effects of change to broader theoretical arguments.

**15-3** Predict the effects of different potential developments in international politics.

In Chapter 1, we identified three broad goals:

- To improve your understanding of international politics
- To prepare you to make informed evaluations about important questions
- To enable you to engage in intelligent, active debate on important public issues

With the hope that these goals have been achieved, this conclusion looks to the future and asks what international politics might look like in the decades ahead. As Chapter 1 pointed out, our expectations about the future will determine the choices we make on important questions.

The contemporary era of international politics is defined by change. The collapse of communism in 1989–1991 brought the Cold War to an abrupt end. The terrorist attacks of 2001 ended the post–Cold War era even more abruptly. A digital revolution has reshaped the way we see the world, think, and interact. New concerns such as terrorism, climate change, and globalization are shaping the international agenda. Economic and political power seems to be shifting from the United States and Europe to Asia. We are still struggling to identify the fundamental characteristics and questions of this era.

To reiterate the themes that have driven this book, power and purpose are both evolving. The distribution of power is changing as resources, technology, and economic vitality move around the world. The sources of power are also changing as terrorism and technology empower the weak while debt crisis redefines what it means to be strong. Purpose is evolving as well, as China envisions global great power status, Europe rethinks the wisdom of integration, the Islamic State aspires to build a fundamentalist Islamic Caliphate, and people around the world contemplate the relative importance of sovereignty, international law, human rights, environmentalism, and economic well-being.

# CONTINUITY AND CHANGE

Previous chapters have stressed the links between history and the present as well as the ways in which the present has diverged from the past. If "everything has changed" since September 2001, to what extent can the lessons of the past be applied to the future? Is the nature of international politics changing in such a way that the five major theoretical approaches are becoming irrelevant? Or does international politics continue to be defined by the same underlying patterns explored in this book? The answer is yes, in part, to both questions. International politics today is defined by both continuity and change.

Robert Gilpin wrote in 1987 that modern realists know little more today about international politics than Thucydides knew when he was writing in the fifth century BCE.[1] Gilpin's point is that although much had changed in twenty-five centuries, the underlying nature of international politics had not. It was still a competition for security in a dangerous world in which power determined outcomes. Even if Gilpin was right in 1987, is that still true today? Is international politics changing in fundamental ways, or is it changing in ways that retain the basic characteristics of the system? Evaluating potential changes in international politics demonstrates one important use of the conceptual tools discussed in this book. We can use them to think about the changes we are witnessing and to assess how fundamental these changes really are.

# THE HISTORY CONNECTION

## THE HISTORY OF THE FUTURE

This chapter considers contemporary views of what the future will look like. Have past attempts to predict the future had any success? Looking back, we can find examples of both impressive prescience and errant forecasting.

Writing in 1795, Immanuel Kant predicted that eventually the horrors of war and the spread of liberal democracy would compel humankind to develop less violent ways of resolving their disputes. At the time he wrote, there were many wars and few democracies, and yet by the late twentieth century, many were claiming that Kant's perpetual peace had come into existence, at least among the advanced industrial democracies.

Norman Angell, a British journalist, published *Europe's Optical Illusion* in 1909. Responding to the wave of economic integration and globalization then taking place, Angell argued that war among the powers of Europe would be so economically destructive that it was pointless, obsolete, and "a great illusion."* Only a few years later, World War I broke out. Looking back, many critics have seen Angell's book as demonstrating the folly of basing predictions on idealism, rather than on realism, although it could just as easily be argued that the economic disaster caused by World War I proved Angell's point. Angell won the Nobel Peace Prize in 1933.

The advent of nuclear weapons in 1945 began a revolution in military thinking. It was unclear what effect nuclear weapons would have on military strategy and on diplomacy. In 1946, a year after the first nuclear weapons were used, a strategist at Yale named Bernard Brodie wrote *The Absolute Weapon: Atomic Power and World Order*. Brodie sought to deduce the effects of nuclear weapons on international politics, and he accurately predicted the shift of strategy from fighting to deterrence, writing, "Thus far the chief purpose of our military establishment has been to win wars. From now on its chief purpose must be to avert them. It can have almost no other useful purpose."[†] It took some time for leaders in the United States and the Soviet Union to accept this point of view, but by the 1960s, it was widely acknowledged to be so.

In recent years, which have seemed revolutionary to many people, there has been a new series of attempts to predict the future of international politics. Francis Fukuyama, in *The End of History and the Last Man*, asserted that the triumph of liberal democracy and capitalism had brought ideological conflict to an end.[‡] Samuel Huntington, in *The Clash of Civilizations*, argued that conflicts between nation-states would be replaced with culturally driven conflicts between civilizations.[§] Thomas Friedman, in *The World Is Flat*, predicted a new world politics based on economic globalization.[¶] Jared Diamond wrote *Collapse*, about the potential for ecological catastrophe to dominate the future.[**] They all make plausible arguments, but they cannot all be completely accurate at the same time.

---

*Norman Angell, Europe's Optical Illusion (London: Simpkin, Marshall, Hamilton, Kent, 1909).

[†]Bernard Brodie, The Absolute Weapon: Atomic Power and World Order (New York: Harcourt Brace & Company, 1946).

[‡]Francis Fukuyama, The End of History and the Last Man (New York: The Free Press, 1992).

[§]Samuel P. Huntington, The Clash of Civilizations and the Remaking of World Order (New York: Simon & Schuster, 1998).

[¶]Thomas Friedman, The World Is Flat: A Brief History of the Twenty-First Century (New York: Farrar Straus and Giroux, 2005).

**Jared Diamond, Collapse: How Societies Choose to Fail or Succeed (New York: Viking, 2005.

*(Continued)*

# CAUSES AND CONSEQUENCES OF POTENTIAL CHANGES

Preceding chapters have identified several emerging sources of change in the international realm that might be viewed as revolutionary—as making the present (and future) fundamentally different from the recent past:

- The rise of transnational terrorism as a central problem in international politics
- The globalization of trade and finance
- The shift toward a system with only one military superpower
- The dramatic change in the pattern of global inequality
- The spread of democracy and resistance to it
- The erosion of the power of the sovereign state relative to societal, international, and transnational actors

The question is whether each of these developments is really novel, with no precedent, or whether it evolved from existing conditions. To the extent that developments are revolutionary, there will be relatively little experience to use in assessing them. On the other hand, to the extent that new developments are linked to phenomena already understood, there is some basis from which to generate expectations.

The prospect of fundamentally new developments in the workings of international politics can lead to both hope and fear about the future. Some of the changes we see raise the hope that the traditional constraints will be weakened, allowing greater scope for collaboration, greater participation by disadvantaged actors, or greater opportunity to resolve conflicts without war. For example, the weakening of the sovereign state and the growth of shared international norms provide, in some people's view, the prospect for greater international collaboration, strengthened global governance, and reduced conflict. To others, globalization seems likely to spread prosperity. Still others focus on the increased chances for global peace brought on by the spread of democracy.

From a different perspective, however, change seems to be a threat rather than a source of hope. The potential emergence of nonstate actors wielding weapons of mass destruction has undermined the assumption that only states can present a fundamental security threat to other states. "The playing field is not being leveled only in ways that draw in and super empower a whole new group of innovators. It's being leveled in a way that draws in and super empowers a whole new group of angry, frustrated, and humiliated men and women."[2] Seen this way, the demise of the Westphalian system would be bad news. Of course, the premise that the state is weakening is itself controversial.

If scholars, policy makers, and citizens are to deal adequately with the challenges of coming years, we must exercise judgment in assessing what is fundamentally new and what represents continuity with the past. By mistaking the old for something new, we overlook important lessons based on existing knowledge. By mistaking the new for something old, we become overconfident in thinking we understand a phenomenon that, in fact, may have substantially changed.

The six broad developments in international politics listed previously will shape the coming decades in essential ways. Each identifies an issue or debate already discussed in this book. This chapter aims the discussion squarely at the future and engages in a bit of speculation. The goal of this speculation is to explore the logical consequences of different assessments about how international politics works and how it is changing.

## TERRORISM: HOW IS IT CHANGING INTERNATIONAL POLITICS?

As recently as the 1990s, international security was almost exclusively about the dangers states posed to other states. After September 2001, this narrow focus seems quaint. Terrorism has fundamentally changed the focus of most discussions of international politics. Today, discussions of security are as likely to focus on terrorist groups as on states. Perhaps the most vexing question at this point is whether transnational terrorism is now a permanent part of international politics. Terrorism might be thought of not as a new kind of war, but as a new weapon. Just as the atomic bomb could not be "undiscovered," the tactics and techniques of terrorism are now widely known and can be used by any aggrieved group (or individual) with sufficient organizational skills.

What has changed less, perhaps, is how political actors deal with international security threats. Since 2001, military force has been at the center of efforts to combat terrorism. This has been especially true in the policy of the United States. The United States invaded Afghanistan and ousted the Taliban government in 2001 as a direct result of the September 11 events. Although the link between terrorism and the 2003 invasion of Iraq is more controversial, it is clear that the perceived threat from terrorism led to the widespread support for that attack among the American public.

Will terrorism empower a whole new group of actors, and if so, with what effects? By provoking the U.S. invasions of Afghanistan and Iraq, terrorism has had widespread economic, cultural, and political effects. But it remains unclear that it can be used to do more than disrupt. Thus, the power of terrorism—the ability to accomplish particular goals—remains in question. Although it may be very powerful at raising the costs of an occupying power, it is likely much less effective in pursuing other kinds of change.

One of the most ominous developments in recent years has been the rise of the Islamic State, which appears to be an effort to use the tactics of terrorism to rule over a wide swath of territory. This is not entirely unprecedented, as the Soviet Union under Joseph Stalin, Cambodia under the Khmer Rouge, and North Korea under the Kim dynasty are all states in which political power was, and in the case of North Korea is still, maintained by the widespread use of violence. Will the Islamic State show that terrorism, rather than consent, can underpin state power in the 21st century? If so, others might try to emulate the tactic.

Terrorism has blurred the lines between international and domestic security. The erosion of the distinction between international and domestic has long been recognized in economics, but until recently most analysts maintained the national/international distinction in security. That is now much harder to do. As a result, many countries have passed new antiterrorism laws that have altered long-held notions of civil liberties. Is it possible that the effort to combat terrorism will lead to a fundamental and long-term curtailment of civil liberties? Civil liberties have often been limited during wars in the past, but those wars were of finite duration. Even as democracy spreads, might it come to be defined differently than it traditionally has been?

**global war on terror**

The George W. Bush administration's term for the U.S. response to the 2001 terrorist attack on the World Trade Center.

Similarly, the **global war on terror** has led to questioning long-held notions about human rights and international law. Governments widely admired for their commitment to human rights are now engaging in thinly veiled operations to torture suspected terrorists, and the vast majority of citizens are untroubled. What are the longer-term effects of democratic societies' becoming comfortable with the idea of government-sponsored torture? We do not yet know. Similarly, as the war in Afghanistan bogged down, and as terrorist threats emerged in Yemen, Libya, and elsewhere, the United States and its allies relied increasingly on air attacks on suspected terrorist sites, often with civilian casualties. A heightened sense of insecurity can have far-reaching societal effects. The Cold War permeated every aspect of the societies involved, sometimes in ways that look incomprehensible in retrospect. The same could come to be true of the struggle against terrorism.

Here are some possible keys to the future.

- Do transnational terrorist groups obtain weapons of mass destruction? If so, terrorism will become much more important than it is even today. The sacrifices societies make to combat it will likely increase dramatically. The willingness of states to use military force to attack suspected supporters of terrorism will also likely increase. Torture may become more widely tolerated. On the other hand, if weapons of mass destruction, and nuclear weapons in particular, come under more effective control, the level of anxiety may decrease.

Petty Officer 1st class Shane T. McCoy/U.S. Navy/PA Wire URN:6787709 (Press Association via AP Images)

Suspected Taliban and Al Qaeda members are detained at Camp X-Ray, Guantanamo Bay, Cuba, January 2002.

- Do scholars and politicians arrive at a more thorough understanding of the sources of terrorism? If so, do states have greater success in combating terrorism, limiting the number and scale of attacks? If it appears that terrorism is a "manageable" problem, then there could be a shift in focus to other problems.

- Does terrorism become more useful as a tool for holding and governing territory than it has been in the past? If so, we may confront new kinds of state actors.

## GLOBALIZATION

To many observers, the most important long-term change now under way is globalization. Globalization is undermining several long-standing assumptions about the international system. Enormous flows of trade and finance mean that more and more economic activity now occurs across, rather than within, states. Reductions in barriers to trade and the ease with which goods, money, people, and information can now move are making geographical distance less relevant than it previously was. The control that individual states have over their economies has diminished.

In more and more economic sectors, the relevant market is global, rather than local, in scope. People with vastly different costs of living, wage expectations, and political rights are now competing economically. Moreover, as technology and education spread, societies that used to compete primarily through low wages are now competing by acquiring skill and knowledge. Rather than a "race to the bottom," some contend there is now a "race to the top," in which firms and workers in Asia compete with the traditional leaders in the most lucrative, knowledge-intensive parts of the economy, such as software development and biotechnology.

Is this really a revolution? The process of globalization is an old one. Disruption arising from changing trade and migration patterns has occurred for centuries. However, many people argue that the world is not just experiencing more change, or more rapid change, but qualitatively new conditions, most notably a fundamental reduction in the ability of states to control economies.

If this is a revolution, is it inevitable? International trade began sharply expanding after World War II because the advanced industrial states, led by the United States, made free trade a high priority and sacrificed other goals to achieve it. If state policies led to an increase in trade, could state policies lead to a decrease? Historically, international trade has increased in some eras and decreased in others. Trade among the European states was very high before World War I but collapsed during that conflict. Similarly, global trade underwent a substantial reduction during the depression of the 1930s. It therefore seems possible that globalization could be slowed or even reversed. Antiglobalization activists hope to achieve this, and free trade advocates warn that if trade is not expanded further, it may recede in the face of various challenges.

Other people argue that states can no longer control globalization—that it has taken on a life of its own.[3] Because the global economy is so big relative to national economies, states now find it difficult, if not impossible, to resist it. Moreover, global competition may drive further globalization, as states that seek to "get ahead" of others are pushed to accept freer trade, even if they have reservations about its effects. Thus, in 2015, Greek leaders found themselves accepting a set of reforms that both the government and its citizens stridently opposed in an effort to avoid having to leave the single European currency. States that are less open to free trade might fall behind economically until they change course. Thus, economic competition may be driving globalization whether states like it or not.

Again, globalization has elements of both continuity and change. There is nothing new about increasing international trade, migration, and intercultural influence; these have been happening since the beginning of history. What is new is the difficulty states are having in controlling this process and the influence it is having on domestic affairs. If it was once fairly easy to distinguish international from domestic economics, that is clearly no longer the case.

What are the likely consequences of these changes? How will states react if their control over international economic affairs continues to diminish? Might they try to regain control? What would be the consequences of

Immigrants arriving at Ellis Island get their first glimpse of the Statue of Liberty, New York Harbor, early twentieth century.

Edwin Levick/Hulton Archive/Getty Images

such attempts? If state control of international economics continues to diminish, what might be the consequences for other state functions?

Most important, perhaps, if states do not govern the international economy, who will? What are the implications of tying national economies to a global economy that is essentially unregulated? In the economic crises of recent years, states have struggled to find joint solutions for shared problems. If government intervention is commonly used to avert crisis in domestic economies, how will crisis be avoided at the international level? In terms of effective governance, might the international economy be moving "back to the future"?[4]

Here are some possible keys to the future.

- Will citizens rebel against globalization? Will citizen pressure force governments to reduce their free trade commitments?

- Will globalization alter the global distribution of wealth and power? If so, how will the losers respond? What will the winners do with their expanded power?

- Can an unregulated and unmanaged international economy avoid crisis? Will states be able to collaborate to prevent or at least manage crises? How bad can crises get if there is insufficient collaboration?

## THE EROSION OF U.S. POWER

In Chapter 8, we pointed out that the United States retains a dominant military position in the world. In nearly every other respect, however, the basis for U.S. leadership in the world has eroded. The U.S. economy, which accounted for half of global GDP at the end of World War II, accounts for roughly a fifth today. Although that decline is natural—in 1945 the leading industrial powers of Europe and Asia had been decimated by war and most of the rest of the world had yet to begin industrializing—it represents a substantial diffusion of economic power. U.S. moral leadership, or "soft power," has also diminished, as many people around the world question whether U.S. international influence is benign. In 2008, the political commentator Fareed Zakaria wrote a popular book called *The Post-American World*, which argues that the change currently under way is as consequential as the rise of Europe during the Renaissance.

To some analysts, China's rise, both economically and militarily, seems inevitable[5] (see Figure 15.1). Others see power diffusing much more broadly to include not only the "BRICs" (Brazil, India, Russia, and China) but also numerous smaller powers such as South Korea, South Africa, and the countries of Latin America. This trend can be seen in the evolution over the past two decades of the G-7 into the G-20, as leading states recognized that seven states could no longer make decisions for the entire global economy. Many people would welcome a world in which no single country has the influence that the United States has had for the past seven decades. If democracy is good domestically, why not internationally? However, one might fear the erosion of U.S. power for three reasons.

First, many people are skeptical of the realist view that it does not matter who the hegemon is. Constructivists, feminists, and many liberals and economic structuralists argue that the *purpose* to which power is put is just as important as the distribution of power. From this perspective, Chinese hegemony might be very different—most assume much less benevolent—than U.S. hegemony. China's authoritarianism and its dismal human rights record prompt some to worry about what kind of world it would promote. Others might welcome a hegemon less interested in democracy and less inclined to intervene in other states' internal politics. This raises a question explored in Chapter 5, "Does

In GDP and military spending, China is closing the gap with the United States but is still well behind. Can we assume that present trends will continue?

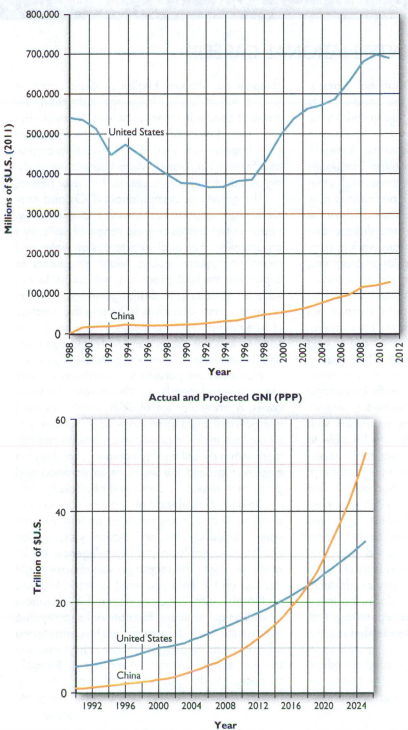

**U.S. and Chinese Military Spending, 1988–2011**

**Actual and Projected GNI (PPP)**

Source: Based on data from the Stockholm International Peace Research Institute (SIPRI), SIPRI Military Expenditure Database.

## THE CONNECTION TO YOU

## INTERNATIONAL CAREERS

For people interested in international careers, these are the best of times, and the future will only get better. In every country, foreign ministries, militaries, and intelligence agencies continue to hire people with an array of expertise. A degree in international relations or foreign languages provides a stepping-stone to these and other careers, and a wide array of professions now demand a global focus. Economists analyze the world economy, geographers map disease and economic patterns, mathematicians work in cryptography, linguists improve translation programs, and computer scientists work in cybersecurity.

Private firms dwarf governments in the number of people with a background in international affairs they hire. Most large firms have operations in more than one country, or are buying and selling in multiple countries. They require not only salespeople or procurement specialists, but lawyers and accountants with knowledge of the legal and tax issues involved in importing and exporting, and senior managers with enough international experience to be able to handle international and cross-cultural issues. Most multinational corporations now consider it essential for employees to have had at least one international posting if they are to be promoted into senior management. The largest, most international corporations now very deliberately select their managers from countries around the world, and move them around the world, to create a leadership group that is completely comfortable internationally and at ease in global business. The ability to work within or to supervise a multinational team is an essential leadership quality.

Education is also internationalizing. At the secondary level, schools around the world are adopting the International Baccalaureate curriculum developed in Europe and stressing international competence. Although English-speaking countries tend to lag in foreign language instruction, the desire of people in other countries to learn English has created a steady supply of jobs for native English speakers trained in TEFL (Teaching English as a Foreign Language). More students are studying outside their home countries than ever before.

The growth of international NGOs and non-profit organizations has also led to expanding opportunities across a wide range of skills. Aid organizations hire engineers to design water and sanitation systems, public health specialists to implement medical programs, educators to run schools, consultants to design government reform programs, and journalists to help in the creation of free media. Doctors, nurses, and other health care workers are also in demand by aid agencies, and these careers can take one almost anywhere.

How does one pursue an international career? The answer depends on the career. In some cases, a particular set of skills that is not itself international might open many opportunities. For example, a major in geology can lead to employment with a global energy company, sending the employee around the world on exploration and production missions. Command of a foreign language and study abroad experience can prepare a student in almost any major for an international career. Language skills and in-country experience can be essential for a job in intelligence, diplomacy, or sales. The language you choose might depend on the field you want to enter. Chinese and Arabic are in heavy demand by business as well as government. For national security and intelligence, the U.S. government has established a list of critical languages that are in high demand but low supply: Arabic, Azerbaijani, Bengali, Chinese, Hindi, Indonesian, Korean, Persian, Punjabi, Russian, Turkish, and Urdu. Willingness

*(Continued)*

to go to less glamorous locations—and endure some hardship—might be a key asset. Once you spend enough time in a country to know it well, you have a big advantage in getting work related to that country. For that reason, a lengthy study abroad experience can be a great beginning.

2. In what ways are careers likely to be international even if one rarely or never leaves one's home country?

3. What other kinds of qualifications besides education might play an important role in international careers?

## Critical Thinking Questions

1. What determines whether a language is considered critical? Why do business and government priorities on language differ?

being a democracy or a nondemocracy substantially influence a state's foreign policy?" More broadly, the prospect of Chinese hegemony raises the question of whether a state's foreign policy is determined more by internal or external factors. If China becomes a hegemon, will it simply behave as other states in the same position have behaved?

Second, and perhaps more disturbing, hegemonic stability theory finds that shifts in hegemony are often accompanied by **hegemonic wars**. This concept has been offered as the explanation for wars from the Peloponnesian War through World War I. According to this view, the United States would not give up its hegemony without a fight. Already, there are signs of tension. Prominent U.S. politicians and strategists have made maintaining U.S. preeminence a central political and military goal. China is viewed as the primary long-term threat to that preeminence. The 2006 "National Security Strategy of the United States of America" pointed to several areas of potential conflict between the two countries.[6] A Chinese general, speaking in July 2005, warned what would happen to the United States if it defended Taiwan in a war with China: "The Americans will have to be prepared that hundreds … of [their] cities will be destroyed by the Chinese."[7] Is a war between China and the United States inevitable? Probably not. But already both countries are viewing each other more seriously as military adversaries.

**hegemonic wars**
Wars contested to determine who will be the dominant state in the system.

Third, some people fear that a world without a hegemon would have little ability to solve common problems. We know from collective action theory that as the number of actors involved increases, arriving at agreements becomes harder. From this perspective, the expansion of the G-7 to the G-20 is not good news. In addition, the G-7 had the benefit of consisting of states with similar political and economic systems and geopolitical interests. The G-20 is a much more diverse group, and although it represents a much broader swath of international society, reaching agreement on major issues may be difficult. Ian Bremmer, a political scientist who runs an international consulting firm, published a book in 2012 called *Every Nation for Itself: Winners and Losers in a G-Zero World*. Bremmer argues that the important result of the relative decline of the United States will not be a competition between the United States and China for global hegemony, but rather a world without a hegemon. No group of states will be coherent enough to get together to solve problems jointly, and this, Bremmer argues, is an unfamiliar kind of international politics.

We can imagine several possible scenarios.

• China rises, but the United States overcomes its recent problems and stops its decline. This might lead to bipolarity, which characterized the period of the Cold War

Russia's President Dmitri Medvedev, Brazil's President Luiz Inacio Lula da Silva, China's President Hu Jintao, and India's Prime Minister Manmohan Singh met at the BRIC summit in Brazil, April 2010.

(1945–1989). Would bipolarity necessarily lead to the intense political conflict of that period? Would China and the United States have the same level of ideological hostility as the Soviet Union and the United States? Could the mutual hostility be successfully managed without a great power war, as it was in the Cold War? With only one modern case of bipolarity to learn from, it is difficult to predict what the consequences of bipolarity would be in the twenty-first century.

• The United States continues to decline, but China does not rise far enough to dominate. Such a scenario would likely lead back toward multipolarity, which many states, such as France and Russia, have vocally promoted. How would the substance of international politics change if the system shifted to multipolarity? Would collaboration become easier or harder? Would free trade expand or contract? Would the UN become more or less relevant?

• The United States reestablishes its hegemony. Militarily, the United States remains far ahead of any rival. It is conceivable that the United States could solve its domestic fiscal problems and reduce the drain of its international military commitments. If so, the traditional dynamism of the U.S. economy might again take hold. A booming U.S. economy might help reestablish the ability of the United States to take the kinds of steps necessary to provide economic and political leadership.

Here are some possible keys to the future.

• Can the United States solve the economic problems that threaten to undermine the basis of its global power? These problems include legislative gridlock, high budget deficits, low domestic savings, high trade deficits, the potential insolvency of the Social Security system, and heavy reliance on imported petroleum.

• Can China continue to rise without further democratic reform? Can capitalist authoritarianism thrive, or will further economic development require political liberalization?

• Will traditional U.S. allies such as the United Kingdom, Germany, and Japan help offset the decline in U.S. power? Can the United States find allies among the rising powers to help it lead?

• How well can states cooperate to solve problems in the absence of a hegemon?

## GAPS IN WEALTH

Global poverty persists, but its patterns are changing dramatically. Moreover, the consequences of poverty, including immigration, disease, environmental degradation, and political instability, spread much further and more quickly today than in years past. Although poverty and inequality will continue to exist, a shared purpose on global poverty has emerged in recent years. As the Millennium Development Goals indicate, many have come to view the alleviation of extreme poverty as a moral responsibility that cannot be ignored. Reduction of poverty has become a major priority for societies around the world. What will be the consequences if this goal is not achieved? What will be the consequences if it is?

Chapter 12 distinguished between two kinds of gaps in wealth: those between states and those within states. In recent years, we have seen an important shift in trends: After

# THE GEOGRAPHY CONNECTION

## PROJECTED POPULATIONS, 2050

These maps show countries according to their relative populations in 2000 and as projected for 2050.

### Critical Thinking Questions

1. Which countries will see substantial population changes?

2. How might changes in the relative populations of countries affect world politics?

3. What effects will overall population change have?

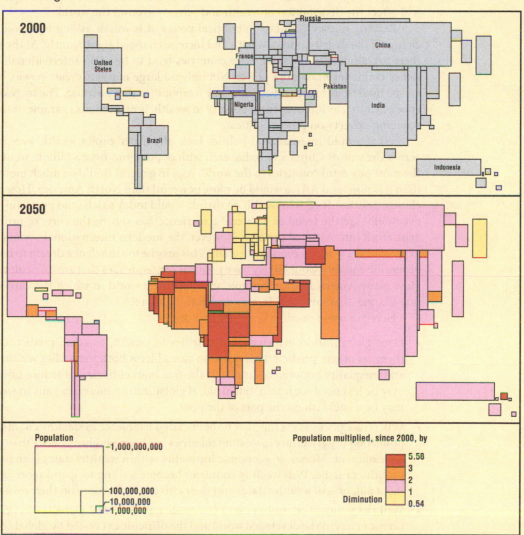

**2000**

Russia
China
United States
France
Pakistan
Nigeria
India
Brazil
Indonesia

**2050**

| Population | | Population multiplied, since 2000, by |
|---|---|---|
| —1,000,000,000 | | 5.58 |
| | | 3 |
| —100,000,000 | | 2 |
| —10,000,000 | | 1 |
| —1,000,000 | | Diminution 0.54 |

Source: These maps are published by the Institut de Recherche Pour le Développement (IRD) in *Population et Développement Durable. Des Cartes Pour Voir* (P. Peltre 2003, 32 p. + CD-ROM Mac/PC, 20 #). The data are taken from the UN Population Projections, 2000 edition. UN Population Division, World Population Prospects: The 2000 Revision.

decades in which gaps between countries were increasing and those within countries were decreasing, we now see the opposite pattern. Countries like China, Brazil, and India are closing the wealth gap with the developed states, but inequality within many states is now increasing. Both of these trends will have important consequences.

The problem of growing inequality within states afflicts wealthy states as well as poor ones. In the United States, for example, income inequality has been growing in recent decades for the first time in history. How well will democratic, market-based systems endure if ever-increasing inequality becomes normal? Because relative deprivation appears to increase the risk of internal conflict, growing inequality might have a profound effect on other key goals, such as democratization.

What will be the consequences of a reduction in inequality between countries? As workers in the poorest countries close the income gap, how will workers in the rich countries react? To some extent, it may be that the poor in the poor countries will become more prosperous partly at the expense of the poor in the rich countries. Economic liberals, of course, strongly reject this view. Theory aside, it remains to be seen how globalization will affect the distribution of wealth and poverty around the world.

Because money is linked to political power, it is worth asking how politics would change if the distribution of wealth and income changed significantly. At the state level, there are already some hints: Poor countries tend to be weak internationally, whereas richer countries have more power. Not only do large markets create power, but wealth can be used to influence others or to buy weapons for that purpose. The increasing influence of China, as it moves from poverty to wealth, is an obvious example of the effect of reducing poverty on power politics.

What would international politics look like if per capita wealth were more even across the world? China and India, each with populations over a billion, would likely be the most powerful countries in the world. Asia in general would be much more powerful than it is now, and Africa would be more powerful than North America. How might this change politics? If gaps in wealth do shrink, would today's rich (and powerful) countries eventually see the trend as a threat? Experience has shown the sorts of problems that arise from international poverty. However, the modern international system has never experienced a world of economic equals. This may be too much of a dream to hope for, but economic equality would likely have political consequences that are difficult to imagine. How many Americans, for example, can imagine a world in which the United States is just a larger-than-average country and nothing more?

Here are some possible keys to the future.

- Does globalization help reduce disparities in wealth, as some predict, or increase them, as others predict? This question can address both inequality within countries and inequality between countries. If the free market begins to reduce poverty, there may be less need for international aid. If globalization increases gaps in wealth, there may be a backlash on the part of the poor.

- Will strategies to assist the poor be politically sustainable in wealthy countries? So far, protection of agriculture in wealthy countries has been a higher priority than promoting development. Moreover, economic inequality within wealthy states is an increasingly prominent issue. Will wealthy countries become willing to spend more on development aid, or will wealthy states and their citizens focus more on their own problems?

- Will the political commitment to free trade and financial globalization erode? Economic crises in the developed world and the difficulties created by global competition appear to be undermining enthusiasm for free trade. What would be the consequences of deglobalization?

## THE SPREAD OF DEMOCRACY

The spread of democracy has been one of the major stories in international politics in the past three decades. Prior to 1989, democracy was still geographically confined, predominating only in western Europe and North America. With the collapse of communism in eastern Europe, the so-called **third wave of democratization** gained momentum. Democracy has become the norm in eastern Europe and in Latin America. A significant change in the contemporary era is that no other model of government is seriously viewed as a good alternative. In contrast to previous eras, there is no credible argument that authoritarian government is superior to democracy. In that sense, a key ideological battle has ended. In practice, of course, much authoritarianism remains, and democracy remains seriously flawed in many places.

Although many states have adopted democracy in recent decades, others have started down that road but ended up elsewhere. In most of the post-Soviet states, democratic practices such as elections have been subverted to support autocratic rule. The states that threw off autocratic rule in the Arab Spring have either readopted some new authoritarianism or, in the case of Libya, descended into civil war. Russia and China have seen attempts to spread democracy as efforts to constrain their influence internationally and to weaken them domestically.

Will democracy continue to spread? Chapter 5 examined in detail the argument that democracies are more peaceful than other states and found that the argument is only partly true. Democracies go to war as often as other states, but they rarely go to war with each other. As a result, a **zone of peace**, composed of states that will almost certainly not go to war with one another, appears to be expanding worldwide. On the surface, this would seem to be a momentous development, especially because the zone has expanded most rapidly in Europe, where history's most violent wars have been fought.

Paradoxically, this trend may itself be a source of new conflicts. If democracies do not fight each other, much is at stake in promoting new democracies. It might be worthwhile to use force to overthrow an authoritarian government in order to establish a democracy that would safeguard peace in the future. This logic was used by the U.S. government to help justify its invasion of Iraq. Is it possible that the main source of international conflict in coming years will be a battle to spread democracy? Or will the U.S. experience in Afghanistan and Iraq, along with the aftermath of the Arab Spring, deter states from pursuing such a strategy in the future?

There is also some uncertainty about whether the "democratic peace" that has existed until now will survive the wider spread of democracy. Some research has indicated that new democracies are especially vulnerable to becoming aggressive.[8] Moreover, it appears that authoritarian leaders in several states are adopting much more moderate international policies than their populations would choose under democracy. In Pakistan, for example, it often appeared that its government was straining to resist a more combative policy toward India, which would have been popular. Many people also fear that in places like Pakistan and Saudi Arabia, support for terrorism would be more likely to increase under democratic regimes than under authoritarianism.

The implications of democratization are especially interesting when considered together with the rise of China. The consequences of China's rise might depend on what kind of government evolves there. For realists, of course, this question is irrelevant: The rise of China will lead to rivalry with the United States regardless of what form of government China has. For advocates of the democratic peace theory, it does not matter how powerful China gets, as long as it becomes more democratic. We will simply have to wait and see which of these factors proves more influential.

**third wave of democratization**
The series of transitions from autocracy to democracy that began with a democratic revolution in Portugal in 1974.

**zone of peace**
A group of democratic states among whom war has become unthinkable.

An even more speculative question is whether democracy will survive as the only legitimate form of government. In some parts of the world, extremists are gaining adherents to the argument that theocracy (rule by religious leaders) should be established. Other countries, including Russia and China, combine rigged elections, partly free markets, and authoritarian control. To the extent that this "illiberal" democracy succeeds, will it come to challenge the liberal democratic model? And what will result from the failure of the Arab Spring and of efforts to build democracy in other societies? Will the world return to the notion—once considered conventional wisdom—that some societies simply are not yet ready for democracy and would be better off ruled by autocrats?

Here are some possible keys to the future.

- Will pro-democracy protests continue to spread transnationally, or will authoritarian regimes get better at combating the technologies and tactics that have empowered protest movements?

- Will efforts to promote democracy become a new source of international conflict?

- Will peace between democracies survive the spread of democracy to less stable regions of the world?

## THE DEMISE OF THE SOVEREIGN STATE?

Perhaps the most far-reaching changes in the field of international relations involve the most basic actor in the analysis: the sovereign state. Today, many actors besides the state affect international politics. The state remains central, but its role is clearly changing. The question for the future is whether the state will continue to play essentially the same role it has for the past 500 years, or whether some fundamental change is taking place. Many people have asserted that the state is losing its importance. Others find it as important as ever, even as its roles change.

Globalization means that many more of the problems states face extend beyond their geographical boundaries. Chapter 11 demonstrated that trade and finance now occur on a scale that cannot be governed by any single state government. State control is segmented territorially, but markets are not. Migration, environmental problems, health problems, and crime are also beyond the control of any single state. Threats to states often come from actors other than states and from groups that easily cross state borders. To deal with these issues, states must work together in ways they have not before. This can mean collaborating more extensively with others or surrendering some decision-making power to international organizations. These problems can also prompt states to turn over some missions to nongovernmental organizations. These trends have convinced many observers that states are losing their power to other actors.

States seem to be losing power to actors from below as well. Domestic interest groups and nongovernmental organizations are becoming more and more involved in foreign policy issues. As business becomes more international, firms have a greater interest in foreign policy. Also, as more states become democratic, citizens may be gaining greater control over foreign policy. Finally, the adoption of market economics around the world means that a much greater share of economic activity is now out of the hands of states and is controlled instead by private entities.

However, some analysts see the state getting more powerful, not less. They point to the fact that states take advantage of advances in communications and information technology just as other actors do. Many key functions of state control, including surveillance, information storage and retrieval, and tax enforcement, are made easier by

# THE POLICY CONNECTION

## THE USE OF SCENARIOS TO PREPARE FOR THE FUTURE

Governments, international governmental organizations, nongovernmental organizations, and firms all seek to prepare for the future by predicting the challenges to which they will need to respond. However, because the future is uncertain, they are reluctant to base policies on a single prediction about the future that might turn out to be wrong. Instead, many planners generate a range of scenarios, each based on different assumptions about how key variables will change. Generating scenarios still requires theory and predictions. Theory tells the scenario developers which variables to include in the scenarios, and predictions link different values for those variables to specific challenges. Several examples illustrate this approach.

Shell, a global energy company, produced a scenario document in 2013 that examined the future not only of energy but of water and of global regulation, stretching out to the year 2100. In contrast to many other energy predictions, these authors did not focus only on predicting the supply and price of different energy sources. Instead, they produced two scenarios of different economic/political orders relating to energy. One scenario imagined a world of strong global collaboration to limit $CO_2$ emissions. That collaboration, the authors reasoned, would be based on strong national governments and tight regulation, and the assumed consequences were slower economic growth and higher stability. A contrasting scenario imagined a world in which individuals and firms were empowered, and economic growth was higher. These conditions, however, were based on weaker governments and less regulation, which meant lower collaboration on $CO_2$ emissions, increased climate change, and less stability. Ominously, even the most optimistic scenario envisions significant global warming.*

The World Health Organization (WHO) created its scenarios for the future by looking at challenges that have arisen in recent years, focusing on three crises in particular. Looking at the anthrax scare in the United States in 2001, the WHO report pointed to the growing threat of biological attacks and the difficulty that existing public health systems have in facing them. The 2009 H1N1 virus spurred similar fears. The illicit dumping of toxic chemicals in Cote d'Ivoire in 2006 highlighted the health hazards of moving chemicals around the world for disposal. As thousands were sickened, the public health system was overwhelmed, and the country, already on the verge of civil war, was left with an environmental disaster it was unprepared to handle. The WHO expects these kinds of problems to define the coming years.[†]

Intelligence agencies use scenarios to assess the scope of future challenges. The U.S. National Intelligence Council sponsors a series of studies, the latest of which, published in 2012, speculated on what the world might look like in 2030. The analysis began with four "megatrends"—"individual empowerment," "diffusion of power," "demographic patterns" (aging and urbanization), and a "food, water, energy nexus"—in which demand for these overlapping resources increased. It followed with questions such as whether the global economy would become more resilient or collapse-prone, whether governments and international institutions can cope with change or will be overwhelmed by it, and whether regional conflicts in the Middle East will spread to the rest of the world. The study then produced four potential worlds in 2030: "stalled engines," in which globalization ebbs, conflict increases, and the United States withdraws; "fusion," in which the United States and China collaborate on global problems; "Gini out of the bottle," in which increased inequality (note the pun on "Gini coefficient") drives conflict; and

*(Continued)*

a "nonstate world," in which nonstate actors eclipse states.[‡]

The purpose of writing scenarios is not to predict the future accurately. Rather, it is to make perceived trends explicit and to consider their outcomes. Creating scenarios is perhaps more useful for highlighting the extent of uncertainty, and hence the range of possible future policy problems, than for providing targeted policy advice.

## Critical Thinking Questions

1. What are the strengths and weakness of using scenarios to inform policy debates?

2. How might the creation of different scenarios complicate efforts to deal with emerging issues such as global warming?

3. In what areas is it most important to consider alternative scenarios?

*Shell, "New Lens Scenarios: A Shift in Perspective for a World in Transition," 2013, http://www.shell.com/global/future-energy/scenarios/new-lens-scenarios.html.

[†]World Health Organization, The World Health Report 2007—A Safer Future: Global Public Health Security in the 21st Century, Chapter 3, "New Health Threats in the 21st Century," http://www.who.int/whr/2007/chapter3/en/.

[‡]National Intelligence Council, "Global Trends 2030: Alternative Worlds," December 2012, athttp://www.dni.gov/index.php/about/organization/global-trends-2030.

technology. For example, immediately following the London Underground bombings in July 2005, British authorities circulated pictures of the bombers taken by closed-circuit television cameras posted throughout the system. Within days, several accomplices had been arrested. Similarly, although the Internet and cell phones and applications for them such as Twitter make it easy for criminals, terrorists, and protesters to communicate, they are also easily intercepted or shut down by authorities. Improved surveillance means that governments know more about their subjects than ever before.

Although states have surrendered decision-making authority over many issues in recent years, they may be able to take it back. Moreover, international collaboration should not be seen as always weakening states. In some cases, it appears to strengthen the state at the expense of the society. For example, it has been argued that one effect of the EU is to empower European states to create new rules at the European level that they could not get approved at the domestic level. Moreover, terrorism may strengthen the state by providing justification for surveillance and law enforcement measures that otherwise would not be tolerated.

What would be the consequences of a vastly weakened state? In places where the state has disintegrated, such as in Afghanistan and Somalia, the consequences have been negative: anarchy, violence, and sometimes starvation. Some analysts fear that the weakening of states will shift the balance of power even further away from the poor and weak and toward powerful corporations. Others argue that the shift of economic control from states to unregulated markets was a major cause of the global financial crisis. As a result, support for state regulation of the economy has made a comeback. For those who believe that the state is already the tool of greedy corporations, its weakening is seen as opening up room for influence by citizen groups and nongovernmental organizations. Those who support a radical free market perspective also welcome the weakening of the state because they see it as an entity that creates regulations that needlessly interfere with freedom and productivity.

Whatever evolution the state undergoes, it will most likely be slow, and it will vary across states. It may be that in some places the state will weaken or collapse, whereas in others it will strengthen. It might also be that even within individual states, some aspects of "stateness" might be augmented while others are eroded. For example, state surveillance of citizens might increase even as state involvement in certain parts of the economy decreases. These changes will undoubtedly influence who makes foreign policy and how states deal with the challenges they face.

However, one important element of continuity in the nature of the state should be stressed. The state, as a set of political institutions, has *never* been static. It has been constantly evolving since its emergence centuries ago. The idea that the state has some essential character, which is now being shattered, is based on a drastically oversimplified view of history. Therefore, the question to ask is which specific areas of state power are being augmented or eroded, and what happened in similar circumstances in the past.

Here are some possible keys to the future.

- Do states seek to take back the authority they have granted to international institutions? If so, do the states that do this suffer any disadvantages, or do others follow suit?

- Will the EU, the avatar of international integration, continue to broaden and deepen, or will one or both of those processes end (or even be reversed)? Will the EU model be adopted elsewhere?

- Will corporations and nongovernmental organizations continue to expand their influence, or can states insulate themselves from these actors? If the state weakens, will relatively more power accrue to citizens and nongovernmental organizations or to corporations?

- Can some other entity fulfill the functions of the Westphalian state? Or is it the case that if the state did not exist, it would have to be invented?

## ★ POWER AND PURPOSE IN THE PAST, PRESENT, AND FUTURE

Will the world of 2050 look fundamentally different from the world of 2000? Undoubtedly; change has always been a normal part of international politics. By comparison, the changes in the first half of the twenty-first century may well be less revolutionary than those that characterized the first half of the twentieth century. At the beginning of the twentieth century, Britain dominated world politics, most of the world's population lived under colonial rule, and military technology had advanced as far as the horse and the machine gun. By 1950, the United States and the Soviet Union were engaged in a global standoff, colonialism was ending, and military technology consisted of missiles and long-range aircraft carrying nuclear weapons. Perhaps the difference between that era and this one is that the changes in place at the end of World War II were clearly visible to observers, and their implications seemed clear. As this chapter has indicated, the essential qualities of the twenty-first-century international system are subject to considerable uncertainty.

The sources of power in world politics are changing. In some respects, we will see the same roots of power that have existed for millennia—the military power to destroy, the economic power to create and to buy, and the cultural power to persuade. However, as more common problems emerge, another definition of power—the ability to collaborate—may become more salient. Moreover, if the sources of power are familiar, their distribution is not. Whereas historically the primary question was about the distribution of power among states, today military power is diffusing to nonstate actors such as terrorists and to for-profit military contractors. Economic power is spreading away from states to billions of consumers and to global corporations. The power to collaborate is strongest, perhaps, in transnational advocacy networks, international organizations, and global corporations.

Similarly, purpose is evolving. Human rights have moved from the periphery to the center of global debate. Disagreement about the role of the global community in individual states' human rights practices is a central issue in world politics today. Whether that dispute is resolved, and how, will be crucial. Environmental collaboration, especially in the area of climate change, is a relatively new issue on the agenda, and one that so far has not attained the high priority that many people think it should. Whether states decide to collaborate on global warming will have an important effect on international politics in coming decades, both directly (in the degree of collaboration we see) and indirectly (in the widespread consequences of severe climate change).

This chapter has asked how international politics will evolve during the lifetimes of today's students. The answer is not predetermined. The evolution of the system will depend on the policies of states, organizations, and individuals. People, and the choices they make, will determine whether there will be more or less conflict, more or less poverty, more or less environmental degradation.

Throughout this book, nearly every question was found to have more than one good answer. Students, citizens, scholars, and leaders, therefore, have a task that is doubly difficult. They need not only to understand how the world works now but also to assess how much of what is true today is likely to be true tomorrow. It might seem like a hopeless task, but it is not. And it cannot be avoided. Policies can be based either on ignorance or on well-informed thinking—but they will have to be made one way or the other.

This book has aimed to inform the reader about some of the implications of different possible choices. Although it is not possible for any individual to shape the global situation as much as he or she might like, anybody—especially any citizen in a democratic society—can attempt to engage the problems discussed in this book. As citizens, volunteers, advocates, and leaders, we can all make choices to try to influence outcomes.

## SUMMARY

- The contemporary era of international politics is defined by change.
- Power and purpose are both evolving.
- The distribution of power is changing. Economic and political power seem to be shifting from the United States and Europe to Asia, Latin America, and Africa.
- The sources of power are also changing, as terrorism and technology empower the weak.
- Enormous flows of trade and finance mean that more and more economic activity now occurs across, rather than within, states, undermining the traditional state basis of economic policy.
- The United States retains a dominant military position, but its economic and moral influence are weakening.
- Hegemonic stability theory predicts that cooperation will be more difficult without a single dominant power.
- Some versions of hegemonic stability see the transition of power as a likely cause of war.

- Collective action theory predicts that if the world moves toward multipolarity, collaboration will be more difficult.

- The consequences of poverty, including immigration, disease, environmental degradation, and political instability, spread much further and more quickly today than in the past.

- After decades in which economic inequality between countries was increasing and inequality within countries was decreasing, we now see a very different pattern. Countries like China, Brazil, and India are closing the wealth gap with the developed states, but inequality within the many states is now increasing.

- In the post–Cold War era, democracy has spread to eastern Europe and Latin America and has made significant inroads in Africa, Asia, and the Middle East.

- The power of the sovereign state is eroding in some respects relative to societal, international, and transnational actors, but is strengthening in other areas.

## STUDY QUESTIONS

1. A fundamentally new development in international security is that
   a. military technology is changing.
   b. a major security threat to states is coming from nonstate actors.
   c. the United Nations is controlling the use of military force.
   d. traditional force is no longer useful.

2. Which theory predicts that a war may erupt if China threatens the dominance of the United States?
   a. Embedded liberalism
   b. Expected utility theory
   c. Theory of comparative advantage
   d. Hegemonic stability theory

3. Which theory predicts that the world may have a reduced ability to solve problems if we move toward multipolarity?
   a. Complex interdependence theory
   b. Collective action theory
   c. Prospect theory
   d. Hegemonic stability theory

4. How is the gap in wealth changing?
   a. The gap between countries is shrinking, but the gap within countries is growing.
   b. The gap between countries and within countries is shrinking.

   c. The gap between countries is growing, but the gap within countries is shrinking.
   d. The gap between countries and within countries is growing.

5. Since the end of the Cold War, democracy has increased in
   a. Eastern Europe.
   b. Africa.
   c. Latin America.
   d. All of the above.

6. Globalization of trade and finance has resulted in
   a. overall economic growth.
   b. economic disruption in many states.
   c. decreased ability of states to control their own economies.
   d. All of the above.

7. How is power evolving in the world today?

8. How is purpose evolving in the world today?

9. What are the most crucial problems facing the international community?

10. What solutions do the theories presented in this book propose to these problems?

[correct answers: 1. b; 2. d; 3. b; 4. a; 5. d; 6. d]

## END NOTES

1. Robert Gilpin, "The Rich Tradition of Political Realism," in Robert O. Keohane, ed., *Neorealism and Its Critics* (New York: Columbia, 1987), pp. 308–309.

2. Thomas Friedman, *The World Is Flat: A Brief History of the Twenty-First Century* (New York: Farrar, Straus and Giroux, 2005), p. 8.

3. This argument has long been made by economic structuralists, beginning with Karl Marx. It is now made also by liberals, such as Thomas Friedman in *The World Is Flat*. The connection between Marx and the liberals on this matter is emphasized by John Gray; see "The World Is Round," *New York Review of Books* (August 11, 2005): p. 14.

4. Paul Krugman, *The Return of Depression Era Economics* (New York: W. W. Norton, 1999).

5. See Clyde Prestowitz, *Three Billion New Capitalists* (New York: Basic Books, 2005).

6. "The National Security Strategy of the United States of America," March 2006, www.whitehouse.gov/nsc/nss/2006/nss2006.pdf, pp. 41–42.

7. "Sizing Up the Dragon," *The Economist* (July 23, 2005): p. 28.

8. Edward D. Mansfield and Jack Snyder, "Democratization and the Danger of War," *International Security*, Vol. 20, No. 1 (1995): 5–38.

## A

**anarchy**  A condition in which there is no central ruler.

**apartheid**  A system of official discrimination in South Africa in which the African majority was controlled by the white minority.

**appeasement**  A strategy of avoiding war by acceding to the demands of rival powers.

**asylum**  The granting of permission for people to enter and remain in a country to protect them from persecution in their home country.

**asymmetric conflict**  A conflict between actors with very different strengths, vulnerabilities, and tactics.

**attribution**  The process whereby individuals attribute the behavior of others to one cause or another. Attribution can create unmotivated bias in decision makers.

**audience costs**  The costs in loss of public support paid by leaders of democracies when they renege on a commitment.

## B

**balance of power**  A system in which no single actor is dominant; also, the distribution of power in such a system, which is not necessarily equal.

**balance of trade**  Exports minus imports (measured in dollar value); a net accounting of how much in the way of goods and services is exported from a country compared to how much is imported.

**Baltic states**  Refers collectively to Estonia, Latvia, and Lithuania, which lie on the Baltic Sea in northern Europe, just to the west of Russia.

**basic human needs approach**  A development strategy focusing on the short-term alleviation of poverty as a prerequisite for further progress.

**Berlin Wall**  Erected in 1961 to prevent citizens of communist East Germany from migrating to West Germany, the Berlin Wall became a symbol both of the division of Europe and of the lack of freedom in the communist-controlled areas.

**blended enforcement**  A model for implementing international law in which the authority for penalties comes from a recognized international organization and is clearly recognized by treaty, but the actual enforcement is carried out by the aggrieved state or by others acting on its behalf.

**bolstering**  The tendency of decision makers facing a difficult decision to increase their certainty once a decision is made.

**bounded rationality**  A theory that decision makers try to be rational but face several inherent limits on their ability to do so.

**bourgeoisie**  In Marxist jargon, the owners of capital.

**Bretton Woods system**  The system that guided economic arrangements among the advanced industrial states in the post–World War II era. It included the GATT, the fixed exchange rate system, the IMF, and the World Bank. Bretton Woods was a resort in New Hampshire where the negotiations took place.

**Bush doctrine**  A set of principles, formed during the administration of U.S. President George W. Bush, asserting the necessity of waging preventive war against potential aggressors possessing weapons of mass destruction.

## C

**capital**  Resources that can be used to produce further wealth.

**city-state**  A state that centers on a single city, rather than a larger territory or a nation.

**classes**  In economic structuralist theory, groups of people at different places in the economic hierarchy.

**climate change**  Changes in long-term weather patterns that result from global warming; the overall warming of the atmosphere may have very different climactic and weather effects in different places.

**coercion**  The use of a threat to change another actor's behavior.

**cognitive dissonance**  A theory that holds that individuals tend to construct internally consistent views of the world and that psychological discomfort, or "cognitive dissonance," results when some new piece of information does not fit with an individual's existing beliefs.

**Cold War** A conflict between the United States and the Soviet Union during which no actual war broke out between the two superpowers. The Cold War dominated world politics from 1946 until 1991.

**collective action problem** A situation in which a group of actors has a common interest but cannot collaborate to achieve it.

**collective security** A doctrine nominally adopted by states after World War I that specified that when one state committed aggression, all other states would join to attack it.

**colonialism** A type of imperialism in which the dominating state takes direct control of a territory.

**competitive devaluation** Competition between states to have the lowest-valued currency in order to boost domestic employment.

**Concert of Europe** An agreement reached at the Congress of Vienna in 1815 in which major European powers pledged to cooperate to maintain peace and stability.

**conditionality** The requirement that an aid recipient agree to a set of conditions that the donor believes will help promote development in the country.

**conflict spillover** The spread of a domestic conflict across state borders.

**Convention on Anti-Personnel Mines** Agreement signed in 1997, officially called the Convention on the Prohibition of the Use, Stockpiling, Production and Transfer of Anti-Personnel Mines and on Their Destruction. Also known as the Ottawa Convention.

**Convention on Biological Diversity** An international agreement aimed at conserving biodiversity, signed in 1992.

**costs of adjustment** Financial burdens that are imposed on a country as a result of changes in the international economic system.

**Council of the European Union** The body within the EU that represents the governments of the member states and, along with the European Parliament, acts on legislation.

**credibility** The ability and will to carry out a threat.

**crisis stability** The likelihood that a crisis, once it begins, will have dynamics that tend to lead toward war.

# D

**debt crisis** A crisis that occurs when a debtor country is no longer willing or able to make the scheduled payments on its debts.

**declining terms of trade** Conditions of international trade that force countries that primarily produce raw materials to export ever-increasing amounts of raw materials to earn the revenue needed to buy the manufactured goods they require.

**decolonization** The disbanding of nearly all colonial relationships between 1945 and 1975.

**democracy** The doctrine that the entire population of a nation, rather than a small elite or a single monarch, should control government.

**deterrence** A policy aimed at convincing a potential opponent not to attack by raising the costs of attack so that they are higher than the perceived benefits.

**developmental state** A state that takes an active role in economic development by fostering the accumulation of capital to invest in particular industries and building the legal and bureaucratic infrastructure necessary for capitalism to thrive.

**diffusion** The spread of protest and tactics through the process of observation and copying.

# E

**Economic and Social Council (ECOSOC)** The UN council that oversees work on economic and social issues.

**economic determinism** The assumption that political behavior is driven by economic motivations and that political outcomes are determined by economic power.

**economic imperialism** Efforts by states to improve their economic situation through military expansion, usually to gain better control of resources and markets.

**electromagnetic pulse (EMP) weapons** Weapons that use a powerful burst of energy to damage electronic circuits.

**embedded liberalism** According to John Ruggie, the normative consensus that guided international economic arrangements after World War II. It combined a commitment to expansion of free trade with acceptance that states would have to intervene domestically to protect themselves from some of the effects of free trade.

**energy security** Protection against the threat of energy shortages either because of supply problems or because of deliberate efforts by others to inflict harm.

**European Commission** The body within the EU that carries out many executive branch functions.

**exchange rate** The price of one currency in terms of another.

**expected utility theory** A variant of the rational action model. The theory asserts that leaders evaluate policies by combining their estimation of the utility of potential outcomes with the likelihood that different outcomes will result from the policy in question.

**export-led growth** A development strategy that focuses on exporting to the global market.

# F

**fair trade** A narrower approach to free trade that advocates retaliation against states that are perceived as "cheating" on free trade.

**fascism** A doctrine in which the rights or goals of individuals are subservient to those of the nation, which is viewed as a single organism.

**feudal system** A political system in which legal and political subservience is owed to multiple overlapping authorities, such as local nobles, emperors, and the Pope, rather than being defined territorially.

**first-mover advantages** Advantages enjoyed by firms or countries that first enter a new industry, including advantages gained from economies of scale, network effects, and access to investment funds.

**fiscal and monetary policies** The two major ways in which governments can influence their economies. In fiscal policy, a government uses a budget deficit or surplus to stimulate or slow economic growth. In monetary policy, a central bank raises or lowers interest rates to stimulate or slow economic growth.

**fog of war** A phrase coined by Prussian strategist Karl von Clausewitz to characterize the difficulties in controlling war once it starts.

**force** The use of violence or the threat of violence to achieve a political goal.

**foreign policy** Policy (actions or statements intended to change behavior or outcomes) aimed at problems outside of the policy-making state's borders.

**foreign policy analysis** Analysis that attempts to understand states' behavior in terms of actors and processes at the domestic (state and substate) level.

**fundamental attribution bias** The tendency to believe that if adversaries make a concession, they were forced to, but if they make an unwelcome move, they did so freely with bad intentions; and the tendency to have the opposite bias about ourselves.

# G

**G-7** Shorthand for the "Group of Seven" industrial countries formed in the 1970s to coordinate economic policies. Members are Canada, France, Germany, Italy, Japan, the United Kingdom, and the United States. Russia was added in 1997 and removed in 2014.

**gender** A set of ideas that society has attached to the biological categories of male and female.

**Gender Development Index** A measure, published by the UN, of the economic equality of men and women.

**gendered ideas** Ideas that take "masculine" perspectives as "normal" and neglect "feminine" perspectives.

**General Agreement on Tariffs and Trade (GATT)** The main trade provision of the Bretton Woods system.

**Gini coefficient** A statistic developed by Italian statistician Corrado Gini to compare the incomes of the top and bottom fractions of a society.

**global war on terror** The George W. Bush administration's term for the U.S. response to the 2001 terrorist attack on the World Trade Center.

**global warming** The increase in the overall temperature of the planet that results when an increase in certain gases in the atmosphere traps more heat in the atmosphere; a source of climate change.

**globalization** A process in which international trade increases relative to domestic trade; in which the time it takes for goods, people, information, and money to flow across borders and the cost of moving them are decreasing; and in which the world is increasingly defined by single markets rather than by many separate markets.

**gold standard** A system in which each currency represents a specific weight of gold. This facilitates stability but is highly inflexible.

**good governance** Governance that is transparent, controlled by the rule of law, accountable, and effective.

**Great Depression** The global depression that lasted from 1929 until World War II, during which the economies of the United States and Europe declined by as much as 25 percent. In economics, a decline in output of less than 10 percent is referred to as a *recession*; a deeper contraction is called a *depression*.

**great powers** The UN Charter ascribed this status to Britain, China, France, the Soviet Union (Russia), and the United States.

**greenhouse gases** Gases in the atmosphere that trap heat in the earth's atmosphere. As they increase in concentration, the atmospheric temperature rises, causing climate change.

**guerilla warfare** Warfare in which tactics of harassment and ambush are favored over direct battle.

# H

**hegemonic wars** Wars contested to determine who will be the dominant state in the system.

**hierarchy of goals** A clear ranking of goals.

**Human Development Index (HDI)** A measure of poverty produced by the United Nations Development Programme that supplements per capita GDP (at purchasing power parity) with measures of life expectancy, literacy rates, and average years of schooling.

**human rights** An array of "inalienable" individual rights, including civil liberties and political rights. Some advocates include economic rights and cultural rights as well.

## I

**identity** In constructivist theory, actors' and others' perceptions of who they are and what their roles are.

**imperialism** A situation in which one country controls another country or territory.

**import substitution** The strategy of producing domestically those goods that a country has been importing.

**institutions** Sets of agreed upon norms, rules, and practices.

**insurgency** An effort to overthrow the political power in a territory through violence.

**interests** In constructivist theory, socially constructed goals that groups of people together define for society.

**Intergovernmental Panel on Climate Change (IPCC)** An international body that assesses scientific research on climate change for decision makers.

**intergovernmentalism** Making international decisions by negotiation and agreement between state representatives.

**International Court of Justice (ICJ)** Also known as the World Court, the body that adjudicates disputes that arise over treaty obligations.

**International Criminal Court (ICC)** International court for the prosecution of war crimes and other heinous crimes.

**international governmental organizations (IGOs)** Organizations whose membership consists of three or more nation-states.

**international law** The set of rules and obligations that states recognize as binding on each other.

**international norms** Shared ethical principles and expectations about how actors should and will behave in the international arena; and social identities, indicating which actors are considered legitimate.

**international organizations (IOs)** Organizations formed by governments to help them pursue collaborative activity; a type of nonstate actor. More specifically known as international governmental organizations (IGOs).

**international political economy (IPE)** The two-way relationship between international politics and international economics.

**international regimes** Shared understandings about how states will behave on a particular issue.

**intervention** The involvement of outside actors in contentious politics or civil war.

**isolationism** The doctrine that U.S. interests were best served by playing as little role as possible in world affairs. From the founding of the republic until the Spanish-American War of 1898, the doctrine was largely unquestioned, but the Japanese bombing of Pearl Harbor in 1941 is widely viewed as destroying any credibility that the doctrine had left.

## J

**just war theory** The theory of the circumstances in which it is ethical to go to war and the kinds of practices that are ethical in the prosecution of war.

## K

**Kyoto Protocol** An international agreement that was signed in 1997 and went into effect in 2005 that aims to reduce greenhouse gas emissions to prevent global climate change.

## L

**late development** The economic challenge faced by developing states because of economic competition from more advanced states.

**law of war** A doctrine concerning when it is permissible to go to war and what means of conducting war are (and are not) permissible.

**League of Nations** An international organization formed after World War I intended to resolve disputes without force, and to use military force against aggressors.

**lender of last resort** An actor that is committed to continuing to lend money to stressed economic actors when market institutions would refuse to do so.

**lesson of Munich** The lesson learned from British attempts to appease Hitler at the 1938 Munich peace conference—namely, that costly wars can be avoided by confronting hostile leaders promptly.

**levée en masse** A draft, initiated by Napoleon following the French Revolution, which allowed France to vastly expand its army.

**level of analysis** The unit (individual, state, or system) that a theory focuses on in its general explanation.

**liberal approach** Political approach focusing on the ability of actors to govern themselves without surrendering their liberty. International liberal theory focuses on the ability of states to cooperate to solve problems.

## M

**mainstream effect** The tendency for the public to follow political leaders and the media when those actors have consensus on an issue.

**maximum sustainable yield** The maximum amount of a renewable resource that can be harvested each year without reducing the amount that can be harvested in future years.

**media** The different means through which news and entertainment are conveyed.

**mercantilism** A trading doctrine that focused on state power in a conflictual world. It was based on the idea that the overall amount of wealth in the world was fixed by the amount of precious metals. Therefore, international trade was a zero-sum game, and the goal of every state was to run a trade surplus in order to accumulate more money.

**methodology** The set of principles, strategies, and practical steps used to evaluate competing hypotheses.

**military-industrial complex** A term made popular by President Dwight D. Eisenhower that refers to a group consisting of a nation's armed forces, weapon suppliers and manufacturers, and elements within the civil service involved in defense efforts.

**ministries** The main institutions of the executive branch of government. In the United States, these institutions are called "departments."

**mixed-motive game** A situation in which actors have incentives that partially overlap with and partially contradict those of their partners. The prisoner's dilemma is one representation of a mixed-motive game.

**monetary crisis** A crisis that emerges when rapid sales of a particular currency cause its value to collapse.

**Montreal Protocol** An international agreement, signed in 1987, that commits the signatories to reducing the production and use of gases that deplete the ozone layer.

**motivated bias** Bias that occurs as a result of some psychological need, such as the need for all of one's beliefs to be consistent with one another or the need to believe that a good solution to a problem is available.

**multinational corporation (MNC)** A company with operations in more than one country; a type of nonstate actor; also called a transnational corporation.

**multiplier effect** An economic effect whereby an increase in spending (for example, of funds provided to a country by a donor) produces an increase in national income and consumption greater than the initial amount spent. When aid flows out of a country, the benefit of aid may accrue to the donor rather than to the recipient.

**Munich Crisis** A crisis in 1938 precipitated by Germany's demand that it be allowed to occupy part of Czechoslovakia. War was averted when Britain and France agreed to Germany's demands.

**mutual assured destruction (MAD)** A situation in which each side in a conflict possesses enough armaments to destroy the other even after suffering a surprise attack.

## N

**national interest** A foreign policy goal that is objectively valuable for the overall well-being of the state. The concept is important in realist theory and in foreign policy discussions, but some dispute that there is any single national interest.

**national self-determination** The doctrine that each state should consist of a single nation and each distinct nation should have its own state.

**nationalism** The doctrine that recognizes the nation as the primary unit of political allegiance.

**natural selection** The tendency for traits that increase the likelihood of an individual's surviving and producing offspring to become more common in future generations of a species.

**neomercantilism** The belief that states should seek a trade surplus. This focus on the balance of trade makes trade a zero-sum game, as it was for traditional mercantilists.

**Niccolo Machiavelli (1469–1527)** A government official in the medieval city-state of Florence who wrote about the "laws of politics" for the "wise statesman," focusing on how the state could defend itself from domestic and foreign enemies.

**nondiscrimination** A principle guiding tariff policy that requires a country to apply equal tariffs on all of its trading partners; also referred to as the *most favored nation* principle.

**nongovernmental organizations (NGOs)** A broad category of diverse organizations, including groups similar to domestic interest groups but with transnational concerns and organizational structures, and groups that focus not on influencing government but on conducting activities in different countries.

**nonrenewable resources** Natural products whose supply is fundamentally limited, such as oil, minerals, and rare earth metals.

**nonstate actor** A political actor that is not a state, such as an advocacy group, charity, corporation, or terrorist group.

**norm entrepreneurs** Individuals or groups who seek to promote a new international norm.

**normative theory** A theory that aims to establish the proper goals of political action.

**norms** Shared rules or principles that influence behavior.

## O

**one state, one vote** A voting system in which each state has one vote, regardless of its size, population, or other characteristics. Used in the UN General Assembly and many other international organizations.

**operationalizing** Translating a theoretical concept into attributes that can be measured.

**ozone layer** A layer of ozone in the upper atmosphere that reduces transmission of ultraviolet radiation. Ozone is a form of oxygen with three atoms per molecule ($O_3$) rather than the typical two ($O_2$). At ground level, ozone is a respiratory irritant.

## P

**paradigm** A theoretical approach that includes one or more theories that share similar philosophical assumptions.

**peace enforcement** The application of force (or the threat of force) to compel states to stop fighting.

**peacekeeping** The introduction of foreign troops or observers into a region to increase confidence that states will refrain from the use of force.

**Peloponnesian War** A war between Athens and Sparta from 431 BCE to 404 BCE. Thucydides's study of this war has been influential on later thinking about international relations.

**Pentagon Papers** A series of secret Defense Department reports on the origins of the Vietnam War that raised serious questions about U.S. involvement in the war.

**per capita GDP** The average income of the people in a country.

**pluralism** The presence of a number of competing actors or ideas.

**portfolio investment** Investments made by purchasing stocks rather than physical assets.

**poverty** The lack of sufficient income, often accompanied by insufficient nutrition, housing, and other necessities. Poverty can be defined in absolute terms as "income poverty" or in relative terms, with a focus on the range of choices open to individuals.

**Powell Doctrine** A set of criteria guiding military engagement, including establishing clear goals and using overwhelming force.

**power** The ability of an actor to achieve its goals. Exactly what constitutes power and how to measure it are vexing problems in international relations.

**power transition theory** A theory that postulates that war occurs when one state becomes powerful enough to challenge the dominant state and reorder the hierarchy of power within the international system.

**precision-guided munitions** Weapons with guidance systems and maneuvering capability that allow them to strike individual targets with a high degree of accuracy. Also known as "smart bombs."

**prisoner's dilemma** A game theory scenario in which noncooperation is the rational strategy but leads to both players being worse off than if they had cooperated.

**proletariat** In Marxist jargon, the working class.

**prospect theory** A theory that contends that how individuals weigh options is heavily influenced by whether a particular outcome is seen as a gain or a loss.

**protectionism** Measures taken by states to limit their imports.

**proximate cause** An event that immediately precedes an outcome and therefore provides the most direct explanation of it.

**purchasing power parity (PPP)** A measure used to calculate GDP that takes into account that goods cost different amounts in different countries.

**purpose** The goals that actors pursue, including the notion of "national interest." Whether actors see themselves as having shared or competing goals is a central concern.

## Q

**quota** A numerical limit on the amount of a certain item that can be imported.

## R

**radiological weapons** Weapons that use conventional explosives to distribute radioactive material, which has long-lasting poisonous effects. Also known as "dirty bombs."

**rally around the flag effect** The increase in popular support often gained by leaders of a country in times of war.

**rational action model** A model that bases explanations of decisions on the assumption that decision makers have clear goals, calculate the costs and benefits of various courses of action, and choose the action that will best serve their goals.

**rational choice theory** A theory that bases explanations of decisions on the assumption that decision makers have clear goals, calculate the costs of various courses of action, and pick the policy that will best serve their goals.

**reciprocity** An arrangement whereby two states agree to have the same tariffs on each other's goods; or the strategy of matching the other player's previous move.

**recognition** The acceptance by the international community of a state's sovereignty over its territory.

**refugee** A person who leaves his or her country of nationality due to war, natural disaster, persecution, or the fear of persecution.

**relative gains** A problem with free trade arising from the fact that if one state can gain more wealth from a given transaction, it can potentially increase its military power vis-à-vis the other state. This implies that even if both sides gain, the side that gains more may increase its power over the side that gains less.

**renewable resources** Natural products that can be sustained indefinitely, as long as the rate of consumption does not exceed the natural rate of replacement.

**reparations** Payments that Germany was forced to make as a result of starting World War I. Reparations caused serious economic problems in Germany and were deeply resented by the German people.

## S

**SALT-I and SALT-II** Agreements between the United States and the Soviet Union to limit nuclear weapons.

**secretary-general** The head of the UN bureaucracy and the personification and public face of the UN.

**Security Council** The fifteen-member council within the UN in charge of dealing with threats to international security.

**security dilemma** The difficult choice faced by states in anarchy between arming, which risks provoking a response from others, and not arming, which risks remaining vulnerable.

**self-enforcing** International law is self-enforcing when states have incentives to obey, even when there is no sanction for violating the law or agreement.

**sovereignty** The principle that states have complete authority over their own territory.

**spillover** A process by which small, incremental steps toward cooperation create the impetus for even further integration.

**standard operating procedures** Procedures that bureaucracies adopt to deal efficiently with a large number of similar tasks.

**state** An entity defined by a specific territory within which a single government has authority; or the government and political system of a country.

**state socialism** A strategy for development in which the state rather than the market allocates resources.

**state strength** The degree to which a state is independent of societal influences.

**state structure** The form and function of state institutions.

**status quo bias** The tendency of leaders to take considerable risks to avoid a perceived loss.

**structural adjustment** A strategy adopted by the World Bank in the 1980s and 1990s aimed at strengthening the financial basis of a country's economy.

**subsidies** Direct payments to producers to help them remain profitable.

**supranationalism** Delegating international decisions to an international organization.

**surplus value** In economic structuralist theory, the difference between the value of raw materials and the value of the final product; presumably this is the value added by laborers.

## T

**tariff** A tax on imports, used to protect domestic producers from foreign competition.

**terrorism** Use or threat of violence by nongovernmental actors to change government policies by creating fear of further violence.

**theory** A generalized explanation of a set of comparable phenomena.

**theory of comparative advantage** A theory developed by the English economist David Ricardo to show logically how and why trade is beneficial to both partners.

**third wave of democratization** The series of transitions from autocracy to democracy that began with a democratic revolution in Portugal in 1974.

**Third World** A term coined during the Cold War to describe those states that were neither in the group of advanced industrial states nor in the communist bloc; typically, it refers to the many poor states in the Southern Hemisphere. The term is generally considered synonymous with "underdeveloped."

**Thomas Hobbes (1588–1679)** Author of the influential work *Leviathan*, in which he argued that government had to be autocratic to prevent a slide back into anarchy.

**tied aid** Aid that must be spent on goods or services from the donor country.

**tragedy of the commons** A version of the collective action problem in which a shared resource is overconsumed.

**Trans Pacific Partnership** A proposed agreement to reduce barriers to trade among twelve countries in North and South America, Asia, and the Pacific, including Australia, Canada, Chile, Japan, Mexico, Singapore, and the United States.

**transgovernmental relations** Direct interaction between bureaucracies in different countries without going through their heads of state.

**transnational actors** Actors whose activities cut across state boundaries.

**transnational advocacy networks (TANs)** Groups that organize across national boundaries to pursue some political, social, or cultural goal.

**transnational corporations (TNCs)** Corporations with operations in more than one country; also called multinational corporations (MNCs).

**transnational relations** Interaction between societal actors across nation-states.

**Treaty of Rome** The 1957 treaty that established the European Economic Community, the predecessor of the European Union.

**Treaty of Versailles** The agreement ending World War I that set up the League of Nations.

**Treaty on the Non-Proliferation of Nuclear Weapons (NPT)** An agreement that states without nuclear weapons will refrain from obtaining them and will allow detailed inspections so that other states can be certain they are fulfilling their obligations.

**Triple Alliance** A pre–World War I agreement by Germany, Austria-Hungary, and Italy that if one state were to be attacked the others would come to its aid.

**Triple Entente** A pre–World War I agreement by Britain, France, and Russia that if one state were to be attacked the others would come to its aid.

## U

**UN Millennium Development Goals** A set of goals and accompanying targets set by the UN, aimed at addressing poverty and inequality.

**unmotivated bias** Bias that occurs as a result of the simplifications inherent in the process of perceiving an ambiguous world.

## W

**war crimes** A set of transgressions established by the fourth Geneva Convention, including willful killing, torture or inhumane treatment, willfully causing great suffering or serious injury to body or health, unlawful deportation or transfer, and unlawful confinement of a protected person.

**War Powers Resolution** A 1973 law that limits the U.S. president's ability to go to war without permission of Congress.

**Washington consensus** A development strategy favored by leading donor countries and organizations that advocates open economies, free trade, and minimal interference by the state in the economy.

**Westphalian system** The system of sovereign states that was recognized by the Treaty of Westphalia in 1648.

**WTO Dispute Settlement Body** The enforcement body of the World Trade Organization, which can empower aggrieved states to impose retaliatory tariffs against countries that violate the organization's rules.

## Z

**zero-sum game** A situation in which any gains by one side are offset by losses for another.

**zone of peace** A group of democratic states among whom war has become unthinkable; or a group of states that tend not to go to war with each other because they are democratic.

Page numbers followed by "f" indicate figures.

Schröder, Gerhard, 138
Schumann, Robert, 198
Schwartz, Herman, 360
da Silva, Luiz Inacio Lula, 456f
Singh, Manmohan, 456f
Sirleaf, Ellen Johnson, 193f
Smith, Adam, 208, 294
Snowe, Olympia, 141
de Spinoza, Benedict, 230
Stalin, Joseph, 172, 230, 449
Straw, Jack, 173, 385

**T**

Thant, U, 194
Thucydides, 22–231, 60, 108, 109, 229
Tillerson, Rex, 137f
Tolstoy, Leo, 26
Truman, Harry, 173
Tsipras, Alexis, 89
Tusk, Donald, 201
Tzu, Sun, 256

**V**

Varoufakis, Yanis, 60

**W**

Waldheim, Kurt, 194
Wallerstein, Immanuel, 29
Walt, Stephen, 69
Waltz, Kenneth, 64, 267
Weber, Max, 29
Wilson, Woodrow, 59, 123, 129
al-Wuhayshi, Nasser, 254

**X**

Xiaoping, Deng, 21, 288

**Y**

Yunus, Muhammed, 112, 311

**Z**

Zakaria, Fareed, 452
Zarif, Mohammad Javad, 243f
Zedong, Mao, 21, 44, 94, 270–271, 288
Zinser, Adolfo, 165
Zuckerberg, Mark, 79f
Zuma, Jacob, 445f

Page numbers followed by "f" indicate figures.